Dvorak's Guide to Desktop Telecommunications

Dvorak's Guide to Desktop Telecommunications

John C. Dvorak
Nick Anis

Osborne **McGraw-Hill**

Berkeley   New York   St. Louis   San Francisco
Auckland   Bogotá   Hamburg   London   Madrid
Mexico City   Milan   Montreal   New Delhi   Panama City
Paris   São Paulo   Singapore   Sydney
Tokyo   Toronto

Osborne **McGraw-Hill**
2600 Tenth Street
Berkeley, California 94710
U.S.A.

For information on translations and book distributors outside of the U.S.A., please write to Osborne **McGraw-Hill** at the above address.

Dvorak's Guide to Desktop Telecommunications

1234567890 DOC 99876543210

ISBN 0-07-881668-8

TAB BOOKS is a McGraw-Hill Company. TAB BOOKS offers software for sale. For information and a catalog, please contact TAB Software Department, Blue Ridge Summit, PA 17294-0850.

For all mankind

CONTENTS AT A GLANCE

CONTENTS

Telecommunications is a diverse and growing technology. Through on-line data services, bulletin boards, electronic mail, and remote PC operation, vast amounts of information are only seconds away from anyone with a modem. For example, there are over 10,000 electronic bulletin boards in the United States alone, devoted to almost any subject you can imagine. Electronic mail and fax transmissions are also growing in popularity. Stock quotes, software support, and even computer-simulated "aerial dogfights" with other users are just a few examples of the wide range of offerings in telecommunications. Yet, even now, the full range of telecommunications possibilities remains to be exploited, and we can expect some exciting developments in the near future.

Many people like you are in a position to take advantage of this emerging technology; recent estimates suggest that there are over 18 million modems installed around the world. Probably fewer than one million of these modems are being used to their fullest potential. With all that telecommunications has to offer, we have to wonder why the other 17 million aren't being used as effectively as they might be. The answer, in part, is probably "telecommunications phobia."

Millions of computer users have overcome "computer phobia" and are now computer-literate. I like to think that the dozens of excellent books available on the subject have had a big hand in educating people about computers. There has been a crying need for similar materials to educate users about telecommunications—until now.

I am delighted that a writer of John Dvorak's stature has taken up the challenge of bringing to the world an authoritative reference on the subject of telecommunications. Dvorak's style and wit make this a refreshing and accessible sourcebook. Its breadth of coverage is impressive, thanks in part to the contributions of many of the telecommunications field's best and brightest.

While other application categories such as word processors and data-bases are pushing the limits of their capabilities, telecommunications is still in its infancy. For those who missed many of the early events in the computer revolution, here is an opportunity to get in on the ground floor of a rapidly growing but still misunderstood new technology. The rewards to be gained are substantial. For corporations, basic training in telecommunications can save thousands of dollars. Mail and courier expenses can be cut, while vital information can be rapidly transferred in ways most folks haven't yet imagined. This book will show you how. It is an indispensable resource for anyone who is serious about telecommunications.

—Peter Norton

ACKNOWLEDGMENTS

This book, the Desktop Edition of the best-seller *Dvorak's Guide to PC Telecommunications*, is the cumulative work of many people. The telecommunications scene is too diverse to be known in complete detail by any one person—or even a team of ten.

To make the original edition as definitive as possible, the authors called on the field's top experts for help. Each chapter was produced by as many as ten people, and was edited and approved by still others. The Desktop Edition enjoys the benefit of all that effort, and adds the efforts of Craig Menefee, writer and telecommunications expert. He reorganized and reworked some of the sections, adding new research. A special thanks goes to him. As usual, the text was expertly copyedited by Carol Henry and the staff at Osborne/McGraw-Hill, and overseen by Osborne/McGraw-Hill editor in chief Jeff Pepper.

Thanks also to Deborah Wilson, Judy Wohlfrom, Stefany Otis, Lance Ravella, Marcela Hancik, Roger Dunshee, Nan Rohan, Lynda Higham, and all the folks of Osborne/McGraw-Hill's production department who put in the big OT to help us make our deadline. We would never have made it without incredible efforts from Madhu Prasher and Erica Spaberg, who organized the production of this book. Special thanks also to Emily Rader and Laura Sackerman for their efforts on the book, and to Ann Pharr for making all the right connections.

In the midst of the typical last-minute insanity of getting a book this size through production, Jeff and Martha Pepper welcomed their new daughter, Anne Mackenzie Pepper, into the world. It was Nick Anis' wife, Patty, who had a baby during the writing of the first edition of this book.

As usual, Mimi Smith-Dvorak again had the thankless chore of applying her magic simplification pencil to the more complicated new material. Patty Anis again helped keep Nick in line and cared for their new baby. Menefee's wife, Sami, did much "green-penciling" on chapters that were renumbered and updated for this Desktop Edition.

Many of the previous edition's contributors stayed with the project, earning field commissions for steadfastness and courage. Maria A. Forrest of Crosstalk contributed new material on communications programs that work in MS Windows. Author Tom Sheldon also helped us "open up the Windows" as a general communications environment. Chapter 17 thus contains a very complete overview of telecommunicating in MS Windows—and it all addresses Windows Version 3, which was released just days before the Desktop Edition went to press.

Werner Feibel, who edited the User Guides included with the original book, again came to our support by helping with this edition's new chapter on communicating in UNIX. Bud Aaron covered communicating in OS/2. Pete Maclean, author of *PC Magazine*'s EMMA agent program for MCI Mail, provided new material on how a modem works. Marshall Dudley, author of the influential BBS utility program DOORWAY, was our source on doors, agents, and front-ends. (We're not talking about houses, real estate salesmen, and automobiles here—see the new Chapter 10.) For the straight scoop on Amiga, we turned to Harv Laser, highly regarded Amiga program developer. Scott Smith of Pacific Bell helped us expand our coverage of ISDN and other exciting new technologies. Don Stoner, publisher of the National Amateur Radio Association newsletter, *The Communicator*, helped us with packet radio and satellite BBSs.

All the aforementioned team members stood on the shoulders of the original group, whose efforts have been so central to the first book's continuing success. If you ever see any of these names on a resume, pay attention. Let's start with the people who helped the most on each individual chapter. First there's Jack Rickard of *Boardwatch Magazine,* who worked on the Introduction to Telecomputing chapter. Thanks to Maria A. Forrest of Crosstalk Communications/DCA (Digital Communications Associates) for the chapter on Installing Modems and Software. Kudos to Stan Hayes of Adworks whose help was invaluable in getting other people to help us! When you see Stan, buy him some Chateau Lynch-Bages. He can toast Ed Girou and the staff of R.A. Kottmeier for their help on telecommunications programs. Regina Whitley, Jane Levene, and Doug Brackbill of MCI, Pete Maclean, and Dr. Ron Albright helped us with our E-mail chapter. Thanks to Alfred Glossbrenner on Dow Jones, as well as John McGovern, Carla Gaffney, and the folks at Dow Jones. Thanks to Anthony Lockwood and Steve Laliberte for the BIX material. Steve Haraznak and John Weaver helped us with GEnie. Thanks to Richard Baker, Kitty Thomas, and all the folks at CompuServe for their help. Mary Dee O'Jolla, O'Jolla Associates, and Paula Dell helped us with DIALOG. Thanks to Sandy Lunner of *USA Today* for her help. Thanks to Bob Huntsinger and Pat

McFarland of NewsNet for their work on the "Information Utilities" chapter. Big thanks to Chris Barr and the staff of *PC Magazine* for their help on PC MagNet.

Tom Foth, Howard Luxenberg, and Mindy Littman of Microcom helped us with a bunch of different things. Thanks to Nancy Jones and Lowell Coulson of DCA for their micro-to-mainframe expertise. Big thanks to Tim Stryker of Galacticomm for his BBS knowledge and practical tips. Thanks to Jim Harrer of Mustang Software (makers of Wildcat!) for coding our Master Control Menu and for giving us the definitive list of software. Thanks to Mike Callahan, sysop alias —"Dr. File Finder"— who helped with the "BBS Software" chapter, the reading list, and the recommended shareware list. Software virus information credit goes to Rich Levin. Thanks also to Ed Zintel of Les Goldberg Public Relations, who helped with the "Telecommuting" chapter. Charlie Bermant, John Frank, Gina Carter, Glen Eric Nelson, and the folks at Zenith Data Systems helped with the "Notebook Computers" chapter. The master of the Mac, Scott Watson of Freesoft (makers of Red Ryder) and Steve Waechter helped us with our "Communicating by Macintosh" chapter.

Thanks to Bruce Page of Magnetic Press International Telecommunications for his expertise on calling from Europe. A big wave and thanks go to David Lytel, an international telecom expert and Ph.D. candidate, and to Holly Atkinson, Jane Hurchalla, and the folks at CTL, who all helped us with Minitel. Geoffrey E. Moore, Edward Nanas, Brian Ek, and the staff of PRODIGY came to our aid with the PRODIGY section. Dr. Aaron G. Filler of Harvard University, Phil Marcello, Pete Maclean, Marty Michael of National Semiconductor, Stan Horzepa, Dale Walsh of US Robotics, and Jim Defriend of Software Bits and Bytes helped us with "How a Modem Works." Matt Gray of Hilgraeve and John Erickson of Eric Labs helped us transfer protocols in "File Transfer Protocols."

Donald Ware did an outstanding job of getting our ISDN chapter into shape! Thanks to Frank Derfler for his help, too. Brad and Debbie Schepp, Bill Grubb, and Joel Borden of the Complete PC helped put together a great section on fax, and Stan Horzepa also worked on packet radio in our "Important Technologies and Advancements" chapter.

Someone told us Jim Button was the man to call if you wanted to know about shareware, and they sure were right. Dee Dee Walsh and Jim Button of ButtonWare were a great help on our "Shareware" chapter, telling us the real story.

Brian Miller and Tess Heder of Channel One helped us come up with those cute emoticons. Paul Roub, author of TelixFonEd, helped Nich Anis turn the glossary into English. (Paul speaks a few languages himself—including computerese.) Again, one more kudo to Mike Callahan, who helped find, sort, and lay out thousands of BBS numbers.

Bob Mahoney of Exec PC and Judy Getts helped also with important BBS systems, including Bob's. Ed Girou and the staff of R.A. Kottmeier, and Harv Laser helped with "Cable Diagrams." Alfred Glossbrenner, Ron Albright, Tess Heder and Brian Miller also gave us their nominations for our Recommended Reading appendix.

Folks like Lynn Ecklund helped us with information brokering, and Phil Katz of PKware, author of PKZIP, helped with understanding data compression. Mike Fay of Fleshman, Hillary and Harv Laser, and the folks at Commodore helped with Commodore.

Kudos to: Joseph Sheppard, sysop extraordinaire; Samuel Smith, The Tool Shop, author of ProDoor; Kelley Stanonik, programmer; Matt Thomas, author of Lynx; Jimmy Pearson, programmer; Herb Swanigan, consultant; Tom Tcimpidis, sysop and volunteer; Rob Rosenberger, programmer; Darin May; Merlin R. Null; Dan Bricklin; Vern Buerg; Paul Roub (this time for the nifty TelixFonEd); Otto Ruppel, sysop; Henry Senk, Jim Summers, Jon Zakin, and Mark Smith of US Robotics; Tom Scott and T.M. McArthur of Galaxy; R.P. Aditya, David Foley, and Rich Levin for his classy Checkup program. Also kudos to Mark Foster, Julian James, Bill Beers, and Tom Foth. Special thanks to Phil Becker of e-SOFT for his support. Thanks also go out to Joseph Webb at Link-up for his support, and to Richard Peterson of PC-SIG for his support.

We don't want to forget the great people at The WELL. Stewart Brand, a great guy and one who makes the impossible happen, Cliff Fiegello, and John Coate all helped us out. We have to thank author T.S. Bennett, Cindy Genusa, and Rob Brun, for helping Nick each and every time he asked for help. Then we have to thank Michael Cahlin for turning us on to Matt Gray of Hilgraeve, who we tapped for his expertise on protocols. A big thanks to Fabin Gordon, Hugh Mitchell, great guy John Newlin of New-Ware, author of ArcMaster. Thanks also to Jere Greene, along with Daniel Gross, and Matt Palcic. We want a big thanks to go out to super-programmer Eric Cockrell of Thumper Technologies for doing our install program (all 35 revisions!). He's the guy who did the masterful EZ-Reader.

And yet more people whose help was invaluable: Dan Parsons of Robocomm; Kevin Collins, sysop, Jim Derr of SHEZ, and one of the most talented programmers in the world; Jim Holloway, sysop; Marshall Dudley, DOORWAY; Sean Dudley, sysop; Stan Horzepa, our resident packet radio expert; Allan Dumaine, author; Gordon Huyck, Lynn Edklund, Jerry Jaeke, superhack; John Jacobson, superhack II; Brian Eggers, and Arnold Jagt.

(Sometimes acknowledgment lists like this are tedious, but these people are important.) There are programming talents who helped us, such as Mark Ellis, author of DIRCOPY, and Phil Katz. There's also Chris Epler, John Erickson, and Dave Krause to thank, along with Mike Kruss, Mark Eppley, and his Traveling Software crew. I'd like to thank Paul Somerson for the inspiration to do a book this large.

Onward with thanks to Steve Tilson, Mark Turner, Mike Weaver, Berne Wu, Livingston Hinckley, Ron Saxton, Paul Miners, Faith Bohnke, Ronald J. Bandy, William Beers, Wayne Bell, Philippe Kahn, Stephen Kahn, Nan Borreson, Glenn Weyhousen, and Sal Manaro. Special recognition goes to Chris Severud of Bourbaki, Justin Boyan, author of Boyan, and Chuck Bradford (alias "Mr. Macintosh").

Kudos to Isaac Ash and Sandy Green of Buyer's Resource for miscellaneous help. We want to thank Margaret Killeen and all the folks at California Freeware for their support. More thanks go to Tom Sherrard and David Carson of Toshiba, and Valerie Strickland Ward of Datavue. Let's make sure to mention David Terry and Fred Clark of Clark Development, makers of PCBoard, the BBS system we used for the project. More thanks go to Steve Gibson and Michael Miller of *Infoworld* for their help and suggestions. Thanks to the guys who helped repopularize telecommunications: Tom Smith and Bruce Barkelew of Datastorm.

More thanks go to the following fabulous people: Fleshman Hillard, Enzo Renari, Donna Gates, Trish Warner, Becky Hitchcock, Dr. Terry Deacon, Mark Stein, all the folks at Delta Airlines' *In Flight Magazine*, Audry Chitoff, John McGovern, Chuck Forsberg, John Friel, Jack Alwise, Mike Lough, Sharon O'Brian, Bob Jones, Nick Sullivan, and Donna Faulkner. The biggest thanks goes to all those who, for whatever reason, we forgot to thank! We'll give you all a big plug in the next revision of the book, for sure!

There are a lot of companies large and small that helped out. In particular, we'd like to thank: Citizen for the use of their computers and great printers; NEC and Tom Martin for the use of their superb UltraLite notebook machines; Willow Peripherals for that special video card of theirs; WordStar Corporation for word processing software for the staff. Thanks to Bernie Woo and Ron Sexton of Archive who came to our rescue with a marvelous SCSI 150MB tape unit to back up our BBS. Artisoft provided us with technical information and evaluations of their popular Lantastic network and Network Eye software. H-P got us the laser printer we needed, thanks to Mike Lowe. A big thanks goes to Avery labels, too. Thanks to

Data Based Advisor for their support. Thanks to Multitech for helping us out on the high-speed modems chapter. Thanks to Borland for software. A big thanks to Peter Norton Computing for its software and support. Thanks to Pacific Data Systems for a font cartridge and Caere for a copy of OmniPage. A big plug to Microsoft and Tanya Van Dam and Mike Poole for getting us important software needed to do this book: three cheers for Microsoft. A big thanks to Bruce Brown at Para Systems for the use of the Minute-Man UPS, which kept the board running 24 hours a day. Also, let's thank Tandy Corporation for the slew of photos they sent us at their expense—thanks, guys.

Thanks to Mark Perkel, the author of Mark's Menu, for software. Special thanks to Tom and Dave Freeman of Advanced Computer Products. Thanks to Mike Peak and the folks at Relyisis for the fax machine. Xtree Corporation and King Lee helped us out with software, too. Thanks also to US Robotics and Telebit for supplying modems, and to Zenith for a computer. A huge thanks to Princeton Graphics and Sharon Cuppett for special equipment. Thanks also to Susan Call at Frost and Sullivan, and Gale Research's Tom Romormig for research help. Finally, thanks to Chuck Guzis at Sydex for free coding.

—John C. Dvorak
Nick Anis

Years ago, when computer industry observers talked about important software applications, they always cited four categories: spreadsheets, word processing, database management, and communications. More recently, as the industry started to cater to the business user, these categories changed. Communications was dropped, and local area networks (LANs), desktop publishing, and even paint programs seemed more important. Lately even computer games are discussed more than communications. It has almost seemed like a plot to limit the machines—keep them at home, as it were, and keep them from calling other computers.

Meanwhile, MCI, GEnie, CompuServe, and all sorts of international networks swept the world. Telecommunications was more important than ever, but you'd never know it if you were reading the newspapers and magazines. The invention of the high-speed modem allowed users to move files to and from remote computers more quickly than ever. The laptop computer demanded telecommunications, thus increasing sales of communications software and modems. Even so, telecommunications has become the second-class citizen of the PC world. I've always been fascinated by this phenomenon. I wondered why communications was only talked about by the experts and power users. I realized that it was actually the success of the telecommunications scene that created the problem. Success without strict standards makes for a mess—there are too many things you have to know in order to get things to work. Only a power user or computer nutball would be interested.

Confusion and frustration do indeed exist in this environment. Newcomers buy a modem and never figure out how to hook it up or use it. The fact is that it's not easy. To make matters worse, new users discover there are peculiar idiosyncrasies and mysterious incompatibilities that may result in a well-planned, expensive system not working at all. Usually the problem is some silly thing—a detail, a switch setting, or a communications program parameter. It's no secret that the first months of modem use can be exasperating.

That's why we decided to do this guide. It's also why we wanted to make it as complete as possible.

ABOUT THIS BOOK

You will learn about modems and how they work. You will read about telecommunications software and what it does. You will find out about on-line services that you can call to get information or programs. We will teach you about bulletin boards, telecommuting, information services, remote databases, electronic mail, and much more. When you read this book, you'll be an expert.

To make it easier, the original software edition of this book contained a great disk tutorial called the Modem Tutor, plus a special edition of the remarkable new telecommunications program, Telix, and a bounty of important computer utilities to boot. These programs are not included with the less-expensive Desktop Edition, but we heartily recommend them. Computer Business Services of Diamond Bar, California, is making them available in a set of three diskettes for $20; there is a coupon at the end of this Preface to use in ordering. Since the programs come in compressed form and the diskettes are chock full, the collection is well worth the minor cost—especially if you're in need of a first-rate modem tutor, telecommunications program and assorted utilities. It really is a fine collection, assembled for the software edition by my coauthor, Nick Anis.

Once you recognize the importance of telecommunications in the years ahead, you'll see that this guide is an important contribution to revitalizing mainstream interest in telecommunications. We want to get *everyone* on line! Those of you already familiar with telecommunications have known for a long time how valuable it is for a computer to have these capabilities, and it's important that this knowledge be transferred to all users, so that the telecommunications scene can expand. This book will help the cause.

We hope *Dvorak's Guide to Desktop Telecommunications* becomes a permanent addition to your PC library.

HOW THE BOOK IS ORGANIZED

The book has four parts. Part One, "A Layman's View," and Part Two, "Telecommunications: Environments and Systems," give you a broad overview of many of the elements of telecommunications, and include a "Quick

Start" section for those of you who haven't yet got your modem up and running. This material is written so that anyone can understand it, and all will find it useful. Part Three, "A Technical View," deals with some of the more technical details of telecommunications. It includes sections on major programs, on communicating with different computer "platforms," and on new technologies. Part Four, "Appendixes," offers a wide array of reference materials.

Use the coupon at the end of this Preface to take advantage of the Computer Business Services diskette and tutorial offer. For $20, you will receive both of the MS-DOS-compatible diskettes that were included with the original software edition of *Dvorak's Guide to PC Telecommunications*. The diskettes contain a comprehensive tutorial program on how to telecommunicate with BBSs and on-line services . . . and the special Telix SE telecommunications program developed for distribution with the software edition. In addition, Computer Business Services will send a third, bonus diskette containing a raft of great public domain and shareware utility programs.

These programs are yours to try for 30 days. If you like them and expect to continue using them, you then register the programs with the authors; this gets you continuing support, as well as notification of new and updated versions. The $20 fee covers the handling, mailing, and other distribution costs of Computer Business Services. It does not purchase the right to use the programs indefinitely, but you are not expected to register any program you do not use.

To obtain Telix SE and the Modem Tutor, plus the telecommunications and other utilities, fill out the attached coupon and mail it, together with a check or money order (NOT cash or postage stamps) to the given address.

DVORAK Telecomm Offer
Computer Business Services
1125 Bramford Court
Diamond Bar, CA 91765

[] YES, send me the original 2 Dvorak diskettes, plus a FREE bonus
disk. I enclose a $20 check or money order. I understand that if I keep
and use the programs, I will need to register them with the authors.

Check one:

[] Five 5 1/4-inch disks
[] Three 3 1/2-inch disks

Name: _

Street Address _

City, ST: _ _ _ _ _ _ _ _ _ _ _ _ _ _ _ _ _ _ (ZIP) _ _ _ _ _ _ _

Daytime Phone Number: _

(California residents add sales tax)
Please mail any comments or suggestions for this book to:

Dvorak Modem Ideas
Computer Business Services
1125 Bramford Court
Diamond Bar, CA 91765

Please allow 4 to 6 weeks for delivery. This is solely the offering of the
authors.
Osborne/McGraw-Hill takes NO responsibility for the fulfillment of this
offer.

Why This Book Is for You

This guide was written to give a complete overview of the world of telecommunications. Whether you are just exploring the idea of buying a modem, or have been using one for years, we think you will find this book to be a great resource.

The beginner will learn how to log on and will be exposed to the enormous variety of services and options available on line. The experienced user will discover a terrific reference, and fun reading with much new information.

LEARN MORE ABOUT DESKTOP TELECOMMUNICATIONS

Here are two other excellent Osborne/McGraw-Hill books that will help you build your computer skills and maximize the power of the hardware and software that you have selected.

If you are a beginning computer user, look for *PCs Made Easy* by Turley, a step-by-step, in-depth introduction to computer software and hardware that explains all the terminology you'll encounter when you buy a computer system.

For terrific reference on shareware try *Dr. File Finder's Guide to Shareware* by Mike Callahan and Nick Anis.

If you're looking for a handy intermediate-level book that covers popular shareware programs, see *The Shareware Book: Using PC-Write, PC-File+, and PC-Calc+* by Zamora, Saito, and Albrecht, a fast-paced, hands-on guide that covers basics, intermediate techniques, and advanced topics pertaining to these programs.

PART ONE

A Layman's View

CHAPTER ONE

Introduction to Telecomputing

Two trends in technology are rapidly coming together to change your life: the evolution of the ordinary telephone system, and the increased use of personal computers. Anyone familiar with these two technologies, and anyone who can combine them with a modem, will be able to access a worldwide library of information beyond anything yet available in the history of mankind. Thousands of mainframe computers and millions of personal computers will someday be networked together via a global communications network to produce a planetary supercomputer of incalculable size and diversity that will contain the knowledge collected and catalogued over the past thousand years. Almost all known facts and ideas will be available from the desktop of any individual who knows how to locate and access information from this global database. Of course, what anyone will do with all this data is still a mystery. Nonetheless, it's nice to know we will be able to get it if we want it.

Unfortunately, not everyone will have the knowledge necessary to access this extensive source. We are slowly evolving toward a two-class computer society. Inevitably, the group that masters the basics of PC communications and the emerging related access tools will be the information "have's." Those who can't, or won't take the time to learn about this trend, will be the "have-not's." Indeed, one of the existing barriers to widespread use of telecommunications technology has been user fear of, or frustration with the modem and telecommunications link.

This book provides you with the basic survival skills you need to get started in PC telecommunications.

THE PAST: TELEPHONES

The telephone has brought us all closer. Alexander Graham Bell invented the telephone a bit over a century ago. He envisioned the day when the music of symphonies and orchestras in one city could be piped to another concert hall in an entirely different city, via telephone wire. As commonly happens, the actual application of the invention varied from the original vision of the inventor. The first telephones were expensive, used mostly by businesses and the very wealthy. Today almost everyone has at least one telephone at home, and more and more people are installing phones in their automobiles.

According to the Census Bureau, there are now over 247 million Americans, who each make an average of six calls a day. The United States has over 118 million telephone lines, and 92 percent of all its residences have at least one line. Our nation is crisscrossed with a communications system of copper lines, fiber-optic cables, and satellite uplinks and downlinks.

PERSONAL COMPUTERS

The personal computer appeared at the same time in history as a generation of baby boomers who were turned into gadget fanatics by television and the electronic revolution that followed World War II. When the microcomputer was suggested, thousands of would-be entrepreneurs jumped on the idea in hopes of striking it rich. Bill Gates, the programmer for Ed Robert's Altair 8800, went on to become the billionaire head of Microsoft Corporation. Steve Wozniak, the technical brains behind the original Apple computer, made his millions, held a rock concert, invested fifteen years trying to get a four-year college degree, and now teaches elementary school. His partner Steve Jobs, put out to pasture by the corporation he helped to found, is currently producing the NeXT computer. Many of the main players faded from sight (George Morrow, Adam Osborne, Don Tarbell, Bill Godbout), while new faces took their place (Michael Dell, John Sculley, Mitch Kapor). All the while various microcomputer designs came and went.

Through all this evolution, the smart computer user found the machines to be quite useful—especially for word processing, spreadsheets, databases, accounting, and telecommunications. Over the years the telecommunications capability of the PC has taken a back seat to the flashier desktop publishing fad and, recently, to desktop graphic presentations. The latest hot ticket is multimedia, where a laser disk is hooked to a PC or a Mac.

As the dust settles, we find that telecommunications has been forgotten by the general press and short-sheeted in the trade press. The commonplace local area networks (LANs) garner more attention. A cynic might suggest that the telecommunications world is so grass roots that it doesn't generate enough advertising to deserve the magazines' consideration. This is nonsense. More likely at fault are the trade paper workers themselves, who seldom take part in the PC telecommunications scene, and who therefore are probably less than knowledgeable about it. Dealing with telecommunications can be difficult, even exasperating.

Furthermore, the promised benefits of connecting your PC to the world of on-line databases, E-mail, and inexpensive software have unfortunately fallen a bit short of expectations. This is due to two factors: low modem speeds, and technical complexity due to lack of consistent standards. These two technical weaknesses have hamstrung the development of PC communications.

Modem Speeds

The current analog telephone system cannot carry the DC voltage level changes required for digital data transmission. Telephones are constructed to carry the voice-modulated information generated in human conversation. Digital data, therefore, must first be converted to audio tones that the telephone lines can carry. This conversion of the digital 1s (nominally 5 volts DC) and 0s (nominally 0 volts DC) to audio tones is called *modulation*.

Converting the tones back to digital levels at the other end is called *demodulation.* A device to perform such conversions is called a modulator/demodulator, which of course has been shortened to *modem.*

British Telecom, in 1954, developed the first unit that corresponds directly to our modern concept of a modem. The unit sent data over telephone lines at the then remarkable rate of 110bps (bits per second). During the late 1970s, when the personal computer scene was born, modems from Hayes and other manufacturers were in use. The standard high speed was 300bps, with some modems achieving a nonstandard 600bps. The advent of the IBM PC saw modem technology essentially stuck at the 300bps stage; such modems were available for around $300. They painted characters on the screen at 30 characters per second, a rate equivalent in speed to a 300 words-per-minute typist. This was considered very fast at the time since there were no 300 wpm typists.

Unfortunately, using 300bps modems to access databases, download programs, or even chat on line became maddening after a very brief period of use. A 100K file (one kilobyte = 1024 characters) required nearly an hour to download, during which time the machine could not be used for anything else. Text from a service such as CompuServe was displayed across the screen at about two and one-half seconds per line. Most individuals could read the text more quickly than it typed out.

The 1200bps modem helped somewhat; lines appeared on the screen at a rate of about two per second. Text scrolled up the screen one line at a time, rather than creeping across one character at a time. But a 100K file still required about 17 minutes to download, and the early 1200bps modems cost between $600 and $800.

As modem prices fell, the 1200bps unit became the standard for speed. The then pricey new 2400bps modem arrived, and became the "Cadillac" of modems, at $600 to $800. Data now appeared as full, scrolling screens, rather than scrolling lines or characters. And the 100K file transfer time was reduced to a nearly bearable seven or eight minutes.

Currently, 2400bps modems cost $125 or less and seem to be the standard modem speed. Newer, "high-speed" modems (9600bps and up) are appearing in the $600 to $800 range. At 9600bps, data appears on screen at high speed, with just a glimpse of a scrolling screen. A 100K file transfer is accomplished in around two minutes.

The evolution in modem speed/price ratios is in large part the driving force behind the current reemergence of PC telecommunications from its closet of obscurity. As modem speeds increase, the utility of downloading software, on-line communications, database access, and so forth, becomes more important. The trend toward even greater speeds will undoubtedly continue, until personal computers can communicate over a national telecommunications system at essentially the bus I/O speed of the computer. At that point, you won't be able to detect any difference in operation between data retrieved from your own disk drive, and that from another machine a thousand miles away.

The current horizon in communication speeds is linked to the development of the Integrated Services Digital Network (ISDN) currently just coming to market via the local Bell operating companies. These essentially digital telephone links, capable of 64,000bps communication, eliminate the need to modulate data into tones (see the ISDN discussion in Chapter 25). At 64Kbps (kilobits-per-second), PC communication should become nearly effortless. Senator Albert Gore of Tennessee is advocating the development of a national data communications highway connecting universities, laboratories, and educational facilities, transmitting at a rate of 3 gigabits (10 to the ninth power) per second. That's fast enough to send the Encyclopædia Britannica over the telephone from one computer to another in less than a second!

Communications Standards

The other problem stunting the growth of PC communications is telecommunications complexity. This complexity has been caused by a lack of real standards. Actually, there are far too many standards. This is partly a by-product of the technological advances. We could have all settled for some very standard 300bps technology but the lure of 1200bps, 2400bps, 9600bps, and now even higher speeds such as that achieved by the Telebit 19,200bps modem has been too much to resist.

For example, some computers communicate by sending seven data bits, a stop bit, and a parity bit to represent a single character/byte of data. Others use eight data bits, a stop bit, and a parity bit, but ignore the parity bit entirely. Others use the parity bit to check if the sum of all data bits equals 0 (even parity) or 1 (odd parity). (These terms will be explained in detail later in the book. For now, just consider that there are a number of ways to transmit a single byte of data.) When two systems use different formats for transmitted data, no accurate communication takes place. The screen displays garbage or nothing at all.

One standard that developed early and helped save the telecommunications arena from complete chaos was the Hayes AT (ATTENTION) command set, popularized by Hayes Microcomputer Products. It was developed to allow commands to be sent from a PC keyboard to a modem, in order to control modem operation. You can dial a telephone number, or disconnect, or answer an incoming call just by typing from the PC. This command set is also used to *initialize* or set up a modem to work with your particular software program. Since the popularization of the Hayes AT command set, few modems are sold without this capability. The command set has been expanded by some manufacturers and minimized by others.

The disparity in standards worsens each year as modem manufacturers add new features and capabilities to their products. The biggest hurdle the new modem user must face is divining the "initialization string" required to get a modem to work with a particular communications software program. This sometimes requires that the user actually read the documentation that comes with both the modem and the telecomm program. People hate to do this. Thousands of perfectly intelligent and capable individuals give up in disgust or frustration after an afternoon of fiddling with the modem.

If you have faced this hurdle yourself, be assured that *you are not the problem.* This initialization/installation chaos is ridiculous. The bad news is there is no relief in sight. Additional options, increased capabilities, and more speed unfortunately result in more difficult installation/initialization procedures. The good news is that once you do get the modem and software working together at least once, the software then automatically sets up the modem for each subsequent use. You will be free of these tasks until you change software or change modems. This book will make modem installation and use a lot easier, and give you the confidence you need.

Once you're ready to go, PC telecommunications offers you a real treat. It may be the most fun you can have with a computer, and the most valuable use for the machine.

THE TELECOMMUNICATIONS REVOLUTION

Today you see statistics that tell you the amount of recorded "knowledge" in the world is doubling each six years. However, this growth of information is rapidly decreasing in usefulness, because facts needed by a particular individual or business are frequently lost in the deluge of billions of pages of information. The new tools for dealing with this inundation of information must allow near instantaneous data transmission and powerful means of selecting the particular item of interest from the flood of information noise. Once these are developed, you will be able to obtain the answer to just about anything. Bringing order to this chaos requires improved data com munications and hordes of "information specialists."

Luckily, this process is beginning. There are now over 3000 databases of information available on line, via hundreds of commercial on-line services. There are over 10,000 public electronic bulletin boards—most of them operating free of charge or at very reasonable annual rates. On-line information is already a multibillion-dollar industry. You will learn about these services in later chapters of this book.

For the entrepreneur, PC telecommunications is a new way to make money. Thousands of individuals are making a good living by learning how to navigate complex on-line services to extract information for businesses.

In business, if none of your competitors know anything, you have the advantage. Unfortunately, this never lasts. Individuals have the option of remaining aloof from the PC telecommunications developments. They can continue to work in the same way for some years with little sudden impact other than an uncomfortable feeling that they may be missing something. For the manufacturer, information is vital to continuing in business. Those who can access the information quickly and efficiently have a powerful advantage over those who choose not to.

In another arena, PC telecommunications technology allows any individual to inexpensively set up shop and publish information electronically for a profit. In this way you can become an on-line service/database and charge others for access to *your* information. How can you possibly compete with the giant database corporations? Quite easily. You simply specialize in one narrow field of knowledge. Believe it or not, most of the giants have a difficult time acquiring, organizing, and maintaining specialized information. Generally, they just buy it from individuals who have created it. For a few thousand dollars and a few years of diligent effort, you can become the authority on a specialized field of study, collect and organize the information into an accessible and presentable form, and then mine that database of information.

Once you become known as the central organization point for information on wild mushroom hunting, hot air ballooning, gourmet rice recipes, pheasant hunting, sculling, model airplane flying, bocce ball, home winemaking, ballroom dancing, ceramics, fly fishing, the history of the Yale presidents, or wilderness survival, data will become progressively easier to gather, as others with similar interests will actually bring information to you. Of the 250 million people in the nation, those interested in your specialty will pay you to gather and organize information for them.

And the combined technology of PCs and telecommunications will help you do this. As long-distance communications become easier, and more individuals join the PC telecommunications revolution, someday instantaneous access will become a reality, via a national telecommunications network. Postage and ink and paper and printing expenses that previously made it difficult to launch a successful specialty publication will be reduced or eliminated by electronic publishing. With a couple of PCs, a couple of telephone lines, and a couple of modems, you will be able to serve a nation of mushroom hunters quite profitably. This will likely lead to an explosion in specialty publishing via electronic media.

ON-LINE COMMUNICATIONS

So what exactly is the advantage of hooking up a modem to your desktop computer this afternoon? Why go to the trouble of learning to use a technology that is changing and evolving so quickly? There are so many advantages to on-line communications today that you're cheating yourself if you don't use them. Available services include current information databases from newspapers, information archive databases, electronic mail, communications utilities, software available for downloading, social contact services, employment services, and want ads.

The key to understanding electronic media is understanding the appeal of immediacy. Headline news is delivered on line with the same immediacy as television, but in a format you can save, combine, collect, print, catalog, or otherwise retain and use as you see fit. A number of newspapers are available on line right now: *USA Today, The Wall Street Journal, Investors Daily,* the *St. Louis Post-Dispatch, The New York Times,* and *The Washington Post.* The actual newswire sources for most of the newspapers in the country are now available on line, including Associated Press, United Press International, Reuters, Dow Jones News, Xinhua Press from China, Agence France Presse, TASS News from USSR, Kyodo News of Japan, Deutsche Presse Agentur of West Germany, and Notimex of Mexico City. Additionally, numerous on-line sources provide stock quotes, either up-to-the-minute or delayed fifteen minutes. A number of vendors provide National Weather Service data, including software to produce amazing color weather maps on line, with real-time radar weather data.

Another inherent advantage of electronic media is that it can be used to archive large amounts of data. An entire year of a print publication can be stored on an area of magnetic media the size of a half-dollar coin. Once stored, electronic text data is accessible through an array of search tools.

With just a few well-designed search commands, you can scour literally thousands of pages of text, covering many years of data, to locate specific information you need.

DATA TIMES of Oklahoma operates an on-line service specifically to archive over 200 local, regional, and national newspapers, and is becoming a favorite research resource for journalists from many of those same papers. NEWSNET operates an on-line archive containing several hundred newsletters on a fascinating array of specialized topics—many of which are expensive ($500 or $600) investment newsletters in their print format. Dow Jones News offers an immensely valuable archive of historical stock quotes you can use to quickly find the daily closing price for the past year of any particular stock. Other services have selected stock data going back 50 years.

There are over 3000 on-line databases currently available offering both archived and up-to-the-minute data on medicine, law, legislation, business regulations, economic data, and so forth. Services such as WESTLAW and LEXIS have forever altered the field of legal research. On-line legislative information services are also becoming popular; they contain the voting records of legislators, the complete text of proposed bills, and even data on monies received by legislators from each Political Action Committee (PAC). One service now publishes the *Federal Register* on line each day by noon. The listing of available information services is nearly endless.

SOFTWARE DOWNLOADS

The commercial software industry provides the programs needed to accomplish tasks more efficiently with desktop computers. Often, however, it's difficult to tell if a package is appropriate unless we buy it and try it out. This drawback, combined with high prices and an endless selection, make it difficult to choose software; and for the software developer, the million dollars or more required for an effective marketing campaign may mean an unsuccessful product—no matter how technically elegant and useful a program may be.

Shareware

Andrew Fluegelman is credited with originating the concept of *shareware* software distribution, with his PC-Talk program. (As discussed in Chapter

11, Jim Button was just as responsible for this idea.) People who use software have a tendency to "share" it, by making copies for their friends. Although in violation of copyright law, this software "piracy" became extremely widespread. Most commercial software companies spoke of piracy in terms of "lost sales," and it became an excuse in firms that had suffered real financial losses for any of the normal business reasons. Actually, the piracy was creating sales. Many individuals tried out a friend's software. If it did the job, they would purchase a real copy, to get on the list for updates, documentation, and telephone support.

Seeing this scenario of software "testing," Fluegelman and Button both encouraged people to copy and share their programs. If users liked the program, they were asked to send in a small payment for continued use. Many users did, and the shareware concept was born. Today, many fledgling software publishers distribute shareware. Rather than $795, the "registration fee" for shareware is typically in the $35 to $75 range. In return for your fee, you usually receive printed documentation and some telephone support.

Over time, an interesting dichotomy has appeared. Shareware authors who don't make much money claim that "everyone" is using their software and not paying for it. They say they're being cheated, and the system stinks. Meanwhile, a good number of shareware producers pocket over a million dollars a year; they like the concept quite well.

Shareware has since been tied to on-line services. The fastest way to distribute shareware is by uploading it to a few major *electronic bulletin board systems* (BBSs) or on-line services. One of the immediate advantages you will have with a modem is access to a vast library of software programs you can download and test. The programs you will find and use are easily worth the $35 to register your copy for future updates.

The shareware download function has become one of the driving forces behind on-line communications. Nearly all the popular consumer-oriented on-line services, such as GEnie, CompuServe, and Delphi feature large libraries of shareware software available for download. Many people join such services solely for access to these software libraries. Almost all of the thousands of BBSs offer some shareware for download, often at no charge. One system, Exec-PC in Shorewood, Wisconsin, has a library of over 100,000 titles stored on three gigabytes of hard disk space. The cost for access to this software treasure trove is $60 yearly.

ELECTRONIC MAIL/COMMUNICATIONS UTILITIES

Electronic mail is here. It is not yet perfect, but it is getting better, and a number of accessory functions have been added to make it more useful. Electronic mail (or E-mail, as it has come to be known) allows you to send messages, memos, and reports to another individual on line. This is inherently more efficient than telephone tag or even voice message services. You compose and send a written message, and it waits in the addressee's mailbox to be read. With this inherent storage capability, time and distance lose some of their power over your activities.

Until just recently, the recipient typically had to have a mailbox on the same E-mail service as the sender. Now many of the larger E-mail services are forming gateways between services, so that you can send messages to someone on another service. In addition, utilities are being added to connect E-mail to the real world more effectively. For example, on most services, you can have an E-mail message delivered by E-mail, telex, or facsimile, or even printed out on a laser printer and sent through the regular mail. In this way, you can reach someone who has an E-mail account, a fax machine, or just a metal mailbox in rural Georgia.

SOCIAL AND PROFESSIONAL CONTACT

Currently, about 20 percent of the households in the country have some form of personal computer, and roughly 20 percent of those are equipped with modems. This would indicate that roughly 5 percent of the entire national population is capable of operating on line, or about 12 million individuals. Roughly 10 percent of those could be considered "active" on-line users, leaving us with an estimated universe of perhaps 1.5 million people on line. Although this is a small percentage of the population, it is a very select group. These people are usually educated, technical, and have a high income. Many of these people interact, develop relationships, and even launch various joint business ventures—without ever meeting face to face.

There have even been numerous marriages of couples who initially met on line. We assume that they met in person after their nuptials, and liked what they saw, but who knows? In some cases the actual ceremonies have been held on line, with the minister typing in the vows!

Even in more conventional settings, you quite likely will meet others with interests similar to your own. Most BBS and on-line services offer "forums" or Special Interest Groups (SIGs). People of similar professions can exchange tips and discuss mutual concerns. Many people establish entire networks of friends and business associates, often entering into work agreements on line. It is becoming quite acceptable to transact business with a network of individuals entirely by on-line messages, voice telephone, and facsimile transmission.

A popular forum is emerging on virtually all commercial consumer services; it revolves around what is becoming known as the *homebased professional.* This is a small but growing segment of the labor force that operates businesses or otherwise works from home.

ACCESS TO SERVICES

A growing number of service businesses are entering the on-line field as a way of catering to their clientele. It is now possible to perform many banking functions from your desktop computer, including paying your bills by having a service actually print and mail the checks, and deduct the funds from your bank account. You can make airline travel reservations, arrange for rental cars and hotels, and even order a delivery of flowers. You can buy and sell stocks with your computer. And a growing number of mail-order firms are finding it easier and less costly to fill orders entered and stored on a computer, than to use real live people on the toll-free order lines. So far, haircuts haven't done too well on line and gardening services have been slow to automate.

ENTERTAINMENT

On-line entertainment is another popular application for modem use. Games, derided by "serious" on-line aficionados, are nonetheless a popular pastime for many. And games are growing more sophisticated.

Commercial services are implementing state-of-the-art games that require callers to use dedicated software to participate in interactive simulations. GEnie now has an "airwars" game that lets one caller be the bombardier, another the pilot, and another the tail gunner on a World War II bomber. Other callers occupy fighter aircraft, and the software creates a visual scene quite like what you would see from that position. This simulation is completely interactive. If another caller makes a left turn, you see it on your screen. If another player veers toward you and begins firing, you see that, too, and your countermoves and returned fire are seen by the other players. As modem speeds increase, these games will improve even more.

A number of multiline BBSs are running interactive pseudogambling operations, in which several callers can play roulette, blackjack, and craps on line. The graphics for many of these games are improving dramatically.

Of a more conservative bent are the adventure-style games, in which you receive text messages on screen and reply with instructions. Role-playing games are a popular variation, such as Dungeons and Dragons where players assume identities and react in a manner consistent with their characters. A text adventure game popular on many BBSs is TRADE-WARS, an interactive, galactic space war/science fiction simulation, in which you must trade the cargo you receive at one planet for the produce of the next.

Finally, on-line chess games are available for the truly unhurried who prefer the invisibility of on-line play.

This first introductory chapter has given you a short overview of what you will experience in the world of PC telecommunications. The remaining chapters of this book provide a more detailed examination of electronic bulletin board systems, commercial services, shareware software, and many of the other subjects mentioned in this overview. Hopefully, you'll become one of the modem literate, and join the crowd of advanced computer users.

CHAPTER TWO

Quick Set-Up

The goal of this chapter is to familiarize you with the basics of telecommunications hardware and software, and to get you on line.

THE FASTEST START OF ALL: ASK AN EXPERT

Like any other area of human knowledge, the fastest way to learn is to find a good teacher. This book is an excellent reference for some of the complexities of telecommunications, and you'll find the answers to most of the problems you may come up against. Keep in mind, however, that some problems require the assistance of an expert. In that case, this book gives you enough information to find and communicate your needs to a mentor.

THE FIRST STEP: DOS AND YOU

Okay, maybe you don't know much about DOS, or you haven't a clue to the amount of RAM your machine has, or what processing chip is in your machine. It's important to know these things in order to purchase new software intelligently, and to communicate with others successfully. You can ask the computer store where you purchased your machine, or look in the documents that came with it.

To learn more about these "techie" details, read a few magazines, join a user group, purchase new software or add-on hardware, or talk to a computer-rabid friend. Let's face it, you probably know what make your car is, whether it's foreign or domestic, and if there's a four-, six-, or eight-cylinder engine in it. For a computer user, DOS and a computer's internals are the basics that need to be learned.

There are some excellent programs that check your system internally and report what you have installed. Call around and find a computer store that will point you toward such a program, or ask a local user group. (See Appendix G for suggestions on how to find a user group.)

The DOS operating system is a set of instructions consisting of a few hundred commands. There is no need to memorize all of them. You'll need to understand 10 or 15 fundamental commands to set up a modem and telecommunications program.

One DOS command you probably already know is the "log to drive" command. Each PC disk drive is designated by a letter followed by a colon, such as A:, B:, or C:. Drives A: and B: are usually reserved for floppy disks. Drive C: and any additional drives are usually reserved for a hard disk or RAM disks. To log on to Drive C: from Drive A:

A>	This is the DOS prompt
A>**C:**	You enter **C:** and a carriage return to change drives
C>	This is the new DOS prompt

So now you know about the DOS commands, drive letters, the DOS prompt, and logging on to different drives. You are ready for the most commonly used DOS command, the DIR command. This command gives you a detailed listing of the files on the disk. With it, you can figure out exactly what's on each hard drive or floppy disk.

C>   Here is your DOS prompt

You probably should change your prompt at this point. Today everyone is using the pg prompt, which gives a more detailed DOS prompt so that you can tell what subdirectory you are in. The installation program does this for you.

C>	This is the standard DOS prompt
C>PROMPT PG	This is the command you type to enhance your DOS prompt
C:\>	This is the enhanced DOS prompt. The :\ has been added to the standard prompt to indicate you are in the root directory. If you are in a subdirectory such as \modem, your prompt will look like this: C:\MODEM>

Now back to the favorite DOS command, DIR. To get a list of what is on your disk, enter the following command at the DOS prompt:

C:\>	This is your DOS prompt
C:\>DIR	This is the command to enter for a directory list

Your system responds by showing five columns of information about the files you have on the disk. At the beginning of the list are the volume label (name of your disk) and the drive letter designator. The five-column DIR list follows.

On this list, you will find your subdirectories and files. A subdirectory will have a sixth item that looks like this: <DIR> (take a look at the list below).

```
Volume in drive C is ZENITH_286#
Directory of C:\
BATCH        <DIR>              9-15-89      7:28a
CONFMT       <DIR>              9-15-89      7:01a
COPYIIPC     <DIR>              9-15-89      7:01a
COPYQM       <DIR>              9-15-89      7:01a
DOS          <DIR>              9-15-89      6:47a
DOSHELP      <DIR>              9-15-89      7:06a
DOSLF        <DIR>              6-11-89      6:16a
DOSLH        <DIR>              6-11-89      6:16a
MODEM        <DIR>              9-15-89      7:20a
MTOOLS       <DIR>              9-15-89      7:20a
NU45         <DIR>              9-15-89      7:08a
MODEM        <DIR>              9-15-89      7:12a
AUTOEXEC BAT           177      9-15-89     12:24p
COMMAND COM          25532     10-31-88      2:54p
CONFIG SYS              59      9-15-89      3:11p
15 File(s)        2084864 bytes free
```

The following diagram shows some of these columns with labels to give you an idea of what this information is

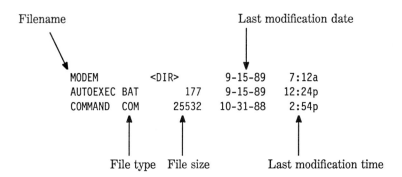

To change subdirectories, enter

```
C:\>
C:\>cd \modem
```

To format a floppy disk, enter

```
C:\>
C:\>Format A:
```

This should get you started with some basics of DOS. If you are new to these systems, read any good book on MS-DOS.

STEP TWO: SELECT YOUR HARDWARE

For telecommunications you need a computer, a modem (external or internal), software, and a telephone line. If you haven't already selected a computer, it's time to shop around to find one that fits your specific needs.

External Modems

To communicate, you will need either an external or internal modem. External modems reside outside of the computer system and are connected to your computer with a cable.

Advantages of External Modems

The advantages of having an external modem are

- *Easy installation* An external modem is self-contained. You put it on a desk, plug it into an AC outlet, hook up to the phone, and use a cable to connect the modem to the serial port of your computer.

- *Status lights* Most external modems have a row of LED indicator lights that let you know the modem is doing something. If the RD (for "Receive Data") light is lit, a file transfer is in progress. When it turns off, the data flow has stopped.

- *External Controls* Most modems have a row of very tiny switches (DIP switches). These switches are used to adjust the various modem settings. (Newer modems are able to modify switch settings through the communications software.)

- *Portability* External modems can be used on various computers. If you are planning to change your computer, or if you have several machines, one of which is used to communicate only occasionally, save some cash and buy one external modem.

Disadvantages of External Modem

The main disadvantages of having an external modem include

- *Separate Power Supply* External modems need electrical current to operate. The competition for outlet space may include the monitor, the computer, one or more printers, a lamp, the telephone answering machine, and a radio. An external modem is one more thing to remember to turn on and turn off.

- *Spaghetti-Cables* An external modem adds several more wires and cables under your table or desk. A tangle of wires can be easily damaged, or accidentally unplugged.

- *Serial Port Requirement* An external modem must connect to the serial port. If you also have a printer that uses the serial port, you must unplug the printer to plug in the modem.

Portable Modems

Small, palm-sized, external modems are now on the market. These modems are designed for use with laptop and notebook computers. They plug into the serial port and are battery powered, or can use power in the phone line itself.

Internal Modems

An internal modem is a printed circuit board. This board, or card, is designed to plug into an empty expansion slot inside your computer. There are a wide variety of modem cards.

All modem cards are machine specific. (You cannot use an old Apple IIe modem board in a new IBM PC.) There may be DIP switches, or a combination of jumpers and switches, that must be appropriately adjusted before installation.

Advantages of Internal Modems

The main advantages of using an internal modem are

- *No Clutter*   Once installed, an internal modem becomes part of the machine.

- *No Separate Power Supply*   Internal modems use power from the computer itself. When the computer is off, the modem is off.

- *Free Serial Port*   Internal modems do not use the serial port. The card has a built-in modular telephone jack that acts as the modem's own COM port. The serial port can thus be used for a printer, a mouse, or other device.

Disadvantages of Internal Modems

The disadvantages of an internal modem include

- *Difficult to Service*   To check the modem or change a setting, you have to open the computer case.

- *No Status Lights*   There is nothing visible to tell you that the modem is working when it's supposed to be. It's not as flashy and problems may not be as immediately obvious.

- *Machine Specific*   Internal modems cannot be passed around. If you change machines, you will most likely need to change modems, too.

How Fast Do Modems Run?

Modems communicate in bits per second (bps), which is also referred to as the baudrate. There are some very slow (usually very old) modems that slog

along at 300bps. Anything slower than 2400bps is on its way to obsoles-
cence.

There are some great deals on 1200bps modems. Keep in mind, however,
that if you plan on regular, long-distance data transfers, you'll quickly pay
in telephone connect charges the price difference between the 1200 and
2400bps modems. Modems with speeds of 9600bps and 14400bps are also
available. The faster the modem speed, the shorter the connect time—and
of course, the greater the initial cost.

For most uses, 2400bps is standard. With their improved technology,
these modems transmit data more reliably than the older 300 or 1200bps
modems. The 2400bps modems are able to connect with slower speed
modems if they need to.

MODEM INSTALLATION

The challenge of telecommunications is the initial setup. To get that first
connection is usually the most difficult. After that, it's really not much more
complicated than using a telephone.

Sometimes the computer store will install the modem for you, especially
if you buy the computer and modem together. If not, most modems come
with some sort of installation instructions. There will be a diagram of the
right switch settings. There should also be a telephone number for technical
support if you have a question or need help.

Set the switches, and make sure they are firmly set. They are like little
light switches and must be either ON or OFF; "in between" is the same as
OFF.

Internal Modems

Internal modems are plugged into the inside of the computer. Slide the case
off carefully, and plug the modem into an open slot. Note which COM port
you've plugged it into. (The telecommunications software will need to look
for the proper COM port to work correctly.) Most modems connect to
COM2. (Newer machines may have ports up to COM8 available.) If you are
in doubt about what all this means, refer to the computer's manual. It will
have diagrams of the slots, and a description of the COM (communications)
port setup.

Try not to bump or wiggle any other existing cards. The modem card should fit snugly in. The slot will resist the card, so firmly, but gently, pop the card in. It's like the connection of an electrical plug into a wall socket. If for some reason someone instructs you to "reseat" the card, what they mean is to pull the card out of the slot and put it back in again. Remember, it usually won't slip out easily.

Once the card is in, replace the computer cover. Now plug a telephone line into the "To Line" jack. Connect the telephone to the modular jack opening labeled "To Phone." If your telephone wiring is an old-fashioned four-prong connector, get an adapter or put in a modular jack.

External Modems

The external modem attaches to the serial port of the computer with a cable. Plug the modem into an electrical power source and into the telephone line. (These modems use a small square transformer like those with many small household appliances. These transformers feel warm to the touch when they've been plugged in for a while.) There are two square female jacks in the modem. One is to connect a telephone, if you desire, and the other is the "To Line." Use the "To Line" to connect your modem to the outside world.

INSTALLING YOUR TELECOMMUNICATIONS PROGRAM

Some modems are bundled with a telecommunications program, also known as communications software, or a "comm" program. The modem and comm program are guaranteed to work with each other. It seems pretty simple, and is probably a good way to begin. On the downside, as with many "free" product bonuses, the program may not have many desirable features. Happily, you aren't locked into any one program, because your modem—ANY modem—will work with a variety of telecommunications software.

Telecommunications programs are constantly rewritten and upgraded. Few of these programs are difficult to learn, so installing new versions is not as complicated as changing to a new spreadsheet program or learning about desktop publishing. Chapter 4 has a wealth of detailed information on communications programs and their features.

Modem Software

Don't let new software paralyze you. Every new program can seem completely foreign, confusing, and frustrating. Software vendors try their best to provide attractive and understandable manuals. The best advice is to play with the program, thumb through the manual, and call for help (to the technical support offered by the software manufacturer, or a friend who uses the program).

Telecommunications software, like most software, must be configured for your system. Some comm programs have a simple step-by-step installation program that asks you many questions, which may not make sense to you at all. (Choose the default when in doubt.) The purpose of this software is to tell the modem how and what numbers to dial, how to transfer data (called *protocols*), and when to hang up. That's pretty simple—the seemingly vague "information" that modems require in order to pass data back and forth are the *parameters* (which only a few real techies understand) and other "little details."

Command Menu Help Screens

Any good telecomm program includes a command menu that doubles as a Help screen. If you read nothing else in the program's manual, take the trouble to find out how to get to that menu. Often, as in Qmodem (see Figure 2-1) and Procomm, the primary Help screen leads into secondary help systems. Other programs, such as Telix (see Figure 2-2), rely on a multilayered menu system in which selecting a command leads to other menus.

Setup Screens

All telecomm programs need to be configured and will have setup screens to help you do it. Qmodem uses a series of pull-down menus; Figure 2-3 shows part of a long list of modems that Qmodem will set up automatically. Picking "Configure" from the Telix command summary pulls up a selection box (see Figure 2-4). Procomm uses a similar selection box, from which the "General Options" screen is shown in Figure 2-5.

Dialing Directories

Though you can dial any number directly from the terminal screen with most modems, it is easier and much more reliable to use a dialing directory. A directory for Procomm is shown in Figure 2-6. It shows names, numbers, and settings for each entry. Note that to the right, a column is reserved for

Figure 2-1

Qmodem command menu

```
═══════════════════════ COMMAND MENU ═══════════════════
──────────────── BEFORE ───────────────        ──────── TOGGLES ────────
Alt-D  Phone Directory  Alt-G  Term Emulation   Alt-0  Session Log
──────────────── DURING ───────────────        Alt-1  Backspace DEL/^H
Alt-C  Clear Screen     ^Home  Capture File     Alt-5  Host Mode
Alt-F  Execute Script   ^End   Send BREAK       Alt-8  Hi-Bit Stripping
Alt-Q  QuickLearn Mode  PgUp   Upload Files     Alt-9  Printer Echo
Alt-S  Split Screen     PgDn   Download Files   Alt-B  Beeps and Bells
Alt-T  Screen Dump      ^PgUp  PgUp (alternate) Alt-E  Half/Full Duplex
↑      Scroll-back      ^PgDn  PgDn (alternate) Alt-I  Order Information
──────────────── AFTER ───────────────         Alt-M  ANSI Music Playing
Alt-H  Hang-up Modem    Alt-X  Exit Qmodem      Alt-U  Scroll-back Record
                                                Alt-Z  Xon/Xoff Flow-ctrl.
──────────────── SETUP ───────────────         Alt-=  DoorWay Mode
Alt-A  Translate Tables Alt-N  Configure Qmodem Alt--  Status Line
Alt-J  Function Keys    Alt-P  Change Baud Rate ShTab  CR/CRLF Mode
Alt-K  Change COM Port                          Alt-2  80x25 (EGA/VGA)
                                                Alt-4  80x43/50 (EGA/VGA)
──────────────── DOS ───────────────           ──────── COPYRIGHT ────────
Alt-L  Change Drive     Alt-V  View/Edit File   The Forbin Project, Inc.
Alt-O  Change Directory Alt-W  List Directory   Post Office Box 702
Alt-R  DOS Shell        Alt-Y  Delete a File    Cedar Falls, IA  50613

═════════════ Qmodem SST Version 4.1b Production  Compiled 10/06/89 ═══F1 Help═
▓▓▓▓▓▓▓▓▓▓ Select a function,  F1 for Help  -or-  [ESC] to TERMINAL Mode ▓▓▓▓▓▓▓▓
```

Figure 2-2

Telix command summary

```
┌──────────────────────────────────────────────────────────────────────┐
│                  Telix SE v1.00 Command Summary                        │
│                                                                        │
│          Main Functions                        Other functions         │
│                                                                        │
│ Dialing directory..Alt-D  Queue Redial #s....Alt-Q │ Local echo.......Alt-E│
│ Send files.........Alt-S  Receive files......Alt-R │ DOS command......Alt-V│
│ Exit Telix.........Alt-X  Run script (Go)....Alt-G │ Run editor.......Alt-A│
│ Comm Parameters....Alt-P  cOnfigure Telix....Alt-O │ Screen Image.....Alt-I│
│ Key defs./macros...Alt-K  Terminal emulation.Alt-T │ Chat Mode........Alt-Y│
│ Capture on/off.....Alt-L  Scroll Back........Alt-B │ Printer on/off...Ctrl-@│
│ DOS Functions......Alt-F  Jump to DOS shell..Alt-J │ Translate Table...Alt-W│
│ Hang-up modem......Alt-H  Clear screen.......Alt-C │ Add LF on/off.Shift-Tab│
│ Usage Log on/off...Alt-U  Misc. functions....Alt-M │ Send BREAK.....Ctrl-End│
│                                                                        │
│             Select function or press Enter for none                    │
│                                                                        │
│ Telix Copyright (C) 1986-89 Exis Inc., P.O. Box 130, West Hill, Ont. M1E 4R4│
├────────────────────────────────────────┬───────────────────────────────┤
│  Time .. 10:02:12    Online .... No     │ Capture ... Off               │
│  Date .. 05-07-90                       │ Printer ... Off               │
│  Baud .. 38400       Terminal .. ANSI-BBS│ Script .... None             │
│  Comm .. N,8,1       Port ...... COM2   │ Reg. Key .. TELIX.KEY         │
│  Echo .. Off         Add LF .... Off    │ Dial Dir .. TELIX.FON         │
└────────────────────────────────────────┴───────────────────────────────┘
```

Figure 2-3

Qmodem setup screen

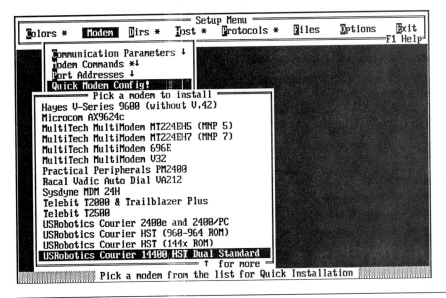

Figure 2-4

Telix selection box

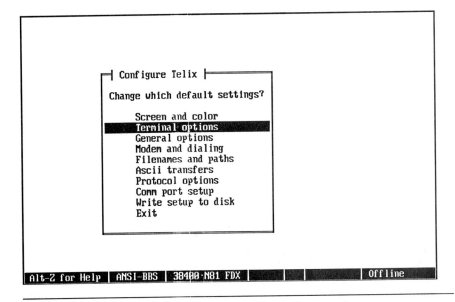

Figure 2-5

Procomm general options

```
PROCOMM PLUS SETUP UTILITY                              GENERAL OPTIONS

A- Exploding windows ... ON        K- Menu line key ....... \

B- Sound effects ....... OFF       L- Snow removal ........ OFF

C- Alarm sound ......... ON        M- Remote commands ..... OFF

D- Alarm time .......... 1   seconds   N- Enhanced kb speedup . ON

E- Translation table ... OFF       O- ANSI compatibility .. 3.x

F- Pause character ..... ^

G- Transmit pacing ..... 0   milliseconds

H- Call logging ........ ON

I- Filename lookup ..... ON

J- Menu line ........... ON

 Alt-Z: Help      Press the letter of the option to change:      Esc: Exit
```

Figure 2-6

Procomm dialing directory

```
DIALING DIRECTORY: BWATCH

      NAME                          NUMBER      BAUD P D S D   SCRIPT
 101 Osprey's Nest             (301)989-9036   1200 N-8-1 F
 102 PDSLO BBS                 (516)938-6722   1200 N-8-1 F
 103 Personal Resource System  (501)442-8777   1200 N-8-1 F
 104 Photo*Life                (301)270-2638   1200 N-8-1 F
 105 PHYSICS Forum BBS         (413)545-1959   1200 N-8-1 F
 106 PKWare BBS                (414)352-7176   1200 N-8-1 F
 107 Popular Mechanics Online  (212)502-0369   1200 N-8-1 F
 108 ProComm Support BBS       (314)474-8477   1200 N-8-1 F
 109 Public Brand Software BB  (317)856-2087   1200 N-8-1 F
 110 Publishers Information    (312)342-6919   1200 N-8-1 F

PgUp Scroll Up    ↑/↓ Select Entry   R Revise Entry    C Clear Marked
PgDn Scroll Dn    Space Mark Entry    E Erase Entry(s)   L Print Directory
Home First Page   Enter Dial Selected F Find Entry       P Dialing Codes
End Last Page     D Dial Entry(s)     A Find Again       X Exchange Dir
Esc Exit          M Manual Dial       G Goto Entry       T Toggle Display

Choice:

PORT: COM2  SETTINGS:  2400 N-8-1  DUPLEX: FULL  DIALING CODES: AB
```

script names. Any good telecomm program will let you create "scripts" to log you on to a BBS automatically by sending it your name and password when prompted.

When you start to dial one of the entries, most programs report their progress on the screen.

Session Settings

Your program will come with certain default parameters or settings, which you may change from one session to the next depending upon whom you call. The settings most likely to change can be adjusted individually for each entry in the dialing directory. For now, just remember that the default settings on most telecomm programs are N-8-1, for no parity, 8-bit words, 1 stop bit. This is the setting for nearly all BBSs.

Figure 2-7 shows the Procomm settings window. The speed is set for 2400bps, N-8-1, com port 2.

The best settings for general use are N-8-1, the highest speed your modem can support (usually 2400bps), and the proper com port. If you seem to have a problem talking to your modem, make sure that last setting is correct.

Figure 2-7

Procomm session settings window

```
Session settings window:

                      CURRENT SETTINGS:  2400,N,8,1,COM2

       BAUD RATE    PARITY        DATA BITS   STOP BITS    PORT

       1)    300    N) NONE       Alt-7) 7    Alt-1) 1     F1) COM1
       2)   1200    E) EVEN       Alt-8) 8    Alt-2) 2     F2) COM2
       3)   2400    O) ODD                                 F3) COM3
       4)   4800    M) MARK                                F4) COM4
       5)   9600    S) SPACE                               F5) COM5
       6)  19200                                           F6) COM6
       7)  38400                                           F7) COM7
       8)  57600    Alt-N) N/8/1                           F8) COM8
       9) 115200    Alt-E) E/7/1

       Esc) Exit    Alt-S) Save and Exit   YOUR CHOICE:


                           LINE/PORT SETUP
```

Software set for the wrong com port is the single most common problem users encounter.

Upload and Download Protocols

When you send or receive files from another computer, you need an error-checking routine or *protocol* to make sure telephone line noise doesn't hash the file. Snaps, crackles, pops, and line echoes can result in disaster. To catch such errors, all telecomm programs should offer a variety of protocols. If your program doesn't offer at least Xmodem, get another one. Figure 2-8 shows protocols available for up- and downloading in Telix.

The difference between uploads and downloads is important. If you confuse the two, a file transfer will go haywire. Here's the difference: the

---

Figure 2-8

Download protocols in Telix

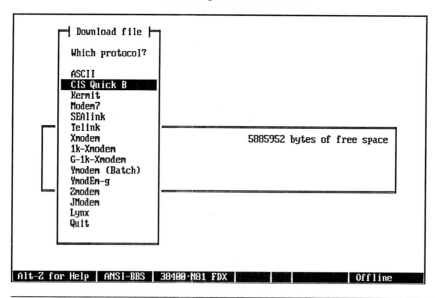

Caller is always DOWN, because he or she always calls the host UP. Put another way:

- *Downloads* send files from the host down to the Caller. If you call a BBS or information service to get a file, you will be downloading from the host.

- *Uploads* send files from the Caller up to the host. If you make the call and send the file, you are uploading to the host.

Chat Mode

Sometimes you and the person on the other end of the connection will need to type messages back and forth. That's called "chatting," for obvious reasons. The problem with chatting is that if one of you interrupts the other, the letters on the screen will get scrambled. Many programs include a Chat mode to help overcome this problem. When in Chat mode the screen is split in two, with messages from the other person displayed on top. You type your replies in the bottom window and, when the other person is finished, you press ENTER to send the entire message line at once, with no garble. Chat mode makes on-line conversations easier for both parties.

READ.ME

Good Manners: Don't Interrupt

How can you tell during a chat whether the other person has finished? If you guess wrong and they're simply pausing to think for a moment, the result can get pretty garbled.

Telecommunicators use a couple of signals to tell each other when they're through typing. The first signal is to hit the ENTER key two or three times. This leaves a blank space before the next person's remarks. The second signal is to add "ga" at the end, standing for Go Ahead.

When you see the cursor drop a couple of lines, or if the other person sends a line ending with "ga," that means it's your turn.

WHEN YOU'RE READY TO GO ON LINE

Once your software is installed and your modem is hooked up, you're ready to go on line. Go ahead and tell your modem to dial a number; if you don't seem to be getting any response, first make sure you have plugged the modem into the phone line. If that's not the problem, refer to Chapter 27, "Troubleshooting Your Modem." Most problems are easily solved with a little thought and patience.

One last thing—when you get everything running, *don't forget to save your settings*. The comm software manual will tell you how to do that. There are few things more frustrating on a PC than to get a new program up and running just the way you like it, and then turn off the computer— only to realize you'll have to do it all over again the next day.

CHAPTER THREE

Installing Modems and Software

Setting yourself up to communicate using a PC isn't easy, but it's not hard, either. It's just that nothing seems to work properly the first time you try it. Your communications hardware and software are designed to work smoothly, and they will. It's only when something is slightly out of kilter that you might run into a snafu. As emphasized throughout this book, this is a common problem; you're dealing with something more complicated than a fax machine, after all. But take heart, and remember the power and usefulness of your new system.

Think about the car you drive. You probably are not intimately familiar with all aspects of the car's operation, but you know the fundamentals well enough to operate it. It's possible to also take this approach when you are setting up your PC, modem, and software: You don't have to be an expert to get everything working and get on line. Nevertheless, all the technical details are included in this book and if you encounter a problem, this information can help guide you to a solution.

To telecommunicate using a PC, you need specific equipment—both hardware and software. The hardware consists of a modem. The software is a program that will command the modem, and perform the various other functions of *terminal emulation.* These programs, called telecommunications or comm programs, range from the inexpensive to the very expensive. They're built into integrated programs such as Microsoft Works and even some of the more powerful utility packages such as PC Tools. They're available as powerful stand-alone commercial programs such as Crosstalk. Comm programs are among the very best shareware offerings, including such best-sellers as Procomm, Qmodem, and Telix. And many modems come with comm programs such as Bitcom or simple, proprietary "modem drivers." It's a buyer's market and if you can't find a comm program that's right for you, you're probably not looking very hard.

Let's start with some basics. If you want more detailed information, refer to Chapter 23, "How a Modem Works." For the most specific details, read the appropriate sections in your modem and communications software manuals.

ASYNCHRONOUS COMMUNICATION SOFTWARE

Many large computer systems consist of a CPU (central processing unit) with terminals attached. To use an application on the computer, a user communicates with it via a terminal. The computer in this case is referred to as a *host.*

A terminal is a dumb device consisting of video display, a keyboard, and the circuitry required to communicate with the host. It is capable of only two things: sending characters you type on its keyboard to the host, and displaying on the screen characters it receives from the host.

Terminals are still in use, but many have been replaced by PC systems running terminal emulation software. This system has many advantages. Among these are the ability to "capture" data received from the host, to exchange information, and to emulate more than one type of terminal without making a single hardware change. This arrangement also allows you to download information from the host and process it locally.

Many communication programs feature a programming language that can be used to automate a variety of tasks, such as logging in to the host. A couple of programs have more sophisticated languages that give you substantial power and versatility. Chapter 4 is about telecommunications programs and is a guide to their respective features.

There are also specialized PC communications programs that allow you to take control of another PC at a remote location. The uses for this type of communication are many, and include remote application software support.

ASYNCHRONOUS COMMUNICATION HARDWARE

Asynchronous communication hardware for PC systems is either built into the PC or added with an expansion card. The type of interface provided by this hardware is known as an RS-232 interface, commonly referred to as a port, a COM (communication) port, or a serial port. IBM originally called this a serial adapter, and sometimes it's called the serial card or serial interface card.

The original IBM PC standard defines two communication ports, COM1 and COM2. Most PC expansion cards can be configured as one of these two ports. PC systems that have a built-in serial port define it as COM1, and it usually cannot be changed. The new PS/2 systems define eight ports, COM1 through COM8. Most of the newer machines say they can address, or "talk to," these extra ports too. At this point, you don't need to be concerned with how many ports you have.

MODEM INSTALLATION

Telecommunication using a PC involves using an internal or external modem. The differences between the two styles will be covered later in this chapter, but first, let's take a look at some of the features found on both modem types.

A modem (whether internal or external) performs the function of converting information from your PC into a form that can be transmitted over a telephone line. It also converts the signals it "hears" on the phone line into information that is sent to your PC.

Most modems have two telephone jacks, one for the line that connects to the wall plug (usually marked "line" or "telco") and one that connects to a telephone. Your modem was probably shipped with a phone cord that connects it to the phone jack on the wall. If you have a spare phone, you can connect it to the other modem jack. This allows you to use the same line for both voice and data calls, although you can't do both at the same time. It is helpful, however, if you can't connect to a remote modem by direct dialing because you may first have to ask an operator to connect you to an extension.

Most modems are equipped with a speaker that lets you monitor the progress of a call. Volume level on some modems is set with a knob; others use a command (modem commands are covered in Appendix C).

External modems usually have status lights to indicate what the modem is doing. Internal modems do not have lights, but some software packages make up for this by simulating these lights with a clever screen display.

Preparing for Installation

Before beginning a modem installation, it's a good idea to take an inventory of the expansion cards you have in your PC. For your purposes, you are really only concerned with the number of serial devices in the system, but it's handy to have a complete inventory for general use. You'll need to take the cover off the PC to do this; if you need instructions for this, refer to your PC user guide.

Start the inventory by writing down the types of cards you have in your system. If a card has a serial port on it, check its settings to see what COM port it's assigned to, and write that down too. (Refer to the expansion cards' documentation to determine their settings or use the procedures suggested in Chapter 27, "Troubleshooting Your Modem.") If you can't figure out the cards and their settings, take the computer to a dealer or friend who can run tests to determine what ports are used. The card inventory will be used in both modem and communication software installation.

Caution: If in the process of making the inventory you find that more than one device is configured for the same COM port number, you'll have to change a few switch settings. In a PC, each serial port must have a unique COM port number. If not, things won't work properly.

If you're using an internal modem, you'll need to know how many serial ports already exist in your PC, so that you can configure the modem. If you're installing an external modem, you'll need to know which serial ports (if any) you have available, and the COM number for which they're configured, because you'll be hooking the modem directly to the connector of one of these ports.

Your modem will likely have to be configured to work with your software. Some modems have physical switches you can set; others have "soft switches" that are set by the software in its configuration process. This isn't something to fret over—most Hayes-compatible modems usually work right out of the box, with the factory settings intact.

If you're installing an internal modem, look in its documentation to see if it has physical switches to set. The most important ones are the ones that define the COM port used, and the one telling the modem if it is hooked to a multiline phone. The other settings are not as important, and the factory (default) setting will usually work. In any case, don't be afraid or annoyed if you have to take the modem out of the computer and change some switch settings more than once.

External modems also have either physical or soft switches. Since the modem is external, it can be configured at any time.

Internal Modems

An internal modem is an expansion card that occupies a slot in the PC. Like any other adapter card, it gets its power from the PC. Internal modems require no cabling. All that is needed is the phone cord to connect the modem to the phone line.

Since many PC systems already have one serial port, and it's usually COM1, most internal modems are shipped from the factory configured as COM2. If you have only one serial port, and it's configured as COM1, then installing your modem card is just a matter of plugging it into an empty slot. If you have a COM2 port but no COM1, just change the modem's switches and/or jumpers so that it's configured for COM1.

If you find that you already have both a COM1 and COM2 in your system, you have the following options. You can disable one of the existing ports, and configure the modem to take its place, or you can check to see if the modem can be configured as COM3 or COM4. You'll also need to make sure that the communication software you plan to use supports this new setting.

Installation of the modem is explained in detail in the modem's manual, so refer to it for more information and to look up settings.

External Modems

External modems are packaged in enclosures, ranging from very nice aluminum cases to inexpensive plastic ones. Use of an external modem requires a serial port in the PC, cabling from the port to the modem, and a power supply.

The power adapter provided with most external modems is a small cube that plugs into the wall, and has a wire that plugs into the modem. Power adapters of this type can sometimes be a bit bulky. Fortunately, a few modem manufacturers now use an adapter that sits on the floor and has two wires — one that extends to the wall plug and one that goes to the modem.

Cabling

A cable is a bundle of wires which, in this case, is used to carry electrical signals from the PC to the modem and vice versa. Cables are manufactured for just about every PC need.

The type of connector used for a PC serial port and most modems is known as a D-type connector (it vaguely looks something like the letter *D*). There are two types of D connectors: male (with pins) and female (with sockets). D-type connectors are labeled so that each pin or socket has a number from 1 to 9, or from 1 to 25. A serial connector on a PC is usually male. Some have 9 pins, others have 25. Modem connectors are usually female and have 25 pins. The 9-pin connector is also known as a DB-9; the 25-pin is called a DB-25.

Computer stores can supply you with a cable manufactured specifically for connecting a PC serial port to a modem. There are two types of cables: ribbon and shielded. Shielded cables are preferred because they prevent radio frequency interference with other equipment such as televisions, radios, and VCRs.

A properly manufactured off-the-shelf cable should work with your setup. If it doesn't, check it against the connection information provided in "Technical Details" later in this chapter. Fifty percent of the problems people have with modems have to do with the cables. Some printer cables, for example, have the pin assignments switched around to work only with certain printers. Since the printer cable looks like a modem cable, it is often used as one. The result, of course, is that your modem won't work.

Connection to the PC

Now that you have determined which COM port you're going to use, you have the correct cable, and you have your external modem, it's time to connect everything together. This is a simple matter of plugging one end of the cable into the PC, and the other end into the modem. If your cable has screws, tighten them just enough to make the connectors fit snugly.

SOFTWARE INSTALLATION

There are many communication programs available, each with unique commands and operating characteristics. For this reason, this chapter includes only general directions for software setup. Some of these products will be easier to configure than others. Fortunately, most packages have a program for installation or configuration, or both.

The first thing to determine before you install the program is the port number of the internal modem or serial port you will be using. (You should already know this if you've read the "Preparing for Installation" section of this chapter.) Some programs can concurrently use more than one device. If your program has this ability, and you plan to use it that way, you will also need to know the port number of the additional devices.

When you install communication software on your PC, the program must be configured for the type of modem you have and the COM port to which the modem is attached. Some software packages accomplish this as part of the installation program; others do it as part of a separate configuration step. The latter is preferred, since this method allows you to define a different setup should you change the modem or configuration of your PC.

Most communication packages have a method of storing a configuration for each service you call (CompuServe, a local bulletin board system, and so on). It's a good idea to set up a configuration for any service you plan to use. You'll then be able to test your setup by using one of these configurations to place a call.

TECHNICAL DETAILS

As mentioned previously, you probably won't need the information in this section. It is useful, however, if your system setup is a little out of the ordinary, or if you simply wish to know some of the technical details.

COM Port Addressing

Think of the communication (COM) port definition as the *identity* of a port. This identity is the combination of an address and an IRQ (interrupt request number). Each port in a PC must have a unique identity; that is, no more than one port can have the same address and IRQ combination.

The *address* is what tells the software where the port is. When the software needs to communicate through COM1, for example, it knows the address for that port, and sends the information there. It's really very much like the street address of your house; when someone needs to send information to you, they use your address.

Various parts of a PC system use signals known as *interrupts* (or IRQs) when they have something to say. For example, a port generates an interrupt when it has received a character. This tells the software that it needs to address the port to get the character and process it (put it on the screen, for example).

The original PC systems defined only two ports, COM1 and COM2. As PC users needed more serial ports, hardware and software manufacturers responded by creating their own definition for two more ports, COM3 and COM4. Since there is no official standard for these ports, however, not all software and hardware products support COM 3 and COM 4. The current PS/2 systems define eight ports, COM1 through COM8.

Most programs refer to the communication ports in your PC as COM ports. You do not usually need to know the actual address and IRQ of a port to make things work, but it can be handy to know the standard settings. The following chart lists the standard addresses used for PC and PS/2 serial ports.

Port	PC Address/IRQ	PS/2 Address/IRQ
COM1	03F8h/4	03F8h/4
COM2	02F8h/3	02F8h/3
COM3	03E8h/4*	3220h/3
COM4	02E8h/3*	3228h/3
COM5	n/a	4220h/3
COM6	n/a	4228h/3
COM7	n/a	5220h/3
COM8	n/a	5228h/3

* Remember, although they are the most common, not all hardware and software products support these address/IRQ combinations for COM3 and COM4.

The UART

The UART (universal asynchronous receiver transmitter) is a specialized IC (integrated circuit) that handles asynchronous communication. It is responsible for sending and receiving data, and handshaking with the attached device. Older PC systems use the 8250 UART. AT-class and better machines (those with 80286 and 80386 processors) use the 16450 or 16550 UARTs. The older 8250 design has had problems at high speed. The newer 16450 and 16550 devices offer better performance, and fewer problems.

There are several "support" chips for the UART, but you need not usually be concerned with these. It can be useful, however, to know which UART is in your system. If you don't know what you have, look at the expansion card for a large, 40-pin IC labeled with one of the numbers listed above. If you can't find the chip or a number that matches, look it up in the documentation or contact the hardware manufacturer.

The interaction between your communication software and the UART is largely transparent. The software tells the UART to send and receive characters, and to start and stop the flow of data (flow control). Some programs actually detect the type of UART with which they are working and make appropriate adjustments.

Serial Port Cabling

Although serial connectors have as many as 25 pins, only 9 of them are actually used to carry signals. These 9 signals are listed in the following table.

Mnemonic	Name	Source	Purpose
TXD	Transmitted Data	PC	Carries characters from the PC to the modem.
RXD	Received Data	Modem	Carries characters from the modem to the PC.
RTS	Request To Send	PC	Used for flow control.
CTS	Clear To Send	Modem	Used for flow control.
DSR	Data Set Ready	Modem	Used for flow control.
SG	Signal Ground	n/a	An electrical reference point for the other signals.
CD	Carrier Detect	Modem	The modem makes this signal active when it has connected to another modem. Some software programs monitor this signal to know when they're on line.

Mnemonic	Name	Source	Purpose
DTR	Data Terminal Ready	PC	Some programs make this signal active when they are about to place a call, or are in "local" mode.
RI	Ring Indicator	Modem	Becomes active when a ring is detected. Can be important when answering calls.

There are two categories of serial devices: DTE (data terminal equipment) and DCE (data communications equipment). Terminals and PCs are DTE devices; modems are DCE devices. This gives you some idea of how the equipment interconnects. Generally, if you're connecting a DTE device to a DCE, and both have 25-pin connectors, a straight-through cable can be used.

The following sections show the connections for a 25- to 25-pin cable and for a 9- to 25-pin cable.

25-Pin PC Connector Signals

A cable of this type is said to be wired "straight through." This is because pin 2 on one end connects to pin 2 of the other, pin 3 goes to pin 3, and so on. Most cables used for the purpose of connecting a 25-pin PC port (DTE) to a modem (DCE) are wired this way.

Signal	PC Pin	Modem Pin
TXD	2	2
RXD	3	3
RTS	4	4
CTS	5	5
DSR	6	6
SG	7	7
CD	8	8
DTR	20	20
RI	22	22

9-Pin PC Connector Signals

The 9-pin AT-type serial port pinout is quite different from that of a standard DTE port's. For starters, there are only 9 pins. Also, the signals are on different pins from what you might expect. This table shows the correct wiring for a 9-pin AT-style port to a 25-pin modem.

Signal	PC Pin	Modem Pin
TXD	3	2
RXD	2	3
RTS	7	4
CTS	8	5
DSR	6	6
SG	5	7
CD	1	8
DTR	4	20
RI	9	22

How Software Communicates with the Modem

This subject is covered in more detail in Chapter 23, "How a Modem Works," but here are some salient facts just to get you familiar with the subject.

Each modem has a set of commands. The most widely used one, the AT command set, was originated by the Hayes Microcomputer Company when they began manufacturing their Hayes Smartmodems. When a modem is said to be "Hayes compatible," that usually means it supports some part of the Hayes command set. Because of these command sets, it is important for your software to know the type of modem you're using, so that the software knows how to "talk" to your modem.

Most modems available today are programmable to an extent. Usually a modem will function just as it is, fresh from the factory, but there are many settings that you may wish to adjust for better performance in your particular environment. *Modem registers* are used to configure a modem's operation. For example, registers set the modem's dialing speed, and how long it waits to get an answer after dialing a number. Your modem's manual lists the modem registers and explains their use.

To set a register on the modem, you need to talk directly to the modem. This is usually done by telling the communication software that you want to "go local." Instructions for this procedure are available in the software's documentation. You can use the software's local mode to give commands to the modem.

The dialing process is usually somewhat transparent. When communication software commands the modem to dial, it sends three pieces of information (strings): a dialing prefix, the telephone number, and a dialing suffix. You usually don't see this data going to the modem, although the software will report that it is placing a call.

The dialing prefix usually contains the actual command to dial. In the case of a modem that uses the AT command set, this is usually *ATDT*. The *AT* gets the modem's attention, the *D* is the Dial command, and the *T* tells the modem to dial using tones. If you need to pulse dial (that is, use a rotary dial instead of push button phone), you would use a *P* instead of a *T*. The telephone number is the number of the remote host's modem, and was entered by you when you set up the software to call the host. The dialing suffix, usually a carriage-return character, terminates the dialing command.

After the modem dials, it will wait to "hear" another modem answer the call. After the modems connect, the software makes you aware of this, and you're on line.

Note: Once on line, the modem can still respond to the AT commands when typed in as, say, a message. It is therefore a good idea to familiarize yourself with commands such as + + +ATH, which hangs up the phone (terminates the connection). This is covered in Appendix C.

You should now be on line and communicating when you command the modem to dial out to another number. Even if there is only garbage coming over the screen (meaning you haven't yet properly set the software parameters), you have at least made the all-important connection! You are now ready to do some serious work.

CHAPTER FOUR

Telecommunications Programs

This chapter discusses the characteristics and capabilities of the leading commercial telecommunications (or modem) programs. The concepts of terminal emulation, file transfer protocol, and scripting are important to the selection of a modem program appropriate for your needs. Throughout the chapter, you will find handy Product Profiles of available software that you can use for reference. At the end of the chapter is a section on remote PC communication.

COMMERCIAL TELECOMMUNICATIONS PROGRAMS

You can't telecommunicate without a telecommunications program, which coordinates activity between the computer, the modem, the telephone line, and the remote computer or host. The best of the telecommunications software constitutes some of the highest-quality programming you can buy.

Modems and Software

Your word processor program displays characters on the screen, monitors the keyboard, and manages the memory and disk drive. If the word processor program isn't *compatible* with your screen, keyboard, memory, and disk drive, then you can't use the program. That magic word—compatible—is of prime importance in telecommunications, too.

Your modem program must perform all the functions of a word processor; in addition, it must manage the communications port (usually COM1 or COM2), and talk compatibly with your modem. Not all modems are the same, and Hayes compatibility, though a key factor, doesn't mean the same thing to all people. You will explore these and other concepts in depth in several chapters of this book.

Carefully inspect the modem program you are considering to see if it will work with your modem. If the program says it requires a "100 percent Hayes-compatible modem," that does not mean "Hayes-compatible AT command set." Smartcom II and Smartcom III, for example, require a "100 percent Hayes-compatible modem," but some programs support almost any full-duplex asynchronous modem.

Important Features in a Modem Program

Some people say the most important feature of a telecommunications program is Zmodem protocol; others will insist that background downloading is more important. Some want a full-featured scripting facility. The person buying his or her first computer may just want the cheapest solution. What really is important is for the program to perform the functions you need with your modem. Ask plenty of questions from experienced users before you decide.

This sounds like a pretty basic requirement, but some of the most well known programs are very limited in compatibility. For instance, if you need to access the company mainframe computer using IBM3101 Block mode, then you absolutely will need a program that provides IBM3101 Block mode terminal emulation—there isn't any alternative.

Scripting

Scripting automates the keystrokes you have to enter each time the telecommunications program is used. This automation provides greater accuracy and shorter connect times.

Electronic funds transfer (EFT) is a common use for modem programs in corporations. The process of logging into the bank's computer system and typing the EFT request is very brief. Obviously, accuracy is important. A very simple script is advised. Many modem programs have a scripting facility that provides this level of support—some even provide an *automatic* scripting facility!

Heavy users of pay services like CompuServe, GEnie, and Dow Jones News Retrieval, or users who access bulletin boards through long-distance connections can really benefit from a full-featured scripting language. Smartcom II provides a bare-bones scripting facility (called "macros") that is only good for logging onto a system. Several modem programs provide excellent scripting languages to allow brief and unattended connections to these services. HyperACCESS includes several superior scripts for accessing CompuServe and other fee-based services. Users of the Crosstalk Mk.4 and Professional-YAM products have written complete navigation scripts for CompuServe; the scripts are available on CompuServe for downloading, with no fees requested by the authors.

SYSTEM COMMUNICATION HARDWARE REQUIREMENTS

Let's start by listing your minimum hardware communication needs. How much computer memory will be available to run the modem program? How much disk space is available for the modem program and its supporting files? What brand and model modem will you use?

Memory

This is the amount of memory left for the modem program after starting DOS and loading any multitasking and/or memory-resident programs (like Notepads, disk caches, pop-up calculators, and so on).

Even with 640K of memory installed and a very limited amount of memory-resident programs, I cannot run Smartcom III, because it requires 512K of available memory. Unloading two of my memory-resident utilities, commonly called *TSRs*, allows me to run Smartcom III without any problems; fortunately, these two TSRs aren't necessary while Smartcom III runs.

On your machine, execute the DOS command CHKDSK, and inspect the last line: "*nnnnnn* bytes free." The number shown must be larger than the minimum RAM configuration listed for your chosen modem in this chapter's Product Profiles. Be cautious, however; for optimum performance many programs need much more than minimum recommended memory.

TSRs

It is important to mention that some TSRs behave poorly with some communications programs. There is no definitive list of the problem-makers, because it depends on the individual configuration. (I *can* tell you that I have never been able to run a no-squint-cursor TSR program and send any files using Procomm at the same time.)

Crosstalk XVI, Crosstalk Mk.4, Procomm Plus, Telix, Professional-YAM, and Relay Gold are generally known to work reasonably well with TSRs. If you have a favorite TSR that you must have loaded with the modem program, contact the developer's Customer Service or Technical Support department for advice.

Disk Space

When the first PC programs were developed, they were very small; each one usually fit on a 360K floppy disk. As the needs of computer users increased, program developers met their demands with superior and more efficient products that required not only more memory to operate, but more disk space to store the programs. Your disk space has to hold the modem program and its supporting files, as well as any disk-capture buffers and files you want to download. Floppy-disk users can juggle diskettes, but there are practical limits to this exercise. I have a system with an enormous hard disk drive, but must still be careful in selecting software, because it also has to operate on my laptop computer.

Remember: the Product Profiles, listed later in this chapter, reflect the amount of disk space required to perform a standard installation; most of the disk space requirements can be reduced.

COM Port

Fortunately, all the programs listed in the Product Profiles will work with the standard computer chip that operates the communications port (the

UART). There are several replacement UARTs available that provide higher performance with programs like Professional-YAM and Crosstalk Mk.4. If you plan to use high-speed connections (19,200 baud or greater), consider a replacement UART, and select a program that takes full advantage of the higher-performance chips. (Don't worry about this now, though.)

TERMINAL EMULATION

If this chapter were written in French, you would have to read and understand French for this written communication to be transferred to your mind. Modem programs "talk" to other modem programs and devices (primarily terminals), and the language they use is called *terminal emulation.* For instance, if one modem program sends in ANSI-BBS, then the modem program on the other end of the connection must receive the discussion in ANSI-BBS.

All modem programs talk at the most basic level: TTY. If the computer to which your modem program connects expects to find a Wyse/50 or a Televideo/950 terminal, then your modem program must have an option to provide Wyse/50 or Televideo/950 terminal emulation. Make a list of the terminal emulations that you will need. Corporate users will probably have wider requirements than the hobbyist. To access GEnie, CompuServe, and local bulletin board systems (BBSs), you will probably only need TTY, DEC VT100/102, and ANSI-BBS terminal emulations.

There are two variants of the IBM 3101 terminal emulation: Block mode and Character mode. Only Crosstalk Mk.4 and Relay Gold support both variants. The other modem programs only support Character mode.

If you have an unusual terminal emulation requirement, there may only be one modem program that fulfills that requirement. If that modem program is unacceptable, contact the manufacturer and see if an alternative emulation is available.

FILE TRANSFER PROTOCOL

A file transfer protocol like Lynx, Mpt, or Zmodem, all discussed extensively in Chapter 24, is a necessary addition to any contemporary modem program. Any of these can be implemented within (built into) the modem program, or the modem program can be temporarily suspended while another (external) program provides the protocol. The process of suspending the modem program while an external program works is called "using an external protocol." The external protocol program for Zmodem, for example, is available as a shareware program; it is not a free program. You should weigh the benefits and costs of using an external protocol program against selecting a modem program with built-in Zmodem support.

One advantage to using an external protocol is its upgrade potential. Program authors constantly update their products. The bad news part of this "good news/bad news" story is that you are charged with the responsibility of purchasing, registering, and keeping the software at the current release level. Using an external protocol can be confusing at first. Often the combined cost of the external program and the modem program that uses it is greater than that of selecting a modem program with built-in support. Also, it can be difficult to determine which vendor to contact when problems develop, because some modem programs do not support external protocols. I prefer to have Zmodem built into the system, and that's the way it comes with Telix.

Another important file transfer protocol is CompuServe B, which was developed to handle the problems of using multiple computers in a time-sharing, packet-switching environment. There are several variants of the CompuServe B protocol, and only Crosstalk Mk.4 and Professional-YAM currently support the full implementation. The other modem programs that provide CompuServe B do not have the ability to recover from an aborted download.

In the early fall of 1989, CompuServe introduced Ymodem support. Ymodem on CompuServe is about 90 percent as efficient as CompuServe B. CompuServe is a fee-based service and it doesn't take too many downloads before that 10 percent difference is cost-justified by using a CompuServe B program. There are several CompuServe B external protocol programs available; the tradeoffs here are the same as for other external protocols.

Nearly every modem program provides one or more "proprietary protocols", that is, special protocols unique to that vendor's product line. These provide very efficient file transfers after you make sure that both the sending and receiving modems are using the protocol. Using a proprietary protocol can provide some additional security from hackers if you are developing a communications network in a corporate environment.

OTHER NEEDS

If you work in a so-called "environment," such as Windows, then your modem program must work in that environment. DESQview and Microsoft

Windows are common environments; they are useful in allowing a long download to run as one session, while you work on a spreadsheet function in another session.

Some modem programs allow background file transfers. These programs become TSRs and work without disturbing the keyboard or display; if sufficient memory is available, you can start another program.

Other modem programs offer multiple concurrent sessions. For example, one session can be connected to a mainframe, another to a local BBS, and a third to MCI Mail, while the user is editing a file in a fourth session. Crosstalk Mk.4, HyperACCESS, Relay Gold, and Smartcom III provide exceptional multisession support without the need for any additional multi-tasking software.

Heavy users of a large number of BBSs will need dialing queues and the ability to have significant dialing directory entries.

SUPPORT AND UPDATES

Quality documentation is important, but documentation is subjective. Certainly Relay Gold has 960 pages of good documentation, but if you can't locate how to download a file, then the documentation isn't worth very much. The script developer working with an 88-page insert for SmartCom III would probably prefer the detailed examples in HyperACCESS, and the secretary retrieving the company's electronic mail from MCI could probably not care less about the 88-page insert.

Thankfully, all these modem programs have voice support. Many of them operate Technical Support BBSs, and some offer support on GEnie and/or CompuServe.

Communication programs are constantly changing, and you should plan on regular updates, probably once a year. Professional-YAM has the most sophisticated updating mechanism—the entire program is encrypted for downloading by registered users as required. The Professional-YAM author regularly posts updated versions on GEnie, CompuServe, and his support BBS. Crosstalk Mk.4 and HyperACCESS developers can release enhancements and fixes easily, because their programs are distributed in modules.

PROFILES OF POPULAR COMMUNICATION PRODUCTS

This chapter mentions several successful telecommunications programs that are on the market today. Each has hundreds of features. To give you the most information in the least painful manner, the following Product Profiles have been assembled in a standardized list form. The commercial products are listed first; shareware products are listed later in the chapter.

Crosstalk XVI

DCA/Crosstalk Communications
1000 Holcomb Woods Parkway
Roswell, Georgia 30076
(404)998-3998

Current Version: 3.71
Retail Price: $195

Hardware Required

Minimum RAM required:
  Foreground operation-128K
  Background operation-160K
Minimum disk space: 250K

Terminal Emulations

TTY
BBS-ANSI
DEC VT-52
DEC VT-100, VT-102
IBM3101, Character mode only
Televideo/910, Televideo/920
ADDS Viewpoint
Texas Instrument 940

File Transfer Protocols

Xmodem
Xmodem CRC
Kermit
Proprietary

Scripting   16 commands in script language.

Other

64,000 directory entries allowed
Background file transfer
Windows/386 support
DESQview support
Command-oriented, no menus
Works with almost all full-duplex asynchronous modems

Support

Manual: 230 pages
Voice Support: 9A.M.-6P.M. EST, Monday-Friday, (404)998-7798
Support BBS: (404)998-8048
CompuServe Forum: GO XTALK

Crosstalk Mk.4

DCA/Crosstalk Communications
1000 Holcomb Woods Parkway
Roswell, Georgia 30076
(404)998-3998

Current Version: 1.1
Retail Price: $245

Hardware Required

Minimum RAM required: 320K
Minimum disk space:
   Minimum configuration-will fit on 360K floppy
   Normal configuration-740K
   Full configuration-1100K

Terminal Emulations

TTY	AT&T Model 513
BBS-ANSI	Data General DASHER D210 and D211
DEC VT-52	Datapoint Datastation 3601
DEC VT-100, VT-102	Hazeltine Esprit II
DEC VT-220, VT-230	DCA REMOTE 2

IBM3101, Character or Block mode
Televideo/912, 920, 925, 960
Lear-Siegler AD 3a
ADDS Viewpoint
TYMNET78

DCA IRMA 327X coax adapter
  card
DCA Smart Alec 525X twinax
  adapter card

File Transfer Protocols

Xmodem
Xmodem CRC
Ymodem
Ymodem batch
Ymodem-G
Kermit
X.PC
Proprietary
Zmodem
CompuServe B

Scripting Over 250 script commands. Extensive window and string handling facilities. Support for intersession communication. Built-in LEARN facility.

Other

Virtually unlimited directory entries allowed
Windows/386 support
DESQview support
Command, menu, and/or ALT key-oriented
Works with almost all full-duplex asynchronous modems
Supports up to 15 concurrent sessions
Supports, in addition to modems:
  TYMNET X.PC via async serial port, most modems
  Local Area Network (LAN) interface module
  Any device supported by BIOS Interrupt 14
  Netware Asynchronous Services Interface (NASI), Network
    Communication Services Interface (NCSI), and Ungermann-Bass
    Network Interface (UBNI)

DCA IRMA 327X coax adapter card
DCA Smart Alec 525X twinax adapter card
Modular design
Host mode

Support

Manual: 2 volumes, totaling 620 pages
Voice Support: 9A.M.-6P.M. EST, Monday-Friday, (404)998-7798
Support BBS: (404)641-1803
CompuServe Forum: GO XTALK

HyperACCESS

Hilgraeve Inc.
Post Office Box 941
Monroe, Michigan 48161
(313)243-0576

Current Version: 3.32
Retail Price: $129

Hardware Required

Minimum RAM required: 128K
Minimum disk space: 330K

Terminal Emulations

TTY
DEC VT-52
DEC VT-220
Televideo/925, 950, 955
Heath/Zenith 19

BBS-ANSI
DEC VT-100, VT-102
IBM3101, Character mode only
IBM 3278, asynch
Wang VS2110

File Transfer Protocols

Xmodem
Xmodem CRC
Kermit
Proprietary

Scripting   100 script commands.

Other

127 directory entries allowed
Windows/386 support
DESQview support
Function key-oriented menu system
Works with almost all full-duplex asynchronous modems
Extensive user training provided in Computer Assisted
   Instructions (CAI) training course that simulates on-line sessions
Uses device driver in CONFIG.SYS file
Extensive host capabilities
Highly functional drop to DOS facility
Modular design

Support

Manual: 239 pages
Voice Support: 8A.M.-6P.M. EST, Monday-Friday, (313)243-0576

Procomm Plus

Datastorm Technologies, Inc.   Current Version: 1.1b
Post Office Box 1471   Retail Price: $89
Columbia, Missouri 65205
(314)474-8461

Hardware Required

Minimum RAM required: 192K
Minimum disk space: 335K

Terminal Emulations

TTY	BBS-ANSI
DEC VT-52	DEC VT-102
IBM3101, Character mode only	Televideo/910, 920, 925, 950, 955
Lear-Siegler ADM 3/5	ADDS Viewpoint

IBM3270, asynch   Wyse/50/100
Heath/Zenith 19

File Transfer Protocols

Xmodem   MODEM7
Xmodem CRC   TELINK
Ymodem   CompuServe B
Ymodem batch   WXmodem
Ymodem-G   IMODEM
Ymodem-G batch   SEALINK
Kermit

Scripting   96 script commands.

Other

Unlimited number of 200-entry directories
Windows/386 support
DESQview support
ALT key-oriented
Works with almost all full-duplex asynchronous modems
Host mode

Support

Manual: 372 pages
Voice Support:
   5 calls within 90 days free
   10 calls within 6 months $40
   20 calls per year $70
   9A.M.-5P.M. CST, Monday-Friday, (314)474-9468
Distribution BBS: (314)474-8477 (not support BBS)
CompuServe Forum: GO PCVENA, Section 14

Professional-YAM

Omen Technology, Inc.   Current Version: 17.25
17505-V Northwest Sauvie Island Road   Retail Price: $139

Portland, Oregon 97231
(503)621-3406

Hardware Required

Minimum RAM required: 256K
Minimum disk space:
   Demo modules-211K
   On-line help modules-204K
   Program and support modules-300K

Terminal Emulations

TTY	Lear-Siegler ADM 3a
BBS-ANSI	Heath/Zenith 19
DEC VT-52	
DEC VT-200, VT-102	
IBM3101, Character mode only	
Televideo/910, 920, 925, 950, 955	

File Transfer Protocols

Xmodem	WXmodem
Xmodem CRC	MODEM7
Ymodem	TELINK
Ymodem-G	SEALINK
Zmodem	Kermit
CompuServe B	

Scripting   Extensive scripting facilities for manipulating text strings, review buffer, telecommunications session, and security. Scripts developed for the DOS version of Professional-YAM can be used in the UNIX version of Professional-YAM.

Other

Windows/386 support
DESQview support
Command line, function key-oriented
Works with almost all full-duplex asynchronous modems
Host mode

Unmatched on-line help facility
Extensive demo of program features
Definite UNIX flavor; intended for serious telecommunicating

Support

Manual: 300 pages
Voice Support: (503)621-3406
Support BBS: (503)621-3746
CompuServe: 70007,2304
GEnie: CAF
BIX: cforsberg
UUCP: !tektronix!reed!omen!caf

Relay Gold

Relay Communications Inc.
41 Kenosia Avenue
Danbury, Connecticut 06810
(800)847-3529

Current Version: 3.0
Retail Price: $295

Hardware Required

Minimum RAM required: 192K
Minimum Disk space: 792K
Could be configured for a 360K floppy

Terminal Emulations

TTY
DEC VT-52
DEC VT-220
IBM 3101, Character or Block mode
Extensive support for 327X asynch

BBS-ANSI
DEC VT-100
DEC VT-240 in Color Text
  mode
Extensive support for 327X
  coax adapter cards

File Transfer Protocols

Xmodem
Xmodem CRC
Kermit
Proprietary

Scripting About 200 commands and functions. Script language-oriented for handling mainframe 3270-type sessions.

Other

Virtually unlimited directory entries allowed
DESQview support
Command- or menu-oriented
Works with almost all full-duplex asynchronous modems
Supports up to 15 concurrent sessions
Supports, in addition to modems, 327X coax adapter card
Uses EMS

Support

Manual: 2 volumes, totaling 960 pages
Voice Support: 9A.M.-5P.M. EST, (203)798-3900
Support BBS: (203)797-0595

Smartcom II

Hayes Microcomputer Products, Inc.
705 Westech Drive
Norcross, Georgia 30092
(404)441-1617

Current Version: 3.0
Retail Price: $149

Hardware Required

Minimum RAM required: 192K
Minimum disk space: 255K

Terminal Emulations

TTY
DEC VT-52
VT-100, VT-102

File Transfer Protocols

Xmodem
Xmodem CRC
Proprietary

Scripting   Very limited macro creation facility. Smartcom III is the recommended product for users needing scripting facilities.

Other

Limited to 25 directory entries
Menu-oriented
Works with 100 percent Hayes-compatible modems

Support

Manual: 198 pages
Voice Support: 8A.M.-8P.M. EST, Monday-Friday, (404)441-1617

Smartcom III

Hayes Microcomputer Products, Inc.
705 Westech Drive
Norcross, Georgia 30092
(404)441-1617

Current Version: 1.1a
Retail Price: $249

Hardware Required

Minimum RAM required: 512K
Minimum disk space: 1375K
Could run on dual 720K (3½-inch) floppy drives

Terminal Emulations

TTY
BBS-ANSI
DEC VT-52
DEC VT-100, VT-102

File Transfer Protocols

Xmodem
Xmodem CRC
Ymodem
Ymodem batch
Ymodem-G
Kermit

Scripting   61 language statements in script language.

Other

Virtually unlimited directory entries allowed
Menu-oriented
Works with 100 percent Hayes-compatible modems
The only program that is shipped with both 3½- and 5¼-inch diskettes
Supports up to 8 concurrent sessions
Supports, in addition to modems, TYMNET X.PC using Hayes X.25 modems. Computer Based Training (CBT) is a $99.95 PC-based learning facility using simulated communications. A single SCOPE script is presented.

Support

Manual: 182-page manual, and 88-page supplement on script-programming
Voice Support: 8A.M.-8P.M. EST, Monday-Friday, (404)441-1617
Support BBS: (404)874-2937

Other Programs

Many good commercial programs are not in these Profiles. For example, Whisper, an interesting and specialized "secure" system based on the DES encryption coding, isn't covered. (You can call L.P. Mika in Rosewell, Georgia at (404)993-4021 for information.) Also, I have seen HyperACCESS V; it's fairly spectacular and worth a look. The exclusion of other programs is not a comment on their quality; the list is simply limited to the most common programs.

SHAREWARE TELECOMMUNICATIONS PROGRAMS

Some of the most creative programming and design efforts are appearing in shareware software products. Without the costs of diskette and documentation duplication, or the overhead of administrative and marketing services, the developer can offer the program at a lower cost. The six shareware programs presented in this chapter are serious efforts that required significant time investments on the part of their authors. Please, if you use one of these programs, register it promptly.

The pricing of shareware programs is very difficult to provide in a product summary like this, without going into all the terms and conditions the developer offers. The prices in these Product Profiles reflect the minimum shareware registration fee for the program.

Product profiles are provided here for Boyan, Commo, GT Power, Procomm, Qmodem, and Telix.

All of these programs are widely available on BBSs, which are supported by the programs' authors, and on pay services like CompuServe and GEnie.

Boyan

Boyan Communications
Post Office Box 71
Woodstock, Maryland 21163
(no voice number)

Current Version: 4.01
Shareware Fee: $40

Hardware Required

Minimum RAM required: 256K
Minimum disk space: 322K

Terminal Emulations

TTY
BBS-ANSI
DEC VT-52
DEC VT-100

File Transfer Protocols

Xmodem
Xmodem CRC
Ymodem
Ymodem batch
Ymodem-G

Scripting   Over 200 commands and variables in a macro programming language.

Other

Unlimited number of 200-entry directories
ALT key-oriented
Works with almost all full-duplex asynchronous modems
Host mode
20-entry circular dialing queue
No built-in editor

Support

Manual: 123 pages
Voice Support: None
Support BBS: (201)794-7125

Commo

Fred P. Brucker   Shareware Fee: $25
Post Office Box 9103
Santa Rosa, California 95405

Hardware Required

Minimum RAM required: 35K
Minimum disk space: 100K or less (in a DESQview window)
Can support up to 115,200bps and can detect 16550A UART

File Transfer Protocols

DSZ
BiModem
Mpt
Jmodem
Other external protocols

Scripting   Has a built-in Macro Processor, used as a way of replacing script languages found in larger programs. Built-in editor to alter macros "on-the-fly."

Other

DESQview aware
Chat mode and Doorway mode
Can shell to DOS
Dials multiple numbers
Sound toggles on and off

Support

Documentation is provided

GT Power

P & M Software Company
3104 East Camelback Road #503
Phoenix, Arizona 85016
(602)285-9914

Current Version: 15.00
Shareware Fee: $70

Hardware Required

Minimum RAM required: 384K
Minimum disk space: 727K

Terminal Emulation

ANSI-BBS
DEC VT-100

File Transfer Protocols

Xmodem	TELINK
Xmodem CRC	TELINK-1K
Ymodem	CompuServe B
Ymodem batch	SEALINK
MEGALINK	

Scripting   79 script commands.

Other

Unlimited number of 999-entry dialing directories
ALT key-oriented
Works with almost all full-duplex asynchronous modems
Full-feature Host mode
Supports BASIC style PLAY for single voice music
200-entry circular dialing queue

Support

Manual: 87 pages
Voice Support: 8A.M.-5P.M. PST, Monday-Friday, (602)285-9914
Support BBS: (602)285-1146 or (713)772-2900

Procomm

Datastorm Technologies, Inc.   Shareware Fee: $50
Post Office Box 1471
Columbia, Missouri 65205
(314)474-8461

Hardware Required

Minimum RAM required: 130K
Minimum disk space: 175K

Terminal Emulations

TTY	BBS-ANSI
DEC VT-52	DEC VT-100
IBM3101, Character mode only	Televideo/910, 920, 925, 950, 955
Lear-Siegler ADM 3/5	ADDS Viewpoint
IBM3270, asynch	Wyse/100
Heath/Zenith 19	

File Transfer Protocols

Xmodem	MODEM7
Xmodem CRC	TELINK
Ymodem	CompuServe B
Ymodem-G	WXmodem
Kermit	

Scripting Command language for writing scripts, fewer than 50 commands.

Other

Dialing directory limited to 100 entries
DESQview support
ALT key-oriented
Works with almost all full-duplex asynchronous modems
Host mode

Support

Manual: 101 pages
Distribution BBS: (314)474-8477 (no support BBS)
CompuServe Forum: GO PCVENA, Section 14
GEnie Roundtable

Qmodem SST

The Forbin Project, Inc.
Post Office Box 702
Cedar Falls, Iowa 50613
(319)232-4516

Current Version: 4.0
Shareware Fee: $30

Hardware Required

Minimum RAM required: 384K
Minimum disk space: 900K

Terminal Emulations

TTY
ANSI-BBS
DEC VT-100

File Transfer Protocols

Xmodem
Xmodem CRC
Ymodem
Ymodem batch
Ymodem-G

Scripting   75 commands.

Other

Unlimited number of 200-entry dialing directories
Windows/386 support
DESQview support
ALT key-oriented
Works with almost all full-duplex asynchronous modems
Host mode
Professionally-oriented tutorial on Qmodem installation, script
  recording features, and installation of external protocols

Support

Manual: 258 pages
Voice Support: 8A.M.-4:30P.M. CST, Monday-Friday, (319)232-4516
Support BBS: (319)233-6157
GEnie Roundtable

Telix

Exis, Inc.
Post Office Box 130
West Hill, Ontario, M1E 4R4,
Canada
(416)289-4641 (Voice)

Current Version: 1.00
Shareware Fee: $30

Hardware Required

IBM PC, XT, AT, PS/2, or any true compatible
Minimum RAM Required: 170K (for some functions, more memory is help-
    ful)
Hayes-compatible modem using Hayes AT command set
Supports up to 8 defined COM ports (COM1 through COM4 are pre-
    defined), any number of disk drives, and a printer connected to the
    parallel port

Terminal Emulations

TTY
ANSI-BBS
VT-102
DEC VT-52

File Transfer Protocols

Internal:
  Zmodem
  CompuServe Quick B
  Xmodem

  Ymodem-G
  Kermit
  SEALINK

Xmodem-1K	TELINK
Xmodem-1K-G	MODEM7
Ymodem (true)	ASCII

External:
4 kinds are allowed and called from within Telix
Almost any kind of file transfer is possible

Scripting   Uses extensive SALT script language to perform automatic logons and other, more complicated functions.

Other

Chat mode
Keyboard macros
Scroll-back buffer
Session capture
Usage log
Translate Table
Full access to DOS, including a DOS shell, a DOS command option, and full path support
Host mode with file transfers, operator paging, a remote DOS shell, and two access levels
Powerful, multiple dialing directories
Automatic queue redialing

Support

Manual is included
Voice Support: (416)289-4641
Fax communications: (416)289-4645
Support BBS: (416)439-8983

Additional Popular Programs

ASCII Pro (ProDOS, MS-DOS)
United Software Industries

8399 Topanga Canyon Boulevard
Canoga Park, California 91304
(818)887-5800

ASCOM IV
Dynamic Microprocessor Associates
545 Fifth Avenue, #1103
New York, New York 10017
(212)687-7115

Freeway Advanced (MS-DOS)
Kortek, Inc.
505 Hamilton Avenue
Palo Alto, California 94301
(415)327-4555

MicroPhone II (Macintosh)
Software Ventures Corp.
2907 Claremont Avenue
Berkeley, California 94705
(415)644-3232; (800)336-6477

MIRROR III
Softklone Distributing Corp.
327 Office Plaza Drive
Tallahassee, Florida 32301
(904)878-8564; (904)878-9884, BBS

Microsoft Access (MS-DOS)
Microsoft Corporation
16011 Northeast 36th Way
Redmond, Washington 98073
(800)426-9400

PC TALK4
Headlands Communications Corp.
1624 Tiburon Boulevard
Post Office Box 8
Tiburon, California 94920
(415)435-0770

Red Ryder (Macintosh)
The Freesoft Co.
10828 Lacklink
St. Louis, Missouri 63114
(314)423-2190

SIDETALK
Lattice Inc.
Post Office Box 3072
Glen Ellyn, Illinois 60138
(312)916-1600; (800)533-3577

TELIOS
Genasys Corp.
11820 Parklawn Drive
Rockville, Maryland 20852
(301)770-4600

Windows InTalk (MS-DOS)
Palantir
12777 Jones Road, Suite 100
Houston, Texas 77070
(713)955-8880

SPECIALTY PROGRAMS FOR PERSONAL USE

There are a number of programs available that help to simplify or enhance your use of telecommunications. They vary in function, but they all augment the use of telecommunications programs. Two of the most popular of these programs follow.

Qanalyst

This is a program for use with Qmodem 4.01. The program analyzes the log file that Qmodem keeps. It is able to keep very close tabs not only on how much time has been spent on line but also on what the cost will be. Qanalyst is easy to set up. While connected, you can pop up Qanalyst and find out just how much your current call has cost you. It can even calculate the cost of your connect time to a regularly called on-line service.

Another one of Qanalyst's many features is its ability to generate reports on usage for your review. Qanalyst can be found on most systems under the name QANA???.ZIP (where ??? represents the version number, for example, QANA202.ZIP).

Author   Rob Rosenberger

Address   Barn Owl Software, Post Office Box 74, O'Fallon, Illinois 62269

Registration Amount $15 disk, $7.50 manual

File Size   200K

Estimated Number of Users   4500 plus

TFE 2.00 — TelixFonEd

The TelixFonEd is usually found under a filename such as TFE_200.ZIP. This utility is designed for use with the TELIX 3.1x communications program. With TFE you can sort and alter multiple Telix telephone .FON directories. Entries can be copied, deleted, rearranged, and so on. The best use of this program is to clean up a crowded dialing directory.

Author   Paul Roub

Address   Post Office Box 141583, Coral Gables, Florida 33114-1583

Registration Amount $10

File Size   40K

Estimated Number of Users   2000 plus

REMOTE PC COMMUNICATIONS

Most every computer user at a remote site has, at one time or another, been stuck—unable to progress and without available help. The most obvious aid is through a phone call, but the solution usually involves a lengthy discussion of "what did you do?" and "what happened then?" The helper is unable to see the user's computer screen, and has to carefully reconstruct the user's situation mentally or on another computer. For difficult problems, other means—travel to the site or a search for a more educated user—are needed, resulting in frustrating, infuriating, and expensive delays.

An innovative answer to this dilemma is *remote control* or *remote communications*. With remote communications, it is possible to operate a PC from a different PC. When support is needed, two people at different locations are able to link together interactively, so both may simultaneously see and operate a single central processing unit (CPU). The helper is able to see what is on the user's screen and can show the user what to do. The helper and user are looking at the same screen—even though they are in different locations—and are both able to enter commands and see the results.

All this is accomplished either through a modem, allowing the distance between the two PCs to be thousands of miles, or by direct connection (hard wired) between two computers in the same office.

History of Remote Control

The concept of remote communications began with general purpose communications programs such as Crosstalk XVI and Ascom IV. The remote features in these programs were extremely limited, but they did allow a remote caller to run DOS commands and some applications on the host computer. However, the remote caller was limited to only "well-behaved" applications.

A well-behaved program is one that goes through DOS for screen output, rather than talking to the hardware directly. With well-behaved programs, the communications program can read data going to the screen, and redirect it out the communications port so that the remote caller can see it. Unfortunately, many of the more popular programs at the time were not well-behaved, so remote control was limited regarding general communications software.

With modern remote control programs, screen output can be redirected to the communications port even from programs that are not well-behaved. Because programs of this kind are not as varied or numerous as in other software genres, there is room available for a heavy hitter. As yet, however, no single remote control product has been able to dominate PC communications in the way that Lotus 1-2-3 has dominated the spreadsheet business.

One product did come close. Meridian Technology Inc., now the Microcom Software Division, developed Carbon Copy 2.14 in 1985. Carbon Copy represented a startling improvement over the only other existing remote control product, MicroStuf's Remote. Remote was the first remote control package to hit the retail market, but it was never well accepted. On the other hand, Carbon Copy was a strong product with an aggressive marketing plan.

Crosstalk Communications' REMOTE2 is another program that lets users of modem-equipped personal computers, portable computers, laptops, and terminals dial in to other modem-equipped PCs and operate them remotely. R2LAN, a LAN-compatible version of REMOTE2, provides similar access to computers that are connected by any IBM NetBIOS-compatible LAN, and to other REMOTE2-equipped PCs.

REMOTE2 was designed to make call-in access easy for users of IBM PCs and compatibles. Using REMOTE2, a PC user can call another PC and, once connected, operate that PC (the host) remotely. Any software present on the host may be used. Combined with REMOTE2's support of modem speeds up to 115,200bps, this breadth of application support makes the product especially attractive to people who support software users at other locations. REMOTE2 uses a "call-back" security feature that may be enabled as desired for each user. When it's enabled, the REMOTE2 host calls users back at the numbers stored in its user database. This prevents unauthorized access to the host system, and allows long-distance tolls to be charged to the host.

The Host/Remote Relationship

Remote programs have two elements—the host side and the remote side. This is a master/slave relationship, where the remote side is the master/controller, and the host side is the slave/observer. To achieve true remote control, the process must be a transparent interaction between two PCs. The remote side views and controls the host side, still allowing the host side total use of the machine. Once connected, the remote PC is usually the only one capable of file transfers to and from the host machine.

While much of the PC communications world struggles to decide which data transmission protocol will become the industry standard for transferring error-free data, vendors on the leading edge are bypassing the protocol standards debate entirely. Remote control packages have implemented proprietary transmission protocols.

The remote/host relationship in remote control packages creates a tightly paired, identical, and interactive set of computer software. When in the remote control mode, the paired units are not intended to perform the varied functions of general purpose communication. Therefore, no reason exists to implement a widely-used protocol, because identical software is provided for both ends.

The tight link between two PCs that implement remote control requires not only that files be exchanged error-free, but that screen graphics, user keystrokes, and remote printing commands be passed as well. Because of these unique transmission requirements, the new and proprietary protocols are used to get all that information across the line most efficiently. Since there is no need to use industry-accepted protocols, vendors are free to optimize their transmission and error-correction schemes in any way that works. Transmissions between host and remote computers are encrypted to some extent, to prevent eavesdropping and data theft.

The goal in data transmission is to reproduce information exactly on each side of the line; therefore, an error-checking protocol is employed by all types of remote control software. (Error-checking is needed when the line has noise or other interference, which is typical of most public dial-up lines commonly used to send information.) Error-checking protocols give the receiving PC an idea of what the incoming data should look like. The receiving PC can then detect distorted data and request retransmission. Protocols are transparent to the user because the same protocol is in use at both ends.

All remote programs continually scan video memory on the host for changes, so that they need only transmit screen updates to the remote PC. They also use some degree of data compression before sending graphic information. Some of the data compression methods used are so streamlined that, when applied to straight file transfer, they can outperform standard file transfer packages by 300 percent.

What Remote Control Can Do for You

Once connected by a remote control package, one PC can do anything the other PC can do. The screens at each end display the same images, the keyboards operate as one, and users at both ends may work with the application at the same time. With this capability, workers on the road can hook into a database on a central computer, access software they don't have with them, and print out invoices and reports at the central computer site if they don't have a printer on hand. They can also operate the host computer just as if they were sitting in front of it. They may access a word processor package, create a file, save it, transfer it to their hard disk, and print on either end.

One of the best uses of remote control is training. Computer classes in corporations have always been expensive, cumbersome, and of questionable value. Numerous other approaches—help lines, videotaped classes, on-site consultants, and expensive, written procedure manuals—have also been tried.

With remote control, a business can train new users from a central location. The student is able to learn while working, and seek help when it's needed—in the context of the job. PC-support technicians and trainers can call remote-control-equipped PCs and monitor both software performance and user interaction, acquiring on-the-spot information to use as the basis for their advice and instruction to the system's users. Both the host's and the calling computer's screens and keyboards are live; either user may control the host, and discuss what is going on. If the host is connected to a LAN, the user can also log onto the network and run any software to which access has been authorized.

Security

Many corporations have found benefits in remote control software. However, corporate users are uncomfortable with the possibility of unauthorized personnel remotely accessing confidential data. Steps have been taken to minimize the risks; data encryption is used, and most packages have passwords.

For maximum security, some packages (like REMOTE2, mentioned earlier) tie the passwords to a telephone list call-back feature. With this option, a remote operator calls in to the host machine and enters a password. The host machine then hangs up the phone line and dials the phone number previously assigned to that password. This keeps intruders off the system; remote users must have the proper password associated with the phone number they are calling from.

Business users of PCs were the first to learn that call-in access can greatly improve the productivity of any user who needs to operate another PC from home or on the road. Now PC users with other interests have also discovered the convenience of this kind of access.

CHAPTER FIVE

E-mail

A decade ago many of us thought that E-mail was going to be what made the personal computer an essential instrument for everyone. It turned out that spreadsheets grabbed the computer revolution, and E-mail was for the most part forgotten. Then the inexpensive fax (facsimile) machine came along and E-mail really became secondary to fax technology, which had the advantages of being outfitted with new worldwide standards and being incredibly easy to use. With the advent of the local area network and the interoffice E-mail system, the value of E-mail is being rediscovered. This return to prominence has been helped along by systems such as MCI Mail, AT&T Mail, and all information utilities such as CompuServe that carry E-mail.

WHAT IS E-MAIL?

E-mail is the transmission of correspondence (such as letters and memos) from computer to computer over a network of some sort. Since this book concentrates on telecommunications, the emphasis will be on wide area networks—the ones you call with a modem. Today many E-mail systems (MCI, for example, when used with an MCI Mail-oriented program) can even send graphics and programs from user to user. Links into the netherworld of telecommunications networks mean you have access to almost every country with this medium.

I'm a big fan of E-mail in general and MCI Mail, specifically. At Ziff-Davis, for example, MCI Mail is used by all its magazines. The editors and the writers are always connected with MCI Mail whether they are in the office or in the field. Other large corporations use MCI as their only E-mail system to save the expense of installing a LAN. Where there is a phone line, there is E-mail.

E-mail has its roots in telex, a worldwide system for sending messages between teletypewriters that has been going strong for close to a century. Telex transmits text at the sluggish pace of ten characters per second and frequently delivers it with characters garbled here and there because of transmission errors. Nevertheless, telex remains an important form of business communication in many less-developed parts of the world, and is even used to carry E-mail on some international services. E-mail grew up in the seventies with systems based on mainframes and minicomputers.

The great thing about E-mail is the convenience. The receiver doesn't need to be at the computer when the message is sent. E-mail's ability to store and forward messages makes it easy to communicate worldwide.

Anyone with a computer, a modem, and a telephone line can use MCI Mail to communicate electronically with others anywhere in the world. MCI Mail can be sent to other MCI Mail subscribers, electronic mail systems (EMS connected to MCI Mail), telex subscribers, postal addresses, or fax devices worldwide. You can also receive electronic mail from MCI Mail subscribers, other EMS systems, and telex terminals.

There are two main classes of E-mail service: private and public. Private E-mail serves the internal needs of an organization and is based on a multiuser computer system such as a mainframe or LAN. Public E-mail services are available to individuals or organizations by subscription and are usually national or international in scope.

Private E-mail Systems

E-mail is the number one application on local area networks. Multiuser computer E-mail systems are also popular with products such as IBM

PROFS, DEC All-In-One, and WangOffice; these typically support a variety of office-automation functions, including E-mail.

Some network systems for PCs, like Torus Tapestry, incorporate E-mail as a standard feature. Certain LAN-operating-system vendors, Banyan and 3Com for example, offer E-mail as an extra-cost option. For the rest, third-party packages are available. The most popular include cc:Mail from the company of the same name, Network Courier from Consumers Software, The Coordinator II from Action Technologies, and WordPerfect Office.

Public E-mail Systems

Public E-mail systems are operated as commercial ventures and sold by subscription. The chief examples are MCI Mail, AT&T Mail, and Western Union's EasyLink in the U.S.A., and Telecom Canada's Envoy 100. MCI Mail is the most popular choice for individuals and will serve as our main example of what one can expect from such services. MCI Mail not only delivers messages to the mailboxes of other subscribers, but can forward them to certain other E-mail systems, such as PT Postel in Italy, Telemail in the U.S., and Missive in Italy, and can also channel them to telex and fax machines worldwide. Last but not least, MCI Mail can arrange for your message to be printed and then either delivered by courier or injected into the regular paper-mail system. One benefit of using MCI Mail to handle paper mail is that, for expediency, the printing is done at a location close to the delivery point.

Other E-mail Systems

There are even more E-mail systems than those already categorized. Semi-public mail services based on computer networks such as CompuServe, FidoNet, and Internet are very popular. (CompuServe will be discussed thoroughly in the next chapter.) Let's examine a few of these systems and their capabilities.

MCI MAIL

In 1983, MCI Communications Corporation became the victor in a court battle with AT&T's telecommunications monopoly. MCI could now introduce new services. E-mail, a way for corporations to communicate internally, wasn't yet offered to the general public. There was a need for the average computer user to communicate electronically. MCI answered this need with MCI Mail.

In nine months, largely through the efforts of telecomm pioneer Vint Cerf, and Bob Harcharik who came to MCI from ARPANET, MCI Mail was produced and implemented. In its brief history, MCI Mail has become established as one of the most innovative telecommunications products offered.

Uses of MCI Mail

MCI Mail is a new business tool. Whether you use it as an individual or as part of a company, it will prove indispensable. And as you become more familiar with it, you will very likely find your own unique uses. People are using MCI Mail today to:

- Distribute hot leads to the sales force in an instant
- Avoid playing telephone tag
- Receive ordering information more quickly and efficiently than by regular mail or phone
- Instantly distribute reports or memos to key people throughout the U.S. and the world
- Send price changes and product announcements to clients across the country
- Send proposals or follow-up letters from anywhere—even from on the road—to get the jump on the competition
- Share spreadsheets and graphics among PCs that use Lotus Express or similar MCI mail oriented programs (see Chapter 10)
- Distribute instant newsletters to MCI Mail subscribers across the country
- Expedite communications with dealers and distributors by eliminating paper backlogs
- Send finished chapters of a new book to a publisher
- Arrange travel or work schedules while moving from location to location across the U.S.

- Create a bulletin board to gather or distribute information on a new project
- Send newspaper stories to an editor from remote locations
- Send a fax to an associate from a streetcorner pay phone, using a laptop computer and modem
- Send up-to-the-minute press releases to everyone on a client list
- Set up an E-mail network by getting business associates to become MCI Mail subscribers

MCI Services

In addition to a full menu of electronic and paper delivery options, MCI Mail also offers a comprehensive range of other services. You may access public and private bulletin boards, or start one of your own. You can use MCI Mail for toll-free access to the Dow Jones News/Retrieval database (you are charged by the minute for using this service). The following are the primary services offered by MCI:

MCI Instant Letter   Delivers messages in seconds from your terminal to the terminal of any other MCI Mail customer, or subscriber to CompuServe, PT Postel, or Missive throughout the world. MCI is also linked to various corporate internal E-mail systems and to Internet, so you can send to and receive from these, too.

MCI Overnight Letter   Laser-printed (paper) copies of your messages are hand-delivered by noon of the next business day for less than the cost of standard couriers. There is an option of using your own letterhead and your signature.

The MCI Letter   To speed up postal delivery, messages are electronically transmitted to the MCI Print Center nearest the recipient. Laser-printed copies of the messages are then sent by local first class mail.

MCI International Courier   Your document is electronically transmitted to an overseas laser print site. A hardcopy is then delivered by courier the next business day to many cities in Europe and Australia — and, usually, in one to four business days in other parts of the world.

MCI International Letter   From an overseas print site, a hardcopy of your document is transported via the local postal service for delivery three to five days faster than normal postal delivery from the U.S.

Fax Dispatch   This feature lets you use MCI Mail to communicate with more than 4.2 million Group III fax machines worldwide. You no longer need to print out a document before faxing it. With Fax Dispatch, you just enter simple commands and your document is quickly transmitted to the receiving fax machines. If necessary, MCI Mail will automatically make several attempts to deliver your message and will notify you when the message is delivered.

Telex Dispatch   Send and receive telexes from the privacy of your own computer terminal, and communicate with over 1.8 million Telex subscribers worldwide.

Special MCI Mail Features

MCI offers interesting features and services besides the delivery of E-mail and paper messages. Some of these include the following:

Bulletin Boards   MCI Mail Bulletin Board is the perfect way to exchange messages. It lets you create, maintain, and search electronic bulletin boards. MCI Mail can turn your terminal into an electronic bulletin board. You can post information that you'd like people to read, and you can control who's allowed to view it by creating an access list.

Shared Lists   You also have access to Shared Lists. These are the names of E-mail users (both individuals and companies) with whom you can share messages. As an "owner" of a list, you can "publish" it to all MCI Mail users worldwide, or create a separate access list that indicates who can use the Shared List.

Private Lists   Unlike the Shared Lists, a Private List is available only to you. It's a handy feature when you correspond with the same people regularly.

Scripts   Script service is the ability to custom-design interactive data-entry forms for users to fill in. All delivery options and formats are available.

Information Services You may access the Dow Jones News/Retrieval (DJN/R) with MCI Mail. DJN/R offers more than 40 services. These include the latest quotes on stocks and bonds and business databases. There is also a section where you can read and place classified ads.

MCI Mail users are billed at DJN/R's standard membership rates. (By calling during non-prime-time hours, you will save money.) See Chapter 6 for detailed information on DJN/R.

Directory Services MCI Mail has a complete and easy-to-use directory. Users are identified by name or MCI ID, so there are no complex code numbers to memorize. In addition, E-mail addresses and postal addresses are stored to facilitate delivery. If you want to send the authors of this book a memo on MCI, all you have to do is type Dvorak or Anis at the prompt asking for the recipient's name or mailbox number.

Return Receipts You may indicate that you want a return receipt, so that you know that your message was received.

Broadcast Hardcopy/RJE This is an option for high-speed, cost-effective handling of hundreds, even thousands, of letters.

Interconnected Services

MCI Mail currently has over 100,000 subscribers around the world. These include both large and small institutions, as well as individuals. MCI Mail subscribers are a part of the largest combined E-mail user base in the world. There are over 550,000 active mailboxes.

MCI Mail provides access to worldwide postal and delivery service, 4.2 million fax machines, and 1.8 million telex machines.

Enhancements to MCI Mail

There are a number of different software programs and gateways designed to enhance the use of MCI Mail.

MCI Agents There are several agent programs for MCI Mail (see Chapter 10). These agents allow the entire electronic mail process to be automated. These agents use a special error-correcting protocol called X.PC that can detect phone line noise or electric glitches and correct any problems that may result.

The key feature is the ability to transmit and receive binary files. Programs, spreadsheets, databases, and fully-formatted word processing files can be sent through the MCI Mail System. With Lotus Express, you can also exchange files with Desktop Express (Macintosh), providing there are the appropriate peripherals at each end.

Desktop Express   Desktop Express is a program designed for use with MCI Mail on the Apple Macintosh line of computers. Desktop Express can transfer any kind of message, including images and programs. You can exchange spreadsheets, word processing documents, and files from such programs as Excel, Lotus 1-2-3, Microsoft Word, and dBASE. And, Desktop Express is the only program in today's software market that can take an image and print it out on MCI Mail's own Apple LaserWriter printers, for delivery by mail or courier. It can also send high-resolution, laser-printed documents from PageMaker, MacPaint, MacWrite, and more, even if you (or the recipient) don't have a laser printer.

VAX Mailgate   This is a program designed to let DEC All-In-One electronic mail users access MCI Mail. With it, both systems function as a single integrated E-mail system. It allows information to be quickly exchanged and easily accessed. It also permits MCI Mail subscribers to exchange messages with All-In-One users.

MCI Gateway for Microsoft Mail   This new software package enables users of Microsoft Mail to add the delivery and handling options of MCI Mail to their AppleTalk LAN system. Microsoft Mail users can then send messages for worldwide postal, courier fax, and telex delivery. They also have the ability to send messages to any MCI Mail subscriber or to EMS subscribers connected to MCI Mail.

MCI Mail Link To PROFS   This is a software interface that provides IBM PROFS users with a transparent gateway to the delivery options of MCI Mail. From their PROFS terminals, PROFS users may communicate with users outside the PROFS environment. Because MCI Mail Link To PROFS was designed to be fully integrated with PROFS, the two systems appear to the user as a single mail system because of the ease of message exchange.

The MCI and IBM E-mail Link MCI and IBM have announced their intent to provide a commercial interconnection between MCI Mail and the IBM Information Network's Screenmail electronic mail service.

The interconnection is expected to be introduced initially as a limited offering available to the U.S. aerospace industry. MCI and IBM will evaluate the move toward later general availability of the interconnection.

The interconnection, using the X.400 message handling standard (discussed later in this chapter), will allow customers of the IBM Information Network (including those using PROFS, DISOSS, AS/400 Office, System/36, System/38, 3270s, and PCs) to exchange electronic messages with subscribers of MCI Mail and its interconnected systems (such as CompuServe, Telemail, and Dialcom).

MCI Mail and CompuServe MCI Mail and CompuServe introduced the first interconnection between major electronic mail companies. As there was no "standard" for such interconnections at that time, CompuServe and MCI Mail used MCI Mail's proprietary LINK. Thus, messaging between the two systems is as simple as (from MCI Mail, for example) stating the destination service (CompuServe) and the destination mailbox.

Unlike the interconnection between CompuServe and MCI Mail, the MCI Mail-Telemail link (as well as all future interconnections) uses the X.400 message handling standard.

Getting Connected to MCI Mail

Obviously you'll need a PC, a modem, and the telecommunications software of your choice to use MCI Mail. For subscription information, simply call the MCI Mail customer service number Monday through Friday, between 9:00A.M. and 8:00P.M. EST: 1-800-444-MAIL (1-800-444-6245). In Washington, D.C., call 1-202-833-8484.

An MCI Mail representative will ask for the appropriate information to help you open an account. You'll be able to select some of the available service options and decide which billing plan to use. In seven to ten days you'll receive the MCI Mail Starter Kit with all the details of your account, including your user name, ID number and password. If you're eager to get started, you can arrange to have your account opened within 24 hours.

MCI Mail Costs

There are no charges for connect time and no service minimums. MCI Mail can be reached anywhere in the U.S. by using the following toll-free numbers. (For more on MCI access numbers, see Chapter 10.)

1-800-234-MAIL (1-800-234-6245) for 300 and 1200bps modems
1-800-456-6245 for 2400bps
1-800-825-1515 for Lotus Express users (all modem speeds)

The only fixed charge is an annual $25.00 subscription fee. The alternative is the special MCI Mail Preferred Pricing Option, which carries a basic monthly charge. Individual messages are charged by message length and the type of delivery option used.

Cost Breakdown

MCI Mail is especially attractive because of its pricing structure. Here's a breakdown of some of the costs:

Instant Letters

Up to 500 characters total length	$0.45
501 to 2500 characters total length	$0.75
2501 to 7500 characters total length	$1.00
Each additional 7500 characters	$1.00

Paper Mail

	U.S.	INTERNATIONAL
MCI Letter up to 3 pages	$2.00	$5.00
Overnight Letter up to 6 pages	$9.00	$12.00-$30.00
Each additional 3 pages	$1.00	$1.00

Fax Dispatch

	U.S.	INTERNATIONAL
First 1/2 page	$0.50	*
Each additional 1/2 page	$0.30	*

*Price varies by country of destination. While on line, type **HELP** and the country's name to get current rates.

Telex Dispatch   Telex messages are billed by the minute based on output time to the receiver Telex terminal. Rates are based on the destination country. Refer on line to HELP TELEX PRICING.

MCI Mail Preferred Pricing Option   If you select this option, for $10 a month you will receive one mailbox and up to 40 messages free, including electronic messages and/or domestic Fax Dispatch. If an electronic message is greater than 7500 characters, then each additional 7500 characters (or portion thereof) is counted as a message. Additional messages (after the first 40) are billed at regular MCI Mail rates.

Letterhead and Signature Graphics   You can register for this for $20 and receive up to 15 graphics.

MCI Mail Alert $1 per message

Receipts   These are automatically generated by Fax Dispatch or Telex Dispatch. The Return Fee is 25 cents. There is no charge for receipts.

General MCI Mail Information

MCI Mail's user-friendly design makes it easy for anyone to become an electronic mail expert, without extensive computer training.

If you do run into problems, consult the "Quick Reference to MCI Mail" found in the Starter Kit, or call MCI's Customer Support service at 1-800-444-MAIL (6245) or at 1-202-833-8484 in Washington, D.C.

International Access to MCI Mail

To sign on to MCI Mail from Canada requires use of the Datapac system. MCI Mail can also be accessed from many other countries. To use MCI Mail from outside the U.S., you must subscribe to that country's packet-switching service. Signing on is different in every country, so it's not possible to give you a universal set of instructions. Chapter 15 will give you some information on how to connect from Europe. You should also refer on line to "International Access" on the MCI Mail Bulletin Board to receive a list of countries where MCI Mail is available, and country-specific contacts and information. (Be sure to do this before leaving the U.S., or you may not know how to sign on.)

Using the Service

MCI Mail is designed to let you move easily through each of the functions by typing a simple English-language command. And, unlike other E-mail systems, MCI Mail's open directory service allows you to find users easily. The FIND command will help you identify or locate other MCI Mail users, whether they are individual MCI Mail subscribers, entries on Shared Lists, or linked to MCI through another system.

In addition, messages that you receive or create on MCI Mail are stored within the system and are easily retrieved. Here are some of the storage commands you'll need to know:

INBOX   stores unread messages. After the message has been read, MCI Mail sends it to DESK.

DESK   stores messages that you have already read. Messages remain in DESK for five days.

DRAFT   stores any message that you have written, but not sent. Only one message can be stored in DRAFT. Any messages written and stored after the first one will be held in PENDING.

OUTBOX   stores messages that you have sent.

LISTS   stores address lists that you have created.

PENDING   holds DRAFTS that you have not yet delivered.

TRASH   stores messages that you have deleted. After all, you may have a change of heart.

GRAPHICS   holds signatures and forms to be sent through paper mail.

Basic MCI Mail Commands

Now that you know where your messages will end up, you can focus on commands. Advanced Service is "command driven," which means you don't see menus before each prompt, as you do in Basic Service. Instead, you see the command prompt alone, so you need to be knowledgeable about which command performs each function. The following list defines some of the most frequently used commands (you only need to type the first two letters).

CREATE creates a DRAFT message.

READ reads incoming messages or DRAFTs, pausing every 25 lines until you press a key.

PRINT makes incoming or outgoing messages scroll up your screen without pausing every 25 lines.

SCAN scans a list of stored messages—you can scan any of the storage areas.

EDIT edits your message on line.

SEND sends your message to another MCI Mail mailbox. The message will appear in the recipient's INBOX, and a copy is sent to your OUTBOX. For INSTANT mail users, the following specific options can be attached:

- ONITE   Your message is marked PRIORITY, and it goes to the top of the recipient's message list.

- RECEIPT   The sender is informed of the date and time the recipient picked up the message.

- ALERT   The recipient is telephoned with the news that an important MCI Mail message is in the INBOX.

- EMS   The recipient gets the message through E-mail link or through the Fax Dispatch feature.

- TELEX   The recipient gets the message through a telex system.

HELP gives you a description of Mail options open to you at any given command prompt. Type **HELP** or **?**.

EXIT signs you off MCI Mail. You can exit at *any* command prompt by simply typing in **EXIT** or **EX**.

Reading Your MCI Mail

With MCI Mail, viewing messages is an easy process. As soon as you sign on, one of the first bits of information you'll see is the number of messages in your INBOX. To get an immediate overview of what's in your INBOX, just type **SCAN**. A numbered list of your messages, including subject, sender, and number of characters, will appear on your screen. PRIORITY mail will be listed first, followed chronologically by all other messages. You can READ or PRINT (to screen) any or all of your messages by typing **READ** or **PRINT** and the message numbers (for example, **READ 1,2,3,4**).

Creating an Instant Message

To address an envelope to an MCI Mail subscriber for instant delivery, just follow these steps:

1. At COMMAND, type **CREATE**.

2. At TO, type the recipient's name, and then press ENTER.

3. At TO, repeat step 2 to enter more electronic recipients, or press ENTER to skip this prompt. (You may send the same message to other EMS, fax, telex, or paper recipients.)

4. At CC, repeat step 2 if you want to send Courtesy Copies, or press ENTER to skip this prompt.

5. At SUBJECT, type a subject, or press ENTER to skip this prompt.

To create the text for your instant message:

1. At TEXT, enter your message or upload a file (based on your communications program specifications). Lines may contain up to 255 characters and must end with a carriage return. Most users limit their message line length to 80 characters. Longer lines can be useful for sending spreadsheets or other large tables.

2. End the text by pressing ENTER after the last line and typing **/** (slash) at the left margin. Press ENTER again.

You may send your instant message immediately after creating it or you may edit the text or the envelope prior to printing. To send your instant message if you have just ended your text:

1. At HANDLING, type in any handling option listed in the user's guide (you should receive this when you subscribe), such as DOC, ONITE, RECEIPT, and so on. Press ENTER if you want to skip this prompt.

2. At SEND?, type **YES**.

Detailed information on all MCI Mail commands and features can be found in your Starter Kit. You can also request information whenever you're on line by simply typing **Help** followed by the name of the command or topic (for instance, Help CREATE, Help FAX, or Help SCRIPTS).

Cellular Access to MCI Mail

MCI Mail has become a necessary part of many people's lives. Now, those addicted to MCI Mail may access the service wherever there is cellular telephone coverage.

Cellular phones provide the capacity to make and receive ordinary telephone calls by "radio" rather than by wire. These phones generally come in three sizes.

- *Vehicular*   This is installed in your car or boat.

- *Transportable*   This is about the size of a large lunch box.

- *Portable*   This is often small enough to fit in your pocket.

Cellular phones communicate with the phone system via a series of adjacent transmitters/receivers (called *cells*) that work in tandem to provide coverage over a broad geographic area. The systems automatically pass a call from one cell to another, usually without your knowledge, as you travel along your route. Many of the cellular companies have joined together to allow the subscriber of one service to *roam*, or to make calls in another company's area. Until recently, this has worked well only for voice access.

The growing popularity of electronic mail has encouraged a number of companies to offer interfaces (usually RJ11C—the same interface that connects your telephone to the wall plug) that can be used by modems. This can be accomplished in three ways.

1. You can put the RJ11C directly into the phone. (NYNEX, General Electric, and Radio Shack units offer this option.) The restriction to this is that you must first dial the MCI Mail number on the phone. Once connected, the modem can start communicating with MCI Mail. This technique will work with most general-purpose communications programs. However, it will not work with agent programs like Lotus or Desktop Express. These programs expect to dial out directly themselves.

2. Tellular Inc. offers another answer—the Celjack. This is a "black box" that is electrically set between the main unit and the handset (obviously, it will not work with portable phones). The modem is plugged directly into the Celjack. It provides all of the signals that your modem expects from the phone company. As such, Lotus/Desktop Express will dial out to access MCI Mail. (For more information contact Tellular Inc., at 1-312-256-8000.)

3. The third option is the Intelligence Technology Corporation's laptop computer (model 286 CAT) that features a built-in cellular phone and modem. (This is the most expensive option—its price tag is over $7000.) This does provide the space and weight benefit of merging the cellular and PC technology into one laptop-sized box. (For more information contact ITC at 1-800-356-3493.)

Some of the current restrictions on cellular/modem use are

• 1200 baud is about tops. Although the Celjack is rated for 2400 baud, the quality of the analog radio signal cannot support it. As some of the phones and cellular companies switch over to digital processing, this may improve.

• The device should not be in motion (that is, your car or boat should not be moving) when communicating. Switching from cell to cell is nearly instantaneous, but the transition can result in a loss of carrier.

- If signal strength is weak, you may need to shift to 300 baud. The communication will take four times longer than 1200 baud.

- One carrier may have better coverage in a local area than another. Before subscribing to a specific carrier, check which carrier has the closest cells.

- If at all possible, try to use the battery to your car or boat or an AC converter as a power source, instead of the internal batteries, to get the best possible signal strength. It is also important to use a cellular phone that outputs a full 3 watts (the maximum output).

- If at all possible, use external antennae.

Remember that the cellular companies charge for *any* calls made or received—even those to MCI Mail's 800 numbers.

X.400 Compatibility

Developed by the CCITT, X.400 is a series of recommendations that sets guidelines or standards for transferring messages between electronic mail systems. The X.400 standards define, for example, the format of the "envelope" of a message so that it may be delivered successfully by all electronic mail systems that support X.400.

Last year MCI Mail unveiled XChange 400, a gateway that allows users to exchange messages with X.400 communities connected to the MCI Mail network. Sending messages to connected X.400 communities is easy, since the gateway follows the addressing conventions already familiar to you as an MCI Mail subscriber. MCI Mail—not you—reformats the message so that it complies with the X.400 standards for delivery.

If your company has made the investment to upgrade its internal communications system to X.400, MCI Mail can help you reach those business partners and customers who haven't yet upgraded. MCI Mail XChange 400 connects you to other private and public X.400 systems. Any MCI Mail user can send messages to your X.400 system—MCI does the conversion. You can even send X.400 messages to MCI Mail for delivery to fax and telex devices or for postal and courier delivery.

An Overview of X.400 Service

Generally, an X.400 E-mail address consists of a mail system name (such as Telemail), the country in which the mail system operates (such as the U.S.), and a personal name, which is broken into surname and given name. (Note that MCI Mail does not require you to supply the name of the country.)

Addressing Terminology

In order to properly exchange messages with X.400 mail services, it is important to understand a little X.400 addressing terminology.

O/R Name is a common term. It means originator/recipient name. It is made up of three components.

- **ADMD** stands for Administrative Management Domain. This is a public E-mail service. MCI is an ADMD. Telemail and Dialcom are also ADMDs.

- **PRMD** stands for Private Management Domain. This is a private—usually a corporate—electronic mail system that is connected via X.400 to an ADMD.

- **Country** is the country in which the domain (PRMD or ADMD) resides.

Personal name is made up of four components.

- **Surname** is a person's last name.

- **Given name** is a person's first name.

- **Initials** are a person's initial(s).

- **Generation Qualifier** Examples of a Generation Qualifier would be Jr. or Sr.

Organization is the name of the organization to which a person belongs. *Organization Unit* is the department or division of an Organization.

Domain-Defined Attribute (DDA) is a special field that helps the receiving system know how to deliver a message to the recipient.

Sending Messages to a Telemail Subscriber

To send messages to a Telemail subscriber, you need to know your recipient's Telemail E-mail address (also known as the O/R Name). The best way to guarantee you have the correct information is to check with your correspondent.

If the Telemail subscriber has a fairly common name, you should also include the Organization. To ensure delivery, include the Telemail Username, which is similar to an MCI Mail user name—usually the person's first initial followed by the last name.

To send a message to a Telemail subscriber, type **CREATE** at the command prompt. Then enter the recipient's name, followed by **EMS** in parentheses. At the EMS prompt, enter **Telemail**. In the MBX lines that follow, type the rest of your Telemail recipient's name, as shown here.

```
CREATE

TO:    Recipient's Last name    (EMS)
EMS:   Telemail MBX:  GI=Recipient's First name
MBX:   OR=Recipient's Organization  {Optional}
MBX:   DDA=UN=Recipient's Telemail Username  {Optional}
MBX:                                         {RETURN}
```

You must label the information you enter. Place an equal sign between the label and the information. Note that there *cannot* be any spaces before or after the equal sign. MCI uses the following labels:

- SU = Surname (or last name)
- GI = Given Name (or first name)
- IN = Initials
- GE = Generational Qualifier
- OR = Organization
- UN = Organization Unit
- PR = Private Domain (PRMD)
- DDA = Domain-Defined Attribute

When a Telemail subscriber's name and organization are not unique, it is necessary to supply his or her Username in the address. This is done by providing a Domain-Defined Attribute (DDA). However, Telemail will not deliver a message when it contains both a surname and the subscriber's Username. Because MCI Mail requires that the recipient's surname be supplied in the TO: (or CC:) line, a blank surname must be entered in an MBX line. This cancels what has been entered in the TO: line. Here is an example of an address for a message to a Telemail subscriber using his/her Username.

```
CREATE

TO:     Recipient's Last name    (EMS)
EMS:    Telemail
MBX:    SU=                                          {RETURN}
MBX:    DDA=UN=Recipient's Telemail Username
MBX:    OR=Recipient's Organization          {Optional}
MBX:
```

Sending Messages to a Private E-mail System

You can also address a message to someone on a private E-mail system (PRMD) connected to Telemail. You need to enter the X.400 address information that the private system requires to deliver the message to your correspondent. Check with your correspondent to determine exactly what components of the X.400 address are required.

A message to an electronic mail system (PRMD) connected to Telemail is created in much the same way that a message to a Telemail subscriber is created. Note that an additional X.400 component, the PRMD, is now required and is placed in an MBX line.

Once you have prepared your message in a PC file, you have to import it into the mail system. This is no problem for a LAN-based system where the E-mail program runs on your PC, but if you have to upload the message to some other computer, as is normally the case with a public system, the procedure may not be straightforward.

Agent Programs

Let's consider strategies for uploading messages to public E-mail systems via a modem and a phone line. Your concern should be to choose a method that ensures your message is transferred reliably, without the chance of any data being corrupted or lost. The same issue applies to downloading messages from the private service. It does seem incongruous that one uses an E-mail service to ensure that mail is delivered reliably

---

READ.ME

How to Prepare E-mail

Here are some tips on preparing mail messages with a word processor:

- If your word processor has an option for producing pure ASCII output, then use it. With WordStar, for example, work in the non-document mode. With WordPerfect, use Text Out.

- Do not use output that is prepared for printing. You do not want to mail text that is formatted with margins, page breaks, underlines, and so on.

- Watch the width of your text. Set the right margin to 68, a line length that will fit any mail system.

- Leave a blank line between paragraphs but otherwise do not double space. It may also be a good idea to indent paragraphs.

- When preparing text for delivery to a telex machine, bear in mind that such devices have small character sets. They print capital letters, digits, and basic punctuation marks only. You can write your message in both upper- and lowercase—the mailer will certainly take care of converting that for you—but unsupported symbols (such as square brackets and backslashes) will probably be discarded.

---

and, in many cases, instantaneously, yet the process of getting the message to and from the service may be awkward, slow, and error-prone.

The best option, if it's available, is to use an *agent program* that runs on your PC and provides an automatic and reliable interface with the E-mail service. Using such a program is like having a postal substation right on your PC. Each agent program is targeted to a particular E-mail service and may cost a few dollars. Western Union offers a choice of two—Instant Mail Manager and Office Access for the PC, for EasyLink subscribers who use PCs. MCI Mail agent programs are described in Chapter 10.

Agent programs not only automate the interface with the E-mail service and guarantee reliable message transfer, but may also provide enhanced features that are unavailable when using the same service via a terminal interface. With MCI, for example, you must use an agent program in order to send binary files as mail attachments.

Agent programs relieve you of the need to do everything in a single session. Instead, you can handle messages in batch mode—the agent program automatically downloads your messages and uploads your replies, using the MCI Mail Exchange Protocol, MEP-2. Your calls to MCI go to a toll-free 800 number, so there's no penalty for calling in twice.

The MEP-2 system lets agent programs send binary files safely using the 8-bit X.PC file-transfer protocol (see Chapter 10). This means you can send formatted spreadsheets, word processing files, graphics, and even executable programs to your recipient. Without the X.PC protocol, such files would normally choke MCI's electronic channels because of the non-ASCII characters they contain.

Remember, though, that agent programs need your MCI User ID and password to work properly. If security is a problem, take any necessary steps to keep others from using your copy of the agent program.

MCI has a different access number to accommodate these agent programs. It uses 8-bit communications settings instead of the 7-bit settings used on its normal access lines. So don't just casually change the default MCI telephone number that comes with an agent program.

The second method of uploading or downloading a message is by means of a file-transfer protocol. AT&T Mail, for example, supports Xmodem transfers, and CompuServe offers several protocols. Some services, however, have none. While this method is as reliable as an agent program, it involves extra steps for the user in initiating each transfer.

File Transfer Protocols

The simplest way to upload or download a message is to have your terminal program send it as if it were text entered at the keyboard. All terminal emulators offer a way to do this. With Telix, for instance, you press ALT-S to send a file, and then select ASCII from the protocol list. ("Protocol" is misleading here; selecting ASCII means that the file is sent *without* a protocol.) You can still ensure reliable transfers if you have an error-correcting modem that is compatible with the modems used by the E-mail service. MCI Mail, for instance, supports the popular MNP (Microcom Networking Protocol) on some of its lines. In the absence of modem-based error-correction, you are at the mercy of the phone lines. To safeguard your mail in such circumstances, it is wise to observe these hints:

- After sending each message to the E-mail system, list it back and check to see that it arrived intact.

- Set the flow-control options in your communications program to suit the E-mail service. In most cases, CTRL-S and CTRL-Q (also known as XOFF and XON, respectively) can be used to regulate the flow of data in each direction. Such flow control ensures that no data is lost because one side is sending it faster than the other side can receive it.

- You may be able to speed up transfers slightly by turning off echoing.

- If you upload a message and find that it is double spaced, it means the E-mail system is adding a line feed at the end of each line when there is one there already. Your communications program should have a means of turning off the transmission of line feeds within files.

- When reading mail, be sure that you have capture mode on in your communications program. "Capture" means that your session is transcribed to a disk file from which you can later extract copies of your messages. With Telix, capture is toggled on and off with ALT-L. Some programs capture to the same file each time they are run and overwrite whatever was on the file before; in such cases be careful to save any messages you want to keep before you run the program again.

DASnet

One of the problems that users of electronic mail services must deal with is lack of interconnectivity. With the exception of MCI Mail and CompuServe's EasyPlex, it's difficult to send a message from one network to another. While you wait for the X.400/X.500 protocols to remedy the problem, you can find a service such as DASnet to do the job of linking you. For a monthly fee of $4.75 and a variable charge per message (depending on the length of the message and the destination), DASnet will forward your E-mail across systems. Contact them at DA Systems Inc., 1503 E. Campbell Ave., Campbell, CA 95008 (1-408-559-7434) for more information about details and pricing.

The following are some of the systems that are compatible with DASnet: ABA/net, AT&T Mail, BIX (an electronic edition of *BYTE* magazine), DASnet Network, Dialcom (another large E-mail network), EIES (from the New Jersey Institute of Technology), EasyLink, Envoy 100 (a Canadian service), Fax, GeoMail (a service for users of GeoMail software), INET, MCI Mail, NWI (a teleconferencing system run by Networking and Information), PeaceNet/EcoNet (a network operated by the San Francisco-based Association for Progressive Communications), Portal Communications (a system used by members of the Sierra Club), The Meta Network, Telemail, ATI's

Telemail (Japan), Telex, TWICS (Tokyo, Japan), UNISON, UUCP, and The WELL (a popular conferencing and E-mail system). DASnet serves as the United Nations for 60 warring E-mail systems.

These networks allow DASnet to accept and forward messages to and from their subscribers. You can do this easily. There's no need to learn anything about another E-mail network to get your messages to it. Simply leave a message on your favorite network to the specified DASnet mailbox address and let DASnet know the address of the recipient (who has to be on one of the other supported systems). The recipient does *not* have to be a DASnet subscriber. If you've made an error and sent an ID or name that does not exist, DASnet will notify you within two to eight hours, and the text of your message will be returned.

DASnet connects to the addressee's network, and sends your message there. The correspondent can then reply using the DASnet account on their system, and their reply is billed to your account. DASnet maintains an account on each of the supported networks. Each account's mailbox is checked about every four hours by DASnet. If DASnet finds a message, the service transfers it to the appropriate recipient's mail system.

Messages are billed per 1000 characters (about 20 lines of text). For example, an MCI Mail subscriber can send a 200-character message to a GeoMail subscriber for 64 cents. An MCI Mail user can send a 2000-character message to a GeoMail recipient in London for $1.69. DASnet also offers fax (a typical one-page letter costs about $3.70 for domestic delivery and $5.70 internationally) and telex services (you even get a telex address for yourself to give out to others). With your subscription, you get a DASnet subscriber directory and a listing in the directory.

DASnet now has an even more useful enhancement. Binary files could be sent across systems. With this upgrade, users can send spreadsheets, formatted word processor documents, graphics, and EDI documents from one system to another. No longer confined to just ASCII messages, DASnet can handle almost any type of file you need to exchange across any of the systems that are part of the DASnet family.

FIDONET

Finally we get to FidoNet, a unique network of BBS systems (see Chapters 7 and 8 for more details concerning BBSs). I've decided to write about FidoNet in this chapter because it's more like an E-mail system than a bulletin board.

FidoNet can be used to swap notes with your sister across the country, converse with fellow "Star Trek" fans, and debate politics and many other subjects, all at little (if any) cost. FidoNet is an amateur network—unlike systems such as CompuServe and Dow Jones News/Retrieval, FidoNet is geared toward hobbyists.

FidoNet may be called a "loosely-coupled" network. That is, the member systems are not interconnected all the time. They call each other when there is mail to be exchanged, usually in the middle of the night when costs are low.

When you call a FidoNet BBS, you'll find many message areas. Some will be local to the system you've reached, but others will allow you to send messages to systems other than the one you've called. These message areas fall into two broad categories. The first is something loosely called *Netmail.* The second is often called *Echomail* or *conferences.*

READ.ME

E-mail Registry

Another unique way to deal with the lack of integration is to have a directory of E-mail users listing their addresses and the systems they use. The National E-mail Registry, Suite 110, Two Neshaminy Interplex, Trevose, PA 19047-9905, offers free registration by modem to anyone. You connect to their network with an 800 number, and register with a password and two security codes (your mother's maiden name and the year of your birth). You then enter any E-mail, fax, and telex numbers you have. These are then placed into the Registry's database. To find another party, you call 1-203-245-7720 by modem. After entering your identifying account information, you enter the name (company or individual) of the party you seek. The database is scanned. The charge is 50 cents for each successful search. Unsuccessful searches are free. You can buy 20 searches for $10, and unlimited use of the system is available for $95 per year. You can update your registry information—add or delete addresses for E-mail, fax, or Telex—by calling 1-800-622-0505. While not an ideal solution to interconnectivity (you would still have to have some way to send messages to individuals on the systems they use), the National E-mail Registry gives us a view of the future: directory assistance for electronic addresses.

Netmail

Netmail is person-to-person mail sent from its author directly to its receiver. To send electronic mail with FidoNet, you must know the name of the person and the "network address" of the BBS the person uses (more on FidoNet addresses in a little while). In addition, you must set up a Netmail account with the sysop (systems operator) of the BBS you call. The Netmail account is used for billing purposes.

Netmail typically costs much less than a voice conversation. It takes very little time to deliver a text message over the phone line. (Certainly, less time than people take when talking.) Most sysops pass the cost of these calls directly on to the users of their systems, without adding in a profit. Some sysops don't make Netmail available to their callers. (If you want to use Netmail, and the FidoNet system you call doesn't offer it, leave a message to the sysop, asking if they know of another local FidoNet system that does make Netmail available.)

Echomail

Echomail is available on almost every FidoNet system. Echomail was originally developed by Jeff Rush, and is largely responsible for the explosive growth of the network over the last few years. Echomail is a conferencing system. A *conferencing system* is simply a set of messages organized around a particular topic, with many people participating in a public discussion about the topic. (Some conferences allow private messages, but this is not the norm in Echomail.) There are "echoes" (as the individual conferences are often called) on many topics. A few of the topics are gardening, "Star Trek," movies, television, books, languages, alternative lifestyles, politics, cooking, and many aspects of personal computing and personal telecommunications.

New echoes are formed and old ones periodically expire. Every system varies in the style and content of its echoes. Here is an example of the echo topics found on one system.

- General Messages (Local)
- AIDS/ARC
- Amiga Video
- DESQview

- ECPROG (Programmers)
- PCjr
- IDI
- Politics
- Science Fiction
- Science Fiction/Fantasy
- Star Trek
- FidoCon
- Binkley Support
- Democracy in FidoNet
- Sysops Conference
- Echomail Coordinators
- QuickMail Support
- Netmail Area

The selection of Echomail conferences will be as unique as the system. Sysops are sensitive to the interests of their callers. They will often add a conference if there are requests for it.

At each echo conference new messages are added to the message base. Like a chain letter, the messages from one system are sent to the other systems. Each system makes a copy for their message base and passes it on. New messages are added to the set of messages making the rounds from system to system.

There is usually no charge for participating in the echo conferences. Sysops use echo conferences to make their BBS systems more interesting and to increase the number of topics under discussion. Since the exchange of Echomail is often done with neighboring systems, the phone charges are often much less. Many people read conferences for a long time before they decide to leave a message, so echo conferences benefit lots of folks who never actually write a message.

Echomail/Netmail—the Differences

Echomail is different from Netmail in several ways. Physically, it works the same way as Netmail—messages from one BBS system are sent to another BBS system. The similarity ends there. Echomail is more like a town hall—it's a place where a number of people get together to discuss a topic of mutual interest. Netmail is like a letter—you send a memo to Enrico, Genevieve, Elbert, your Mom, or whomever.

Fido as a BBS and a Network

Tom Jennings was the original author of Fido, the BBS software. When he first began work on his software in November of 1983, he had no idea that it would someday grow to network capability, or become FidoNet. The name comes from the original computer that Tom's BBS ran on—a hodgepodge, mongrel system, hence the name "Fido." Originally the software itself had no name other than "BBS" (it was called "BBS.EXE"). Jennings' system was called the "Fido BBS," and over time, the software took on the name by association.

Jennings built a simple message exchange capability into Fido to exchange debugging information with a friend in Baltimore who was also testing the BBS software. As they continued to exchange messages and debug Fido, word spread quickly about the BBS that could "network."

In February of 1984, there were 20 systems, although not all of them were able to exchange messages with each other. The number grew quickly—to 160 in September, and 250 by the following February.

A routing capability was developed in 1984. By 1986, there were so many *nodes* (individual systems in the network) that they began to organize into local networks. FidoNet was on its way. Today, FidoNet has over 5000 nodes.

Uses of Fido and FidoNet

Lots of system operators run Fido, although they are not part of FidoNet or any other network. A Fido system is not required to be part of FidoNet, but the capability is there for anyone who wants to use it.

The networking power in Fido may be used to create private networks for special purposes. You don't even have to use Fido itself. There are several programs compatible with FidoNet's architecture.

As a user you may encounter many different kinds of BBS software that allow participation in Echomail and Netmail via FidoNet. Some BBS packages that are now network-capable are Opus by Wynn Wagner (freely

---

READ.ME

The FidoNet Plan

Tom Jennings' plan for FidoNet is based on four points:

- Implementation must be inexpensive
- Compatibility with normal BBS operation must exist
- Required hardware must be domestic and affordable
- The sysop must be in control of the system

In retrospect this may seem tame, but in 1983 there were scores of people saying it couldn't be done. The concept of a network was a group of large interconnected (hard-wired) computers. UNIX systems were exchanging newsgroups in a UNIX-to-UNIX Copy Program (UUCP), but there was no precedent for FidoNet in the BBS community.

---

available), TBBS by Phil Becker (eSoft), Wildcat by Mustang Software, QuickBBS by Adam Hudson (freely available), and RBBS-PC (a freely-available program by Tom Mack and other members of the Capital PC Users Group), and more will soon follow.

Front-Ends

A category of software called "front-ends" has recently become available. A *front-end* is a program that answers the phone for the BBS. It determines (through a set protocol) if a caller is another electronic mail system. If it is, the two systems exchange electronic mail.

If the caller does not respond as an E-mail system would, the front-end program loads the call into the BBS. There are variations on this method (in some cases the BBS loads the mail handling program instead). The idea is to add network capability to BBS programs. See Chapter 10 for more on front-ends.

How to Use Netmail and Echomail

First of all, find a FidoNet member system. If you've called any BBS systems, you've probably noticed that most of them maintain a list of "other systems." It's likely that one of the systems will be a FidoNet member. Once you find one FidoNet system, you'll find the rest.

The FidoNet's phone directory is called the *nodelist.* This is the means by which FidoNet systems know the network address and telephone number of other nodes. Many FidoNet systems have a downloadable listing of the nodelist. The sysop should be able to help you.

If you are unable to locate a FidoNet system near you, write to the International FidoNet Association (IFNA), P.O. Box 41143, St. Louis, MO 63141.

Once You've Found a System

You've found a FidoNet system, logged on, and become familiar with the operation of the BBS software in use. There are so many different participating BBS systems in FidoNet, it would be impossible to discuss each, but all of them will have the following in common:

- Multiple message areas dedicated to specific topics
- A Netmail area (although not always available in all cases)
- Help files
- A systems operator

This is a volunteer, hobbyist effort, and if you don't like one system, try another.

How to Use Echomail

Although Echomail is complicated from the sysop's point of view, it's easier for the user. The user enters a message, either to an individual or to all. There's no need to know about network addresses. In a few days the message will travel to the other systems. Other people will read and reply to your message.

Quoting

Some BBS systems have sophisticated editors. These editors allow quoting. *Quoting* is a way to include a piece of the message that you're replying to. This is helpful because of the time lag in echo conferences. (Sometimes a time lag of as long as several weeks may pass before a reply to a message comes back to you.) This delay is often due to the time it takes people

READ.ME

PCBoard Echo Relay Mail Systems

Message bases, or conferences, may be linked and shared with hundreds of other systems. Messages left on a member system go out over the net (as Echomail), and get replies echoed back from other systems. Messages appearing on the home system are identical to messages entered directly, except for *origin* and *seen-by* tags, which identify the originating system and the intermediate "echoing" BBSs.

Echo networks may vary in size, organization, and features. In contrast to the defense/academic networks—Arpanet or InterNet or UseNet—the PC BBS networks are both more primitive (for example, in message handling and verification) and simultaneously friendlier and more accessible. Together these BBSs constitute an information service used daily by tens of thousands of callers.

For five years, FidoNet and its recent clones—Alternet and Eggnet—were the only PC BBS networks available. Recently, PCBoard BBS software, a product of Clark Development Corp. in Salt Lake, has become something of a standard among medium and large PC-based BBSs, and has gained the support of third-party developers offering, among other enhancements, Netmail engines to link systems into small-to-large networks. PC-Netmail systems now include InterLink, SmartNet, RelayNet, Hypermail, and Netmail.

PCBoard-Compatible Netmail Systems

Following are the largest PCBoard-compatible Netmail systems:

InterLink   The first PCBoard Echomail system with strong technical conferences and positive sysop leadership. InterLink is led by Andy Keeves of Exec-Net BBS in White Plains, NY.

SmartNet   Organized by Paul Waldinger of the Sound of Music BBS on Long Island, SmartNet offers good product support conferences and an emphasis on professional issues.

RelayNet   The largest PC echo network, RelayNet supports private mail, encryption, file sends, a universal interface to other systems, and over 150 conferences and more than 200 systems.

The newer networks are all young compared to FidoNet, but are growing

READ.ME

PCBoard Echo Relay Mail Systems *(continued)*

and evolving rapidly. They have as member systems the large, high-performance multiline systems made possible by sophisticated, network-compatible BBS software such as PCBoard (Fido lacks network support). Here's a sample message from a RelayNet Computer Tech conference.

```
-------------------------------------------------------------
Date: 07-26-89 (20:11)      Number: 2486
  To: GREG EIGSTI           Refer#: NONE
From: DAN MORAN               Read: NO
Subj: UPGRADE               Status: PUBLIC MESSAGE

GE>I own a Compaq Deskpro (PC 8088), and would like to upgrade to 286, or
GE>preferably 386. Can this be done economically, and if so what hardware
GE>changes does it entail?

There are any number of 286/386 accelerator boards out there.
Intel makes some nice (but expensive) ones. I'm using a PC
Express board made by some folks here in Ann Arbor, MI.
You're probably talking $200-250.
---
EZ-Reader 1.14  Louis Antoine De Saint Just  1767-1794
PCRelay:PATCH -> RelayNet (tm)
Strawberry Patch * (606) 432-0879 * HST/V32
----
```

"EZ-Reader 1.14 Louis Antoine De Saint Just 1767-1794" is a *tagline.* "EZ-Reader" is the program used to create this message off line from a BBS (more on this shortly). "Louis Antoine ..." is a *personal statement* made by Dan, which may or may not have some relevance to the message.

Greg and Dan are probably not writing on the same host system. Their interchange was read by conference participants on over two hundred systems across the country and in Europe, within a day or two of the messages being sent.

While Echomail and BBS E-mail have been around for a while, a new set of communications tools—the combination of downloadable, compressed messages from the BBS and an off-line message read-and-reply program at home or work—has already revolutionized the BBS "lifestyle."

Here's how it works. In the case of PCBoard, one of the functions permitted by the BBS software is the running of other programs while connected to the system. To the user, this means additional functionality, whether it means playing chess on line, accessing a database, or transferring messages through a mail "door."

```
READ.ME
```

PCBoard Echo Relay Mail Systems *(continued)*

The off-line reader—examples are Qmail by Mark Herring, EZReader by Eric Cockrell and Relaymail by Kip Compton—is a program run on the home or office PC that frees the caller from having to write on line, saves money, allows the use of a favorite editor, and provides a local simulation of the BBS environment. Economy and convenience (you can get a snack in the middle of a message) are an irresistible combination. Often users report that they actually end up writing more messages—using their time to communicate more effectively with more people.

Many users have automated their interactions with the host BBS system either by using the capability of their communications program to run a *script* (sequence of commands) while unattended, or by using a program such as Dan Parson's Robocomm, which is a kind of programmable VCR for calling PC-Board systems and performing specific "agendas" on each one.

The result is that Robocomm will write a script for you in the middle of the night. Or you can push one key on your keyboard and go make coffee while your PC gets your morning's BBS E-mail.

to read and respond. If your system allows message quoting, use it sparingly. Quote a sentence or two, for context. More than that is an irritation to sysops and other users.

Moderator

A *moderator* is found on some echo conferences. The moderator is usually a sysop of a participating system. The moderator sets the rules and enforces them.

Rules

The rules are usually posted in the system on a regular basis. Pay attention to the rules of the conferences. Infractions of the rules first result in a warning. Repeated infractions result in a message from the moderator directly to the sysop of your BBS, who has the ability to bar you from using it.

Netmail

Netmail was the original reason FidoNet was created. But, because few people know someone else on a BBS in another city, Netmail didn't grow as Echomail did. This service may yet grow as networking and gateways between networks become more common. FidoNet already has a gateway to UNIX systems.

ZONE   To understand Netmail, you must understand network addresses and how the network is organized. The nodelist is FidoNet's "phone book." The network address is like a telephone number with its area code and international access code. FidoNet's network address looks like this:

```
ZONE:NET/NODE.POINT
```

Zone is the highest organizational level of the FidoNet address and *Point* is the lowest. The current FidoNet zones are

- Zone 1: North America

- Zone 2: Europe

- Zone 3: Oceania (Australia and the Pacific)

- Zone 4: Latin America

Many other networks are patterned on the FidoNet model, and can communicate with FidoNet nodes. They use unique zones to indicate that they are separate from FidoNet. These will not be discussed here. (Information may be found on your local FidoNet-capable BBS system.)

Net and Node   *Net* is the local network. This is the original grouping of nodes that were necessary when FidoNet began to grow. A network serves a fairly limited geographic area, although there are exceptions. The *node* is the number of the BBS system itself. The number 0 is always the routing address for the zone, or net. The routing address will forward mail to an individual node within its organization. (For example: Net 204's routing address is 204/0.) Usually, the sysop handles this detail.

POINT   This is the last part of the address. *Points* came about for two reasons: users of BBS systems became more sophisticated, and the number of conferences and messages became too lengthy for the average person to have time to read them.

The solution was for the sophisticated BBS caller to become a "mini-BBS." Instead of reading messages on line, the caller's software downloads messages like a BBS system. The caller then disconnects, reads the messages off line, and replies. New messages and replies are sent back to the BBS system with which the user has a "point arrangement." The point number is present in all addresses. If it's not in use, a zero is used. (BBS systems in the nodelist should always have a point number of zero.)

Using this model, the full FidoNet address of Fido Software in San Francisco is

```
1:125/111.0
```

This means: Zone 1 (North America), Net 125 (San Francisco Bay Net), Node 111 (Fido Software), Point 0 (a placeholder—no special meaning). In practice this address would usually be shortened to "125/111" within Zone 1. (Zone and point can usually be ignored.)

Joining FidoNet

If you're a BBS sysop and want to join FidoNet, you'll need to find your nearest FidoNet system. Call and log on to the system. Leave a message for the sysop.

To be assigned a FidoNet node number, you'll need to meet some technical qualifications. One of the qualifications is to prove you know how to make FidoNet work. The test is to send a Netmail message to the proposed net host. To send a message by Netmail shows that your system is functional. Some net hosts will send a return message before assigning a node number.

The *net host* is the holder of the /0 address in the network. The net host is usually referred to as the *NC*, or network coordinator. The system is responsible for routing mail to others and verifying new nodes. Some networks are better organized than others. Some abide by strict local network rules, and some have almost none.

Zone Mail Hour

Originally FidoNet systems didn't have the capability of sending mail any time the user wanted to send it. (The front-end programs described earlier were developed only recently.) All mail was exchanged during National Mail Hour (NMH—later renamed Zone Mail Hour or ZMH). ZMH is from 1:00A.M. to 2:00A.M. (PST), and this was not modified during daylight saving time. In order for FidoNet to function, BBS callers weren't allowed to call during this one hour of the day. This is still a requirement, although it's much less important now.

As a sysop, the NC will probably choose to send you a message during this hour as part of the verification procedure to put you on the nodelist. You are officially prohibited from allowing BBS callers on your system during this time. To do so could result in your being removed from FidoNet.

Joining a BBS to FidoNet

The BBS software must be FidoNet compatible. If you've never been a FidoNet sysop, contact your NC by logging on as a BBS caller. Be sure to read the chapters on BBSs and their operation.

THE USENET NETWORK

Usenet provides news, information, and communication for UNIX users worldwide. (UNIX, a trademark of AT&T, is the name of an operating system.) Usenet is something like the DOS world's BBS networks, something like an information utility, and something like an E-mail system. If that seems a bit fuzzy, it might be because the UNIX world is different from the DOS world. This difference springs partly from the minicomputer "flavor" of the system, and partly from the fact that UNIX came from the U.S. university system whereas DOS was designed for business use.

News and information found on Usenet are distributed from one UNIX site to another by means of a program called UUCP, for UNIX-to-UNIX Copy Program (or Protocol). If indeterminate acronyms seem a bit strange to you, chances are you haven't been around UNIX much. Many DOS users, when hearing about UNIX, think you're talking about a harem, not a computer system. To those familiar with the UNIX command set, however, the system offers power and flexibility not available in DOS. It really is a matter of what you're used to.

Because of interconnections to MS-DOS-accessible systems like CompuServe, Usenet is also an important part of some MS-DOS systems'

E-mail. Some of these interconnections are described shortly. See Chapter 20 for more detail on communicating in UNIX.

Access from Outside UNIX

If you don't have access to a UNIX system, you can get to Usenet through several other information utilities, including CompuServe (enter GO UNIX-FORUM for details), DASnet, Channel 1, and The WELL (see Chapter 6). You can also join a separate service called UUNET. UUNET Communications Services, Inc. facilitates access to Usenet for MS-DOS and other systems for a fixed monthly fee, plus connect charges.

The UUNET Connection

Hooking up to Usenet used to be next to impossible without access to a minicomputer or mainframe that had its own site address or domain. This was fine in the days when traffic involved mainly universities and other huge computer users. These days, however, many people outside this province also need access. People work at home. Small businesses lack access to UNIX computers. People need Usenet for dozens of other reasons.

Enter UUNET, a nonprofit company whose primary role is to act as a "backbone network" communications link to Usenet. Founded by the Usenix Association in 1987, UUNET hooks into Usenet via a 56 Kbps X.25 leased line from TYMNET, leased lines to CompuServe, and X.25 public data network access. It also provides access via both 800 and 900 phone numbers. The X.25 hookup allows international sites to connect directly. Only a standard UNIX UUCP program is required.

UUNET uses a Sequent Symmetry S81 and multiple 80386 CPUs as host processor units, and can easily handle 50 simultaneous transfers. The system is monitored 24 hours a day. Because it is dedicated to Usenet as a communications relay, there is no delay or waiting until others give up priority system use.

UUNET subscription costs include a variable monthly fee, plus variable hourly usage fees. Subscribers receive free Usenet domain registration. However, for a one-time fee of $35, UUNET will provide a domain registration even if you do not subscribe.

For more details, contact UUNET Communications Services at 1-703-876-5050 (voice) or 1-703-876-5059 (fax). They may also be reached by Usenet at info@uunet.uu.net, or by CompuServe, as described next.

Access via CompuServe

CompuServe subscribers cannot directly access Usenet newsgroups, but can send EasyPlex mail back and forth to Usenet users. The interconnection is handled via Internet; there is no surcharge for this service.

To send a message, first create it just as if you were sending mail to another CompuServe subscriber. At the "Send to (Name or User ID):" prompt, enter **INTERNET:** followed by the user name, an @ symbol, and the domain or site name. For example, you could mail a letter to John Doe at Georgia Tech by entering the following:

```
>INTERNET: jdoe@gatech
```

To send mail in the opposite direction, from the net to CompuServe, the address is composed of the recipient's CompuServe ID (with the comma in the ID replaced by a period), followed by this domain address: compuserve-.com. For example, using the imaginary CIS ID 12345,123, the message address in Usenet would look like this:

```
12345.123@compuserve.com
```

It is essential to change the comma in the CompuServe ID to a period, and to use the compuserve.com domain address. When a message arrives via CompuServe, it contains routing information that it picked up on its way to the recipient. CompuServe translates the electronic address into the more familiar form and sends it on.

Transmission Time

As a result of the way systems in Usenet interact, the time needed for a message to get to its destination varies from half an hour to a couple of days. As with the BBS mail networks, a message goes from node to node, getting passed along in the right general direction at each stopover.

THE FUTURE OF E-MAIL

As electronic mail becomes ever more widely used and important, it will also become more powerful. There are two areas in particular in which we can look forward to improvement: interconnectivity among E-mail systems, and support for multimedia mail.

Public and private types of electronic mail systems have grown up isolated from one another. You cannot communicate with anyone and everyone using E-mail as you can by telephone or paper mail. Links do exist here and there between services—for example, many E-mail packages for LANs can channel messages to and from MCI Mail, and CompuServe and MCI Mail subscribers can correspond—but these are the exceptions, not the rule. In the future E-mail services are expected to gradually unite into one global system. The worldwide E-mail network of the year 2000 may well be composed largely of the same bits and pieces that we know today—MCI, EasyLink, and so on—but they will operate with seamless connections among them.

The CCITT's international standard X.400 Message Handling Service will serve as the technical foundation for interlinking E-mail services. X.400 dictates a standard format for electronic envelopes and a uniform addressing scheme that simplifies the relay of mail from one service to another. Multimedia mail, also supported by X.400, will allow us to compose messages that combine text with images and recorded speech. Only the nontechnical issue of figuring out how to assess charges for internetwork messaging is holding back the introduction of X.400. Hopefully that will vanish and we can get on with it.

CHAPTER SIX

Information Utilities

We don't know who coined the term "information utility," but it's the only way to describe a group of services that provides information in electronic form to users of modem-equipped desktop computers. These services can be arbitrarily divided into three groups. They are the large mass market group (described in this chapter), the small mass market group, and the premium services group, typically used only by professionals who can afford the high fees. Our discussion of these services is by no means all-inclusive, and we hope that you'll discover many of the specialty services on your own as you explore this on-line world.

We differentiate these services from programs such as PRODIGY and Minitel, and all the other systems that require specialized software. The services are typically more graphics-oriented and do not make it easy to transfer large blocks of ASCII text using just any old telecom program such as Telix. In fact, few of these services offer downloading. See Chapter 16 on Minitel for a description of a typical graphics-oriented system.

Traditionally, the most important companies providing services to personal computer users were CompuServe and The Source. Recently The Source was bought by CompuServe. The newcomer on the block is a system called GEnie, funded by General Electric. It now shares the upper tier with CompuServe, the popular Delphi system, The WELL, BIX, PC-Magnet, and the Executive PC, which will all be discussed in this chapter.

COMPUSERVE

Since its introduction in 1979, the CompuServe Information Service (CIS) has become the largest general on-line information service in the world. More than half a million members reach CompuServe by a local phone call and have access to more than 1400 databases, including electronic mail, personal computer support, financial and stock market information, news services, educational and reference services, entertainment, computer games, and much more.

Getting Started

To get started, you'll need a CompuServe membership kit, available at most computer stores or through CompuServe by calling its toll-free number 1-800-848-8199. The kit provides everything you'll need to use CompuServe, including a user's guide, a membership booklet containing a User ID number, a password, and detailed instructions for accessing CompuServe. In addition, CompuServe offers a $25 on-line usage credit to allow new members time to explore the service. The fee for the service depends on the modem speed and time of day. A screen from CompuServe showing the "connect rates" is shown in Figure 6-1.

Logging On

If you haven't yet received a password from CompuServe, call them at the 800 number given above and order a starter kit. This gives you a password to use when first accessing the system.

Figure 6-1

CompuServe's connect rates

```
BILLING Info                                              CONNECT

CONNECT RATES (per connect hour)

            Prime/        Standard/
            Daytime       Evening
   BAUD     $/Hour        $/Hour
   ─────────────────────────────────
   up to 300 $6.00        $ 6.00
   450*      $6.00        $ 6.00
   1200      $12.50       $12.50
   2400*     $12.50       $12.50
   4800**    $32.50       $29.00
   9600**    $47.50       $44.00

   * Not available from all locations
   ** Requires hardwired network connection and is not available from all
   locations.


   Connect time is billed in one minute increments, with a minimum of one minute
   per session.  Connect time rates do not include communication surcharges and

Press <CR> for more !
  Alt-Z FOR HELP| ANSI      | FDX |  2400 E71 | LOG CLOSED | PRINT OFF | ON-LINE
```

Once you have your starter kit, obtain the local CompuServe phone number in your area, again by calling the 800 number given previously, and following the voice mail prompts. Because the CompuServe network reaches most cities in the United States, you'll probably be able to access the service with a local phone call, keeping communication charges to a minimum.

We recommend starting with a 1200bps or 2400bps access number depending on your modem's capabilities. Set your communications parameters to 7-E-1, or you'll see garbage characters on your screen. (7-E-1 means 7 databits, Even parity, and 1 stop bit.) When your modem makes the connection, enter CTRL-C. Your screen shows these characters:

^C

and the system asks for your User ID.

If you make a mistake and press the ENTER key, the way you would on a BBS, instead of entering CTRL-C, the system asks:

HOST NAME:

Just enter **CIS**, and the system will then ask for your User ID.

Enter your User ID and then your password, and you'll be on line to CompuServe.

Once you enter the system, you'll be guided by a simple and concise menu format until you find the desired information. As you become more experienced, you can use quick reference words and the Go commands to bypass the menus.

In CompuServe, all the information sections have both a name and a page number. You can, for example, type **GO TRAVEL** at the prompt (an exclamation mark [!]), to jump to the travel section and a new set of menus. You can also type something like **GO PAGE 560** and end up in the middle of some other section, using that page of the database. Explore these two techniques of moving through the database.

Communications and Bulletin Boards

Some of CompuServe's most popular services are the communications services: electronic mail, special interest forums, and CB Simulator.

As an enhancement to the basic service, CompuServe also offers an Executive Service option. If you select this option, you'll receive access to exclusive financial databases, a special news-clipping service, discounts on CompuServe merchandise, and other amenities.

CompuServe Electronic Mail

This is the most popular section in CompuServe—the E-mail system. CompuServe electronic mail allows members to send and receive messages 24 hours a day, regardless of distance or time zone. CompuServe comprises the largest group of potential recipients of any electronic mail system in the world. In addition to communicating with other CompuServe members, you can communicate electronically with users of CompuServe's electronic mail service for corporations, and with MCI Mail users. You can also send messages to both Telex and facsimile (fax) machines worldwide with CompuServe. Although the system is rather simple and elementary, with menus that guide you through each step, you should know that you have to have the exact account number of the recipient (CompuServe number, MCI number, Telex number, or fax phone number) to use the system.

To access the E-mail function at any time you simply type **GO EMAIL** at any system prompt (!), and you'll jump into the E-mail menu.

Special Interest Forums

With CompuServe's 170 special interest forums, you can attend on-line conferences, share information, and benefit from the expertise and enthusiasm of others who share a common interest. Hundreds of topics are covered by CompuServe's forums, which bring together literally thousands of members sharing ideas and information about careers, hobbies, health, personal computing, music, games, investments and travel, among other topics.

CompuServe forums provide three ways to communicate: a message board, where you can post messages, ask questions and carry on non-simultaneous discussions; live on-line conferences, where you can communicate with other members in real time by typing messages on your keyboard; and libraries, which contain software and information files you may download. At any one time, CompuServe has 27,000 user-contributed software programs available for downloading from the forums.

This sharing of information in the forums is one of CompuServe's greatest assets. For example, if you are having a problem with your printer, you can post a message describing the problem in the appropriate hardware forum. Within a day or so, often within a few hours, you'll receive several responses with potential solutions to your problem. The response may be from a member who had a similar problem, or it may be from a representative of the hardware manufacturer who monitors the forum for questions and problems such as yours.

The forums provide a unique medium where all members, both novice and veteran, benefit from the sharing of information.

CB Simulator

CB Simulator is the ultimate in on-line interactive communications. It is called CB Simulator because communication is similar to that of a citizens band radio. By "tuning in" to CB, you can chat electronically with others across the country in "live" on-line dialogue. Although CB has practical applications, such as business conferences, most members log on to chat with anonymous members, socialize, or actually make pen-pals. To explore CB type **GO CB-1** at the system prompt. You'll be asked for a "handle," which is the name people will know you by when you type into the system. For a complete list of commands type **/?** at the beginning of a line. All commands are preceded by a forward slash in CB and in most conferences done on CompuServe.

News, Weather & Sports

CompuServe offers a variety of services for accessing the latest in world, business, and entertainment news, sports information, and weather reports and forecasts.

Members choosing the Executive Service Option have access to CompuServe Executive News Service (ENS). ENS is an electronic clipping service that brings to your personal computer the power and scope of the Associated Press and United Press International newswires that are updated throughout the day, *The Washington Post, Reuters Financial Report, McGraw-Hill News, NewsGrid,* and *OTC NewsAlert.* National, state, regional, business, political, and entertainment wires provide an up-to-the-moment look at what's happening in the world. When you choose ENS from the menu you'll be asked if you want to set up a "folder," where you enter keywords or phrases and specify which wires are to be scanned. Stories are then "clipped" as they come across the wires and filed in your folder for review at your convenience.

Weather Services

The National Weather Service (NWS) weather wire provides state, marine, and sports weather forecasts, weather warnings, and aviation weather updated hourly. CompuServe also provides ski reports from various ski resorts during the season.

Travel Services

CompuServe's travel services give you the ability to manage your business or personal travel, including selecting itineraries, booking flights, and making hotel and car reservations. Some people don't like do-it-yourself travel arrangements, and some people love it. I usually use the services as an adjunct to a travel agent.

Airline Information and Reservations   TRAVELSHOPPER, Official Airline Guide Electronic Edition (OAG), and EAASY SABRE provide continuously updated information on schedules and fares for virtually every published airline in the world. On all three services, you can shop for the lowest fare that meets your schedule, and book the flight on line. These services also provide hotel and rental car information.

Hotel Services   The ABC Worldwide Hotel Guide Index provides complete reservation information and lodging descriptions for more than 35,000 hotels worldwide. Search the database using a variety of criteria including price range, hotel chain name, location, and other factors.

Electronic Shopping

Electronic shopping on a personal computer, while not a new concept, is slowly growing in popularity. One advantage of electronic on-line shopping is the ability to shop at any time of the day or night, from your home or office. On the other hand, you don't get to see and feel the merchandise, so it seems unlikely that on-line shopping will totally replace modern retailing.

The Electronic Mall   CompuServe's Electronic Mall provides a convenient alternative to the long lines, crowded parking lots, and restrictive business hours associated with a traditional mall. More than 100 merchants, including Brooks Brothers, Waldenbooks, and Pepperidge Farms, offer merchandise ranging from Florida fruit to BMWs, from computer equipment to flowers. Products can be ordered on line and shipped directly to you.

Discounts with Shopper's Advantage   Shopper's Advantage is a discount shopping club that allows comparison shopping for more than 250,000 brand name products at the lowest price; you can browse for everything from air conditioners to computers to microwaves.

Money Matters and Markets

CompuServe offers a broad range of investment data available on stocks, mutual funds, bonds, commodities, and money markets, allowing you to plan an investment strategy with the information obtained on line. Then, utilizing

CompuServe's on-line brokerage services, you can implement your investment decisions immediately.

Market Information   Current price quotes and historical pricing is available for stocks, bonds, options, and foreign exchange rates. For commodities traded on North American exchanges in which there is significant trading interest, historical price, volume, and open interest are available. In addition, cash prices, market news, and analysis from industry experts can be found on line. For mutual funds, members can obtain daily net asset values extending over 12 years, along with hard-to-obtain distribution data that is vital to analyzing historical performance.

On-line Brokerage Firms   With CompuServe's on-line discount brokerage services, you can place, buy, and sell orders electronically 24 hours a day. Orders placed after the market closes are executed the next business day. Electronic portfolio management is an optional feature that automatically updates the investor's portfolio to reflect every transaction.

Entertainment and Games

Not only is CompuServe a valuable reference resource, it provides a variety of entertainment services for relaxation and fun.

Multiplayer Games   CompuServe's most popular games are interactive multiplayer games that take full advantage of the on-line medium. You can pit your mental talents against opponents thousands of miles away.

Multiplayer adventure and fantasy games include MegaWars, The Islands of Kesmai, and British Legends. There are also several forums on line for computer game enthusiasts.

Parlor Games and Other Entertainment   Trivia buffs enjoy "You Guessed It!", an interactive game show fashioned after traditional television game shows, and the Science and Showbiz Trivia games. These are sometimes hard to find. Just type **GO GAMES** at the prompt. There are many CompuServe users addicted to these games.

There are also sports, card games, and board games available on line, as well as a variety of word games.

CompuServe also offers Entertainment News for the latest in Hollywood gossip, movie reviews and soap opera updates, biorhythm charts, and daily horoscope readings.

Hobbies and Lifestyles

Issues concerning your everyday life and that of your family are addressed in CompuServe's Hobbies and Lifestyles area. From food and wine forums to personal financial information, from the photography forums to RockNet, you can find something — or several things — of interest on line.

On-line wine tastings sponsored by the Bacchus Wine Forum allow connoisseurs and novices alike to sample specific vintages in their homes and compare notes in lively on-line discussions. The data libraries of this forum contain good listings of wine-tasting notes.

The Cooks On-line Forum allows those interested in cooking to exchange recipes and gather cooking tips from other forum members. Recipes range from the very simple to the gourmet.

A variety of health-related databases provide up-to-date information written for a lay audience. For members who want first-hand medical news and research data from professional journals, PaperChase offers access to the Medline database, an electronic library of more than 3000 indexed and abstracted publications with over 3.5 million references.

You can access other health-related services and forums on line including the Disabilities Forum, Handicapped User's Database, the AIDS database, and the Cancer Forum for information and for support.

In addition, CompuServe offers a whole range of general-interest forums including the Religion Forum, National Issues Forum, Military Veterans Forum, and the Working From Home Forum for lively discussions on a variety of topics.

Many personal hobbies have their own forum on CompuServe: photographers, coin collectors, sailors, scuba divers, ham radio operators, and model builders have a home on CompuServe. Other hobby forum topics include tropical fish, comic books and animation, astronomy, genealogy, and model trains.

If you're in the market for a car, use CompuServe's automotive databases to research the model of your choice. A good place to start is *Consumer Reports* on-line magazine and the New Car Showroom. Both provide research information on crash tests, costs, and optional items available on cars of interest.

Buick, Ford, Chevrolet, and Nissan provide on-line information for their current model lines. If you're interested in learning more about this year's models, you can order catalogs from these Mall merchants for further review. And when you're ready to buy, you can even order your new car and arrange for delivery on CompuServe, through AutoVision, another Mall merchant.

Education and Reference

CompuServe provides educational and reference resources for students of all ages and educators at all levels.

IQuest   Over 900 bibliographic and full-text databases are available to you through the IQuest gateway. Supplied by a variety of vendors, the information is derived from all types of publications, and covers subjects ranging from business and technology to humanities and the social sciences. Type **GO IQUEST** to get into this system.

Grolier's Academic American Encyclopedia   Updated four times a year, the on-line edition of *Grolier's Academic American Encyclopedia* is filled with the latest in science, technology, politics, business, law, the arts, and social sciences, as well as a whole range of historical data.

Peterson's College Database   Peterson's offers a comprehensive database of detailed descriptions of over 3000 accredited or approved U.S. and Canadian colleges that grant associate and/or bachelor degrees. You can search colleges by characteristics, college name, or location. This is a perfect resource for the indecisive student.

Computer Library   CompuServe's Computer Library consists of two parts: Computer Database Plus, a collection of computer-related articles and article summaries from leading computer trade publications; and Computer Directory, a collection of listings of computer and communications products and their manufacturers.

U.S. Government Information   The Information U.S.A. database tells you about the free or nearly free government publications and services that are available to taxpayers. It also provides an explanation of the art of obtaining information from the government once you find something of interest.

CompuServe also provides access to the Government Publications Office via an on-line catalog of government publications, books, and subscription services. In addition, the database provides consumer information articles from various government publications and is updated weekly.

Education Databases   A wide variety of other services and forums are available for students and educators including Computer Training Forum, Dissertation Abstracts, Education Forum, Foreign Language Forum, Students Forum, and the Science and Math Education Forum.

Business and Other Interests

CompuServe also offers databases and services to those involved in the business world, from a corporate vice president to a working-from-home entrepreneur.

Business Management   CompuServe provides several services which directly support decision-making in large and small businesses. SuperSite demographic reporting systems, investment decision support, and access to a variety of professional organizations are a few of the services for business people.

Professional Forums   Professionals from a variety of fields and disciplines exchange information, solve problems, and generate new ideas through forums that support journalists, public relations, health care and safety professionals, entrepreneurs, attorneys, and other professional groups.

Aviation Services   CompuServe equips corporate and private pilots with complete flight services, including local and en route weather briefings, and flight plan filing with the FAA. The Aviation Forum gives pilots a place to discuss private and commercial aviation issues with experts and peers.

GENIE

While CompuServe is king of the services, the newcomer GEnie is getting more interest each day. GEnie, which stands for General Electric Network for Information Exchange, is a product of GE Information Services, a component of General Electric Company. GEnie is an on-line information service that offers hundreds of products and services for personal computer users. Headquartered in Rockville, Maryland, GEnie provides local access phone numbers to subscribers in the U.S.A., Canada, and Japan. There are over 150,000 subscribers to GEnie worldwide. GEnie's products range from RoundTables (discussed later in this chapter) to travel services to business and financial services. The number and scope of GEnie services almost guarantees that there will be something of use for everyone.

The cost of using GEnie is a combination of a one-time subscription fee of $29.95 plus a basic rate based on the time you spend connected to GEnie and the speed of your modem. A remote access surcharge of $2 applies in some areas which do not have a local GEnie number. The basic rate in the U.S.A. is summarized in the following table:

Modem speed	Prime-time rate	Non-prime-time rate
300bps	$18.00/hour	$5.00/hour
1200bps	$18.00/hour	$6.00/hour
2400bps	$18.00/hour	$10.00/hour

The prime-time rate is in effect from 8:00A.M. to 6:00P.M. weekdays. The non-prime-time rate is in effect from 6:00P.M. to 8:00A.M. weekdays, and all day on the weekends and national holidays. The subscription fee includes a $10 usage credit, a subscription to GEnie's *Live Wire* newsletter, and a GEnie User's Manual.

Logging On to GEnie

If you want to talk to a representative about signing up for GEnie you can call GEnie Client Services toll-free at 1-800-638-9636 (in the U.S. and Canada). Their office hours are 8A.M. to midnight weekdays (EST) and noon to 8P.M. on weekends and national holidays. To sign up:

1. Get a major credit card out of your purse or wallet (your checking account number can also be used).

2. Start up your favorite telecommunications program and set your modem to half duplex.

3. Set your modem speed to 300 or 1200 baud.

4. Dial 1-800-638-8369 using your program's dialing directory, or give your modem the command **ATDT18006388369** and wait until you connect.

5. Once you have connected with GEnie, type **HHH** and press ENTER. GEnie will respond by giving you the prompt "U#=". Type **XTX99694,GENIE** and press ENTER. (This string of symbols is similar to the one you will use to log on to GEnie once you have an account.) GEnie will now take care of creating your account. You will immediately be assessed a one-time subscription fee of $29.95.

Figure 6-2

The GEnie main menu

```
 *   Brand Name 5.25" Disks at Bulk   *
     Prices! "DIRECTMICRO" in GEnieMall

****************************************
 *    Internal Beta Test Products    *
****************************************

Galaxy Multi-player game - p. 925

No letters waiting.

GEnie          TOP          Page   1
       GE Information Services

   1. GEnie Users' RT  2. Index - Info
   3. Billing/Setup    4. Communications
   5. Computing        6. Travel
   7. Finance          8. Shopping
   9. News            10. Games
  11. Professional    12. Leisure
  13. Reference       14. Logoff

Enter #, or <H>elp?
Communication ready.         ▌ BOYAN v4.0 ▌ 0:00:59: GE Genie
```

Navigating the GEnie System

GEnie is organized into a hierarchical menu structure. From the main menu you can choose one of thirteen submenus, and from those menus you can choose other submenus or services. A reproduction of the main menu is shown in Figure 6-2.

Each menu or service is identified by a page number. Usually each menu or service is also identified by a mnemonic keyword for that area of service. The page number and the keyword are two of the four ways of navigating GEnie (I'll explain what the other two are in a moment). If you look at the sample menu above, you will find the page number in the upper-right corner and the keyword in capital letters in the top center of the menu.

To use a keyword to get to a specific service, just type the keyword from anywhere in the system when you are given the system prompt, which is

```
Enter #, or <H>elp?
```

for the main menu, and

```
Enter #, <P>revious, or <H>elp?
```

for all the other menus. For example, the keyword for the main menu is TOP because it is at the top of the menu structure. From just about anywhere in GEnie you can type TOP at the prompt and you will move to the main menu. Similarly, GROLIERS is the keyword for the Grolier's Encyclopedia menu, and TIS is for Traveler's Information Service. The page number for the TOP menu happens to be 001, which is the only page number that is easy to remember, since it makes sense. Page numbers for the other menus and services probably only make sense to the person(s) who created the menus. The page number for Grolier's Encyclopedia, for example, is 365.

You can get to Grolier's Encyclopedia by typing **m365** at the menu prompt. The *m* in **m365** stands for MOVE. This should make it easy to remember how to use the page number method of navigation—otherwise you might want to type **p365** (*p* for page) or **n365** (*n* for number), which would result in an error message from GEnie.

A third way of navigating GEnie is simply to pick one of the numbered choices given to you at each menu. That is what the "Enter #" part of the prompt is telling you to do.

The <P> in "<P>revious" is giving you the option of moving back or forward one menu in the menu tree by typing a P at the prompt. This is the fourth way of navigating GEnie and is one you will use frequently at first. Once you learn what areas are of interest to you, you will probably use the keywords to go there directly and then use the numbered choices and the "<P>revious" option to move around the local area.

GEnie Products and Services

Information is the heart of GEnie. The heart of the information is found in the forums called the RoundTables.

RoundTables

A RoundTable is a place where computer users can exchange information and ideas. Essentially it is the same as the forums on CompuServe.

RoundTables can have a narrow spectrum (for instance, the Atari 8-Bit RoundTable is for owners of Atari 8-Bit computers), or a wide spectrum (such as the Religion and Ethics RoundTable), or an even wider spectrum (such as the Public Forum*Nonprofit Connection that covers any topic of public interest from computers to religion to ecology). GEnie RoundTables, or RTs, are described and classified into five categories. The keyword given to each RT is the one you use to move directly to the RT's menu from anywhere in the system where the system prompt appears:

```
"Enter #, <P>revious, or <H>elp?"
```

Personal Computing RoundTables The Personal Computing RTs are for anyone who uses a computer. The student, the business computer user, and the recreational computer user will all find answers here to questions about their particular machine. All these RTs have lots of public domain software to offer. Product support for your computer hardware and software is available, either from fellow users, on-line experts, or from the company that makes the product. Table 6-1 summarizes the RTs in this category.

Programmer's RoundTables There are four RTs especially for those who write programs for PCs. Here programmers will find discussions of topics suited to their interests. The software libraries contain source code as well as executable programs. Table 6-2 summarizes the RTs in this category.

Professional Services RoundTables These RTs serve the interests of groups of professionals such as lawyers and musicians but are open to anyone. Table 6-3 summarizes the RTs in this category.

Product Support RoundTables Many questions about computer products can be answered at an RT which specializes in information on that product. For instance, if you use Procomm Plus as your communications software and have a question, go to the Datastorm Technologies, Inc. RoundTable to get it answered. Many companies provide product support through these RTs.

Special Interest RoundTables The rest of the RTs cover a broad range of special interests from aviation to genealogy to radio and electronics.

Financial Services
There are a variety of services to assist you with financial matters.

Table 6-1

Personal Computer RoundTables

Keyword	Name	Comments
A2	Apple II RoundTable	For owners of the Apple II family of computers
AMIGA	Amiga RoundTable	For owners of the Commodore Amiga
ATARI8	Atari 8-Bit RoundTable	For owners of the Atari 8-Bit computers. Staff of Atari Corp. are on line
ST	Atari ST RoundTable	For owners of the Atari ST computers. Staff of Atari Corp. are on line
CBM	Commodore RoundTable	For owners of Commodore 64 and 128 computers
IBMPC	IBM RoundTable	For owners of IBM PCs, compatibles, and clones
MAC	Macintosh RoundTable	For owners of Macintosh computers
TANDY	Tandy RoundTable	For owners of Tandy computers
TI	Texas Instruments RoundTable	For owners of Texas Instruments, Adam, Vic-20, and Commodore+4 machines

Dow Jones News/Retrieval You can access the Dow Jones News /Retrieval service through a gateway offered by GEnie just as you can access it through a gateway offered by MCI Mail. The DJN/R is a source of business and financial information. Stock quotes (delayed by fifteen minutes), as well as current and back issues of *The Wall Street Journal, The Washington Post*, and other publications are available. The cost of the DJN/R is $35 to register (a one-time fee) plus fees which vary anywhere from 44 cents to $2.75 per minute depending on the product you use. Type DJNS at the system prompt for this service. There is more information concerning this service later in this chapter.

VESTOR VESTOR is an electronic investment advisor. VESTOR gives users an analysis of current market conditions and projections, including actual buy/sell signals and evaluations for over 6000 individual securities.

Table 6-2

Programmer's RoundTables

Keyword	Name	Comments
PRO/AM	Pro/Am RoundTable	Devoted to the interests of Amiga programmers
A2PRO	Apple II Developers RoundTable	Product support from companies that publish languages for the Apple II family of computers
ATARIDEV	Atari Developers RoundTable	A RoundTable of Atari developers, supported by Atari Corp
MACPRO	Macintosh Developers RoundTable	For developers of software for the Macintosh

The cost of using VESTOR is $5/hour, regardless of the speed of your modem or time of day, plus the basic connection fee, plus the cost of each report, which is variable and depends on the analysis performed. Type **VESTOR$** at the system prompt.

GEnie Quotes Securities Database   This service provides current (previous day's closing) and historical information relating to over 67,000 security issues of all types. Information is gathered from the NYSE, AMEX, NASDAQ and other sources. GEnie Quotes is searchable by Ticker symbol, CUSIP, Company name, or Industry code. In addition, portfolios can be entered that will provide convenient updates of your market position. Over 20 standard reports can also be requested to give you a stock's current status, three- to five-day history, its high and low for the past year, and other information. QUOTE$ is the keyword for this service.

News and Information Services

GEnie's news delivery system is outstanding; they even have a clipping service similar to the one found on CompuServe.

Newsgrid Headline News   NewsGrid is a real-time news service compiled from the dispatches of some of the largest U.S. and international wire

---
Table 6-3

Professional Services RoundTables

Keyword	Name	Comments
ALERT	A Law Enforcement RoundTable	For those who work at any aspect of law enforcement, or anyone with an interest in, opinion, or problem with law enforcement
ERT	Education RoundTable	For anyone in the educational community, professional trainers, and interested public
LAW	Legacy Law RoundTable	For legal professionals and anyone interested in learning about the law
MEDICAL	Medical RoundTable	For those who work in the field of medicine and anyone interested in medicine
MIDI	MIDI WorldMusic RoundTable	For users of MIDI-based computer music systems as well as anyone interested in MIDI-based systems. Supports most major computers (IBM, Macintosh, Atari, Commodore, and so on)
NADTP	National Association of Desktop Publishers RoundTable	For anyone interested in desktop publishing. Software library includes clip art files and other sources of graphic images
NPC	Public Forum*Nonprofit Connection	This RT covers a broad range of topics of public interest from computer technology to ecology to politics
PHOTO	Photography RoundTable	For beginners and expert photographers. Information on equipment, techniques, business management, and so on
RELIGION	Religion and Ethics RoundTable	Discuss any religion or religious idea here. Take the religion I.Q. test and see how well you score
WRITERS	Writers' Ink RoundTable	For any and all writers—poets, journalists, humorists, etc. Learn how to get published, share resources or just have fun

---

services. NewsGrid is comprehensive in scope, covering world affairs, political issues, sports, business, entertainment, and feature items ... even the weather. It is updated continually, throughout the day. You can set up your own electronic clipping service, which will select articles for you based on a profile you create. You can even keyword-search for articles. There is no surcharge for this service. The keyword for NewsGrid is NEWSGRID.

QuikNews News Clipping Service   GEnie QuikNews is designed to save you time and effort while keeping you up to date on the news and information you want to see. Based on a profile of "search terms" and "standing stories," all incoming stories are scanned, and those which are appropriate are transmitted to you via GE Mail. There is a $25/month fee for this service, which includes up to ten search terms and/or standing stories. Additional terms and standing stories can be added for an additional fee. The keyword is QUIKNEWS.

USA Today DecisionLines   USA Today DecisionLines is provided by Gannett News Media Services. It is a collection of 18 news summaries that are updated at 8:00 A.M. EST each weekday. Topics include:

Advertising	Banking	Energy
Business Law	Health	Insurance
International	Investing	Real Estate
Technology	Telecom	Market Trends
Travel	Weather	Sports
Issues & Debates		

Genealogy KnowledgeBase

Here's an unusual database worth exploring. The Genealogy Knowledge-Base is a growing collection of documents about available sources for genealogical research. Its purpose is to let you rapidly find materials or organizations that can help you in your own research. Among the resources described in the Genealogy KnowledgeBase are

- Genealogical and Historical Societies

- Computer Interest Groups

- Books and Magazines

- Publishers

- Family or Surname Associations

- Family or Surname Newsletters

- Software

- Libraries

- Professional Researchers

- Sources for Vital Records

You can search the KnowledgeBase by asking for any word or sequence of words in the text of the documents. The cost of using the KnowledgeBase is $5/hour over your basic rate, and begins the moment you select

```
1. $Search Genealogy KnowledgeBase
```

and ends when you respond with Q or Quit at one of the prompts within the KnowledgeBase. The keyword for all genealogical information is GENEAL-OGY. The KnowledgeBase can be accessed directly by using the MOVE command and moving to page 543 (that is, **m543**).

Miscellaneous Related Services
GE offers a superb variety of miscellaneous services to its subscribers.

Cineman Entertainment Information   Cineman Entertainment Information is a source of reviews of current movies, as well as an extensive database of reviews for recent and old movies. There are also reviews and information about current and future books and records, and a weekly column that reviews recent video releases. The keyword is CINEMAN.

Hollywood Hotline Movie Reviews   Hollywood Hotline Movie Reviews concentrates on the top 50 current movies. Each review is 500 to 600 words long and covers the major credits, a summary of the film's story line, and the observations of the reviewer. The keyword is HOTLINE.

Rainbo Electronic Reviews   Rainbo Electronic Reviews covers popular books, books for children, cookbooks, computer books, and books on audio cassettes and video cassettes. Their reviews are light and informal. The keyword is RAINBO.

RockNet Entertainment News   RockNet offers the latest, most accurate information in the world of rock and roll. Radio and record industry personnel, musicians and DJs all contribute to the daily news columns. Each day RockNet updates four columns: Late RockNet News, Backstage Chatter, Reviews, and Miscellaneous. You can also send feedback to RockNet to share your views, complaints, and ideas. The keyword is **ROCK**.

Soap Opera Summaries   Here's a unique use for computer technology. Soap Opera Summaries provides current and past summaries on 12 daily soap operas and 6 prime-time soap operas. Also provided are updated information on news and gossip within the soap industry, soap opera cast lists, the capability of writing to soap opera stars, soap opera birthdays, and a look at what has evolved in the soaps in the previous year. The keyword is SOAP.

Dr. Job   Dr. Job is a weekly question-and-answer column covering career and employment issues, written by business journalist, Sandra Pesmen. Topics discussed range from corporate politics to communications to career decisions. Questions or comments can be left at electronic mail address DR.JOB and will be answered privately via electronic mail. Some of these questions will be used in future Dr. Job columns, but names will not be included in the columns. The keyword is DR.JOB.

Travel Services

GEnie offers its users several travel-related services that are found by entering the keyword TRAVEL.

Adventure Atlas   Adventure Atlas is a comprehensive vacation database. The database can be searched by trip type, country, month, and other criteria in order to help you find a vacation that is everything you want it to be. From road trips in the rural U.S. to expeditions to Mt. Everest in Nepal, you can find anything you want. There is no surcharge for this service. The keyword is ATLAS.

EAASY SABRE   The same as CompuServe. EAASY SABRE from American Airlines lets you look directly at schedules for over 650 airlines worldwide and over 13,000,000 fares. At the same time, you can make room reservations at over 12,000 hotels, rent a car at your destination, and check the weather at hundreds of places in the U.S. and around the world. There is no surcharge while using EAASY SABRE. The keyword is SABRE.

The Official Airline Guide's Electronic Edition   The Official Airline Guide's (OAG) Electronic Edition Travel Service lets you view schedules for over 600 airlines and over 37,500 hotels in North America, Europe, and the Pacific. In addition, information is available on tours, cruises, and discount vacation packages. A recreation guide is available to help you with ideas for having fun. There is a surcharge of $10/hour non-prime time and $28/hour prime time in addition to the basic GEnie rate for this value-added product. The keyword is OAG.

The Travelers Information RoundTable   The Travelers Information RoundTable is designed to be a one-stop travel information service. It offers regional travel recommendations, an on-line travel newsletter, and information on how to travel free, discount tickets, and more. There is no surcharge for this service. The keyword is TIS.

Shopping

GEnie has an electronic mall where you can shop at over 35 stores ranging from "Apparel Concepts For Men" to "Tiffany & Co." The paragraphs that follow explain how to shop at the mall and what the mall policies are. All the stores' descriptions are contained in Table 6-4.

Shopping at the GEnie Mall is similar to shopping at your local supermarket. First you must enter one of the stores by either starting at the GEnie Mall main menu and choosing the store you want to enter, or by going directly to the store you want to shop at by typing the keyword for that store at the system prompt. (The keyword for the main menu is GENIEMALL.) After you enter the store you can begin selecting the items you want and they will be put into your electronic shopping cart. Figure 6-3 shows a screen used to make a selection for your electronic shopping cart. If you decide you don't want an item in your basket, you can type **RE-MOVE** and you will be given the chance to remove it. If you want to know what is in your basket, just type **DISPLAY**. If you decide you no longer want anything in your basket (this is really convenient), you just type **EMPTY**. When you are done shopping, type **CHECKOUT**. You will then be asked for all the information needed to complete your purchase. You can type **QUIT** at any time during the checkout procedure to cancel any or all items in your order. Payment can be made by VISA, MasterCard, the Discover Card, American Express, COD, personal check, or from a mailed invoice, depending on the merchant.

Table 6-1

GEnie Mall merchants

Keyword	Merchant Name	Description/Products
ACE	A-Comm Electronics	Fax machines, modems, and other communication products. General information on suppliers of hardware, software, and peripherals. Accepts American Express, MasterCard, VISA, and personal checks
APPAREL	Apparel Concepts For Men	Fine quality men's furnishings and apparel. Accepts MasterCard, VISA
AUTO-QUOT-R	Autoquot-R Store	Dealer price quotes on all new cars. Accepts MasterCard, VISA
BITS	BITS-N-BYTES, Inc.	Hardware and peripherals for IBM PC/XT/AT and compatibles, and some items for Apple, Macintosh. Accepts VISA, MasterCard, COD, company checks, personal checks
CAREFREE	Carefree Shopping	Specializes in gift items from the Southwest and England. Accepts MasterCard, VISA
COFFEE	Coffee Anyone ???	Coffees, teas, and other gourmet delights. Accepts MasterCard, VISA
CUS	Comp-U-Store On-line	Over 250,000 different products at guaranteed low prices. Accepts MasterCard, VISA
DIRECT MICRO	Direct Micro	Discount microcomputer supplies. Accepts VISA, MasterCard
ELITE	Elite Eyewear	Sunglass and eyeglass sales. Accepts American Express, VISA, MasterCard, personal checks
ENGRAVING	Engraving Connection	Engravable items—desk sets, trophies, name plates, etc. Accepts American Express, Discover, MasterCard, VISA
EXPRESS	ComputerExpress Products	Computer hardware, software, and accessories. Accepts MasterCard, VISA, Discover, and personal checks
FFS	Florida Fruit Shippers	Fresh Florida fruit shipped to your home. Accepts American Express, MasterCard, VISA

Table 6-1

GEnie Mall merchants (*continued*)

Keyword	Merchant Name	Description/Products
GODIVA	Godiva Chocolatier	Godiva confections. Accepts American Express, MasterCard, VISA, and personal checks
HOBBIES	21st Century Hobbies	A complete hobby store. On-line help from expert hobbyists. Accepts MasterCard, VISA, and personal checks
HYPERMAIL	Hypermail	Order print catalogs from over 50 mail-order merchants. Accepts MasterCard and VISA
INVESTMENT	Investment Software	A large selection of investment related software for the IBM PC and compatibles. Accepts VISA, MasterCard, and American Express
IVORY	The Ivory Cache	Authentic Alaskan gold, ivory, jewelry, and gifts. Accepts MasterCard, VISA, American Express, and Discover
KNOLL	Walter Knoll Florist	Live and silk florist products. Accepts MasterCard, VISA, American Express, and personal checks
LATHROP-SPORT	Lathrop Sports Vacations	Windsurfing and skiing camps, clinics, and vacation packages. Accepts American Express, Discover, and personal checks
LDROSES	Long Distance Roses	Roses, orchids, and FTD bouquets via Federal Express. Accepts MasterCard, VISA, Discover, and American Express
LEGAL-SEAFOOD	Legal Sea Foods	Live lobsters and other seafood shipped to you. Accepts MasterCard, American Express, and Discover
MAGALOG	Video Magalog	A magazine and catalog of movies, special interest, and how-to videos. Accepts VISA, MasterCard, and American Express
MARYMAC	Marymac Industries	Discount prices on Tandy computer products. Accepts MasterCard, VISA, American Express, and Discover

Table 6-1

GEnie Mall merchants (*continued*)

Keyword	Merchant Name	Description/Products
MUSICALLEY	Music Alley Online	Keyboards, synthesizers, and other musical equipment. Accepts MasterCard, VISA, and COD
NOTEWORTHY	Noteworthy Music	A selection of over 7500 compact discs. Accepts MasterCard, VISA, Discover, COD
OAGMALL	Official Airline Guide Mall Store	A comprehensive, up-to-date electronic travel information and reservation system. Check fares, flights, seat availability, and make reservations. Accepts MasterCard, VISA
ORVIS	Orvis	America's oldest mail-order catalog. Accepts American Express, MasterCard, VISA
PC-SIG	PC-Sig	IBM shareware for sale at low prices. Accepts VISA, MasterCard
RENT	Rent Mother Nature	Rent a maple tree, a lobster trap in the Atlantic Ocean, or a bee hive, and collect the harvest without doing any work. Accepts American Express, MasterCard, VISA
SAFEWARE	Safeware, The Insurance Agency Inc.	Protect your computer equipment and accessories from fire, theft, electrical blowouts, and more. Accepts MasterCard, VISA, personal checks
SDA	Software Discounters of America	Over 1300 software products at discount prices. Accepts MasterCard, VISA, personal checks
SPIRITS	800 Spirits	Wine, champagne, and spirits. Accepts MasterCard, VISA, American Express
TALLTAILS	Tall Tails	Quality pet products. Accepts MasterCard, VISA, personal checks
TIFFANY	Tiffany & Co.	Order Tiffany products on line; open a charge account. Accepts MasterCard, VISA, American Express
VIDEO-SIG	Video-Sig Video Library	An extensive video library of current and hard to find movies. Accepts MasterCard, VISA, personal checks, purchase orders

---

Table 6-1

GEnie Mall merchants (*continued*)

Keyword	Merchant Name	Description/Products
WSJ	Wall Street Journal	Order the Wall Street Journal at GEnie member prices. Accepts MasterCard, VISA, American Express, personal checks, and mailed invoices

---

Figure 6-3

A selection is made through electronic shopping

```
   *=*=* GOURMET HIGHLIGHTS *=*=*

 1. Alaskan Sourdough
 2. 8 Oz Alaskan Smoked Salmon
 3. 1 Lb Alaskan Smoked Salmon
 4. Alaskan Crab/Shrimp Sampler
 5. Salmon Sampler
 6. Seafare in a Wooden Box
 7. Smoked Salmon/Smoked Halibut
 8. Smoked Sockeye Fillet

Enter #, <P>revious, or <H>elp?4

Alaskan Crab/Shrimp Sampler


4 ounces each of Alaskan shrimp and Alaskan crab each in
separate pouches. These are not smoked, just their own nice,
rich flavor.


Our Price: $   22.00

Do you want to order? (Y/N)?
Communication ready.            █ BOYAN v4.0 █ 0:14:20: GE Genie
```

All merchants adhere to the following policies:

1. All merchandise orders must ship within 12 days of order unless otherwise displayed in the store's "ordering and shipping policies."

2. Your credit card will not be charged until the merchandise is shipped.

3. Your credit card number is not available to anyone except the store from which you ordered. Your security and privacy are assured.

4. All stores have liberal return policies. (So your satisfaction in a purchase is guaranteed.)

5. If the product you order is not available, you will be notified within two business days after placing your order. If you have a problem with an order, take your complaint to the GEnie Mall Manager, whose electronic mail address is MALL.

6. All merchants will respond to any electronic mail inquiry within three business days.

If you would like to open a store on the GEnie Mall (or for more information), you can write to: MODEM MEDIA, P.O. Box 2573, Westport, CT 06880 or call 1-203-853-2600.

GEnie also has a classified ads section. Viewing the ads is free and placing an ad is inexpensive. The cost depends on the duration of the ad and the number of 80-character lines. Charges at the time of this writing are ten cents a line for seven days, and twenty cents a line for 30 days. The keyword for the classified ads menu is ADS.

Games

GEnie has many on-line games. There are single-player or multiple-player games, as well as graphics-and text-based games. In the multiplayer games you can play against one or more people on line anywhere in the world where GEnie is available. The single-player games are played against yourself or GEnie's computer. A few of the games, such as those that give you a graphic display instead of a text display, require that you download "front-end" software. This software is run from your computer during play and provides the graphic interface. If you want to play a game, type the word **GAMES** at the system prompt; from there you can choose any game in the system. Once you find out which games you like best, learn their keywords so that you can go directly to them and bypass the main games menu (see Figure 6-4). Besides these on-line games, there are many games available for download from the software libraries.

GEnie Electronic Mail

GEnie's electronic mail service provides a way for you to send mail in seconds to anyone with access to GEnie. You can also send paper mail, called a GEnie Quik-Gram, to anyone in the U.S. The cost of a Quik-Gram is $2 for the first page (40 lines) and 75 cents for each additional page (50 lines each) up to five pages total. Xmodem is available for binary file transfers.

Uploading and Downloading Software

There are thousands of files in GEnie's many software libraries that you will want to download. Protocols supported at the time of this writing are Xmodem, Xmodem-1K, Ymodem, and Zmodem. Use Zmodem whenever

---

Figure 6-1

A screen from one of many games that are available on GEnie

possible. During a download you are charged at the regular rate for the time period of your call. Uploading is free during non-prime-time hours, but you are charged your basic rate during prime-time hours.

GEnie Livewire CB Simulator

The CB simulator is similar to the one found on CompuServe. You choose a "handle," or nickname, for yourself and talk to several people at once—just as you would on a citizens band radio. You can also have a private, one-on-one conversation with your GEnie friends. Muffy's Gossip Corner is a RoundTable where you can discuss anything you want—maybe even spread a rumor or two. Type **cb** at the menu prompt to get to the main LiveWire menu. Type **MUFFY** to get to Muffy's Gossip Corner.

Special CB Club rates are available for addicts who can't find any better way to spend their time. The reduced rate plan costs $30/month and allows you to use the CB Simulator only during non-prime-time hours for $3/hour at any modem speed. The special rate begins after you enter the CB Simulator, not after you log on to GEnie. The Nightly User Plan costs $100/month and allows you to use the CB Simulator only during non-prime-time hours with no hourly fees. The special rate begins after you enter the CB Simulator, not after you log on to GEnie.

As you explore GEnie, you'll discover new services that are constantly being added. This is an outstanding information utility that is highly recommended.

DELPHI—A PROGRESSIVE ON-LINE COMMUNITY

Now we get to Delphi. Delphi is one of the pioneers in the telecommunications field. It was founded in 1981 and was the first full-service system to offer 1200bps access at no surcharge. It was the first to offer a surcharge-free 2400bps access, and the first to publish an on-line encyclopedia.

Members who opt for Delphi's Advantage Plan enjoy the lowest evening connect rate of any major national information service ($4.80/hour including access via TYMNET or Sprintnet).

Signing Up

With any computer or terminal and modem, you can sign up though a special procedure available to buyers of this book. Set your telecommunications parameters to 8-N-1 and use 300, 1200, or 2400 baud (depending on your modem). Then:

1. Dial 1-800-365-4636.

2. Once connected, press the ENTER key once or twice.

3. At the Username prompt, type **JOINDELPHI**.

4. At the Password prompt, type **DVORAK**.

5. Have credit card information handy.

Cost   There is a sign up fee of $49.95. Members do not pay any monthly fees, only connect charges. There are no surcharges for remote areas.

The Delphi Advantage—
More to Your Advantage

Advantage Members enjoy the lowest Delphi access rates available. Delphi Advantage Rates are as low as 8 cents per minute—that's only $4.80 per hour—for domestic U.S. access via TYMNET, Sprintnet, or direct dial (and access from Canada via TYMNET) during the evenings and weekends. International access for Advantage Members will be 12 cents per minute, 24 hours per day. And there are no premium charges for access at 1200 or 2400bps!

To join the Delphi Advantage there is a one-time membership fee of $19, with a commitment to use $24 worth of Delphi connect charges per month.

Information from Delphi

For more information, call Delphi Member Services at 1-800-544-4005 or at 1-617-491-3393 from within Massachusetts. Telephone support is from 8:00A.M. until midnight on weekdays. On weekends the hours are from 10:00A.M. until 10:00P.M. Members may use Delphi mail to send questions or requests to SERVICE 24 hours a day. Delphi's mailing address is Delphi, Three Blackstone Street, Cambridge, MA 02139.

The Delphi Services

Delphi is known for its relaxed and friendly atmosphere, which gives the service a sense of community similar to that found in the BBS world.

Delphi offers computer-specific computer groups. The groups are packed with valuable hints that will help you to get the most out of your computer. Thousands of useful programs are available for you to download. Delphi has been designed for ease of use to make it simple to find the programs you need.

Delphi also has an entertainment area. There you may try some of Delphi's multiplayer games. Unlike many other services' complex games and rules, Delphi's games are easy to play. Many are familiar games, such as poker. Delphi has five different variations of poker, with tables set aside for beginners and hustlers. You may play against other members, human-looking robot players, or both. There's a place to pit your knowledge of trivia against other members in TQ Trivia. Another popular game among Delphi users is FlipIt, a strategy game similar to the board game Othello. With all the Delphi games available, new members and beginners are always welcome.

Of course, Delphi also offers all the features of a leading information service: electronic mail, real-time conferencing, news wires, comprehensive business information, extensive travel information (with an instant reservation system), and on-line shopping.

The On-Line Community

Delphi likes to think of itself as more than a service or a resource. It's an on-line community. The service has grown because it responds to the comments and suggestions of its membership. You won't find thousands of seldom-used or obscure services on Delphi. There is a healthy selection of quality, useful services.

On Delphi you are able to ask the experts questions about hardware and software, or discuss today's issues. There is also a place to just chat in Conference. Any time of the day or night there's someone on line for you to talk with.

"Real-time" Conferences make it possible to converse with friends from the other side of the world. Japanese members have to get up pretty early in the morning to chat, but they do. Other Conferences feature special guests from around the globe and informal meetings to discuss specific computer types.

The Clubhouse Log on and check out the groups and clubs menu. You'll see groups for most major types of computers, and special interest groups for hobbyists, writers, science fiction fans, photographers, and business people.

The Forum In each group you'll also find a forum or a "bulletin board" feature. To take part in an ongoing discussion, place a permanent message in the Forum. Other members will respond. All the messages on a specific topic are linked for easy reading. Delphi also has an on-line color computer expert to aid members in adjusting screen tints, among other things.

The Color Computer Group The Color Computer Group is one of Delphi's most active areas. It is devoted to the users of the Tandy Color Computer (called the CoCo). This club is sponsored by *Rainbow the Color Computer Monthly Magazine.* Its resources include thousands of files to download, scheduled conferences with industry experts, files on upcoming RAINBOWfests, and daily news bulletins from RAINBOWfest shows.

Macintosh ICONtact Group Delphi Macintosh ICONtact Group is an information exchange for the Apple Macintosh Computer. Here is a wealth of expertise, ideas, and public-domain software for the Mac. It's a place to find out how to use HyperCard to your best advantage, and to get the latest from the emerging world of desktop publishing.

Tandy PC Group The Tandy PC Group is an international forum for users of Tandy's personal and business computers. This is the place to share ideas, access more than 1000 public-domain programs, and find software for the popular PC-compatible computers, the Tandy 1000, 1200, and 3000.

Science Fiction Group If your interests gravitate toward the crazed or the fantastic, look up the Science Fiction Group, dedicated to readers, writers, and fans of science fiction. This is a place to share a common interest in fantasy. Access a convention calendar and book and film reviews. Topics of conversation range from television series such as "Dr. Who" and "Star Trek" to comics, books, and films.

On-Line Entertainment

Games seem to be getting more and more popular. The ones found on Delphi are quite unique. The Entertainment Menu offers trivia, vote-in polls, movie reviews, and horoscopes. Meet your match on line when you play Delphi's four great multiplayer games: TQ Trivia, SCRAMBLE, Poker Showdown, and FlipIt. The games are social; you may talk with other players between rounds and even chat *during* a game to give hints or to distract your opponents.

TQ Trivia   Capitalize on your gift for knowledge of trivia and bump heads with hundreds of on-line players in TQ Trivia Contests. Questions range from movies to politics, sports, religion, and TV characters. Stay on your toes as the contest progresses through several rounds. Early correct answers will help to accumulate points that you can wager with in later rounds. You may converse freely except while a question is outstanding. As the responses come in, a tally is displayed to compare how everyone answered each question. At the end of each round, you are given an in-progress ranking and score. Scheduled games take place weekly and organized tournaments are frequent.

TQ Anytime can be played 24-hours-a-day, seven days a week, except when the scheduled TQ Trivia contests are in progress. TQ Anytime proceeds automatically. You are presented with a category and asked to bet. When the bets are in, the question is asked and you have to make a guess. A summary of all players' answers is shown before the correct answer is revealed. If your answer is correct, you win your bet. TQ Anytime points are kept separate from TQ Trivia Contest points, so TQ Anytime will not affect your chances of winning TQ Trivia Contests and the prizes that come along with victory.

SCRAMBLE   SCRAMBLE is a game of sharp observation, quick thinking, and nimble fingers. You have 90 seconds to come up with as many words as possible from a grid of 16 letters. The longer the word, the more points you gain. Compete with other Delphi members who are trying to get the "best" words first. After 90 seconds, scores are displayed.

Poker   Meet with players skilled in the art of on-line wagering. Introduce yourself and "talk" with your opponents before the game and between hands. Even if you don't find people playing, you can hone your skills against Delphi's "robots"—some very cagey opponents. Sit down at one of several tables and play any of four types of poker including Five Card, Seven Card Stud, and Five Card Draw. There are also poker tournaments. The wagers are purely for fun, but if you lose all of your chips, you are eliminated from the tournament.

FlipIt   Pick your moves carefully in the exciting game of reversals. FlipIt is played like the board games Othello or Reversi. As in poker, you may play against other members or one of two robot adversaries. The game is easy to learn and fun to play. Novices may watch others' games to learn winning strategies.

Some members thrill to the challenge of scheduled tournaments. The winners are chosen by the best records on ten-by-ten boards, eight-by-eight boards, and best overall record.

Travel

Delphi is home to Travel+Plus, one of the most comprehensive and unique travel services offered on line. Like the rest of Delphi, Travel+Plus offers easy access to a wealth of informative and useful materials. Unlike services on other networks, Travel+Plus connects you directly to travel professionals specially trained to assist you with on-line services. These are people who are dedicated to helping you learn how to take control of your travel options and how to get the most out of every itinerary.

With instant world wide communications, Travel+Plus gives travelers a special advantage in obtaining current information on the latest fares, special offers, last-minute sales, and other rapidly changing aspects of travel.

Travel+Plus has neatly organized information by destinations. By selecting the profiles for the country and city you plan to visit, you have immediate access to useful details. If your destination is an obscure one and not shown, Travel+Plus will find it for you.

Travel+Plus incorporates services so that it is possible to confirm reservations immediately. Use American Airlines' EAASY SABRE, The Official Airline Guide (OAG), or PARS TravelShopper. You may book airline seats, reserve hotel rooms, and confirm car rental arrangements in minutes. Use a toll-free voice and on-line support to help you ensure the correct reservation and at the best rates available.

Merchant's Row—On-Line Shopping

Use Delphi's shopping services with Comp-u-Store Online. You find over 250,000 name-brand products to choose from, and most are available at guaranteed savings of 10 percent to 50 percent off manufacturers' list prices.

Shop with Delphi's Merchants' Row vendors like the following:

- Boston Computer Exchange is for IBM, Apple, Apple GS, and Macintosh software plus computer peripherals and hardware for your computer
- Chocolates by Godiva will ship chocolate anywhere
- Long Distance Roses will send floral displays
- Coffee Anyone??? offers a fine array of gourmet products
- Investment Software offers financial software
- Softwhere Bargains Report gives you facts about software
- MaryMac Industries offers many Tandy products
- UNICEF Greeting Cards and Gifts for those special occasions

Communications

Use Delphi's communication services to get your message out immediately, on line. Delphi's electronic mail is easy to use. Send, instantly receive, forward, reply to, and file private messages of unlimited length, and search mail by date or keyword. You'll have a personalized member name which also serves as a mailbox address. Mail is organized into files, folders, and messages.

In addition to text messages, members may send binary files including programs, spreadsheets, word processing files, graphic images, and sounds. There is no per-message charge for electronic mail. You're only responsible for connect-time charges.

You may also send and receive messages via Telex. Delphi offers a variety of other connections to public communication networks. A message or text file may be sent to a fax machine anywhere in the world. Messages may also be sent to Easylink subscribers in the U.S.A. or the United Kingdom.

Translation Services

Wordet is a professional translation service for translation to and from Spanish, French, German, Italian, Portuguese, and other languages. The text is translated, sent by electronic mail or telex, and a copy is sent to your Delphi mailbox.

The Resource of Choice for Business

Delphi offers a solid package of business information that is designed for businesses or personal investors. Delphi provides continual stock quote and mutual fund updates for all issues traded on the New York Stock Exchange, American Stock Exchange and NASDAQ. Stock and Commodity Quotes are the current prices for over 9000 stocks and are delayed by 15 minutes. MarketPulse, an exclusive Delphi service, provides an immediate snapshot of the market with current Dow Average, most active stocks, advances/ declines, and percentage of gain and loss.

There is TrendVest to track your financial portfolio and analyze stocks. With VESTOR and Security Objectives Services you'll have access to market analysis.

If you invest in CDs or money market funds, Delphi provides CD InfoLine and Donoghue's Money Fund Report. CD InfoLine ranks financial institutions by the highest CD rates. Donoghue Money Fund report provides weekly rates for tax-exempt, government, and general purpose money funds.

Read UPI for the latest corporate and economic news. Consult the BusinessWire for press releases that cover new products, company earnings, dividends, management changes, and other information on the rapidly changing business world.

DIALOG

Back before there were personal computers, before on-line bulletin boards existed, before electronic mail was commonplace, there was DIALOG.

DIALOG grew out of a Lockheed Missiles and Space Company research and development program begun in 1963. Contracts with government agencies such as NASA and the U.S. Office of Education followed. In 1972, DIALOG was established as a commercial search service. Its first customers were scientific and technical libraries, but business libraries soon followed. The database was accessed by use of dumb terminals, most of which operated at 300 baud. In 1981, the rapidly growing DIALOG became a wholly-owned subsidiary of the Lockheed Corporation.

The growth of on-line databases was fueled by the growing popularity of personal computers. As more individuals bought PCs, there was more demand for the electronic research capabilities DIALOG could provide. Business executives, scientists, teachers, doctors, and individual investors realized the value of the ability to search databases. DIALOG responded by adding more databases, by refining its search software, and by branching out into related information products and services, such as databases on CD-ROM. DIALOG was purchased by Knight-Ridder, Inc. DIALOG is now part of Knight-Ridder's Business Information Services Division.

Without DIALOG Information Services, today's world of information retrieval would be significantly different. For one thing, DIALOG exemplifies the concept of the *databank*. A databank is a collection of databases. As a databank, DIALOG facilitates quick and easy access to a broad range of information. And DIALOG is not resting on its laurels. Instead, DIALOG is looking for new technologies to better serve existing customers and to attract new individuals who need the information DIALOG has to offer.

On-Line Databases

Suppose you have serious research to do. In the days before microcomputers and modems, there would be the necessary trip to the nearest research library. There would be hours of searching through reference books, some periodical indexes, and the card catalog. Then there would be the endless notes, and numerous photocopies at a quarter each.

Now your best bet, if you can afford it, is to access DIALOG Information Services. There are on-line equivalents to many of the tools you use in libraries, and other services. Because of the processing power of the computer, you are able to focus in on the information you really need. On-line research is a much faster process. DIALOG may not keep you out of the library, but it should enable you to spend less time there.

What Is DIALOG?

DIALOG represents itself as the "World's Largest On-line Knowledgebank." This is no idle boast. DIALOG has over 325 databases, ranging in subject from aerospace to zoology. There's information on art, music and the humanities, business articles, company news, and industry assessments. Research resources include the hard sciences: biology, chemistry, and physics.

DIALOG covers a wide variety of source material. There are some databases in full-text format (the entire text of journal and newspaper articles may be retrieved on line). Many newswire services, such as AP, UPI, and *Knight-Ridder Financial News,* are full-text searchable on DIALOG. Other DIALOG databases are the on-line equivalents of corporate directories, a great help if you need to know a company's address and phone number or some obscure fact such as how many software producers there are in the state of Missouri.

Other Resources On Line with DIALOG

DIALOG's on-line information includes directory entries, journal articles, conference papers, patents, books, trademarks, and statistics. DIALOG offers the full text of articles from more publications than any other on-line service in the world.

There is information on more than 12 million companies from sources such as Dun & Bradstreet, Standard & Poor's, and Moody's. You can find information on over 15 million patents from over 56 patent-issuing authorities. There are summaries of articles from more than 100,000 journals, and the complete text of over 800 journals and newsletters.

Graphics may be retrieved from DIALOG. Both trademark design images and chemical compound drawings can be reproduced from DIALOG databases.

DIALOG subscribers are able to access almost any database on the system. Connections can be made between disparate pieces of information found in different databases. Information can be put together in ways which would be impossible without computer access.

DIALOG Subscribers Worldwide

DIALOG's content is worldwide, and so is its customer base. Worldwide access is possible with DIALOG. There are over 100,000 subscribers in nearly 100 countries.

These subscribers are a unique group. Over 75 percent of *Fortune* 500 companies maintain DIALOG passwords. Employees at government agencies, libraries, universities, and research institutions around the world regularly search DIALOG databases. DIALOG is also for lawyers, business consultants, engineers, students, medical professionals, information brokers, and small-business owners. Although there are no figures available for the number of children who use DIALOG for help on their homework, probably the numbers are impressive.

DIALOG's Computers

At its Palo Alto headquarters, DIALOG has four large mainframe computers, plus disk drive storage for over 700 billion characters. That's roughly equivalent to the storage capacity of 70,000 IBM XTs. The storage capacity is increased by about 20 billion characters per month, to accommodate the new data on DIALOG. There are over 190 million items on line, and that number is growing.

Availability of DIALOG

DIALOG is accessible 157 hours per week. (There is scheduled maintenance downtime from 3:00A.M. to 2:00P.M. EST on Sunday.) DIALOG is available through the major public telecommunications networks, as well as through DIALNET, DIALOG's private network.

Customer Service

Customer service is available in the U.S. on toll-free numbers, 24 hours a day from 6:30P.M. EST Sunday through midnight Friday. On Saturday the hours are from 10:00A.M. to 6:00P.M. EST. Local support is available in DIALOG offices in Boston, New York, Philadelphia, Washington D.C., Chicago, Houston, and Los Angeles. DIALOG also has representatives in Europe, Asia, Latin America, Australia, and Canada.

Getting Started

Signing up for DIALOG is simple. Customers pay a nominal annual service fee ($35 as of this writing). There are no monthly minimums. There is a connect-time charge. This ranges from 25 cents to $2.75 per minute. The charge varies by the database accessed. A typical DIALOG search costs from $5 to $25, and discounts are available for extensive usage.

DIALOG does not have on-line sign-ups for its service. The toll-free number is 1-800-3-DIALOG (or 1-800-334-2564). A recorded message will answer. The message is very clear and precise. The instructions will tell you to press the 1 on your touchtone telephone for the Marketing Department. For those without a push-button telephone, wait on the line and someone will assist you.

DIALOG's Marketing Department will be happy to send out all the necessary paperwork. If you prefer, write: DIALOG Information Services, Marketing Department, 3460 Hillview Avenue, Palo Alto, CA 94304.

You may also contact DIALOG by facsimile machine (fax). The fax number is 415-858-7069.

Telecommunications Software Requirements

You can use any standard telecommunications software to access DIALOG. DIALOG also offers its own personal computer communications software called DIALOGLINK for IBM or IBM-compatible microcomputers. DIA-LOGLINK has two different programs. You can buy just the "Communications Manager," which offers one-step logon to all DIALOG services, or you can add on the "Account Manager," which helps track DIALOG on-line costs for subaccounting and charge-backs to clients. DIALOGLINK also lets you capture images, something you can't do with most other telecommunications packages. For Macintosh users, DIALOG has ImageCatcher to download images.

DIALOG's Customer Training

Once you've signed up and received your password, you will be introduced to DIALOG's excellent customer service. With the great number of databases to choose from, new users can quickly become overwhelmed. Customer service is very helpful to the new user.

DIALOG also offers training classes held in most major cities in the United States and abroad. The basic training, called the System Seminar, covers how to search DIALOG.

Special ONTAP (ON-line Training and Practice) files are available at 25 cents per minute for customers to practice their search techniques. Passwords for complimentary access to the ONTAP files are given to all attendees at the system seminar. Your regular password allows you to access all ONTAP files at the 25-cent rate.

Other classes are also offered in both full- and half-day sessions. Some training concentrates on special features; others focus on subject areas such as patents, legal information, and competitive intelligence. You may also buy an instructional videotape from DIALOG (Introduction to DIALOG) or their self-paced manual (Searching DIALOG: The Tutorial Guide). There are also DIALOG Field Guides, self-instructional manuals which are analogous to DIALOG's advanced subject seminars. DIALOG also has a complete user manual, *Searching DIALOG: The Complete Guide*. The cost is only $80. DIALOG documentation is extensive.

In addition to these manuals, there are overviews for each DIALOG database called "Bluesheets." Bluesheets range from one sheet of paper to manuals of more than twenty pages. They are free with your password. Bluesheets give the basic information to search the database.

For an in-depth look at the individual databases there are the Database Chapters. These can be dozens of pages long, and explain every intricacy anyone could possibly want to know. The Database Chapters may be ordered individually, or a standing order may be placed if you need them all. The Database Chapters cost $6 per chapter. For frequently searched databases, it's a worthwhile investment.

DIALOG sends subscribers a monthly newsletter called *Chronolog*. It updates DIALOG documentation, informs customers of new features and new databases, and provides helpful search tips and techniques. It also includes a calendar of upcoming training sessions and a list of new Bluesheets available.

The Bluesheets and the *Chronolog* newsletter are also available on line in separate databases. The on-line versions are often more current than their printed equivalents. Most DIALOG databases are accessed via a file number. The number for the Bluesheets is 415. The number for *Chronolog* is 410.

Choosing a Database

DIALOG is not really a database producer. Its role is to make others' databases available to you. DIALOG provides powerful search software and interfaces that allow users to select the information they need. DIALOG does have a few databases that are aids to use the system. Two examples were just given: Bluesheets—415, and *Chronolog*—410.

DIALOG also offers an aid to find which database to search. This is DIALINDEX, file 411. Just as you dial 411 to ask a telephone operator for someone's phone number, you search file 411 to find the DIALOG database most likely to have the information you need.

Choose one of the predefined DIALINDEX categories. These include topics such as market research, computer science, daily news, biotechnology, and public affairs. Databases that contain related information are selected for you. DIALINDEX will tell you how many items you may retrieve from a number of different databases. Keep in mind that you are not actually searching the individual databases when you're in DIALINDEX. You will still need to access the files to get to the actual information.

DIALOG OneSearch allows you to search up to 20 different databases simultaneously. These databases may be of your own choosing or from a DIALINDEX category. One particularly helpful category is FIRST. FIRST contains the DIALOG FirstRelease newswire databases that are updated continuously throughout the day. OneSearch saves time and money because of its global search approach.

What Do You Do with a Knowledgebank?

Most corporate users of DIALOG have business, professional, and technical questions that need answers. Typically, business executives use DIALOG to

- Investigate the current competitive situation
- Get market research information on demographic changes
- Compile lists of potential customers and generate telemarketing lists and mailing labels
- Find ways to streamline the business and make it more efficient
- Discover economic statistics to aid business decisions
- Locate financial information to support merger, acquisition, and divestiture activities
- Compare one supplier with another
- Research the track record of a company

DIALOG Search

Since its very inception a distinguishing characteristic of DIALOG has been the powerful command-driven search language. DIALOG has always allowed its customers to use full Boolean operators in search statements. This means you may use AND, OR, and NOT in your search. Early on, DIALOG made use of adjacency commands, letting you search one term within a given number of words of another term. DIALOG also has a command it calls Super Select (SS), which gives searchers the freedom to mix and match commands. Newer DIALOG products use menu-driven systems. But DIALOG offers the choice of either menus or commands.

DIALOG's powerful search software allows your search to be as narrow or as broad as you like. You are in command. Just decide what you want your search to retrieve. Keep in mind, however, that search strategies may not be universally successful. What works for one search may not work on another search. The following are some things to consider when formulating your search:

- Is this a full text database? If so, you'll need to use the adjacency commands, rather than simply using AND to string together the concepts.

- Is this a directory database? Use DIALOG's additional index terms to search the proper field.

- How current is this database? If it's several months old, yesterday's news won't be in it.

- Does the database have more than one type of record? Some databases combine text and numeric records. Others have both directory and review records. You must designate which type of record you want.

- How far back in time does the file go? To locate something that occurred in 1980, don't search a 1985 database.

- Does the database originate in the UK? If so, use British spellings, for example, colour instead of color.

If your search doesn't work and you don't know why, call DIALOG's Customer Service toll-free number. They'll be happy to help you figure it out.

DIALOG Business Connection

To learn DIALOG commands is no more difficult that any software program. But it does take experience to become proficient with the ins and outs of a DIALOG search. In fact, many people turn DIALOG expertise into a career. I've seen amateurs do well on the system, but in the hands of an expert it's amazing what can be retrieved.

Not everyone has the time, or desire, to become proficient at DIALOG. Business executives, for example, want solutions to their problems. For these people DIALOG created a simplified search mechanism called DIALOG Business Connection.

Many business questions are repetitive. That is, some business applications need the same type of repetitive search. DIALOG Business Connection takes advantage of this. It's the sole applications-oriented approach to a comprehensive group of authoritative business databases. Included in DIALOG Business Connection are the heavy hitters of business databases, which include: McGraw-Hill, Dun & Bradstreet, Moody's, and Standard & Poor's.

DIALOG Business Connection requires no special training and no knowledge of DIALOG's command-driven search software. There's no need to know what database has what you need. You simply pick an application off the menu.

If you have a DIALOG password, you may access DIALOG Business Connection by typing **BEGIN DBC** at the prompt and pressing ENTER.

You may also subscribe to DIALOG Business Connection as a stand-alone product. There is a $145 start-up fee, which includes a private password to DBC, $100 of free on-line orientation in the first month, DIALOGLINK communications software, and a comprehensive user's guide. There are no monthly minimums or annual subscription fees. You pay only for actual usage.

If you will be using DIALOG for nonbusiness searches, you would be better served with a full DIALOG subscription. For many users DBC is their main use of the system. If you find that the DIALOG Business Connection is what you use most, ask DIALOG to change your default file to DBC. This will put you directly into DBC when you log on.

There are six major categories of applications on DBC: Corporate Intelligence, Financial Screening, Products and Markets, Sales Prospects, Travel Planning, and News.

DIALOG Medical Connection

DIALOG created a simplified search approach tailored especially for physicians, biomedical researchers, and other health professionals. It is designed to provide fast and easy access to comprehensive medical information. There are 28 selected databases divided into four libraries: medical, bioscience, science/technology, and general reference.

The medical library focus is on clinical medicine and medical research. The bioscience library is a collection of databases that concentrate on life sciences (biology, biochemistry, microbiology, agriculture and food science). The science/technology library is a complete overview of scientific and technical literature from the areas of engineering, geophysics, and organic chemistry. The general reference is current information on technology, news, business, and computers. It also contains full text, as well as an index to thousands of newspapers and magazines.

Like DBC, DIALOG Medical Connection is available to all DIALOG subscribers. Enter **BEGIN DMC** and press ENTER at the prompt to gain access. Or, you may subscribe to DMC as a separate service. DIALOG Business Connection is menu driven. With DMC there is a choice of menus or commands.

You don't need to be a medical specialist to be interested in a search of DMC. Much of the information is general, and frequently needed by those other than medical professionals. A legal firm may use medical literature to research issues that pertain to a malpractice suit or to locate medical expert witnesses. A bank may need to assess the financial future of a medical product manufactured by one of its borrowers. A parent may simply want more information when the pediatrician talks about a child's tendency toward ear infections.

KNOWLEDGE INDEX

DIALOG introduced its KNOWLEDGE INDEX service in 1981. This was created to meet the needs of individual personal computer users for information on topics such as medicine, engineering, and education. KNOWLEDGE INDEX offers more than 75 databases that contain 40 million items from thousands of publications. Available nights and weekends, KNOWLEDGE INDEX costs 40 cents per minute. A typical search can be done for under $5. KNOWLEDGE INDEX customers pay a one-time start-up fee of $35, payable by credit card. Users receive a complete self-instructional manual and two hours of free time to be used during the first month. There are no monthly minimum charges.

The most recent innovation with KNOWLEDGE INDEX has been the addition of menus. You may choose a command search, which is a simplified version of DIALOG search software, or menus may be used. With KNOWLEDGE INDEX you may not access all 325+ DIALOG databases. There is, however, a very good selection of files.

With its low price and convenient search facilities, KNOWLEDGE INDEX is a winner. As Peter A. McWilliams, syndicated columnist and publisher of the *McWilliams Letter,* says, "If I had only one reason to buy a modem, it would be for KNOWLEDGE INDEX."

The wealth of information available from DIALOG is incredible. Much was written in the 1960s about the "information explosion." This explosion continued in the 1980s and will not slow down in the 1990s. What DIALOG has done is to rescue data users from information inundation, while allowing them to systematically collect, synthesize, and analyze useful information. What follows is one of its primary competitors.

BRS/AFTER DARK

BRS (Bibliographic Retrieval Services) is a pioneer of the database industry. BRS/After Dark is a subset of the full BRS/Search system, an information database system. It offers an array of resources for professionals.

BRS/After Dark is a low-cost database service that operates during evening and weekend hours. The system is open during restricted, non-prime-time hours and there are a limited number of databases. The cost for use is less than for the full BRS network. For the purposes of this book we'll only discuss the After Dark mode of BRS. Professional information hounds can get hold of the company to obtain information about the full service.

There are nearly 100 databases on the system. Databases range from business to science and medicine to general reference.

Getting Started

First you have to contact Maxwell On-line, Inc., 8000 West Park Drive, McClean, VA 22102 or call them on their sign-up line at 1-800-468-0908. The customer support numbers are 1-800-345-4277 (8:00A.M. to 1:00A.M. Monday through Friday; 8:00A.M. to 5:00P.M. Saturday and Sunday).

The service currently has about 5000 subscribers. You pay a $75 one-time subscription fee, which covers manual, password, and associated materials. There is a $12 per month minimum usage fee. Access charges are based on a varying fee structure based on connect time and display charges. Both vary widely, depending on which of the 100 or so databases you search in. The system is available only between the hours of 6:00P.M. and 6:00A.M. (your time zone) Monday through Thursday, and 6:00P.M. Friday until 6:00A.M. Monday. There is no surcharge for access at 1200 or 2400 baud. There are no specific BRS/After Dark software aids as of this writing, although the company does provide a manual and quick reference card when you sign up. Seminars are available from the company, too.

Database Access and Display Charges

Database charges vary. The per-hour access charge can range from a nominal $8 (for "ERIC" and several practice search files) to $81 (for the "CA Search" file). The display charges may be as little as 3 cents per citation viewed, to as much as $11.20 for data in the "Disclosure/Spectrum Ownership Data." The charge for each database is available when you select to enter the area. *Be aware* of price differences between the databases.

Logging On to BRS/After Dark

Once you've signed up for the service, BRS will forward your account number and password along with the After Dark manual and quick-reference card.

BRS/After Dark is accessible through both Telenet and TYMNET packet-switching networks. If your area isn't served by one of these networks, there will not be an 800-number telephone access to BRS/After Dark. (Connect rates include Sprintnet and TYMNET charges.)

TYMNET Log-On Procedure

Set your modem and software parameters to 7 data bits, even or odd parity, 1 stop bit, and full duplex. Call the local TYMNET number with your modem. At the message

```
please type your terminal identifier
```

type the letter **A** (upper- or lowercase). You will now see

```
please log in:
```

Type **BRS** (upper- or lowercase) and press ENTER. You will now see

```
host: call connected
ENTER BRS PASSWORD
MMMMMMMM:
```

Type in your assigned account number. (You will not see what you type in.) Next, you will see

```
ENTER SECURITY PASSWORD
: MMMMMMMM
```

Type in your password. (Again, it will not show on your screen.) If you make an error, you will be asked to reenter the codes.

Sprintnet Log-On Procedure

Set your modem and software parameters to 7 data bits, even or odd parity, 1 stop bit, and full duplex. Direct the modem to call the local Sprintnet number. When connected, hit the ENTER key twice. You will see

```
SPRINTNET
```

followed by your local node's identification code, and the message

```
TERMINAL =
```

Enter **D1** and hit ENTER. Next, Sprintnet will send you a caret (^) symbol. Enter BRS's destination code (which is C 31520b), followed by ENTER. (Notice the space between the *C* and the numbers.) You will be prompted for your account number and password, as in the TYMNET procedure.

Tips for Navigating BRS/After Dark System

Many of these tips, which were provided by the company, apply to all expensive database services.

Study the Manual   After Dark is more expensive than the usual general communications system like CompuServe or GEnie. It is essential to study the manual.

Read the Information on Charges Carefully   Some of the databases carry surcharges in excess of the standard connect fees. BRS indicates these on-line charges with an appropriate message. Look for them.

Read About How Boolean Operators Are Handled   These are the terms AND, OR, and NOT. Before your first on-line session, understand what these mean and how they are used to expand and limit your search results.

Know How to Use Your "log to disk" Function   By using the "log to disk" function of the communications software you will have the ability to capture everything that passes across your screen. Don't waste time and money by not remembering to save your costly data as it comes flying across from BRS.

Plan Your Visit   The key to using electronic information services – any pay-as-you-go system, really – is moderation. If there is an easy alternative to electronic information, try to find what you want there first. Weigh the cost of a trip to the library versus connecting to After Dark and collecting your information from there. Think about what you want to find and where you might find it. Read the database descriptions in the After Dark manual carefully. Know exactly where you want to go, what commands are needed to get there, and how you can get the system to display your results.

Stay Flexible   Be prepared to change directions and strategies. Be prepared to deal with too much or too little information and know the maneuvers needed to solve the problem.

Use Macros, or a Pencil   Write down your search phrase and keep it handy. If you understand the macro function of your software, set up some macros for the search phrases you want to use. No one can type at 1200 baud. By setting up long phrases, you can save time (and time is money). Set up a macro for the logoff sequence, the proper display command for citations you want to view, and other repetitive commands. Until you are an expert at the system, avoid long scripts to search for you. They would speed things along, but until you are proficient they are more likely to lead to trouble early on.

Keep a List of Commands   Keep a list of the commands to disconnect from the system and to stop the system in its tracks – the "break" command. With Procomm, it is the ALT-B key. (Nothing is as frustrating, or expensive, as watching the system display results that are not what you wanted, and being unable to stop the display process.) Customer Service recommends sending a break command. If that is not effective, hang up and call customer service immediately. They will disconnect you and stop the charges.

Practice   After Dark offers a practice library containing cut-down versions of some of their most popular databases (including ABI/Inform, a business database). These practice databases function just as their full-fledged parents do but are limited in content. The charge for mastering on-line searching in these areas is only $8 per hour. There are no additional charges for displaying the documents found. Since they are smaller, searches are faster. You can spend an hour in one of these databases and get some useful, hands-on experience in manipulating on-line databases. Electronic databases can be overwhelming in the extent of their contents. It takes study and practice to master them.

BRS/After Dark is a superb system. It offers a rare combination of a menu-driven system to get you where you want to go, with a full-featured command system once you arrive there. The system is well supported and documented. It is also reasonably priced. In fact, BRS/After Dark offers some of the cheapest access rates available.

DOW JONES NEWS/RETRIEVAL

Now let's explore one of the most popular and easiest to access high-end systems in the country. Dow Jones News/Retrieval (DJN/R) has nearly 50 different databases and services. It offers everything from the full text of *The Wall Street Journal* (back to 1984) to the latest 10K reports from every publicly held company. (These are the same reports that the company must file with the Securities and Exchange Commission.) DJN/R also has rating reports from Dun & Bradstreet, Standard & Poor's, *Business Week*, insider trading filings, a discount stock broker for round-the-clock on-line trading, a gateway to the MCI Mail electronic mail system, and Dow Jones News for up-to-the-second news and information—all of this is available through DJN/R.

Dow Jones has high-quality information, carefully focused to meet the needs of business people and investors. DJN/R boasts a subscribership of 300,000.

Dow Jones has three membership plans: standard, Corporate, and Blue Chip. The standard membership kit is available from Dow Jones or from your local computer retailer at a cost of $29.95 for individuals and $49.95 for companies. Individual membership kits include five free introductory usage hours on the system. Standard members are charged an annual $18 service fee.

The Corporate version includes multiple passwords and eight free hours. Both the standard and the Corporate packages include the *Dow Jones News/Retrieval User's Guide*, the main system manual. Corporate membership subscribers receive a one-third discount on both prime- and non-prime-time usage, but the fee is $75 per month for each location on a one-year contract.

Blue Chip memberships sell for $95 per year and entitle you to a one-third discount on usage during non-prime-time hours.

For subscription information contact Dow Jones News/Retrieval Service, P.O. Box 300, Princeton, NJ 08543, or phone 1-609-452-1511. For customer service call 1-609-452-1511 between the hours of 8:00A.M. to midnight EST Monday through Friday, or 9:00A.M. to 6:00P.M. Saturday. DJN/R hours of operation: 24 hours a day, 365 days a year. Prime time begins at 6:00A.M. EST. Non-prime time begins at 6:01P.M. your local time. Weekends and holidays are non-prime as well. Access is through Sprintnet and TYMNET. You may also use ConnNet, for access from any city in Connecticut.

The connect-time rate you pay on Dow Jones News/Retrieval varies. In addition to the type of membership you have, rates also depend on the time of day, the speed of communication, and the specific database or service you want to use. You'll find a complete rate table in the //FYI feature that will be described shortly. But as an example, Dow Jones News (//DJNEWS) standard membership prices range from 20 cents a minute (non-prime time at 300 baud) to $2.80 per minute (prime time, 2400 baud). Some databases involve specific additional charges as well, such as $5 per screening in //TRADELINE, plus 25 cents per issue listed. Some involve "document charges," such as $6 per company search in Disclosure or Standard & Poor's. And some databases levy an "information unit" charge for each 1000 characters transmitted. InvesText, for example, charges you $1.25 for each information unit transmitted.

Customer Support

Dow Jones also operates an active customer support and training program with frequent seminar dates in major cities around the country. Morning sessions typically focus on the system's major news and business offerings. Afternoon sessions concentrate on //TEXT. The cost at this writing is $45 for the first representative from a company or organization and $25 for each additional person. All attendees receive a free full day on line. Customized on-site sessions are also available. Call Customer Service for schedules and details.

How to Make the Most of Dow Jones

Dow Jones News/Retrieval can be a powerful tool. Here are a few masters' tips to get you off to a good start.

The //FYI Feature Should Be Your First Stop   This is a free facility to download information such as pricing, tutorials, and seminar schedules. Print out this information and keep it with your system manual.

Plan Which Features You'd Like to Access   Every on-line system is different.

The Stock Symbol is Crucial   If you want to investigate a company, the command //SYMBOL can locate any stock symbol.

Menus and Commands

As you may have noticed, many of the commands in DJN/R are preceded by a double forward slash (//), which is located on the question mark key of many keyboard configurations.

The DJN/R system uses either menus or commands. If you'd rather have a menu-driven system, type //**MENU** at the sign-on. The other option is to use commands. Do this by entering the name of the feature you'd like to access at the sign-on.

The command to instantly end your DJN/R session is: DISC (with no slashes); it's short for Discontinue Service. DJN/R does not use BYE or OFF as do many other systems. Should you need help with any feature while on the system, key in the feature's name followed by HELP (//**SYMBOL HELP**, for example).

Keying in //**DJNEWS** at the Enter Query prompt (and at most other system prompts) takes you directly to the Dow Jones News feature. Keying in //**SYMBOL** will take you to the system's security symbol look-up feature, and so on. Additional help for many features can also be found in the //FYI section.

What's Available on DJN/R?

Let's start with the master menu. Type in //**MENU**, and then hit the ENTER key. The following Master Menu appears on the screen:

```
PRESS   FOR
  A     News
  B     The Reference Library
  C     Custom Profiles and Reports
  D     Company, Industry Statistics & Forecasts
  E     Quotes & Market Averages
  F     Business Services
  G     General Services
  H     On-line Reference Tools
```

Let's start at the top and key in **A** for "News." The following menu then appears:

```
                    News
     FOR                                 ENTER
Up-to-the-minute Dow Jones News
on Companies and Industries              //DJNEWS
Up-to-the-minute
international Dow Jones News              //DJINS
Top Business, Financial, Economic News   //BUSINESS
Credit Markets, Financial Futures News   //CMR
News, Trading Alerts, and Statistics
From The Professional Investor Report    //PIR
Japanese Business News                   //KYODO
National and World News                  //NEWS
Press Release  Wires                     //RELEASE
Sports                                   //SPORTS
Weather                                  //WTHR
Help For Individual Data Bases           //CODE HELP
```

//DJNEWS //DJNEWS, the first item on the News menu, contains articles and special features from *The Wall Street Journal* and *Barron's,* two Dow Jones publications. But the backbone of the database is the Dow Jones News Service, also known as the Broadtape or the Ticker.

Dow Jones News stories are filed by Dow Jones reporters and bureaus around the country. Stories appear on line within 90 seconds of being filed by a reporter, and they are kept in the database for 90 days. (After that, they are moved to a different database for permanent storage.) Dow Jones News is therefore the place to turn for fast-breaking, current stories on companies, industries, government agencies, international financial markets, the stock market, and news of general interest.

Your manual will explain the ins and outs of searching this feature, but briefly, if you want a list of the latest headlines about a company, key in a period, the stock symbol, a space, and 01, like this: **.IBM 01**. This produces a menu of current stories, any one of which you can then read in its entirety by choosing it from the menu.

Similarly, you can get a list of stories concerning topics of interest by keying in a period followed by a Dow Jones News Category Code. For example, keying in **.I/AUT** would focus on stories about the automobile industry; **.I/TEL** would focus on the telephone industry, and so on. All DJNEWS codes are given in your manual. If you like, you can go directly to the most recent story by keying in a period and a stock symbol or a news category code.

//DJINS   //DJINS is the Dow Jones International News Service, a feature that is quite similar to Dow Jones News. Different category codes are used for news stories, however (see your manual for a list), and stories come from Dow Jones reporters stationed in 16 bureaus around the world, plus the European and Asian editions of *The Wall Street Journal.*

//BUSINESS   //BUSINESS is the Business and Finance Report, a news database for people who need a quick update of what's happening in the world of business at any given moment. Stories here come from the Broadtape and Dow Jones Capital Markets Reports newswires, plus the *Journal*, and the *Associated Press*. //BUSINESS is not searchable. It is intended instead to give you a continually updated "front page" of business news and the latest financial statistics.

When you key in **//BUSINESS**, the first thing you see will be a list of headlines for the five top stories of the moment. At your option, you may choose to read one or more stories, type **N** for list of additional stories, or type **F** to go to a menu of up-to-the-minute financial statistics. Financial statistics covered include the Dow Jones Industrial Average, volume, and most active issues, foreign exchange news, precious metals markets, and more.

//CMR   //CMR stands for the Dow Jones Capital Markets Report (CMR) newswire. This feature offers comprehensive coverage of the fixed-income and financial futures markets, including news, statistics, forecasts, and expert commentary on Federal Reserve Board actions, U.S. government securities, money markets, financial futures and options, and corporate, municipal, and mortgage-backed securities.

//PIR   The Professional Investor Report, or //PIR, monitors every common stock traded on the New York and American stock exchanges, as well as the National Market System portion of the over-the-counter market. Should the price or the volume of an issue break out of that stock's normal trading range, the system generates an alert. Dow Jones reporters immediately begin investigating the reasons behind such behavior and quickly transmit their findings as a story that appears on line in //PIR. You can search by stock symbol, industry group code, or //PIR News Code.

//KYODO   The Japan Economic Daily, made available through Kyodo News International (//KYODO), contains domestic and international news items and feature stories relating to Japan and Pacific Basin countries, including Korea, Taiwan, and China. Financial news and tables on the Tokyo stock, bond, commodity, and currency markets are included, as are Japanese and world political and economic news and lifestyle features. The //KYODO feature on Dow Jones concentrates on financial developments. The full text of every story carried by the Japan Economic Newswire may be found in the Business Library of the //TEXTM feature, which will be discussed later.

//NEWS   //NEWS is to national and foreign news what //BUSINESS is to business news—that is, //NEWS instantly gives you a constantly updated "front page" of late-breaking stories. The difference is that the emphasis here is not so much on business topics as it is on politics, economics, and other major events covered by the Associated Press and Dow Jones news-wires, and the broadcast media.

//RELEASE   As you can see from the left side of the menu, //RELEASE gives you access to press release wires. The feature is, in fact, the Business Wire supplied by the PR Newswire. Here you will have instant access to press releases from over 9000 companies, educational institutions, and other organizations. And when we say "instant," we mean you get the information 15 minutes after the news media does. You can search //RELEASE on the basis of company stock symbol, industry code, market sector, product, news subject, geographic area, or the name of a U.S. government body. New releases are added continually between 7:00A.M. and 7:00P.M. each business day.

//SPORTS   Professional, college, and amateur events of every sort are covered here, including regular reports on the NBA, NHL, and NFL, major league baseball, golf, tennis—you name it.

//**WTHR**   The //WTHR database is supplied by Accu-Weather, Inc., the nation's largest private weather forecasting company. Eight U.S. regions, 15 major U.S. major metropolitan areas, and three-day forecasts for 100 domestic and 65 foreign cities are included, plus ski reports, in season.

DowQuest: A Revolution in On-Line Reference

Now look back at the Master Menu and notice that the next selection is B, The Reference Library. When you select it, the following submenu appears:

```
                    The Reference Library

FOR                             ENTER
A news archive                  //TEXT
A menu-driven archive           //TEXTM
Natural-language searching      //DOWQUEST
Help For Individual Data Bases  //CODE HELP
```

The Reference Library includes *The Wall Street Journal*, selected Dow Jones News, *Barron's*, *The Washington Post*, *Business Week*, *PR Newswire*, *Business Wire*, and local, regional, and national publications.

The Reference Library is among the most powerful of Dow Jones offerings, and we would not recommend starting here. Wait until you've had a little experience. Then make an appointment with yourself to really get to know //DOWQUEST and the text databases. You will thank your lucky stars that you did.

We should begin by saying that all of the features listed above give you access to the same databases. (There is one exception, which we'll discuss in a moment.) These include the following full-text selections:

- *The Wall Street Journal* dating from January 1984 to 6:00 A.M. EST, each weekday morning

- *Barron's* back to January 1987

- Dow Jones News (the Broadtape) back to June 1979 (this is where //DJNEWS stories go once they are more than 90 days old)

- *The Washington Post* back to January 1984

- *Business Week* back to January 1985

- The Business Library, including *Forbes, Fortune, Financial World, Money, Inc., American Demographics,* and the Japan Economic Newswire (full text of //KYODO)

- Business Dateline, from UMI/Data Courier, with news from over 150 regional business publications in the U.S. and Canada. That means publications such as *Boulder Business Report, Focus* (Philadelphia), *Nashville Business Advantage,* and *Western Ontario Business*

- The McGraw-Hill Library, with the full text of some 25 leading industry-specific publications, including *Byte, Aviation Week, Chemical Engineering,* and *Electric Utility Week*

- Press Release Wires, *The PR Newswire,* and the *Business Wire* from July 1989 onward

In addition, through the //TEXT feature, you can traverse a gateway to the DataTimes system with its 37 regional, 6 national, and 16 trade publications (at this writing). This is the place to search papers such as the *Chicago Sun-Times,* the *Louisville Courier-Journal,* and the *St. Petersburg Times.*

Now, let's look at the major differences distinguishing the three features //TEXT, //TEXTM, and //DOWQUEST. Briefly, //TEXT is the most difficult to use. It is really designed for information professionals who have the training to make use of its powerful, precise search features. At this writing, Dow Jones publishes a separate manual for using //TEXT (available free of charge), but that material is scheduled to be incorporated in the next edition of the main system manual.

Unless you are an information professional, the only reason to key in //TEXT is to gain access to the DataTimes gateway cited earlier. Otherwise, you'll be better off with the menu-driven version of the feature, //TEXTM. //TEXTM doesn't lend itself to the rifle-shot precision of //TEXT, but it is far easier to use, and with it you can locate exactly the same information you would have found in //TEXT.

But the real gem in the Dow Jones crown is //DOWQUEST. DowQuest is so powerful and so easy to use that this is where we would recommend most people start. In fact, you may find that DowQuest does such a superb job tracking down elusive facts that you will never need to go anyplace else.

DowQuest is truly a revolution in the information retrieval field. No other on-line system has anything like it, and to my knowledge, none has announced plans to implement a similar feature.

Relevance Feedback

Behind the scenes is a $5 million parallel processing computer called a Connection Machine from Thinking Machines Corporation. (In fact, there are two Connection Machines at Dow Jones's Princeton headquarters — one for backup should the main one go down.) The raw power of this computer's 32,000 separate processors makes the so-called relevance feedback technique of on-line searching a practical reality. (Each search takes only about 74 milliseconds.)

Relevance feedback is easier to describe than to explain. Basically, after you key in //DOWQUEST you will be asked to enter your query, which you can do using completely conversational English. To wit: "What's the impact of health consciousness on fast food companies?" or "Which athletic shoe brand is the current market leader?" or "What's the demand for golf clubs and equipment in Japan?"

The system accepts your request, conducts a search of the text databases, and returns with the 16 articles it thinks will answer your question. The article list is presented as a series of headlines, and you are free to read any and all of them. When you select an article, you can either start at the beginning or use the BEST command to call up the paragraph that best satisfies your search request.

Each paragraph in each article is numbered, and here's where the real magic begins. When you find one or more paragraphs that closely approximate what you're looking for, you can key in a command such as SEARCH 9 to tell the system to use paragraph 9 for its *next* search. By entering this command, you tell DowQuest to use *every* word in the specified paragraph(s) as a key word and conduct the search on that basis.

The results of this second search will be 16 articles, as well. Some of them may have appeared on the first list, but some will undoubtedly appear here for the first time. You can repeat this relevance feedback search process as many times as you like.

Aside from being easier to use than almost any other search method, DowQuest also has the potential to turn up stories and concepts you may not have thought of initially. It may alert you to ideas you will want to pursue, while making it easy to do just that. In a word, DowQuest is the closest thing yet created to HyperText for on-line databases. It is one of the most remarkable features on Dow Jones — or any other system.

Saving Keystrokes and Money with Custom Profiles and Reports

The third selection from the Master Menu is C, Custom Profiles and Reports.

```
          Custom Profiles and Reports

FOR                                  ENTER
Complete Company Reports             //QUICK
Company, Industry Tracking Service   //TRACK
Help For Individual Data Bases       //CODE HELP
```

Though not in the same league as DowQuest, both the //QUICK and the //TRACK features on this menu grow from the same root—a desire to make Dow Jones News/Retrieval as easy as possible to use. //QUICK is the less sophisticated of the two, but it can be used instantly. Its purpose is to save you keystrokes (and connect time) by making it easy to conduct a cross-database search. You need only key in //QUICK followed by a stock symbol (for example //QUICK IBM) to cause the system to generate a complete report on your company of interest.

//QUICK   //QUICK reports include composite current quotes (15 minutes delayed), the latest business headlines and stories from //DJNEWS, company profiles from //SP (Standard & Poor's), earnings estimates from //EPS (Zacks Investment Research), price, volume, and comparative statistics from //MG (Media General), S.E.C. filings from //DSCLO (Disclosure, Inc.), insider trading summaries from //WATCH (an expanded version of the Insider Trading Monitor), and investment reports from //INVEST (Investext).

The //QUICK selections for your target company appear as a menu from which you may select individual items or the entire report (all items). You can enter the //QUICK command followed by a stock symbol from any location within the DJN/R system.

//TRACK   The best way to think of //TRACK is as a feature that lets you track complete portfolios of stocks. The first step, logically enough, is to create a portfolio (actually a list of stock symbols) of the issues you want to follow on a regular basis and give the portfolio a name (COMPUTER, UTILITIES, STEEL, and so on). You may also include Dow Jones News codes.

There is a charge of $8 per month for storing your portfolio on the system. But that fee entitles you to store up to five separate portfolios, each of which may contain up to 25 stock symbols and news codes.

If you simply key in //**TRACK**, you will be taken to a menu of options. But the quickest way to use the feature is to key in //**TRACK** followed by one of your portfolio names (//**TRACK STEEL**, for example). Dow Jones will then immediately retrieve the current composite quote (15 minutes delayed) for every stock in your portfolio, plus any news stories relating to those companies or to the DJNS codes you may have included. Additional command switches (explained in the manual) can be used to limit retrieval to just current quotes or to focus //**TRACK** on some particular time period.

Corporate and Industrial Forecasts

Selection D from the Master Menu yields Company, Industry Statistics & Forecasts, a rich mine of facts and figures that can be tapped via the following submenu:

```
          Company And Industry Statistics And Forecasts

FOR                                  ENTER
Dun & Bradstreet Reports
   On 750,000 Companies              //DB
SEC Filing Extracts                  //DSCLO
Canadian Corporate Reports           //CANADA
Earnings Forecasts                   //EPS
Technical Analysis Reports           //INNOVEST
Insider Trading Filings              //WATCH
Analysts' Reports On Companies
   and Industries                    //INVEST
Statistical Comparisons
   Of Companies & Industries         //MG
Economic, Currency, Debt
   And Stock Market Trends           //MMS
Standard & Poor's Earnings
   And Income Estimates              //SP
Help For Individual Data Bases       //CODE HELP
```

//**DB**   When you key in //**DB** you will reach a database called D&B Dun's Financial Records. This database contains non-credit-related information on some 750,000 public and private companies. Coverage includes up to three years of balance sheet and income statement data and 14 key business ratios, plus corporate profile information (history, operations, and financial summary). //DB is not cheap—there is a document charge of $73 for a financial records report and $39 for each company profile. If you opt for both reports on a given company, the total cost is $89.

//DSCLO   The next database on the list, //DSCLO, is provided by Disclosure, Inc. It includes 10K, 8Q, and other financial reports made to the Securities and Exchange Commission by some 12,000 publicly traded firms.

//CANADA   //CANADA is Corporate Canada On-line, a database of business news and financial and market information on more than 2200 public, private, and Crown Canadian companies. Most information in the database is provided by the *Globe* and *Mail*, Canada's national newspaper.

//EPS   //EPS stands for "earnings per share," and it gives you access to forecasts compiled by Zacks Corporate Earnings Estimator. The Zacks survey consults some 2800 securities analysts at 125 U.S. and 25 Canadian brokerage firms. Forecasts cover some 4800 companies, plus estimated EPS growth for 100 industries and key companies within those industries.

//INNOVEST   //INNOVEST is the Innovest Technical Analysis Reports database, and it provides technical opinions on some 4500 stocks trading on the New York, American, and OTC markets. Opinions are based on computer analysis of daily price and volume data for each stock.

//WATCH   If you want to keep track of insider trading activities—stock bought and sold by corporate management, for example—key in //WATCH to access The Corporate Ownership Watch, an expanded version of the Insider Trading Monitor. Over 80,000 corporate insiders in some 8000 U.S. companies are covered, as are five percent ownership and tender offer activities.

//INVEST   Next is //INVEST, short for InvesText, a database that features comprehensive research reports prepared by analysts at more than 30 leading brokerage, investment banking, and financial research firms. Firms such as Merrill Lynch; Bear, Sterns; Dean Witter; Kidder, Peabody, and Donaldson; and Lufkin & Jenrette are represented. These are the reports such firms normally make available only to their very best customers.

//**MG**   //MG stands for Media General Financial Services. This is the database to tap for price, volume, and fundamental data on over 5400 exchange-listed companies and composite statistics on more than 180 industries. //MG is particularly useful for comparing two companies, two industries, or a company and its industry.

//**MMS**   MMS International (formerly Money Market Services, Inc.) is the database accessed by keying in //**MMS**. This is the place to go for analysis of the debt, currency, and equity markets. Three forecasts are included: Weekly Economic Survey, Foreign Exchange Dealer Survey, and Survey of GNP Forecasts. Data is compiled from interviews wth economists, traders, and dealers from more than 50 financial institutions for each survey. There are also Debt Market Analysis, Currency Market Analysis, and Equity Market Analysis features.

//**SP**   Finally, there is //SP for Standard & Poor's On-line, a database derived from the firm's S&P Marketscope database. Here you'll find descriptions and statistics on more than 4700 companies. Included in most cases are an overview of the firm, EPS forecasts, dividends forecasts, current earnings and dividend information, and income history and balance sheet information.

Securities Quotes and Market Averages

It isn't until we get to Master Menu selection E, Quotes & Market Averages that we reach the information most people assume is the sum total of what Dow Jones offers. But as you can see from the following submenu, there is much more to stock quotes than, well, stock quotes.

```
              Quotes And Market Averages

FOR                                  ENTER
Current Quotes                       //CQE
Real-Time Quotes                     //RTQ
Up to 15 years of Pricing
   on Securities and Indexes         //TRADELINE
Historical Quotes                    //HQ
Futures and Index Quotes             //FUTURES
```

```
Historical Dow Jones Averages      //DJA
On-line Brokerage                  //FIDELITY
Help for Individual Data Bases     //CODE HELP
```

//CQE and //RTQ Let's look at the first two features together. //CQE stands for Current Quotes Enhanced, and //RTQ stands for Real-Time Quotes. The difference between the two is that the "current" quotes are actually delayed a minimum of 15 minutes while the markets are open. This is in accordance with exchange requirements that apply to all on-line systems offering a quote wire. Instantaneous "real-time" quotes are available, as you can see. But gaining access to this feature requires the signing of a separate contract and the payment of special fees to the exchanges. (Current pricing information can be found in the //FYI feature.)

Other than this, //CQE and //RTQ are virtually identical. The exchanges covered are the New York, American, Pacific, Midwest, and NASDAQ-OTC traded companies. Composite quotes are also available from trading reports from the New York, American, Midwest, Pacific, Philadelphia, Boston, and Cincinnati exchanges, as well as trades reported by Instinet and the National Association of Securities Dealers. Stock prices and prices for options, corporate and foreign binds, U.S. Treasury issues, mutual funds, and more are available.

Both features are equipped with a "news alert." That's the "enhancement" noted in //CQE. If there is any breaking news on the companies for which you request stock quotes, the system will present you with a list of current headlines. At your option, you can then read the stories of interest.

//TRADELINE and //HQ Now let's consider the next two features, //TRADELINE and //HQ. //HQ is a database of historical stock and securities quotes. Here you'll find a full year's worth of daily volume and high/low, and closing stock prices for common and preferred stocks, warrants, and rights. Monthly summaries are available back to 1979, quarterly summaries back to 1978.

Before using //HQ, you must have already decided upon a specific stock to research. With //TRADELINE, however, you can "screen" for issues that meet your special criteria. //TRADELINE covers more than 120,000 issues, with daily pricing through the previous day's close dating back as far as 15 years for stocks, mutual funds, bonds, government securities, and most market indexes. (Option prices go back one year.) //TRADELINE also includes extensive technical, descriptive, and fundamental data, as well as pricing and dividend information.

The feature's screening function allows you to specify a set of criteria, which produces a set of issues. If the set is too large, you can keep adding criteria until you have reduced it to a manageable number.

//FUTURES   //FUTURES, the Dow Jones Futures Quotes database, offers current and historical quotes on more than 80 commodities and financial futures traded on major North American commodity exchanges. Quotes date back to January 1970. Current quotes are delayed 10 to 30 minutes, depending on the exchange.

//DJA   //DJA is the historical Dow Jones Averages database. This includes daily summaries of the industrial, transportation, utility, and 65 stock composite indexes. //DJA provides high, low, close, and volume trading information dating back to May 24, 1982. You can ask for the average of a particular date or all of the averages for a 12-day trading period. The 12-day trading period averages are available for one year.

//FIDELITY   The //FIDELITY feature is your connection with Fidelity Investors Express, an on-line stock brokerage service from one of the leading firms in the industry. You'll have to set up an account, of course, but once you do, you can use Dow Jones News/Retrieval to access the system and place buy and sell orders at any time of the day or night. Orders placed in the evening are executed at the opening bell of the next trading day. Fidelity Investors Express is a discount brokerage firm, meaning that in some cases investors can save up to 75 percent on commissions.

Of course with savings like that, you can't expect to receive the kind of research and hand-holding offered by a full service firm. But then, that's just the point. With Dow Jones News/Retrieval at your disposal, you can do your *own* research and make your own decisions.

Business Services

The next selection on the Master Menu is F, Business Services, and here is what its submenu looks like:

```
            Business Services

FOR                               ENTER
Airline Schedules, Fares,
  Reservations And Ticketing      //OAG
```

```
Electronic Mail And Communications    //MCI
Wall $treet Week Transcripts          //WSW
Help For Individual Data Bases        //CODE HELP
```

//OAG   //OAG is the old familiar Official Airline Guide, a database containing comprehensive information on world-wide flight schedules for more than 600 airlines.

When you find the flight you want, you can tap a few keys and make your reservation. You can reserve hotel rooms and rental cars as well, all while you are on line. I still prefer using it as an adjunct to a travel agent.

//MCI   The next item, //MCI, is your gateway to the world's leading electronic mail system (see Chapter 5 on E-mail). You'll need to set up an account on MCI Mail before using this feature from Dow Jones, but once you do you'll be able to send E-mail letters to other MCI subscribers, and telexes and TWX messages anywhere in the world. You can also arrange for MCI to print your messages and deliver them by U.S. mail or express courier. (There's even an option to have letters printed on your own customized, laser-printed letterhead.)

You can also use your DJN/R-MCI Mail connection to send messages to any fax machine anywhere in the world. And, if you use Lotus Express or Desktop Express, you can send graphics and spreadsheet files to correspondents who also have that software.

There are no Dow Jones charges associated with using MCI Mail. All costs are based on the delivery options you select and the number of characters you send.

//WSW   If you're a fan of "Wall $treet Week with Louis Rukeyser," you will be happy to know that complete transcripts of the last four programs are available via the //WSW option on the Business Services menu. The database is updated each Tuesday at 8:00P.M. (EST).

General Services

The next selection on the Master Menu is G, General Services. Here's what its submenu looks like:

```
General Services
```

```
FOR                                  ENTER
Shopping Service                     //STORE
Encyclopedia                         //ENCYC
College Selection Service            //SCHOOL
Movie Reviews                        //MOVIES
Book Reviews                         //BOOKS
Help For Individual Data Bases       //CODE HELP
```

//STORE   Man does not live by news and investment information alone, so Dow Jones has included a variety of services focused on other aspects of life. The first is //STORE, a gateway to Comp-u-Store, one of the country's leading discount shopping services. Comp-u-Store offers over 250,000 brand name products at savings of up to 50 percent. You can order from your keyboard. Equally important, you can scan the entire database for the specific products with the specific features you want. Even if you don't order from Comp-u-Store, scanning for products can be an invaluable aid in any purchase decision.

//ENCYC   The //ENCYC feature gives you access to Grolier Electronic Publishing's Academic American Encyclopedia. This is a full-blown encyclopedia offering everything on line but the pictures and charts published in the print edition. The encyclopedia is updated four times a year, in March, June, September, and December.

//SCHOOL   //SCHOOL accesses the Peterson's College Selection Service, a database that lets you scan for colleges and universities on the basis of your specified requirements. Search criteria include location, selectivity, total enrollment, costs, and areas of study, among others.

//MOVIES   //MOVIES is a feature provided by the Cineman Syndicate. It offers weekly reviews of the latest films, highlights of soon-to-be-released films, and the top ten films ranked by gross revenues. Since the database goes back to 1926, you may want to use //MOVIES as a guide for videotape rentals.

//BOOKS   //BOOKS is the Magill Book Reviews database produced by Salem Press, Inc. Here you'll find more than 300 reviews of current fiction and nonfiction titles, plus essays on more than 500 literary classics (novels, plays, short stories, and poetry). The reviews typically include an abstract of the work and about 300 words of commentary. In addition to satisfying an adult's literary tastes, the database also offers students an excellent place to start assigned school reports.

On-Line Reference Tools

Finally, Master Menu selection H leads to the On-line Reference Tools submenu:

```
              On-line Reference Tools

FOR                                 ENTER
Customer Information And Updates    //FYI
Menu Of Data Bases                  //MENU
Directory Of News/Retrieval Symbols //SYMBOL
Definitions Of Financial Terms      //DEFINE
News/Retrieval System-Wide Help     //DJHELP
Help For Individual Data Bases      //CODE HELP
```

//FYI //FYI or "For Your Information," is Dow Jones' free system news-letter and tutorial guide. There is no cost for using this feature and we strongly advise all new users to come here first. //FYI not only gives you information on new databases and enhancements, it also includes all pricing and membership information, the current schedule of Dow Jones training seminars, and extensive tutorials for selected databases.

//MENU //MENU is your command for accessing the Master Menu.

//SYMBOL //SYMBOL takes you to a database for looking up stock and security symbols. You can key in as much of a company's name as you can remember and the system will generate a list of potential matches. The //SYMBOL database also covers Dow Jones News Codes and Media General Industry Group Codes. These are published in your manual, of course, but it is handy to use //SYMBOL should your manual not be available at the moment.

//DEFINE //DEFINE is a database of financial and investment terms adapted from *Words of Wall Street*, a book published by Dow Jones Irwin, Inc. Should you ever run across a Wall Street term that is unfamiliar, as might happen when using one of the reference text databases, simply key in //**DEFINE** and look it up.

//**DJHELP**   This on-line help feature gives you a quick summary of how to use the system and a brief explanation of each of its features and databases. For more detailed information, key in //**CODE HELP**, where **CODE** is any of the // features, for example //**DJNEWS HELP**.

There are other on-line information utilities of note. One of them is NewsNet, another fairly expensive gathering of news sources. Contact NewsNet, 945 Havorford Rd., Bryn Mawr, PA 19010.

MEAD DATA CENTRAL

This is the last of our important information providers. Mead Data Central, Inc. is one of the oldest service companies selling computerized searches of unique databases. Headquartered in Dayton, Ohio, the company offers information services in 50 nations and has more than 50 sales and training offices in North America and abroad.

The company is a pioneer in the on-line information industry. In 1972 — three years before the personal computer was launched — Mead Data Central introduced the first custom terminal and printer for database searching. LEXIS, the first full-text database, was introduced in 1973, and NEXIS, the full-text news and business information database, was introduced in 1979.

LEXIS

The LEXIS service is the world's leading computer-assisted legal research service. It contains major archives of federal and state case law, codes, and regulations. LEXIS also has 29 specialized libraries covering virtually every field of practice, including tax, securities, banking, environmental, and insurance law.

The LEXIS service also contains libraries of English and French law, and other legal materials from Australia, New Zealand, Ireland, and Scotland. In addition, LEXIS offers Shepard's and Auto-Cite citation services. (Shepard's Citations is a service of Shepard's/McGraw-Hill Inc.; Auto-Cite is a service of VERALEX INC.)

NEXIS

Mead Data Central's other primary database is NEXIS, an information service of general and business news. More than 650 news sources are searchable in full text in the service. These include *The New York Times* (on line exclusively in the NEXIS service), *The Washington Post, Los Angeles Times, Business Week, Fortune, U.S. News & World Report, Financial Times, The Economist, Manchester Guardian Weekly, TASS, Zinhua,* and the AP, UPI, and Reuters newswires.

In addition, more than 2000 sources of abstracts, including *The Wall Street Journal,* are searchable in the service. The NEXIS service is used by a wide range of professionals in corporations, investment banks, public relations and advertising agencies, law firms, libraries, and the news departments of print and electronic media.

Other Services

The following services are also available on Mead:

- The LEXISR Financial Information service provides company and industry information from leasing brokerage firms, filings with the Securities and Exchange Commission, business news, economic forecasts, and earning projections.

- EXPATR is a computer-assisted patent research service that contains the full text of U.S. patents issued since 1975. About 75,000 new patents are added each year, usually within three days of issue.

- The LEISR Private Database Services provide litigation support files, private libraries, other proprietary databases and related support services for law firms and corporations.

- The MEDISR service contains the full text of more than 40 current medical journals and textbooks. It also contains Medline, a bibliographic database produced by the National Library of Medicine, with citations from thousands of clinical and research journals.

- NAARS, the National Automated Accounting Research System, is a library of annual reports, proxy statements, and reports of the American Institute of Certified Public Accountants.

Customers may gain access to Mead Data Central services through a variety of equipment, including personal computers and terminals manufactured by IBM, Apple, AT&T, Wang, and Digital Equipment. In addition, some mainframes and minicomputers can be used to gain access to the services. Dedicated terminals and printers can also be leased from Mead Data Central.

Mead Data Central's services are used by about 225,000 active users. An average of 75,000 searches are performed each day.

For subscription to this service contact Mead Data Central Inc., P.O. Box 933, Dayton, OH 45401 or phone 1-513-865-6800. Customer service is available 24 hours a day. For more information call 1-800-227-4908.

SMALL INFORMATION UTILITIES

Just beneath the tier of major information utilities there exists a group of smaller commercial services that do not offer all the service of a big system like CompuServe, but instead offer specialized subsets of interest to many users.

The WELL

One important system is the WELL. Started in 1985 by Whole Earth and Network Technologies (NETI), the WELL was designed as an inexpensive on-line meeting place, and it has been described as a "people's think tank."

There are over 90 WELL conferences. Some are computer specific, others are technical, and some are purely entertainment. Anyone may start a discussion topic in a conference, and topics may be linked between different conferences. The conferences are well organized because every conference has a conference host who manages and keeps continuity in the discussions.

The WELL has a minimum number of rules which are enforced in a low-key style probably stemming from the many social and cultural elements of the varied membership. Its character comes from an odd assortment of hackers, writers, artists, knowledge workers, fugitives from the counterculture, businessmen, educators, programmers, lawyers, musicians, and many more.

There is a strong San Francisco Bay Area tilt to the WELL, although that seems to be changing. There is no advertising in the WELL and no surcharges for any information. The participants work to keep the information accurate and objective.

The WELL's staff often talk on line to their users. They keep track of who's logged. In fact, members of the WELL staff know most of the 5000 users personally. WELL users and staff have frequent social gatherings, from which many friendships have developed. The WELL also welcomes visitors to its facilities to meet the staff, and take a look at the Sequent minicomputer.

Electronic Mail

The WELL has a fast and sophisticated electronic mail facility. Mail may be sent to an individual or a group. There is also a "send/reply" facility that allows real-time dialogue between users.

Access through the CompuServe Packet Net (CPN)

At this writing you can reach the WELL through CPN. This may reduce the long distance access charges. The rate is $5 per hour, which is added to your WELL bill. To reach the WELL via CPN, call 1-800-848-8990 and ask for your local CPN number. When you are connected it will prompt:

L 6-21   Host Name:

Type **WELL** then press the ENTER key. You will be connected with the WELL.

Access to UNIX

The WELL uses the UNIX BSD 4.3 operating system. WELL subscribers have the ability to use UNIX utilities and programs. There are several ways to customize your account. It's also a great place to learn. The UNIX manual is on line (some specific conferences are devoted to it) and there are some real UNIX hackers logged in much of the time.

Access through UUCP and Usenet
The WELL has full access to the worldwide UNIX community through UUCP and Bitnet mail, and carries a large selection of Usenet news groups. There is a choice of user interfaces for Netnews. The WELL is one of the few places where any individual with a computer and modem can become a terminal in this huge international network that connects universities, businesses, and research institutions.

File Storage and Transfer
As a WELL user you will get up to 500K free file storage. You may create files and subdirectories, and your own directory is created when you register. The charge for storage above 500K is $20 per megabyte per month. File transfer facilities include Xmodem, Kermit, and XON/XOFF.

Direct Access, Modem Speed, and Settings
For direct access use one of the following numbers:

Sausalito: 1-415-332-6106 1200 BPS   1-415-332-7217 2400 BPS
East Bay: 1-415-848-0841 1200 BPS   1-415-848-0842 2400 BPS

The default setting on most communications programs is eight bits per character, one stop bit, and no parity. This usually works fine for the WELL. If you see garbage on the screen, switch to seven bits per character and even parity. The WELL supports a large variety of terminal emulations.

Cost
The WELL charges a monthly fee of $8. There is also an hourly charge of $3, billed to the nearest minute. The rates are among the lowest in the country for comparable facilities. Payment may be made by VISA or MasterCard, but credit card use does require a $25 advance payment.

If you live outside of the San Francisco Bay Area, you may be able to save substantial money on the phone call by reaching the WELL via CompuServe. The WELL is unique in that it is one of the few places where an individual account has full access to the worldwide Usenet and UUCP mail.

Getting Started

For more information call 1-415-332-4335 (voice). To register, simply call the WELL's modem number 1-415-332-6106. When you get connected you will see the Logon Banner. Type **NEWUSER** then press ENTER at the prompt. You create your own user ID and password when you register. After your account is established you can reach the WELL directly or through CompuServe or PC Pursuit and also through StarLink. At this writing the WELL can handle up to sixteen direct callers and up to seven callers through CompuServe. In the San Francisco Bay Area there are four direct lines from Berkeley and Oakland, plus three new direct South Bay lines through Pacific Bell's PPS packet-switching network.

Their mailing address is: The WELL (Whole Earth 'Lectonic' Link), 27 Gate Five Road, Sausalito, CA 94965.

Conferences on the WELL

The following will give you some idea of the conferences available.

General Conferences

Best of the WELL (g best)

Business and Education Conferences

Classifieds (g cla)	Legal (g legal)
Consultants (g consult)	Library (g lib)
Consumers (g cons)	Stock Market (g stock)
Design (g design)	The Future (g fut)
Desktop Publishing (g desk)	Translators (g trans)
Education (g ed)	Word Processing (g word)
Homeowners (g home)	Work (g work)

Social and Political Conference

AIDS (g aids)
Archives (g arc)
Berkeley (g berk)
Central America (g centro)
Drugs (g dru)
Gay (g gay)
Health (g heal)
Irish (g irish)
Jewish (g jew)
Liberty (g liberty)
Men on the WELL (g mow)
Mind (g mind)
Nonprofits (g non)
Parenting (g par)

Peace (g pea)
Philosophy (g phi)
Poetry (g poetry)
Politics (g pol)
Psychology (g psy)
San Francisco (g sanfran)
Sexuality (g sex)
Spirituality (g spirit)
True Confessions (g tru)
Whole Earth (g we)
Women on the WELL (g wow)
Words (g words)
Writers (g wri)

Arts, Recreation, and Entertainment Conferences

ArtCom Elec.Net (g acen)
Audio-Videophilia (g aud)
Boating (g wet)
Comics (g comics)
Cooking (g cook)
Crafts (g craft)
Eating (g eat)
Flying (g flying)
Fun (g fun)
Games (g games)
Gardening (g gard)

Jokes (g jokes)
MIDI (g midi)
Motorcycling (g ride)
Movies (g movies)
Music (g mus)
On the Air (g ota)
Pets (g pets)
Science Fiction (g sf)
Sports (g spo)
Television (g tv)
Weird (g weird)

Grateful Dead Conferences

Grateful Dead (g gd88)
Deadplan (g dp)
Feedback (g feedback)

Tapes (g tapes)
Tickets (g tix)
Tours (g tours)

Computers

Amiga (g amiga)	Laptop (g lap)
Apple (g app)	Macintosh (g mac)
Art & Graphics (g gra)	Mactech (g mactech)
Atari (g ata)	Microtimes (g microx)
Computer Books (g cbook)	Programmers (g pro)
Desktop Publishing (g desk)	Programmers' Net (g net)
Forth (g forth)	UNIX (g unix)
HyperCard (g hype)	Word Processing (g word)
IBM PC (g ibm)	

Technical and Communications Conferences

Info (g boing)	Science (g science)
Media (g media)	Technical Writers (g tec)
Netweaver (g netweaver)	Telecommunications (g tele)
Packet Radio (g packet)	Usenet (g usenet)
Photography (g pho)	Video (g vid)

Conferences on The WELL Itself

Deeper (g deeper)	Help (g help)
Entry (g ent)	Hosts (g hosts)
General (g gen)	System News (g news)

Exec-PC

Another interesting system started out as an overgrown BBS dedicated to downloading. While the owner of the system still thinks of it as a BBS, I think of it as a small commercial system posing as a BBS. Be sure to read the chapters on BBSs and their operations for more details.

If you believe that one can never spend too much time on the phone or have too much software, The Exec-PC Network BBS is for you. Exec-PC went on line in 1983. It began in the basement of Bob Mahoney's home in Shorewood, Wisconsin. He decided that there was a need for his service after spending too many long nights alone on the phone with his computer modem downloading software from electronic bulletin boards. In an attempt to get some time to socialize he decided to turn his PC into a BBS. As it often does, one thing led to another, and before he knew it he had the largest computer bulletin board in the world with the biggest MS-DOS software library ever assembled for modem callers.

Bob Mahoney is Exec-PC's owner and chief librarian. His wife, Tracey, handles the bookkeeping and administrative chores. They have no other employees. Although they've recently moved the service from their basement, maintaining the system is still a full-time job for both Mahoneys. It's strictly a "Mom and Pop" enterprise.

Over the years, Exec-PC has grown into a national archive for downloadable software. Its well-stocked library offers over seventy thousand public domain and shareware software titles. From spreadsheets to fortune-telling programs, from desktop publishing utilities to program editors, practically every downloadable software title may be found there. Many shareware and public domain software authors use Exec-PC as a central distribution outlet for their wares; new versions of popular programs often appear here before they can be found on other on-line services.

Old titles are rarely deleted from the collection. It's a regular history lesson of the personal computer industry to search through the text files. There are files from bygone days that divulge rumors of a mysterious machine under development at IBM, code named "Peanut" (it was eventually released as the ill-fated PCjr). Then there's the old gossip about the then-pending releases of the IBM PC-XT and AT.

Exec-PC also offers the entire PC-SIG California software collection.

The History of Exec-PC

Since Exec-PC first went on line in 1983, its main slant has been towards the business PC user. In the early days of the BBS, most systems were geared for techies or home computer users. Bob Mahoney, a manager of information systems at an appraisal company, thought it curious that no BBS existed solely for the distribution of business software. He began his system with an IBM PC, a 30MB hard disk (30 megabytes was an enviably large hard disk at the time) and a 1200 bps modem. He began with a wide collection of downloadable software that he'd amassed from other bulletin boards. The BBS was called The Business Knowledge Exchange.

Within six months, the BBS's single phone line was chronically busy. Mahoney set about to find a way to rig the BBS to handle several modem callers simultaneously (multiuser bulletin boards were rare). After many months he discovered TurboDOS. He outfitted Exec-PC with TurboDOS and new bulletin board software. He added two new modems and accompanying phone lines. The board could now handle an impressive three modem callers simultaneously. Mahoney thought his problems were finally licked.

Within two weeks, however, all three phone lines were constantly busy. Mahoney quickly added three more phone lines and modems. Again they were busy. Word spread fast that there was an extraordinary free software collection for downloading.

Mahoney decided that he had to renovate the system. To finance this he decided to charge a subscription fee. The callers didn't seem to mind much. The lines were still constantly busy.

He decided to make the bulletin board his career. Within three years, Bob and Tracey Mahoney had nurtured Exec-PC into a service that boasted 52 incoming phone lines and a gigabyte of hard disk storage. Bob Mahoney says, "Every time the telephone linemen would come out to the house to install more lines, they'd laugh. It wasn't your ordinary residential installation."

The original single-computer Exec-PC had been replaced by four tightly packed power chassis holding 52 networked Z-80 boards—the equivalent of 52 PCs. Their corresponding 52 modems were stacked above on industrial steel wire-mesh shelving designed to promote air flow and prevent overheating. The whole concoction was powered by an ingenious contrivance of golf cart batteries and a power inverter. Should the Mahoneys' neighborhood suffer a blackout, the continually recharged golf cart batteries could provide Exec-PC with up to 24 hours of uninterrupted power. An Ethernet computer network link connected the bulletin board to the personal computers on Bob and Tracey's desks in another part of the basement.

Unfortunately, with each new phone line the Mahoneys added to their service, the communications software weakened. It was designed to handle a dozen, not 50+. There was no way to avoid it: it was time to upgrade, again.

The big problem was what to upgrade to. Bob Mahoney investigated. He eventually chose the computer operating system that is the pet favorite of mainframe programmers, UNIX—specifically, SCO XENIX 386. He teamed that with turbo-speed 80386-based personal computer boards.

The new Exec-PC made its debut in fall of 1988. It boasted seven super-fast networked 80386 PCs serving as XENIX multiuser servers, each handling 15 callers and capable of many more. The new system was not without problems. It took more than two weeks to install the system and nearly three months to get the kinks out.

The power lines strung across the back yard were humming at a low 60-cycle frequency in response to the heavy load of power flowing into the basement. The circuit breaker box in the house soon started humming as well. Before long, the Mahoneys couldn't run the vacuum cleaner or plug in the coffee maker without popping fuses.

In addition, heat problems were mounting in the basement. The big window air conditioner near the computers was running constantly, even in the zero chill of the Wisconsin winter. (The immense heat generated by the machines cut the Mahoneys' winter heating bills by 30 percent.) To keep them cool in the summer, however, would require an air conditioner of 30,000 BTUs. If the Mahoneys wanted to continue expanding the service, they would either need to install a huge new power system in the house, or move the system.

In the summer of 1989, the Mahoneys moved Exec-PC to rented office suites in a suburb outside of Milwaukee. The phone company installed 600 phone lines in a direct link to the phone company's central office. Exec-PC now has 3.5 tons of air conditioning and its own air filtration system. Snaking through one wall is a three-inch thick telephone cable. Each of the service's server PCs, each with multiple cooling fans, sits on industrial steel shelves along the walls. Above them on wire-mesh racks sit dozens of computer modems. Its processors crunch data at a brisk 75 million instructions per seconds.

Exec-PC can service 150 modem callers simultaneously, to be increased to 300 by mid-1991. Many of its phone lines offer data transfer speeds of up to 19,200 bits per second. The rest operate at speeds up to 2400 bps.

You can contact Exec-PC at the following address: Exec-PC, Inc., P.O. Box 57, Elm Grove, WI 53122, 1-414-789-4200 (voice), 1-414-789-4210 (data). Exec-PC is accessible via StarLink, PC Pursuit, and always through direct dial.

The Exec-PC Menus

When you log on to Exec-PC the menu that greets you (see Figure 6-5) is as straightforward as a baseball score. Simplicity is the key to Exec-PC's user interface and one of its secrets to popularity. All menus are self-explanatory and layered in such a way that you will never get lost (see Figure 6-6).

Figure 6-5

The greeting menu of Exec-PC

```
The following ARE SCREEN SHOTS

YOU ARE ON NODE# : 36        SUBSCRIPTION LEFT: 316 days
CALLER NUMBER    : 1,967,573
YOUR LAST ACCESS : Monday, 07/31/89
YOUR TOTAL CALLS : 2062
YOUR UPLOADS     : 127        YOUR DOWNLOADS: 239
DOWNLOAD LIMIT   : 4000000 characters per week (0 used this
week)
SECURITY LEVEL   : 10
-------------------------------
Exec-PC  T O P   M E N U
<?>help ....... Help with this menu
<S>ubscribe ... Subscribe or Renew for Exec-PC full access
<B>ulletins ... Info about this BBS
<H>elp ....... Help on the most often asked questions
<R>ead mail ... Read all pending messages addressed to me
<F>ile ....... File Collections
<M>essage ..... Message system
<E>nvironment . Change my password, default protocols, etc.
<A>nsi/color .. Turn on/off color and graphics from BBS
<L>ist users .. Info on other users
<W>ho ........ Who is on the system right now?
<X>pert ....... Toggle expert mode (short or long menus)
<G>oodbye ..... Log off system (hang up)
(420 minutes left) TOP (SBHFMREALWXG, ?=HELP) ->
```

Figure 6-6

The opening menu to the Exec-PC conference area

```
C O N F E R E N C E S  Available
-----------------------------------------
    <*> ALL COMBINED       <B> Amiga                 <C> Apple
Macintosh
    <D> Atari ST           <E> Communications    * <F>
Corporate Accts
    <H> Exec-PC Comment    ?<I> MS-DOS Systems      ?<J> Non-
Computer
    <K> OS/2               <L> PC Applications      ?<M>
Private
    <N> Programming        <O> Unix & Xenix          <P> Want
Ads


Conferences marked '*' are non-public.
You have mail waiting in '?'-marked conferences.

    <?> Get some help
    <T> Show conference tree
    <Q> Quit to main menu
    <G> Goodbye, logoff


(419 minutes left) CONFERENCE (*QGT?BCDEFHIJKLMNOP, ?=HELP) -
>
```

For those more familiar with the system there is an expert mode that will abbreviate the menus. Commands may also be chained together "programmer-style." For those who need it, help is always available at the touch of the question mark (?) key at any menu. There is also a complete tutorial for the service that may be downloaded at the introductory menu through use of the help function.

Cost

Software downloading is the primary function of Exec-PC. It's designed to be both fast and easy. A menu from the Mahoney Software Collection is shown in Figure 6-7.

The Mahoney Software Collection is the largest library of programs for IBM PCs and compatibles ever assembled for modem callers

```
Exec-PC   F I L E   S Y S T E M
path>> TOP:FILE

<?>help ..... Help with this menu
<H>elp ...... Help on the most often asked questions
<C>hange .... Collection selection
<L>ist ...... Directory of files
<N>ew ....... Files since your last call
<U>pload .... Transmit file(s) from YOU to BBS
<D>ownload .. Transmit file(s) from BBS to YOU
<S>can ...... Hyperscan(tm) for text phrases in file list
<A>ccess .... Access a .ZIP or .ARC file (view dir, read,
download members)
<T>ype ...... Type out the contents of an ascii file
<W>ho ....... Who uploaded that file & what else did they
upload
<E>xtra ..... Extra detailed info about a file
<Z>recover... Resume an aborted Zmodem upload
<F>iddle .... Delete files, modify descriptions
<Q>uit ...... Quit this menu
<G>oodbye ... Log off System (hang up)


Mahoney MS-DOS Collection  CPS=1712   4000000 bytes left
(423 minutes left) FILE MENU
(H,C,L,N,U,D,S,A,T,W,E,Z,F,X,Q,G,?=HELP) ->
```

For $60 a year, a subscriber to Exec-PC receives seven hours a week in which to download all the software desired, with few restrictions. Over 200,000 software downloads are transacted on the board each month. Subscribers call from all over the globe.

"We can tell when a country has climbed the PC evolutionary scale high enough to be able to reach out across national boundaries to dip into the shareware software pool in the U.S.," says Mahoney. "Even language differences don't seem to bother foreign callers," he says.

What's Offered

Exec-PC offers seven major software collections. The Free Collection provides telecommunications utilities and text files free to nonpaying callers. Software for Apple Macintosh, Commodore Amiga, Atari ST, and UNIX/XENIX-running computers is available in file collections for each of these machines. But the service's crown jewels are the Mahoney Software Collection and the PC-SIG one, both for IBM PCs and compatibles. Over 30,000 popular shareware and public domain programs are available in the PC-SIG collection from the California software distributor of that name. Another 100,000 software titles are found in the Mahoney Collection, almost all of them uploaded by subscribers.

To encourage users to post new software on the system, Mahoney exchanges free access time for uploads. (For 10 minutes of uploading, a program user receives 40 extra minutes to download software.) Subscribers post over 1000 new software titles on Exec-PC each month.

Trojan Horse and Virus Concerns

With all the media attention many subscribers are concerned about Trojan horse and destructive virus programs. (A Trojan horse is vandal software that masquerades as something benign, such as a video game or screen picture. A virus is a program with the ability to invisibly self-replicate, often spreading itself from computer to computer. See Chapter 12, "The Software Virus and You," for more details.) Exec-PC offers several remedies:

Ask Questions   Before you download a software title ask the service who posted it and when. Ask if they are still a subscriber, and if so, ask their security level.

Know What You're Getting   Exec-PC will also tell you what's inside a compressed file before you download it. If it's a text file, Exec-PC can type it out for you on line.

Be Cautious   Wait for new software to "age" on the board before downloading it. This will allow time for other, braver souls to try it out.

In the past, whenever a Trojan horse has appeared on Exec-PC it was only a matter of days before someone discovered it and alerted the Mahoneys, who promptly removed the software, along with its uploader, from the service. Mahoney does test any software uploads that strike him as suspicious. However, because of the great volume of software deposited on the board each day, he is unable to test everything.

Search and Scan for Software

Exec-PC's search and scan features make software hunting a breeze (see Figure 6-8). Scan through software titles and descriptions for key words and phrases, like "database" or "accounting." Exec-PC can scan 20,000 file entries in under two seconds, and will list on the screen software matches within seconds after a search is begun (see Figure 6-9).

You may focus the hunt with AND/OR operands as well as date parameters, and even ask Exec-PC to give you a list of all the new software posted since the last time you logged on. For those who'd rather search the software library off line, you can download Exec-PC's complete software directory and apply to it a program called Maximum Overkill (by W. Charles Taylor). This is a sophisticated search program designed specifically for hunting through Exec-PC library lists. Maximum Overkill is shareware and is available in the Free Collection on Exec-PC. Once you've located files you wish to download, query the board for an in-depth description of the software, if one has been provided. Among the board's unique flourishes is a function that will remember a list of software titles that you wish to download, then automatically transfer them to you on cue.

Figure 6-8

Exec-PC's Hyperscan function can hunt through 20,000 software titles in two seconds

```
H Y P E R S C A N(tm)  for PHRASES

<?>help ..... Help for this menu
<S>earch .... Begin entry of search phrases now
<&>AND/OR ... Toggle ANDing/ORing of search phrases
<D>ate ...... Set a date filter (files before/after selected
date)
<Q>uit ...... Return to main file menu
<G>oodbye, <T>op menu of system

              Logic between phrases: AND
(403 minutes left) FILE SCAN (PHRASE) Command (S&DQTG,?=help)
-> S

                    Enter search phrases now.
                    Finish entry by hitting RETURN key on
blank line.
                    |------------------|
Search phrase #1  AND:LASERJET
Search phrase #2  AND:FONT
Search phrase #3  AND:


Searching  Press S or Q to stop the first pass
First Search Pass:  70 . . .
```

While the software library is the soul of Exec-PC, its message section is equally energetic. Public conferences range in topic from UNIX to OS/2, from spreadsheets to computer-aided design to purely recreational interaction.

A scene from a software hunt. After Hyperscan locates entries that match the search words entered by the subscriber, it lists them on the screen

```
Collection:  Mahoney MS-DOS Collection
Search for:  LASERJET & FONT
Filename     Size   MMDDYY Description ("+" means there is extra info)
Exec-PC
-------------------------------------------------------------
QFONT15.ZIP  123186 072689 SOFT FONT EDITOR FOR HP LASERJET FONTS
(7/22/89 REL)
DJFONT.ZIP    57321 071389 CONVERT LASERJET FONTS TO DESKJET FONTS
CHANALL.ZIP  206555 091088 CHANCELER FONT FOR HP LASERJET. MANY POINTS.
NYTR-SFP.ZIP 139101 050288 COLLECTION OF LASERJET TIMESROMAN FONTS
FONTFILT.ZIP  15107 042088 HP LASERJET FONTS.
DOWNSOFT.ZIP  70720 040888 XLNT. H/P LASERJET SOFTFONT LOAD UTILITY
POSTER.ZIP    82537 020288 MAKE LARGE-FONT "POSTERS" WITH HP LASERJET2
ROCKLAND.ZIP  76919 122287 ROCKLAND FONT FOR HP LASERJET
GARGLYX.ZIP   66803 121287 GARAMOND FONTS FOR HP LASERJET
ZEP100.ZIP    14007 120987 HP LASERJET - TSR SOFTFONT PROGRAM
CENTURY.ZIP   73778 110987 FONT FOR LASERJET/VENTURA PUBLISHER
FONTPAK2.ZIP  48211 083187 LASERJET FONTS
HELSOFT.ZIP  118972 080187 HELVETICA SOFT FONT FOR HP LASERJET
FONT10.ZIP     8912 053086 DOWNLOADABLE FONT FOR HP LASERJET+
>>END OF LIST.
Y=N=Q=S=quit/DL/UL/Remem/Access/Extra/Type/Who/Fiddle/?=help)
```

Message System

Exec-PC's message system is as painless to use as a corkboard. Full-screen menus appear when you enter a public conference. Conference trees that display where you are on the service may be activated at any time. Subscribers may read through messages by date, follow conversational threads, jump to reference numbers, and mark messages for later retrieval, as well as join and exit conferences. There are other features such as message copying, and notification of receipt of messages. The public message collect may be scanned for topics. Even past conversations—years past—may be scanned.

The message system's ease of use together with its many electronic office-oriented features make it popular among corporate clientele. Numerous businesses rent private message and file areas on the service to communicate with customers and clients. A banking investment advisory firm, for instance, deposits time-sensitive information for bond investors on the service each morning, and banks from around the country call within the hour to pick it up. Another firm uses Exec-PC to disseminate customer information to its satellite offices.

The BYTE Information Exchange

The BYTE Information Exchange (BIX) is an on-line conference and electronic offshoot of *BYTE* magazine. BIX's emphasis is on the personal and career growth of computer professionals. Since its founding in November 1985, it has become a gathering place for more than 30,000 hardware and software engineers, system designers, independent consultants, technology buffs, and computer industry celebrities. BIX offers a global community with users from six continents. All types of computers, programming languages, and disciplines are welcome. Nearly all proceedings are in English, although French and German are spoken along with C, LISP, and Pascal.

BIX users, many of whom call themselves "BIXen," have access to features such as private electronic mail with binary file capability, program listing uploads and downloads, a daily microcomputer industry newswire, an on-line chat facility, and more than 150 focus areas, called conferences.

BIX's Bulletin Board Exchange (BBX) allows members to call Monday through Friday to collect a file of news and features about computers and technology. This information may be republished on the member's own BBS or, in a corporate environment, E-mail system. The file includes a daily news service called Microbytes Daily along with excerpts from BIX conferences, news of new hardware and software products, product reviews, and articles from *BYTE*.

Another service offered by BIX is the User Group Exchange (UGX). The UGX provides private conferences for user group presidents and newsletter editors, discount subscriptions to the group's members, and access to the BBX and other materials.

Cost

BIX is a subscription-based service. An annual subscription is $156, which is charged in quarterly installments of $39. BIX is not charged by hourly usage, although *access* to BIX is charged at a rate of $2 an hour for off-peak use. Flat-rate TYMNET accounts are available from BIX at $15 a month. The BBX subscription is $196 per year, which includes all other public BIX areas and services.

BIX maintains direct-dial numbers capable of speeds up to 9600 baud in the Boston area. The Boston area numbers are without telecommunications charges.

BIX has two premium services: DASnet electronic mail and McGraw-Hill News. DASnet (based in Campbell, California) is also a subscription-based service. It allows BIX users to exchange private electronic mail with users of other electronic services. DASnet may be purchased separately or along with other BIX subscriptions. McGraw-Hill News is a general-purpose business newswire that generates 100 to 200 news items each business day.

BIX has made some recent changes. It has become FidoNet compatible, users may now get the BBX files as echo-mail, and there is now 9600bps access for US Robotics HST users.

Getting Started

Registration to BIX is done on line. Users who pay the quarterly subscription fee by American Express, MasterCard, or VISA credit cards may use BIX immediately. Payment by invoiced account is also available. Two user's manuals (one on menus, the other on command interfaces) and a disk-based tutorial will be mailed within one week. (However, if you wish to use BIX before the manuals arrive, BIX has—as a default—a menuing system for new users.)

Follow these three easy steps to sign up for BIX:

1. Set your computer's telecommunications program for full duplex using either 7-bit words, even parity, and 1 stop bit, or 8-bit words, no parity, and 1 stop bit. BIX is able to receive and send at a baud rates of 300, 1200, or 2400.

2. BIX is accessible from within the United States, some of its territories and possessions, and major Canadian cities, through local TYMNET numbers. To reach BIX via TYMNET, contact the BIX Customer Service Line 1-800-227-2983, or call TYMNET at 1-800-336-0149.

   Call your local TYMNET number. Depending on your baud rate, TYMNET will respond with "garble" or will request a terminal identifier. Enter the letter **A**.

   If, after you enter the letter **A**, your terminal is still receiving unreadable data, change the terminal parameters. The two choices for BIX are 8 bits, no parity, 1 stop bit; or 7 bits, even parity, 1 stop bit. You may need to switch from one set of parameters to the other.

   TYMNET will ask you to log in. Type **BIX**, then hit the ENTER key. You will then be connected to the BIX computer.

3. The BIX logo should now scroll onto the screen and a prompt will ask you to enter your name. Respond with the word **NEW** (for new user). If you wish to use the service immediately, BIX has a built-in default for new users so that they are directed through the necessary commands with a menu.

To reach BIX from outside the U.S., you need a packet network account with your local Postal Telephone & Telegraph (PTT) company. From your PTT, enter **310690157800**. Then follow instructions starting at Step 3. A list of PTT addresses and contacts for most countries is available by calling or writing BIX.

BIX has a direct-dial number in suburban Boston. The number is 1-617-861-9767. Type in **BIX** at the prompt. Then follow the instructions beginning with Step 3.

If you follow these instructions but still are unable to log on to BIX, or if you require further information, callers from the United States and Canada can telephone the BIX Customer Service Line at 1-800-227-2983. Help is available from 8:30A.M. to 11:00P.M. EST Monday through Friday. For those in New Hampshire or outside the continental United States call 1-603-924-7681.

The mailing address for BIX is: One Phoenix Mill Lane, Peterborough, NH 03458.

New Users

New users are defaulted into a menu mode. This is an aid to new users until the user's manuals arrive.

BIX maintains help files that are available at every system prompt (except the .More.. prompt). On-line help is also available privately through BIXmail to "helper."

CTRL-C is your abort key. Please use it only in emergencies, such as to break a long message or an inappropriate search. CTRL-C may take a second or two to take effect. This is due to delays inherent to packet-switching networks. The BREAK key supplied with your modem software should work more efficiently than CTRL-C. BIX recommends that you use the modem software's BREAK key, or disconnect sequence.

The Main Menu

BIX has three primary areas: electronic mail, conferences, and listings. After you sign on to BIX, the BIX main menu is displayed.

Select OPTION 1 and press ENTER to go into the BIX Mail Subsystem. In Mail, you can send and receive private memos, learn the status of your mail in- and out-baskets, and privately send and receive binary files, such as Excel worksheets.

OPTION 2 puts you into the BIX conference subsystem. Here you can see lists of conferences, join and resign from conferences, read and post public messages, and search the BIX Index for specific words, phrases, or topics.

Listings, OPTION 3, gives you access to the BIX program upload/ download area. BIX Listings has all the files that complement *BYTE* magazine articles, beginning with the September 1984 issue, and dozens of areas of public-domain and shareware programs. BIX has listings areas for computer languages, stackware, and for machines ranging from the Apple to the Zenith and for Sun to DEC. BIX routinely screens all files for computer viruses.

OPTION 4, CBix, the BIX Citizen Band Simulator, is where you may converse with other users in real time. (No part of your conversation is recorded.) When you first type in **CBix**, information on your terminal type and backspace character is requested. Once successfully logged into CBix, you precede commands with the slash character. To send a message, type it, press the ENTER key, and the message will be sent. Type /**quit** to leave CBix.

Convenient access to the MicroBytes Daily News service is provided by OPTION 5.

OPTION 6 is access to McGraw-Hill News for articles on general business topics.

The Subscriber Information menu, OPTION 7, allows you to see who is on line, search the BIX user list, and check billing information.

The BIX Individual Options menu, OPTION 8, allows you to tailor your BIX environment to your personal preferences. You can change the screen length and width, make up a new password, and edit your on-line resume. You may also select upload and download protocols. Changes to your BIX operating environment may be permanent or one-time-only.

The Quick Download menu, OPTION 9, saves time with a quick and easy way to download your conference and mail messages. These materials may then be viewed off line, at your convenience. BIX supports ASCII, Kermit, Xmodem, Ymodem, and Zmodem protocols.

Use OPTION 10 to abandon menus and try out the BIX command interface. The command interface uses words or phrases. Type a **?** at any prompt to get help. Turn the menus back on by typing the phrase **OPT MENU ON QUIT**.

OPTION 11 ends a BIX session.

BIX Electronic Mail Menu

When first connected to the BIX Mail subsystem, there will be a listing of any unread messages. ITEMS 3 and 4 allow you to see the status of both sent and received mail. ITEM 5, Delete Mail, is to clear the mail in- and out-baskets.

ITEM 1 is to read any incoming messages in chronological order. You may also specify a selected message by number.

Use ITEM 2 to send mail to another BIX user. BIX prompts you for the name of the person that you want to send the message to. You may specify up to a dozen names at one time. BIX asks for a subject name. You will then be in the workspace to type your message—this area is called the "scratch-pad" by this system. While in the scratchpad, limit your lines to 60-65 characters and use a return carriage at the end of each line. (Use the ENTER key.) You cannot edit the message in this mode, except for use of the BACKSPACE key on the line the cursor is on. Once the message is written, exit the write mode, and then you may edit. After editing the message, press ENTER to activate the Mail Send Action menu. Use OPTION 1 to deliver the message.

On the Mail Send Action menu, OPTIONS 2 and 3 allow you to send copies of the message to as many as 12 additional BIX users. If there are more than 12 people to whom you wish to send the message, reenter the command and specify another 12 users.

To change the subject of your message, select OPTION 4 on the Mail Send Action menu. BIX will prompt you for a new subject name and redisplay the Mail Send Action menu.

ITEMS 5 through 7 allow you to discard, review, or edit your memo. The BIX editor is not a complicated application. For lengthy or complex messages, write the document off line and then upload it to BIX.

Use ITEM 8 to attach a binary file, such as a Lotus spreadsheet, to your message. The size limit is two megabytes. Only one file can be attached at a time. Multiple files must be uploaded and mailed individually.

ITEMS 9 and 10 are an aid if you've forgotten someone's city, state, or last name.

Enter QUIT from this menu to return to the BIX main menu without mailing or discarding your message. The commands P and MM clear your scratchpad. P returns you to the Electronic Mail menu, and L returns you to the BIX main menu.

The Mail Read Action menu appears after you've read an incoming mail message. Your options here are to reread the message, reply to or delete it, forward the message to another user, or let it remain in your in-basket. If your message is part of a long, ongoing correspondence, use OPTION 6 to read a previous memo to refresh your memory.

BIX Conferences

A *conference* is a structured discussion made up of topics and messages. Like a single book in an encyclopedia, a *topic* is a single element of the conference. A topic contains messages on the theme of both the conference and the topic itself. The messages are text files readable by all members of that conference. A BIX conference message can range in size from one character to 80,000 characters.

A line of equal signs (= =) divides one message from another, indicates the start of a new message, and marks the beginning of the header that BIX applies to each message.

A line of dashes (--) is the end of the header, and tells you that the message is about to begin.

The first line of text in the header (after the equal signs) contains the following information:

- Conference/topic name

- Message number

- Author of the message

- Number of characters

- Date and time posted

The second and third lines of the header are additional status reports, and may not always be present.

Message threading is the term that describes the relationship of the original message to the comments mode to it. A series of linked messages is a *thread.*

Each BIX conference has one or more topics. Joining a conference automatically makes you a participant in all its topics. You can leave a conference any time you choose, move from topic to topic, or resign from a particular conference or topic. Every BIX conference has a moderator whose job is to answer questions and help newcomers. By selecting ITEM 2 at the BIX main menu, you enter the BIX conference subsystem, and the Conference Subsystem menu is displayed. (ITEMS 2, 3, and 4 of this menu are better left for when you are more familiar with BIX).

In the Conference Subsystem menu, use ITEM 1 to browse through a list of BIX groups and exchanges. BIX divides conferences into such groups as computers, graphics, and programming languages. Exchanges include Amiga, IBM PC, Macintosh, and Writers. When prompted, enter the number of the group or exchange to display a list of conferences in that group.

All BIX conferences belong to a group or to an exchange. Exchanges differ from groups in that they offer a range of conferences on a particular theme, such as the Amiga computer, and have a full-time editor coordinating activities.

Groups and exchanges are both categories. You can browse through a group as you would the sections of a library, to see what's available under a particular category, but you do not enroll in that category.

To Get Into a Conference   To enroll in a conference, move into the Conference Subsystem menu (as described above), use ITEM 1 to look through the list of groups and exchanges, and then enter the corresponding number of the conference that you wish to join.

When you first join a conference, BIX displays a welcome message, a list of topics in the conference, and the TOPIC? prompt. You can respond to the prompt by typing in the name of a topic, or you may enter a carriage return. In response to the latter, BIX goes to the first topic in the conference.

Once in a topic, use the ENTER key to begin. At the end of each message a prompt is displayed.

```
Return for next, m for menu, or message number:
```

As you read messages, BIX employs a pointer that marks messages that you read. This ensures that only new messages are displayed when you next join that conference. It is possible to reset this pointer, and BIX lets you read forward, backward, or only those messages posted after a specific date. At the end of a message, you may enter the command **REFERENCE** to read the message in conversational order rather than in chronological order. (This is a message thread.)

To attach your comments to someone's statement, and thereby add to the thread, use the command **COMMENT**. Enter the command **SAY** to add an original message to the conversation.

A variety of commands are available within a conference. Enter **HELP** to see the commands. Enter the letter **M** to see your menu options. A double M (**MM**) will return you to the BIX main menu.

BIX Keyword Indexer   The BIX Keyword Indexer finds a discussion you're interested in. It scans all open BIX conferences for a keyword or phrase and reports back to you if it's found. You may then view or download its findings.

When you join the Keyword Indexer, BIX displays this prompt:

```
BIX Index    Word or phrase to look for (or 'quit'):
```

Type in the word or phrase that best describes what you are looking for. Be as specific as possible in your requests: words such as "Amiga," "computer," or "IBM" are much too general. Instead, use words or phrases such as "CLI," "model 100," and "BIOS."

The FILE command tells the Indexer to put its search results into your scratchpad. You can download them from there once you leave the Indexer. The BIX Keyword Indexer will let you search and file any number of keywords.

To download the entries, first exit the Indexer by entering **QUIT** at the Indexer search prompt. This returns the Conference Subsystem menu. Enter **MM** to go back to the BIX main menu.

In the main menu, select ITEM 9, which will produce the Quick Download menu. From this menu, choose OPTION 3 (Download your SCRATCH-PAD). Then it's off to the Download Scratchpad menu. Set your telecommunications software to capture ASCII screens. Then, choose OPTION 1 (ASCII transfer). All the entries will scroll by. When complete, save the captured data and enter **MM** to leave the Quick Download Subsystem. BIX will clear your scratchpad automatically.

If you prefer to use a protocol to download the messages, select OP-TION 2 (protocol transfer) from the Download Scratchpad menu. The default setting is Xmodem. To use Kermit, Ymodem, or Zmodem, it must be set beforehand by the use of OPTION 5 in the Individual Options menu.

The BIX Listings Subsystem

The BIX Listings Subsystem consists of a general area and conference-specific areas. You can download files from or upload files to most areas. Enter the BIX Listings Subsystem by selecting ITEM 3 from the BIX main menu or the topic Listings topic in a conference.

In the main Listings area, you'll find the source code associated with most of the articles that have appeared in *BYTE,* beginning with the September 1984 issue, and a wide assortment of public domain and shareware files. It has separate divisions covering specific brands of computers, language types, operating systems, and disciplines. Listings subareas are topics such as applications, leisure, and utility.

BIX Listings has three operating modes: Menu, Verbose prompts, and Terse prompts. The default setting is the Menu mode, and all the modes use the same commands. BIX listings are flexible. BIX lets you choose the length of file descriptions, preset download and upload protocols, and set the area to enter when you join Listings. Enter your commands at the Selection: prompt. You may use the number, the word in uppercase letters, or the first three letters of a command. Enter the command **LIST ALL** to produce a list of all the files in the file area.

PC MagNet

PC MagNet is an on-line information service to provide *PC Magazine*'s readers instant access to *PC Magazine*'s programs, articles, databases, and editorial staff. It also gives *PC Magazine* editors and readers discussion forums where they can share their opinions, experiences, and expertise. PC MagNet users can also get expert advice on how to configure and use the programs provided in *PC Magazine*, and the forums are the source for cutting-edge information on new hardware and software, especially OS/2.

PC Magazine's first on-line service, the Interactive Reader Service (IRS), was established in 1985. It was based on one PC-AT and had two incoming lines. Over the next few years that system was expanded to eight ATs, forty-four modems, and systems on both coasts. It used DMA's CHAIRMAN BBS software, and Arnet's multiport serial adapter to access six communications ports per AT. *PC Magazine*'s IRS was flooded with callers who wanted to download their utilities, and in 1988 they moved the IRS to a fully interactive system on PC MagNet. Now *PC Magazine* is capable of more than 400 simultaneous callers.

PC MagNet offers a variety of features, including fast and easy access to utilities, benchmark programs, forums, and libraries and databases.

Utility Programs

PC Magazine utilities in one place — hundreds of programs — are available in the PC MagNet Utilities Database. These free programs have been published in the pages of *PC Magazine* and are designed to help you get more out of your computer. Some of the more popular utilities are CO.COM, which will help you move and copy files, TED.COM, one of the tiniest editors you'll ever see, and the *PC Magazine* Reviews Index, a downloadable index to past articles.

Benchmark Programs

PC Labs Benchmark Series of Tests — the same tests used to analyze computer hardware and software — are available to you.

Forums

One of the most popular aspects of PC MagNet are its forums.

Editorial Forum   Here you can talk with *PC Magazine* editors about the latest offerings in the magazine. Discuss the fast-breaking trends in the computer industry with *PC Magazine* columnists such as Will Zachmann, Stephen Manes, and yours truly, John C. Dvorak.

Tips/Utilforum   This is the place to go for expert advice on how to use your hardware and software. You can ask *PC Magazine* veterans about your configuration, and get answers almost immediately. And the forum libraries are filled with *PC Magazine* programs and the latest shareware programs.

Programming Forum   In this forum you can get the latest news on OS/2 from Charles Petzold, power programming tips from Ray Duncan, and questions answered from on-line experts.

After Hours Forum   This popular forum is where users talk about topics that don't necessarily have to do with computers. Discussions about beer seem prevalent.

Practice Forum   Here's where you can learn the on-line structure without being charged $12.50 an hour. While you are in the Practice Forum, no charges accrue except your network (TYMNET, Sprintnet, or CompuServe, whichever you dialed in on) access charges. The normal $12.50/hour charges are suspended.

Libraries and Databases

Also note there are more than 30 Forum Libraries, for the exchange of files and utilities uploaded by *PC Magazine,* and PC MagNet users.

The Computer Library family of on-line databases is designed to provide a complete reference resource for you. It includes Computer Database Plus and Computer Directory. Computer Database Plus is a comprehensive collection of computer-related article summaries and full text from leading publications in the computer industry. Computer Database Plus provides comprehensive coverage of major computer industry publications in the areas of hardware, software, electronics, engineering, communications, and the application of technology.

Over 130 magazine, newspaper, and journal titles are covered in Computer Database Plus. Coverage includes *PC Magazine, BYTE,* and *MacUser* as well as trade and professional titles such as *Communications of the ACM* and *PC Week*. Coverage for most titles begins as of January 1, 1987, and is updated weekly. Every article contains either a summary or full text; most have both. Computer Database Plus contains both a connect surcharge and an article/summary surcharge.

The Computer Directory is an on-line reference for information on computer products and their manufacturers. This new service helps you find virtually any hardware, software, or telecommunications product sold in North America. More than 55,000 products are listed, along with profiles of more than 9000 companies that manufacture those products.

Searching the Computer Directory is easy, using criteria such as product name, company name, product type, and price range. It uses the same powerful search tools as its companion product, Computer Database Plus, so it's also possible to search on any words contained in product or company listings.

Computer Directory carries surcharges above standard PC MagNet rates.

PC MagNet is administered by CompuServe Information Service, which means PC MagNet is located on CompuServe's computers. CompuServe handles the customer support and administrative support for PC MagNet. When you receive your bill it will probably list the billing source as CompuServe/Ziff (Ziff-Davis publishes *PC Magazine*). It costs $12.50 per hour (not including network charges) for 1200 and 2400bps service.

When you have questions about PC MagNet, you can ask Customer Service. Customer Service makes it easy to get the help you need, either on line or by voice. If you send an electronic message to Customer Service, a representative will respond via EasyPlex as quickly as possible. You are not billed for your connect time while using the Feedback area.

If you would rather call Customer Service, representatives are available from 8:00A.M. to midnight Monday through Friday, and from 2:00P.M. to midnight on weekends (EST). Holiday hours will vary. To reach Customer Service dial 1-800-848-8990 within the contiguous United States, except Ohio. Dial 1-614-457-8650 from within Ohio or from outside the contiguous United States.

How to Get to CompuServe from PC MagNet

To access the CompuServe Information Service from PC MagNet, select "CompuServe Information Service" from the PC MagNet top menu or type

218 Dvorak's Guide to Desktop Telecommunications

GO CIS at any ! prompt. If you know the name of a specific CompuServe service, you may also type **GO CIS:XXXX**, where XXXX represents the CompuServe Quick Reference Word.

To return to PC MagNet from CompuServe, type **GO PCMAGNET** at any ! prompt. You may also go directly to a PC MagNet service from CompuServe by typing **GO PCM:XXXX**, where XXXX represents the PC MagNet service name. For example, **GO PCM:EDITORIAL** would take you directly to the Editorial Forum.

Getting Started

You can sign up on line for no additional charge. To join PC MagNet, set your communications software to 1200bps, 7 data bits, even parity, 1 stop bit, and full duplex.

You can access PC MagNet through Sprintnet, TYMNET, or any of the CompuServe access phone numbers (there are more than 300). These are a few of the CompuServe numbers for 1200bps access. (Appendix G lists some BBS access numbers.) The network charge is 30 cents per hour, in addition to the $12.50 per hour that PC MagNet costs. Other networks tend to charge more.

Atlanta	1-404-266-7014
Boston	1-617-542-1796
Chicago	1-312-693-0330
Dallas	1-214-953-0212
Houston	1-713-462-0202
Los Angeles	1-213-739-8906
Miami	1-305-266-0231
Minneapolis	1-612-342-2207
New York	1-212-422-8820
Newark	1-201-643-0404
Philadelphia	1-215-977-9758
Pittsburgh	1-412-391-7732
San Diego	1-619-569-8360
San Francisco	1-415-296-0375
Seattle	1-206-241-9111
St. Louis	1-314-241-3102
Washington	1-202-388-4280

When you get a prompt, the procedure is the same as for CompuServe.

1. Hit CTRL-C or ENTER and you'll either get a HOST NAME prompt or a USER ID prompt.

2. At the HOST NAME prompt, enter **CIS**.

3. At the USER ID prompt, enter **177000,5000**.

4. At the PASSWORD prompt, enter **PC*MAGNET**.

5. At the ENTER AGREEMENT NUMBER prompt, enter **Z10D8900**.

6. Register your name and enter your MasterCard, VISA, or American Express card number. For information about direct corporate billing, call 1-800-848-8199.

7. Your personal User ID and Password will be displayed at the end of the registration process. Please record them and have copies in a secure place.

8. A new password will arrive in the mail within ten days to confirm your subscription.

At the end of the registration process you will go directly into PC MagNet and see the main menu:

```
PC MagNet                    PCM-1
1 What's New on PC MagNet
2 PC MagNet Assistance
3 Search for PC Magazine Utilities and Programs
4 Forums--talk to PC Magazine
5 EasyPlex (Electronic Mail)
6 Free--Participate in a PC Magazine Survey
7 Computer Library (Full-Text Search)
8 CompuServe Information Service
Welcome to PC MagNet!
```

Channel 1, the Shareware Network

Creators Brian Miller and Tess Heder started the Channel 1 network in 1986. It is now the largest LAN-and-microcomputer-based interactive service in the U.S., with 35,000 constantly updated IBM, Amiga, and

Macintosh public domain and shareware programs. Besides an array of conferences (over 120, with 25 exclusive to Channel 1), E-mail capabilities, and other services, Channel 1 provides a full-color on-line environment. Brian and Tess take a shareware approach to their interactive service. They figure if people like it, they'll register as members and keep coming back for more.

Channel 1 tries hard to maintain the largest assortment of new daily files of any system in the U.S. The files are stored in easily searchable file directories designed with the novice user in mind. (Busy users will find the quick search feature useful.) An on-line file viewing feature allows the member to read part or all of most programs' documents before downloading. This saves download time.

The Channel 1 network components are

- High-speed Novell LAN network

- More than 2.5 gigabytes of on-line system storage

- PCBoard Multi-Node Software

- 31 access lines, including members-only lines

Tweaked for Fast Access

Channel 1 supports most 9600bps modems. There is no surcharge for connecting at this speed. If you connect late at night, you can direct dial and browse this system for considerably less per hour than an on-line service like CompuServe at 2400 baud. Without a fast modem, if cost is a major concern, unless you're near Boston you may do better with one of the large 2400bps services.

Access and Modem Settings

To call Channel 1, set your modem to 8-N-1 and call 1-617-354-8873. Once you are connected, follow the instructions to receive your free trial membership. Remember, there is no additional surcharge for 9600bps modems.

The Channel 1 voice phone is 1-617-864-0100. If you prefer to make a written off-line inquiry, address it to

Channel 1 Communications
P.O. Box 338
Cambridge, MA 02238-0338

Getting the Manual

Channel 1 doesn't send you any fancy manuals, but the system is set up to be extremely easy to search and to use. Your first time on, go to the conference covering your type of computer, and download the file named CHAN1HLP.ZIP. This is all the user's manual you should ever need—it's the complete set of help bulletins and gives detailed instructions on how to use the system.

Here is the exact procedure for getting the manual if you have an MS-DOS machine:

1. Sign on and get your trial membership.

2. At the main system prompt, enter **J 5** to join the MS Conference.

3. At the main Conference menu, enter **D CHAN1HLP**.

4. Follow the prompts to set your protocol and then download the file. Print it out, and you've got a complete, if not terribly fancy, system manual.

Getting Started

As part of its commitment to keeping up-to-date files, Channel 1 provides limited free access on a shareware, try-it-and-see basis.

New subscribers are invited to try out Channel 1 on a three-month free trial basis. Starting access time for validated new callers is 26 minutes per day. This limited access lets new users explore the system.

There are 16 Amiga, 28 Macintosh, 3 Microsoft Journal, 2 CAD, and other conference-specific directories available.

Membership Requirements and Costs

Trial account-holders must maintain a ratio of one upload for every four downloads. Full members have extended access, with no upload requirements and private lines. The Deposit Door, which enables you to store time from one session for use in another, is available to all members. So are certain Games Doors, conferences and file directories.

Trial members who contribute good uploads to the system may request extensions of free access, as may software authors and callers who don't download but who call only to participate in the conferences. All time spent uploading in Prodoor or ZDoor is matched by equal extra time for the uploader for that session.

Full membership allows complete access to all Channel 1 resources. Memberships of 45 or more minutes per day have priority access on phone lines reserved for members' use. Some system functions are available only to members.

At the end of the trial membership, users are invited to join as full members. Full memberships to Channel 1 range in price from $20 to $150, and last from two months to one year. You can sign up online with VISA/MasterCard/American Express, or mail a check to Channel 1. Bulletins #3 and #4 contain all the information you need.

Memberships are limited to a rather large but specific number of downloads: 100-600 files. You can pick a plan especially tailored to your needs, depending on the amount of on-line time you will need. By this time you'll have had three months to play around on the system and find out what your use needs are, which should make it easy to decide.

Company memberships offer priority access on members-only lines, use by several of your staff, and full access to all of Channel 1's resources. Bulletin #4 has more information about company memberships.

Other Services

Channel 1 supports a wide variety of on-line, single-, and multiplayer games—all available in color and graphics. Other features available include on-line shopping for computer equipment and peripherals, corporate services including E-mail, private and support conferences, public domain and shareware library services for companies and institutions, file ordering by mail, and daily industry news from *Byte* magazine.

Channel 1 is an active member in RelayNet, a growing association of over 250 national and international BBSs. All conference messages are transferred daily. Channel 1 also relays Interlink and Smartnet network conferences.

NewsNet, the Newsletter Database

NewsNet is an information network which carries more than 350 newsletters in 30 different fields, from defense and aerospace to computers and electronics. NewsNet also carries UPI, AP, Reuters and eight other newswires with late-breaking news.

News Service and Other Coverage

NewsNet coverage is full text, not archive-oriented, and ready to be read on line or downloaded. Usually information is on NewsNet before it's available in print. Wire service stories are available as soon as NewsNet gets them. Everything in the service is completely searchable as soon as it's on line.

NewsFlash—Hot Off the Wires   The service offers NewsFlash, what it calls an "electronic clipping service," a keyword-oriented search program that monitors some or all services on a 24-hour basis. Material containing your keyword is saved for retrieval. Once on line you can read the items, cull the headlines, delete anything unneeded, and download the rest. It's an information-access tool because there's no need to do any complex on-line searching. Tell NewsFlash what to look for, and let it catch the stories as they break.

NewsFlash is particularly useful for writers, analysts, and others who need a complete monitor of breaking news.

Gateway Services   As a subscriber you can access various gateway services right from NewsNet.

- TRW Business Profiles, carrying detailed credit reports and analyses of more than 13 million U.S. business addresses

- Vu/Quote Stock and Commodity Quotes, with complete quotes from the New York Stock Exchange, NASDAQ, and AMEX exchanges

- The Official Airline Guide (OAG), to let you make and review airline reservations and get current travel and frequent-flyer information.

Command Structure and Finding Help

The NewsNet commands are straightforward and easily learned, although the service does offer periodic training classes. Commands are common sense English words that reflect their functions. For example, to scan newsletter headlines you would use the command SCAN. Help files are available from any prompt.

Signing Up for NewsNet

NewsNet will sign you up immediately if you want, but they prefer that you have their introductory packet on hand before you actually go on line. If you prefer, they will set up a demonstration account for you, to give you a shareware-like preview of the system before you shell out any hard-earned money.

To get the introductory packet, sign up for a demonstration account. Or—if you're headstrong—to go immediately on line, call NewsNet at 1-800-345-1301. International users call 1-215-527-8030.

CHAPTER SEVEN

The BBS Scene
and
Teleconferencing

The computerized bulletin board was invented shortly after the first micro-computer appeared on the scene. During the late 1970s, CP/M systems and Apple computers hosted slow systems whose popularity was limited due to access problems. To this day, most single-user bulletin board systems (BBSs) are often tied up by one guy hogging the line with long downloads. Appendix G explains how to find and access BBS systems.

COMPUTERIZED BULLETIN
BOARD SYSTEMS

The idea of a *computerized bulletin board system* (CBBS or BBS) is simple. A computer enthusiast sets up a computer, modem, and phone line to act as a central point for information exchange. Some BBSs are used as a cheap way to exchange E-mail. Some are used to store files for downloading.

Some are real-time sources of information for computer clubs or even cults. BBSs are used for many purposes—even the distribution of pirated software, which is not recommended.

Some bulletin board systems have gone beyond the hobbyist level and have almost become true service bureaus, with multiple lines—something like CompuServe. Many systems have gone big-time. These are discussed in Chapter 6.

This chapter discusses the serious BBS—the one that exists somewhere in between a professional system and the hobbyist system. The BBSs least likely to go out of business are the *multiline* or *multiuser* BBSs run by serious sysops around the country.

How big do they get? The number of incoming phone lines and modems determines the maximum number of users a BBS can support simultaneously. This number is the most widely adopted measure of the size and popularity of a multiuser BBS. A 4-user system is generally "better" than a 2-user system, and a 16-user system is usually pretty hot stuff. This is true merely because phone lines are expensive, and a sysop whose lines are frequently unoccupied is wasting money. Simply put, a 2-line system only has to be popular enough that at least two people at a time want to access it. A 16-user system must be so popular that an average of sixteen people at a time want to use it, or there would be no point in having sixteen lines. Of course, this example is a slight oversimplification. In neither case are we talking about constant usage, 24 hours a day, and there may be degrees to which a busy signal is intolerable, so that the relevant criterion becomes not average usage but rather peak usage.

Even though a multiuser BBS may have many individual phone lines, there are normally just one or two master phone numbers. This is because the sysop has usually acquired what is called a *rollover*, or *hunt group*, or *rotary* line from the phone company (these terms seem to be used interchangeably). Often there is a separate rotary for "free sample" callers, as opposed to registered, or paying, subscribers. When you call the BBS for the first time, you call the master number for the "free sample" rotary. Then, once you have signed up, or provided a credit card number, or otherwise registered as a member, you are allowed to log on via the master number of the subscriber rotary.

The Advantages of Multiuser BBSs

Certainly BBS operators have various economic reasons for running multi-line systems. For instance, by sharing the same computer hardware among multiple users simultaneously, they are getting more value for the dollar. Also, the volume of messages and file upload/download traffic can be much higher when there are multiple lines in use. But these are merely economies of scale. You might gain the same qualitative advantages by calling a series of single-user systems. The major advantage that a multiuser BBS offers to you, the user, is real-time interaction with other people.

Real-time interaction means that you can talk directly with other people on line, without the time delays of single-user BBS conferencing. You can talk with other users in a variety of ways, from one-on-one "chats" to open-channel "simulated CB" or "on-line seminar" formats. You can even make use of numerous electronic "environments." For example, Moonshae Isles, a 24-line BBS in Fort Lauderdale (305-928-1640), offers many nonverbal communication possibilities like "nod," "shrug," and "grin." All these features allow large or small groups of people to participate in a teleconference with almost the full impact of being physically present, but at a fraction of the travel cost.

Why is this interface so important? Think about it: If you are a normal person (as opposed to a computer nut!), a large portion of your life involves real-time interaction with other people. Although you may not often need to access computer file libraries and message bases, you probably enjoy talking on the telephone with your friends. Your work no doubt involves plenty of real-time interaction, too, whether you retail vacuum cleaners, develop new semiconductors, or teach elementary school.

Imagine a world in which you could only use your telephone to call machines. Various automated data services would provide your bank balance or the weather forecast. In order to talk to your friends and business associates, however, you could only call into special voice mail systems and leave messages. Your friends would have to respond by calling into the same voice mail systems later, and leaving messages for you. Suppose, too, that sophisticated methods existed for combining and preserving message bases, and for scanning them for pertinent information. This is the world of single-user BBSing.

Now, imagine that someone invents a way for people to talk together directly by telephone, in real-time. But it is very expensive technology, and its economic viability is so heavily dependent on the economies of scale that only a few centralized sites exist around the country—each of them boasting tens of thousands of subscribers. A new access service industry grows up around these systems, allowing long-distance access to these sites at cheaper rates. Still, the relatively high cost of the underlying service, combined with the long-distance access charges, puts the cost of direct, real-time interaction out of reach for most people. This is the world of mainframes, and services such as CompuServe and GEnie.

As technology has progressed, the cost of providing communication service has dropped, but the long-distance access charges have remained relatively fixed. The cost of providing the underlying service has become a fraction of the long-distance access charges. The real-life result of this imbalance is that small-scale services have mushroomed all over the nation, only a local phone call away from most users. This is the world of the multiuser BBS.

Real-time interaction is not the only benefit of a multiuser BBS. It also offers message bases, file libraries, and person-to-person electronic mail; in fact, these facilities are easily offered on a multiuser BBS due to the economies of scale. You can generally expect access to larger file libraries, more diverse bulletin boards, and more of a "one-stop shopping" approach to E-mail on a multiuser BBS than on a single-user system. Additional, more specialized forms of database access, such as classified advertising, order entry, product line catalog browsing, and product support are much more likely to be found on a multiuser BBS.

The most important feature, however, that multiuser systems provide, and that single-user systems by their very nature are prevented from providing, is real-time multiuser interaction. It is the need for this capability that has fueled the growth of high-cost mainframe services. And it is real-time multiuser interaction that today's multiuser BBS is uniquely qualified to provide at reasonable cost.

Drawbacks of Multiuser BBSs

The one major drawback of multiuser BBSing, for many users, is that it is rarely free of charge. A single-user BBS requires the sysop to dedicate just one phone line, which is typically obtained at the phone company's "residential" rate of about $20 a month. This is pocket change for most single-user BBS sysops who want the personal satisfaction of providing a useful community service. In contrast, an 8-line system, even at residential rates, would cost more like $160 a month. Moreover, if the sysop wants to recoup these costs by charging users for the service, the sysop must then pay the phone company's business rates—around $400 a month for eight lines!

Different sysops deal with this dilemma in different ways. Exec-PC—the largest BBS in the world, with 90-user capability (414-964-5160)—charges a yearly subscription fee of $60, but limits each user to a maximum seven hours of use per week. The 32-user Multi-Comm of Las Vegas (702-362-9224) offers unlimited access at a rate of fifty cents per hour. Others, such as Viewline (403-467-8509), offer you a choice: either a flat-rate subscription or a variable hourly fee, either of which may be charged to your credit card.

Although having to pay for access to a BBS may run against your principles, the fact is that most multiuser BBSs are a great deal cheaper than the nationwide mainframe-based services. Response times are generally quicker. Also, if the BBS of your choice is local to you, the on-line friends you make are more likely to be local to you, too. You might even meet them in person at the system get-togethers, picnics, and other events often sponsored by multiuser BBS sysops for exactly this purpose.

Many systems use a nifty arrangement whereby you have unlimited "free sample," or "non-live" time on one number (which is usually busy, of course!), but you must have "credits" or "live" time in order to call another bank of lines reserved for paying customers only. When you can get through on the non-live lines, you can get the feel of the system before you spend a dime on it. There are usually massive restrictions on your privileges when you are in this non-live mode, but you can at least talk a few times in teleconference, view certain message bases (but not write to any), and send E-mail to the sysop (but not to other users). Also, you are limited to only ten minutes or so per call, which frequently puts you back in the pool of demon dialers trying to get at those free sample lines. If you like what you see in your first couple of non-live sessions, go ahead and send in the small payment that the sysop suggests, for full system access through the "paying customers only" number.

The main exception to the pay-for-use rule among public multiuser BBSs is the customer support system. A growing number of companies, such as Ashton-Tate (213-324-2188), AST Research (714-852-1872), and Sierra Online (209-683-4463), provide unlimited, 24-hour customer support by modem. This is an excellent trend. Your cost to access these support services is just the cost of the phone call.

TELECONFERENCING

Let's take a look now in some detail at some of the possibilities for real-time interaction on a multiuser BBS and use as a model the program The Major BBS by Galacticomm, which currently runs at hundreds of sites around the United States, and on the bulletin board systems referenced in this chapter.

Teleconferencing allows several users to converse with one another over their terminals. Whatever each user types is sent to all other users on the same teleconference channel, with identification as to the sender. The cost of this type of teleconference is far less than that of presently available video teleconferences, or of assembling all participants from across town, or across the country, in the same room.

Compared to voice "conference calls," multiuser BBS teleconferencing offers these advantages:

- Many more users can participate.

- There is no "fading away" of a conferee's voice when too many people are on line.

- With the appropriate communications software, each conferee can automatically capture a complete transcript of the entire conference.

- Words don't get lost when two people "speak" at once—all messages eventually get through.

- Private messages can be "whispered" between conferees.

The two disadvantages of BBS teleconferences when compared with voice conference calls are

- Terminals are not yet as widely available as telephones.

- People cannot type as fast as they can talk. Nor can they easily convey on a terminal screen subtle nuances of the voice, such as amusement, sarcasm, or friendliness. These must be expressly spelled out.

How to Conduct a Teleconference

Teleconferencing on a Galacticomm-based BBS operates much like a citizens band (CB) radio. When you first enter the teleconference (typically, by typing **T** and pressing ENTER from the main menu), you "tune in" to channel 1. You are notified of all other users on that channel. If you want to confer with one user in particular, or a small group of users, you suggest to them that they "switch" to some other channel, say 22. While a conference is in progress on that channel, you can invite other users to join you with the PAGE feature.

To talk in a teleconference, you simply type in whatever you want to say, and press ENTER. There are also some special commands you can type that are interpreted directly by the teleconference program itself:

WHISPER TO *User-Id message*   With this command, you can send a private message to just one user. No other users on the teleconference channel will be aware of the exchange (see Fred's screen in Figure 7-1).

/User-Id message   This is the shorthand form of the WHISPER command (see Barney's entry beginning "/FRED UH-OH..." in Figure 7-1).

CHANNEL *number*   The CHANNEL command switches you to the channel number you specify. There are 65,535 channels to choose from.

SCAN   Shows a directory of all users in the teleconference, and what channels they are using. The following is an example of the SCAN command:

```
        :SCAN USER-ID ..... CHANNEL ... TOPIC Betty    ... 22
Bargains in 2400 bps Modems Judy        ...  22      Bargains in
2400 bps Modems Farley    ... (Chat) Wilma    ... 22 Bargains
in 2400 bps Modems Bilbao    ...  (Chat) Fred    ...(Unlisted)
Barney    ... (Unlisted)
```

In this example, channel 22 is associated with a permanent *Special Interest Group* (SIG) whose topic is "Bargains in 2400bps Modems." (Users may also establish transient teleconference topics of their own choice on channels not already nailed down this way; see the MODERATE command below.) Farley and Bilbao are in chat mode with each other (see the CHAT command). Fred and Barney are both unlisted (see the UNLIST command). We can't tell what channel Fred and Barney are on, but we can presume they are talking to each other and do not wish to be disturbed.

Figure 7-1

Sample teleconference session

Barney's Screen	Fred's Screen	Wilma's Screen
:	:	:
Fred and Wilma are on teleconference channel 1 with you.	Barney and Wilma are on teleconference channel 1 with you.	Fred and Barney are on teleconference channel 1 with you.
:***	:HELLO	:***
From Fred: HELLO	— Message sent —	From Fred: HELLO
:***	:***	:FRED, WHERE HAVE YOU BEEN?
From Wilma: FRED, WHERE HAVE YOU BEEN?	From Wilma: FRED, WHERE HAVE YOU BEEN?	— Message sent —
	:WHISPER TO BARNEY DON'T TELL WILMA THAT WE WENT BOWLING.	
:***	—Message sent only to Barney —	
From Fred (whispered): DONT TELL WILMA THAT WE WENT BOWLING		
:***	:UH, HI, HONEY	:***
From Fred: UH, HI HONEY	— Message sent —	From Fred: UH, HI HONEY
:OK, FRED, I WONT TELL WILMA THAT WE WENT BOWLING	:***	:***
— Message sent —	From Barney: OK, FRED, I WONT TELL WILMA THAT WE WENT BOWLING	From Barney: OK, FRED, I WONT TELL WILMA THAT WE WENT BOWLING
:***	:***	:FRED!
From Wilma: FRED!	From Wilma: FRED!	— Message sent —
:/FRED UH-OH FRED, SEE YOU LATER	:***	
—Message sent only to Fred —	From Barney (whispered): UH-OH FRED, SEE YOU LATER	
:***	:BARNEY GET BACK HERE!	:***
From Fred: BARNEY GET BACK HERE!	— Message Sent —	From Fred: BARNEY GET BACK HERE!
:X	:***	:***
Exiting teleconference mode, returning to main menu. . .	Barney has just exited the teleconference.	Barney has just exited the teleconference.
		:NOW SEE HERE, FRED, IF YOU THINK YOU CAN GO BOWLING EVERY NIGHT OF. . .
		— Message sent —
	:***	
	From Wilma: NOW SEE HERE, FRED, IF YOU THINK YOU CAN GO BOWLING EVERY NIGHT OF. . .	

UNLIST   Issuing the UNLIST command makes your channel number show as *unlisted* when other users issue the SCAN command. By default, you are automatically unlisted except when on channel 1, or a SIG channel, or when moderating your own channel topic. Note that the sysop can always tell what channel you are on, even if you are unlisted.

LIST   This is the inverse of the UNLIST command, and allows your channel number to be seen when other people use the SCAN command.

PAGE *User-Id message*   This broadcasts a message to the specified user ID, identifying you by your user ID and by the teleconference channel you are paging from. Normally you use PAGE without an express message. For example:

```
:PAGE FRED
```

If you are logged on as Wilma on channel 22, the previous PAGE command causes this message to appear on Fred's screen:

```
:***<beep!> Wilma is paging you to teleconference channel 22!
```

Fred can then either switch to channel 22, or page you back, so that you will see his channel number and switch to it. Or, Fred can just ignore your page altogether. In fact, if he is feeling especially antisocial, he can issue the command PAGE OFF.

PAGE OFF   This automatically turns a deaf ear toward users who may be trying to page you or chat with you (see the CHAT command), so that you will not be bothered if you have work to do. If Fred sets his terminal to PAGE OFF, he will be unaware of your page. You receive the message:

```
:PAGE FRED Sorry, Fred has shut off incoming paging and chat
requests.
```

PAGE ON   PAGE ON (the default condition) means you will receive incoming pages, but no more often than once every two minutes or so. This handy feature ensures that you won't get pestered to death, but you can be reached if someone needs to speak with you.

PAGE OK   This disables the two-minute waiting period between incoming page and chat requests, so that you can be paged continuously, if desired. Some people like to use paging as a form of interchannel whisper for ongoing conversations.

CHAT *User-Id*   This command allows two users to enter chat mode with each other. In chat mode, every keystroke from each user is immediately echoed to both users. This is in contrast to the regular teleconference condition, in which the ENTER key must be pressed to send a line of input to others on your channel. Chat mode is suitable only for two users at a time; with three or more people using chat mode simultaneously, it would be difficult to tell who was talking.

To begin chat mode, both users must consent. The first user requests, and the other consents, using the same command. Figure 7-2 shows an example of two users entering, using, and exiting chat mode. Note the confusion that can result if both users type simultaneously. In the regular teleconference this can't happen because output from other users is always "buffered up" for you when you are in the process of typing a line of your own.

MODERATE *topic*   Use this command to set the *transient topic* for the channel you are on, and to make yourself the moderator of that channel. As moderator, you have the following privileges:

- Changing the topic of the channel (see the SCAN command)
- Squelching (silencing) other users on the channel (see the SQUELCH command)
- Unsquelching other users on the channel
- Appointing another moderator for the channel

The moderator can change the topic of the channel by simply reissuing the MODERATE command with a new topic name. If the moderator types MODERATE by itself, without a topic, then that channel has no moderator.

SQUELCH *User-Id*   This command can only be used by the moderator of a channel (or the sysop). It is used to silence a specified user, to eliminate heckling or other disruptive activity on channels in use for serious business

Figure 7-2

Chat

Wilma's Screen	Betty's Screen

```
:chat betty
Ok, Betty has been notified of
your request to chat.


:***
Betty has accepted your
request to chat
TELECONFERENCE CHAT ACTIVATED.
Type 'X' on a blank line to
exit.
hi betty, how are you?
Fine thanks, Wilma, and you?
Oh, I'm fine.
SSaayy WBieltmtay
Say Betty, have you seen Fred?
I was just going to ask you
about Barney.
Those two are up to something!
Don't you know it!
x
. . .Okay, exiting chat. . .
:
```

```
<BEEP>Wilma is requesting
you join her in chat! Type
"chat Wilma" within the next
two mintues to accept.
:chat wilma



TELECONFERENCE CHAT ACTIVATED.
Type 'X' on a blank line to
exit.
hi betty, how are you?
Fine thanks, Wilma, and you?
Oh, I'm fine.
SSaayy WBieltmtay
Say Betty, have you seen Fred?
I was just going to ask you
about Barney.
Those two are up to something!
Don't you know it!
x
. . .Okay, exiting chat. . .
:
```

or academic purposes. The anonymity and unaccountability available to users of these systems can sometimes foster irresponsible behavior.

UNSQUELCH *User-Id*   This is the inverse of the SQUELCH command. It allows the specified user to speak on the channel again.

APPOINT *User-Id*   The moderator of a channel can name another user as moderator.

EXIT or X   This takes you out of chat mode and back to regular teleconferencing mode. If you are already in regular mode, you exit the teleconference altogether.

HELP or ?   This command displays a summary of The Major BBS system commands.

Teleconference Etiquette

Unlike almost anything else you have ever done with your computer or modem, multiuser BBS teleconferencing involves other real people in real-time. In almost any other computer activity, if you get up from your keyboard to get a soda, or answer the doorbell, it doesn't matter. If you are involved in a teleconference, however, interruptions like this can annoy or inconvenience several people.

In most situations, using a computer is rarely a real-time activity. You become accustomed to the idea that the computer exists solely for your personal convenience, and rightly so. It is a tool, a machine. Its feelings cannot be hurt if you leave it sitting there while you go and watch the latest installment of "Murder, She Wrote." When the computer offers you an unfamiliar prompt or error message, it is not the least bit bothered if you sit there for several minutes thinking over your possible responses, or talking about the football game with your brother-in-law. Even if you are using the computer to send E-mail to another user, you are not doing it in real-time; the recipient of your E-mail message cares very little about how long you took to type it.

When you enter your first teleconference, your instinct may be to treat the environment like any other computer environment you are used to. However, there is a major difference: out there in Modem Land there are at least several other real people who will be affected in real-time by your actions. When one of them says "Hello!" and waits for a response, you will be considered impolite if you don't answer.

Dvorak's Rules of Teleconference Etiquette

Dvorak's First Rule of Teleconference Etiquette is

Be responsive!   Don't make your listeners wait while you think about possible ways to answer. Don't type lengthy dissertations before hitting ENTER: your listeners may grow impatient enough to actually abandon their keyboards. If you are a slow typist, enter very short phrases, one at a time.

If you frequently change your mind about what you want to say, and need to backspace over whole phrases and clauses, first send at least what you have typed so far, so your listeners won't wonder if they're communicating with a dead line.

Dvorak's Second Rule of Teleconference Etiquette follows readily from the first one:

If you do have to leave your keyboard, even for a moment, say so on line first!   A simple entry like "(phone call)" or "(doorbell)" alerts your co-participants not to expect your answers to their queries until further notice.

Dvorak's Third Rule of Teleconference Etiquette could be phrased

Emote!   Always consider the relatively cold nature of the digital communications stream, and go out of your way to be friendly.

One popular method for doing this is to liberally sprinkle your conversation with little doodads called *emoticons*. There are several kinds, for example:

`:-)`

Tilt your head to the left and visualize this as two eyes, a nose, and a mouth. There is also the wink:

`;-)`

and the mischievous grin (with bozo nose):

`:o>`

You'll think of your own variations, and Appendix D lists dozens you can use. Or, throw in some action verbs and expressions from time to time, like "(grin)" or "(sticking out tongue)," or even "(making lewd gesture)."

The use of emoticons can take the sting out of what might be considered a sharp or negative remark. Because, often, too few words are used in a teleconference dialogue, emoticons can be quite helpful.

Many systems (including Moonshae Isles, mentioned earlier) use the Entertainment Edition of The Major BBS, which has a built-in action verb handler. You can "smile," "grin," "wink [at] Eldridge," and so forth. You can even "sneeze," "pout," "growl," or indicate any other emotions the sysop has seen fit to configure for that particular system. For each emotion verb, an appropriate message is sent to the other users on your channel, in place of the verb or verb phrase you actually typed. For example, if Fred types the word "laugh" in an Entertainment Edition teleconference, the other users on his channel see

```
:*** Fred is laughing his fool head off!
```

This makes for very satisfying communications if you know the ropes.

Dvorak's Fourth Rule of Teleconference Etiquette is more about the absence of a concern than the presence of one:

Don't worry about typos, worry about message content! In fast-paced real-time multiuser interplay, nobody thinks less of you because you hit a few wrong keys. If they can understand what you are saying, that's what matters. Taking an extra five seconds per line to backspace over typos so that you're always picture perfect cuts into the pace and spontaneity of the whole process.

Lastly, Dvorak's Fifth Rule is one that becomes important only when someone forgets it:

Don't use ALL UPPERCASE! The ideal is mixed upper- and lower-case, saving uppercase for emphasizing particular words. In the heat of open teleconference you may forget the extra keystroke required to capitalize words like the pronoun "I," but an "e e cummings" style of all lowercase is acceptable, even mellow. Never set CAPS-LOCK on and proceed; it appears that you're shouting at everyone all the time. All uppercase brands you as ONE OF THOSE YO-YO'S WHO HAS NO REGARD FOR HOW HE SOUNDS TO THE OTHER PEOPLE ON LINE.

Linking Teleconferences

The next step beyond multiuser BBS teleconferences is linking them. Originally unveiled in July 1984 by Bill Basham in his Apple-based DiversiDial program, this idea is now catching on in a big way with programs like OraComm and the Entertainment Edition of The Major BBS.

The concept of linked teleconference calls is for telephone lines and modems to be used not only for linking users to systems, but also for linking systems to other systems. We saw this in Chapter 5 in the discussion of FidoNet, which allows different BBSs to trade messages in the

middle of the night. In linked teleconferences, the phone connection between systems is left active, so that you can talk in real-time to other people
who may be logged onto other BBSs.

No effort on your part as a user is required to link up. The sysop
establishes one or more links to other systems on one or more channels—all
you do is talk! For example, Figure 7-3 is a diagram showing five linked
systems. Suppose you are logged into Logicom, on the linked teleconference
channel, as Jsmith. (Let's simplify and assume that all links tie into the
same teleconference channel number.) If you enter **HELLO** on your keyboard, Galaxy users will see

```
:*** (Logicom) From Jsmith: HELLO
```

Figure 7-3

Sample teleconference link-up

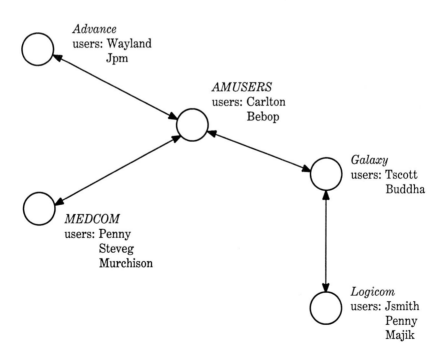

Users on AMUSERS, to which Galaxy is linked, will see

```
:*** (Galaxy) (Logicom) From Jsmith: HELLO
```

Users logged into both Advance and MEDCOM will see

```
:*** (AMUSERS) (Galaxy) (Logicom) From Jsmith: HELLO
```

Similarly, if Penny on MEDCOM says "long time no see!," your screen will read

```
:*** (Galaxy) (AMUSERS) (MEDCOM) From Penny: long time no see!
```

The displayed "genealogy" of the message serves to distinguish people with the same user ID on different systems, and gives you some feel for the routing delay involved. For example, Wayland on Advance might witness the following exchange:

```
:*** (AMUSERS) (Galaxy) (Logicom) From Penny: hey that's my
                                  handle!
:*** (AMUSERS) (MEDCOM) From Penny: no, i had it first
:*** From Jpm: ladies, ladies, let's take this calmly
:*** (AMUSERS) From Carlton: i remember medcom penny from '88
:*** (AMUSERS) (MEDCOM) From Penny: hah, you see there! ;-)
```

Incidentally, on the subject of routing delay, seldom do you find conversations coming out as neatly ordered in time as shown in the preceding example. This is because it may take several seconds for a message to be transferred over the phone lines, responded to, and transferred back. During this interval, the other people on line are not likely to be just sitting idly at their terminals. They will be generating their own comments and witticisms. The resulting transcript tends to read like a somewhat chaotic series of subconversations, threads of which dwindle and reappear, constantly twisting and branching. Here is how the interchange might appear from Bebop's point of view:

```
:*** (MEDCOM) From Murchison: she did not
:*** (Galaxy) (Logicom) From Majik: really? when was that?
:*** (Advance) From Jpm: by the way Carl, I forgot to tell
                 you...
```

:*** (Galaxy) (Logicom) From Penny: well i've been online
                         since 87!
:*** (Galaxy) Tscott is laughing his fool head off!
:*** From Carlton: i think it was november, majik! what, j.p.?
:*** (MEDCOM) Penny is slapping Murchison across the face!
:*** (Advance) From Wayland: this is getting kind of wild...

CHAPTER EIGHT

Running a BBS

Operating a BBS makes you an automatic big shot in your local computer community. Some people will throw tomatoes at you. Others will deify you and hang on your every electronic utterance. Others will stand on you, using you as a soapbox from which to advocate their own peculiar philosophies. And, always, there will be rumors, rumors, rumors — scuttlebutt about how you deleted so-and-so's account, or how you made such-and-such remark, or how you plan to raise your rates, or lower your rates, or abolish your rates.

Actually, it's very satisfying work. You are often able to provide a forum for businesspeople, hobbyists, students, consultants, and assorted hangers-on. On a multiuser BBS, users are able to share advice, tips, and insights, just as they can on a single-user BBS. More importantly, however, they can interact in real-time. They can "teleconference," or participate in various real-time multiuser simulations. And they can get to know one another on line, widening their social and professional horizons in ways never before possible. It's the multiuser BBS that is discussed in this chapter.

TYPES OF MULTIUSER BBSs

Few sysops are independently wealthy and can operate a multiuser BBS as just a hobby. Virtually all multiuser systems are run by a business, as a business. Sometimes it's a hobbyist-owned business, but it's nonetheless a business! Some systems are operated by a church or government. There are four categories of the multiuser BBS.

Special Purpose BBSs

These are generally very private systems, run by a company for some specialized internal purpose. MCI, for example, runs a 64-user BBS for electronic mail and file transfer between its nationwide field sales force and the home office. The Census Bureau has an 8-user system to upload housing statistics data to Washington, D.C. from its branch offices. Epson America runs a private 8-user system for the benefit of its printer dealers, to disseminate price updates, diagnostic programs, confidential dealer promotional information, and so on. Access to these systems is strictly prohibited to the public, and any usage that is "charged for" is a matter of internal accounting policy.

Public Service BBSs

Operated by computer user groups (such as the Borland Turbo User Group; 206-697-1151), government agencies (such as the City of Alexandria, Virginia; 703-838-4793), or charitable or religious organizations (such as the Celebration Station; 207-374-2303), these systems provide forums for their unique clientele to trade ideas and files, and to keep abreast of upcoming meetings, social activities, and special events of interest to members. Usage may or may not be free, but is typically regulated to exclude nonmembers — though there are many exceptions.

Customer Support BBSs

Operated by companies such as Central Point Software (503-690-6650), Abel Supply (615-453-0643), and Sho-Tronics (602-495-0000), these systems serve as public relations tools, order takers, technical support centers, software update distributors, "app note" repositories, and much more. In many cases, the sponsoring organization provides specialized forms of database access, such as backorder status or part number cross-reference. A customer support BBS is usually free to users (except for the phone call), but a few companies do charge for access.

For-Profit BBSs

Unlike the previous BBS types, systems run for profit are generally the whole focus of the business, rather than a support feature for some larger function. As a result, they must be financially self-supported. They tend to offer a wide range of personal and business services, and constantly add new features and functions to remain competitive. This is where the main action is in BBSing, since these systems are simultaneously the most visible, the most rapid to evolve, and the most difficult to keep alive. The remainder of this chapter is devoted to the special concerns of running a profitable BBS.

THE MATTER OF CASH FLOW

The key to operating your own multiuser BBS is, to be succinct, staying in business! As discussed in Chapter 7, the cost of supporting a large number of phone lines makes it impossible to offer your services for free. A typical 8-line system needs a steady cash flow of around $400 a month just to break even; for a 16-line system, you'll need to pull in about $800 a month.

There are two ways to raise this money: you can charge users to use the system, or you can charge advertisers to advertise to the users. (Or both.)

Systems do survive and prosper on what they charge advertisers—but these systems are few and far between. Successful ad solicitation requires excellent sales and marketing skills, and a willingness to make continuous sales visits to businesses in your area. You will also need deep pockets, because many businesspeople are skeptical, and will tend not to put their money into an unproven advertising medium. In the long run, charging your users is the easier path.

For all of your paid customers, you will want to establish some sort of "free sample" policy that allows a small taste of what you have to offer.

If your paying customers are advertisers, post a few free ads on their behalf for a week. If your paying customers are the users, let them log on for a limited time for free, with restricted privileges.

You may be tempted to offer a half hour or so of free "live" time to each new sign-up, as a way of attracting new users—live time spent in a fully "validated" status. Don't do it. A few people are sure to figure out that if they repeatedly call back and sign in as a new user, they get the same level of access as if they pay. The result is likely to be that your system will accumulate dozens of "new" users a day, none of whom ever send in any money. Limit full access to fully paid customers.

Make it easy for your users to transfer money from their pockets to yours. Keep your rates reasonable—perhaps $5 to $20 a month—and avoid any hassle in the payment arrangement. Accept credit cards. Accept cash, in person. Consider a 976 number hookup that spits out "chit codes" that can be cashed in for time on your system. Have picnics, bowling tournaments, and general get-togethers from time to time, where people can meet one another, swap war stories, and buy on-line time.

Above all, don't bill users for system time. The clientele that is attracted to this type of system tends to be young and Not-Especially-Fiscally-Responsible (the "NEFR" type). Unfortunately, NEFR is when they will get around to paying your bill—if they can continue to use your system in the meantime. You may find that some users hesitate to use a system whose bill they haven't yet paid, so they put off using it until they have paid the bill. Then they never get around to paying the bill—and the result is that you've lost both the money and the user.

Per Hour or Flat Rate?

You may want to avoid the flat-rate subscription plan. This is an explosive issue with some BBSers, who don't want to "keep an eye on the clock" while they are on line. Let's look at the pros and cons. The theory is that a flat-rate subscription for unlimited usage over a month or a year works for everybody. Users don't have to fret over making utmost use of every minute they are on line, and sysops benefit by having more users who are satisfied. A quick calculation produces some heady figures: $10 a month from 200 users yields $2000 a month—enough to cover a 32-line phone bill and then some!

On the other hand, how much on-line time does each of those 200 users want for $10? Consumption differs dramatically among BBS users, from five hours every night to only one call a week. The people calling in only once a week are not likely to want to pay you $10 a month, and would prefer to pay by the hour. Those who argue for a flat-rate charge say that these light users wouldn't produce much revenue anyway—even if you charged them by the hour. Losing them from the flat-rate contingent won't harm that market base, either.

So, let's assume every one of those 200 users on the $10-a-month subscription plan are high-volume users. No problem! says the flat-rate argument. Even among heavy users, there is an average level of use. For every subscriber who logs on for five hours a night, there is one who only logs on for an hour every couple of days. Still, this totals to an average of almost three hours a day per user, and the prospect of busy signals begins to rear its ugly head. No problem! says the flat-rate argument. Just limit the daily users to only an hour per 24-hour period. This reduces the average usage—between high-volume and low-volume customers—to less than an hour per day. That leaves plenty of room on those 32 lines to accommodate everybody.

There is a negative side to imposing usage time limits on frequent, high-volume users. A person is enthusiastic about your service (five hours a night!) and is probably willing, even eager, to pay a little extra for additional time on the system, yet you tell that user you won't allow him or her to purchase that additional time. This will not be a plus for your marketing strategy.

The problem worsens if you encourage high-volume users to take out additional, burdensome subscriptions under troublesome alternate account codes. Or you could introduce "Multi-Tiered Access Plans," under which users pay different subscription rates for different monthly levels of use. This last idea actually amounts to an hourly rate, although it's more complicated—and less advantageous for users, as there will always be some fraction of time every day or every month for which they have paid but not used.

The best approach to this problem is to treat each user-hour of on-line time as a resource. You, the sysop, have a certain amount of this resource to dispense every month, and you also have certain monthly expenses to cover. Clearly, not every user-hour is of the same value to your customers: usage outside of "prime time" will be nearly zero. Let's assume that prime time lasts about six hours a day (which six hours these are will depend greatly on the nature of your BBS and your clientele).

Suppose you run a 16-line system, with the phone company charges around $800 a month for hunt-grouped lines at business rates. You have 2880 (16 × 6 × 30) user-hours a month to dispense, so your raw cost is about 28 cents per user-hour. Of course, you won't sell all 2880 every month. Specials, free samples, and sign-up time will cut into this. And remember the natural peaks and valleys in usage; you can't take advantage of the peaks, when more than 16 people want to call in, but you are fully vulnerable to the valleys. Figure that approximately half of available user-hours will sell, so your real cost is then around 56 cents an hour. (We are assuming the hobbyist mentality here, that capital, space, electricity, and people's time as a "hobbyist" all cost zero.)

If you sell these user-hours at, say, $1 an hour, you will make a small profit. Patterns of usage will show that approximately 20 percent of your users contribute 80 percent of your financial support. But then the same 20 percent of your users derive 80 percent of your total system benefit. This is a more equitable equation than the flat-rate concept, in which these percentages are dissociated.

All of your users will appreciate this, in the long run. Most complaints about charges come from the 20 percent of your users who are shouldering 80 percent of the load. They would like to shoulder only 20 percent of the load, so they have a vested interest in some of the less pragmatic aspects of the flat-rate "standard argument" outlined above. In the strictly logical way this argument is presented, this couldn't happen, but there are a variety of twisted offshoots of the basic theme in which they can (if only temporarily, as the system spirals into bankruptcy) achieve their aim. And, since they are among the biggest enthusiasts of your system, you will hear their views expressed more often, and more forcefully, than the views of others.

Not all flat-rate subscription plans, with limitations on usage per unit of calendar time, will fail. Obviously, Exec-PC does quite nicely. But it is possible that Exec-PC succeeds in spite of its subscription policy, not because of it. A sufficiently outstanding service will prosper regardless of difficulties. As you set up your own multiuser BBS, consider all the factors presented in this chapter, to give yourself the best possible chances of success.

PACKET SWITCH OR DIRECT DIAL?

An upheaval is taking place in the communications industry. Traditionally, setting up a BBS has always meant buying a modem and a phone line, and hooking up your computer. Meanwhile, the big systems like CompuServe and MCI all use "packet switching," an international networking standard, referred to technically as X25.

The hardware and software needed to communicate using X25 are very different from that of the direct-dial network. Instead of a separate modem for each user, you have just one high-speed modem for your whole system. Instead of many separate direct-dial phone lines into your building, you have just one line—a special "leased line" that is not accessible over the regular telephone network.

The big companies have gravitated toward X25 mainly to save money. The cost per hour of long-distance communications over standard voice lines is $10 to $20 or more. X25 services such as Sprintnet and TYMNET have a sliding scale of charges that averages out, in typical scenarios, to between $2 and $6 per hour. The catch is that these typical scenarios all involve large numbers of "virtual circuits" (the X25 lingo for individual phone lines, or, in BBS context, users). There are steep up-front costs involved in connecting to an X25 network, and hefty monthly minimum charges. These costs are negligible, however, in comparison to the total charge if you have large numbers of virtual circuits passing huge volumes of data every day.

A single-user BBS is not in this ball game. Even a multiuser BBS (up to four lines) is not a good candidate for X25. But in the 8-line-and-above category, X25 becomes a possible advantage. In addition to the raw cost issue, there are six key factors to consider:

1. *Does your BBS have national appeal, or are you interested mainly in your local users?* You can't be all things to all people. The national scene may be much more competitive than your local one. As far as phone line costs, you can't get any cheaper than free, which is what your local users pay for their calls. If you're making a good living running a local system, keep it up. The volume of calls you take, and the number of people you please, will surely increase as society becomes more computer-literate every day.

2. *Do you have deep pockets?* Going national is not something you should do halfway. Your fixed costs will immediately rise dramatically if you do it, so be certain that you have the resources to stick it out. Like any new venture, the going is especially rough at first, until news of your service starts to get around. Be prepared for that period during which your resource is underutilized.

3. *Who gets charged for the call?*   When someone calls your BBS long distance on the direct-dial network, they pay for the call. When someone calls your BBS over Sprintnet or TYMNET, you pay for the call. Be careful that your rate structure reflects this cost; the idea of offering "free sample" time to your prospects, prior to arranging payment, becomes problematic. Actually, there is an exciting twist to this on the horizon—the bill-through concept—which is discussed later in this chapter.

4. *Does your BBS offer sufficient value to justify the cost of communicating with it?*   A dollar-an-hour for BBS time looks pretty silly coupled with $2-an-hour for the communications charges. Given that your prospects will likely have a selection of local options, is your service unique and valuable enough to deserve their preference?

5. *Is your target market familiar with packet switch network use?* On a packet switch network, there is an extra level or two of menus for your user to deal with. Also, since the number that your user will call is different in every city, you can't publish literature and ads listing just your BBS phone number. You must offer a network "address," and your users must be savvy enough to know how to respond to the various network prompts to get to your phone number in their own city. The alternative is to provide complete phone number listings and detailed instructions in hard copy, as CompuServe does.

6. *Will your users tolerate the slow speed of a packet switch system?* The packetizing process, satellites, and other factors all lead to greater delays in both character echoing and response time. Also, the relatively inexpensive X25 arrangements described here assume the use of a single 4800 or 9600bps modem, for up to 16 users. The bps figure is divided as needed and as available, between all contending user channels. Thus 4 users, downloading files at 2400bps each, would completely saturate a 9600bps link; the other 12 users on line would experience sluggish or no response. If, instead, you go with individual phone lines and modems for each user, you could have 16 people all downloading files simultaneously at 9600bps each, and never miss a beat.

With all these negative considerations, is there any point to X25 for the independent sysop? The answer in the future may be an overwhelming yes, because of one key factor: *bill-through.*

Bill-Through

The terms of the AT&T divestiture have permitted each of the Regional Bell Operating Companies (RBOCs) to construct what most of them now call a "gateway": a means whereby they can handle the data traffic, and act as the billing agent, for information service vendors (ISVs) such as yourself.

The reason this is so critical becomes clear when you compare the fate of the American *videotex* industry with that of the French. Videotex is the generic term applied to unfortunate ventures like Miami's Viewtron, San Francisco's original Gateway, and England's Prestel—as well as to the profitable French Minitel network. Minitel began as nothing more than a way to cut telephone directory printing and distribution costs, and has become quite successful. This is in direct contrast to the other such attempts, which lost tens of millions.

Some try to explain Minitel's success with statements about the difference between American and French preferences for information services. Others cite the massive Minitel terminal giveaway as the critical factor, despite the huge base of installed, modem-equipped PCs in the United States.

The true critical difference is *convenience of payment.* American videotex experiments are considered failures only financially: they didn't make enough money to stay in business. For a business to make money with a high-volume, low-cost, mass-appeal service, it is absolutely critical that the end-user can easily pay the small amounts involved. Otherwise, the "cost" to the end-user is much more than the price charged by the vendor. Imagine how few hamburgers McDonalds would sell if the only way the customer could pay for a hamburger was by registering ahead of time, by credit card or through a monthly "hamburger subscription." Few people realize the importance of the convenience factor, because paying cash for a purchase in a normal retail business is such a familiar procedure. It's so simple that it tends to be ignored.

In France, a phone call starts a meter ticking, and you pay for your access by writing a monthly check to the phone company, which acts as a billing agent for the various ISVs. There is no extra effort for the consumer. There is only a familiar phone bill to pay, which contains some additional charges. Preregistration with each individual ISV is not necessary, as it is in the U.S. Consumers don't have to hand out their credit card numbers, for potential misuse or abuse. They don't have to make a "minimum buy" from each vendor to sample its wares, or be subjected to "demo modes" or "trial subscriptions" while their registration is processed. Upon placing the phone call and linking up with a service, consumers are instantly full-fledged members of the service, with full access to its information. For 30 seconds of usage, a user is billed for 30 seconds of usage.

The RBOCs now realize the desirability of this approach. Experimental gateways are springing up in New York City, Atlanta, San Francisco, and elsewhere. As these first ones take off, new services will be extended throughout the nation. It is unfortunate that they are all X25-based. This means that to operate a profitable BBS under a bill-through gateway, the sysop will have to charge users a minimum of 15 cents a minute, and give about 12 cents to the phone company. Still, the convenience to the user of being able to access the service so easily, without prearrangement, will be worth the higher price. And the NEFRs mentioned earlier in this chapter might not have paid *your* bill, but they will certainly pay their phone bill, or suffer disconnection.

As a financial proposition, operating a bill-through gateway makes enough sense to more than overcome the other drawbacks of X25. If only the RBOCs would offer this kind of arrangement on ordinary direct-dial lines! (Although 976 numbers offer some of the necessary characteristics, they are generally still controversial and somewhat restrictive.)

Hardware Considerations

There are two basic architectures for multiuser BBSs: multi-CPU and single-CPU. CPU stands for central processing unit, the main "brains" of any computer. In a multi-CPU design, there are as many PCs, physical or virtual, as there are incoming phone lines or virtual circuits. The PCs are all linked together in a LAN (local area network), so that they can share a common file database, user account structure, E-mail message repository, and other features and utilities. PCBoard and Wildcat are examples of products adopting this architecture.

In a single-CPU multiuser BBS, all the incoming phone lines or virtual circuits connect to a single PC. No LAN need be involved (although there can be, if necessary for other reasons). The entire task of managing up to 64 simultaneous users is handled by a single desktop machine, whose software is intrinsically multiuser. The Major BBS by Galacticomm, and TBBS are examples of products built using this architecture.

The advantages of multi-CPU operation are primarily these:

- Since each caller has his or her own private PC, the programming of the BBS itself is much simpler. The programmer can write code as though for a single-user BBS, and with some minor enhancements this single-user code can be made to operate on several machines at once, sharing a common group of database files through the LAN.

- Doors to DOS are elementary and always form part of the package. This means that other software not designed with BBS or multiuser operation in mind may be copied into the BBS with very little effort. Often this is done to provide on-line access to sophisticated single-user database programs or single-player games.

- External protocols are also simple to set up, using the same mechanism as that behind doors. This means that newly published file transfer protocols can quickly be added to an existing system, without any modifications to the underlying program.

- The architecture may be, in principle, expanded at your discretion. To add users, you can simply add nodes to your LAN. A practical limit is imposed only by the bandwidth of the LAN.

In contrast, the advantages of single-CPU operation are these:

- A much higher degree of interaction is possible among the users. This is because the delays inherent in LAN use are not present. For one on-line user to directly communicate with another, no disk files need be opened, no "pipes" come into play, and no LAN activity is generated. Data is simply moved from one memory buffer to another.

- Your job as sysop is easier and more efficient, because you can tap into any on-line session at any time, or view across-the-board input activity, all from a single console. This way you can monitor your system for people who need help, or for anomalous activity, with just a couple of keystrokes.

- System security can be higher for those third-party software applications that you do install. Doors are generally not possible; if you did turn over control to one user, everyone else on the system would be frozen out until that person was finished, because DOS is not multitasking. On the other hand, by not using doors to add features, you also sidestep the serious security risk of doors that is inherent in the transfer of full console-level (CTTY) control to an external program.

- Much lower operation and expansion costs are possible, because you don't have to buy a whole PC or its equivalent for each user. You just add modems or virtual circuits, as needed. Also, expenditures on LAN interface circuitry and software licenses are eliminated.

If you opt for X25 interface, your software vendor will recommend a specific X25 board or PAD (packet assembler/disassembler). In a multi-CPU architecture, you also need some form of X25 "server" software, so that the packet data can be properly distributed among the various CPUs on the LAN. Keep in mind that the combination of X25 with a multi-CPU architecture greatly increases traffic on the LAN, since all character I/O to or from every on-line user has to pass over the LAN. Make sure your LAN bandwidth is sufficient for the task.

If you interface with your users through an individual user modem and phone line, there are several options open to you. In a multi-CPU environment, each PC will require just one port—either a serial port connected via RS-232 cable to an external modem, or an internal modem card configured as COM1 or COM2. Alternatively, in a single-CPU multiuser environment, you have three choices:

- Multiport serial cards connected over RS-232 cables to a set of external modems

- Multimodem cards, in which the card that plugs into your PC actually contains 4, 8, or 16 modems

- An interesting new device called a "GalactiBox," from Galacticomm, which allows up to 16 standard internal modem cards to become addressable "in parallel" without conflict. You can thus plug in up to 16 internal modems, all addressed as, say, COM1, and treat them as a single "channel group"—without consuming any more of the PC's precious I/O port space than would a single conventional COM1 card

Another important issue you will encounter is the type and speed of CPU to buy, based on your projected number of users on line at one time. Consult your software vendor for detailed advice on this point. Each package is different in terms of the number of users it can support at one time and in terms of CPU class, disk speed, and user baudrates.

The question of how many users is "too many" for a given hardware configuration is difficult to address. The issue is really one of response time; that is, how long does it take after the user hits ENTER for the BBS to respond? Is half a second too slow? Two seconds? Five? This depends not only on what the user is doing, but on the individual's expectations of BBS performance, based on other systems used over time.

ON-LINE SERVICES

What kinds of BBS services attract users? File download libraries and message bases have been the mainstay of BBSs for years, and you will certainly want to support them. However, there are many other bells and whistles. Don't fall into the common misconception that the size of your file database will be a competitive edge to attract paying callers. It is a unique conceit among BBS sysops that the number of megabytes of hard disk storage supported is a measure of overall system quality. This is a myth left over from the early days, when all anyone did with these systems was upload and download files. File loading and messaging remain the only two basic functions of a single-user system.

Today you can buy a CD-ROM player for $700, and a disk for $100, with thousands of fully tested, high-quality public domain (PD) and shareware programs on it. One CD-ROM distributor, Quanta Press, even offers an entire BBS system complete with a full shareware library. Spend a week indexing and cataloging these programs, and you've got half a gigabyte or more of the greatest free software of all time on tap. If it's that easy, figure that anybody can do it, and will. You should too. So files are not going to offer you a competitive edge, unless you dedicate yourself to being among the very first to offer virtually every new PD and shareware title that comes out. The best of these programs spread like wildfire. Your only hope of getting people to consistently call you when they're looking for the latest and greatest is to be the first to have it. Keep in mind, though, that your competition is all the local, free, single-user BBSs, whose sysops are trying to beat you to the punch.

Messaging is a little easier area in which you might gain an edge. Although the contents of your message bases will depend on your unique clientele, you can promote good postings with these techniques:

- Highlight the message information in your literature, and in your system help messages.

- Read and respond to all postings of interest within a day or so of their appearance.

- Cull inappropriate postings quickly, or forward them to more appropriate areas.
- Forward to your public areas any private communications (E-mail) of general interest, and invite comment.
- Offer an award for "Message of the Week" with free live time as the prize.

Even with all this going for you, you will be fighting an uphill battle if you rely on messaging to draw users. The reason is simple: Users don't want to pay for a service they can obtain for free by calling other numbers. Your particular message base may even be unique, but the general nature of the service is widespread, and many single-user boards specialize in this kind of thing.

Other frequently touted concepts for smash-hit BBS money-makers are classified ad services, matchmaking services, and on-line employment agencies.

Classified ads seem like a natural: Newspapers take in millions of dollars daily for listing four-liners that are often lumped together in such large categories that a reader has to scan hundreds of tiny entries just to find a specific one. You could charge a small fraction of what the newspapers do, and offer keyword search capability, an updates-only service, two-directional messaging...how can it miss?

But it does—at least in today's marketplace—because of the relative scale of the enterprise. Newspapers print millions of copies every day, 99 percent of which are thrown away unread except for the front pages of each section and perhaps the comics page. The one percent who read the classifieds is further subdivided by area of interest, so that an ad might be seen by 0.01 percent of the readership, and responded to by another one-tenth of that number. Still, 0.001 percent of a million people is ten respondents—not bad if you're charging $100. Even if you can generate ten times this degree of responsiveness on your system, and assuming you have 1000 active users, .01 percent of 1000 users is 0.1 responses to a typical ad... well, you can see the odds are ten to one that there will be no response at all!

Matchmaking services may be another losing proposition. Operating a matchmaking service generally implies the use of questionnaires, and a program of some kind to match up the individuals with the best "fit." This is single-user BBS thinking. Multiuser teleconferences offer the true golden opportunity for users to get to know one another—gradually, in an amusing and risk-free electronic environment. You'll be amazed at the number of strong relationships—amorous and otherwise—that eventually form in this way on your system. You provide the forum, and your users will do the matchmaking.

The employment agency concept is a kind of hybrid of classified ads and matchmaking, with a hefty dose of dollars thrown in. There are many variations: you can charge employers to post open jobs, charge employees to search the posted jobs, or both, or just charge when a connection is made between employer and employee. Another approach is for employees to post their resumes while employers search the postings. Or both can post, in which case a "matchmaker" program comes into play. What makes these ideas work is the money participants can save. Professional search firms typically get $5000 to $20,000 or more for a single placement. Do a couple of these a month and you're in fat city. Interestingly enough, a large proportion of the people these employers are looking for are modem-aware, open to fresh ideas, and likely to call your system given the appropriate incentive.

This is another labor-intensive undertaking, like cultivation of a nationwide clientele. The employment agency field is subject to cut-throat competition (they don't call them "headhunters" for nothing). The service you provide is hardly unique, and hundreds of established firms precede you. Be careful that your listings don't turn into a prospect-generating resource for your more conventional competitors. And if you box your participants in with extensive legal paperwork, it will only alienate the legitimate ones.

If none of these get-rich-quick schemes work, then what will? Remember that the common vitality underlying all of the foregoing proposed services is that what you are offering to users is interaction amongst themselves. If you have some new concept for a specialized on-line service that will set the world on fire, so much the better. But the coming mass market for BBS services is people who want to interact with one another in new and productive ways.

So do offer file upload/download services, and file libraries of outstanding free software. Do offer extensive message bulletin boards, categorized by topic, with "threading," keyword searching, and "quickscans." Try classified ads, user registries, and employment services, too, if you like, along with any other specialized on-line services you think may have potential.

However, be prepared for the fact that the newest main attraction of a multiuser BBS will revolve around teleconferencing, as predicted by Tim Stryker of Galacticomm—a dependable source, to be sure. Your users want features that distinguish a multiuser BBS from its single-user kin. They want unique features that take advantage of the fact that many people can be on line together, simultaneously. Your users will pay you only for computer experiences they cannot have for free. Thus, it is teleconferencing and multiplayer, real-time games that offer the greatest mass market profit potential.

Look at the size of two theoretical groups (pools) of people. Pool One knows all about Zmodem, and why it's better than Xmodem or Ymodem. Pool One users like to experiment with programs for their own sake; they constantly download the latest and most amazing programs using the latest and most amazing protocols. Pool Two contains everyone else who has a computer or might be about to buy one. Pool Two people wonder whether an "X" modem is maybe one step "sexier" than an "R" modem. Furthermore, they're not into programs, they're into people.

Pool Two is much larger than Pool One. It is where the major action is, now and in the future. Because they are people-oriented, Pool Two folks are unimpressed by on-line banking, stock quotes, and newswires. They are equally immune to protocols, kilobauds, and gigabytes. On the other hand, they do get excited about talking to their friends, en masse, on line. Give them a chance to drop into the middle of an on-line poker game at midnight, or any other time they please. Let them begin to make new, good friends on line, and be free to come and go, anonymously or not. You will gain a customer for life.

The trick is getting them to try it! Most Pool Two folks are too busy to try something new unless they know for a fact that there's a point to it. BBSing is a whole new archetype for this group; introducing them to it is what the next section is all about.

DRUMMING UP BUSINESS

Never forget that the main thing you offer users is each other. This means that your system development and marketing plans must go hand in hand. You can take two different approaches: the gradual crescendo or the big bang.

In the gradual crescendo approach, you will begin with some grassroots, techie-oriented publicity methods directed toward Pool One. When you first open for business, nobody knows about you. If you were to advertise first to Pool Two, any of them who logged on would likely find themselves all alone, causing them to log off in disgust and perhaps never try your system again. So target existing BBS users first—Pool One people who like file downloads and message bases. Then, as you accumulate a core group of steady users, you can gradually expand your advertising to include the less technical types. Methods to accomplish this will be described later.

The big bang approach is more suitable for big companies, and sysops with rich uncles. The idea is to simultaneously advertise and create an environment where users will meet many new friends on line. You mount a giant advertising effort that causes hundreds of new users to try your system for the first time. Because so many people are doing the same thing, the large pool you advertised for is, in fact, created. The rest is history. Your PR can take the form of the usual press coverage, direct mail, radio, TV, and newspaper advertisements. But, if you have the money to do this sort of thing, you probably don't need this advice!

Necessary to both of these approaches is "critical mass": plenty of people to participate in your program. Concentrate on building a core group of ten or twenty users, from either Pool One or Pool Two, as long as a few of them will generally be on line during the period you consider prime time.

In the gradual crescendo approach, your biggest problem at first will be to reach the point where incoming calls overlap, so that users don't log off out of boredom while they wait for someone to talk to. Once you reach critical mass, virtually any time someone logs on, there will be another caller already on line. This will keep both users on line together, so that the next person to log on finds people already there, and so on. Getting started with your publicity campaign is simple: you post notices on other BBSs in your area that announce your new system and encourage people to give it a try. Word travels fast and far this way, among the technical elite. But don't expect a huge response right away; many new sysops make the mistake of overestimating the appeal of their announcements, and then lose heart when the response fails to meet expectations. People will have a variety of reasons for not trying your new system, including the fact that it's unproven, and they may be happy with what they have.

When one or two adventurous souls do give you a try, roll out the red carpet for them! They will enjoy the chance to contribute to the seminal stages of a thriving future enterprise, so ask them for their suggestions, and respond. Make it clear how much you appreciate their business, and sign them up as quickly as possible. Too much live time given away in a startup effort can dog your attempts to get properly underway on a paying basis. A few free hours judiciously granted here and there can prime the pump, but don't allow prospective paying customers to get used to give-aways. (In addition, don't confuse this with the "free sample" policy outlined earlier, which should be maintained indefinitely as a marketing tool. Offering free samples of non-live time in small increments, with significant restrictions, is the key to maintaining an ongoing flow of new signups.)

It is a good idea, as your system gains momentum, to make the members of your core group SIG-Ops. SIG (Special Interest Group) capability may or may not be part of the software you are using, but there is generally some way for you to delegate responsibilities and special privileges to certain users. Make your core group feel involved by giving them some of these special privileges. Consult them on key business decisions, such as software enhancements or an increase in your phone lines. If chosen wisely, these people can become your ambassadors of goodwill throughout the area. Make them feel that your system is their system.

Once you have reached critical mass, you can begin to target Pool Two users in earnest. Encourage your users to bring their friends on line. Offer bonuses for this. Call your local computer user group chairpersons and ask to give a presentation at their next meeting. Offer a special deal of some kind at these meetings, for people who respond within a few days. Announce a "parents drive," with special bonuses for kids who bring their parents on line.

Have picnics, bowling tournaments, and general BBS get-togethers, and encourage users to bring their nonuser friends and partners. Coordinate these events with other sysops in your area. Get as many people as possible caught up in the BBS social whirl, so that it becomes talked about as the "in" thing to do.

Make up flyers, with discount coupons, for distribution to computer store owners in your area, asking them to include one flyer with each modem they sell. This technique works with store managers, because it lends added value to their sales, at no cost to them. You might even code the coupons, and offer the store a small premium for each user they refer to you. Make sure, too, that you give each store a demo account on your system, for salespersons who are demonstrating modems in the store.

Don't expect any one of these measures to have a pivotal impact. Success in business generally comes after patient waiting, contrary to the glitzy stories of the rich and famous you have heard. Above all, continue to operate a consistently superior BBS, so that word-of-mouth advertising has enough time to work its magic. Each user won through quality service is worth ten window shoppers. These faithful become a group in which peer pressure demands loyalty to your system.

CONCLUSION

The success or failure of a multiuser BBS depends on, more than anything else, the personality of its sysop. If you project a genial, helpful on-line persona, users will be naturally drawn to you. If you are into control and ego gratification, they will be naturally repelled.

Be careful—running a BBS gives you a chance to "play god" in many ways. You hold the absolute power to maintain or destroy this miniature "universe" that you have created. You dispense time and privileges in this universe, as you see fit. It is easy to get carried away in demonstrations of your power—disconnecting dubious users, snooping into people's E-mail, deleting messages from people you don't like, demanding conformance to arbitrary rules in exchange for permission to log on—but don't fall into this role.

Be Mellow

Maintain an upbeat tone in your messages. Let users know you are pleased to be of service when answering their questions. Greet them by name whenever possible, and make them feel welcome on your system, freeloaders or otherwise.

CHAPTER NINE

BBS Programs

In this chapter we will discuss some very good BBS software packages. The ones covered are a good representation of what's available and do not all take the same approach. Some are message based, others are file oriented, and still others emphasize interaction with the caller. You can use any one of these programs with full confidence in its reliability.

To get a feel for the different types of bulletin boards, sign onto a few operating systems and find one that appeals to you. Sysops welcome interested visitors. Since most BBS program vendors keep lists of systems that use their products, you can contact them for more information. BBS-oriented magazines are another good way to keep abreast of what's out there.

THE BULLETIN BOARD PROGRAMS

The following is a nearly complete list of available systems. Due to constant price changes and updates, prices have not been included. They may vary from $25 for a shareware registration up to $1000 for an elaborate 99-line commercial system.

READ.ME

Boardwatch Magazine: A BBS Resource

Each month *Boardwatch Magazine* editor Jack Rickard packs this valuable resource with some of the most concise, comprehensive information available on the BBS scene and its related technologies. He covers new developments and fills each edition with interviews, articles, first looks at new pertinent technologies, and whatever else he thinks will be of interest to either sysops or BBS rangers. Rickard writes most of each edition himself, in a straightforward, informative style. He also does most of the research himself. It's an eccentric, enjoyable magazine to read.

Boardwatch Online Information Service, a multiline service that carries the electronic edition of *Boardwatch*, keeps a finger on the BBS pulse and provides extensive listings of other on-line services. It also offers downloadable dialing directories, terminal programs, and utilities, plus a wealth of on-line periodicals — including a daily newspaper.

For more information, contact *Boardwatch Magazine*, 5970 South Vivian St., Littleton, CO 80127. Or call 303-973-6038 (voice) or 303-973-4222 (data).

PCBoard

PCBoard is probably the best known and most popular BBS software sold today. Written originally in BASIC, new version 14.5 scheduled for release during 1990 has been rewritten completely in C and Assembler. It now incorporates almost all the features of ProDoor (Chapter 10), including a full-screen editor. PCBoard features a single menu for all system functions, rather than the more common separate menus for messages and file functions. Menu text and display characteristics are configurable. Multilingual support is also available.

PCBoard is controlled with the PCBSysMgr program, which in turn can call the PCBSetup program, the PCBFiler program, and the PCBDiag utility. Many of the changes made in the PCBSysMgr can be executed while users are connected. Other batch changes require nodes in a multiline system to be dropped to DOS prior to operation. PCBoard also packs the user file to permanently remove deleted users and create a smaller file with proper indexing. All user and file maintenance is performed from within the external utility.

The SysMgr also lets you create a table to adjust the user's security level based on file transfer activity. Security level changes may be triggered by ratios of uploads to downloads, the total number of downloads, or just the number of uploads. Conference maintenance is also handled from within the SysMgr and allows the sysop to move or delete users from conference sections.

The PCBFiler utility is used to create the DIR listings file, stored as text descriptions in an ASCII file. It eases file maintenance by making list changes as the actual disk files are moved or altered.

Up to 65,000 conferences may be defined. Each conference may include a related file transfer area and may have specific or shared doors, bulletins, news files, or script questionnaires. PCB supports up to 32,767 messages per conference, with an individual message length of up to 99 lines. Interaction with Netmail and Echomail is supported through front-end programs and separate message reading programs. Messages to a caller are checked upon entering a main board or conference.

A large number of doors have been written specifically for PCBoard. It can address an unlimited number of doors and offers an external program to monitor for CTRL-C, CTRL-BREAK, and CTRL-P, although it does not monitor for loss of carrier. Exiting from a door entered from within a conference returns the caller to that same conference.

The PCBoard file system internally supports file transfer using ASCII, Xmodem (checksum), Xmodem-CRC, 1K Xmodem, and 1K-Xmodem-G. No batch transfer protocols are internal to PCBoard. An additional 21 protocols may be added externally through a shell procedure.

Multiline versions of PCBoard make use of DOS 3.x file sharing and perform the necessary file locking for up to 99 nodes. Two nodes may be operated on one AT system utilizing any COM port from COM1 through COM8. Cross-node chat (CB Chat) is supported. The network/multiline version of PCBoard includes an additional Network Node Monitoring utility (PCBMoni) that can be operated from a command line or by pressing ALT-M at a live PCB node. It provides information about each node, including its status and the user connected.

PCBoard requires a hard disk. A 99-line version is available.

Address   Clark Development Company, Inc., P.O. Box 71365, Murray, UT 84157

Voice Phone   1-801-261-1686

BBS Phone   1-801-261-8976

Wildcat! BBS

The Wildcat! BBS System is a full-featured electronic BBS. Connection speeds, using normal phone lines, range from 300 to 38,400 baud on any COM port address.

Wildcat! can be installed as a single-line BBS or a multiline system. The configuration program MAKEWILD is the heart of the install process. Wildcat! provides a point-and-load system for modem setup. Your only chore is to highlight your modem model from a window list and press ENTER.

Rather than maintain text lists or data files containing the valid user names, files available, or messages, Wildcat! saves this information in databases with fast B-Tree ISAM sorting and multiple indexed fields for virtually instant data access. A second advantage to the database concept is record-based locking rather than full-file locking. Major manipulation of files, messages, and users in a multiline or network system is possible even while callers remain on line.

The caller's options (while connected) include the standard BBS fare. The menu system revolves around the main menu, allowing access to a file menu, bulletin menu, message menu, and questionnaire menu.

Wildcat!'s questionnaires are custom designed by the sysop using a special full-screen editor. Real-time branching to other questions (based on how a caller responds) provides great flexibility. Question types include free-form text, phone numbers, four different credit card types, social security numbers, dates, and customized multiple choices. Up to 9999 questionnaires may be created.

The message section allows callers to place messages in sections referred to as folders. Each folder may be used to separate messages by content, user type, or any criteria desired. Each security level is given access to any combination of message folders. Wildcat! offers a number of other message options, including a local "snapshot" to the printer, forwarding to third parties, notification to the author when mail is received (return receipt), and import of the text of a file into a message at any point. Importing allows the sysop to create a text file of any length and include reference to the file with a single text-coded message line. It saves space in the message file since the text is dynamically sent to the caller when the message is read. When a sysop wants to change the message text, a single file change reflects the revision in all messages.

The file section also has the standard BBS fare—downloading and uploading using ASCII, Xmodem, Xmodem-CRC, and 1K Xmodem. Internal support is also included for multiple file downloading using Ymodem and Ymodem-G of up to 50 files, and uploading of up to 200 files. External protocols also extend batch file transfers using Zmodem, Kermit, Jmodem, Bimodem, SEAlink, and many more. The file area also offers the ability to view the contents of files that have been compressed.

Other Wildcat! features of interest are

- The sysop menu offers access to the databases.

- The User Database menu choice displays a full-screen record for each user.

- The File Database option displays complete information on each file in the system.

- The Event Manager schedules automatic system maintenance at any time on a daily or weekly basis.

- The CATEYE utility (a small TSR program) may be run on any LAN workstation, or in a foreground application under DESQview when multiple lines are installed.

Versions after 2.0 require an IBM PC, XT, AT, or 100-percent compatible, any monitor type, 234K RAM, and MS-DOS 3.1 or higher. A hard disk is recommended. A shareware version is available. Source code is not available.

The 250-page WILDCAT! manual comes in a three-ring binder with slipcase. Almost half of it addresses the setup program MAKEWILD, covering much the same information as you'll find in the help screens. The rest of the manual explains program features, including details of available display files. There are separate sections for server-based LANs, peer-to-peer LANs, DESQview, and slave cards.

Support is available by phone, on the multiline Mustang Software BBS, and on CompuServe in the PC Vendors Forum.

Address   Mustang Software, Inc., 3125 19th St., Suite 162, Bakersfield, CA 93301

Voice Phone   1-805-395-0223

BBS Phone   1-805-395-0650

RBBS-PC

Remote Bulletin Board System-PC is one of the oldest BBS programs available for the PC. There have been 32 releases since the first release in July of 1983. It includes the major features of many other BBS systems, including bulletins, electronic mail (public and private), file exchange (uploading and downloading), on-line questionnaires based on "scripts" written by the sysop, and access to other applications from RBBS-PC (that is, doors). Support is included for 300-19200 baud.

RBBS-PC allows an unlimited number of conferences, each with its own set of files, messages, questionnaires, doors, and more, and a user's security level that can be changed for each conference.

Messages may be as long as 99 lines and may be public, private, or addressed to a group of callers. Text files may be uploaded into messages, and the sysop may import text to a message.

File transfer protocols available internally include ASCII, Xmodem (Checksum and CRC), and Ymodem. An unlimited number of external protocols are allowed. Access to files may be set based on the subdirectory, disk drive, filename, file extension, or a wildcard file list. Questionnaires are composed of script commands edited by the sysop using a standard text editor. External system events are configurable for any number of batch processes, at any time of day. Up to 99 bulletins may be defined. The menu structure is sysop definable and may be presented as a single large menu or with submenus for functions such as files and messages.

RBBS-PC requires an IBM PC, XT, AT, or 100-percent compatible, any monitor type, 320K RAM (640 recommended), MS-DOS 2.0 (3.1 or higher recommended), and a single floppy disk (a hard disk is recommended). It supports 300-19200 baud. The compiled program is available for $8 through Capitol PC Software Exchange. Source code in BASIC is also available.

Author   Thomas Mack

BBS Phone   1-203-268-5315 and 1-203-268-0129

Coauthor   Jon Martin

BBS Phone   1-415-689-2090

Coauthor   Ken Goosens

READ.ME

RBBS-PC in a BOX

Through the cooperation of the authors of RBBS-PC, Tom Mack, Jon Martin, and Ken Goosens; the sysop of RBBS-PC of Chicago, Loren Jones; PKware and others, Quanta Press has produced the first CD-ROM that actually installs itself as a complete, operating, fully functional bulletin board system for IBM PC and compatibles.

The disk contains over 7000 verified public domain freeware and shareware programs. It can also be used as a databank library and accessed off line.

The disk is available directly from the publisher, Quanta Press, by phone or fax.

Coauthors   Tom Mack, Jon Martin, and Ken Goosens

Address   Quanta Press, 2239 Carter Avenue, St. Paul, MN 55108

Voice Phone   1-612-641-0714

Fax   1-612-644-8811

BBS Phone   1-703-978-6360

Address   Capitol PC Software Exchange, P.O. Box 6128, Silver Springs, MD 20906

The Major BBS

This multiuser BBS was originally developed as a part of a software/hardware package manufactured by Galacticomm, Inc. The earlier versions of the Major BBS ran only in conjunction with Breakthrough, a multimodem plug-in card for the IBM PC family. The current offering functions in Multiuser mode on a single PC or AT with a variety of multiport cards. The software can be configured to support up to 64 simultaneous users, depending on hardware. Its specialty has been the connection of multiple phone lines to a single PC without the need for multitasking programs such as DESQview and DoubleDOS, or network hardware. It offers fully configurable port base addresses for each channel when modem or serial connections are used.

User accounting and statistics are a prominent feature of The Major BBS. Users may be charged for many specific services and features, and the BBS will deduct specific credit amounts from the user's account.

Teleconferencing is a system similar to the internode chat on many BBS systems. Callers can select from over 65,000 separate channels to hold their conversation, much like an expanded citizens band radio system.

SIGs (or special interest groups) are built around a message database for users to exchange messages and files. Uploading and downloading files are performed within any SIG to which a user has access using Xmodem (Checksum and CRC) and Ymodem.

Other features include a separate text area for Classified Ads, and private E-mail with return receipt and file attachment options. Polls and questionnaires (up to 10 with 20 questions each) can be created with the configuration utility, which the sysop can use to configure the system at four levels:

- Quick setup

- Normal configuration

- Detailed configuration

- C source-code modification

A built-in configuration editor called CNF provides full-screen support for the first three levels. At the C source level, the programmer has full control to add or modify every feature in the system. Several companies offer third-party add-ons to The Major BBS at the C source level. Packages include a FidoNet Echomail interface, forums, multiplayer poker, and several other advanced games.

Doors, external file-transfer protocols, and other programs operating outside of the BBS are not supported due to the internal multiuser operation. However, The Major BBS is compatible with multitasking DOS-like environments like DoubleDOS and DESQview. It also can be operated remotely through piggyback products such as PCAnywhere.

In addition to the standard system, Galacticomm offers four Extended Editions, any one of which may be added to the program. Incorporating more than one edition requires purchasing source code and performing recompilation to add the additional features.

- The Entertainment Edition adds two real-time multiplayer games— Androids and Quest for Magic.

- The Shopping Mall Edition adds the ability to set up vendors with specific listings of items for sale or services.

- The MenuMan Edition adds the ability to create custom menus and on-line information.

- The File Library Edition provides enhanced file transfer and mainte-nance to the standard edition.

Version 5 requires an IBM PC, XT, AT, 386 or 486, or 100-percent compatible, any monitor type, 512K RAM, MS-DOS 3.0 or higher, and a hard disk. It supports 300-9600 baud. The price varies depending on the version purchased.

Unlimited support (within reason) is available by phone, fax, and BBS. The 220-page paperback documentation included with the package answers most users' questions.

In addition to the BBS, Galacticomm offers several hardware platforms that support multiple (up to 64) modems or serial ports on a single PC. Small systems can start with one or two standard Hayes-compatible COM1/COM2-type modems, and expand from there.

Address   Galacticomm, Inc., 4101 S.W. 47th Ave., Suite 101, Ft. Lauderdale, FL 33314

Demo BBS   1-305-321-2410

Voice Phone   1-305-583-5990

TBBS (The Bread Board System)

TBBS is one of a few BBS programs that can be configured as a multiline system using only a single PC/AT without the assistance of multitasking programs such as DESQview and DoubleDOS, or a network configuration. All multiport addressing is performed internally. It is a system with tremendous flexibility and power that requires a degree of software and DOS sophistication to master. It will function with up to 32 lines at speeds from 300-19200 baud (depending on hardware) and is written in assembly language.

TBBS uses a series of editors (CEDIT, MEDIT, and QAEDIT), each responsible for constructing a specific portion of the overall program. Once configured, TBBS offers the functions of 40 separate menu commands and may be used to support up to 63 separate or combined, public or private, message boards. The program derives much of its power from the fact that the main program does not have any hard-coded structure as such, but takes its structure from the control files defined by the system operator.

An accounting system provides the ability to place callers into Billing Classes used to limit or account for time spent in certain menus. Time accrues while the caller is in the menu, and billing is then easily computed.

Message features include carbon copies, return receipts, distribution lists, files attached to messages, and threaded reply chains.

The file section supports transfers using Xmodem, 1K Xmodem, Ymodem, SEAlink, Kermit, Super Kermit, and Zmodem.

TBBS features a questionnaire and voting system that allows text answers and can tally answers from a voting file.

Doors are not available due to the method of multiline control. The Integrated Mail System (TIMS) runs multiline automated mail sessions for systems up to 32 lines. It provides store-and-forward FidoNet-compatible mail handling that makes TBBS into a 24-hour multiline mail hub. It can also process incoming file requests, message exchanges, and Echomail.

Another powerful enhancement to TBBS, The Data Base System (TDBS), provides an extension language for TBBS with a full-power database engine included. This opens the door to true on-line remote transaction processing.

TBBS requires an IBM PC, XT, AT, or 100-percent compatible, any monitor type, 512K RAM, and MS-DOS 3.0 or higher; a hard disk is recommended. It supports 300-19200 baud. Pricing varies depending on the version purchased. Source code is not available.

Address   eSoft, Inc., 15200 E. Girard Ave., Suite 2550, Aurora, CO 80014

Voice Phone   1-303-699-6565

Fido

Fido is both a specific bulletin board system and the largest amateur mail system in the world. The BBS system was once a shareware program, but now is distributed as a commercial product. It offers full connectivity to the FidoNet mail system with additional local message support and file transfer capabilities. FidoNet is covered in more detail in Chapter 5, so it will not be discussed here.

Address   Fido Software, Inc., 164 Shipley, San Francisco, CA 94107

Magpie

If one word describes Magpie BBS, it's "unique." Most BBS software offers some form of message threading in order to provide a contextual framework for messages, but Magpie takes it one step further and creates formal links between messages and their replies.

Logically, Magpie's message base is a large, upside-down tree. A tree structure would be an academic feature if the Magpie didn't also provide users with commands to move around the BBS using these linkages. You navigate messages on Magpie in much the same way that you navigate menus in other software. In fact, Magpie is mostly modeless in operation and largely devoid of chatty menus.

Magpie's strength is in organizing discussion. Users can move freely around the message base, accessing older messages as easily as newer ones. This enhances Magpie's usefulness as a public information BBS for product support systems and the like. Many private sysops also appreciate Magpie's structure because it allows them great control over their BBS's appearance and topical design. Magpie supports 200 discussion areas, each of which may also support a secured "internal" discussion area with separate read and read/write permissions for all users. This is convenient for applications where you may want everyone to be able to read a certain subdiscussion, but only certain people to be able to write or post replies to it.

Magpie is a novel system in several other ways, too. One is its download file interface. Where most BBSs whisk users off to another area of the software to display and download files, Magpie employs the same tree structure and the same message base commands for its download file library. An added benefit: Because download files are "attached" to messages, file descriptions may be as long as the maximum length of any Magpie message—10,000 characters!

To enhance Magpie's usefulness as an archival information system, there's a very powerful message searching function that allows users to search for messages by text phrases, author, recipient, attached filename, date, or any combination simultaneously.

Yet another novelty is Magpie's handling of private mail. Each user creates and owns a public mailbox, which can be personalized by the user to introduce himself or herself to others.

External programs may be hosted in Magpie's open window, with a control file limiting program execution to given times of day for users with a given access level.

Like many BBSs, Magpie employs a fossil driver for compatibility with a growing number of third-party programs that require one, and also to simplify the chore of writing custom programs for Magpie.

Magpie is one of the few BBSs supporting multiple operating systems. Currently, Magpie runs with DOS, SCO XENIX, and with SVR3 UNIX supporting the unified 80386 COFF. Under SCO XENIX, Magpie may support up to 128 simultaneous users on appropriate hardware.

Author   Steve Manes

Address   Roxy Recorders, Inc., 648 Broadway, Suite 300, New York, NY 10012

Searchlight

Searchlight is a BBS that offers single and multiline operation with several unique features. The most notable of these is the ANSI support for cursor movement throughout the program, which allows built-in full-screen editing similar to the WordStar commands. This feature extends to the menus, messages, and all other areas where single-letter command selection is usually the choice.

Netmail and Echomail are not directly supported, but front-end programs (see Chapter 10) can be used with the program. Electronic personal mail is a separate, independent function.

Bulletins in Searchlight also function differently from most other systems. Bulletins are simply system messages that are stored in a special message base, one that lets users with a high enough access to enter more "bulletins."

Door support is provided in each sub-board up to a maximum of 40. Like most other BBS sytems, programs using direct video writing will not operate properly even with Searchlight's port management turned on. Questionnaires are not directly supported, but may be implemented through a door interface.

The multinode version operates each node as a separate task or on a separate PC on a network. File locking is used to prevent conflicts, and an internode chat system is supported.

File access is security controlled, and file transfer may be done with Xmodem, Xmodem-CRC, and 1K Xmodem, with an additional nine external protocols. Batch uploads are also supported. File directories may be displayed in alphabetical or date order. Automatic filename completion lets the user type only the first few characters of a long filename. Searchlight then prompts with the matching filename, or presents choices if there are two or more matches.

Searchlight requires an IBM PC, XT, AT, or 100-percent compatible, any monitor type, 250K RAM, MS-DOS 3.0 or higher, and a hard disk is recommended. It supports 300-19200 baud. Searchlight is distributed in a shareware version. Source code is not available.

Author   Frank LaRosa

Address   Searchlight Software, P.O. Box 131, Plainview, NY 11803

BBS Phone   1-516-724-0971

WWIV

Wayne Bell designed WWIV to let callers access as many options with as few keystrokes as possible. Callers can view a caller's log, vote on sysop-specified topics, and view a list of other BBSs. The system offers context-sensitive help, but most users need to know only a few commands to feel comfortable.

WWIV uses external programs for many functions, making configurations and upgrades flexible and easy for the sysop. External file-transfer protocols like Zmodem and SEAlink can be added in minutes (Xmodem, Ymodem, and Ymodem-Batch are internal). WWIV can support up to four archiving programs (like ZIP, ARC, PAK, and LZH), allowing users to list files, extract files, and create temporary archives for downloading files.

The system supports external full-screen editors. This gives greater flexibility than internally designed full-screen editors. Since sysops can specify multiple editors, users can choose their favorite or go with the internal line-oriented editor. WWIV also supports external door programs for games and other purposes.

Unlike other BBSs, WWIV stores private mail and public messages separately. WWIV BBSs are compatible with FidoNet and can be linked with 300 participating WWIVnet systems in the U.S. and Canada.

From the sysop's point of view, WWIV is very flexible. It allows up to 32 different public message areas, with some message areas and file sections requiring special security access. System abilities such as sending mail, posting public messages, working with archives, and downloading can be given or restricted on a user-by-user basis.

WWIV supports 300/1200/2400 baud. Executable source code (23,000 lines of Turbo C) is available to registered users. Registration is $50 (plus $5 for the code disk).

Author   Wayne Bell

Address   P.O. Box 636, 904 Silver Spur Road, Rolling Hills Estates, CA 90274

BBS Phone   1-213-208-6689

Opus

Opus is a BBS program placed in the public domain by Wynn Wagner III, and it is "militantly public domain," according to the author. It is primarily used by long-time FidoNet sysops who are accustomed to writing complicated text control files with the accompanying extended batch files. If anyone profits from the use of Opus, or recommends it to another and profits, then a $50 donation to the Shanti Project (an AIDS support group) is mandatory.

Although Opus has been used for some time as a method of implementing both Netmail and Echomail, the program is complex and not very well supported. The documentation includes completely new terminology for standard BBS functions—such as CBCS (Computer Based Conversation System) rather than BBS, BARK rather than the more standard File Request in a FidoNet system, and Matrix Mail as a substitute for the standard Netmail.

Opus provides a complete FidoNet-compatible mail system without the need for a front-end program such as D'Bridge or SEAdog. All mail functions, with the exception of making or unpacking mail, are included. A separate program, OMMM (Opus Matrix Message Masher), is added to the batch-file process to perform this function.

Message sections in Opus may be flagged as public, private, anonymous, or password protected. Features include forwarding and import and export of messages from disk files.

The file section of Opus supports transfers using Xmodem, Ymodem, Zmodem, Telink, and SEAlink. Up to 10 additional external protocols may be added.

Opus requires an IBM PC, XT, AT, or 100-percent compatible, any monitor type, MS-DOS 3.1 or higher, and a serial-port fossil driver; a hard disk is recommended. It supports 300-9600 baud.

Author Wynn Wagner III

BBSXpress

Also known as The Personal BBS, it is targeted at the single-user system operator who is being abandoned by many other professional BBS systems, according to the author. It's an easy-to-set-up system that offers most of the standard BBS features, including doors. It allows an unlimited number of multiple SIG (special interest group) areas for both messages and files.

BBSXpress requires an IBM PC, XT, AT, or 100-percent compatible, any monitor type, 200K RAM, and MS-DOS 2.0 or higher. A hard disk is recommended, and it supports 300-9600 baud. BBSX is distributed in a shareware version. Source code is not available.

Author Richard B. Levin

Address P.O. Box 14546, Philadelphia, PA 19115

BBS Phone 1-215-333-8275

Professional OLEcom

Professional OLEcom is a very configurable BBS system written in C and assembler. The sysop makes use of four special editors, one each for the system configuration, the menus, the user log, and the message base.

The configuration editor defines up to 128 separate message bases, 32 terminal types, new user default privilege levels, authorization flags, and all systemwide features. The strong point of the configuration is the ability to fully customize user terminal definition.

Menus in OLEcom offer immediate keystroke response and are totally configurable. The message bases are each configured as E-mail (private only) or Standard (public and private access).

The file section in OLEcom lists files with 35 character descriptions. It supports Xmodem, Ymodem, Zmodem, SEAlink, and MegaLink protocols.

OLEcom includes a Survey Command Language for questionnaires and surveys that is a rather complex program-oriented method of preparing questionnaire files. It operates well, but does require some programming or script file language knowledge.

OLEcom requires IBM PC, XT, AT, or 100-percent compatible, any monitor type, 512K RAM (640 recommended), MS-DOS 3.1 or higher, and a hard disk. It supports 300-2400 baud. A shareware version is available. No Netmail or Echomail. Source code is not available.

Author   John T. Oleson & Associates

Address   P.O. Box 290951, Temple Terrace, FL 33687

BBS Phone   1-813-980-2981

TCOMM

TCOMM, written in Microsoft C and assembler, offers standard BBS fare in both a shareware and registered user package. An extremely flexible system, it supports from 300-38400 baud and allows setup of up to 100 caller "groups," of which 36 may be private. Groups, similar to conferences, may include bulletins, remote programs, and download files. Only preregistered callers can access these groups.

Message handling includes message threading and forward and backward reading. Up to 90 lines per message are allowed, with each message stored as a separate file. Messages are automatically deleted after a predetermined period of time.

The file system offers Xmodem, Ymodem, and Kermit, with nine others added as external protocols. Users may view compressed files or perform downloads from within a compressed file using external programs. TCOMM has support for Netmail or Echomail through external front-end programs, and mail is imported to the TCOMM message groups.

One unique feature of TCOMM is the inclusion of a smart terminal program that may be executed without exiting, and the ability to make use of any other terminal program without exiting.

Questionnaires can be implemented through external programs via the door interface. Doors are supported with program monitoring to ensure the connection has not been lost.

TCOMMnet is the multiuser version of TCOMM and is available only as a registered release.

TCOMM requires IBM PC, XT, AT, or 100-percent compatible, any monitor type, 256K RAM, MS-DOS 2.1 or greater, and two disk drives. It supports 300-38400 baud. A shareware version is available. Source code is not available.

Address The CommSoft Group, P.O. Box 3652, Gaithersburg, MD 20878

BBS Phone 1-301-428-7931

TPBoard

TPBoard was designed for easy setup and low maintenance. It is written in Turbo Pascal and makes use of database indexed files for storage of system information on files, messages, and users. Baud rates include 300-38400.

TPBoard allows up to nine conferences, each with its own set of messages and files available to callers. The message section supports the standard features and adds a line editor with ANSI cursor movement support for making single-line corrections. It will connect to most front-end mailer programs for access to Netmail and Echomail.

The file section supports transfer using internal versions of Xmodem (Checksum, CRC, and 1K), Ymodem, and Zmodem, as well as 1K-Xmodem-G and Ymodem-G for error-checking modems. No external protocols are implemented. Contents of a compressed file (.ARC, .ZIP) may be viewed or sent using external programs. After a time set by the sysop, files uploaded by users are automatically moved from an upload directory into a directory selected by the uploader. The sysop can change the destination directory, of course.

TPBoard supports RBBS-type doors and can also run other programs using external utilities. It does not support questionnaires, but does allow programmed maintenance at predetermined times.

TPBoard requires IBM PC, XT, AT, or 100-percent compatible, any monitor type, 200K RAM, MS-DOS, and two disk drives. It supports 300-38400 baud. A shareware version is available; registration information is included with the shareware release. Source code is not available.

Coauthors   Jon Schneider & Rick Petersen

Address   Southwest Systems Group, 5436 Van Horn, El Paso, TX 79924

BBS Phone   1-915-592-4976

MiniHost

MiniHost was specifically designed to perform basic BBS functions while remaining a small, easy-to-operate program. Although it has grown in features over the years, it remains a system for basic host functions.

The notable features in MiniHost include a callback mode that allows the sysop to specify a phone number for MiniHost to dial back when a specific user calls in. It also has a "ringback" feature for sharing the BBS, and a voice phone line. Ringback instructs the program to ignore any calls unless they are immediately preceded by a single-ring call.

MiniHost allows basic messages and file transfer, making use of the major protocols available in DSZ, such as Xmodem, Ymodem, and Zmodem. The number of users is limited to 500.

MiniHost requires IBM PC, XT, AT, or 100-percent compatible, any monitor type, 200K RAM, MS-DOS 3.0 or higher, and two floppy drives. It supports 300-2400 baud. A shareware version is available. Source code is not available.

Author   Don Mankin

Address   3211 Crow Canyon Place, #A296, San Ramon, CA 94583

BBS Phone   1-209-836-2402

Phoenix

Phoenix BBS is an outgrowth of the former Colossus and Collie BBS systems. It is written in Turbo Pascal and supports the basic BBS features. Up to 9999 Bulletins may be made available, and it handles 300-9600 baud.

Like WWIV, Phoenix supports its own net, called Phoenix Net, a group of BBSs linked in the same manner as the better-known and larger FidoNet.

Phoenix requires an IBM PC, XT, AT, or 100-percent compatible, any monitor type, 512K RAM, and MS-DOS 2.0 or higher, and will operate on a two-floppy system. A shareware version is available. Source code is not available.

Address   The GeneSys Project, Box 190, Willingboro, NJ 08046

Auntie

Auntie was developed with the primary objective of a user-friendly attitude. It includes up to 32 threaded message sections, with a rich set of "message tree" traversing commands. Each of these "sections" or "topics" has the ability to ARChive or ZIP messages for downloading.

Both upload and download make use of Omen Technology's DSZ program (no protocols are internal to Auntie), and both require that the sysop obtain a registered copy for operation. All DSZ protocols are supported including Xmodem, Ymodem, and Zmodem, with batch transfers where allowed. Other external protocols that can be added include Kermit and Jmodem.

Users may easily search the file listings with a DOS-like DIR command that supports wildcards.

Auntie will operate doors, but only those written specifically for version 14.x of PCBoard. It also offers questionnaire files that are created by the sysop as text strings and will prompt callers for information. No branching or output formatting is implemented. Up to 99 bulletins are supported.

A rather unique feature is the Rating System that rates users based on number of logons, number of messages entered, and number of uploads and downloads.

Auntie requires an IBM PC, XT, AT, or 100-percent compatible, any monitor type, 512K RAM, MS-DOS 3.0 or higher, and a hard disk. It supports 300-9600 baud. A shareware version is available for a 30-day evaluation. Source code is not available.

Author W.J. Meier

Address M&M Associates, 230 Park Lake Circle, Suite B, Walnut Creek, CA 94598

Spitfire BBS

Spitfire, a single-line system written in Turbo Pascal, has most normal BBS features. The message system allows reading in any of 40 areas and has an option to set up a "queue" of message areas to access. It supports carbon copies for up to three other users. Messages are limited to 60 lines.

It is DESQview aware, and will allow running the BBS in the background while another application is in the foreground if enough memory is available.

File transfer supports ASCII, Xmodem (Checksum, CRC, and 1K), SEAlink, Telink, and batch download using Ymodem and Ymodem-G for modems with hardware error-checking. External file-transfer protocols are also supported.

Up to nine questionnaires are configurable using text line prefixes for command direction, and can be created using any text editor.

The sysop can configure up to 24 doors internally, with expansion capabilities through third-party utility programs.

Spitfire is totally compatible with front-end programs like FrontDoor and BinkleyTerm for Netmail and Echomail processing. However, it lacks event support and so cannot guarantee that the BBS will go off line to callers during the national mail hour. For this reason it is not commonly used with Netmail and Echomail.

System display files may use ANSI color and control codes.

Version 2.7 requires an IBM PC, XT, AT, or 100-percent compatible, any monitor type, 256K RAM, MS-DOS 3.1 or higher, and a hard disk. It supports 300-9600 baud. Spitfire is distributed as shareware and can be used for a trial period of 30 days or 500 callers. Source code is not available.

Address Buffalo Creek Software, 913 39th Street, West Des Moines, IA 50265

BBS Phone 1-515-225-8496

GAP

GAP is a full-featured system written in C and assembler that includes a number of unique concepts. GAP's loyal following benefits from its impressive update record. It is available in single and multiline configurations. It can handle an unlimited number of users, files, and messages. It supports 99 nodes, record locking, 90 forums, and over 9000 bulletins and questionnaires.

The user file can hold up to two billion user names, indexed by both name and security level. GAP's caller database includes total bytes uploaded and downloaded, files uploaded and downloaded, number of messages left and read, number of bulletins read, birthdays, and a sysop-maintainable comment field.

The files system on GAP is perhaps its most powerful feature. File searches are lightning fast, due to the use of keyword indexes. An external Filebase Editor is provided that allows full-screen, interactive editing of individual files. The editor provides searching capability, listing of subjects, moving and deletion of files, and listing of archive contents. The Utility section lets the sysop update files, create a master file listing, perform global moves, and add any stray files on the disk to the filebase. Callers can view files based on subject matter, keyword searches, filenames, or recently uploaded files. GAP displays files either in a condensed or an enhanced format, depending upon caller preference.

GAP gives callers a true internode chat mode that lets them chat directly with other callers. No gimmicks like temporary disk files are required, so there is none of the delay usually experienced with internode chats.

There is internal support for ASCII, Xmodem, Xmodem-CRC, Xmodem-1K, Ymodem-Batch, and Zmodem protocols and up to eight external protocols. It supports two external events and unlimited doors.

Questionnaires make use of an intelligent script language. The files system internally supports archived file viewing and reading.

GAP requires an IBM XT, AT, or 100-percent compatible, any monitor type, 240K of memory, MS-DOS 3.1 or higher, and a hard disk. It operates up to 38400 baud and supports the 16550 UART chip. GAP is distributed commercially or in a shareware version. Source code is available as a separate programmer's kit.

Support is available by phone or from one of four support BBSs that serve GAP sysops. The GAP Development Co. maintains a forum on the National Echo Mail Network to provide local support to users.

Address   GAP Communications, GAP Development Company, 24242 Porto Fino — RT7715, Laguna Niguel, CA 92677

BBS #1   1-714-493-3819

BBS #2   1-714-493-9851

CHAPTER TEN

Front-ends, Doors, Games, and Agents

This chapter describes several types of programs designed to interact with you, or the host system, or both, to make life on line easier and more fun.

- *Front-ends* automate BBS mail networks
- *Doors* let BBSs safely transfer program control to callers
- *Games* have proliferated in the BBS doors environment
- *Agent* programs help callers collect, read, and reply to mail and messages, and navigate large information systems

You will run across one or more of these programs at some point in your electronic travels. Here is what they are about.

BBS FRONT-ENDS

When calling a BBS, you may sometimes find that a program other than the BBS itself seems to have answered the call. You'll have to wait a few seconds, or enter an escape code to load the BBS software and continue with the session. Your call has been answered by a *front-end program*. One of the most common front-ends is called BinkleyTerm. Front-ends are used to handle Netmail on a BBS. When the front-end answers the phone, it queries you to determine, through a special protocol, if the call is coming from another electronic mail system. If it gets the response that indicates this is a mail transfer, the front-end transfers the mail to and from the calling system. Otherwise, it simply exits and loads the BBS software.

FidoNet mail runs are usually done through a front-end as described, but there are variations on the theme. Other Netmail or Echomail systems log on to the BBS as a user and then drop into a door (see below) to execute the mail transfer. In others, the BBS itself may directly load the mail handling program. In all cases, the idea is to give automated network mail capability to BBS programs.

DOOR PROGRAMS

Many BBSs offer something called *doors*. What are they and what do they do? The term came from the idea that a door program can let you leave a BBS and pass through a "door" into a new and different independent program. The new program may be a game, an editor, or any other function not governed directly by the BBS itself.

It is a brilliant idea that sweeps away the limiting horizons of the sysop's BBS software. With doors, sysops can personalize their bulletin boards in previously unimagined ways. The power and scope of what a sysop can offer are hugely expanded, and a small industry has quickly developed to supply a growing demand for new and interesting door programs.

How Doors Work

Most BBS programs now support the door function, though the name of the technique may differ from board to board. For example, Wildcat BBSs call them *live programs*, which may be more descriptive from a user's point of view. The function, though, is always the same—to leave the BBS and run another program while you are on line.

Doors have become tremendously popular on BBSs across the country. There are literally hundreds of available door programs, not all of them aimed at the caller. They have many uses and come in many levels of complexity. Doors range from the utilitarian, like databases to look up other BBS phone numbers, to the fanciful, such as games that let you compete interactively with other callers. Some doors are expressly designed to simplify the job of the sysop by automatically handling Netmail and other administrative chores.

The First Door Programs

Originally, BBS programs provided a limited selection of functions—if a sysop needed any additional capability, there was little that could be done. The original doors were attempts to get around these built-in limitations. Programs were written to run on line, using a little-known DOS function called CTTY to redirect the screen and keyboard functions to the COM port. In effect, they transferred control to the caller.

Too often, this proved disastrous. If the carrier signal were lost, or a backspace entered, the system would lock up, and neither user time nor keyboard time would be monitored. Everything was redirected, so nothing would appear on the sysop's monitor to announce that something was wrong. If the sysop did suspect something wrong, there was no help for it; any sysop keyboard entries would be ignored. To make matters worse, if the user entered a CTRL-C several times, one of the keypresses was likely to remain in the keyboard buffer. If this got transmitted to the BBS after the door program terminated but before control was returned to the BBS, the user was returned to DOS. Once there, the caller could do anything, including format the BBS drive or get into other mischief.

A few antisocial hackers had a field day. A way was needed to prevent (or at least break out of) such situations, but with the CTTY command, transfer of control was too complete. Another way to let callers run independent programs was needed.

At this point, a few very talented programmers began writing programs to run as doors. The goal was a program to read both the local keyboard and the COM port, while sending output to both the screen and the COM port. It must check for carrier loss, track both the keyboard and the user's time left, and talk to the modem at the correct baudrate. It must send and receive ANSI escape sequences (arrow key codes) to control cursor movement, or paint colors on the remote caller's screen.

Keeping all these balls in the air at once meant the early door programs often lost control when things got too complicated. The BBS would lock up or issue an error message, pausing for the sysop to enter a key before continuing. This was not a desirable state of affairs—even with the sysop present. If the sysop was gone, the system would go down.

First, Build a Door

To simplify the writing of door programs, several people wrote modules that could be compiled with specialized source code to produce a door. Those writing doors in QuickBASIC often used a module called DOORPCH written by Clint Labarthe and Terry Shotkley. This module is simply a set of QuickBASIC subroutines used by the main program to provide COM port support and time checks. For Pascal programmers, Sam Smith wrote Pro-KIT, containing a set of Pascal library functions that serve the same purposes. Both DOORPCH and ProKIT simplified the door writer's job immensely, and added reliability to their code.

Yet, even programs using these modules ran into problems. For example, QuickBasic resets the baudrate when it opens the COM port and will not work at transfer rates faster than 9600bps. Also, unless the code is patched, QuickBASIC drops the carrier when exiting. It also had a bad habit of putting error messages on the BBS screen and locking up until the sysop pressed ENTER.

Then Marshall Dudley released his DOORWAY program (see next section), which largely solved such problems. It gave door authors a reliable interface between the caller and the BBS program. One cannot credit DOORWAY alone with the doors revolution, but together with ProKIT and DOORPCH it has had a large effect on the BBS world. Door programs are now so popular that several door products exist solely to provide callers with menus of the other available doors. Two good examples of such "doors into doors" are DorMenu, by Don Cheeks, and SuperDor, by Stephen L. Cox.

The rest of this section will describe some current doors on BBSs and give information on how to obtain them. Remember, though, that the number of available doors is expanding rapidly. Today's stars may be replaced by something new tomorrow.

We'll start the descriptions with DOORWAY itself.

READ.ME

Instant Registration

One DOORWAY invention has made ripples throughout the shareware world: the ability to instantly register programs. Before, it might have taken weeks to receive a registered program copy after sending in a check. This delay is no longer necessary.

With DOORWAY registration installed in a program, you can simply call the program author's home board, register (often by credit card), and receive your registration number on the spot. You then type **DOORWAY REGISTER** with your name and registration number when you next use the program. The program tests the registration number, usually by generating a number based on the registered name. If it gets a "good" test, the program changes itself into a fully registered version.

There's a satisfying electronic immediacy to registering a program this way. No cash changes hands, and there's no daily wait for the mail.

DOORWAY

Marshall Dudley's DOORWAY is an ultradoor. It is used to change another program into a door. DOORWAY runs the selected program in a shell while redirecting the screen and keyboard to a COM port. The running program is controlled by the caller while DOORWAY sits at a distance, monitoring what goes on. If trouble comes—if the running program hangs, or the carrier signal drops out, or the caller's time limit runs out—DOORWAY aborts the program and returns control to the BBS. The BBS keyboard and monitor remain alive and active throughout the process, not blocked as with the DOS command CTTY.

Like any enhancement program, DOORWAY has become useful in ways not originally intended by the author. Sysops often use it to turn programs never intended for on-line use, such as full screen editors, into doors. If a program locks up, DOORWAY simply aborts it and returns control to the BBS, so sysops are free to experiment.

Telix, Qmodem, and other shareware communications programs are now providing built-in DOORWAY modes. These let the user send function keys, cursor keys, and ALT keys to the host computer. Many users are delighted they can remotely control the host machine using their favorite comm program. With Qmodem, DOORWAY also provides the host (answering) mode of operation.

Many sysops use the DOORWAY drop-to-DOS function to do remote maintenance. They prefer DOORWAY to programs like Carbon Copy or PCAnywhere, which were designed specifically for this task. DOORWAY is fast and smooth, and it's already installed in most BBSs.

Author   Marshall Dudley

Address   406 Monitor Lane, Knoxville, TN 37922

BBS Phone   (Public) 1-615-966-3574 (Hayes 9600V)

Sysop   Sean Dudley, Data World BBS

File Size   85K .ZIP file, total program

Registration Amount $30

Estimated Total Users   10,000 plus

BBS Mail Doors and Agents

The large on-line information and E-mail services have separate agent programs to help callers navigate their mazes. In the BBS world, mail doors and agent programs are closely tied. The major mail doors and agent programs are described together, below.

Qmail

The Qmail door lets PCBoard users download waiting messages quickly, so they can hang up and read them later. The system is very efficient; a user calling at 1200bps can typically receive 300 messages in five minutes. A companion agent program, Qmail Reader, lets the users read and reply to their messages off line, saving both time and money for long-distance callers. They can then upload their replies to the PCBoard.

Author   Mark Herring

Address   Sparkware, P.O. Box 38216, Germantown, TN 38183-0216

Voice Phone   1-901-386-0100

BBS Phone   1-901-382-5583

File Size   600K (total system with utilities)

Registration Amount $50

Estimated Installed Base   395 systems

Estimated Total Users   28,000 plus

Mark-Mail

Mark-Mail is a mail-handling door based on the QMail system and, like QMail, is used solely on PCBoard BBSs. You can use either the Qmail Reader or EZ-Reader described next to read and reply to messages downloaded from a Mark-Mail door. Mark-Mail makes it easy for users to configure for the conferences they want to read. Sysops also find it easy to configure their side of the Mark-Mail door when installing it on their systems. If the user logs on using Graphics, then Mark-Mail uses the ANSI escape codes to give smooth screen writing.

Note: Users of Procomm Plus and the Everex 2400 modem need to reconfigure the S7, S10, and S11 registers to avoid problems while using the Mark-Mail door. See Mark-Mail documentation for details.

Author   Mark Turner

BBS Phone   1-714-677-0570 (leave message for Mark Turner)

File Size   320K

Registration Amount $50

Estimated Installed Base   40 bulletin boards

Estimated Total Users   3000

EZ-Reader

EZ-Reader is an agent program and off-line message reader for PC-Board bulletin boards running either Qmail or Mark-Mail. It allows you to download your mail, read and reply off line, then upload your messages and replies later. EZ-Reader lets you use your own editor to compose replies, so you don't have to learn a new program. It repeats commands easily, stores an unlimited number of addresses with mailing lists, and is highly configurable for colors, hotkeys, compression programs, and regular actions (you can check for new bulletins, read the new ones, and so on).

Author   Erik Cockrell

Address   Thumper Technologies, P.O. Box 471012, Tulsa, OK 74147-1012

Registration Amount $25 (includes free upgrades)

Program Support   Via networks such as InterLink, SmartNet, and PC Relay

ProDoor

ProDoor is a door program that offers many of the features of PCBoard along with an astonishing number of enhanced and added features. ProDoor is used for batch file transfers using file transfer protocols such as Zmodem, Ymodem-G Batch, 1K-Xmodem-G, Lynx, and many others. Another feature of ProDoor is that it has the ability to manipulate a variety of archived files with formats such as .ZIP, .ARC, .PAK, .LZH, .ZOO, and others. ProDoor also gives the sysop a full set of commands that are not available through PCBoard itself. With ProDoor, a user can extract individual files from a large archived set, test the integrity of packed files, and even repack them. In addition, ProDoor allows the user to view the contents of any packed file.

ProDoor allows multiple-line file descriptions in addition to batch protocols where as many as 50 files may be downloaded in one session. The program also supports extended conferences, auto-joining of conferences, downloading of mail packets, and much more. The author, Samuel Smith, is also the creator of ProKit, a program that is used by many other program authors to write durable and dependable door programs.

Author Samuel H. Smith

Address Send your voluntary contributions to Samuel H. Smith, 5119 N. 11th Ave. #332, Phoenix, AZ 85013

Voice Phone Not available

BBS Phone 1-602-264-3969

File Size 180K

Estimated Installed Base 500 plus

Estimated Total Users 10,000 plus

ZDoor

ZDoor is an enhanced file-transfer door that allows batch Zmodem file tranfers. It also has an enhanced directory search. Using ZDoor, a user can view the contents of an archived file in both .ZIP and .ARC formats. You can also extract specific files from an archived file for download. ZDoor allows the sysop to see who has done uploads and downloads, as well as the contents of these transfers.

Author Richard Byrne

Address 5 Twin Elm Terrace, Sparta, NJ 07871

BBS Phone Software Society South BBS 1-201-846-9664

File Size   200K

Registration Amount $35 required for business and government; optional contribution for hobbyist use

Estimated Installed Base   700 plus

Estimated Total Users   10,000 plus

TextView

TextView is a system that allows PCBoard sysops to display written information to callers by modem. It is often used for on-line magazines such as *USA Today, NewsBytes,* and other electronic publications. Many systems use TextView for product support. It allows the caller to read about new enhancements to a program and then download from a selected list of files. TextView can be protected by password or security level, so it may be configured in a way that lets only paying customers have access to a supported commercial program.

Author   Joseph Sheppard

Address   P.O. Box 10, Tajunga, CA 91043-0010

BBS Phone   1-818-352-3620 (HST)

File Size   49K

Registration Amount $15

Estimated Installed Base   300 plus boards worldwide

Estimated Total Users   3000 plus minimum

MULTIPLAYER AND INTERACTIVE GAMES

Games, in many ways, drive the computer industry. Games are not just "kid stuff"; they are of real significance to the computer world. The first three mass-produced microcomputers—the Commodore PET, the Apple, and the

TRS-80—were all designed with games in mind. If they hadn't been, they wouldn't have sold, and the entire microcomputer industry as we know it might not exist today.

Games instruct the mind, hone the reflexes, and build friendship. Games capture the interest of kids, who will become the supercomputer designers of tomorrow. Games provide a profitable avenue for technology to explore without having to do anything truly useful in the meantime.

There are immense possibilities for fundamentally new types of games designed for multiuser BBSs. As Tim Stryker pointed out in the 1980 *BYTE* article, "Multimachine Games," three key factors when brought together offer tremendous entertainment potential:

- More than one human player is involved in the game. Rather than having the user compete against the machine, the machine is utilized to permit two or more people to compete with each other in ways that would be impossible without the aid of the machine.

- Success in the game hinges on the players' judicious use of incomplete information. Although the game may or may not be entirely deterministic in the sense that each legal move a player proposes gets put into effect without the intervention of any randomizing influence, the fact that each player has only a limited notion of what his opponents are up to lends a strong element of suspense and calculated risk-taking to the game.

- The game is played in real-time: your options are constrained not so much by the rules of the game as by your own fleetness of hand and mind (or lack thereof).

Bringing all three of these factors together in a single computer game essentially requires that each player have a separate console. A multiuser BBS provides the ideal platform for development of games of this type.

Some multiuser systems, particularly those with doors, offer a variety of fine single-user games, by using the simple expedient of "shelling out to DOS" and executing the game programs as if on a PC. A related approach is to provide ordinary, single-user game programs for download, so that you can execute them on a PC.

The multiuser games listed here, however, are specifically designed with multiuser operation in mind. Their whole concept is a unique synergy of play action that becomes possible only when Stryker's three key factors of multimachine game design are present. Bear in mind that any listing of games currently available is bound to be out of date by the time it is printed.

Fazuul

Created by Tim Stryker and brought on line in May 1984 in Miami, this early BBS game cast each player in the role of a shipwrecked spaceship captain. Marooned together on the planet Fazuul, players worked together to escape from the planet back to Galaxenter...or did they? The basic text adventure verb/noun command syntax was applied to a collection of alien technology left behind by the long-ago denizens of the planet. Some of this alien technology was helpful, once figured out. A "dongle," for example, allowed you to project your voice to another specified locale. Some of the alien technology constituted weapons: Directing a "scroom" at another player caused the player to drop everything he or she was holding; pushing the button on your "dweezle" caused everything to implode! Players eventually levitated into the "metastatic transfer chamber" and, through an elaborate procedure requiring a minimum of six people and hundreds of separate steps, were able to teleport back to Galaxenter. Unfortunately, this game no longer runs on any known system. However, another Stryker game called Flash Attack is seeing play on TMBBS boards (below).

Flash Attack

This Tim Stryker game is the first of a series of multiuser "flash" games. They use a downloadable program that each player runs in his or her own PC while connected to a multiuser bulletin board running the Entertainment Edition of The Major BBS (see Chapter 9). The action is full-screen, window-oriented, and blindingly fast. Up to six people can play together in one game, and up to ten games can be in progress on one system at one time. The game can also be played solo.

Players begin on an island covered with mountains, forests, and lakes. Each player runs a military base, hosting an array of tanks, lasers, "neutrons," and "seekers." Each tank sports phasers, mines, and "pods." The objective is to destroy all of the other players' bases. While in the game, you see only the immediate environments of four of your tanks, plus your own base. Split-second decisions are crucial, because at any instant another player's tank or base may come into view in one of your tank windows, or your own base may come under attack.

The game builds in a new type of pre- and postgame multiuser "chat." Extensive help screens cover almost every aspect of the game.

Quest for Magic

Written by Scott Brinker in 1986 as an option to The Major BBS, this multiplayer text adventure casts each player as a sorcerer's apprentice in the once magical land of Peyennuu. The quest is to restore the magic, and undo the terrible damage wrought by the evil Duke of Drajorth. Standard text adventure verb/noun syntax is applied to a series of gems, wands, orbs, staffs, and so forth. Magic spells also come into play. In fact, a major portion of the game involves discovering the magic words to do various things. For example, typing **cuunol** cures you of any minor wounds you have received, and **istmagic** detects the presence of any especially magical forces in your vicinity. The game solution—exactly what it means to "restore the lost magic" of Peyennuu—remains a mystery for most of the game, and is kept secret here, too. Suffice it to say that the solution may require the simultaneous efforts of more than one person.

Poker

Although not embodying all three of the above key multimachine game factors (it is not real-time), this package by Dan Hanson in 1987 nonetheless broke new ground in its use of gambling "chips" representing units of on-line time. Chips can be won, lost, or traded between players. Five Card Draw is faithfully re-created here, complete with graphic representations of cards, a built-in miniteleconference for idle game chatter, and a jacks-or-better option. "You bring the beer!," say Dan's ads. The legality of letting players "cash in" chips for on-line time may be dubious in some localities, so Dan made it sysop-selectable.

Galactic Empire

Developed by Michael B. Murdock in 1988, this game combines real-time player-versus-player space battles with a long-term political/economic simulation that may stretch over several months at a time. Players build up entire empires of planets through skillful management of natural resources, soldiers, food, cash, and fighting ships. Individual planetary conditions may or may not favor colonization, so the most attractive planets are also the most hotly contested. You can set up your planets to be self-defending, so that it is not vital for you to be on line when one of your planets is attacked by another player... but it helps! Scoring takes place automatically in the wee hours every day, and is based on factors like the size of the population under your control, the amount of cash in your Galactic Bank Account, the magnitude of your tax base, any recent "kills" you have made, and so forth.

Kyrandia

Arguably the most advanced multiuser text-adventure game created to date, Kyrandia is styled after the "magic users" of the popular role-playing game Dungeons & Dragons. It was developed by Scott Brinker and Richard Skurnick in 1988 as an option for The Major BBS. Kyrandia is filled with elves, dryads, flying dragons, fireballs and lightning bolts, teleportation and shape-changing—and especially, spells, counter-spells, and counter-counter-spells. A currency system based on gold lets you bargain, trade, and gamble with other players, as well as fight them. Magical items range from scrolls (some helpful, some cursed) to special relics from the world's patron goddess to dragon-summoning staves of power!

Sea Battle

The advance into ANSI graphic, real-time multiplayer games is now under way, as demonstrated in this 1989 implementation of the old paper-and-pencil Battleship game. Don Arnel programmed it to display a graphic on-screen grid (for those with PCs or clones) showing ship dispositions and incoming/outgoing hits and misses. Originally intended as a quiet turn-taking game, the play action picks up to cardiac-threatening speed when turn-taking is eliminated and players are free to fire salvos as fast as their fingers will permit. Macros are, of course, disallowed.

MOTU (Master of the Universe)

MOTU offers space warfare and humor. The game allows players to form teams and use mines, fighters, and their wits to beat others. MOTU features a flexible door that will work on many varieties of BBS software. Registration benefits the American Cancer Society. Another related door game is Sequel. (Other games are available as well.)

Author Phil DeWitt

Address P.O. Box 2994, Manassas, VA 22110

Voice Phone 1-703-690-6206

BBS Phone 1-703-590-1441

File Size 285K

Registration Amount Donation to American Cancer Society

Estimated Installed Base 750 plus BBSs

Estimated Total Users 4000 plus

Trade Wars—the "Original"

Trade Wars, by Chris Sherrick, was the *first* space-oriented door game. Chris distributed his source code free with words to the effect of "Take this and use it to make more space games that are even more complex and challenging. I'd like these kinds of games to flourish and prosper." Games such as MOTU, Power Struggle, and other forms of Trade Wars have their basic roots in Chris Sherricks's Trade Wars.

Author Chris Sherrick

File Size 280K

Estimated Installed Base 1000 plus

Estimated Total Users 50,000 plus

Galactic Conquest II

Galactic Conquest and Galactic Conquest II are space-adventure games based many years in the future. In Galactic Conquest II, players must rummage through the Galaxy trading goods, spying on other players, killing, and obtaining intelligence information. As players progress in the game they move from Merchant, to Bounty Hunter, to Spy, and finally to the coveted position of Galactic Overlord. Galactic Conquest II features orbiting reconnaissance satellites, booby-traps, and three different "galactic nations" that trade in different currencies and exchange rates. Galactic Conquest also has an Inter-BBS feature that lets the users of two systems play against each other without leaving their Home Board.

Author   Michael Cleverly

Address   158 E. 1650 South, Bountiful, UT 84010-5229

Voice Phone   1-801-292-0815

BBS Phone   1-801-298-5662

File Size   Test drive version: 210K .ZIP; registered version: 330K .ZIP

Registration Amount $24/U.S. (plus $2 S&H if Canada)

Estimated Installed Base   150 plus systems including Channel 1 in Boston

Estimated Total Users   8000 users and growing

Power Struggle

Power Struggle is a multiplayer space game that puts the player into a three-dimensional universe. The object of the game is to become the most powerful player in the universe by taking and controlling the three Power Planets. There are many ways to build assets.

Coauthors	Stephen Boston	Rick Greer
Address	The MicroMart BBS P.O. Box 59604 Dallas, TX 75229	Trichotomy BBS P.O. Box 17383 Fort Worth, TX 76102
Voice Phone	1-817-572-7913 (Stephen Boston)	
BBS Phone	The MicroMart BBS 1-214-221-7814	Trichotomy BBS 1-817-292-4871
File Size	217K	

Registration Amount $30 (single node), $40 (multinode)

Estimated Installed Base 2000

Estimated Total Users 22,000 plus

LARGE SYSTEM AGENT PROGRAMS

Agent programs make it easier for you to interact with large information and E-mail systems. Each of the programs outlined below is designed specifically for a single system. In one case, TAPCIS, other programmers have paid it the ultimate compliment of writing auxiliary support programs. In all cases, the programs are well designed to get you onto the system and do what you want to do. In all cases but CIM, the programs are also designed to get you on and off the system in the shortest time possible.

The following program sketches are organized according to the system with which they interface. They're intentionally brief—just long enough to give the flavor of the program.

CompuServe Information Service (CIS) Agents

CompuServe, the largest of the information networks, appropriately has three separate agent programs designed for it. The first two are designed to "hot-rod" your sessions and save you money; the last, CIM, is designed more toward easing system navigation.

TAPCIS

This program is designed to simplify your use of CIS. The CIS-B file transfer protocol is built right in, and kept up to date with every new CIS-B release. TAPCIS lets you map your way through any number of forums on CIS and makes their use much easier. The program takes some time to install because there are so many available services on CompuServe, but the documentation is clear and, once you've done it, finding your way around the system is a breeze. TAPCIS does everything possible to get you on and off the system quickly, for significant savings in time and connect charges.

When the CompuServe Information Manager (CIM), a new graphic interface, was introduced in late 1989, some TAPCIS partisans were concerned about the future of TAPCIS. The late Howard Benner, TAPCIS author and one of shareware's success stories, made it known that CompuServe had called on him to help design and test the new interface. In fact, the two programs are not in competition because CIM does not share the TAPCIS "get on, get off fast" design philosophy.

Though TAPCIS is one of the best of the agent programs, future versions are on the drawing board. Upgrades for registered users have always been free of charge when downloaded, but there are minor charges for upgrades mailed to versions registered more than a year or two before. All TAPCIS registrations have a 90-day money-back guarantee. Support is provided through the Support Group, Inc., a commercial program support company formed by Rick and Sandy Wilkes.

One measure of any program's success is whether other programmers jump in with related support programs. TAPCIS has inspired at least two outstanding ones—TAPLEX and TAPMARK (described below).

Author   Howard Benner

Support   Support Group, Inc., P.O. Box 130, McHenry, MD 21541

Support Phone   1-800-872-4768 (USA-GROUP)

Download   Log on to CompuServe and enter **GO TAPCIS**.

Registration Amount $79

File Size   170K without documentation or auxiliary programs

Estimated Number of Users   50,000 plus

TAPLEX is a utility designed for use with TAPCIS. TAPLEX helps to handle mail by way of the CompuServe EASYPLEX system. It keeps track of incoming and outgoing messages.

Author   Tracey Siesser

Address   Program can be found on CompuServe. Enter **GO TAPCIS**.

Registration Amount $5

File Size   50K

TAPMARK is used with TAPCIS to mark message threads. In this manner, it becomes easier for the user to follow a series of notes on any given topic.

Author   Jim Korenthal

Address   Program can be found on CompuServe. Enter **GO TAPCIS**.

Registration Amount $10

File Size   81K

Estimated Number of Users   Unknown

Autosig

Autosig (ATO) is a free communications program for use with CompuServe forums. It makes access, message capture, and file downloads automatic. Up to 10 different CIS hosts and 24 forums are supported. There are on-line help, user defined function keys, a simple script command language, CompuServe's B protocol for file transfers, split screen for conferencing, verbose (menu) and terse (one-line prompt) modes, and a terminal mode for manual operation. It includes a built-in address book to store and retrieve user names and ID numbers. ATO can automatically log onto

CIS through direct nodes, TYMNET, Sprintnet, Datapac, direct connects, and other telecommunications networks.

Autosig is fully supported on the CompuServe IBMCOM forum. There are thousands of users. A new version is released once or twice a year.

Author   Vernon D. Buerg

Address   139 White Oaks Circle, Petaluma, CA 94952

File Size   173K .EXE file, 200K documentation, and 30K help

Estimated Number of Users   10,000 plus

CompuServe Information Manager (CIM)

This program, developed by CompuServe, features a graphics interface with attractive screens, pull-down menus, and mouse support. It makes navigating the service very easy, though it does take its time—which on CompuServe costs $12.50 an hour plus connect charges. The apparent slowness results from the program's paged output; actual data transfer speeds are not slowed. Taking into account a standard $15 on-line credit, the price comes to a net of $10, for which you get the program plus a well-produced, boxed manual. It's a very good deal, but remember the program is interactive, not automated. It is not designed to cut back your on-line charges.

Author   CompuServe Information Network

Address   Obtain from CompuServe (enter **GO CIM**)

Price $24.95 (includes $15 usage credit)

Aladdin: Agent for GEnie

Aladdin, the preferred user interface for GEnie, combines the graphics approach of CIM with the time-saving, get-on-and-get-off approach of TAP-CIS and Autosig. By doubling as a friendly user interface and a time-saving agent program, it tries to give you the best of both worlds. For the most part, it succeeds.

Aladdin lets you do most of your work off line. You can read, write, and reply to messages using your own word processor. You can tag files for downloading. When you're ready, turn Aladdin loose. It jumps onto GEnie, picks up any new mail, sends your prepared messages to their destinations, downloads any files you specified, and hangs up again. There are no wasted motions, no on-line charges while you puzzle over what to do next.

GEnie recently bought the rights to this user-friendly program and has made the full-featured version available for downloading. It is well suited for novices and experienced users alike, and new users will save on-line time by using Aladdin while they learn the GEnie system. On-line support is provided in the Aladdin RoundTable, which is a preset item in the Aladdin main menu. At this writing the new registration amount has not been announced, but it is expected to be about $30.

Author   GEnie IBM RoundTable sysops

Address   Program may be obtained on GEnie

Registration Amount $30 (estimated)

File Size   203K

MCI E-mail Agents

MCI, despite its status as North America's largest E-mail carrier, for a long time limited users to pure ASCII, nonbinary messages. If you tried to send a formatted spreadsheet, word processed document, or executable file, MCI stripped off the high (eighth) bit during transmission. This resulted in an unusable file at the other end.

To overcome this problem, MCI developed a system called Mail Link to let users attach 8-bit binary files to otherwise normal 7-bit ASCII messages. File transmission by Mail Link using MCI's Mail Exchange Protocol (MEP-2) can then take advantage of X.PC error-correction, a protocol developed originally by TYMNET.

The Mail Link system does increase file transmission time. It's a free 800-number call, though, and total message cost is not affected. Slowness is the only penalty, but this is quite noticeable—you may want to use Mail Link binary transfers as an occasional convenience, not as your normal routine.

At this writing, five agent programs take advantage of Mail Link. All will allow you to sign onto MCI, automatically download your messages, and sign off again. You can then prepare answers off line with the benefit of word processing, spell-checking, consultation with colleagues, and calm reflection. Once you prepare your answers, you can sign back onto MCI and send them. The agent program handles all addressing, which eliminates the potential embarrassment of sending a response to the wrong party.

Agent programs for MCI available at this writing are described on the next page.

READ.ME

The Right Connection to MCI

Four different free numbers are available for accessing MCI. The one to use depends upon your MCI agent program and on whether your modem supports MNP error-correction. Here's a guide to MCI access numbers:

1-800-456-6245   Plain vanilla, with no built-in error-correction. Use for sending everyday, non-error-corrected messages without an agent program.

1-800-825-1515 and 1-800-234-6245   Both numbers support X.PC error-correction for binary file transfers. They are *not* compatible with MNP error-correcting modems; if your modem supports MNP, turn MNP off. Use either of these access numbers with Lotus Express, Desktop Express (Macintosh), or Norton Commander.

1-800-333-1818   Supports MNP level 5 error-correction, allowing an effective 4800bps throughput using a 2400bps modem. Use only with MNP error-correcting modems. *MNP is not compatible with X.PC error-correction.* Do not use this number with Norton Commander or Desktop Express (Macintosh); they cannot turn off their built-in X.PC support.

Lotus Express

This program, by Lotus Development Corp., was the first commercial package to take advantage of MCI Mail Link. Lotus Express lets you turn off X.PC error-correction for use with MNP error-correcting modems.

Norton Commander

The Commander offers MCI Mail Link support with X.PC error-correction, as part of the Norton Commander shell program, version 3.0. The X.PC error-correction is built into the software and cannot be turned off. On MNP error-correcting modems, turn off MNP before accessing MCI. Since X.PC is inherently slower than MNP, you may not want to use the Norton Commander MCI agent program if you have an MNP modem.

Desktop Express (Macintosh)

This program for the Macintosh has the same MCI mail characteristics as Norton Commander.

EMMA

EMMA, which stands for Electronic MCI Mail Agent, does not support X.PC error-correction, though it does handle binary file transfers. When sending binary files, use EMMA only on extremely clean phone lines or with an MNP modem. The program was written by Pete Maclean and published originally as a *PC Magazine* free utility program named 1STCLASS. It is available on PC MagNet (see Chapter 6). Written entirely in assembly language, it is extremely small and fast. It also has one very special attraction—it's free.

Early versions of EMMA required a second program named BESS (for BEtter Serial Services) to be installed separately in memory. In version 1.7, Maclean combined BESS and EMMA into a single program. If you get this program from PC MagNet, be sure to download it from the Forum Library. The PC MagNet File Finder may only list version 1.4, which still requires BESS as a separate memory-resident program.

3 + Mail and 3 + Reach

These programs are distributed by 3Com Corporation of Santa Clara, California, for use with 3Com netware. The 3 + Reach/MCI gateway allows 3 + network mail users to access MCI and send messages with binary attachments from PC, PS/2, and Macintosh workstations. It also connects to ALL-IN-1, PROFS, DISOSS, or VMS-mail users who are accessible through other gateways in their networks.

CHAPTER ELEVEN

Shareware

The idea was almost a gimmick: Give people a disk of software or let them make a copy. If they like it, they send you money! Few outside observers thought this idea would ever work, but it did—and still does for many shareware marketers.

THE VERY BEGINNING

Shareware was born simultaneously in two locations. In Tiburon, California, it was born as the *freeware* program PC-Talk, fathered by Andrew Fluegelman. (Freeware eventually became synonymous with *shareware* because Fluegelman trademarked "freeware" and it soon fell into oblivion as a term.) In Bellevue, Washington, shareware sprang to life as PC-File, the "child" of Jim Button. It's hard to say which of the two men actually invented the shareware concept. Andrew Fluegelman died in an unfortunate accident some years ago, leaving Button as the Grand Old Man of shareware.

Button's story has its roots in the late 1970s. Button and his son, John, were computer hobbyists. They built their first computer from scratch—a real "home brew" machine. It wasn't much more than a circuit board with a 6502 microprocessor, and a cassette tape to store data and programs. The input was through a hexadecimal keypad. The Buttons had to program the computer in machine language. A lot of the ideas for building that computer were adapted from electronic schematics designed and published by other hobbyists.

Using the home brew machine, Button wrote a simple mailing list program for a friend, who had a business and needed to keep track of customers and print mailing labels. The friend paid for the program, and Button used the money to expand his hobby. Later, when the Apple computer was unveiled, he purchased one and rewrote the mailing list program in Applesoft BASIC. He also expanded it to a general purpose database program. With some added refinements, he thought he could attract a few more customers and make more money.

Then the IBM PC was announced in November 1981. Button, along with many others, anticipated that IBM would revolutionize the personal computer industry. So he sold his Apple and placed an order for an IBM PC. The first program he converted from Applesoft BASIC to IBM BASIC was the database program. Button found that the conversion was an easy one—it only took a few days to get the database program on the IBM PC.

At this time, Button was also working for IBM in Seattle. He found that many of his co-workers were learning to use their first personal computers. As an "old hand" at personal computing, Button shared his database program with them. It was soon a hit throughout the Seattle area, as enthusiastic users of the free program shared copies with friends and associates. "Easy File" (the early name of PC-File) was born.

Button kept a mailing list of Easy File users, but problems soon developed. It became increasingly expensive and time consuming to notify the users when fixes or improvements became available. There was no way to identify the serious users—those who desired upgrades, enhancements, and fixes—from the casual users. Which ones had ceased to use the program? The list was becoming too long, and mailings too expensive.

Button decided to place a message in each copy of the program. The message requested a voluntary, modest donation to help defray costs and to maintain the user's name on the mailing list. The message also encouraged users to continue using the program and sharing it with others.

The first person to receive the program with its unusual request called almost immediately. He had also received a copy of PC-Talk, which contained a similar message, and he told Button about it. Button read the PC-Talk request for other programmers to join with Andrew Fluegelman in this unique "marketing experiment." Button contacted Fluegelman, and sent him a copy of Easy File in July 1982.

Fluegelman was impressed, and the twosome decided to reference each other on distribution disks. Button renamed his program PC-File, complementing the PC-Talk name. The suggested voluntary payment on each program disk was $25.

Bob Wallace Enters

Soon another shareware pioneer, Bob Wallace, entered the market in 1983. He was one of the earliest employees of Microsoft, and the founder of the Northwest Computer Society. Wallace started a Seattle firm, Quicksoft, Inc., to market his word processor, PC-Write.

Bob Wallace added a new twist to the shareware concept. His idea was simple: If you're a registered user, share your program with someone who then becomes a registered user, and earn a commission. Wallace's new marketing idea soon made his name well known. PC-Write continues as one of the all-time shareware success stories, with over 45,000 registered users.

Marshall Magee

The next big shot to arrive on the scene was Marshall Magee, a college student, in 1983. He had developed a software product called Automenu that helped PC users move from program to program without using DOS commands. When someone offered him $20 for a copy, he started Magee Enterprises. He marketed his product with visits to user groups, distributing thousands of copies. His work paid off; in 1988 sales were reported at $1.2 million.

A FOOLISH OLD MAN?

The shareware concept is a sound one, but that fact wasn't always clear. In the beginning, Button's wife, Helen, chided that he was a "foolish old man" to think that anyone would voluntarily send money. Button had his doubts, as well. The most he hoped for was enough money to help pay for his increasingly expensive computer hobby. However, the events of May 1983 were wilder than his most outlandish dream.

Button and his family were vacationing in Hawaii when *PC World* hit the newsstands with a stunning review of PC-File. The response to the article was overwhelming. A neighbor of the Buttons' had agreed to watch the house and pick up the mail—little did the neighbor know that the mail would begin to arrive in grocery bags. By the time the Buttons returned their entire basement floor was covered with grocery sacks bursting with mail. They worked most of the summer to catch up with the deluge. It was no coincidence that Andrew Fluegelman was the editor of *PC World* at the time.

Button, making ten times his IBM salary selling shareware, continued to work eight-hour days at IBM. Then another four hours—and all day Saturday and Sunday—were devoted to his "hobby business." Finally, exhausted, he realized the truth of what friends and family were saying: "If you can do this well in the software business as a part-time hobby, how well would you do if you took it seriously?" He quit the day job.

ButtonWare eventually moved from the basement office to a modern office in Bellevue. The business now has a staff of 18, a broad range of products, and annual sales of over $2.5 million. Not bad for a hobbyist.

THE UPSIDE: REASONS FOR SHAREWARE'S EARLY ACCEPTANCE

Button cites seven reasons for the immediate hit made by the shareware concept and the companies that used it.

- The software was well written.

- The companies offered support to users.

- The disks were anti-copy-protected—unlike commercial programs at the time.

- The products were available through many computer club disk libraries.

- The programs were available from bulletin boards.

- Prices were moderate—between $10 and $25.

- The press was hungry for new software, unusual ideas, and a new angle on the industry.

Not every shareware product made money. Fluegelman himself said, "Only the good products will survive." Shareware and traditional software are marketed quite differently. Retail software producers have advertising budgets—a mediocre product can be made successful with lavish advertising and promotional campaigns. Shareware, on the other hand, relies on its own virtues to elicit a sale. If users don't like the program, they won't pay for it. They won't talk about it, or give it to others. It will die unceremoniously. Shareware marketing is largely word-of-mouth.

The successful shareware companies responded to user registrations with thank-you letters. They answered their customers' questions and listened to comments. Companies that realized their customers were the best source of ideas for new versions, improvements, and marketing suggestions were the most successful.

Meanwhile, big-time commercial software manufacturers were hell-bent on restricting illegally copied software. The industry dreamed up complex copy-protection schemes, while the public tried to find ways to get around them. Sentiment was something like, "I spent $295 for this program, and I can't even give a copy to my dear old mother, who can't afford to pay that much right now." The public wasn't larcenous; they just wanted to share with others their favorite software program. Imagine the impact on these good-hearted souls when a shareware author actually encouraged them to copy his programs!

When Fluegelman and Button encouraged this sharing of their programs, the rest of the software industry was outraged. Industry leaders proclaimed the idea a poor one, claiming that "these shareware people" would go broke. Even today you will hear that "shareware guys like Button aren't really making any money." After all, who would pay for something after they already had it?

As the "right time, right place" phenomenon goes, one more event coincided for shareware: large computer clubs. They sprang up all over the country. Club librarians needed programs to share with their members. It was a perfect vehicle for assuring wide distribution of shareware disks.

Then there was the contribution of telecommunications to shareware's success. Telecommunications and shareware fit each other perfectly. Bulletin boards quickly took advantage of shareware. BBS operators wanted programs to post for their wide range of users. They posted both public domain programs and shareware. Shareware was especially well received because it was a supported product.

THE DOWNSIDE: EARLY PROBLEMS WITH SHAREWARE

The early days of shareware were invigorating for Button. It was like a dream come true. But there was no road map to show him the way; shareware was a new concept. Every decision broke new ground, and sometimes the decisions were wrong. For example, bulletin boards were a "can't live with 'em, can't live without 'em" problem. They clearly helped spread the word about shareware—but there was a downside, at least in the beginning.

At that time, programs were sent in a standard 8-bit ASCII format. Errors that occurred while the program was downloaded from a bulletin board remained as errors on the user's disk. As a result, the program often didn't work, and the authors were blamed for writing a "buggy" program.

Another problem was incomplete downloads. For instance, PC-File contains several essential files that needed to be downloaded. The files were listed individually on a bulletin board. Unknowledgeable users would download some—but not all—of the files, and would get a "Program Not Found" error message when they tried to use PC-File.

Button's first reaction to these problems was to add the message, "No BBS downloading permitted" on early versions of PC-File. However, later improvements to the bulletin board systems made him change his stance. Error-checking protocols came into wider use, as did methods of grouping all the program's files into a single download file.

Separating Shareware from Public Domain Software

Public domain software was the stock in trade of BBS, disk vendors, and user clubs. Shareware had a lot of the "feel" of public domain software: You couldn't buy it in a computer store, it was available on the bulletin boards, it wasn't copy-protected, and it didn't cost you anything up front. It's not surprising that it was hard to get people to understand that shareware was something different.

Disk dealers—small, "garage" mail-order operations—advertised in magazines that they'd send long lists of programs for a modest sum. Send in a check, and get a disk full of programs—some public domain, some shareware. People were led to believe they need only pay for the disk. Most vendors didn't make any attempt to distinguish between shareware and public domain software. They didn't make it clear that there was an additional financial obligation if the buyer decided to keep and use a shareware program. Button and the other shareware dealers got calls from angry buyers, accusing them of trickery. To the misguided user, the disk dealer and the shareware author were one and the same.

Shareware authors were also guilty of causing some of the public's misconceptions. Essentially, the only difference between shareware and public domain software was the disk message requesting payment. These early messages used words like "voluntary," "contribution," and "donation" in their sheepish requests. Some authors tried to lay "guilt trips" on non-registered users, with laughable phrases like, "Your conscience will bother you until your dying day if you don't pay," or "God will strike you dead!" Unfortunately, these tactics cheapened the image of all shareware products.

When Button eliminated words like "contribution" and "donation" from his solicitation message, and replaced them with "payment" and "registration," his revenues began to improve. The addition of incentives like upgrades, a printed manual, and technical support were also major factors in producing voluntary payments. Another valuable incentive was a monetary bonus for a user who got others to register.

Not all shareware authors went along with these changes. Some authors still believe that payment for their software should be completely voluntary. However, most authors believe they are entitled to payment if their programs are used. After all, they provide *technical support* for their product.

Technical support is an obligation that continues beyond the point of sale; every software company provides it. Commercial software companies support only registered users. If you don't register, there is no support. Someone who makes a copy of your software, and then tries to call for support using your registered serial number, will not only get no support but will get you into trouble. Most computer users understand and accept this concept.

There have also been unfortunate situations where shareware programs were stolen. Back in Button's early years, another shareware author told him there was a disk dealer in California who was selling PC-File as his own product. The plagiarist had printed the manual from the disk, made copies of it, and was advertising in magazines about a great database program and manual for $40. ButtonWare didn't get a penny.

Button contacted the disk dealer and told him he was violating the copyright, that he was only authorized to sell PC-File as a shareware program, and only at a maximum cost of $6. He was not authorized to make copies of the documentation. Button, on solid legal ground, expected this warning to put an end to the dealer's unscrupulous activity. The dealer, however, merely told Button to "get a lawyer."

Button realized that he had to enforce the copyright or lose it by default. He tried to enlist other shareware authors in the legal battle, but was unable to convince them that there was a problem. Left to foot the legal bills on his own, he hired an attorney, who eventually stopped the plagiarist. Button considers the incident a pivotal episode in the shareware story.

Corporate America's Skepticism

Another early problem for shareware companies was lack of interest from corporate PC users. They wanted "professional" software. The shareware concept was somehow unbusinesslike, and the companies producing shareware were not expected to be around for support.

This concern was fueled to a degree by commercial competitors. In one early product review in a major magazine, for instance, PC-File was compared to one of the commercial database programs. The reviewer interviewed the competitor's marketing person, who said, "We're in this for the long haul." The implication was that the shareware program wouldn't be. In fact, both companies are still in business.

Early Disappointments for Some Shareware Authors

Because Button and Fluegelman were successful using the shareware concept, many early authors felt that all shareware programs would be successful. It soon became clear that this wasn't the case.

Shareware is not a good plan for all programs. Complexity sells. General purpose programs sell best. And high quality is a must; users do not pay voluntarily for a shoddy, or even average product. The perceived value must be high.

As a rule, the following genres of shareware programs haven't been clearly successful:

- Games
- Utilities
- Vertical programs

Games

Game players tire of the game and decide not to register. Some see games as trivial—something to play with, but certainly not to pay for. Younger game users just don't have the money to pay for the games.

Utility Programs

Shareware utility programs, for the most part, are still classified with public domain software by many users. There are exceptions to every rule, of course, and some shareware utilities that fill a need not met by the commercial products have been well received.

Vertical Programs

Vertical programs have not generated enough of a user base to create the revenue needed for continued support and upgrades.

WHY SHAREWARE?

A software author makes a huge investment of time, talent, and thought in developing a product. Except for the true hobbyists who write for the public domain, most authors would like to make some money from their work. The traditional approach to marketing and distribution—advertise the product to build name recognition, roll it out and update it, get distributors to carry it and dealers to stock it—is an expensive route not available to everybody. Small software developers can't afford it, and must obtain venture capital, borrow money, or sell the program to a large company.

In contrast, shareware allows the author to control the product, and to test the water. Putting a program into shareware distribution channels can cost only a few hundred dollars. Once the shareware channel is saturated, many companies release a version of their program to be sold through normal retail channels.

It's apparent to many observers that although shareware is as good as anything available from a retail store (usually for more money), the shareware market is somewhat limited. Sometimes there is justification for moving away from 100 percent shareware and toward some percentage of retail effort—complete with fancy packaging, advertising, and all the expenses related to selling through stores. An example of a company that made this transition is DataStorm, with its Procomm telecommunications program.

Procomm—A Blockbuster

In the mid-1980s, Bruce Barkelew and Tom Smith formed PIL Software Systems and introduced Procomm as a shareware communications program. Competing with programs like Crosstalk, which sold for hundreds of dollars, Procomm, then selling for under $50, was a great success. It has been as strong a competitor as any of the commercial programs, and is now available through both shareware and commercial channels. PIL incorporated in April 1986, as DataStorm Technologies.

ACCEPTANCE BY CORPORATE AMERICA

Major corporations make up a giant section of the overall software market. Shareware traveled a long, difficult road before it gained acceptance in major corporations.

Before the PC, mainframe-oriented corporate Management Information System (MIS) departments controlled all computing within their companies. Departments had to ask the MIS department for terminals to access the mainframes, and their requests were frequently denied. A terminal became a status symbol for managers and a few key employees. Then came the PC. Departments could purchase PCs from their own budget, without anyone's permission. PCs began to appear on desks everywhere, and MIS control eroded.

Many MIS departments fought to maintain control over the software purchased for use on the company PCs. Shareware, with no support, company background, or guarantees, was never on the list of "officially purchased" programs. And, shareware wasn't marketed to companies like other commercial software—with marketing people taking the MIS managers out to lunch. Shareware usually crept into corporate offices through the efforts of some individual who would bring in a program, copy it, and share it. By the time MIS was aware of the situation, dozens, sometimes hundreds, of people were using the program routinely, and often illegally. Nervous MIS departments quickly negotiated site licenses, or arranged discounted volume purchases through the shareware authors.

Once corporate users accepted shareware as respectable software, they began to see its virtues. It was inexpensive. Companies could use shareware as an interim step while they were deciding on a commercial program. (The shareware product often became the permanent product.) Because shareware programs could be used before purchase, there was less risk of the company users being unhappy with a selection. And the simple design of shareware programs involved less training time.

Shareware has been so well accepted that many corporations routinely monitor the shareware marketplace for new products. If something looks interesting, they'll try it. If it works for them, they'll negotiate a price with the manufacturer.

A SHAREWARE PRIMER

Hundreds of shareware authors today offer a variety of programs, from simple utilities to complex programming tools. Each of the familiar applications—word processing, spreadsheets, databases—has a number of shareware titles. There's a whole world of shareware available.

Computer Shows

Disk vendors are everywhere at computer shows, bringing with them program disks and lists of other titles, complete with capsule descriptions of each package. Disks usually sell in the $2 to $5 range, with discounts for multiple purchases.

PSL News

PSL News is published monthly, billing itself as "The Monthly Magazine About Free and Low-Cost Software." Loaded with information about new programs and updates to existing programs, the magazine sells for $2 an issue or $18 a year. It is published in Houston by the Public (Software) Library, a disk vendor offering shareware programs on disk for a small fee. Unlike other disk vendors, PSL tests every program before offering it. PSL is a strong advocate of the shareware concept, and is highly recommended. More information is available from Nelson Ford, the editor, at 713-665-7017.

Shareware Magazine

Bimonthly *Shareware Magazine* is available at many stores that sell computer magazines. It is also available for subscription from its publisher, PC-SIG, 1020 East Duane Avenue, Suite D, Sunnyvale, California 94086 (408-730-9291). PC-SIG is a giant disk vendor in California.

PC-SIG's *Shareware Magazine* is devoted entirely to shareware and gives a broad overview of available products. You can order shareware disks through PC-SIG or through other advertisers in the magazine.

Information Utilities

On-line information services, such as CompuServe, GEnie, Delphi, and so forth, have extensive directories of shareware programs for download. For more information, see Chapter 6.

Other Bulletin Boards

There are thousands of bulletin boards that offer shareware programs for downloading, and libraries of shareware programs. Bulletin board operators will advise you of the procedures for downloading shareware from their systems. These services are discussed extensively in this book; with the software provided, you can get just about everything imaginable from on-line downloading.

Computer Clubs and User Groups

Most shareware authors target user groups and computer clubs. They speak to user groups, make sure the clubs have current copies of programs, and encourage the clubs to share the product. If you don't already belong to a user group, you can find out about them through your local computer dealer. Clubs are often listed in the back of computer magazines, and in some of the free computer tabloids. Most clubs have a disk librarian who will show you the club's shareware offerings. You may or may not have to be a member to get a copy of a program through the librarian.

Ask a Friend

Person-to-person contact is still an important way for shareware to be passed along. If you have friends who are computer users, ask them if they have any shareware programs they can share with you. Ask them what they've tried, and what they've heard about. You'll find this a valuable source of information.

CHOOSING A SHAREWARE PROGRAM

With shareware, you don't have to rely on someone else's review to tell you how the product works—you get a chance to use it yourself. Is this the program for you? Here are several questions to help you make that decision.

1. *Does it do what I want it to do?* Obviously, a word processor won't do spreadsheets. An important tool in software evaluation is to put together a list of your specific product requirements. With that list you can effectively judge the shareware, or any software, on its merits that are uniquely valuable to you.

   Caution: Don't judge your needs by the bells and whistles the commercial companies are offering in comparable software. Examine what *you* expect from your software on a daily basis.

2. *Is it easy to use?*   Only you can be the judge on this one; it's a matter of personal taste. Shareware products tend to be easy to use, but a product one person finds simple may be limiting to another. Some people love point-and-shoot menus. Others love multiple key-stroke commands. If you're a heavy computer user, menus may get in the way. If you're a novice, two- and three-key commands may seem overwhelming. Does the product you're evaluating offer the system that's right for you? Is it easy to get into and out of? Do you enjoy using it, or do you find yourself dreading to sit down with it? If the program "feels" right to you, then it probably is.

3. *Is it written in a professional way?*   If you haven't logged a lot of computer time, this may be difficult to answer. If you're a power user, you can tell in just a few minutes. Regardless of your back-ground, however, there are some ways to judge the quality of the writing.

   • Are there noticeable bugs? Does the software always work as expected, or do you find yourself lost in the menus, or bounced around the program, or looking at garbage on the screen?

   • Do the commands always work as they should? How does the software handle errors? Can your errors have disastrous effects (like ruining your opening screen, or hanging up the program), or does the program protect you from your mistakes?

   • Is the system flexible enough to be useful? Does it seem that the author anticipated the way you would use the program?

   • Do the menu options make sense?

   • Is the program fast, or are there long delays after entering com-mands or changing menus?

4. *Is the documentation complete and easy to understand?*   If you can't understand the documentation, there is no sense in installing the program on your system.

5. *Does the company support its product?*   If this is your first time looking at shareware, it may not be clear to you how to judge the level of support. Here are some ideas.

- Take a look at the release number. If it's 1.0, the question of support probably has yet to be answered. If it's a later release, that's usually a sign that the author is working regularly to upgrade the program.

- Find out how long the program has been around. Companies rarely survive if they don't treat their customers well.

- Talk to the person who shared the program with you, and find out what his or her experience has been with the company's support system.

- Call the company and ask them what they offer in the way of support. Do they have a bulletin board for off-hour support? Are they on CompuServe? When is someone available to answer support questions? Can they give you the name of some current users?

- If you're a member of CompuServe or GEnie, check the various forums and find out where the program is available for download. Look to see if any of the messages on that forum pertain to the program you're considering. Leave your own question about support, and follow up to see if anyone can give you some insight.

- Find out if the product has been reviewed. Some computer magazines are in the magazine index available at most public libraries. Look up the program name; then look for a review that says something about support.

THE ASSOCIATION OF SHAREWARE PROFESSIONALS (ASP)

In April 1987, the Association of Shareware Professionals was formed. ASP is a trade group organized to help those actively involved in the shareware community, and to strengthen the future of shareware as an alternative to commercial software. ASP members subscribe to a code of ethics, and are committed to the concept of shareware as a method of marketing. The goals of the organization are to

- Inform users about shareware programs, and about shareware as a method of distributing and marketing software

- Encourage broader distribution of shareware through user groups and disk dealers who agree to identify and explain the nature of shareware

- Assist members in marketing their software

- Foster a high degree of professionalism among shareware authors by setting programming, marketing, and support standards for ASP members to follow

- Provide a forum through which ASP members can communicate, share ideas, and learn from each other

Membership in ASP is not automatic. To become a member, an individual has to have developed a serious shareware product that meets ASP's criteria. There are currently 120 active members representing a diversity of shareware authors.

WHERE ARE WE HEADED?

Now that shareware has established itself as a viable method of marketing and distributing software, it is worthwhile to look to the future. Jim Button of ButtonWare sees shareware continuing to grow in popularity. Good authors will continue to write good programs, and will want to sell those programs. For many of these individuals, the traditional marketing channels will be unavailable. They may get a software publisher to buy their program and distribute it, but only a tiny percentage of programs make it that way. Shareware will continue to be an exciting alternative for building a software company. Shareware is a gamble, but the entire software business is a gamble—regardless of the method used for distribution.

Today shareware is accepted as a sound business concept. Several shareware companies are doing well over one million dollars in annual business. As more companies become successful, the concept will look even better to software authors, and the pipeline should remain full.

Bootstrapping into Commercial Areas

Some companies have already established their software via shareware and then parlayed their success into mainstream companies with prominent positions on dealers' shelves. For example, DataStorm's Procomm is still sold as shareware, but most of its sales now come through dealers. Some people in this commercial audience won't buy and use shareware, regardless of what it costs or how well it is supported. Although the shareware community includes only about a third of potential users, an excellent path for the small software author is through shareware to the dealer shelf. This path helps to accumulate a track record, as well as important feedback from the public.

CONCLUSION

If you always look for quality in your shareware selections, and carefully screen each item for utility, performance, and ease of use, you'll find that you just can't lose. Remember, though, it is important to register any programs that you decide to use, after you have tried them out for a while. Otherwise, the shareware concept will stop working and it will become a vendor's, not a buyer's, market.

CHAPTER TWELVE

The Software Virus and You

Every silver lining has a dark cloud, and in the world of PC telecommunications, the cloud is *rogue software*—programs designed for no purpose other than to destroy unsuspecting users' hard-earned data. In the world of on-line data exchange, the worst software quality troubles you'll probably ever encounter will be buggy, ill-designed programs engineered by well-meaning aspiring programmers. It is possible, though, that you will find yourself among those unfortunate souls who have been duped by a bona fide computer virus, worm program, or Trojan horse program.

TYPES OF ROGUE SOFTWARE

Rogue software (rogueware) has many names and faces; its developers, however, often remain nameless and faceless. Some folks argue that discussing Trojan horses, logic bombs, and computer viruses in the popular press glorifies their anonymous creators. I suggest these people reconsider this attitude. It is always better to expose the facts to the public. If these malicious programmers feel glorified, then they have a skewed sense of reality.

A more serious argument concerns releasing such programs to others. Exposing the truth is one thing, publishing kitchen recipes for bombs quite another. One man in Virginia, for "educational" reasons, sold working viruses and their source code to anyone who wanted them. That probably took education too far, but he thought the more people who knew about viruses, the harder it would be for virus writers to sneak up on the world.

On the other end of the spectrum, it is the opinion of some researchers that rogue code should never be released outside the small world of recognized data security experts. Such a "closed shop" approach may be too restrictive. For one thing, it ignores the need to expand the number of people in the field.

The best approach may be the one used by the Computer Virus Industry Association (CVIA) of Santa Clara, California. The CVIA releases virus simulator programs and disabled, partially disassembled virus source code to qualified researchers. Live viruses and fully disassembled code are released only to researchers known personally to CVIA officers. So far, the compromise seems to have worked well.

Bombs

The simplest form of rogueware is the software bomb. These easy-to-design troublemakers appear to provide some marginally useful functions, such as playing songs or displaying pictures. While these innocuous diversions are taking place, the software bomb secretly erases disk boot sectors (a process that takes less than one second) or performs other destructive actions. Detonating quickly, shortly after they've been launched, bombs then typically mock you by advertising their attacks via taunting on-screen messages, such as "Arf! Arf! Gotcha!" Few of these programs remain on a BBS for more than one or two downloads, if they get posted at all. They are too easy to catch and stop.

Next in line on our tour of the rogue's gallery is the logic bomb. Like their software bomb cousins, logic bombs (also known as time bombs) are easily engineered, and pretend to be useful applications. Unlike their aggressive, land mine-styled brethren, logic bombs are somewhat more subdued; they conceal their true purpose until one or more external event triggers their detonation. For instance, a logic bomb may wait until a specific date arrives (like the programmer's birthday), or until certain sequences of events occur (perhaps the deletion of the programmer's payroll record). Then the logic bomb explosively fulfills its destructive mission.

Worms

A related troublemaker is the worm program, sometimes confused with the virus. A worm is a little program that worms its way around the system, but doesn't replicate itself. Typically, it "grows," taking up more and more processing time until the system is slowed beyond use. Since the invention of the virus, few destructive worm programs have been written. Worms are easy to find and destroy. Viruses, on the other hand, are difficult, and it may take a system manager days to cleanse a large installation.

Viruses

Of all rogue software, computer viruses are, without question, the most feared and most misunderstood. By incorporating key elements of software bombs, logic bombs, and other malevolent software, and adding their own unique twists, viruses alternately amaze and annoy experts and end users alike.

Authors of both software bombs and logic bombs design destructive kernels and harmless-looking disguises for their programs, but virus authors engineer their products to hide inside or around legitimate application programs. Thus, virus authors need only devise deadly program kernels; their viruses automatically adapt and secrete themselves among whatever files are available, effortlessly hiding behind any one of a thousand programs. The computer virus is the latest twist in the never-ending desire of bored hackers and computer crackers to play a global practical joke on computer systems and their users.

So what is a computer virus? It is a computer program that attaches itself to another program, and becomes part of that program—just as a biological virus attaches itself to a host cell. When the host program runs, it also executes the instructions contained in the virus program. Usually the instructions in the virus program include two things. First and foremost, they make a copy of the virus and attach it to another program elsewhere in the system, or even elsewhere on another system, perhaps via a network. In a recent case, the virus was sent by network over a complex mail and intercomputer messaging system. The second thing a virus does, besides copy itself to ensure survival, is to execute some complex computer instructions telling the computer to do something extraordinary, such as erase files, change spreadsheet entries, destroy disk partition tables, or carry out otherwise harmless practical jokes.

A large proportion of viruses seem to do nothing but spread. This is disconcerting because some virus programs are set off by "trigger" events years in the future. Even the "humorous" varieties can cause problems, though—especially when they disrupt serious work. The Cascade Virus has attracted the most attention among prankster viruses. It first surfaced as a Trojan horse that would supposedly turn off the NUM LOCK key light at bootup, but someone soon turned it into a virus that infected .COM files. This rogue program caused all the letters on the monitor to fall into a pile at the bottom of the screen. To restore the screen, you'd have to reboot. Not funny, especially if you lost all your work.

Other prankster viruses leave odd messages on the screen. For example, the Joker Virus, isolated in Poland in December 1989, leaves bogus DOS error messages. Some examples:

"Invalid Volume ID Format failure"
"Please put a new disk into drive A:"
"End of input file"
"END OF WORKTIME. TURN SYSTEM OFF!"
"Water detect in Co-processor"
"I am hungry! Insert HAMBURGER into drive A:"
"Don't beat me!!"
"Don't drink and drive."
"Another cup of coffee?"
"Insert tractor toilet paper into printer."

Such sophomoric pranks are annoying but not ultimately destructive. Unfortunately, other viruses are deadly serious in their intent. These are the ones that have much of the computer-using public in an uproar.

Is there reason to panic, or to refuse to experiment with new programs? Absolutely not. Virus damage, especially for the individual PC user, is not terribly widespread. Also, several antivirus programs, and the security hardware described later in this chapter, can provide a high degree of safety.

Virus damage on corporate LAN systems is a bigger problem. But hardware and software products are coming on the market to help deal with even LAN-environment rogue software.

Knowledge of what you're dealing with is the first line of defense. If you often exchange diskettes with others or if you simply want to stay abreast of the field, you can call the CVIA Homebase BBS at 1-408-988-4004 (1200-2400bps) in Santa Clara, California. Once signed on, browse for virus information. Available files include virus simulators (these are not real viruses!) and some very informative text files. In particular, look for the latest edition of VIRSUM.ZIP. This file contains a text file named the Virus Information Summary List by Patricia M. Hoffman. It has short but very informative descriptions of known viruses, their symptoms, and specific antivirus programs that have proven effective against them.

Some Virus Sidelights

The theory and concept of a modern computer virus was developed by Professor Fred Cohen of the University of Cincinnati. While a graduate student at UCLA in 1983, he first exhibited how a virus code would work, and later discussed the concept in a famous speech he gave in Canada against the wishes of a worried National Security Administration. Before that the idea for such a program was outlined in a novel by John Brunner called *Shockwave Rider* (1975), which is a cult classic for programmers.

I recently interviewed a Russian émigré who was studying computer science as a medical student at the University of Leningrad. He told me that around 1978 there was talk about a Soviet agenda to develop a spy program that could infiltrate Western computer systems. "The description of how it worked," he told me, "was a description of a virus."

AVOIDING ROGUE SOFTWARE DAMAGE

Telecommunication can and should be an informative, rewarding, and enjoyable pastime. But, as with any group activity, a few bad apples can spoil the fun for the rest of us. By understanding how rogue software and its developers operate, and by employing simple yet effective safe computing techniques, users can ensure the integrity of their disk-based data while reaping the benefits of connectivity.

READ.ME

Federal Law and Telecommunications

Although viruses are a relatively recent development, tampering with telecommunications dates back many years. Telecommunications is a complex field; volumes of state and federal laws pertaining to telecommunications have been written. While it would be impractical to list sources for the laws of your particular state, federal laws governing wire and electronic communications can be accessed in a number of ways. Many public domain bulletin boards have text files of such laws. Other fine sources are the on-line services provided by LEXIS and NEXIS.

As you would expect, not all the federal laws appear in one place. Federal law regarding communications has changed with the technology and continues to evolve. Among the documents you should peruse are the Federal Communications Act of 1934, Title III of the Omnibus Crime Control Act of 1968, the Foreign Intelligence Surveillance Act of 1978, and most significantly, the Electronic Communication Privacy Act of 1986. In addition, you may want to browse through the Rules of the Federal Communications Commission.

While none of this is "fun reading," some of the laws may affect you, particularly if you are a sysop for an interstate bulletin board service.

Remember: On single-user systems, the simple process of regularly backing up your data eliminates much of this concern about rogueware damage.

Another commonsense rule is "Don't Use Pirated Software!" Software pirates have the skills, the software tools, and the motivation necessary to create rogue software. In fact, numerous episodes involving bombs and viruses have been linked to pirated software—a high price to pay for a few dollars saved.

Some of the most paranoid users assert that abstaining from the use of public domain and shareware software is the cornerstone of any reliable antivirus policy. This is an impractical and unnecessary move. It's true that the accessibility of downloadable software renders it, in theory, a tempting distribution method for rogue programmers, but there have been few occurrences of infected software transmitted through the nationwide, ad hoc network of PC-class bulletin board systems. Most instances of rogue software strikes have occurred in mini- or mainframe-computing environments, or have been associated with a physical exchange of disks, usually with links to computer software piracy. Moreover, most BBS operators have long since developed antivirus procedures by using antiviral software and by monitoring any virus outbreak. Personally, I've been downloading and using strange disks for 11 years without catching a virus.

ANTIVIRAL SOFTWARE

For the truly cautious, there is antiviral software available, and it does work. Antiviral software falls into two categories: prevention systems ("vaccines") and detection systems. Prevention systems attempt to stop attacks as they happen. Detection systems check software before it's run, looking for infections in the form of hidden messages, "signature" bits of code, and telltale destructive actions buried in legitimate program code. Antivirus detection systems attempt to isolate viral infections after they have occurred in your software.

Prevention Systems

Memory-resident or TSR programs, already infamous for their tendency to conflict with other programs, are even more annoying when applied as antirogueware, primarily because they interrupt work in progress with warnings of attempted disk writes. Furthermore, antirogue TSR programs cannot detect the direct manipulation of disk controllers—a potentially fatal flaw. Worse still, just as utilities like PopDrop, Headroom, the TSR Utilities, and other TSR management systems can detect and disable memory-resident programs on demand, so can rogueware, when it examines hosts before striking. Also, there are some new viruses that avoid DOS calls and hide themselves in memory.

On the other hand, virus writers are handicapped by the need to keep their code as small as possible. If the code becomes too long, a virus cannot go unnoticed. As a result, few viruses are able to bypass DOS function calls completely. So there is some valuable protection in TSR monitoring systems. One widely used antivirus TSR program is FLUSHOT+ by Ross Greenberg. It is available on BBSs, and Greenberg keeps it up to date on Exec-PC (see Chapter 6). Another good program is VACCINE, which, with its companion program SURVEY, provides three different levels of protection, and guards against some operator errors. VACCINE and SURVEY are part of the Paul Mace Utilities, a well-regarded set of commercial data protection and recovery programs.

If you use a TSR antivirus program, remember they're not absolutely effective. They will stop many common viruses—those you're most apt to come across. For more sensitive applications, you may wish to use a postinfection virus detection program, instead of or in addition to a TSR program. For the broadest, most effective antivirus systems possible, you'll probably need to take a hardware approach (discussed later in this chapter).

Detection Systems

Detection systems complement prevention systems; they allow intruders to breach systems and then rely on sophisticated examination algorithms to isolate the intruders. Detection systems fall into two distinct categories: antibomb and antivirus.

Antibomb Detection Systems

Antibomb systems search files for destructive routines (such as file erasure or program reformatting calls) embedded in executable code. Some detectors extract text messages stored in programs, looking for overt indications of rogue activity (statements like "Arf! Arf! Gotcha!"). Unfortunately, most antibomb detection systems share the same, unsettling drawbacks: they sometimes flag legitimate programs as bombs, and they can't locate or display encrypted text messages.

Antiviral Detection Systems

Due to the very nature of viral activity—viruses cause detectable changes to otherwise static (unchanging) files—antivirus detection systems are considerably more effective than their antibomb cousins. Here again, the software falls into two classes: program-specific detectors and generic detectors.

Program-Specific Detectors   Program-specific detectors search for a limited number of known viruses. Thus they require frequent updates as new viruses are discovered or old strains "evolve." Because of this need for updates, you may want to use a shareware virus detector — although several good commercial products are available, including one from IBM. Three of the best programs are

F-PROT, Fridrik Skulason's detector/disinfector
VirScan, IBM's Virus Scanning Program (commercial)
ViruScan, McAfee Associates' ViruScan detector/disinfector

Each of these has special areas of effectiveness. To see which is most deadly against which viruses, sign onto the CVIA Homebase BBS and download Patricia Hoffman's *Virus Information Summary List.* Although all three programs will detect the ten or so viruses that account for 95 percent of reported infections, the sheer number of viruses caught may not be your primary concern. The greater the number of viruses caught, the longer a detector program takes to run.

One problem with program-specific detectors is that some viruses have the ability to self-encrypt. They leave no detectable signature. The nastier viruses do not even change the size of the files they infect. Unfortunately, as detectors get more sophisticated, so do the viruses that play hide and seek with them.

Generic Detectors   Generic detectors take a different approach. Instead of looking for a virus's signature, they try to catch all changes, no matter how small or insignificant, that occur to static files. Such programs generally create checksums for every executable or every user-specified file. Some new viruses can "hide" their changes by preserving original program code in unused parts of the disk, but this is not a common practice.

Two very good examples of this approach are CHECKUP, by antivirus researcher Rich Levin, and the Mace Utility program SURVEY, mentioned earlier. John McAfee's SENTRY program is another good choice. Like program-specific detectors, the generic approach has its deficiencies: generic detectors may take a long time to run; their output data files can consume vast amounts of valuable disk space; and, if stored on the host system, they themselves are subject to viral infections and alterations. Moreover, some generic detectors require time-consuming maintenance of their output data files; others employ poorly conceived detection algorithms capable of being duped by sophisticated viral algorithms.

Still, on balance, this type of program is a reliable software-based way to find changes in your files. Changes do not prove you've caught a virus, but they do suggest something strange might be going on. If your disk access is fast enough, and you're in a position of risk, a CHECKUP-type program is a very good way to counter the virus threat.

The Hardware Approach

As viruses proliferate and LAN users start to feel vulnerable, it's to be expected that antivirus hardware will appear. A hardware solution may appear extreme, but if done right it can stop intrusions that software monitors cannot cope with, even theoretically. Also, hardware detection works much faster than software does, and so can function invisibly to the user—or "transparently," as the experts call it.

For example, as this is written, a new ViroCrypt board is completing beta testing at Digital Safety Technology Corp. in San Mateo, California. The board uses onboard memory and complex firmware programming to monitor disk activity. It also provides password protection and disk encryption. At its higher settings, the system uses message authentication techniques borrowed from the banking industry to detect changes to files.

ViroCrypt has stopped every virus thrown at it so far. One reason for ViroCrypt's effectiveness is its independence from the main operating system. By the time a computer boots up and loads an antivirus program, the meaner viruses have already been loaded into memory. It takes hardware to cope with viruses imported from floppy diskettes.

Another firm, RSA Data Security Inc. (Redwood City, California), has developed a Digital Signature system that verifies without encryption that a given program or message has not been altered. The idea is to give files a signature that changes if a virus makes any alterations. The RSA system was strong enough to be selected by the Pentagon for key management on unclassified material.

As networked systems like Channel 1, Exec-PC, and corporate LANs proliferate, fast hardware solutions may soon become the antivirus tactic of choice.

A COMPREHENSIVE SAFETY PROGRAM

The ideal antirogue software safety net consists of an intelligent and well-tested combination of safe computing methods, plus both prevention and detection software. Safe computing methods work to protect most users from harm. Prevention software erects barriers that stop common rogues from accessing user data. Detection software identifies advanced rogue programs after they've slipped through prevention shields. By adopting this three-pronged defense and by maintaining regular data backups, you can be reasonably certain that your systems are indeed protected from the ravages of software lunacy, and you can comfortably enjoy the extraordinary world of telecommunications.

Here is some more software to consider. A complete security system is available from Sophco, Box 7430, Boulder, CO 80306 (800-922-3001). Called Protec, the system offers everything from virus protection, to password protection, to encryption. It's priced at $295.

In Canada, Orion Microsystems, Box 128, Pierrefonds, Quebec, Canada H9H 4K8 (514-626-9234), created an excellent vaccine program called NTI-VIRUS.EXE. Selling for U.S. $49.95, it is worth a look. The owner of the small firm, Madjid Bourki, has studied viruses as thoroughly as anyone.

RG Software Systems, 2300 Computer Ave. #I-51, Willow Grove, PA 19090 (215-659-5300), added antivirus code to the latest version of their $99.95 utility called Disk Watcher. Disk Watcher actively observes the disk drives and lets you know when they are getting full; it also stops you from accidentally formatting a hard disk.

If you need to be more cautious, the ViroCrypt board will cost $400 to $440, suggested retail. It should do the job until an antivirus disk controller finally comes on the market, and several are rumored to be under development.

The commercial and shareware products mentioned earlier far from exhaust your choices. Many similar products are on the market, and they all seem to catch most of the viruses you're likely to run into. Remember, though, that shareware authors can afford to issue program updates more freqently than can commercial vendors. So if you decide to go for a postinfection virus detection program, shareware is probably your best bet.

Let your wallet and your security needs be your guide. Meanwhile, back up your disks, enjoy your modem, and don't lose sleep over viruses!

CHAPTER THIRTEEN

Telecommuting

Modems and telecommunications give us new freedoms, one of which is the "office without walls" idea. Some call it the office in a briefcase, the home office, or the office away from the office. These terms all fall under the broad category of *telecommuting.*

The idea of working outside a traditional office is not new, as any field sales representative can tell you. Many large U.S. companies such as J.C. Penney, The Travelers Companies, and Pacific Bell, to name a few, have already tapped into the benefits of telecommuting.

In recent years, the practice of telecommuting has boomed. Studies show that an estimated 25 million North Americans in all types of professions already do income-producing work at home. A survey by the Link Resources Telework Group in New York showed that, entering 1990, approximately 3.5 million corporate workers have formal work-at-home arrangements with their employers, and about 16 million corporate employees work at home either part time or full time.

Jack Nilles, president of the management consulting firm JALA Associates in Los Angeles, is credited with coining the term *telecommuting* in

1973. His definition is "the partial or total substitution of telecommunications, possibly with the aid of the computer, for the commute to work." Telecommuting means working at home or at a satellite office, and communicating with the home office or plant mainly by phone, sometimes with a computer. The computer and modem are often combined with wide area network E-mail systems such as MCI, to make an even more powerful combination.

Due largely to increasing highway commuter traffic, more workers during the last decade have looked toward the home office as a viable alternative to the traditional office workplace. This trend has emerged for a number of reasons. Many U.S. companies have become more decentralized to cut expenses and serve markets more quickly. In return, telecommuting allows companies to draw a broader range of talent from employees across the country.

There is obvious appeal to corresponding with the office via fax lines and computer links. The employee usually feels a certain sense of freedom working at home. There is also the advantage of flexibility and independence. Other potential benefits include

- Reduced childcare costs

- Less time wasted in traditional vehicle commuting

- Reduced cost to the company for office space, equipment, and supplies

- Reduced cost to the employee for business clothing, gasoline, and other traveling expenses

- Heightened productivity from the employee, due to increased motivation and personal reward

The remote office has disadvantages, too. There is the drawback of reduced social interaction with co-workers. The employee incurs added costs in equipment that the company does not buy. The employer incurs costs for transmitting and receiving information to and from the off-site employee. There is the potential concern that an employee who is not often visible becomes "invisible." Lastly, some companies think telecommuting creates a security risk, because there is less control and actual supervision of the employee's work.

When all is said and done, however, the benefits of telecommuting far outweigh any perceived drawbacks.

SOCIOLOGY OF THE REMOTE OFFICE

If most of your job is accomplished at a computer terminal, wouldn't it be just as easy to do your work at home? If the terminal can communicate over the telephone, why not call your home your office? Studies show that half the jobs in the nation could be done this way. Here is a sampling of professionals who benefit from telecommuting:

- Writers

- Salespersons

- Real estate agents

- Architects

- Accountants

- Engineers

- All types of managers

- Computer programmers

- Travel agents

Personal computers, cellular phones, voice mail, fax machines, electronic mail, and other electronic communication tools are catching on rapidly, and their use is spreading beyond the traditional office. As the U.S. becomes a country absorbed in these devices, it is beginning to let go of the confinements of centralized group environments. Satellite communications and computer networks began the alteration of corporate organization. The J.C. Penney Company, for example, was able to move its entire headquarters from New York City to Plano, Texas, thanks to the advancements in network communications equipment. (Unfortunately, now the company is stuck in Plano.)

Managers of telecommuters say—and studies substantiate it—that their employees actually work more hours and increase their productivity. The DuPont Co. in Wilmington, Delaware, is one such company where telecommuting is successful. More than 1500 of the firm's sales managers are telecommuting on a regular basis, with favorable results. The administrative workload has been reduced by up to eight hours a week. Just as important, the telecommuters are happy.

As for the isolation issue, many telecommuters say it probably affects full-time telecommuters more than part-time ones. They point out that they are able to cut down on the number of meetings they attend, thus leaving them more time for tasks requiring concentration. Let's face it; too much office time is spent either in a meeting, waiting for a meeting, or wondering what a meeting was about.

Planning for Telecommuting

It is important to plan and develop the telecommuting program. Adequate computer and electronic equipment must be available, as well as user support for the telecommuter. Many companies provide all the necessary equipment: a workstation (typically an IBM-compatible PC), monitor, modem and telecommunications program, word processing programs, perhaps accounting and time management software, and a copy of this book.

The company's data processing department should provide support to the telecommuter for installation, operation, and maintenance of the home system. If possible, a training course in effective telecommuting should be developed and offered. Finally, the telecommuter should be allowed to remotely tap into the company's mainframe. This allows the off-site worker to make extensive use of the electronic mail system to exchange messages, data, and documents with co-workers, just as though he or she were in the on-site office.

A fax machine is an important part of a modern telecommuting office. The fax allows the telecommuter to see all the office memos and messages, in a timely fashion. It also saves some of the transportation costs involved in transmission of important information.

CHANGES IN TECHNOLOGY

It is estimated that among some five million North Americans operating full-time businesses from home, about the only thing most of them have in common is ownership or use of a computer. The reason is simple: computers are relatively inexpensive, and they increase productivity.

Just as the telephone is a fixture of our home lives, and as the personal computer quickly becomes one, modems will soon be equally commmonplace, say the experts. The people at Hayes Microcomputer Products, Inc., one of the largest developers of modems, like to say that a computer without a telephone is like a car without gasoline.

The Portable Computing Breakthrough

Since the invention of the Osborne 1 portable computer in the late 1970s (see Figure 13-1), portable computers have become the fastest-growing segment of the personal computer market. Ranging in price from $600 note-takers to 80386-based machines that cost $8000, and weighing from 3.5 to more than 30 pounds, these machines are the hot ticket in personal computing.

As a nation, the U.S. will purchase nearly one million portables in 1990, according to Data Quest, a San Jose, California, computer research firm.

Figure 13-1

The Osborne 1 portable computer

That equates to a $1.5 billion industry. Portables now claim about ten percent of the PC market. Portable makers such as Toshiba, Zenith, GRiD, NEC, Compaq, Tandy, and others are grabbing significant market shares with inventive, state-of-the-art technological advancements.

The PC market itself, along with the computer tabloids, defined the early model of a laptop product that would be successful—the "dream machine." It was battery powered and small in size, with dual diskette drives, 640K of RAM, a crisp and readable screen, and IBM compatibility. In 1986, Toshiba introduced the ten-pound T1000, a front-runner in the battery-powered laptop arena. Interestingly enough, Toshiba's most popular machine ran on AC power—the sleek T3100. It is essentially a lightweight AT with a plasma screen, and a 1988 Gallup poll of *Fortune* 1000 companies ranked it fourth in microcomputer use among responding companies during 1987. Amazing!

As mentioned elsewhere in this book, portable computers come in two styles: transportable machines and laptop PCs. Transportables weigh about 20 pounds, and their movability is debatable. In fact, they've been nick-named "luggables." They come equipped with microprocessors and memory comparable to any desktop PC, and can almost equal one in features (except for high-resolution color and easy expandability).

Portable Modems

Advancements in modem technology have shrunk the modem's size to go right along with smaller personal computers. Today, modems the size of a cigarette pack contain a 2400bps Hayes-compatible modem and a 9600bps fax unit. The lightweight and compact packaging appeals to portable computer users who need to send and receive fax messages, as well as access company E-mail systems via a data modem.

One such modem, Touchbase Systems Inc.'s WorldPort 2496 fax/data modem, plugs directly into the computer's serial port, or to a serial cable, for ready usage. A software setup program stores the parameters needed for the device to work as either a modem or fax machine. The modem runs on nine-volt alkaline batteries that last three to four hours.

In 1989, Rockwell International Corp. introduced the V22 modem-on-a-chip. The RC224AT chip, a single, 68-pin microchip, is compatible with the AT command and can be attached directly to the PC motherboard. The chip offers 300, 1200, and 2400bps in half- or full-duplex mode. This new technology is in demand by laptop users, who can now transfer data at 2400bps from their laptops.

Networks

Through electronic networking, telecommuters can "talk" to other people in their field. Bulletin board systems, described throughout this book, are set up by many companies to keep tabs on telecommuters and customers. Compu-Serve offers a Work-at-Home Special Interest Group (SIG) for on-line support. You locate it by entering **GO HOM 146.**

For information regarding networking electronically, CompuServe Information Services (800-848-8990) is a good resource.

Support

Probably the leading voice of the home office market is the magazine *Home Office Computing,* formerly *Family and Home Office Computing.* This publication specifically targets the $6 billion working-at-home market, providing tips on setting up the home office, reviews of new products, and case studies of those who have been successful. Other magazines of value to the telecommuter include *PC Magazine,* with its comprehensive reviews of related products, and an outstanding user's point of view; and *PC Computing,* which is written for the kind of person who has always wanted to be a telecommuter.

There are also newsletters directed specifically to the telecommuter, such as Gil Gordon's *Telecommuting Review.*

There are a few organizations, such as the Association of Electronic Cottagers, the National Association for the Cottage Industry, and the National Alliance of Homebased Businesswomen, that aid in the development and promotion of the home-based office worker. The National Association for the Cottage Industry (312-472-8116) provides a complete nationwide list of companies currently using telecommuters.

THE IDEAL HOME OFFICE

The prices of personal computers, fax machines, copiers, telephone answering machines, and other high-tech tools are coming down, so that equipping a home office now involves a reasonable expense of a few thousand dollars. Sales of fax machines are on the rise, with prices as low as $600. Even cellular phones are becoming more affordable—some go for $400.

Here are some of the basic equipment necessities for your home office.

Computer System

The first objective in setting up a telecommuting office is to select a computer system. There are no ultimate standards for connecting personal computers to business computers by telephone. This book does provide a general purpose telecommunication software package. Most people can get by with a turbo 8088-based machine. An EGA or VGA color card with color monitor is a recommended addition. A hard disk is essential; it should not be smaller than 40MB. To get started, 640K of memory is sufficient, but you'll need a lot more in the future. Also, if you really want your computer to be useful for years and years, consider the extra expense of an 80386-based machine.

Printers

Any good dot matrix printer will do the job, but you would be wise to invest in a laser printer. An HP LaserJet or other HP compatible product is the current single standard for PC-based laser printers. If you plan to do desktop publishing and fancier design, you will want to explore the world of the PostScript-compatible printer, although a complete Apple Macintosh system is your best bet.

Laptop Buying Tips

If you want to get fancy, or need to take your computer on the road a lot, read Chapter 14 on notebook computers. Meanwhile, here are the tips I give people who are interested in buying a laptop.

First, remember that the ideal laptop hasn't yet been built, and probably won't be built for a few years, although with each new product generation, the designers are getting closer and closer. Among some favorites at the moment are the Zenith SupersPort 286, the Zenith MinisPort, the NEC Ultralite, and the Toshiba 1000 and 1600 machines. Other laptops such as the Compaq SLT and the Dynabook Laptop (see Figure 13-2) are highly regarded. I do not include as laptops any machines that require full AC power to operate. A laptop should be able to run on batteries and be used on an airplane.

There are four primary considerations you must make when buying a laptop.

Appearance

This may seem a silly thing to worry about, but the appearance and overall design of a laptop is an indication of the amount of care the manufacturer has put into the machine. It also affects your relationship to the machine. If people are going to laugh at you for using the world's ugliest computer, for example, you'll probably be reluctant to use it in public, thus hurting your career and chances for advancement. If, on the other hand, you are proud of your sleek, modern laptop, then you'll probably use it just to show it off, thus putting in extra hours of work. Companies that buy their employees laptops should recognize the status factor of certain machines.

Figure 13-2

Even early pioneers like Adam Osborne are impressed with the speed and performance of today's portables. Osborne is shown here installing and using his Dynabook 286. The Dynabook is easily converted to a laptop by detaching its patented Docking Module

Weight

You have two choices: light and heavy. A new category of machine now growing in popularity, called the notebook computer, should weigh in at four pounds or less. This category was born at NEC in the form of its nifty Ultralite, followed by Zenith's MinisPort. Both these machines are in the $2000-and-up range. The old lightweight classic is the Toshiba 1000. Weighing about 6 1/2 pounds, it includes a 3 1/2-inch floppy, unlike the notebook computers. The NEC uses plug-in storage modules, and the Zenith uses a new 2-inch disk. The Toshiba is quite inexpensive, selling for less than $1000, but suffers from a hard-to-read display.

A possible third weight category may soon emerge: the billfold-sized MS-DOS computer. Poquet and Atari are the forerunners in this category.

Power

As of this writing, the more power you have, the more weight you have to carry. However, many more laptops will incorporate the new 2 1/2-inch hard drive, which can pack 40MB of storage into the size of a cigarette pack. Newer chips and fancier circuits also mean using the more powerful 80286 and 80386 chips in a lightweight laptop. But for now, plan to lug around 11 or more pounds if you want the high-speed, hard disk laptop. The leaders in the category are the Zenith SupersPort and the Toshiba 1600. They can do almost anything a full desktop machine can do, except color graphics.

Readability

This refers to the screen and how readable it is. Flat screen technology has been slowly improving over the years, and now the back-lit, active matrix LCD screen is very usable, even in dark surroundings. Unfortunately, there is a trade-off: just try going to Hawaii and reading the back-lit Zenith display while you're sitting on the beach. It gets washed out by the sun. Meanwhile, the normally hard-to-read Toshiba 1000 looks great with this lighting. Zenith has developed a "combo" screen for its new MinisPort that supposedly corrects this problem, but it will take a trip to Hawaii to test it.

Most important is that you spend as much time as possible with each machine you're considering before you buy anything. With desktop PCs, one

25Mhz 386 VGA machine is about the same as another, but this is not true of laptops. They are all different, in every way, so take your time before you select one. And to be on the safe side, check to see how easily your selection can be resold.

THE FUTURE

No one is saying just yet that we will soon be tearing down all of our office buildings because everyone is working from home. But the tools that make telecommuting feasible are here. They're affordable, and they work. As these products become even easier to use and cheaper to buy, today's home office will become tomorrow's home information center. Copiers and fax machines will soon become as commonplace in our homes as television sets.

Although telecommuting may not be a full substitute for passenger rail, or air travel, it could make a significant contribution to the battle against highway congestion.

CHAPTER FOURTEEN

Notebook Computers

The invention of a viable *notebook computer*—one that packs full DOS functions into less than six pounds of hardware—has the potential to revolutionize telecommunications. With the ability to tap into on-line databases, a user has access to information anywhere. The world, suddenly, is smaller. The notebook computer is small enough to be essentially a terminal, connecting any location serviced by a telephone to all forms of information, bringing data to you in the remotest corners of the world, into your hotel room, or an airport lounge.

The Zenith 181, with its backlit screen, used to be a dream come true. It was surrounded by Toshiba, NEC, and Sharp laptops—all of them weighing in at ten pounds or more. The Toshiba T1000 and its less-than-seven-pound heft led manufacturers to think in terms of weight. Now, the wave of the future is this new category: the notebook computer. In the years ahead, no serious telecommuter will be seen without one.

A state-of-the-art notebook computer will certainly be quite different a year from now, as products never stand still. Even at the dawn of the 1990s, though, certain minimum standards and requirements have established themselves, and the consumer should accept no less than the following:

- A weight of under five pounds
- Compatibility with existing programs, and the ability to exchange data with larger machines
- A readable screen, and a comfortable, durable keyboard
- A battery life longer than the average airplane flight
- A price not exceeding that of the average major appliance

Consumers of the future will probably clamor for a 50MHz, 80486-driven, cellular machine with a 3-D screen that fits in your palm and costs $499. They will know what a desktop can do, and will want laptops to be capable of the same tasks. Thanks to the trickle-down nature of innovation, laptops will soon have more desktop capabilities, but by that time the desktop will have taken yet another leap. Consequently, there can never be a "perfect" small computer. Nevertheless, the notebook computers of today can handily manage the essential telecommunications tasks, and act as portable data- management terminals that can be attached to any phone.

Notebook computers have gone "over the hump" in terms of power, functions, and weight. This opens up telecommunications to many and diverse new applications. Moreover, even if on-the-go computing has always required compromise, these compromises are no longer debilitating. Your notebook computer may not be as versatile as your home machine, but it performs the tasks at hand well enough so you don't mind.

EVOLUTION OF THE NOTEBOOK COMPUTER

The latest crop of notebook computers evolved from three needs: power, portability, and expandability. Since the beginning, manufacturers have recognized the importance of portability, and have tried—in most cases unsuccessfully—to meet that demand. Sometimes, as with the early GRiD, the machine was too expensive to be popular. An advantage of notebook computing is effortless transportation to remote places; but no one will attempt to scale a mountain with a $10,000 machine in a backpack.

In the past, the "portable" label was subjective. Osborne Computers, years ago, scored big with a so-called portable machine weighing 20 pounds. The "portable" designation worked only if you were a weight lifter. Compaq's first success was with a similar machine, and one of IBM's first PC failures was a Compaq look-alike called, deceptively enough, the PC Portable. And let's not forget the Otrona, probably the best designed machine among these "luggables." These products missed the mark because of perceived, rather than actual defects. They ran well enough, but most users left them at home on desks, and moved them maybe twice a year. In addition, the standard five-inch screen was uncomfortably small, and purchase of an extra monitor ultimately destroyed the cost effectiveness of these early portables.

No More "Luggables"

These older portable PCs are now found at swap meets, and sold by second-string companies. Desktop PCs, in general, continue to become smaller, if still not easy to move.

"Portable" evolved to "laptop." The laptop label is also a misnomer. Generally, it is applied to machines that theoretically can be used when sitting down, with your knees as a surface. In practice, however, few people use a laptop on their laps; the posture is hardly comfortable or efficient for typing. It's particularly difficult to use one in a plane, seated in coach, when the seat in front of you is leaning back—but anything is possible. For the sake of argument, we can say that the laptop category includes machines that run standard software and have a clamshell-like design. Beyond this, the category has seen more variety than almost any other personal computing genre.

Throughout the development of laptops, the common denominator has been compromise—between power, portability, and expandability. The most significant problem has been weight; even a 15-pound machine seems unbearably heavy by day's end. Even in the most capable units, the battery life was too short, or the screen was too hard to read, or the keyboard was too small. In some of the more powerful laptops, batteries were no longer used at all; manufacturers assumed that anyone who needed that much computing power would always be close to an electric socket. Finally, laptops have never accommodated expandibility to any satisfaction.

A laptop's power now approaches that of a desktop PC, but users generally pay a 20 percent premium for portability. Some kind of trade-off is always needed, and so far there is no one computer that combines the Big Three of *power*, *portability*, and *expandibility*.

Enter the Notebook

Notebook computers, used primarily for gathering data and sending short files, are nothing new. For years, newspaper reporters have toted around remote terminals to transmit late-breaking stories into their newspaper's computer system. No wonder Tandy/Radio Shack's Model 100 was so popular when it was introduced. Journalists accustomed to dragging around an expensive clunker called a "bubble-term" loved the Model 100. It was lighter, easier to use, and allowed limited storage and retrieval of data as well.

Next came the Convergent Workslate, which has recently popped up in surplus outlets for less than $200. It was a more powerful, but less successful solution. Perhaps the electronic Filofax concept was ahead of its time, or the push-button keyboard was too hard to use. There was a reasonable range of software, loaded through a microcassette, but the LCD screen was too much of an eyestrain for anything besides occasional reference.

While the Model 100 found its niche and the Workslate disappeared from view, no significant notebook-style computers appeared for several years. In 1988, however, British miniaturization king Clive Sinclair came up with the Z-88. Though decidedly nonstandard, the Z-88 was a step in the right direction, and was a bridge between the Model 100 and the full-function notebook units of today. It had no disk drives and could not run DOS software, but files could be easily exchanged with databases on larger machines. The Z-88, which continues to sell, had a sleek look and light weight. Still, its inability to store and back up information on site prompted users to pay a little more for the admittedly heavier standard DOS laptops.

NEC's UltraLite, announced in late 1988, brought several new issues to the table. Weighing less than five pounds, and less than two inches thick, the UltraLite was not only easy to carry, but could run standard DOS software. It included a modem. The UltraLite also promoted the idea of the silicon hard disk. On this disk, up to 2MB of RAM was configured as nonvolatile storage, which could be saved even when the machine was turned off. This hard disk, too small for desktop use, was still large enough to meet most laptop needs.

The UltraLite heralded the debut of two significant laptop features: a silicon hard disk and an embedded file transfer utility. Both will become standard and necessary equipment on the notebook and laptop computers of the future. The silicon hard disk turns RAM into a nonvolatile, battery-backed storage device, and at 2MB it is large enough for fundamental laptop data functions. The transfer utility (UltraLite uses Traveling Software's LapLink) enables files to be sent from a laptop to a desktop through the respective serial ports. This is a more efficient transfer process than copying to and from a floppy disk.

The UltraLite has no installed floppy drive; rather, it uses ROM cards and RAM cards for file and software transfer. These cards have the potential for efficient data transfer and storage, and could evolve into a software distribution medium.

Despite some disadvantages and nonstandard behavior, the UltraLite is clearly a strong product that increased the ante in the notebook computing game.

Getting Lighter

Since the UltraLite bid, the Zenith MinisPort saw and raised the bet. (IBM has been notably absent from the game, and innovation has sprung from the NEC/Toshiba/Zenith triumvirate.) Some innovations that seemed like good ideas have been dropped for more familiar approaches; other experiments are being tried. If you step back a bit, the market sorts itself out. It is moving toward smaller, faster, more practical machines with more storage, better keyboards, and brighter screens.

One innovation dropped is the Zenith MinisPort's internal 2-inch floppy diskette drive. This was a nice little drive with a familiar, reliable means of on-the-road data exchange, but Zenith has replaced it now with an internal 20 or 40MB hard disk. There is still an optional external floppy drive for those who need one.

Laptops, as standard DOS machines, have always been touted as alternatives to desktops. In this endeavor they are already a step or two behind. Notebook computers, on the other hand, have no such burden; no one expects a notebook computer to do everything that a desktop PC can. The appearance of functional notebook computers has changed the concept of portability.

The notebook machines of the future will remain an adjunct to another system. File transfer to a larger computer will take place over a little antenna using low-power radio. (The Japanese have already perfected the technology of wireless RF serial port connections.) We can expect to see the 2 1/2-inch hard disk crop up in superlight machines offering 20MB to 40MB of inexpensive storage, thus turning the notebook computer into a miniature powerhouse.

While the first laptop users traveled in style and faced none of the inconveniences of covered wagons and dust storms, they were nonetheless pioneers. Taking a computer on a trip was exciting, but you also carried along enough obstacles and inconveniences to make you wish for the good old days of pen and paper.

For instance, I remember a colleague who decided to take his PC Portable to a trade show. The machine required electricity, so using it on the airplane was out of the question—even if the seat-tray would have supported it. The computer barely fit under the seat, to the aggravation of my friend and everyone around him. After landing in Las Vegas, where the flight gates are about six miles from the taxi stand, he weathered his first strenuous physical workout of the day. The next obstacle course was at his hotel; when he arrived, there was no bellman in sight. By the time he got to his room, he was too exhausted to compute. In the end, he was able to use the machine for only ten minutes at the show.

Four years later I saw him at the same trade show—this time toting a Zenith SupersPort. He carried it to meetings and around the show floor. However, even at half the weight and twice the power of the PC Portable, the 15-pound SupersPort became quite a burden at day's end.

In the future, then, a notebook computer could be the final trade show solution. It's actually lighter than the press releases you collect on an average day. And carrying it around for a 15-hour stretch won't make your arm longer.

Coming Down the Pike

Some of the newest machines go far beyond the requirements we suggest for notebook computers of the future. Here are some thumbnail sketches of products that are paving the way to the future.

Compaq LTE and LTE/286

Weighing in at six pounds with an 8 1/2-by-11-inch footprint, the new Compaq LTE and LTE/286 notebook PCs are hot. They are a full two-thirds smaller than Compaq's last version, the SLT/286. They have CGA-compatible, backlit supertwist displays, and NiCad batteries that are good for about 3 1/2 hours. Optional battery packs, backups, and quick chargers are available for those who can't just plug into a standard AC outlet before fade-out.

The LTE models are the first notebooks to provide high-speed 20 or 40MB fixed disk drives; a 3 1/2-inch, 1.44MB diskette drive; an 80-key keyboard with standard key spacing; an embedded numeric keypad and 101-key compatibility; and an optional built-in 2400 baud modem.

Both LTE models are the same size and weight. The 286 operates at 12 MHz and can handle all standard applications, including spreadsheets, cost analyses, and account profiles. The slower 9.54 MHz 80286-based LTE is designed more for basic applications like word processing, electronic mail, inventory tracking, and customer databases. Both machines have 3 1/2-inch drives, can read off-the-shelf commercial programs, and can store and transfer data to desktop machines in a standard format.

Toshiba T1000SE

Beating the six-pound goal by ounces, Toshiba released its new T1000SE as the new decade opened. The machine's 1.78-by-12.4-by-10.2-inch size fits nicely into most briefcases. The built-in 11 1/2-ounce nickel cadmium battery is included in the total weight and lasts about two hours before it needs recharging. The AC adapter only adds an extra 10 1/2 ounces.

The T1000SE has a full-size, 82-key keyboard that is pleasant to use. Expansion capabilities abound. The industry-standard 1.44MB, 3 1/2-inch diskette drive makes the machine compatible with existing systems.

Poqet

This little machine gives full service to DOS applications and has a full-size keyboard (or close to it), but would fit in some coat pockets. The Poqet weighs in at just about one pound, making it by far the lightest of the full-service notebook machines. It measures 8 3/4 by 4 1/4 inches and can run for up to 100 hours on two AA batteries! It also uses self-powered static RAM and ROM cards, like the ones used by the NEC UltraLite, rather than dynamic RAM. The LCD display is a full 80 columns by 25 lines and has a glareproof surface. The machine has built-in parallel and serial ports.

Poqet is working with programmers to develop ROM-card versions of major applications. These include WordPerfect, Lotus 1-2-3, and Lucid 3D. AlphaWorks plans an integrated package combining a word processor, a database compatible with dBASE III+, a Lotus 1-2-3-compatible spreadsheet with graphics, and a communications module. The machine comes standard with DOS 3.3, BASIC, PQ-Link (a file transfer ROM utility), and a null modem cable that attaches between your desktop PC and the Poqet's proprietary expansion port.

The Poqet's primary disadvantages are its keyboard and the lack of a built-in modem. If you buy the Poqet, be sure to pick up a plug-in modem. The keyboard was an engineering trade-off. To keep weight down, they chose a nonmechanical keyboard that feels cramped and uncomfortable until you get used to it. Maybe they'll pay the two- or three-pound penalty and offer a future machine with a more familiar mechanical keyboard.

Despite these minor drawbacks, the Poqet is an altogether impressive feat of engineering.

AIRLINE TRAVEL

In the past few years travelers have learned a lot about portable computing—mostly through trial and error. As computers have become lighter and more powerful, the standards for laptop travel have also developed.

Airline travel, for which portable/laptop computing was designed, has its own set of foibles. Should you travel with a laptop, in most cases you'll want to check the accessories—external disk drive, adapter, portable printer, and other peripherals—in your baggage. (The exception to this rule might be the adapter. If you are stuck in an airport on a layover, it would be wise to plug into an electric socket and save battery life.) In general, though, carry as little as possible on the plane itself.

Knowing what to check through and what to carry is only the beginning. Airline policies, international travel restrictions, varying power standards, and hotels inhospitable to modems can all become irritants. To defuse troublesome elements, you need to plan ahead.

Your planning can be as fundamental as researching the carry-on restrictions, and determining how strictly the airline adheres to the two-bag limit. If you want to travel light and avoid checking anything—usually a wise move—carrying a garment bag, briefcase, and portable in a separate case will violate the rules. A lot depends on how zealously the flight attendant decides to enforce the letter of the law. Try using your laptop bag as a briefcase.

While jamming a 12-pound laptop into carry-on luggage presents a logistical nightmare, notebook computers solve this problem. Few flight attendants will nail you for a 12-by-10-inch unit slung inconspicuously across your shoulder. In that unlikely instance, it's easy to slip the notebook into a briefcase, or even into the folds of a newspaper.

It is a fallacy that portable computers emit signals that can interfere with an airplane's operation. Most airline employees, fortunately, know this. Still, the pilot controls all activity on the plane, and if for some reason computing is banned on a particular flight, there is nothing you can do.

Airplane laptop users may face a controversy that has nothing to do with the two-bag limit, and that is the possibility that a portable computer can contain a bomb or other terrorist implement. There was an incident in which a portable stereo, checked through as luggage, destroyed a plane in midair. This tragic occurrence has resulted in attempts to prohibit passengers from carrying any electronic equipment on flights.

Realistically, the hazards of traveling with your laptop are pretty unspectacular. Aside from packing correctly, you'll have to deal with getting through security safely, protecting yourself against theft, and finding a comfortable place to work during a layover. As for security, increased or not, the standard X-ray scan will endanger neither the machine nor the disk data. A less commonplace magnetic detector, on the other hand, might affect your data. When in doubt, ask. (Here is yet another reason for you to back up all your files, all the time.)

Theft

Notebook computers have a sleek, expensive look. As a result, they are prime targets for airport thieves and other shifty characters. The obvious rule of thumb is to keep your unit in sight, the same way you would your camera, but that doesn't always work. A thief only needs a second's distraction. The fact that your laptop is not only expensive hardware, but also contains valuable data, makes extra security measures imperative.

The first security precaution you should take is the all-important data backup. The best procedure is to find a backup system and stick to it. A good one is to copy all data files to a floppy disk at the end of each day, and then mail that disk back to the office. Always copy to a floppy, and keep that disk separate in a place that won't attract a thief—like inside a pair of clean socks. If everything is backed up, a stolen computer won't be quite as heartbreaking a loss.

Protecting the computer is part common sense and part preventive skill. For instance, don't make a conspicuous display of your computer. Another important defense is securing the computer to your luggage, or even to your arm. Sometimes this can be done with the handle, although some of the better-equipped laptops supply a security bracket that can be used to lock the unit to an immovable object. (If your laptop has neither a handle nor a security bracket, you might want to avoid carrying it "downtown" at all.)

Encryption

For those who feel there can never be too much security, look in the back of the major computer magazines for ads about data encryption and security software. For example, Secret Disk, from Lattice Software, will encrypt your files so that they are unusable unless a password is entered.

OTHER TRAVEL CONCERNS

A notebook computer does not pretend to accomplish all desktop tasks; rather, it is the first personal computer in history with the role of a "second computer." It won't, for instance, handle color graphics or give you access to a million records. An effective notebook will give you just enough power to solve the inevitable on-the-road computing problems. So it makes sense to plan ahead for what your laptop doesn't include.

Printers

One typical travel problem is the need to output hard copy. Portable printers are available, but you'll have to carry around at least another four to ten pounds of inefficient weight. In most cases, you won't need to print much material on the road, but when you do, it helps to call ahead. Many hotels and airlines offer access to printers. For instance, you can stop by United Airlines' Red Carpet Club in O'Hare for a beer and a printout.

These airport clubs aren't free; "initiation" fees are $100 and up, with similar annual costs. Still, the first time you're rescued from the hard plastic seats of an airport waiting room, you'll consider the investment worthwhile. The alternative, in many cases, is an expensive hotel room.

Airport travel clubs usually can accommodate a modem, enabling you to telecommunicate en route. Once you arrive at your destination, though, you might not be so lucky. Although this situation is changing, don't assume that the phones in your hotel room will allow easy access to a modem. To prevent theft, hotels have bolted everything down, so in many cases the phone is hard-wired to the wall. There has been some progress; some of the larger hotels now include the standard RJ11 jacks in the rooms. As a courtesy to portable computer users, many of the classier places provide an extra open jack.

Phone Hassles

Solving the hardware struggle may only get you halfway there; a hotel room phone is a breeding ground for software incompatibilities. Telecommunications services like MCI Mail supply toll-free numbers that work throughout the country. As a result, you only have to program your modem to dial one number, regardless of where you travel. That helpful consistency goes out the window as soon as you check into a hotel. Most hotels use the dial number 8 to access a long-distance or toll-free line, but this is hardly universal. Another wildcard is whether a 1 is required before a long-distance call. To accommodate changes you won't know about until you arrive, an on-the-fly mutation of your dial-up file is required.

For this, it helps to choose a communications program that lets you accomplish these dialing tasks easily.

Aside from phone oddities, the notebook computer user must be aware of power aberrations. Some aspects of this problem are only of concern to the international traveler. You'll need to do some research to find out whether your destination country's power standard is consistent with your notebook computer. Happily, most countries share a consistent standard that often extends throughout the entire continent. The French-German

READ.ME

When There Is No RJ11 Jack in the Hotel

Portable computing pioneers by necessity have become telephone mechanics, learning how to dissect and rewire various systems on the fly. But this is not how you want to spend your traveling time, especially when there is the danger of crossing wires and disabling the phone altogether. An acoustic coupler, a unit that clamps over a phone's mouthpiece, will allow data transmission, but it adds weight to your luggage and is a hassle to use.

A better idea is to go to Radio Shack and buy a phone line with an RJ11 plug on one end and four alligator clips on the other. In hotels where the phone is hard-wired, you have to open the phone with a screwdriver and hook two of the alligator clips to the innards. It's not that hard. First unscrew the screws (usually two) on the bottom of the phone. Then take off the top carefully; do not unhook the usually red "message waiting" light. You'll see two to four wires coming out of the wall cord that goes into the phone. Find the green one and the red one. To these, fasten the alligator clips from the matching green and red wires on the cord you purchased. Then pop the RJ11 connector into your laptop modem. Make sure the receiver is on the hook. It can be balanced upside down on the metal bracket that goes up and down and which hangs up the phone. Now, using your regular telecommunications software, you can use the phone with your modem.

connector, for instance, works in approximately 80 percent of Europe and the United Kingdom. Places like Australia, New Zealand, Hong Kong, and Singapore share this standard (perhaps because of their current or former colonial status).

What to Bring

Buying more than one adapter is unnecessary, because multiadapters that can accommodate many different standards are available. For a few dollars more, you can pick up a unit that channels electricity from wall plugs throughout the world to your notebook computer. Check with your dealer about the adapter/charger you already own; most automatically switch to and from 220 volts. (Few say so on the box, though, because UL will not approve the idea.) The newest Zenith power supplies, for example, typically work on 220 and 120 volts.

A cheaper tool, the three-to-two prong converter, may be needed to alleviate incompatibilities in the good old U.S.A. Those irritating two-pronged wall sockets are still around, and they tend to turn up in your room when you are most in need of a recharge. An inexpensive converter is one little lifesaving necessity that should be packed and ready to go with your notebook computer.

Another light and essential item is a length of phone cable (the hotel may supply a jack, but don't bet on the wire). Throw in a list of local logon numbers for your favorite E-mail service, in case the toll-free number doesn't work. And don't forget the system manual.

BATTERY TIPS

Extra floppy disks and battery packs are a good idea. These items add flexibility to media portability and power, making the notebook computer more versatile than its predecessors. Access to a removable battery gives a portable computer an almost unlimited operating time; you are restricted only by the number of packs you can bring along. Based on a three- to five-hour operating time per pack, and "average" computer use time, a practical estimate of battery needs is two packs per day. (Should your task involve traveling to the remote wilderness to compose a *Call of the Wild* sequel, that estimate may increase. In any case, the necessary batteries will surely weigh considerably less than the daily food ration.)

While using a notebook computer, you always need to keep one eye on how much power is being consumed, in the same way you need to stay aware of how much gas is in your car's tank. The smartest power management strategy is to always carry a spare charged battery. An intelligent system like the Zenith MinisPort will do some of the work for you. On this model, nonessential functions like serial ports, controllers, and disks shut off automatically when they are not in use. In addition, you can turn down the video display, turn off the modem, or decrease the processor speed. Cutting the MinisPort back to 4.77 MHz adds another 30 minutes of battery life. Another way to save power is to use fewer programs that constantly access the disk. For instance, disabling any auto-save facility will save power. A disk cache is also a good idea.

A company's battery specifications statistic is similar to a car's miles-per-gallon rating, and should be approached with similar caution. You might not get the sticker rating under standard conditions. Zenith rates the MinisPort's cassette battery life at three hours, using full processor power and full screen illumination, and estimating a higher-than-average level of disk access. Unlike other laptops, it's not necessary to let the MinisPort's battery run down completely before charging it again. The MinisPort's three-hour battery rating is at least close to the Holy Grail of power duration: the length of a cross-country plane trip. If you take battery-saving measures, and turn the machine off while you eat and read the paper, there will be just enough power to do the job.

MASS STORAGE TIPS

One aspect of notebook computers that is new to the genre is the "silicon hard disk," a parcel of battery-backed RAM that acts much like a standard hard disk. This technology has a good deal of potential; comfortable traveling capacities of 10MB and beyond are within reach. For the time being, however, a notebook will offer little more than 1MB of usable space for applications and data. Although you can never have too much space, this is at least a workable minimum.

Developing a workable notebook-computing software environment is a trial-and-error process, and may take a few tries to perfect. Like any computing setup, it depends on what you want to accomplish. You'll want to make the notebook setup as much like your desktop system as possible, and you can use your home system to refine that setup. First, copy to a separate subdirectory all the programs you want to use on the notebook, and see how much space they occupy. Then delete all files that aren't essential to the program's operation, such as printer drivers, thesaurus modules, and some overlay files. After making sure that the abbreviated programs function adequately, transfer the whole subdirectory to the notebook with the file transfer utility.

THOUGHTS ON SOFTWARE

Any self-respecting notebook computer will have one of these programs built into ROM: LapLink, FastLynx, or the Brooklyn Bridge. With these utilities, after the serial ports of a laptop and desktop are connected and the linking software is loaded, both machines' directories are shown on the master system. You highlight the files you want to transfer, and enter the appropriate commands. It is only slightly more complicated than copying data from one disk drive to another.

For a notebook computer to be used in word processing and telecommunications, I assembled a workable, powerful, and compact environment with QEdit and Telix. Try to use the most efficient programs on your laptop. Sometimes it's better to use an editor like QEdit, with all its laptop features such as the big block cursor, than it is to use a regular word processor like XY-Write. You can always transfer the file later to a desktop, and do the final edit with more powerful software.

Another common use for laptops will be data storage and retrieval. For this you'll need some kind of database manager. Unfortunately, though, to manage any standard dBASE-style program, you'll need a hard disk-driven laptop. For the time being, such applications are beyond a notebook's power.

One common application will be to manage a phone list of the people you need to call while on the road. For this, the original SideKick, General Information's Hotline, or Prodex from Prodex Development will all work well. Prodex, which needs less than 100K, has the added advantage of attaching a note field to each name or data entry.

The magic numbers for memory are about 500K if you're using the internal disk to store applications, or 720K if you opt for the floppy. If you want to install a complex environment onto a notebook, such as one that includes a database facility, you will probably need a floppy for each application (word processing, communications, and database).

The ideal software solution for a notebook computer is an integrated program that combines all needed functions into one neat package. About the best choice is Microsoft Works, an inexpensive four-in-one program that uses about 430K without the dictionary. (Software Publishing's First Choice is similar, and is actually easier to learn. However, First Choice uses over a megabyte, making it a poor choice for the modern notebook.)

WordPerfect Executive is another good option, although it has its own set of drawbacks. Though it features a WordPerfect look-alike word processor, card file (another name for a database), spreadsheet, and scheduler, it has no communications module. But if file and command compatibility mean a lot to you, then the WordPerfect solution is a nifty little package, and the entire program fits on one 720K floppy. You can keep the "main" applications based on a single disk, and use the internal disk for your communications program and data.

Notebooks of the Future

The "notebook" label, as it applies to computers, is no accident. To extend the paper metaphor, this computer is like the spiral-bound tablet that fits in your pocket and contains the day's jottings. When you get home, you transfer all the information to a larger sheet of paper, where it is easier to edit, manipulate, and visualize. There are also a number of tasks that cannot be easily performed on the computer version of a notebook. A notebook computer, however, allows the data used by the home machine to be gathered with more precision and accuracy.

No doubt innovation will continue to trickle down from the desktop; hard disk-driven notebook machines should be common by the end of 1990. While it's impossible to guess what a notebook will do a decade from now, you can expect technologies like voice and writing recognition, cellular modems, and facsimile transmission to become integrated into portable systems in the next few years.

Today's notebook computer already gives you more freedom—unchaining you from your desk and letting you compute in the sunshine. Notebook computing now allows information to be intelligently sent and received from every corner of the planet, or from the heart of the world's biggest cities, with the same machine. And remember—if you ever need those files sitting at home on your desktop, you can always have your telecommunications program preloaded at home, and put the computer in Host mode. You can then call it from anywhere with your notebook computer, and download the files.

CHAPTER FIFTEEN

International Telecommunications: Calling from Europe

As you might expect, telecommunicating in Europe offers some unique problems. These problems and some of the unique characteristics of European telecommunications will be discussed in this chapter.

WHAT'S DIFFERENT ABOUT TELECOMMUNICATIONS IN EUROPE?

Europeans use modems less than their counterparts do in the United States. The European telecommunication problem is a complex web of technological, linguistic, and regulatory barriers. As a result, today there are only 172,000 subscribers to public electronic mail networks in all of Europe, in contrast to the estimated 1.6 million in the United States.

Incompatible Services

In Europe there are more than 20 telecommunications authorities. Each operates different E-mail services, and many of these systems are incompatible. What's more, there are about nine different "official" languages in Europe, each requiring its own electronic character set. Sending a message from one system to another is often impossible except by telex or facsimile.

European Modems

European modem hardware is based on a set of standards different from that of their U.S. counterparts. European modems follow the International Consultative Committee for Telephone and Telegraph (CCITT) V-series standards: V22 for 1200bps full duplex, V22 for 2400bps full duplex, and V29 for 9600bps half duplex. This, of course, causes problems in direct communication with U.S. modems. A call between a Bell modem (the U.S. standard) and a CCITT modem doesn't work, because the signaling systems between the two aren't compatible. The newer U.S. modems do have CCITT compatibility. Some Holmes laptop modems, for example, have a switch for turning the modem into a CCITT modem when traveling in Europe.

Modem Registrations

Europe has a highly regulated group of telecommunications administrators. They keep close tabs on who has modems, and where each one is hooked up. Some users are actually required to submit their modem to the telephone company for approval, and to order a special line subscription for connecting the modem. Although these antiquated policies are becoming less prevalent, it's still difficult to use a modem in a country where it isn't registered.

Telephone Equipment

Another problem in Europe is that the telephone jacks are different in each country. Even if you have a modem, you may not be able to connect it to the phone line except via a slow and unwieldy acoustic coupler. Beware also of overstressed and dirty transmission lines.

The quality of European connections is generally good, but some of the less sophisticated networks in Italy, Spain, and Portugal are notorious for their poor quality. These noisy lines can produce errors and increase transmission time; the connection may sometimes be severed. Add to this the fact that European long-distance charges are approximately three times those in the United States, and a bad situation turns worse—particularly if the line is dropped on the 598th block of a 600-block file transfer.

The Italian national telephone company, SIP, can handle only one-half the demand for telephone circuits in a business day. Italian modem users must wait until after their evening espresso before they attempt on-line communications with remote correspondents.

Network User Identification (NUI)

The major barrier to modem use in Europe is the Network User Identification (NUI) requirement. To access international packet-switched networks for international E-mail services, a European telecommunicator must first obtain an NUI, so that usage of the international network can be monitored and billed.

The application for an NUI may take a month to process. There is generally a surcharge for the NUI, sometimes as much as $50 a month. (This is for the same capability you have in the U.S. when you call a local Sprintnet or TYMNET access number.) The high quality and reduced transmission cost of international packet networks can't be accessed without an NUI.

PROGRESS IN EUROPEAN TELECOMMUNICATIONS

Today there are relatively few large E-mail providers in Europe. The CCITT has a plan for an open, unified European telecommunications system by 1992. Here's an overview of some important developments.

British Telecom (Dialcom)

British Telecom's Dialcom offers an international E-mail service. Dialcom services are available in both the U.S. and the U.K. In addition, other services are operated by telephone authorities in Ireland, Finland, Italy, the Netherlands, Spain, and West Germany. The systems are interconnected, so users may send mail internationally by dialing into their local system.

Calvacom

The French company, Calvacom, operates an electronic mail service accessible throughout Europe, but it is used mostly in France. A cross between BIX and CompuServe, Calvacom's primary services are electronic mail and file transfer. Apple Computer uses the network to communicate between its U.S. headquarters and various European offices. Calvacom currently has about 10,000 subscribers.

Minicom

In France, over four million people use the services of the nationwide Minitel information network. The debut of a new electronic mail service promises to make most Minitel owners electronic mail users, as well.

Minicom, as the system is called, is now being rolled out in Toulouse and Grenoble. Minicom will have a capacity of tens of millions of subscribers when it begins nationwide service. By contrast, the biggest U.S. E-mail service, CompuServe, has perhaps 700,000 mailboxes. Even the international telex network has less than two million network addresses. In terms of sheer size, Minicom is more comparable to other telephone networks than it is to other electronic message networks.

France's Minicom initiates a new era in electronic mail: the era of ubiquity. Since it was invented, E-mail has remained a medium for an elite of computer-literate hobbyists and professionals. With Minicom, E-mail will become a medium of the masses. When the Regional Bell Operating Companies begin to deploy E-mail networks in the U.S., you also may participate in more widespread use of E-mail.

Minicom is based on the French electronic directory system, the single most active database on the Minitel network. It handles over one million calls per day. In fact, the Minicom system will operate on the same computers as the electronic directory: a network of 210 Bull DPS6 computers. France Telecom predicts Minicom will be used as much as the electronic directory, becoming the world's most popular electronic mail network in just a few years.

Case Study: ISDN in France

France is also ahead of the pack in the installation of Integrated Services Digital Network (ISDN) capabilities in its network. ISDN service will be available nationwide in France by the end of 1990. France Telecom has introduced ISDN brilliantly, funding dozens of ISDN applications in order to propel the use of the new network. Nearly all of these applications are based on PCs.

In France an ISDN line subscription costs $120 for installation, plus $54 per month. France Telecom expects to have some 150,000 ISDN subscribers by 1992, and 700,000 by 1995. By the turn of century, nearly every professional in France will be an ISDN user.

For a more detailed discussion of ISDN, see Chapter 25.

SUCCESSFUL MODEM COMMUNICATIONS IN EUROPE

Let's look at three types of modem communication in Europe: communication within a single European country, between European countries, and communication from Europe to U.S. E-mail and database services.

Within a European Country

There are few problems in point-to-point communication with a CCITT modem within any European country. (There are dual-standard Bell/CCITT modems that you can carry with you; see the "Useful Tips for Modem Users in Europe" section that follows.) The phone plug problem, however, is the bane of every European traveler. Experienced European telecommuters carry a bag full of various European phone plug cords, each with the U.S. standard RJ11 plug on one end.

Between European Countries

For economy and efficiency, try to transmit most international data calls within Europe over the international packet-switching system. However, because it can be difficult to obtain an NUI, remember that it's always possible to dial directly into a foreign PC or database. This can be expensive, though — particularly if you're dialing from a country with high international toll rates, such as West Germany.

Back to the U.S.

The biggest problem you will have in Europe is calling home to U.S. databases and E-mail systems. Between the telephone lines, the satellite connection, and the line noise, sometimes the two modems simply never connect. This problem can be avoided. Find access to one of the fiber-optic communication links from the United States to the Continent, or set the line delay on your modem to a higher value. (See the section "Useful Tips for Modem Users in Europe.")

One French company, Allocomms S.A., has a service for travelers who need to access electronic communications services. Called Alloconnexion, it offers access to both U.S. and European E-mail services, through a standard Paris telephone number. Without an NUI, you can simply call the Alloconnexion number, enter a credit card number, and select from the list of available E-mail services. These services include CompuServe, Delphi, Dialcom, MCI Mail, and others.

You may find it difficult finding a telephone outlet to plug into for your call to the States. Guests at some European hotels will soon be able to access the Alloconnexion service directly from their rooms, using either RJ11 (U.S.) or the local European phone plugs. This service is now available at three Paris hotels owned by the Accor Group: the Sofitel La Défense, Hôtel Mercure Montparnasse, and Novotel Charles de Gaulle. The Accor Group plans to extend Alloconnexion access in their hotels throughout Europe.

Calling U.S. BBSs via i-Com

A fast-expanding Swedish company named Idioma Communications now supplies a direct interconnect service called i-Com between the U.S. and Europe. For $25 an hour plus an $8 monthly maintenance fee, i-Com connects via TYMNET to outdial modems in various U.S. cities. Access points and technical support are available in points throughout Europe, including Belgium, Denmark, France, Italy, the Netherlands, Sweden, Switzerland, the United Kingdom, and West Germany.

At this time i-Com is rapidly adding more access points. They expected to tie Rome, Madrid, Hamburg, Helsinki, and Oslo into the system before this book's publication date. Outdial modems are available in 38 of the 50 United States, with more being added.

To use the i-Com system, first contact the parent company at the following address:

Idioma Communications
P.O. Box 5125
102 43 Stockholm SWEDEN

You can contact Idioma directly from the U.S. at 011 46 8 611 8402 (where 011 accesses international lines, 46 stands for Sweden, and 8 connects to Stockholm). The people at i-Com are very friendly and speak English fluently. They will send a registration form for you to fill out and return. Your account will start about a week after they receive your registration. Expect a phone call from them, verifying your account.

The procedure for using i-Com is simple. You call the nearest access point (they provide a list), login under your user name, give the outdial interface number, and provide your password. TYMNET (the carrier) will reply that you are connected to an outdial service in the specified destination city. You can then place your call just as you would from the outdial city itself. Any local toll charges are billed by i-Com.

At this writing, an i-Com BBS was being set up in the U.S. for access via TYMNET. This will speed registration and let potential users see what they're getting into before they register. To find out about this BBS, call i-Com in Stockholm, or TYMNET customer service at 1-800-336-0149.

Contact Through CompuServe

CompuServe (see Chapter 6) provides access numbers throughout Europe, with no foreign handling fee. Cost at this writing is the standard $12.50/hour connect fee, plus communication surcharges of $9.50/hour via the U.K., Istel, or Swiss Telepac networks (for a total of $22.50/hour). Billing is done entirely through your CompuServe account.

In many cities a local CompuServe number is available to anyone with a CIS account. Be sure to specify your host as CSF, not CIS, to get the lowest rates. Even so, connection by this method costs $20.50/hour communication surcharge, plus the 12.50/hour usage fee at 1200 or 2400bps, for a total of $33/hour. Billing is through your CompuServe account.

A third way to contact CompuServe from Europe is to establish an account with a local Public Data Netwrok, or PDN. Once you have an NUI, you can access CompuServe through Bern, Switzerland, by entering the Network User Address 228464510003. Charges for this access method are a $12.50/hour (1200 and 2400bps) usage fee, plus $5.50/hour communication surcharge, or $18/hour total (billed by CompuServe). To this, add the local PDN hourly usage fee, which can sometimes be high. (See useful tips in the following paragraphs on how to get or avoid getting a local NUI account.)

For further information, sign onto CompuServe and GO INTERNA-TIONAL for detailed information free of connect charges. You also can GO EUROPE for detailed logon instructions. If you use an MS-DOS machine, GO IBMEUROPE for current information and advice from other members who use the European connection. The message section at IBMEUROPE is very lively. Sysop Earle Robinson, who spent much of his life in France and knows European phone systems inside and out, is very helpful and accessible.

USEFUL TIPS FOR MODEM USERS IN EUROPE

Here are some helpful tips and sources:

The Right Modem

Most American modems are built to Bell 103 or 212A standards, which are incompatible with CCITT modems. Thus, if you try to call a CCITT modem with your Bell modem, it won't work. It's best to have a modem that can handle both CCITT and Bell signals. The WorldPort 2400 is one such modem. It is small, and runs on a 9-volt battery, which eliminates the potential electrical problems. To switch between European and American modes requires a simple software command.

How to Get an NUI

To obtain a Network User Identification (NUI) number, you must be a telephone subscriber in a European country. Make your application to the

Posts and Telecommunications Authority (PTT) in the country in question. Of course most American travelers won't have a European telephone subscription, so an NUI can be difficult to obtain.

British Telecom offers a temporary NUI service for visitors. For a fee of £25 plus a £5 signup charge, you can get an NUI that is active for three months. The charges (7.5 pence per minute, plus 2.25 pence per 64 bytes transmitted) are billed to your home address. British Telecom allows access to any data services on Sprintnet, TYMNET, Accunet, Infonet, or other international packet switching systems.

For more information on British Telecom's NUI Visitor Service, call 800-225-0071, or fax to 44-1-404-5707.

Avoiding an NUI

Many of the international packet networks operate dial-up nodes in various European countries. With these nodes, you can dial directly into Sprintnet or TYMNET, give the full packet-network address of your desired data service, and you're in. Access points are limited.

In Paris, you can also dial into an E-mail gateway service operated by Allocomms. It is available only in Paris, on modem number 45-67-95-70. Alloconnexion gets you into CompuServe, Dialcom, Delphi, MCI Mail, and other services, at rates well below the overseas dialing charge.

Connecting Your Modem

Get a phone plug converter cable. Then your modem can be connected to the telephone network in your destination country. These converter cables can be hard to find, but without one you'll have to use an acoustic coupler—yet another piece of equipment to haul along, and a slow one besides. Visitors to France can get an RJ11 (French) converter from Allocomms S.A. (Saint Germain en Laye, France, 331-3061-1500).

Don't Let Satellites Defeat You

When you make an overseas modem call, you may get connected on a satellite line. If you do, set the line delay on your modem or in your communications software package to a higher value (700 milliseconds, for example). This prevents the time delay of satellite transmissions—the familiar "echo" of international calls—from confusing the modem.

Saving Time

Compress your files before you send them (use a public domain software program such as ARC or ZIP). Text files can be packed down to about 40 percent of their original size; database files can be compressed even more.

Persevere!

Telecommunication from Europe is likely to be frustrating. There are solutions out there somewhere, and once you find something that works, store it, and stick with it.

CHAPTER SIXTEEN

Minitel and PRODIGY

There is a growing market for graphics-based information services. Unlike services that scroll messages on and off the screen in a character-based environment, these systems offer a wide variety of services in a graphics-style environment. End users with little or no computer background can access a world of information, play games, shop, and partake of just about any of the other telecommunications services that the public demands. Generally, use of these services is inexpensive.

Graphics-based services are still in their infancy, but growing fast. Two of the most prominent services, Minitel and PRODIGY, are discussed in this chapter. Minitel, a big success in France, is now gaining ground in the United States. PRODIGY, the flagship U.S. service sponsored jointly by IBM and Sears, expects huge gains in its user base over the next few years.

MINITEL — A DIFFERENT APPROACH TO INFORMATION

Remember the conehead characters of NBC's "Saturday Night Live"? Their heads came to a point about two feet above their noses. Whenever any earthlings suspected that something was amiss, the coneheads would blurt out, in a computer-like monotone, "We come from France!"

We expect the weird and different to come from France. So hello, Minitel! OK, maybe Minitel isn't that weird, but it *is* different, and we must examine France's experience in this unusual mass-scale interactive computing medium to see what is possible elsewhere. In many respects, France is again leading the way with the Minitel system.

Many information services in the United States are now using the French Minitel technology. These services differ from the straight ASCII text of the American services. They use a common set of navigation commands to make the systems immediately easy to use—so easy, in fact, that there are *no manuals*. All you have to do is load the software, enter the phone number of the gateway or network, or the direct-dial number to access the service, and away you go. U.S. on-line services descended from French cousins are unquestionably worth exploration—and you don't need to speak a word of French. Let's back up for a moment and look at what Minitel is all about and how it all happened.

The History of Minitel

In the 1960s the French telephone system was the joke of Europe. Half of France waited for a telephone, while the other half waited for a dial tone. The nationalized telephone system was continually underfinanced during the reign of General Charles de Gaulle.

Then in the 1970s France undertook a massive development effort. The "Telephones for Everyone" program multiplied the number of subscribers by four, in less than ten years. On the heels of that success, France Telecom began an ambitious attempt to equip households with their own terminals. The intention was that people would use the terminals to look up telephone numbers on their own, thus saving money on operator assistance and on the printing and distribution of paper telephone directories.

France Telecom succeeded beyond its wildest expectations. Initial experiments showed that people did have some interest in on-line information, but there was even more interest in on-line interaction with other people. In the early 1980s, users more or less stumbled upon the ability to send messages among themselves, on line, in real-time—using pseudonyms, just like CBers and ham radio operators. Today one-third of the French population uses this on-line system, called "telematics" or, more commonly,

"Minitel," from home or office, and the telematic industry in France generates over $1 billion in economic activity. About 20 percent of the households in France are included in the installed base.

Meanwhile, in the United States, we were breaking up our de facto national communications authority, AT&T, as the French were doing just the opposite.

France built a bigger-than-ever nationalized telephone system. They built a packet-switching network as the foundation of it all—an X25 network, to be specific—to carry computer communications. It now handles more than ten times what either TYMNET or Sprintnet does in the United States. (France is just one-sixth the size of the U.S.) A nationwide set of *gateways* to Minitel—points of entry to the network—all have the same telephone numbers throughout France. Once connected with the gateway, you can search a database that lists all the available services. Then France Telecom takes over responsibility for billing and payment for the services you've used. The independent service providers receive revenue from the phone company for a share of the on-line traffic their services generate.

The Telematic Services

The only services run by France Telecom are the on-line national telephone directory, and a nationwide electronic mail service, on which each telephone subscriber is given a mailbox. There are now over 10,000 different telematic services on privately owned computers available on the French Minitel network.

The Terminal

France Telecom developed a terminal with a set of eight navigation keys, and a graphics protocol—color and pictures are included. So far, more than four million of the terminals have been distributed free-of-charge to telephone subscribers. Technically, the terminal is called a Minitel. The network is called TRANSPAC, the communications protocol is called CEPT 2, and the medium is called Teletel. But the popular name is Minitel, and it's used to describe the whole system.

CTL Arrives—The French in the New World

There are superior and well-crafted services available in the United States that use the French Minitel technology.

The first French company to establish a beachhead here in the United States was CTL (Conseil en Technique des Langages). The head of CTL, Jean-Louis Fourtanier, is bold, imaginative, and has consistently been on the cutting edge of the telematics industry since he began CTL in 1979.

Fourtanier's good fortune began when he adopted the UNIX operating system. UNIX is flexible and well-suited to real-time communications applications (see Chapter 20). With UNIX, Fourtanier was able to upgrade his host hardware, without massive rewrites or replacement of the software he had already developed.

By the mid-1980s Fourtanier understood that the core of business for mass-market telematics was real-time—live interaction among users. He invested in computer systems equipped with (at that time) a huge number of ports. (Ports are the access points to the host computers; they determine the number of people able to access the host at one time.) By the beginning of 1986, one thousand users could be accommodated simultaneously on one of CTL's computers. Meanwhile, Fourtanier's competitors had to settle for a few hundred. Rather than try to duplicate his operations, the most popular services moved to his computers. CTL is now one of the highest ranking host systems on the Minitel network.

Fourtanier is a clever marketer. He cultivates new ways to attract people and attention. One interesting ploy was to make a way for people to follow a transatlantic sailing race as if they were there. Fourtanier and his Minitel were in a trimaran in the water. To "participate," people simply dialed up the service to see the positions of the boats and talk to the skipper of the CTL boat. The dial-in sailors could also race along in an "electronic boat," equipped with on-line maps of the North Atlantic, plus weather, wind, and wave information to help them navigate the course. Dozens of real boats were in the Atlantic, but there were many thousands of electronic boats, as well. Hundreds of hours of usage were logged on each day of the race.

The success of the regatta and other creative applications enabled Fourtanier to try and crack the biggest potential market for on-line services—the United States. In 1986 he set up a host computer in New York City and leased a transatlantic line to connect with hosts in Paris. He offered American users access to one of his services, "CTL-City." In the first year, the service was free to U.S. users, and CTL touted it as the first Minitel service to allow direct communication (from news to games to chat) between the United States and France.

Eventually, CTL-City was connected up with a U.S. network, extending its availability. Local access is now possible in over 325 North American cities; it's the first consumer-oriented service available over AT&T's Accunet packet-switched network. It's also on most of the new gateways operated by the U.S. telephone companies. The New York host now logs about 2000 hours of connection per month. (CTL's bank of computers just outside Paris logs more than 100 times that amount.)

The remarkable thing about CTL-City is pictures. Even with a monochrome monitor, the CTL-City logo is impressive. The next thing you'll notice is that Minitel services are screen-oriented rather than line-oriented. Instead of watching text lines scroll, the service paints in a screen full of information, like a slide. Then it pauses while you decide what to do next.

CTL-City's real-time chatting portion, the BAR, allows communication on a one-to-one basis, or with a number of people at the same time. It's different from CompuServe, where the real-time parts of the system might give a hurried feeling to many users. By contrast, the Minitel services seem calm. This is because the words don't scroll off the screen seconds after you enter them. Also, CTL-City participants typically fill out an introduction message known as a mood message (carte de visite or C.V.) that says something about themselves.

Games on Minitel are also visually-oriented. Some are very colorful video games. CTL changes them routinely, so you may call back every few weeks to find new ones. The typical bulletin board sections are also included. Incidentally, the French method is to post the most recent entry as number one, a reversal of American services.

Another pleasant CTL innovation is to give each user an "answering machine," so that every time someone sends you electronic mail, they get your answering machine with your customized message. It's very much like the mood message, except it's permanent (it's stored when you go off line, although you may change it whenever you want).

Besides offering CTL-City, CTL designs and hosts on-line services for other companies, usually media firms such as newspapers, and radio and TV stations. *USA Today* was one of the first U.S. newspapers to go on line in Minitel format. *USA Today* is hosted by CTL on the U.S. phone company gateways and in France. The *USA Today* service offers its syndicated DecisionLine, an 18-category executive news summary. There are also summaries in the "Money, Sports, and Life" section as well as an opinion forum and E-mail.

Recently CTL has set up an office in Montreal to serve the 23,000 Canadians who have an Alex terminal provided by Bell Canada. It's similar to the Minitel. Bell Canada's Alex system (named for Alexander Graham Bell) is unique in its graphics protocol. The software CTL distributes that allows PC users access to Minitel services also supports the graphics

---

READ.ME

The Minitel Navigation Commands

Minitel-like services are so easy to use because they take advantage of the same eight navigation functions of a Minitel terminal. Minitel emulators for your PC can be either low-budget, specific programs or full-scale communications software packages with Minitel built in. Each sets up your keyboard so that certain keystrokes perform the same eight major functions, although each product may use different keys to perform the commands. A Teletel operator's group (led by CTL) is standardizing the Minitel keyboard emulation. This will require a revision of all the emulators now in use, but once in place will make the eight commands the same on all terminals, with all software, and on all services.

Command (English/French)	Function
Previous/Retour	View preceding page
Next/Suite	View next page
Send/Envoi	Same as ENTER or RETURN key
Erase/Correction	Same as BACKSPACE key
Cancel/Annulation	Cancel a complete line
Index/Sommaire	Return to the last menu
Repeat/Repetition	Redisplay the same page
Guide/Guide	On-line help

The Local/Line key is used to connect or disconnect from a service; for example, you would hit Local/Line to drop one service and return to the gateway menu to select another service. (In French, it is called Connexion/Fin.)

---

protocol used by Alex, which is called NAPLPS (the North American Presentation Level Protocol Syntax—pronounced "nap-lips"). NAPLPS allows higher-quality graphics than Teletel's because it is alpha-geometric (the screen is painted pixel by pixel). Teletel is alpha-mosaic (it uses only the graph defined by the 40 columns and 24 lines of the screen). On Teletel, each box of the graph is called a tile. Each tile can be broken down into six squares, but this isn't a small enough unit for smooth edges to make circles and curved lines.

CTL host technology supports NAPLPS. So if NAPLPS starts to catch on here (PRODIGY uses it), then the progressive French company will already have made the transition. CTL-City is already available on NAPLPS. The fact that users of different communications protocols can communicate directly with one another is yet another accomplishment of CTL that sets it apart.

Baseline—Another Offshoot of Minitel

Jim Monaco was one of the first North Americans to travel to France and investigate the French Minitel network back in 1981. He was a writer who understood the entertainment industry well. He saw the professional research services produced for American lawyers (LEXIS) and decided there was a need for a similar service in the entertainment industry. In 1983, he began a company called Baseline. Baseline now stores more than a million entries on every aspect of the entertainment industry—everything from movies in production to money earned on the opening weekend. In June of 1988, Baseline presented a selection of general interest topics from the database and premiered a service called New York Networks.

New York Networks is new, but is already very popular. In particular, Monaco was astounded by the amount of usage that came from Houston, where the activities of another Teletel operator, U.S. Videotel (USV), were drawing a lot of attention.

Baseline made an early commitment to the Teletel system using Minitels to deliver its entertainment information. Then U.S. Videotel decided to import great numbers of Minitels. Both Baseline and USV enlisted the support of CTL's Fourtanier to bring Minitel technology to the United States, and both companies are now using CTL host software to offer Minitel services on line.

Bell Telephone and USV

Three of the seven Regional Bell Operating Companies (RBOCs or Baby Bells) adopted the French standards for their new gateways, which is a strong endorsement. U.S. Videotel is also committed to the French standards and to the Minitel terminal. USV is the exclusive distributor of

Minitel terminals manufactured by Telic (several companies make them), and plans to place 30,000 Minitels in Houston alone to create a broad user base for on-line services. This move will impact the industry. The results at U.S. Videotel and Southwestern Bell will be watched closely by the other telephone companies.

In six months, USV distributed 14,000 Minitels (called "videotels"; see Figure 16-1). Another 3000 people use PCs with Minitel emulation software for access. USV receives about 6000 calls a day for about 1600 hours per day of connect time. Even New York Networks, available on the Houston gateway, is receiving twenty times the amount of usage that it gets in New York City.

During a one-year trial period, Southwestern Bell adopted the French model of telematics. They chose the Teletel navigation and graphics proto-

Figure 16-1

U.S. Videotel screen

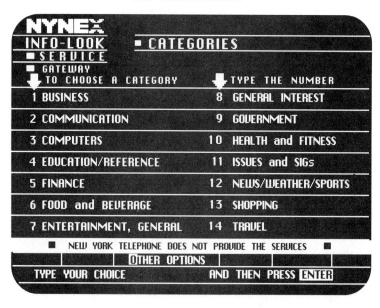

READ.ME

What Can You Read About on U.S. Videotel?

- Business and Finance
- Community Services
- Electronic Mail
- Entertainment
- Health and Fitness
- Learning Center
- Lifestyle
- News
- Sports
- Travel
- Shopping
- "New On The Service"

cols. Though ASCII services were available from the gateway, the assumption is that people have Minitel terminals or software emulators.

In 1989, U.S. West became the second Baby Bell to adopt Minitels. For their trial, the company has chosen Omaha, Nebraska. U.S. West will use Minitel terminals made by Philips Electronics, offering both a lease and a purchase plan to their subscribers. They will also sell emulation software for personal computers. To date, U.S. West has purchased 4000 terminals for distribution at their company store (The CommunityLink Center), with a goal of 7500 by the end of the first year. Eventually, they hope to have between 30,000 and 40,000 users in Omaha alone. They also have plans to create a second gateway.

In March of 1990, NYNEX became the first RBOC to distribute free end user PC software that displays services in ASCII (text only), NAPLPS, and

Teletel formats. The software was developed and customized for NYNEX by CTL Communications, Inc. Establishing a base of end users that can receive NAPLPS and Teletel services should encourage graphics-oriented information services.

At about the same time NYNEX began distributing the new software they added a NAPLPS interface to NYNEX's INFO-LOOK gateways in New York, Boston, and Vermont. Consumers calling INFO-LOOK gateways using NYNEX software (or other NAPLPS emulation software) will view the gateway in NAPLPS. Without NAPLPS emulation software, users will see the same gateway information, but in ASCII (text only) format.

Other Baby Bells, including Bell Atlantic and BellSouth, are in varying stages of gateway deployment. Keep an eye out for one opening in your area.

French Design

All this is still a glimmer of what will eventually become a reality in the United States. France has offered an attractive foundation upon which to build services.

The real-time interaction is essentially the heart of the medium. In France it is used in conjunction with television and radio programs to voice an opinion. It's used to make contacts, both professional and personal. Sexually explicit messages do exist—dubbed "Messagerie Rose" (pink messages)—that may be avoided by simply hanging up.

On the other hand, prayer services are offered on line in Brittany and Alsace. They are referred to as "Messagerie Violet," in reference to the purple robes worn by priests. You can dial up, log in, and follow the blinking cursor along with an on-line priest. You can even leave a confession in the priest's electronic mailbox! These aren't mail-order religious figures, but actual ordained priests. This puts a new twist on religion.

There are also more mundane services available, like ordering food, buying tickets, receiving test results, reading mail, ordering from a catalog, and so forth. You can play games built around real events, like a road race game that coincides with a big road race between Paris and Northern Africa. Politicians are invited on line to answer questions from regular folks, not journalists. Information, communications, transactions, and entertainment all converge in France's on-line services.

READ.ME

For More Information

For CTL-City, call or write:

CTL Communications
611 Broadway, Suite 430
New York, NY 10012
(212)979-8553

CTL's emulator is called CTLink, and it includes Minitel, Alex, and ASCII terminal modes. The full package costs $49.95, and is available for the IBM PC and compatibles. A shareware version is available for trial free-of-charge. A Macintosh version will be available soon.

To communicate directly with the French Minitel Network, call or write:

Minitel Services Company
2900 Westchester Avenue, Suite 101
Purchase, NY 10577
(914)694-6266

Minitel Services Company will send a free emulator for the IBM PC and compatibles, as well as for AppleII, Macintosh, and Commodore computers. They will also send a list of InfoNet access numbers that you may call to establish an account. Payment may be made by credit card. Check out the price; it may be less expensive to use these services through a telephone company gateway if one serves your area.

New York Networks is run by:

Baseline II, Inc.
838 Broadway
New York, NY 10003
(212)254-8235

You don't need to call or write to begin using the service. It is available through Infonet or the telephone company gateways. If you are a Macintosh owner, you may want to purchase their Mac communications software package called MacTell ($97). For the IBM PC, Mirror II with Minitel emulation is available from Baseline ($67).

READ.ME

For More Information (*continued*)

For USV, call or write:

U.S. Videotel
5555 San Felipe, Suite 1200
Houston, TX 77506
(713)840-9777

You may become a subscriber to USV, in which case you must put down a $50 deposit on a terminal and use it for 60 days. After that it will cost $14.95 a month. If you have a PC, you may purchase USV's software for $14.95 and then pay $9.95 a month for the service after the first 60 days. You will still pay an hourly charge for connect time when you use the service.

If you would rather be a casual user, you may use the Southwestern Bell gateway called SourceLine, to gain access. Through SourceLine you will not have a chat line, the RSVP dating club, or access to French on-line services. To get the entire bundle, you have to become a subscriber to USV's The Interactive Network, accessible via a different access number. It does involve additional cost to subscribers, but they offer a 60-day trial period.

Minitel is certainly on the way to making a home in the United States. The companies that offer Minitel in the U.S. are improving it, changing it, and adapting it to American interests. I encourage you to try these systems for yourself.

PRODIGY INTERACTIVE PERSONAL SERVICE

PRODIGY is the most aggressive effort yet to sell a fancy graphics-based system to U.S. computer users. It offers a flat-fee subscription for access to more than 700 features. A flat fee means there is no pay-per-minute host computer connect time; this is a big benefit.

Members (users) can browse leisurely, or set up a personalized list of regular features to access in a certain sequence. Regular features include information, shopping, electronic mail, travel help, financial services, education, bulletin boards, and entertainment. See Figure 16-2.

READ.ME

The RBOCs: Your Local Phone Company Gets into the Act

Most of the Regional Bell Operating Companies (RBOCs or Baby Bells) have learned from France's success with mass-market on-line services, and have opened or are about to open gateways to on-line services. These gateways offer a single local telephone number for access to a number of independent on-line services. The charge is applied to your regular telephone bill. In most cases, you need a PC with a modem and communications software (or a Minitel/Alex terminal), and a telephone company calling card. You may browse through listings of on-line services of all kinds and try out the ones of interest. You do not need to be a subscriber to see them. You may find your local RBOC in the following list.

- NYNEX's INFO-LOOK gateway was launched in Vermont, New York City, and Boston in 1988-89. For information, call 1-800-338-2720 (New York Telephone) or 1-800-328-2717 (New England Telephone).

- BellSouth's TransText Universal Gateway (TUG) opened in Atlanta in late 1988. For information, call 1-800-622-2726.

- Bell Atlantic's Gateway Service made its debut in Washington, D.C. and Philadelphia in early 1989. For information, call 1-800-543-8843 (Bell of Pennsylvania) or 1-800-638-6363 (C & P Telephone).

- Southwestern Bell's SourceLine made a splash in Houston in 1989. For information, call 1-713-865-5777.

- US WEST's CommunityLink service began in Omaha in the fall of 1989. For information, call 1-800-289-4283.

Pacific Bell and Ameritech have no plans for a graphics-based gateway right now. (Ameritech is still concerned about an earlier experiment in Chicago that failed.)

Bell Canada's Alex offers a terminal for lease or purchase, a gateway, great graphics, and hundreds of services to the people of Montreal. They will get started in Toronto in 1990. For information, call 1-514-350-ALEX.

───────────────────────── **Figure 16-2** ─────────────────────────

The national weather map is an example of PRODIGY's graphics capability

PRODIGY Services Company, the developer, emphasized ease of use. They tried to meet the needs of a general audience—family members, college students, and the elderly.

The History of PRODIGY

The PRODIGY service was researched and tested for four years before it began operation in 1988. PRODIGY Services Company is a partnership of IBM and Sears, managed independently. (PRODIGY carries advertising messages. It's not unusual to find advertisements for the parent partnership's competitors.)

PRODIGY's market research polled potential users, and found that, as consumers, they'd prefer a service that didn't have a meter running while connected to a costly mainframe computer over long-distance lines. The goal of PRODIGY was to use the power in today's personal computers to make a service visually attractive at a reasonable cost.

Getting Started

PRODIGY is one of the easiest-to-use systems, because its software is custom-designed around the service.

Equipment Needed

- An IBM PC, XT, AT, PS/2, or compatible; or an Apple Macintosh

- Memory: at least 512K (or 1MB for a Macintosh) of internal memory

- Graphics Adapter: Hercules, CGA, VGA, MCGA, EGA, or compatible. Hercules and CGA display in monochrome only; the others display in full color

- Disk Drive: at least one

- Modem: Hayes or Hayes-compatible 1200bps or 2400bps

- Software: The PRODIGY software (requiring DOS 2.0 or higher) is in the startup kit, along with easy-to-follow instructions and a list of local access numbers. Additional communications software is not necessary.

- Printer: PRODIGY provides a PRINT option on many of its screens. You'll need a parallel printer connected to the parallel printer port (LPT1) of your computer.

READ.ME

Speeding Up PRODIGY

Depending on your equipment, you may find that the PRODIGY screens don't change fast enough. Several factors affect response time: the clock speed of the computer, the complexity of the graphics displayed, and modem speed. Speed may be improved substantially by upgrading from a 1200bps to a 2400 bps modem. PRODIGY Services sells a 2400bps Hayes modem, along with a startup kit and three free months of the service, for about $219.95.

Cost

The PRODIGY service startup kit costs $49.95. It includes all the necessary software, installation instructions, and three months of free service. (The startup kit may also be purchased in retail stores, sometimes at a discounted price.) After the first three months of service, the billing rate is a flat $9.95 a month. A full year's subscription is $89.95.

PRODIGY allows up to six members of a household to use the service under a single membership. Each member has an ID and password, at no extra charge.

PRODIGY'S fees are kept low by three contributing factors: low operating costs; revenue from merchants and service providers; and advertising by merchants.

For More Information

The number to order the PRODIGY service is 1-800-822-6922, extension 205. Or, you can get the PRODIGY startup kits in dozens of computer, software, and retail chains, such as Computerland, Egghead Discount Software, Radio Shack, Electronics Boutique, Software Etc., Software City, and Sears.

The service is now widely available. A few areas are not yet served by a local telephone number. Call PRODIGY's Membership Services department at 1-800-759-8000 to find out your local access number.

READ.ME

Screen Printing with PRODIGY

Not all screens can be printed with the standard PRODIGY software, because even the text part of the screens are actually graphics. Extra resources are required for PRODIGY to convert these graphics to a standard text format. However, a number of utility programs written by independent developers allow printing of PRODIGY screens. These programs are available on many local computer bulletin board systems.

Figure 16-3

Headline News is offered all day long

Screen Commands

PRODIGY's two main commands are the TAB and ENTER keys. For example, with the Headline News screen in Figure 16-3, you can look at the first page (about the Voyager spacecraft) by using the TAB until the blinking cursor is on the NEXT box. Then use the ENTER key or click the mouse to go on to the next story (about a bombing). Or, if you want to see more of the first story, just hit ENTER.

Every time you press ENTER, you issue a command to the PRODIGY service. A WORKING symbol appears in the upper right-hand corner of the screen, and the cursor disappears. When the command is completed, the blinking cursor reappears.

Command Line

At the bottom of the screen is the command line. You activate the commands by moving the blinking cursor to them. They are in plain English, and appear in the same place on every screen in which the command is appropriate.

The function of most of the commands is obvious. EXIT (plus the ENTER key) removes you to a sign-off screen, or to the system prompt, or allows another family member to access the service. BACK, which can also be activated by the PGUP key, moves you to the previous screen of the feature you're in. MENU lets you see the last menu you looked at. HELP is always available. NEXT, equivalent to the PGDN key, takes you to the next element of the current feature.

These commands may also be invoked by typing the first letter of the command, like **B** for BACK, and then the ENTER key. Several of the more frequently used commands are also available by use of an assigned function key. A template for the function key commands is included in the PRODIGY service startup kit.

The Guide

The PRODIGY service is divided into five broad categories: Information, Living, Shopping, Finance, and Travel. You can always pinpoint where you are on the service by pressing the F5 key, or by typing **G** for Guide. This displays a series of three overlapped windows, with your current category highlighted. You can then return to your original screen with the ESC key, or use TAB to move to another option.

The Index

Another way of getting around PRODIGY is with the function key F7, or by typing **I** for Index. This displays an alphabetical list of more than a thousand JUMPwords (described in the next section). You can then use PGUP or

PGDN to select the Index entry you want, or type the letter that corresponds to the feature and jump to that feature.

The Index grows with every new feature and new entry. The Index may be found on line, or in listings that appear in *The PRODIGY Star,* a monthly member newsletter.

JUMP and JUMPwords

Every Index entry is a JUMPword, which corresponds to a feature. The handy JUMP command is available in the command line, by hitting **J** and ENTER, or with the F6 function key. JUMP produces a window, where you type the JUMPword (feature) you want to go to. No imposed sequences get in the way.

There is a DIRECTORY option in the JUMP window. Use this to see a cross-referenced listing of places on the PRODIGY service where you may browse categories and get brief descriptions of the JUMPwords in each category.

Personalization

Many members have favorite features that they like to see in a certain order when they sign onto the PRODIGY service. For example, you might want to check the news headlines, business news, the stock market summary, your own investment portfolio, baseball scores, and travelers' weather, in that order. Children might like to open up with My Weekly Reader, and then Humor, the SmartKids Quiz, and the popular Where in the World is Carmen Sandiego? educational adventure series.

The PRODIGY service can accommodate each of these family members, who can set up *paths* to take them through selected features. A personalized path may be exited or changed at any time. You can also exit and return to where you left off, by means of a REVIEW command that brings up a list of the last dozen features you've accessed. You can then TAB to any of those features.

PRODIGY Services and Features

Here are descriptions of PRODIGY's feature categories.

Information

All general news, weather, sports, business, and financial news services are updated throughout the day. There also are in-depth features on "hot" topics.

Communications/Electronic Mail

This is one of the big benefits of PRODIGY. If one or more new messages have arrived for you since you last signed off the service, the first screen you see when you sign on again will show a flashing NEW MAIL indicator in the upper left-hand corner. You can go directly to your mailbox by pressing ENTER, or defer the mail until later. The system includes an electronic address book for each member to personalize, and allows you to draw up personal distribution lists. You also can send messages to the PRODIGY company for customer service, and inquiries to many merchants about products and the status of orders.

Many bulletin boards, organized along the lines of PRODIGY member interests, are active on the PRODIGY service. Here members can seek and share information, comment on the views of others, and just have a good time. Particularly active bulletin boards are those dealing with computer-related subjects, travel, investments, and food and wine. It's important to note that these are not "chat" features, where a live interchange takes place in real-time.

The PRODIGY company reserves the right, as a family-oriented service, to reject posted messages it considers inappropriate. (This editing of public postings should not be confused with the treatment of private messages, which are sent directly to the recipient's electronic mailbox and never seen by anyone at PRODIGY.)

Shopping

Each time you press the ENTER key, about one-fifth of the screen shows a message from an advertiser or merchant, or an announcement of a contest or service of some kind. The message, often with interesting graphics, does not interfere with what you're doing on the other four-fifths of the screen. You can choose to ignore it.

If you do want to see more of the ad, use the TAB key to move the cursor to the LOOK box within the advertisement, and press ENTER. You can then get a whole range of information on the product or service, investigate as you wish, and actually order on line. It costs nothing to LOOK. In fact, you can even go all the way through the ordering process and still cancel at the last screen in the series. At any point, you can ZIP back to the point in PRODIGY where you were before you LOOKed, by pressing Z and ENTER.

Your purchases of merchandise on the service provide revenue to PRODIGY Services, which allows the PRODIGY service to be priced at a flat rate.

Grocery Shopping

This is an interesting subset of the Shopping feature. It is available in many cities, with more to come.

As an example of how it works, assume for a moment that you're a working parent in New York or Atlanta. It's 9:00P.M. on a Tuesday night, and you need to do your grocery shopping, but you don't want to go out. You can sign on to PRODIGY, check your incoming mail, and go right to D'Agostino's (in New York City) or Kroger's (in Atlanta). In seconds, you see your personalized shopping list, which you've previously stored on the service. You can browse through the list, remove some items, and add some items.

Using the PRODIGY commands, not only can you order your staples (such as eggs, milk, and bread) after checking updated prices and specials, but you can tell the store that you want your bananas not too ripe, your four sirloin steaks cut thick, and a half-pound of salami thinly sliced. You can even choose the time when you want the order to be delivered tomorrow, when someone will be home to receive it. Your grocery shopping is done.

Managing Your Finances

You can gather financial management information from many sources. These include expert information from Julien Block on taxes, Brendan Boyd's Investment Digest and Money List columns, Robert Bruss on real estate, and the Money and Personal Finance section of the *Consumer Reports Library.*

Late quotations on stocks, bonds, and mutual funds, and the latest company news via Dow Jones News/Retrieval (see Figure 16-4), are all

Figure 16-4

You can check financial information as often as you like at no extra charge

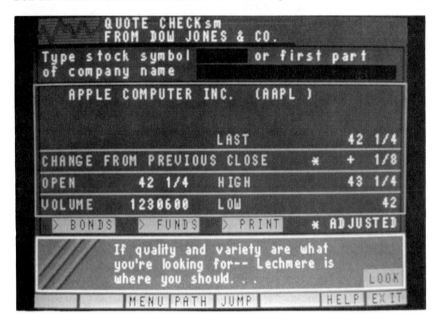

available. Your own portfolio of up to 30 securities can be stored for automatic retrieval. None of this costs anything extra; it's all included in the flat monthly fee. You can also review the latest key economic indicators.

If you want to know what some fellow members are thinking about investments and financial planning, and even specific securities and strategies, JUMP to the Money Talk bulletin boards. Ask questions, if you wish.

Other money-related activities on the PRODIGY service include insurance analysis and sales, auto and home financing services, and credit card services. In several geographic areas, on-line banking services are offered, including bill paying, balance inquiry, funds transfer, and loan applications. Some banking services carry a fee charged by the bank.

Travel Services

A version of American Airlines' ubiquitous EAASY SABRE system allows you to look up all flights between any cities (see Figure 16-5). You

---

Figure 16-5

The EAASY SABRE reservation service accesses 300 airlines, 16,000 hotels, and 40 car rental companies

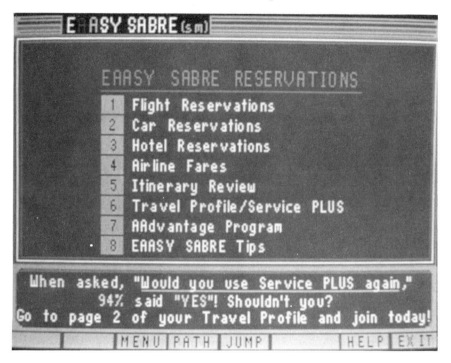

may select a flight for a specific date, and book and confirm reservations. These services are available for 300 airlines, 16,000 hotels, and about 40 car rental companies worldwide.

As with all the shopping services on the PRODIGY service, you may change your mind right up until the last double-check confirmation screen. In fact, you aren't really committed to a reservation until the final screen, even though the system says your seat is reserved. You can go beyond that screen to check the exact fare, and still, if you so decide, cancel the reservation.

PRODIGY also offers Travel Club bulletin boards, segmented by geographical region. Here, members offer their travel experiences and knowledge of their local area. *Consumer Reports* magazine contributes its travel letter and travel tips to the PRODIGY service.

Figure 16-6

Consumer Reports is an example of the many consumer information services

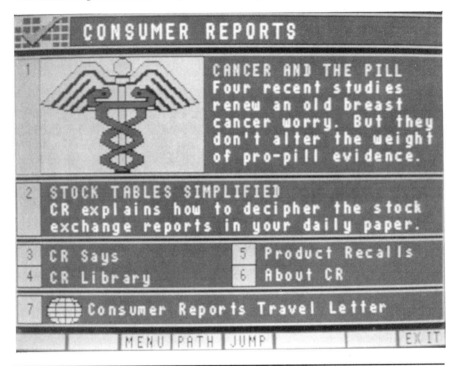

Consumer Information

Consumer Reports also provides product evaluations and several other features (see Figure 16-6). Other databases for consumers are featured, including a versatile on-line cookbook with recipes from the *Los Angeles Times,* and reviews of movies and books.

Experts' Columns

The PRODIGY service has columns by 30 nationally known experts in a variety of fields. In addition to the financial advisers mentioned previously, you have Gene Siskel on movies, and Hints from Heloise. Robert Parker and John Mariani are prominent wine and restaurant experts; Larry Magid and Stewart Alsop talk about computers; and Ask Beth provides a parent-teen advice column.

Education and Entertainment

Elementary school children have an interactive *Weekly Reader* that includes a section called Story World. Youngsters are asked to contribute on line to the story. There is a SmartKids Quiz, a proprietary PRODIGY service feature, which is a challenge-and-reward educational game. There's also a children's bulletin board (The CLUB), a feature that encourages writing.

Older children can read features on science, geography, and other subjects, and weekly in-depth discussions of current events topics, as well as the results of member polls on controversial subjects in the news.

An on-line encyclopedia is expected to be added to the service during 1990.

Games and Entertainment

Two popular free games on the PRODIGY service are Where in the World is Carmen Sandiego? (see Figure 16-7), which provides a new geography/adventure/mystery game each week; and CEO, a business simulation that pits you against real competitors in one of six industries that you select. There are also trivia quizzes, soap opera digests, jokes, horoscopes, and art exhibits.

Making Changes to Your System

If you travel with a portable computer or move your residence, it's easy to make resulting phone information changes from the PRODIGY. If you change your modem to a different bits-per-second rate, or change the communications port setting, you can simply update PRODIGY. These changes may be made from the startup menu, which you see every time you log on.

Figure 16-7

The Where in the World is Carmen Sandiego? game screen

Bigger changes, such as adding an EGA adapter and color monitor, or moving the software from a diskette to hard disk, are made by repeating the installation procedure from the installation disks of the startup kit.

Call Waiting

If your telephone line has a Call Waiting feature, the PRODIGY service will be interrupted if there is an incoming call. In many areas, there is a way to temporarily disable the Call Waiting feature with a special code. Check with your local telephone company.

Summary

PRODIGY hasn't yet provided the depth of a CompuServe or Dow Jones News/Retrieval, but it is inexpensive and easy to use. Its features are aimed at the broadest possible audience. PRODIGY is an excellent and low-cost way for many to get acquainted with on-line services. The PRODIGY service has the solid backing of IBM and Sears, and these companies have made it clear that their goal is to put PRODIGY into millions of homes.

PART TWO

Telecommunications: Environments and Systems

CHAPTER SEVENTEEN

Communicating in DESQview and Microsoft Windows

Multitasking and windowing environments are important features in tele-communications programs. This chapter presents some of those features as they relate to two popular multitasking programs, DESQview and Microsoft Windows. There's not enough room to completely document each program, but there is enough useful information here to give you a sense of how the programs work.

MULTITASKING ENVIRONMENTS

The multitasking environment is perfect for the use of communications programs such as terminal emulators, electronic mail programs, and bulletin board systems (BBS). The communications, (or comm), program operates in the background to get information from a mainframe database, to send electronic memos and letters, or to download a freeware program. Meanwhile, you are able to perform other tasks.

The Basics of Communications

Two important concepts in telecommunications are ports and interrupt request lines or IRQs.

The COM Port

This is the place where data is read and written. When a value is to be sent to the serial line (either to a modem or by a direct connection), the data goes to the communications port. There are several ways to decide which port to use, but most comm programs allow flexibility. You are able to configure the one you want. The most frequently used are COM1 and COM2. The usual port values for these are 3F8 and 2F8. The location for determining the exact port value is at 40:0 and 40:2, in memory locations known as the BIOS data area. A comm program normally looks in this area to find out if a communications port exists, and if so, what port value to use.

The IRQ

An *interrupt request line*, or IRQ, is a way for a device such as the serial line (using a device called a UART), to interrupt whatever the computer is doing in order to handle something important. (One example would be a character coming in on the serial line.) These interrupts are prioritized so that the most important ones are handled first and can interrupt less important ones. The normal IRQs used for communications are IRQ4 (COM1) and IRQ3 (COM2). Yes, this does seem backwards. The educated guess is that when the IBM PC was being designed, only one communication line was envisioned. Some time later, after many programs had already been written with COM1, someone decided that another COM line was needed. The only remaining unused IRQs were numbers 2 and 3. IBM chose IRQ3 for COM2. Normally this wouldn't even be mentioned, except in this case the lower the IRQ number, the higher the priority. Thus, COM2 has a higher priority than COM1.

A Multitasking Summary

Remember these things about multitasking:

- A serial port can be used by only one program at a time
- The number of serial ports is limited
- Most programs receive their serial input using interrupts
- Communications interrupts are prioritized

DESQVIEW

Most programs, unaware that multitasking may take place, are reasonably well behaved. This allows a program such as DESQview to run programs without modification. There are two things that must be taken into account: writing to the video display and keeping a program in memory.

Writing to the Video Display

To work as quickly as possible, many programs write directly to the video display memory. This is the fastest possible video response; however, it is bad for a multitasking environment. If a program in the background writes directly to the video display, it will bleed through to other programs that are also running. This is undesirable for most people.

To make your program "behave" is the solution. Most programs have the option to write directly to the video display, or to use the DOS or BIOS calls. This option is usually found in the initial startup of the program. (Refer to the software manual for startup options.) To make a program behave, reset the program option that allows use of the DOS or BIOS calls provided to write to the display.

There is also a special interface on the market that allows programs to continue to think that they're writing directly to the video display, while the multitasking program accesses another location. One program can then be updated without interfering with the other programs.

DESQview's efficient method for allowing programs to think they are writing to the video display can automatically be invoked by any running program. Many of the most popular programs use it, including Crosstalk XVI and Mark IV, Procomm, ProYAM, PIBTerm, BitCOM, and PC-Talk. On an 80386, DESQview 386 can even make "misbehaved" programs stay away from the video screen using special features available on that chip.

Keeping the Program in Memory

Most multitasking environments allow the programs that run in them to be "swapped" out of memory. A swapped program is usually written to the disk, but it could also be to a RAM disk, network drive, or expanded memory. One problem is that a communications program must *not* be allowed to "swap." Since the serial ports can interrupt at any time, it is essential that the program never leave memory while communications are in progress. Unfortunately, many programs do not say if they do or if they don't permit swapping. The best bet is to ask the software vendor.

Most multitasking programs, including DESQview, allow these comm programs to be set up so that they cannot swap, which brings up another possible problem. If you force a program to be "nonswappable," the memory may become fragmented.

So, let's say you've got a nonswappable program running, and you want to run a new program. You'll need to close the first program, which defeats the purpose of multitasking. DESQview overcame this. By allowing communications programs not currently active to be swapped, it disconnects the interrupt value from the program. Then, if a character happens to come in (maybe the phone rings), it will be ignored. DESQview will reconnect the interrupt location when the program is swapped back in at a later time. It's a cute trick.

Running Multiple Communications Programs

If you can afford it, there is no reason to limit yourself to just one communication session at a time. Keep in mind these technical considerations, though:

- No two programs can use the same port at the same time. The communications ports are like your water faucet; you can make it flow as fast as you want, but only one glass at a time can fit under it. Some special applications programs embed information into the data to say "this is for program A," and then only that program can take the data. This allows a single serial line to appear to be handling multiple sessions. This feature is not commonly used.

- Without separate add-on boards with their own IRQ values, you can only use a maximum of two comm programs at one time. COM3 and COM4 don't usually have their own IRQ values, so they can't be used under DESQview.

Communication Speed

The computer itself only performs one function at a time. DESQview's multitasking capabilities divide the computer's attention between several different programs for short periods. These programs appear to be running simultaneously, but they are not. Thus, when multitasking, each program is running slower than it normally would. This is usually not a major problem. However, comm programs must be ready to take data as it arrives. As mentioned before, interrupts are used to get the computer's attention when the data is ready. If the data streams in too fast, the interrupt routine cannot process the information before the next byte arrives. Information gets lost.

If you run more than one comm program, you must allow even more time. There has to be some extra processing to move between programs, and the interrupts come in about twice as fast. The bottom line is, if you need to keep more than one communications window open at once, especially at higher baudrates (1200bps or higher), you'll need to use a fast 286 or 386 machine.

Using Expanded Memory with DESQview

The difficulty of working in the 640K of memory available with DOS is well known. When multitasking, 640K seems like a very tiny space — especially when each program wants 300K or more. One solution to the DOS memory crunch is *expanded memory*. DESQview manages programs that use much more than a total 640K by running the programs in expanded memory, even if the programs don't know that expanded memory is being used. Comm programs running in expanded memory divert the CPU from what it is doing, transferring control to an interrupt routine in the comm program. DESQview sees the IRQ first, saves the current program's memory mapping, and then maps the comm program into place. Now the interrupt routine can be run. When it's finished, DESQview maps the original program back to where it was and allows it to continue. DESQview is able to do this because it knows when a program needs to use a particular interrupt location, and it can insert itself into the interrupt routine. But the extra processing takes time, and that can interfere with data flow.

To speed up the process of mapping programs that use a lot of memory, many EMS4 boards use *alternate maps* that are saved in the memory board's hardware for quick access. This significantly reduces the time required for memory operations. On 80386 computers, QEMM-386 features can also make these alternate maps available. For efficiency's sake, DESQview keeps one alternate map for each program if it can. Keep this in mind when buying an expanded memory board.

Conclusions

If you've ever gone out for a long lunch while downloading a file, or wanted to have your electronic mail available at a moment's notice, then multitasking is for you. When you understand the potential problems of working in this environment, you'll find that most comm programs on today's computers perform well "in the background" while you do other work. DESQview's special features make comm programs, as well as other software, coexist to create a powerful working environment.

MICROSOFT WINDOWS

Microsoft Windows is a windowing and multitasking environment for personal computers running PC-DOS and MS-DOS. First introduced in 1985, Windows is an enhancement to DOS and to applications that run under DOS. It uses simple pull-down menus, eliminating the need to remember complicated commands. It provides a standardized graphic interface. Programs designed to run under Windows have a similar look and feel, making it easy for you to learn and use many different programs.

All Windows versions discussed in this chapter allow you to:

- Switch between applications

- Transfer data between applications

- Multitask two or more applications in different windows, allowing them to process information simultaneously (normally used only on 80386 and 80486 systems)

While giving a general overview of older Windows versions, this section is written primarily around Windows 3. Version 3 is radically improved over previous versions in power, flexibility, ease of use, and quality of graphic interface. It has many new features, including the ability to handle memory beyond the 640K barrier normally associated with DOS. An enhanced appearance, plus new ways of organizing your programs and working with files, make Windows an all-purpose program. Essentially, the DOS command prompt is a thing of the past.

Windows looks very much like its OS/2 cousin, the Presentation Manager. In fact, if you plan to use OS/2 and Presentation Manager in the future, Windows offers an excellent environment in which to prepare for the transition. (See Chapter 21, "Communicating in OS/2.")

What Windows Can Do

At its most basic level, Windows can organize your programs, as shown in Figure 17-1. Several windows are pictured, each of which holds its own set of program icons. Each icon represents a program or utility that starts when you double-click with the mouse on the icon. Figure 17-1 shows three stackable, overlapping windows that can be opened or closed as you see fit.

Figure 17-1

In Microsoft Windows icons are used to start programs and utilities

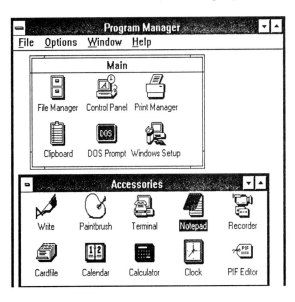

The Program Manager window manages all other windows; the Main and Accessories subwindows organize specific applications and utilities. The Program Manager window (and most others) can be expanded to cover the entire screen or reduced to an icon.

In Figure 17-2, the Program Manager window is smaller, and the Accessories window has been reduced to an icon, along with a couple of other available windows. A window reduced to an icon can be immediately reopened by double-clicking on the icon.

In Figure 17-3, two programs are loaded in separate windows. Window's Paintbrush drawing program is the active top window, and the Windows Terminal communications program is the inactive (but not paused) bottom window. The Program Manager has been reduced to an icon because it is not being used. In this example, the Terminal and Paintbrush windows are both open simultaneously, so the user can work on a drawing while the communications program downloads a file from a BBS in the background.

Figure 17-2

Windows reduced to icons to make more room on the screen

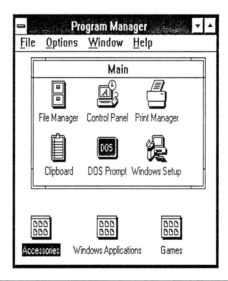

Figure 17-3

Multiple open windows let you run more than one program simultaneously

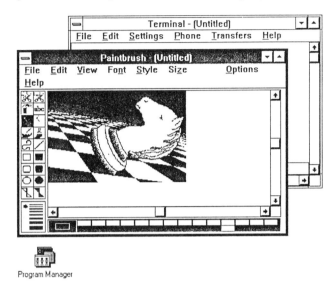

Features and Benefits of Windows

Many Windows features benefit both new and experienced PC users. Some of these features were illustrated above. Here are some other, not so apparent features.

Foundation for Program Development Windows is an excellent programming environment, since the user interface is already in place. Many software applications have been written for the Windows environment, including Aldus PageMaker, Microsoft Excel, and Micrografx Designer.

Consistent User Interface Many applications are designed to fit within the Windows user interface. You'll spend less time learning how to use your applications and more time getting productive work done.

Multitasking Capabilities Multitasking lets you not only load multiple applications in multiple windows, but actually run those applications simultaneously.

Data Transfer Capabilities   The Windows Clipboard makes all your Windows applications (and some non-Windows applications) act as if they are part of a single integrated software package. Clipboard converts images in one format to another during the transfer between applications, and holds this information as you switch between windows.

Dynamic Data Exchange (DDE)   This feature is more automatic than the Clipboard and relies on features programmed into the application being used. DDE allows direct transfer of both ASCII files and graphics between windows.

DOS Compatibility   Windows is a "shell" over the DOS environment and runs most DOS applications by opening a window to the DOS command prompt. The File Manager lets you perform many DOS commands using the familiar Windows interface. You can copy, delete, rename, change file attributes, create and remove directories, and format and label diskettes.

Programs That Work with Windows

This section profiles some of the major communications programs available for Microsoft Windows:

- Windows Terminal (packaged with Windows)
- APE (A Programmable Emulator)
- Crosstalk for Windows
- DynaComm

These products share many basic features, but differ in their presentation. Some of the shared features are terminal emulation, file transfer protocol support, scripting (for automation), and storage of profiles for the hosts you call.

Windows can run several of these programs at once. You can have as many concurrent communications sessions as you have ports and available memory. This lets you communicate with more than one host at a time. You also can have a program answer calls while you use it to call out.

Other Windows applications may be used during the communications session; for example, you can be working in Excel while transferring files in the background, waiting for calls, or running some automated process.

WINDOWS TERMINAL

Windows Terminal is a comm program that lets you connect to other systems and transfer files. You can connect to local systems (connected with special cable) or remote systems (connected through the telephone system using modems). If you use a modem, become familiar with the connecting system's communications protocols. In most cases, these will be published by the host services. If you're not sure of the protocols, contact the other party before making connections.

When connecting two local computers together, you need a special null modem cable, which can be purchased at most computer stores. For best results, both machines should be running Windows Terminal, and the communications parameters should be set identically in both machines. Terminal is easy to use, once you have established the correct communications settings for connecting either the local or remote systems.

Establishing a Communications Session

Since Terminal comes packaged with Windows, you don't need an installation procedure—just double-click the Terminal icon in the Accessories window. A window similar to Figure 17-4 appears.

To prepare for a communications session, determine the connecting system's settings and make appropriate changes to make the Terminal settings match. You may want to call the user at the remote location, or if you are connecting with on-line services like CompuServe, refer to the manual that comes with the package.

Saving and Retrieving Communications Settings

Most of the settings you specify for a communications session can be saved in a file for later use. Save them with the Save option on the File menu. Terminal gives the files a .TRM extension. The settings saved in a .TRM file include the phone number of the remote location or on-line service, communications settings such as transmission speed, and other parameters.

Save the settings for any communications session you may need to use again in the future. Then you can retrieve the settings by opening the .TRM file with the Open option on the File menu.

Figure 17-4

The Windows Terminal program and the Settings pull-down menu

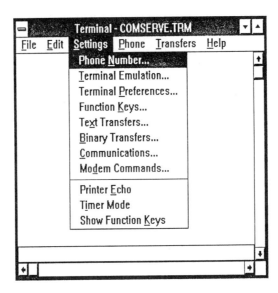

Recording Scripts in Learn Mode

Many communications programs use a scripting procedure to save a series of commands and keystrokes when connecting with a remote system. This lets you script your logon procedure with the logon name and password. Terminal does not have a scripting language of its own, but the Windows Recorder accessory can save any set of keystrokes to be played back later. Recorder can run in a separate window while Terminal is in use.

Basic Settings

Here are the selections on the Settings menu for the required and optional settings you will need to start a communications session.

Session Timer   The Session Timer keeps track of the amount of time you are connected to the remote system.

Phone Number Option Choose this option to display the Phone Number dialog box. Type in the phone number, inserting commas and dashes where necessary. Other Phone Number options:

- *Timeout If Not Connected* tells Terminal how long to wait for a response from the remote system.
- *Redial After Timing Out* lets Terminal continue redialing the number after it failed to connect.
- *Signal When Connected* lets the computer know you want to be notified when a connection is finally made.

Terminal Emulation Option When connecting with some remote computers, it may be necessary to emulate a specific terminal (screen and keyboard). When your system is set to emulate a terminal, its keyboard functions will be like those used on the remote system, not like the ones your system uses. In most cases, only a few keys will be different.

The Terminal Emulation dialog box lets you select between two DEC (Digital Equipment Corporation) terminal emulation modes, or a more standardized TTY mode. If you are not sure, select the TTY mode.

Terminal Preferences Option You can specify how you want your system to perform during a communications session. These settings control sound, line wrap, and other features. Figure 17-5 shows the Terminal Preferences dialog box, where you'll choose from these selections:

Line Wrap	Automatically wraps characters at the 80th column. This is important if the remote system is sending larger width columns.
Local Echo	Displays your keystrokes so you can see the characters you are sending. Most systems operate in full duplex mode, which means the remote system will send the characters back to you so you can verify that they have been transmitted properly. This is known as a remote echo. Leave Local Echo off if operating in full duplex mode.
Sound	Click this option to turn sound on or off.
CR to CR/LF	When characters reach the right border, they usually wrap to the next line. With this option, the carriage return moves the cursor to the left border and the line feed advances one line.

Columns	If you have a 132-column monitor, select 132; otherwise select 80.
Cursor	Lets you specify whether the cursor is a block or an underline and whether it blinks.
Terminal Font	Allows you to select one of the Windows fonts for displaying the characters you type and those received from the remote system. This selection is largely a matter of personal preference.
Translation	Changes data into other languages. Choices are United Kingdom, Denmark/Norway, Finland, France, French Canada, Germany, Italy, Spain, Sweden, Switzerland, and None.
Show Scroll Bars	Use this option to set the scroll bars on or off.
Buffer Lines	Stores incoming lines if your system is temporarily paused or running slowly. You can specify from 25 to 400 lines of buffer storage, depending on the amount of memory your system has. The default is 100.

Figure 17-5

The Terminal Preferences dialog box

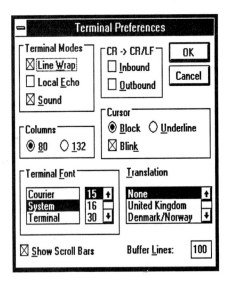

Communications Options   In order to communicate with another system, various protocols and parameters must be set in common. To determine the required settings, you may need to call a user at that system. If you are connecting to an on-line service, refer to the owner's manual that comes with the subscription. Choose the Communications option on the Settings Menu to display the dialog box (Figure 17-6), where you may select from the following options:

- *Baud Rate* sets the speed at which data is to be transmitted over the phone lines. The speed is usually determined by the remote modems used. It can be very high when two computers are directly connected with a null-modem cable.

- *Data Bits* specify the number of data bits in each packet sent between two computers—usually 7 or 8. If Parity is set to None, use 8 data bits.

- *Stop Bits* specify the timing units between characters.

Figure 17-6

The Communications dialog box

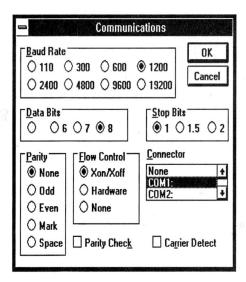

- *Parity* can be set to None, Odd, Even, Mark, or Space, depending on the settings of the remote system.

- *Flow Control* halts transmission when the buffers become full on either side of the session. As discussed earlier in the chapter, XON/XOFF is a software handshaking method. If handshaking is done through the hardware, select Hardware. When None is selected, Terminal uses no flow controls and you may need to set a slower baudrate.

- *Connector* selects the serial port to be used, which can be COM1 or COM2. Select None if a null modem is being used.

- *Parity Check* tells Terminal to display a question mark for every character that was transmitted improperly.

- *Carrier Detect* sets the use of the modem's carrier detect. When set to Off, Terminal's carrier detection method is used.

Dial-up and Connect Procedures

Once communications parameters for a session are set, you are ready to dial the remote system. Choose Dial from the Phone menu. Terminal then dials the number you typed in the Phone Number dialog box and attempts to connect with the remote system.

If the connection is made and works properly, the Save option on the File menu saves the settings for future use.

Transferring Files with Terminal

There are two types of files you can send and receive with Terminal.

- *Text files* contain ASCII characters. Use Notepad or another of the many available programs to create these files. ASCII is a industry-wide standard used to code alphanumeric characters. Every DOS-based PC and most other computer systems are familiar with the coding scheme and are designed to read such files. Text files do not contain special formatting codes or control characters and may be transmitted using simple text-transfer methods.

- *Binary Files* are usually program files, or files with special formatting and control codes that use the extended ASCII character set. Binary files must be transmitted without any type of alteration. If you are sending program files with the extension .COM or .EXE, you must use binary transfer methods.

In most cases, you can transfer all your files, including text files, using the binary method. It has several advantages over text-transfer methods. Errors are less likely to occur and are handled better when they do occur. Only use text transfer when you are connected to a system that does not have its own binary transfer capabilities.

Transfer Methods for Text Files

Figure 17-7 shows the Windows setup with your transfer options. As you click through these choices, other options appear. Select the ones you want and your file transfer is ready to send or receive.

Sending Text Files   After you specify the correct text-transfer settings, choose the Send Text File command on the Transfer menu. When the dialog box appears, enter the name of the file you want to send in the Filename field.

Figure 17-7

Text transfer setup

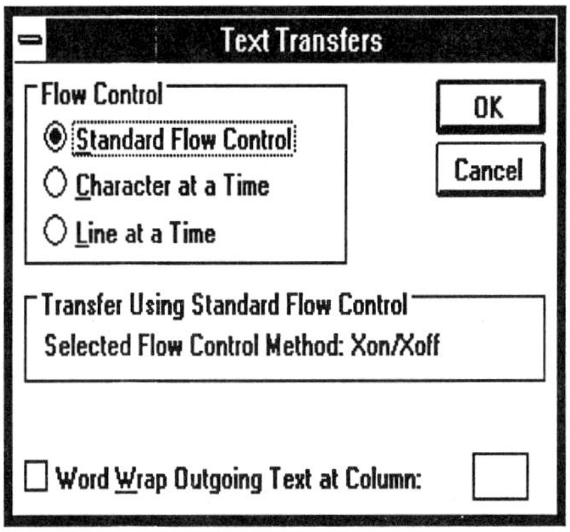

Receiving Text Files   After you specify the correct text-transfer settings, choose the Receive Text File option from the Transfer menu. Enter the name of the file to be received in the Filename field. The Receive Text File dialog box contains options for specifying how the received file should be handled.

Viewing a Text File   The View Text File option on the Transfer menu lets you look at a text file before you send it or after one has been received. You can specify whether line feeds should be added or removed by selecting the Append LF or Strip LF options, respectively. Click on OK to view the file.

Transfer Methods for Binary Files

Setting up a communications session to transmit binary files is easy. All you have to do is select between two standardized protocols on the Binary Transfers dialog box shown in Figure 17-8. Both systems must be using the same protocols, limited to Xmodem-CRC or Kermit.

Xmodem-CRC protocol uses all eight bits as data bits and requires that the Parity option in the Communications dialog box be set to None. The cyclic redundancy check (CRC) error-checking method is used to ensure that data is transferred properly. If the remote system does not use CRC, a checksum scheme is used.

The Kermit protocol uses either seven or eight bits, with Parity specified as Even, Odd, or None. If you are sending files with extended ASCII characters or program files, use the eight-bit setting and None for Parity.

Press OK after setting the appropriate options, and then:

Figure 17-8

Binary transfer setup

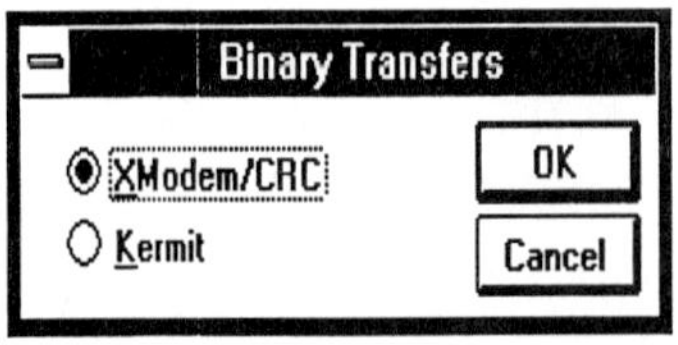

- *To send a binary file,* choose the Send Binary File command on the Transfer menu. Type the name of the file in the Filename box and click on OK to start sending the file.

- *To receive a binary file,* choose the Receive Binary File command on the Transfer menu. Type the name of the file in the Filename box and click on OK to start receiving the file.

Working in the Terminal Window

You can type messages or paste information from the Clipboard in the Terminal window to send to the remote location. To send the contents of the Clipboard, choose Paste from the Edit menu. The pasted information is then sent to the remote site. You can also type text in the window, highlight it, and then choose Send from the Edit menu to send it to the remote site.

Switching Among Applications

As mentioned, multiple windows can be open at once in Windows, so you can switch to another window and work while a file is being transferred in Terminal. To switch to another window, press ALT+ESC, or double-click on the mouse to open the Task List dialog box.

Ending a Communications Session

To end a communications session with a remote system, you may first need to log out of the remote system. After doing so, choose the Hang-up option on the Phone menu to hang up the modem.

APE (A PROGRAMMABLE EMULATOR)

APE's "auto-connect" directory displays available host system profiles. The auto-connect dialog displays setups for hosts like CompuServe and MCI Mail. If you have an account on any system on the list, simply fill in the configuration blanks with the access phone number, your ID, and your password. Then save the new settings. A simple login script is provided automatically. The powerful script language can automate many processes, including logins, communication with other Windows applications (via DDE), and file transfers. A Generate Script learning feature can track your on-line activity and generate a script for any procedure you specify.

You can get information about APE from:

Hi-Q International, Inc.
1142 Pelican Bay Drive
Daytona Beach, FL 32119
1-904-756-8988 (voice)

Setting Up

APE's installation program, INSTALL.BAT, creates a directory where all the program's files and subfiles are stored. APE requires some fine-tuning before the files are usable, but the program leads you step by step through this procedure.

Because the installation program does not allow you to choose your own destination for APE's files, you'll have to move the files later if the APE installation results are not what you want. Doing this also requires some extra work in the configuration file, but the necessary entries are well detailed in the manual.

On-line Features

Some of the program's on-line features include:

- *Scroll bars* for browsing data you've just received

- A *clipboard* that lets you mark, cut, copy, and paste text

- Extensive *mouse support*

- *Learn mode* automatic script generation

In Learn mode, the program records your interactions with the host and saves them in a script file that you can use to duplicate login procedures or any other specified action.

Data Capture

Data Capture saves all received characters into a file, the clipboard, or a device (like the printer). APE supports two capture modes:

- *Imaged data*, the default, stores data with terminal control sequences removed except for carriage returns and line feeds at the end of each line.

- *Raw mode* stores all received characters, including terminal control codes, exactly as they are received.

Selectable capture formats control how the data appears in the capture file.

- *Text format* stores the data as it appears on screen.

- *Table format* replaces two or more consecutive spaces in the text with a tab (ASCII 8) character.

- *List format* converts two or more consecutive spaces into a comma.

File Transfers

APE supports ASCII, Kermit, XMODEM, XMODEM-1K, and YMODEM file transfer protocols. ASCII is used only for text files, where it can simulate fast typing. APE allows you to choose the ASCII file to send from a list box. ASCII text send options control line delay, line prompt, character delay, wait for echo, minimum line length, and EOF timeout. Some ASCII text options apply to text received as well as text sent. The manual explains all this.

Kermit, XMODEM, XMODEM-1K, and YMODEM protocols have the necessary options to vary their operation as required by a variety of hosts. The settings include timing control, block length, and retry limit. These protocols are used for binary transfers like formatted spread sheets or executable programs.

Terminal Emulations

APE supports terminal emulations through scripts. Terminals emulated are TTY, ANSI X3.64, DEC VT52, DEC VT100, DEC VT220, Bull HN PCT, and Bull HN VIP7800.

Scripting

APE's scripts can be used to handle DDE conversations with other Windows applications, automate file transfers, and do just about any other task. The script language is fully documented in about 60 pages of the reference manual. Scripts can call each other, initialize and command the modem, monitor outdial attempts, and respond appropriately to events.

The script language contains familiar programming constructs like IF/THEN/ELSE, along with several, like WAIT and WHEN, that are specifically well suited to asynchronous communications.

APE scripts are ASCII text files that can be created or edited with the Windows Notepad program or with any other text editor capable of producing plain ASCII text.

Dynamic Data Exchange (DDE) Support

DDE support in APE is very good. The package includes sample DDE scripts, which demonstrate APE's ability in this area. There's an entire DDE chapter in the manual. DDE terminology and concepts are thoroughly explained, and DDE statements and variables are listed and described.

APE may be a DDE client or server and has a set of commands for each function. Among other things, DDE variables allow a script to check the name of another application in the link, verify the execute commands, and determine the completion status of the last DDE-related command.

Other Considerations

Miscellaneous features include the following:

- *Character translation* is useful if you live or work overseas. Characters may be translated when received or displayed. Danish, German, French, and Spanish are among the character sets supported.

- *Communications activity* logs maintain a record of when APE is started and shut down. The program keeps a record of hosts called, file transfers, and other information.

- *Analysis aids* display incoming data in mnemonic or hexadecimal formats for debugging purposes.

- A *Communications status* window shows the status of the communications port and its signals.

CROSSTALK FOR WINDOWS

Crosstalk for Windows uses what it calls "phone book entries" to store host connection settings. These settings include the telephone number, terminal emulation, connection speed, file transfer protocol, display characteristics, and function key settings required by the host.

Scripts automate logins and other processes. Crosstalk's script language has over 250 commands, functions, and statements. It includes commands to communicate with other applications through DDE and to work with the Kermit Command Processor. Login scripts are provided in the package for most popular on-line services, such as CompuServe, MCI Mail, and Dow Jones/News Retrieval. There are also login scripts for bulletin board systems and for calling into other Crosstalk products.

Three directories organize Crosstalk's files. One holds phone book entries, another scripts, and the third, file transfers and captured data.

For information about Crosstalk, contact

Digital Communications Associates
1000 Alderman Drive
Alpharetta, GA 30201-4199
1-404-442-4000

Setting Up

When you install Crosstalk, you are prompted for the destination drive and subdirectory. The program also creates directories for scripts and other files, if you so choose.

The first time you start Crosstalk for Windows it runs a script called INTRO.XWS. As its name suggests, this script introduces the program. It explains program configuration, tells how to place calls, and gives an overview of mouse and keyboard functions. You can select to run INTRO each time Crosstalk is launched, or to run it the first time only.

Saving and Retrieving Communications Settings

Crosstalk includes a script called LEARN to create on-line scripts, primarily for logins. It helps you place a call to a host system, tracks your on-line activity, and writes a script that reproduces your steps. LEARN optionally attaches its script to the phone book entry used to place the call.

On-line Activities

Crosstalk's Dialing Directory displays your phone book entries. When you select an entry, Crosstalk loads it and initiates the connection process. Once connected, the login script runs and you're on line.

While on line, you can capture data, print, run scripts, or transfer files. You can review data that has scrolled off the top of the screen by selecting Scroll (Review) mode. In Review mode you can mark text to print, write to a capture file, or copy to the clipboard.

- *Full mouse support* gives you complete latitude while on line. Just point and double-click to send unwanted text back, select from host-oriented menus, or use a full screen editor on the host system.

- Crosstalk provides *48 user-programmable keys* that can be used to execute scripts or send text to the host.

- *Key icons* can be displayed along the bottom of the window, where you can click on them with a mouse. Icons may be color coded by function and may be labeled in a pull-down menu.

Data Capture

The data capture feature lets you to save incoming data in a text file. You can review or record on-line transactions, aid in script writing, or train others to use the program. Default data capture filenames can be defined for each phone book entry.

Four capture modes control the way data is stored in the file:

- *Normal mode* (default setting) captures the information as it is received, with control characters and terminal control sequences removed.

- *Raw mode* captures all data as it is received, including control sequences.

- *Visual mode* captures data as it looks on the screen, rather than in the exact order it is received. This compensates for control sequences that may move the cursor around.

- *Manual mode* lets you to take "pictures" of the screen and send them to a disk file.

File Transfers

Crosstalk for Windows supports ASCII, CompuServe B, CROSSTALK, DART, Kermit (w/KCP), XMODEM, XMODEM-CRC, XMODEM-1K, YMODEM-Batch, and ZMODEM file transfers. Each has its own operations requirements and options. The manual gives detailed guidance. Crosstalk's ASCII upload protocol provides full flow-control. ASCII uploads generally simulate fast typing, and the control settings must be customized for each host.

An optional Kermit Command Processor (KCP) provides a powerful command line interface for interacting with Kermit servers. All KCP commands are documented in the Programmer's Reference.

While a transfer is in progress, Crosstalk displays a file transfer status box that visually shows the progress of the transfer and, depending on the protocol, the time remaining to complete the transfer. If the file transfer window is at minimum size when a transfer takes place, the icon still displays the percentage of the file sent or received.

Terminal Emulations

Crosstalk for Windows' terminal emulations are built in. The program emulates CompuServe VIDTEX, DEC VT102, DEC VT52, IBM PC (ANSI), and IBM 3101 (character mode) terminals.

Scripting

The script language is based on Crosstalk's CASL language found in DCA's Crosstalk Mark IV program. This almost full implementation of CASL has added Windows-specific commands to show dialog and "alert" boxes. The Programmer's Reference Manual gives details about scripting in CASL. It includes a quick reference guide to scripting, plus nearly 300 pages of detailed reference material. Many scripting commands are similar to those in BASIC.

Crosstalk automatically compiles scripts before running them. If a script does not compile properly (as can happen when there is a syntax or logic error), a dialog box appears with an error message describing the problem. Especially with larger scripts, it may take several attempts to correct all errors. Compiled scripts may be distributed to other Crosstalk users.

Dynamic Data Exchange (DDE) Support

DDE support makes Crosstalk for Windows usable within other applications, effectively adding communications capability to other Windows applications. A sample DDE application available from DCA includes a Microsoft

Excel workspace and Crosstalk for Windows scripts. In the demo, Excel tells Crosstalk to dial CompuServe, get stock quotes, and send the information back to Excel.

Host Mode

Use the Answer script to get to host mode. Callers can access limited functions and can transfer files, view, or change the current directory. Restrictions can be imposed on a per-caller basis when more security is desired. Source code for the Answer script is provided.

Other Considerations

A *status bar* displays current capture, printer, on-line timer, and flow control status. The *playback feature* can replay any session for demonstration or educational purposes. An included *conversion utility* converts scripts, command files, and phone book entries written for Crosstalk XVI.

DYNACOMM

DynaComm stores settings in what it calls Setting Files. The program's scripts can automate any number of tasks, like tutorials, logons, and other activities. The DynaComm startup package includes several sample scripts, and a built-in text editor to edit scripts or other files.

For information, contact

Futuresoft Engineering, Inc.
1001 S. Dairy Ashford, Suite 203
Houston, TX 77077
1-713-496-9400

Installation and Training

The DynaComm package includes three disks. The installation program prompts the user when to insert new disks. Directories are created for

Setting Files and scripts. The procedure is flexible, and the number of files copied varies depending on how much of the DynaComm package you choose to install.

DynaComm sets up a script file called the Director, which provides a simple interface for new users. From there you can run DynaComm's Computer Assisted Instruction (CAI) script. This script provides a good introduction to the DynaComm environment and covers every aspect of DynaComm, from Setting Files to script programming.

Learn Mode

DynaComm uses a Recorder feature to track activity in the terminal window. Recorder can be executed from a pull-down menu or from the Director. Once active, Recorder may be paused and restarted as necessary. If done correctly, the resulting script can closely reproduce your on-line steps for later use.

On-line Activities

With the necessary host information set, you can contact the host using a pull-down menu command, or the Director. DynaComm lets you review up to 100 lines of backscrolled text, depending upon the scroll buffer value you specify. The scroll buffer and other terminal preferences are saved in Setting Files. Function keys may be used on line—either to send text and commands to the host, or to execute DynaComm commands.

Data Capture

DynaComm uses a Receive Text File command to capture text to disk. You select the filename to use. You can either append to or overwrite the file if it already exists. You can also save the data in table format for later use in another application.

On line, you can upload or capture a text file, transfer files using one of the binary protocols (XMODEM, for example), run scripts, or use the built-in editor. While capturing text, DynaComm displays status information showing the number of bytes received and the name of the file where the data is saved. The capture process may be paused or stopped by clicking the appropriate button in the display.

File Transfer

DynaComm offers six file transfer protocols: DynaComm, XMODEM, YMODEM, YTERM, Kermit, and CompuServe B+.

The text upload feature simulates very fast typing. A DynaComm dialog lets you specify the file to send. Other options set flow control, maximum width of a line of text, and other variables.

Binary file transfers can be initiated manually or from scripts. Depending on your command, you choose either the file to send or the file to receive. For duplicate filenames, DynaComm asks for confirmation before overwriting. A graph visually indicates the progress of the transfer. If your host supports a Kermit server, the Remote Kermit option lets you perform remote Kermit commands from a special DynaComm dialog.

Terminal Emulations

DynaComm's terminal emulations are built in. Terminals emulated are DEC VT220, DEC VT100, DEC VT52, ADDS VP/60, HP 700/94, IBM 3101, Televideo 925/950, and CompuServe VIDTEX. The documentation contains tables of equivalent keystrokes for the IBM PC keyboard for each terminal, definition of functions, and corresponding sequences.

Scripting

DynaComm offers a very powerful programming language consisting of over 275 commands and functions. Scripts are ASCII text files. Compiled scripts can be shared with other DynaComm users. Several example scripts are included. Errors and bugs get pointed out as the scripts are executed, so you can review the steps and spot any procedural problems.

DynaComm's script language is compatible with both PC versions (the Asynchronous and 3270 Synchronous Editions) and the Macintosh Edition. All use the same Script Reference manual. This language compatibility is an added bonus for those working in an environment with a variety of systems.

Dynamic Data Exchange (DDE) Support

DynaComm can be a DDE server and client at the same time. The DDE implementation is very complete. Script language commands support DDE functions and can handle the asynchronous events required for DDE Advise. Sample scripts demonstrating DDS's capabilities are included with the package.

Host Mode

Pull-down menus activate the answer mode and send commands to the modem to enable it to answer calls. When a call is received, DynaComm answers it and allows the caller to execute commands remotely.

Other Considerations

Function keys send text and commands to a host or execute one of several DynaComm commands.

Network connection is possible with any of several network types. You can communicate from one network PC to another. If your network has an asynchronous communications server (ACS) with modems, you can connect to systems outside the network by addressing the ACS.

CHAPTER EIGHTEEN

Communicating by Macintosh

Hundreds of thousands of Macintosh computers are sold each year worldwide, and it's very likely that you're going to need to telecommunicate to or from a Mac someday—if you haven't already. More often than not, this will happen at the worst possible moment, and if you're unprepared, it could be a grueling experience. The information in this chapter will give you all the background you need and will also introduce you to the Mac's unique communication features.

WHY USE A MACINTOSH FOR TELECOMMUNICATION?

When the Mac was first released, there was a dearth of useful software for it. The first telecommunications programs were primitive compared with what was available in the MS-DOS market. Thankfully, this is no longer true. There are now a number of exceptionally good telecommunication programs available for the Mac within a wide price range, and it is not difficult to find a package that is as good, if not better than its MS-DOS counterparts. We'll look at the major players in detail a bit later.

The best reasons to use a Macintosh to communicate are the same ones that make this a unique machine to begin with. There have been reams written on this subject, so I won't attempt to rehash the Macintosh way of life, but here are some of my own favorite reasons.

Consistency of Operation Between Applications   From the first day the Macintosh was on the market, Apple released to software developers a set of Human Interface Guidelines that would help provide consistency between all Mac application programs. This is not to say that all Mac programs look alike and operate with the same commands, but the user interaction components are similar from program to program. A lot of what you learn from your first Mac program will be useful in other applications. If you've ever been saddled with a new computer and a half dozen user manuals, each as thick as your arm, you'll appreciate that the Macintosh (with well-written Mac software, of course) lets you get to work much sooner.

Built-In Communications Between Programs   The Macintosh allows data to be moved from one program to another with very little fuss. Typically, you select the data you wish to move, use a single menu command (the same command for every Macintosh application) to copy this data to a holding area called the Clipboard, and then choose a second menu command to "paste" this data from the Clipboard to the second program. In practice, this is even easier than it sounds. For instance, it's a simple task to copy a large table of numbers from a word processing document and paste it into a spreadsheet program for calculations or analysis.

Graphic Display   The radical design of the Macintosh system software has resulted in the most eye-pleasing display of any personal computer. Beyond its aesthetic charms, the Mac's display lends itself greatly to an interface based on visual symbols, rather than memorized commands. To widen a spreadsheet column, for example, you might simply move the mouse to "grab" the edge of the column and pull it to the right or left as desired. The author uses word processing software that displays each page symbolically as a piece of paper, and it looks exactly as it will when it is printed out. The intuitive nature of well-designed Mac software means you'll be spending less time digging through user manuals for a forgotten sequence of cryptic commands.

MACINTOSH COMMUNICATIONS SOFTWARE STANDARDS

There are two major differences between communicating with a Macintosh and communicating with other brands of personal computers: file compression and file format.

File Compression

File compression is used widely by Mac telecommunicators to reduce the size of a file, so that the time needed to transmit the file is equally reduced. Upon reception, the compressed file is then decompressed to its original size and content. Compression is also used to join several files into one long file, which reduces the amount of human interaction necessary to transfer the group. Upon reception, the member files are then extracted from the group file.

Just as in the MS-DOS industry, the Macintosh industry has moved through a number of file compression standards. Each compression program was judged widely on its ease of use, as well as the relative merits of its compression algorithms. One program, StuffIt, has clearly risen above the rest, and is now used by nearly all Macintosh telecommunicators. All the major commercial networks have accepted this standard for files uploaded to their libraries. StuffIt has emerged as the compression program of choice, and is highly recommended to you if you intend to use your Mac for telecommunications with other Mac owners. Your local Macintosh user's group, bulletin board system, commercial network, or computer dealer can provide an evaluation copy (shareware). Or you can purchase a copy directly by sending a check for $22 (U.S. funds) to Raymond Lau, 100-04 70 Ave., Forest Hills, NY 11375-5133.

Files compressed using StuffIt are by convention given a filename that ends in .SIT. Therefore, if you see a file titled GRAPHICS.SIT, you will know this file has been compressed using StuffIt, and that you will have to decompress the file using StuffIt after downloading, before the file can be used. Since this file-naming convention is used by the majority of Mac telecommunicators, it is strongly suggested that you adhere to it when uploading files to a public network, to avoid confusing those who later download the files. A public domain version of StuffIt that will do only decompression, called UnStuffIt, is widely available through the aforementioned sources.

In addition to file compression/decompression, StuffIt can also be used for password-protected file encryption, so that only authorized parties can decompress and use a file. The program can also compress several files into one large compressed file; each of the files can then be extracted and decompressed automatically upon reception.

File Format

One of the more marked differences between Macintosh files and files on other personal computer brands is the file storage format. Files on other personal computers typically have their data stored in one long stream. In contrast, a Macintosh file may consist of two different areas of storage called the *Data Fork* and the *Resource Fork*. One or both of these forks may be present in a single Macintosh file, and when either is present, it is a necessary element of the file.

The contents of the Data Fork are nonspecific. Software developers are free to use for any purpose the Data Fork of a file created by their product. The Resource Fork, however, is more closely controlled. The Resource Fork may be compared to a database file, in that it is composed of grouped records, called *resources*. There are literally hundreds of different kinds of resources; common ones are executable software code segments, icons, bit-mapped pictures, and the contents of a program's pull-down menus.

Each resource is given a type designator, to identify what kind of resource it is, and an identification number, to give it a unique specifier among similar resource types. Thus software developers who want a program to display a predetermined picture on the screen can write a very simple piece of code that instructs the Mac system software, for example, to "Load the resource containing picture #128." The Mac software then extracts that resource from the Resource Fork and presents it to the program, which in turn displays the picture. This concept is radically different from anything found on other personal computer brands, and is extremely efficient. It is one of the major factors behind the Mac's success.

A third storage area holds a group of data called the *Finder Information Block*. This data tells the *Finder* (the Macintosh's built-in disk operating system) what sort of icon will represent the file, how to react when a user tells the Macintosh to open that file, and other facts about the file.

MacBinary Format

Because there is no such thing on non-Macintosh computers as a Data Fork, Resource Fork, or Finder Information Block, it was necessary for Macintosh telecommunications software authors to establish a way to move all the information about a Mac file as a contiguous block of data. This would allow the file to reside on non-Macintosh computer systems, and then be automatically recognized and reconverted back to the original three file elements upon reception by a Macintosh. In 1985, a group of telecommunications software authors created what would become known as the MacBinary Format, and all the current Macintosh telecommunications programs use and recognize this standard.

The beauty of the MacBinary Format is its transparency to the user. The Macintosh telecommunications program knows when this format must be used and automatically invokes it. Likewise, the software recognizes when data being received is in MacBinary Format, and automatically does the necessary conversion back to the file's original form and content. Because this conversion is done before the data is actually sent, and again after the data has been received, the MacBinary Format is compatible and will not interfere with any of the file transfer protocols implemented widely on personal computers, including Xmodem, Ymodem, and Zmodem.

A minor revision was made to the MacBinary Format in 1987 to account for some additional information Apple added to the Finder Information Block, and to provide additional protection against a file being incorrectly identified as MacBinary Format. This revision is called MacBinary 2, and has been implemented by most of the major telecommunications programs. The revision is upwardly compatible with the original MacBinary, which means that if a file is uploaded in MacBinary 2 Format, it can still be downloaded by a telecommunications program that only recognizes the original MacBinary Format.

One side effect of the MacBinary Format is that the Finder Information Block contains the original name of the file. The receiving Mac program will always attempt to use that original name. Therefore, don't be surprised if you download a file listed as GRAPH.SIT on a network and it shows up on your disk with the name GRAPHICS PICTURE.SIT.

Most telecommunications programs allow MacBinary Format use and recognition to be turned on or off. The rule of thumb here is to know what sort of file you are receiving. If the file was originally created on a Macintosh, the MacBinary Format must be turned on. If it was created on a machine other than a Macintosh, the MacBinary Format must be disabled.

MACINTOSH COMMUNICATIONS HARDWARE STANDARDS

The Macintosh is equipped with two built-in serial ports, labeled Modem Port and Printer Port. Although either port can be used for telecommunications, Apple's local area network hardware (AppleTalk) is tied to the Printer Port. Therefore, always use the Modem Port for telecommunications whenever possible.

According to Apple, the serial ports are configured to both RS-232 and RS-422 standards. In truth, they are not full implementations of either standard, but they can be used to get at least a primitive compatibility with either standard. RS-422 is a high-speed, externally clocked standard: On the Macintosh, RS-422 has seen limited use by the AppleTalk hardware and some laboratory data acquisition equipment. For telecommunications, only the RS-232 standard aspect of the serial ports is used.

Actually, to refer to the Macintosh serial ports as RS-232 ports is stretching the point. This is because Apple chose to implement only the minimum number of signals necessary to make a connection with *most* RS-232 equipped machines. On the original 128K Macintosh, this meant a ground signal, transmit and receive signals, and one input handshake line. Beginning with the Mac Plus, an additional output handshake signal was added, along with rudimentary software support for hardware (CTS/RTS) handshaking.

It should be noted that the Serial Controller Chip (SCC) in the Macintosh does provide support for the entire RS-232 standard, and there's a reason why Apple originally used only a few of the available signals. The company reasonably assumed (in 1984) that there would be little need for the full complement of RS-232 signals. To save production costs, the unused data lines were employed to control the mouse (an admirable hardware hack in itself). Why this questionable arrangement has endured all the way to Mac's top-of-the-line, multi-megabuck models is anyone's guess.

The proliferation of reasonably priced high-speed modems in the last year or so has revealed this lack of full implementation to be an Achilles' heel. It's simply impossible to monitor the status of the Carrier Detect signal, or properly use the Data Terminal Ready signal, while supporting hardware handshaking. Since most of the current batch of high-speed modems prefer, and some even demand, hardware handshaking between the Mac and the modem, the Mac telecommunications authors may continually find themselves in a position to compromise the quality of their software when working with these state-of-the-art modems.

To make matters worse, there has been no standardization between the dozens of modem cable manufacturers concerning the ground transmit and receive signals. As far as the input and output handshake lines are concerned, it's potluck as to where the manufacturers decide to connect them, if they connect them at all. It's strongly recommended that you buy your modem cable from the same company that manufactures your modem, to avoid potential problems. Macintosh serial port pinouts are shown in Figures 18-1 and 18-2.

TRANSFERRING TEXT FILES TO AND FROM A MACINTOSH

The Macintosh, like all other personal computers, uses the 7-bit ASCII (American Standard Code for Information Interchange) standard as its

Figure 18-1

Macintosh serial port pinouts: DIN-8 (Mac Plus and later)

(Female connector)

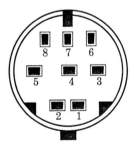

1 - Output Handshake
2 - Input Handshake
3 - RS-232 Transmit data
4 - Ground
5 - RS-232 Receive data
6,7,8 - Not used for RS-232

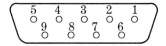

Macintosh serial port pinouts: DB-9 (Mac 128K, 512K, and 512KE)

1,3 - Ground
5 - RS-232 Transmit Data
7 - Input Handshake
9 - RS-232 Receive Data
Other pins not used for RS-232

native character set. However, because the Macintosh uses software (rather than hardware) character generation for on-screen display, a programmer can invent a custom font that deviates completely from the ASCII standard. It is a relatively simple matter, for example, to rearrange the transmitted characters to support IBM's EBCDIC (Extended Binary Coded Decimal) standard, or to write a font that supports non-English alphabets. Because the 7-bit ASCII standard defines characters only for codes 0 through 127, the codes 128 through 255 are not standardized. In fact, they can (and almost certainly will) vary—not only from personal computer brand to brand, but even among the different fonts installed on a single Macintosh. Again, it would not be difficult to program a font that mimics the IBM-PC or Commodore 64 character sets.

Note: As of this writing, only one Macintosh telecommunications program, Red Ryder, allows the use of any font installed in the Macintosh to be used for displaying received data. Other programs ignore system-installed fonts and defer to only those provided in the program itself.

Another problem with file transfer occurs when the connection between computers must be made with less than eight data bits. In this case, it is mechanically impossible to transmit the ASCII codes 128-255. Even with an 8-bit connection, some telecommunications programs automatically strip out the highest order bit of each received byte, which converts characters in the 128-255 range to bogus characters.

Although it would be ideal to have completely equivalent character sets between machines that exchange textual data, the lack of support for diverse fonts will most likely not be a problem for most Macintosh users. You'll need to acquaint yourself with the characters defined in the 7-bit ASCII standard character set, and restrict your use of characters with codes in the 128-255 range. The characters in the 7-bit ASCII standard should prove adequate for all but the most specialized needs.

If you do need to use characters 128-255, there is a simple way to get this across to the destination machine. Simply, define a unique sequence of 7-bit ASCII standard characters for each special character, and then use a word processor's find-and-replace-character feature to replace all occurrences of the special character with the defined sequence. Once the document has been transmitted, the receiver can then use a word processor to find and replace all occurrences of the defined sequence with the special character (or something as close to it as possible).

Typically, these measures will only be needed when transmitting between a Macintosh and a non-Macintosh computer. It's best to avoid any character set conflicts by sticking to the 7-bit ASCII standard.

Control Characters

When it comes to control characters (ASCII codes 0 through 31), use of the ASCII standard becomes quite inconsistent among personal computer brands. Some word processors assign a meaning to almost all the control characters, while others support only a minimal subset. The word processors currently in wide use on the Macintosh all have private data file formats, and use the 7-bit ASCII standard only for importing and exporting files to other word processors. The control characters not recognized by the Macintosh are almost always displayed as rectangles.

Let's examine each of the control characters recognized and used by Macintosh word processing programs.

Line Feeds and Carriage Returns

Perhaps one of the most aggravating aspects of trading files between Macintosh and non-Macintosh machines is the treatment of line feed (ASCII code 10) and carriage return (ASCII code 13) characters. The Macintosh convention is that a carriage return character implies both a carriage return (move cursor to leftmost column) and a line feed (move cursor down one line). Unfortunately, you'll find that a large number of non-Macintosh computers (including the PC-DOS/MS-DOS machines) require *both* carriage return (CR) and line feed (LF) characters to accomplish this function. If a file with only carriage returns is transferred to a machine that requires CR/LF pairs, the word processor may die when it attempts to load that file, or the file may be displayed in some bizarre manner.

When importing files that contain CR/LF pairs to a Macintosh word processor, the Mac software will almost certainly display the LFs as garbage characters at the beginning of each line. Luckily, most of the popular Macintosh telecommunications programs have features to add LFs after CRs in outgoing text files, and to strip LFs after CRs in incoming text files. However, if your telecommunications software lacks these features, there are at least two public domain desk accessories, DeskZap and McSink, and one commercial utility program, Vantage, that perform these tasks after a file has been received, or before it is sent.

A second CR/LF conflict you're likely to run into concerns the placement of CRs. The Macintosh convention is to treat a paragraph of text as one long line of data, and to place a single CR at the end of the paragraph. The prevailing PC-DOS/MS-DOS standard is to place a CR/LF pair at the end of every line in a paragraph. For files outgoing from a Macintosh, this is only a minor problem, since all the current word processors can be instructed to place the CR (often referred to as a line break) at the end of each line in the paragraph. Additionally, several Mac telecommunications programs can word-wrap outgoing files so that these line breaks are automatically added at the proper column number as the file is being sent.

The placement problem may be more severe when importing text files to a Macintosh. Unless the CRs are removed from the end of each line, the paragraphs will not reformat properly when the margin settings are changed. Red Ryder contains a feature to automatically convert an incoming text file to "paragraph" format, but if you are using another Macintosh telecommunications program, you'll have to delete the line breaks inside a paragraph yourself.

Tabs

The Macintosh does not recognize or use vertical tabs (ASCII code 11). Horizontal tabs (ASCII code 9) are supported, but there are some problems inherent with their use. For tabbed (columnar) data to line up properly, it's important that the tab stops be set at precisely the same locations on the machine that creates the document as the one that will receive it. If this is not easily accomplished, use a group of spaces, rather than a tab, to separate your columns.

Form Feeds

Most of the Macintosh word processors ignore or improperly display the form feed character (ASCII code 12), and use multiple carriage returns to simulate this character when saving files for export. Most of the non-Macintosh word processors use the form feed character to cause a page break. There's no easy solution to this, except to compare the number of lines each machine prints on a page of paper, and use multiple carriage returns in the transmitted file to make sure the pages line up properly. Otherwise, you'll need to manually clean up the page divisions on the receiving machine.

Character Width Conflicts

Another problem crops up when the character width is different on the sending machine than the receiving machine. If a document is prepared with a monospaced font (each character in the 7-bit ASCII standard is of equal width) and then sent to a machine that is using a proportionally spaced font (each character may have a width different from others), the document will not display as intended.

Experts suggest, when you're preparing a file for transmission from a Macintosh to a non-Macintosh, that you use a Monaco 9-point font, and set the margins so that the 81st character on a line drops down to the next line. This has proven to be the most reliable solution.

For importing a file from a non-Macintosh computer, set the same margin positions, and then convert the entire document to Monaco 9-point. (On most Macintosh word processors, this is easily accomplished.) Position the mouse to the left of the first character in the document, and click. Then move the mouse to the right of the last character in the document. Hold down the SHIFT key, and click the mouse again. This selects the entire document, so that global font selection and point sizing can be performed.

The Lazy Way to Get It Right the First Time

What you've read in the preceding sections might seem to be an inordinate amount of gymnastics necessary to import and export files between a Macintosh and a non-Macintosh. Your fears are somewhat justified: The truth is that it can be more difficult than you'd like to get a file into shape on the receiving end. If you find yourself frequently communicating with a machine that requires a lot of adjustments to accomplish a file transfer, you might want to consider shopping for a Macintosh telecommunications program that will do most of the dirty work for you.

However, there is a significant ray of hope for those transferring word processing documents between Macintosh and PC-DOS/MS-DOS machines. Microsoft Word, WordPerfect, and PageMaker (among others) all have versions for both the IBM side and the Macintosh side. Each of these programs saves a document in a special format for exporting to the complementary machine's version. Even graphics embedded in the text can be easily transferred, and none of the import fiddling is necessary. If you can swing it, this technique is highly recommended.

Caution: Remember to *turn off* the telecommunication software's Mac-Binary Format option before transferring a file in either direction between a Macintosh and PC-DOS/MS-DOS machine.

ANATOMY OF A MACINTOSH TELECOMMUNICATIONS PROGRAM

This book's resident expert in Mac telecommunications programs is Scott Watson, author of Red Ryder, one of the more popular programs, so you'll now get a guided tour of his product. In the process, you'll see how Macintosh telecommunications products differ from those on other computer brands.

Depending on your needs, Red Ryder may or may not be the best choice for you. If you're planning to purchase a Macintosh telecommunications product, it's important to research *all* the following widely used products:

- MicroPhone II, from Software Ventures Corporation, 2907 Claremont Ave., Berkeley, CA 94705. Suggested retail price $295

- Smartcomm II, from Hayes Microcomputer Co., 5923 Peachtree Industrial Blvd., Norcross, GA 30092. Suggested retail price $149

- MacTerminal, from Apple Computer, Inc., 20525 Mariani Ave., Cupertino, CA 95014. Suggested retail price $125

- VersaTerm-Pro, from Peripherals, Computers, and Supplies, 2457 Perkiomen Ave., Mount Penn, PA 19606. Suggested retail price $295

- Red Ryder, from FreeSoft Company, 150 Hickory Drive, Beaver Falls, PA 15010. Suggested retail price $129

The Terminal Window

When Red Ryder is executed, the program first loads all your settings from the last session. Then it displays the *Terminal Window,* shown in Figure 18-3.

Figure 18-3

The Terminal Window

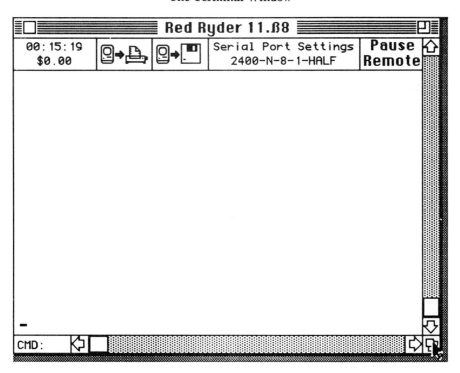

At the top of the window, from left to right, are a number of controls that continually display information or perform a task. Leftmost is the elapsed time clock and billing clock, which tells you at a glance how long you've been on line, and how much you've spent on long distance charges and/or network connection time charges. Next are two buttons for saving received information; the first one sends the current screen of data to the printer, and the second sends it to a disk file. To the right of these buttons is the current serial port settings display. Clicking the mouse in this box allows you to quickly change the baud rate, parity, data-bits, stop-bits, and duplex settings. Clicking in the last box in this row tells the remote machine to stop sending; clicking again instructs the remote machine to resume sending.

Note that the size of the Terminal Window can be enlarged or reduced to whatever size is convenient to you. The horizontal scroll bar at the bottom lets you look at data that is past the right edge of the window. The vertical scroll bar lets you look at data that has scrolled off the top of the window.

Received text appears in the center of the Terminal Window, as in Figure 18-4. It's easy to work with the data in this area. To select text, merely position the mouse cursor over the text, and then hold down the mouse button while dragging the mouse over the desired text. The selected text is displayed as white characters on a black background. Once text is selected, you can send it to the printer; or create a new file on the disk and save the information in that file; or append the selected text to the end of an existing file. You can also copy the selected text to the Macintosh Clipboard so that it can be pasted into a different program.

The appearance of incoming data in the Terminal Window is controlled by an interesting gizmo called a *filter* (Figure 18-5). There are three separate filters in Red Ryder. One filter controls how received text is displayed in the Terminal Window; a second determines how incoming text is saved in a captured file (to be explained later); and a third filter determines how characters are saved that have been received as part of a protocol file transfer.

For each of the 256 ASCII character code values, you can specify that it should be passed through, stripped out, translated to some other ASCII code, or enumerated to show the ASCII code itself rather than the actual character represented by that code (for example: < 008 >). Filters make it easy to deal with unwanted or awkward characters originating from non-Macintosh systems.

Figure 18-4.

Received text

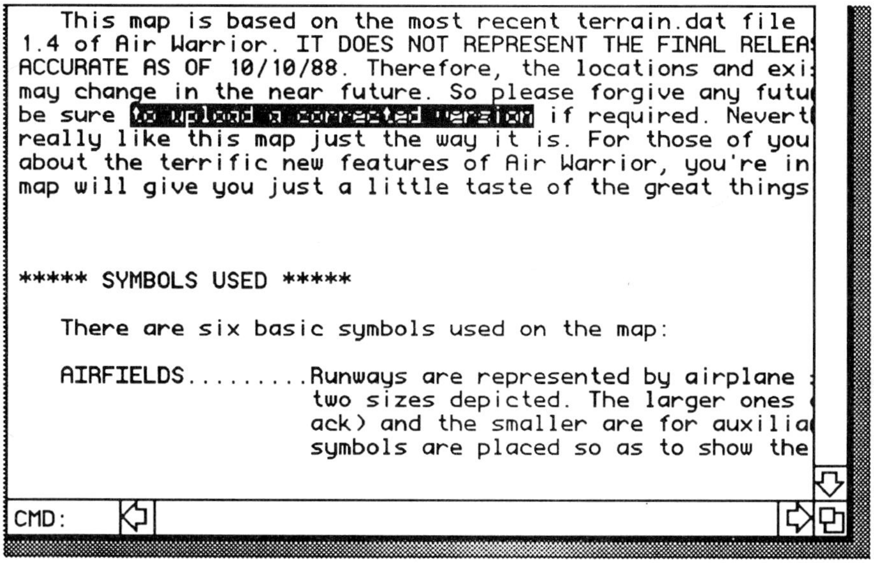

```
This map is based on the most recent terrain.dat file
1.4 of Air Warrior. IT DOES NOT REPRESENT THE FINAL RELEAS
ACCURATE AS OF 10/10/88. Therefore, the locations and exi:
may change in the near future. So please forgive any futu
be sure to upload a corrected version if required. Nevert
really like this map just the way it is. For those of you
about the terrific new features of Air Warrior, you're in
map will give you just a little taste of the great things


***** SYMBOLS USED *****

  There are six basic symbols used on the map:

  AIRFIELDS........Runways are represented by airplane
                   two sizes depicted. The larger ones
                   ack) and the smaller are for auxilia
                   symbols are placed so as to show the

CMD:
```

The received text in the Terminal Window can be displayed using any font and any point size installed on the Macintosh. If you are using a Macintosh that supports Color Quickdraw, you can specify the colors for the foreground, background, and highlighting from a palette of 248 possible colors.

The Terminal Window supports TTY, VT52, VT100, and VT102 terminal emulation. Incoming text can be easily routed to the printer.

Sending Text Files

Red Ryder lets you send a text file without a file transfer protocol, as a byte-by-byte dump over the serial port. You can also specify that the file is to be sent a line at a time, each line to be sent after receipt of a prompt character from the remote system. You can also select an amount of time to delay after each line or character has been sent. If your word processor saves text files with a carriage return only at the end of each paragraph,

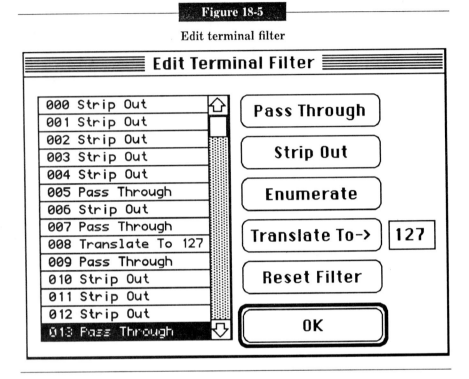

Figure 18-5

Edit terminal filter

you can tell Red Ryder to automatically word-wrap the transmitted lines at a certain column, so that words are not broken in the middle.

Capturing Incoming Data

Red Ryder can be instructed to route all incoming text to a disk file until further instructions. You can even temporarily halt and resume capturing without closing and reopening the file. Through the File Capture Filter, you have complete control over which characters are saved in the disk file, and which ones are stripped out, translated to other characters, or enumerated.

Red Ryder also contains a facility for printing out a captured (or any other text) file. All Apple-approved printers are supported, including AppleTalk printers like the LaserWriter. Printed documents can be in any font and any point size installed on the Macintosh. Red Ryder will also number and time/date stamp each page.

Protocol File Transfers

Red Ryder supports a wide variety of the most commonly used file transfer protocols. Since Red Ryder supports desk accessories and can operate in the background under Apple's MultiFinder operating system, you can use the Mac for another task while a file transfer takes place.

The protocols supported are

- Xmodem - Checksum

- Xmodem - CRC

- Xmodem - 1K blocks

- Xmodem - Supercharged receive (pre-acknowledged blocks)

- Ymodem

- Ymodem - 1K blocks

- Ymodem - G

- Zmodem (with later resumption of interrupted file transfers)

- Kermit

- Long Packet Kermit

- Sliding Windows Kermit

- Flash Protocol

The Flash Protocol is a proprietary (nonstandard) protocol used for highest efficiency file transfers between two Red Ryders connected with error-correcting modems.

Modem Handling

Red Ryder has a number of built-in routines for handling Hayes-compatible modems. This means the user should never have to know the rather obscure commands used by the modem. There are routines for dialing, automatically redialing a busy number, initializing the modem, turning on or off the modem's auto-answer incoming call feature, or disconnecting a connected modem. Red Ryder also supports a special kind of script file (discussed later in this chapter) called a Modem Driver, which allows the program to automatically control a semi- or non-Hayes-compatible modem, or to implement up to ten user-defined commands to take advantage of brand-specific modem features.

Phone Book

Another convenient Red Ryder feature is the Phone Book. You can create as many different Phone Books as you wish, each one with or without password protection. The Phone Book (Figure 18-6) looks much like its real-life cousin found on most desktops.

To connect to a system that has been added to the Phone Book, simply position the mouse over the desired name, click the mouse button, and then click inside the "Call" box. Red Ryder then changes any settings (such as

Figure 18-6

The Phone Book

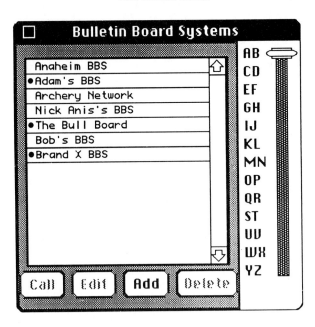

baud rate) necessary for that system, dials the system, and can even execute an auto-logon sequence after a connection is made.

An interesting feature called *gang dialing* is sure to be appreciated by those who frequently call several busy bulletin board systems. In the above Phone Book illustration, the system names marked with a black dot have been specified as members of the gang. When you tell Red Ryder to gang dial the Phone Book, it will attempt to connect with each member of the gang, in round-robin fashion, until a connection is made.

Macro Keys

Red Ryder has 30 Macro Keys that you can define. These keys are displayed as either three sets of ten push-buttons at the top of the Terminal Window, or in a special Macros Window. In the Macros Window, each key can be displayed as a push-button, an icon, a color icon, a double-sized icon, a double-sized color icon, or a picture. The items in this window can be arranged as you wish, and there are script commands for making each individual item visible or invisible in both the Terminal Window and Macros Window displays. This lets you construct your own graphic interface.

By clicking the mouse on any item, the associated Macro Key is executed. A Macro Key can perform one of these user-selected functions: send a preprogrammed string of up to 240 characters; execute a script file; or load a set of Macro Keys previously saved as a disk file.

Script Files

The workhorse of an advanced telecommunications program is its automated programming language, often referred to as a *scripting language.* Red Ryder's scripting language consists of over 200 commands, and it sports a built-in, two-pass compiler, to produce scripts that execute extremely fast. Red Ryder calls these Procedures.

The commands compiled into a Procedure are submitted to the compiler as a text file, as in native software development environments such as Pascal or C. For beginners, Red Ryder provides a point-and-click environment to make the construction of Procedures easy. In Figure 18-7, the lines containing the Procedure commands are shown at the top; at the bottom is

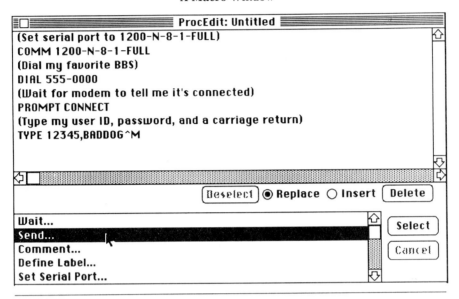

Figure 18-7

A Macro Window

the point-and-click area, which guides the user through plain-English prompts to arrive at a desired command.

Red Ryder's Procedure language includes full support for numeric and string variables. There are many commands for character input/output processing and user interface presentation. Red Ryder's scripting language can also link transparently to external code written by the user in such languages as Pascal or C, to provide unlimited future expansion.

Keyboard Support

You can instruct Red Ryder to supply line feeds after carriage returns when the ENTER key is pressed. The keyboard can also be mapped to support the execution of Macro Keys with a designated key or combination of keys. Additional support is provided for remapping the keyboard to utilize the VT100/VT102 numeric keypad, function keys, and cursor keys.

THE FUTURE OF MACINTOSH COMMUNICATIONS

When Apple released the Macintosh in 1984, the machine was completely isolated from all other computer brands. There were no suitable telecommunications programs available for it. For awhile, it appeared that because of the Mac's unique disk size and format, there would be no way for it to exchange data with any other machine except another Macintosh. In just a few short years, this situation has changed dramatically.

One does not need a crystal ball to see that the Macintosh's future in telecommunications is bright. There are an enormous number of developers working feverishly to expand the Macintosh's communications capabilities, and Apple has committed an exceptional amount of resources and support to assure that this happens.

Future Hardware

A full range of "connectivity" hardware has been announced by Apple, and other developers are working on similar products. Macintosh will soon have the same ability as MS-DOS machines have to connect with mainframes and minicomputers.

Also, the built-in limitation of only two serial ports should be eliminated after the release of System Software Version 7. This version will contain a Communications Toolbox, which will allow drop-in circuit boards containing additional serial ports. At least one manufacturer is already producing such boards, but it's impossible to write software to take advantage of these additional ports without an Apple standard.

As high-speed modems become more common, Apple will have to address the limited number of RS-232 handshaking lines available. The solution to this problem will probably require a radical engineering redesign, and will probably not be tackled until the users demand it.

You can also expect to see facsimile modems come down in price and become commonplace peripherals in Macintosh setups. There are already quite a few existing (and planned) facsimile modems that also contain an on-board Hayes-compatible modem, which offers the best of both worlds to the Macintosh owner.

Future Software

When a Macintosh telecommunications program emulates a DEC VT100 terminal, the effect on Mac's hardware is akin to a lobotomy. Suddenly, you lose nearly all the advantages the Macintosh offers, and are returned to the old world of memorized command sequences and an unintuitive interface. However, the Mac telecommunications program must provide this support, because the DEC VT100 "lowest common denominator" terminal offers a wide range of connectivity possibilities.

What Macintosh users are waiting for is efficient telecommunication without losing the Macintosh interface, and software authors have taken great strides in providing a glimpse of the future in this regard. Two commercial networks currently support a Macintosh interface—AppleLink and MacNet. Although different in appearance, both operate in a similar and intuitive manner that makes it easy for a first-timer to perform complicated tasks. Both suffer from a bit of sluggishness, but that seems to be a design or mechanical flaw, rather than one of concept. You can look for these operating glitches to be removed in future implementations.

Apple has even provided a new program and protocol, MacWorkStation, that allows in-house developers to write mainframe software that presents a Macintosh interface to the user on the mainframe.

Unfortunately, these Mac interface systems limit the kinds of machines that can connect to the network. AppleLink, for example, can only be called by Macintosh computers using the specially designed AppleLink software. What is clearly needed is a standardized protocol that can take advantage of whatever benefits the host and client machines offer, without being brand specific—much like the X Windows protocol has done for the UNIX environment. Commercial network services tend to innovate more slowly than personal computer software authors, but nearly all of the major services have shown interest in this particular improvement.

A second way telecommunications can be made friendlier for Macintosh users is for the telecommunications program to do some intelligent conversion of both incoming and outgoing data. If the network to which you are connected operates in a predictable manner, the telecommunications program can offer an environment that is much more Macintosh-like.

For example, if the network sends out a menu of commands and asks for a selection, the Macintosh telecommunications program might intercept this menu, recognize it, and present a Macintosh-style window containing icons or pictures representing the commands. When you click the mouse over one of the pictures, the telecommunications program intercepts this action and sends the proper data to the network to select that command.

This sort of "intercept and convert" operation is becoming very popular with Macintosh owners. It can be in the form of a network-specific telecommunications program, like CompuServe's Navigator, or it can be offered by a general-use telecommunications program as a sophisticated programming language. Both Red Ryder and MicroPhone II contain numerous commands in their scripting languages to accomplish this conversion process, and additional improvements are underway.

However, this I/O conversion operation has its drawbacks. Because there can be a tremendous amount of redundant information, an "intercept and convert" script may run faster than the network, and performance tends to suffer compared to what could be done with a protocol written specifically to support such an interface. Second, these scripts can be extremely complicated, and in many cases can only be written by experienced programmers and telecommunications specialists. Until we do have the ultimate portable telecommunications environment protocol, most future innovations will probably come from "intercept and convert" scripting capabilities.

Future Communications Protocols

In the past, communications protocols have not been limited to any specific brand of computer, but a machine's particular architecture can limit how quickly a protocol is implemented. For instance, the Zmodem protocol was widely available on MS-DOS machines due to their relatively simple file structure. However, only with the most recent crop of Macintosh telecommunications programs has the Zmodem protocol been implemented on Macs. This is due to the difficulty of working with the MacBinary Format in conjunction with this protocol.

One of the more interesting new developments has been multi-channel protocols. Although several have been proposed, few have worked well in practice. Scott Watson's program, Okyto, allows you to send and receive a file simultaneously, as well as carry on a typed conversation with the remote party while the file transfers take place. All of this is done with only a tiny amount of efficiency loss, as compared to a single-direction file transfer protocol like Xmodem.

Mac users are also clamoring for on-the-fly data compression/decompression schemes that are independent of machine and file transfer protocols. The current batch of algorithms (Huffman, Lempel-Ziv, to name a few) used for this task consumes too much processor time to operate along with a file transfer protocol without severely degrading the file transfer. Hopefully, a new compression/decompression scheme will emerge that offers acceptable compression ratios, or perhaps faster CPUs will allow the current schemes to operate within acceptable limits. It will certainly be to everyone's mutual benefit if the authors of these packages can agree upon a machine-independent standard, much as the Macintosh telecommunications authors did for the MacBinary Format standard.

In the long run, although the Mac will always be in a world slightly different from that of the PC, these differences need not be obstacles.

CHAPTER NINETEEN

Communicating
by Amiga

Commodore Business Machines introduced the Amiga in late 1985. On the face of it, that first Amiga was an innovative and powerful computer, but unfortunately, early buyers had precious little software and even less add-on hardware to choose from. It's a Catch-22 familiar to computer developers: You need software and add-ons to attract buyers, but until you've sold enough units, commercial developers can't justify the cost of creating products for your machine.

Hobbyists and independent developers who appreciated Amiga's potential leaped into the breach. During the months before commercial Amiga products appeared on the shelves, these talented people shared their Amiga work on BBSs and SIGs. Other users who connected modems to their Amigas found a rapidly growing treasure trove of software and information. Soon there was an abundance of freely distributed programs. Today you can choose from four Amiga models, with more in development. Users can find thousands of commercial software titles, tens of thousands more in the public domain, and hardware galore. There is a huge corps of dedicated Amiga users who are convinced that this fast, friendly, graphics-oriented, multitasking little machine has truly found a better way to compute. The Amiga has grown up.

WHY AMIGA FOR TELECOMMUNICATIONS?

All Amigas, including the original model 1000, have qualities that make telecommunications easy for serious PC users. Here's a small catalog of Amiga special features.

True Multitasking   The Amiga can run many programs at the same time. This is not the same concept as the troublesome terminate-and-stay-resident (TSR) programs that MS-DOS users hotkey into. This is full, *real* multitasking, built into every Amiga's hardware and operating system (software).

These multiple programs, even those in windows that are overlapped or completely hidden, don't just sit there and wait for user attention. They're fully active, running on their own. Each program opens its own console with full access to all system resources. If you're doing a download from a BBS, you needn't sit and stare at "block" numbers counting off. You can switch to another screen or window and load any other multitasking program, memory permitting. You could download one file, be unARCing an earlier download, have a ray-tracing program rendering, and be printing a letter at the same time. These built-in multitasking features set the Amiga apart from other desktop PCs.

Custom Coprocessors   Unlike other 68000-based machines like the Macintosh and Atari ST, the Amiga's CPU doesn't do all the work. A set of three custom VLSI coprocessor chips uses its own Direct Memory Access (DMA) channels. This lets them independently operate Amiga's graphics, animation, sound, disk drives, and peripheral control. It takes some of the burden off the microprocessor, which can continue crunching numbers at full tilt. It's the reason an Amiga can outperform some other machines that use the same CPU.

Built-in Ports   All Amiga computers come equipped with just about everything needed to function. Standard equipment includes at least one disk drive, a two-button mouse, and video, audio, serial, parallel, mouse/joystick, and expansion ports. Just plug in your peripherals and go. For telecommunications you'll need only a modem, a serial cable, and some terminal software.

Software Compatibility   Commodore is careful to maintain downward compatibility on the Amiga. You never have to worry that you bought an incompatible program, because all Amigas use the same operating system. Commodore upgrades it about once a year, but makes the new version available to users through dealers at a low price.

Graphics Modes   You don't have the burden of choosing color or black-and-white, graphic or nongraphic modes. No jungle of mono, CGA, EGA, VGA, and "super" everything. Amiga has it all built in for each system. You don't need separate graphics boards or video drivers because all Amigas can operate in all graphics modes and resolutions. Since Amigas are multitaskers and several programs can open their own screens at once, many programs can run simultaneously in different modes of resolution and using different color palettes.

MS-DOS Emulation   Amiga 2000-series owners can install Commodore's XT or AT Bridge Cards. This hardware allows cross-compatibility with XT- or AT-class MS-DOS machines. Its perfect emulation does not disable the Amiga side of the computer, so it is like having an OS/2-style "DOS box" (see Chapter 21) inside your computer. You could use your Amiga terminal program on one screen to call your favorite BBS, while other people call the MS-DOS BBS in your DOS box screen at the same time. The Bridge Card turns the already versatile Amiga into two computers, both running at once.

Macintosh Emulation   The AMAX hardware/software cartridge turns an Amiga into a mock Macintosh. (You will need to supply Macintosh ROM chips.) AMAX lets you use Mac telecommunications programs to talk with other Mac telecommunicators. Unlike the DOS Bridge Cards, AMAX completely takes over the Amiga, and its Mac emulation is almost perfect. Plug in a Mac drive (additional hardware), and you can format, read, and write Mac disks. With AMAX you can run most Mac software, including terminal programs and games.

Setting Up to Telecommunicate

Making your Amiga ready for telecommunication is easy. Buy a modem and a serial cable. Use the cable to connect the modem to the Amiga, add a phone line and electric power, and you're in business.

COMMERCIAL TELECOMMUNICATIONS PROGRAMS

Amiga terminal programs come in two flavors: freely distributable (including public domain and shareware) and commercially produced. All the following programs handle binary protocol file transfers, capture incoming text to disk and handle multitasking. Other features vary from one program to another. Because of software's mutability, version numbers are not included unless specifically referenced in the product description.

While there are other communications software packages sold for the Amiga, the three discussed below—Baud Bandit, Online!, and A-Talk III— offer the widest range of choices for Amiga telecommunicators.

Baud Bandit

Price: $49.95
Progressive Peripherals & Software
464 Kalamath St.
Denver, CO 80204
303-825-4144

If you are familiar with Amiga's standard pull-down menus, don't be confused that Baud Bandit has none. It does have some rather unorthodox gadgets along the top of the screen that resemble menu titles, but are not. If you point your mouse to any of these titles, you can make something happen, such as hanging up the modem, redialing the last phone number, or sending a break signal. Baud Bandit is fast, well written, and inexpensively priced.

Phone Book

Baud Bandit's phone book (Figure 19-1) looks simple, but is very innovative. When you call a window, such as macros or phone book, it slides up from the screen bottom over the main screen. Each disk-based phone book can hold 1000 entries. To create or change entries in your phone book, point your mouse to Phone and click. The phone book fills the screen. Now click on Edit, Insert, or Delete and you can change, add, or remove telephone entries from the phone book. Instead of invoking a separate text editor, Baud Bandit's phone book is the editor. Additions and modifications are created in place and added directly on the screen, rather than requiring the extra action of mouse pointing, clicking, and typing data into small boxes for insertion. The same procedures work in the configuration setup and macro key windows.

Once you've entered the information for each phone directory field, point your mouse and click. The program uses a specific file transfer protocol for each BBS or information service. You can toggle through available baud rates and setup values without having to delete and retype them. Since Baud Bandit stores its phone book files as plain ASCII text, you can easily edit them with your favorite text editor. This also means you can import phone book files from other programs that use a similar format.

As with many other telecommunications programs, numbers may be put into a queue, and the next in line will be auto-dialed when another number is busy or you finish another call.

Figure 19-1

Baud Bandit with the phone book open

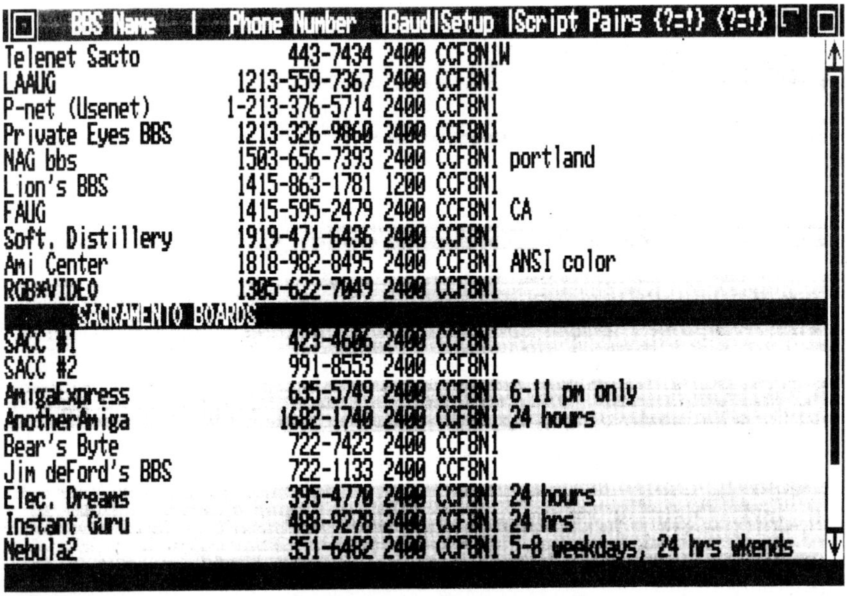

Backscroll Buffer

A slick backscroll buffer-review window lets you use your cursor keys to recall and view text that has scrolled off your screen. Text in this special window can be selected and shot back out through the modem, or saved to disk as an ASCII file. Because of the Amiga's facility with windows, you can be viewing the backscroll in one window while composing text in another—a great convenience when replying to current-session messages.

Point to Chat, and you've opened up an area on the bottom quarter of your screen that is perfect for live, interactive conferencing, or for the chat mode of a BBS.

File Transfer Protocols

Xmodem, Xmodem-CRC, WXmodem, Ymodem, Ymodem-G and -Batch, Xmodem-1K, Zmodem with auto-receive, and CompuServe B protocols all equip Baud Bandit for most file transfers.

Scripting

Besides having its own simple scripting language, Baud Bandit has an ARexx port for interprocess communication using the optional ARexx language (see next READ.ME).

Terminal Emulation

Baud Bandit lacks any VT-terminal emulation but it can load and use different bit-mapped screen fonts for IBM-ANSI graphics (or just to change the way it looks). Owners of Amiga multiserial port boards like the ASDG-DSB can run multiple Baud Bandits and have each talking to a different host on separate serial ports and phone lines at once. This lets you download from one place while uploading to another. With ARexx, you could have two or more terminal programs talking to one another at once, simulating a conference call.

READ.ME

ARexx: Scripting for the Multitasker

ARexx, a commercial scripting/language product published by William S. Hawes, Maynard, MA, is bundled free with the new WorkBench 2.0. It's an extremely powerful macro system that has found wide application in Amiga programs, including telecommunications packages. Reviewers have come to expect ARexx ports, since it is so well suited to the Amiga.

ARexx allows *interprocess communication* for many Amiga programs. This means you can use it to clip text directly from a terminal program, like Baud Bandit, and paste it directly into a text editor or word processor—so long as both programs have the ARexx port. You can also use ARexx to perform multiple tasks within Baud Bandit, Online! Platinum, or other programs using ARexx macros. For example, you can unARC a downloaded file in midsession without leaving the terminal program. ARexx can even filter text through an external language translator, or perform math operations on it. The multitasking Amiga can handle such tasks even if the programs called by ARexx were written by different authors and published by different companies.

ARexx also invites creative users to develop their own sophisticated applications. For example, Selector, by Jeremy Farrance, is a complete front-end written in ARexx for People/Link interactions.

Online! Platinum Edition

Price: $99.95
Micro Systems Software
12798 Forest Hill Blvd.
West Palm Beach, FL 33414
407-790-0770

About three years old, Online! was one of the first Amiga terminal programs. Figure 19-2 shows the main menu on the Amyholics BBS, as accessed with Online! Platinum. The Platinum Edition is the result of many upgrades and offers Amiga users some interesting and unique features.

Configuration Saver

You can save your program's entire configuration, with all its parameter settings, as a .TRM file attached to a WorkBench icon. Later, to run the program with special settings, simply point to that icon and load Online! All those customized parameters are ready and waiting. Different configuration settings can be loaded once Online! is running by opening a requester and selecting one of the .TRM files you've created. It's easy because everything is stored in one file, rather than having separate disk files for phone books, macro keys, and screen/color setups, like other programs. The downside to this scheme is that the .TRM file is binary and cannot be externally edited or changed.

Figure 19-2

Accessing the Amyholics BBS with Online! Platinum

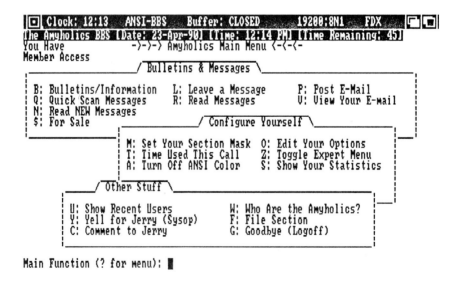

Phone Book

Each .TRM file you create can have a phone book with up to 40 phone numbers, and each phone number may have a unique set of 20 macro key assignments. Once you've created your phone book, Online! will auto-redial a number until it connects. It also lets you queue-dial a group of phone numbers. You can manually force the program to skip to the next number, or remove a number from the queue. A small window monitors your progress.

File Transfer Protocols

Online! Platinum is equipped with Xmodem, Xmodem-CRC, Xmodem-1K, WXmodem, Ymodem and Ymodem-Batch, Kermit, Zmodem, and CompuServe B and Quick-B protocols. It also has a proprietary protocol named Sadie that will let you simultaneously chat with someone else while conducting two-directional file transfers with another Amiga using Online! Platinum. Although transferring two files at once while chatting back and forth slows things down a bit, Sadie works quite well. Unfortunately, no BBS software currently supports Sadie, so it's strictly an Online! user-to-user protocol for now.

Scripting

Powerful scripts and macro processing are available through the ARexx language, incorporated into later versions of Online! Platinum.

A-Talk III

Price: $99.95
Oxxi, Inc.
P.O. Box 90309
Long Beach, CA 90807
213-427-1227

A-Talk III, also called A3, is the latest version of a powerful telecommunications program that, at first glance, seems simple to the point of being generic—but don't be deceived. A3's simple and uncluttered screen hides

many powerful features. Figure 19-3 shows a graphic weather map downloaded from the Accu-Weather service, overlaid by the A3 phone book and a
palette requester window. The "power features" are kept off screen until
you call for them.

Modem Support

A-Talk III has a unique menu for selecting features available in particular brands of modems. It offers specific support for the U.S. Robotics
Courier HST, Telebit T1000, and TrailBlazer+ models.

Phone Book

The A3 Phone Book is a full-screen window that opens to display the
first 30 of a maximum 60-number list. An arrow button switches to the
second 30 slots. You can type your phone numbers, their accompanying
settings, and any short comments directly into the phone book window, or
by entering text in a box.

Figure 19-3

A-Talk III windows over on-line Accu-Weather map

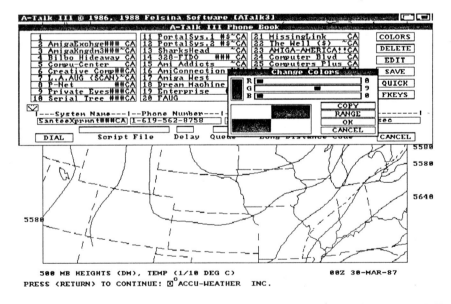

A-Talk III understands the format of phone book files as developed by Chet Solace, and used in his "Final List" of Amiga BBSs (available through numerous sources). However, a major weakness in A-Talk III is that there's no Load button in the phone book window. In order to use another 60-number-limit phone book, you must name it AT3.PHONE and copy it to a specific directory, then quit, and rerun A-Talk III to load it. This procedure may be reworked in the future.

Configuration

Once you have A-Talk III configured to your liking, the total environment is saved to a disk file. This is then scanned and loaded, and sits ready for the next time you run the program. Rather than using the available menus, you can open the Quick Menu, a huge window showing all the pull-down menu choices.

File Transfer Protocols

A3 includes Xmodem, Ymodem, Ymodem-G and -Batch, WXmodem, Zmodem, and Kermit protocols for your file transfer chores. A-Talk III's manual goes into depth on the nuances of using these protocols to your best advantage—a very good write-up.

Special Features

A-Talk III gets its name because of its speech capabilities. Using Amiga's speech synthesis feature, A-Talk III can tell you what it's doing, and can speak whatever is being sent in and out of the modem. Sight-impaired users may find this feature valuable. The speaking parameters are completely adjustable to the user's special needs.

Terminal Emulation

Here's another area where A-Talk III shines. Though it can be used on a novice level as a simple TTY (dumb terminal), you will also find full support for more sophisticated host machines that require ANSI, VT100, VT52, H19, or TEK4014. The Tektronix emulation (Tek mode) requires special menu-selection setup. The screen switches to a 1-bitplane, green-on-black interlace with many setting options and special Tek fonts in different sizes at your command. Plots created in Tek mode can be saved to disk as IFF files or as structured drawings in Aegis Draw Plus format.

PUBLIC DOMAIN TERMINAL PROGRAMS

These are available on disk collections and by downloading. A user group is the best place to get one if you're just starting out, since you won't be downloading without software.

Comm

This little workhorse of a program by Dan James isn't fancy, but it's fast and powerful and doesn't take up much disk space. It may be the perfect beginner's program. Features include a 44-number mouse-driven phone book, 20 macro keys, variable-speed ASCII text send, split screen for "chatting" on national networks, Xmodem, Xmodem-CRC, and WXmodem protocols, and hotkeys. Comm's source code (in C) is available to programmers who want to tear into it for examples or to modify it for custom terminal applications. Many have done this.

Some variations of Comm are described below.

- **AZComm**   Designed purely for high-speed file transfers, AZComm boasts the fastest Zmodem available on the Amiga.

- **NComm**   Written in Europe, NComm adds an activity log, and Ymodem instead of WXmodem. Can interface with special BBS software for automated message gathering and reply.

- **CommPIX**   By using proprietary backslash commands, CommPIX can display and send text in highlighted and reversed colors, italicized, and underlined, while maintaining all of Comm's standard features. Only other CommPIX users will see the striking text modifications.

SHAREWARE TERMINAL PROGRAMS

You can get the programs discussed in this section, and many others for telecommunicating by Amiga, from user groups, from BBSs, and from most major information services that have an Amiga SIG (Special Interest Group).

Access!

Although it doesn't look much like its ancestor, Access! by Keith Young really is Comm under the hood. Access! is the prettiest Amiga terminal program yet—it sports colorful, shaded mouse buttons and file requesters, and text with drop-shadows.

CompuServe B protocol is added to Xmodem, Xmodem-CRC, and WX-modem. Zmodem is not built in, but can be used through an external protocol. Access! also has a rudimentary scripting language and a text reading program.

An Access! screen is shown in Figure 19-4, but you really need to see this one in color to know how well executed its screens are.

JR-Comm

A distinct departure from the Comm-derived group, JR-Comm by Jack Radigan looks like no other Amiga communications program. Xmodem,

Figure 19-4

An Access! screen with multiple windows open

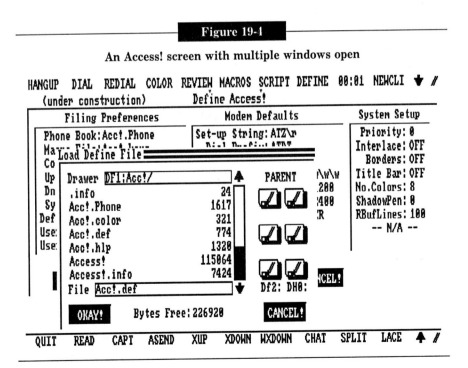

Xmodem-CRC, Xmodem-1K, Ymodem, Ymodem-G, Zmodem, and Compu-Serve B+ protocols are all built in. All protocols are optimized for speed, and JR-Comm's Zmodem is very fast.

You can run JR-Comm in different colors and resolutions. You can configure the program to switch in different colors and macro keys (up to 20) for each listing in its phone book.

JR-Comm sports near-perfect IBM-ANSI graphics emulation for calling PC-based BBSs and host systems. It maintains a disk-based calling log that is updated each time the user dials out or does a file transfer. Although JR-Comm can be found in on-line libraries for downloading, only those who pay the shareware fee will have the latest version. Downloadable versions are always one version behind.

Handshake

Handshake's claim to fame is its flawless VT*nnn* screen emulation. This program, by Eric Haberfellner, is nearly perfect for connecting with mainframe- and UNIX-based hosts and BBSs. Xmodem, Xmodem-CRC, Ymodem, Ymodem-Batch, and 7-bit and 8-bit Kermit are built in. (Zmodem is missing.) Text can be switched into a "smooth scroll" mode. The phone book holds 20 numbers. Handshake can run in many different screen modes and can open up to 132 columns wide.

WHAT'S NEW IN AMIGA SOFTWARE

The entire look and feel of Amiga's WorkBench has changed in version 2.0. It sports a new, more professional-looking color scheme and has added a three-dimensional look to its screens, windows, requesters, and gadgets. Terminal programs that run on WorkBench will inherit the new look in their own windows, requesters, and gadgets. There are many new features, including a mouse accelerator, "SunMouse"-type window-to-front activation, and automatic shrinking and expanding of open windows.

The screen shots in Figures 19-5 and 19-6 are from a pre-release version of WorkBench 2.0. Some details may be changed or revised in the near future.

Figure 19-5

WorkBench 2.0 ready for multitasking

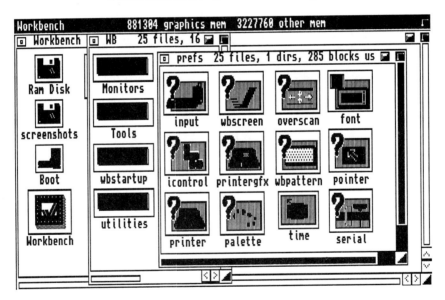

Figure 19-6

WorkBench 2.0 with open windows

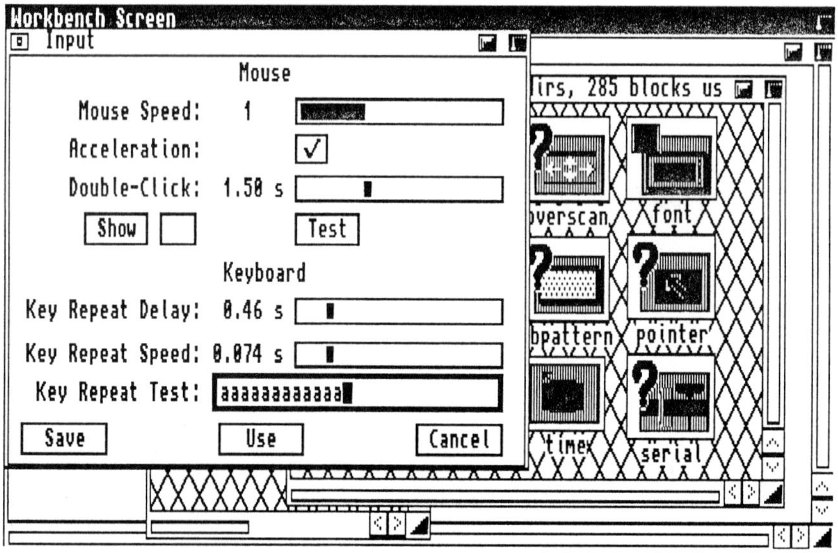

CHAPTER TWENTY

Communicating Under UNIX

In some ways, communicating under the UNIX operating system is more primitive than under DOS; in other ways, it is more sophisticated and advanced. It depends partly on your point of view, because most DOS users don't consider UNIX user-friendly. You give UNIX a command, and it goes about its business, without bothering to report to you. As is typical with computers, this is a design trade-off—the designers had to choose between power and ease of use, and UNIX is very powerful. Communication under UNIX reflects this tilt toward the power user. You lose the variety and ease of use available in the DOS environment, but you get the flexibility to call almost any UNIX machine directly or through other machines. As your work environment dictates, you may not even have to call the machine yourself. All the details of transmission will be handled for you—provided you specify the target machine.

OVERVIEW

The UNIX communications picture involves multiple levels. When UNIX machines are connected by any of several means, including telephone lines or local connections such as Ethernet, several people may be connected to the same machine. These users then communicate with each other on line, even though they may be at different physical locations.

At the top level, communications commands such as **cu, uucp,** and **mail** are available. If it's available on a particular machine, you can even use a Kermit program. These commands rely on protocols to execute the appropriate actions to establish and carry on communications. Such protocols are responsible for breaking a transmission into packets and for making sure these packets are sent and received. A commonly used protocol is TCP/IP (Transmission Control Protocol/Internet Protocol).

The transmission protocols rely on a lower level that establishes the physical connection through which the communications take place. For example, if you're communicating with another PC hooked onto a local area network, you may very well be communicating on an Ethernet. This network standard is popular in the UNIX world because of its extremely fast transmission, on the order of 10 megabits per second!

Local UNIX networks often hook into larger communications nets, called *internets*. One of the best known internets is the DARPA (Defense Advanced Research Projects Agency) internet, which connects and provides access among thousands of computers worldwide.

If you're communicating by modem, the transmission speed is much slower on UNIX, and the protocols involved may be different. For example, if you communicate with another machine using the Kermit protocol, both machines need to be running Kermit. Kermit operates in UNIX the same way as in the DOS environment (see Chapter 24).

COMMUNICATION COMMANDS IN UNIX

The main commands for communicating between UNIX systems are **mail, uucp,** and **cu.** Each command has different capabilities, advantages, and disadvantages.

In the following discussion, different machines are mentioned. The *local* machine is the one from which you initiate the command. Other *remote* machines are given single-letter names.

The **cu** Command

The **cu** command—for call up—lets you call a remote machine, log on to that machine, and execute commands on that machine. You can then interact with the remote system. This remote system might be running UNIX, but it is not necessary. The **cu** command's capabilities include limited terminal emulation and communications (such as the ability to transfer and receive ASCII files). The UNIX environment variable, *TERM,* determines the terminal emulation used in a particular session.

Once connected and logged on, you can execute commands locally or on the remote system. It is as if you were logged on to the remote machine — except that you can also operate on the local machine. Among other things, you can use the **cu** command on the remote machine (A) to call another remote machine (B). Thus, you'll be connected from the local machine to two remote machines: directly to remote A, and indirectly to remote B.

Specifying the Target Machine

There are three ways of specifying the machine you want to call:

- By using the machine's telephone number

- By specifying the line by which the remote machine is connected

- By specifying the remote machine's name

To specify a telephone number, use its digits preceded by special characters to indicate a dial tone or a delay. To specify a remote machine connected by a direct line, you provide the device name (such as *tty0*). To specify a machine name, you need to provide the **uucp** name associated with the machine. The number or line needed to establish a connection with the machine is available in a **uucp** information file — /usr/lib/uucp/Systems.

Here are some sample **cu** command lines.

```
cu -n 9=1123-5551111
cu -1 /dev/tty4
cu zenda
```

The first command dials 9, then waits for a dial tone (indicated by the =), and then dials the remaining digits. The dash between the 3 and the 5 specifies a delay before the 5 is dialed. The second command tells **cu** to use the line connected to a serial port, such as *tty4*. The third sample command line connects you to a machine named *zenda*, whose details (phone or line number) will be obtained by the **cu** command from a predetermined file.

Specifying Other Command-Line Options

The **cu** command provides other options. For example, you can specify transmission speed using the -s option. You can also control whether communication will use half- or full-duplex. Since machines may differ in the parity they use, the **cu** command sets the parity parameter, if necessary. For example, **-e** would specify even parity, and **-o**, odd parity. You can even print the results of tracing command execution.

The following listing shows an example of a command line using some of these options. The example invokes **cu**, sets transmission to 2400 baud, specifies half-duplex mode, odd parity, and dials the number.

```
cu -s 2400 -h -o -n 9=1123-5551111
```

Session Options

Once connected, the **cu** command actually runs as two processes. One process takes data from the standard input (the keyboard) and transmits this input to the remote machine. On this machine, the input is processed and acted upon just as if you had typed it at the remote machine.

The other **cu** process receives data from the remote machine and sends it to the standard output (the screen). To keep buffers at either end from overflowing, **cu** generally uses CTRL-S and CTRL-Q signals to control data flow.

Certain inputs get special treatment. In particular, input that begins with ~ is processed on the local machine—instead of being passed directly to the remote machine as data. For example, the inputs

```
~%take    remotefname
~%put     localfname    remname
```

transfer files between the local and remote machines. The first line copies the file named *remotefname* from the remote machine to the same name on the local machine. The second line copies file *localfname* from the local machine to file *remname* on the remote machine. The command line will include the name of the local machine. This is added automatically, as soon as the program sees the tilde (~) at the start of the input.

The following command ends the session, and disconnects the machines from each other:

```
~.
```

Once you've used **cu** to call another machine, your default working environment is on the remote machine—even though you're typing on the local machine. The tilde commands let you work on the local machine.

What happens if you log on to another remote machine from the first remote machine? That is, what happens if you call remote A from the local machine and then use **cu** to call remote B from remote A? After giving the **cu** command from the remote A environment, you are connected to the remote B machine, but you still input from the local machine. This (local) input passes first to remote A, and then on to remote B.

To execute on the local machine, use a single tilde at the start of the input; to execute on remote A—that is, on the "local" machine for remote B—use two tildes. For example, to transfer file *bfile* from remote B to remote A, enter

```
~~%take bfile
```

Limitations of cu

The **cu** command lets you work on multiple machines at once, adding flexibility to what you can do as well as where you can do it. There are limitations to **cu**, however.

First, you must be able to log on to the remote machine. Second, you can only transmit or receive ASCII files. To transfer binary files, you need to convert them to ASCII on the source machine and then convert them back to binary files on the target machine. Needless to say, this is an inconvenience.

Another limitation is the lack of error detection and correction capabilities. Furthermore, special characters (such as non-printing ones) may not be transmitted reliably with the **%put** and **%take** commands.

The uucp Command

The **uucp** command—for UNIX to UNIX copy—is the central process in a whole subsystem used to transfer files between machines. This process does all the administrative work needed to copy a file from one machine to another. Such a transfer can involve ASCII or binary files, and uses error detection and correction to ensure an accurate copy.

The **uucp** command actually calls a UNIX daemon, which transfers the file as a background process. The transfer takes place only if several conditions are met: The file to be copied and the destination directory must both exist. Also, you must have the necessary user permissions to transfer a file and to write it to a new machine.

The basic syntax for **uucp** is shown in the following listing. You can include various options when invoking this command.

```
uucp source  destination
uucp source1 source2 source3  destination
```

Here the command copies the files specified by *source* to the file specified by *destination*. The last file specified is the destination, and all filenames before that are interpreted as files to be sent. Both the *source* and the *destination* names include a machine specifier (which may be implicit in the case of the local machine).

Theoretically, this command allows you to specify files on the remote machine as sources, and copy from the remote machine to the local machine. Using such a transfer, you could transfer files containing passwords, or you could accidentally copy a file over an existing one with the same name. For this reason, the **uucp** command requires that you have permission to be working with the specified files and directories. This helps restrict the kinds of files you can copy.

All the work of the **uucp** command takes place in the background, although you can tell the command to report when it has copied the files. The simplicity of the **uucp** command actually covers a great deal of activity. The command first checks a predefined file to see what other files or information the command needs. These files provide information about the systems involved, about the devices that connect the machines, and about the "dialing" methods and protocols that must be used to establish and maintain a connection.

For example, a *Systems* file specifies all the connections that exist between the local machine and any other machines. Such connections can be via modems, direct cable links, and so forth. If there are restrictions on calling times for specific machines, this information is also contained in the *Systems* file. (Thus, if a machine is removed from a net for maintenance, there is no point in calling the machine until it is back on the network.) The transfer rate for each connection is also provided in the *Systems* file. This file will also contain information required to log on to the remote machine to establish a connection.

A *Devices* file stores the location of the connections between the local and remote machines. For example, the local machine may be connected to remote A via modem on *tty1* (the UNIX name for COM2), and with remote B via a direct connection on *tty0* (that is, COM1). This file also contains information on the transfer protocols.

A *Dialers* file contains special information needed to carry out communication between two particular machines based on the type and location of the connection, and the machine type. For example, the file may specify that certain characters must be converted to others during the copying process. The *Dialers* file may also specify any special passwords needed to get through the remote machine's security (provided the permissions exist).

The **uucp** command gathers and processes all this information, and then calls a daemon to establish the connection and copy the files.

Options for **uucp**

The **uucp** command understands several options that provide feedback to the user or notification for the recipient of the file copy. Here are some of these options.

-C   Ordinarily, the specified source files are not touched until the copying is about to occur. This means you can keep editing and changing the file, but also that the file must be available when it's ready to be copied. The -C option tells **uucp** to copy the files immediately to the spool directory, from which they will be copied at the appropriate time. With this option, the file versions current when **uucp** was invoked will be copied — regardless of any changes you make in the file between the time you give the **uucp** command and the time the file is actually sent.

-g *grade*   This option is used to establish a *grade*, or priority, for the copy. The grade is specified using a single letter or number. Files with lower grade values will be copied earlier.

-m   This option tells **uucp** to send a mail message to the sender, reporting when the copy process is done.

-n *user*   The **user** option tells **uucp** to inform the specified *user* on the remote machine that the copy process is done.

Selecting Transfer Protocols

The **uucp** command can use several different transfer protocols, depending on the machines involved. When **uucp** is invoked, it tries to use the default protocol (the **g** protocol), which is supported by all versions of **uucp**.

If the *Devices* file specifies other — perhaps faster — protocols to try for a particular connection, **uucp** tries to establish one of these as the protocol to be used. This effort continues until a protocol is found that both machines support.

Commands Related to **uucp**

The **uucp** subsystem includes several additional commands that retrieve information or carry out simpler copying processes.

uuname	Determines the names of the machines to which your current machine is connected.
uulog	Lets you examine the contents of the **uucp** activity log.
uustat	Determines the status of the transfer queue for the files you're transferring.
uuto	Lets you copy files from the source machine to a public directory on the target machine. The command actually uses the **uucp** command, but always transfers to public directories. This command can only copy files directly to another machine. It cannot copy files from the local to a remote that is connected to the local through a third machine.
uupick	Once files have been transferred to a public directory using **uuto**, the **uupick** command can be used by the recipient to retrieve these files from the directory.
uux	This command (UNIX to UNIX execute) lets you execute commands on the remote machine, provided the necessary execute permissions exist. This can be a very dangerous command in the hands of someone with the necessary permissions who is malicious or clumsy. The **uux** command is therefore generally very restricted on most machines.

Advantages and Disadvantages of the **uucp** Subsystem

The **uucp** command, with its files and related subcommands, provides a very powerful and flexible transfer capability. The command copies files quickly (depending on the connection) and error free (because of error detection and correction).

The command runs in the background, which means you can continue with your work without having to wait for the copying to be completed. This can be very convenient when you want to copy files to another machine but you don't know when that machine will be available. With the command in the background, the files will be copied as soon as the target machine can be called.

uucp's drawbacks and restrictions arise from its power and potential for disrupting the system. Different machines may have different restrictions. To implement such restrictions, machines often use different versions of the **uucp** command, which can cause difficulties and frustration.

The **mail** Command

The **cu** command lets you call and log on to a remote computer. The **uucp** command is most useful for sending material from one machine to another. Because this command works in the background, it is suited for transmitting long files.

The **mail** command is also useful for sending material to other machines—or even to other users on the same machine. This command operates in the foreground, and so is best suited for material that is composed on the spot or that needs to be delivered right away. The command is also used to read material received from other users.

The **mail** command always sends material to a recipient's mailbox. The material sent is saved as a new message, distinct from any messages that may already be in the recipient's mailbox. The recipient need not be on an interconnected machine. The mail will reach the person as long as both your machines are on the same internet. Because UNIX allows you to specify aliases, you can use a simple name to represent a long internet address.

Here is the basic syntax for the **mail** command.

```
mail recipient
mail recipient1   recipient2   recipient3
```

The first command sends mail to the person whose address is specified or aliased by *recipient;* the second command sends the same piece of mail to several people at the same time. There are also several options you can use when sending or reading mail. In fact, you can even forward your own mail to other people.

Passing Along the Mail and Information

Each network site (see the READ.ME on Usenet) has a predetermined number of other sites to which it transmits new information as it becomes available, or on a set schedule. The **uucp** command handles the transfer of intersite electronic mail. To communicate with a user at any other network site, address the message to the other person's site name or to a more general "domain" name, adding the person's user name. Specific information about how to use intersystem mail is available in UNIX system manuals and in third-party directories and manuals.

Delivery Time

As a result of the interaction among Usenet systems, a message's delivery time varies from half an hour to a couple of days. As with DOS BBS mail networks, a message goes from node to node, getting passed along in the right general direction at each stopover.

FILE TRANSFER PROTOCOLS: TCP/IP

UNIX machines may be connected to complex networks, and these networks may themselves be connected to an internet. Transfers between machines in such a topology may take direct or roundabout paths. As a result, the logistics of UNIX communication can become chaotic. For this reason, transfer protocols need to be selected with care.

The protocol must be able to handle packets coming from many different sources, and going to many different destinations. Moreover, the protocol must allow rapid transfer, and must be able to avoid collisions between packets. (A collision occurs when two packets are sent out at the same time to the same network.)

The TCP/IP protocol—developed as part of the research that led to the DARPA Internet—fulfills these requirements nicely. TCP/IP actually contains two different types of protocols.

At the transmitting end, the TCP (Transmission Control Protocol) breaks files into packets, adds required header information (packet number, destination, source, and so forth), and sends the packets onto the network.

Because of the way an internet works, packets from the same transmission may reach their destination through very different routes. Thus, it's possible for packet 100 to reach the destination machine before packet 50 does; thus packets may not arrive in sequence. For this reason, the TCP protocol at the receiving end must be able to reassemble the packets in the correct order. The packet sizes are determined by the TCP/IP protocols on the machines involved. The largest packet size common to both protocols is used.

The IP (Internet Protocol) is responsible for *connectionless delivery* of packets. A delivery is connectionless if there is no direct connection between the source and the destination machines. In such a case, the IP must find an indirect path from source to destination. The shortest path of this kind depends on what else is happening on the internet when a particular packet is being routed. Because of this, packets from the same transmission do not always take the same route to the destination.

The IP knows the source and the destination, but knows nothing about the contents of the packet it is delivering. This is why the TCP at the receiving end must be able to reassemble the file.

READ.ME

Usenet

Usenet, the UNIX network, was created in 1979 as a BBS-type exchange for mainframes and minicomputers between Duke University and the University of North Carolina. At a UNIX conference in 1980, the system was described in a paper; soon other UNIX sites joined the network, and Usenet rapidly grew. Today it is a well-organized system maintained by volunteer administrators.

Usenet Newsgroups Usenet has *newsgroups* somewhat like the conferences or message areas found on BBS systems. A large number of newsgroups cover interests ranging from computing topics to music, art, taxes, religion, and even rumors. Many newsgroups are moderated, which helps to organize and control the type of information appearing in them.

News and information found on Usenet are distributed from one UNIX site to another by means of **uucp**, the Unix-to-Unix Copy Program.

SUMMARY

In general, UNIX is a silent operating system. Commands do their work, and they don't talk much about it. This silence is part of the UNIX design philosophy. Theoretically, it is easier to do things by stringing together existing commands.

One consequence of such silence is that you won't see many UNIX menus. This means that options and settings for a command must be specified on the command line. This makes UNIX commands much more complex and cryptic than DOS commands—DOS programs simply ask you when they need more information.

This difference makes UNIX a bit daunting at first, but its advantages become clear when you begin to see the system's power and flexibility. For example, with a single command, you can send several files to a machine halfway around the world, without ever dialing the machine directly.

This chapter barely scratches the surface of UNIX communications. Many issues have not been addressed here, and many capabilities have not been described. We hope the brief description of these three communications commands gives you an idea of the kinds of things you can do with the UNIX system.

READ.ME

Finding Your Way onto UNIX
A Directory to Electronic Mail Addressing and Networks

O'Reilly and Assoc.
632 Petaluma Avenue
Sebastopol, CA 95472
300+ pages, $24.95

Networking in UNIX, as with MS-DOS networks and BBSs, is exploding worldwide. Authors Donnalyn Frey and Rick Adams are on the second edition of this resource book about UNIX networks and are scheduling updated editions every eight to twelve months. An O'Reilly and Assoc. "nutshell handbook," the book is a directory of over 100 research, educational, and commercial UNIX networks.

READ.ME (*continued*)

The directory is useful to system administrators, researchers, conference attendees, and others who routinely send UNIX E-mail. Each network's section contains general information, address structure and format, connections to other sites or networks, facilities available to users, contact names and addresses, cross-references to other networks, and the date of the last directory update. There is also a three-way index to network name, network type, and country, plus a list of many of the world's second-level domains. Each network listing is complete on two facing pages, in a short reference format. The directory also has sections on UNIX resources, Usenet programs and file libraries, and guides to system usage.

For further information, contact O'Reilly and Associates at 1-800-338-6887 (in California, 1-800-533-6887). The international number is 1-707-829-0515. The Usenet E-mail address is nuts@ora.uu.net.

CHAPTER TWENTY-ONE

Communicating in OS/2

Operating System/2, or OS/2, arrived on the computer scene in April 1987 with 300 man-years of development effort already expended. There are still conflicting opinions about whether OS/2 is a failure or an incredibly flexible operating system. Many OS/2 users keep a "DOS box" section of memory and switch back and forth; the two systems are not incompatible. The main benefit to using OS/2 is that it takes full advantage of 80286 and 80386 processors, operating in what Intel calls "protected" mode.

To put the additional capabilities into perspective, consider the additional memory capacity of these fast chips. The 8088 and 8086 chips used in PC- and XT-class computers were grand achievements when they were introduced, providing 20 address lines and about 29,000 transistors on a single chip. They could address 1MB of RAM. The new 80386 processors provide 32 address lines and 275,000 transistors, and can control more than 4 billion bytes of physical RAM. OS/2 is able to tap all that power; DOS cannot.

This chapter introduces you to some of the ins and outs of using OS/2 to enhance your telecommunicating abilities.

TECHNICAL OVERVIEW OF OS/2

The information-handling capabilities of OS/2 make it one of the most powerful systems ever invented for computers, including mainframes and minicomputers. OS/2 is very complex, which accounts in part for the time OS/2 has taken to get up a head of steam.

Technically, OS/2 is a preemptive, time-slice, multitasking operating system. It runs in protected mode on computers containing an Intel 80286 or 80386 chip. Current versions operate on a "Desktop" similar to the Microsoft Windows desktop. From there you can start Presentation Manager (PM) applications (available with more recent versions of OS/2), full-screen or windowed character-based sessions, or the DOS session.

Once started, any session except the DOS box continues to run, no matter what is showing on your screen. (The DOS session goes into a pause state when you leave it.) In OS/2 you can "detach" background programs like DOS TSR applications, eliminating many of the conflicts and side effects that make TSRs unruly. You can activate detached programs with a hotkey, just like you can activate a TSR under DOS. All sessions and running applications make use of virtual memory and "Dynamic Link Libraries," or DLLs. These terms are described briefly below.

Virtual Memory

Computer instructions are executed in physical memory—in your computer's actual RAM. This memory is a finite resource, even if you have a full 16 MB of RAM in an AT-class computer. If you could arrange to remove code or data from memory when it's not being used and put it in a disk file, you would wind up with a logical address space much larger than your actual physical RAM. This extra address space is called *virtual memory*.

Virtual memory makes a large difference in your computer's capabilities. For example, an 80286 can address 16MB of actual physical RAM. In protected mode, though, it can manage up to a full gigabyte (1,073,741,824 bytes) of logical or virtual memory. An 80386 can address 4 gigabytes (4,294,967,296 bytes) of physical RAM. In protected mode it can manage 64 terabytes (over 70,000 million bytes) of logical or virtual memory. That's like putting the power of a mainframe on your desktop, and it's one of the principal strengths of the OS/2 operating system.

Dynamic Link Libraries

Dynamic Link Libraries (DLLs) are relatively new. In DOS applications, a programmer links all executable code into a single application program. This program is loaded in its entirety when it runs. This is called *early binding*, because everything is linked together in memory when the program starts.

Using DLLs, the link operation installs pointers to the DLL modules it will need when it executes a program, instead of installing the actual code. When the program runs and a call is made to a DLL function, the system first checks to see if the DLL is in RAM. If it is, it uses the RAM-resident copy; otherwise, it loads the required DLL from disk. This process is called *late binding*, and helps conserve RAM memory. It also improves the overall efficiency of the system, because only code that is actually needed gets loaded.

INSTALLING OS/2

To install the OS/2 system, you insert the diskette marked Install, and reboot your computer. That's all. Installation really is that simple. OS/2 loads a basic version of itself, checks the hardware you have installed in your computer, and prompts you for disk changes and required information as it proceeds. Screens of text tell you what is happening as the package is installed, and prompt you to choose various options. Help is available on screen for virtually every option.

To install *dual-boot* capability under OS/2 Version 1.2, you must have DOS installed, with DOS AUTOEXEC.BAT and CONFIG.SYS files already in the root directory when you begin installation. With this requirement satisfied, OS/2 will automatically install the dual-boot feature. When installation is complete, you are asked to remove the diskette from your A drive and reboot your computer. After 30 to 60 seconds, the OS/2 Desktop Manager screen appears.

To boot in DOS, go to a full-screen windowed session and type **boot /DOS** at the prompt. You will be asked to confirm your intentions. A yes answer causes the system to move some files around and reboot in DOS.

If you now take a look at the files in the OS2\SYSTEM directory, you'll find COMMAND.OS2, AUTOEXEC.OS2, and CONFIG.OS2. The OS/2 system files are, by default, installed in an OS2 directory. It is good practice to have a separate DOS or BIN directory for your DOS files. Don't mix DOS and OS/2, and don't put the OS2 directory in your DOS PATH.

BOOT.COM is a "bound" program that bridges OS/2 and DOS. It will run in either DOS or in OS/2. Make a copy of BOOT.COM and keep it in your DOS or BIN directory. That way you can type **boot /os2** from your DOS root directory to reboot the system in OS/2.

This completes installation. You now have a choice between running under DOS or under OS/2, and you can reboot from one to the other at any time.

OS/2 CONFIG.SYS

The OS/2 CONFIG.SYS file is far more extensive than the DOS equivalent. The OS/2 configuration file serves as both CONFIG.SYS and AUTOEXEC-.BAT for OS/2 operations. Under OS/2, AUTOEXEC.BAT is used for the DOS box or DOS session. The first time you double-click the DOS icon in the lower-left corner of the Desktop Manager screen, or select it from the Task Manager, AUTOEXEC.BAT is executed. After that, double-clicking will simply switch you to the DOS box.

Your CONFIG.SYS file is set up when you install OS/2. It establishes PMSHELL as the Presentation Manager shell, and CMD.EXE as the character-based shell (equivalent to COMMAND.COM in DOS). It also indicates the .INI files (like Windows' WIN.INI) that will be used.

Most of OS/2 runs from the Dynamic Link Libraries mentioned earlier. You will probably find close to 100 files in your OS2\DLL directory. Many entries and commands allow you to involve the DOS session, the display, and the mouse. Check your OS/2 manual to find out how to do all the necessary functions.

COMMUNICATIONS STARTUP

Setting up your machine for communications in OS/2 is similar in many respects to setting up in DOS. Here is a comparison of their respective approaches.

OS/2 STARTUP.CMD

When OS/2 starts, you have the icons for Desktop Manager, Print Manager, Group-Main, and the DOS session available on the Presentation Manager Desktop. From the Group menu in the Desktop Manager, you can select additional groups.

You also can set up other programs from the Program menu. It's a good idea at this early point in startup to set up other programs. This will make them easier to select later on, from your Desktop, on the fly. For example, you can set up a group of programs in a file named STARTUP.CMD, as shown here:

```
mode com2:9600,n,8,1
START "File Manager" /PM /I C:\OS2\PMFILE.EXE
START "Process Status" /PM /I C:\PROFILER\PS.EXE
START "Clock" /PM /I C:\OS2\DIGCLOCK.EXE
detach qh -120 -m50 -q
```

This file first runs *mode* to set COM port 2 for serial communications. Next, a series of START commands contains program names in double quotes; these will appear with icons on the Desktop. The /PM entries indicate a Presentation Manager application; /I means the program will start with its own icon; and the final segment of each command line specifies the path and program name. Finally, the file starts Quick Help (qh) as a detached (background) program. Like a DOS TSR, Quick Help shows itself only when you press the appropriate hotkey.

Once this file's named, in this instance with the filename STARTUP-.CMD, you can move it to any Group you want and activate it when the system starts.

DOS AUTOEXEC.BAT

AUTOEXEC.BAT applies only to DOS and is run just once, when you first activate the DOS session. You will have a number of options available at boot-up. (For details, see your OS/2 manual.) In essence, though, your DOS AUTOEXEC.BAT file needs to establish the serial communications variables for the DOS session. As with OS/2, you will use *mode* to establish the COM port. If your DOS session communications software sets its own communications parameters, you'll only need to use

```
setcom40 com2-on
```

to activate the same port for DOS.

Additional COM Ports

There is an internal driver configured to run COM1 and COM2 in most versions of OS/2. OS/2 will support additional ports if you get appropriate software and drivers. If you need extra COM ports and you happen to find the accommodating hardware at an acceptable price, be sure to ask if a compatible OS/2 driver is available to manage the extra ports.

General Suggestions

When you start the OS/2 Control Panel, you will see the Control Panel dialog box with the Options menu selected. When you enter Communications port, the screen shows the Communications Port dialog box. Clicking on HELP brings up the help screen.

You can check your COM ports from an OS/2 full-screen or windowed session. Simply type **mode com1** or **mode com2** at the prompt. OS/2 will report that the port is unavailable or not installed, or it will report the current settings for the port if settings have been established.

COMMUNICATION SOFTWARE UNDER OS/2

There are dozens of software packages available for OS/2 networking. The OS/2 Applications Guide from IBM lists many of them. It would take more than this book to cover them all.

It's important to remember that, multitasking system or not, OS/2 won't let you share a modem between sessions. Once a modem is on line, it's on line—it can't switch around from task to task the way a printer or a monitor can. If a modem could handle several different connections, sharing one might make better sense. Modems can't usually do this, however, so trying to multitask one would simply chop your telecommunications session to pieces.

There are at least four software packages available for use with OS/2 Presentation Manager, listed at the end of the chapter. (If you have a favorite DOS communications program, you can use that instead.) Products like QModem, Procomm's PCPlus, and other DOS communications programs all run well in the DOS session of OS/2. Using a communications program designed specifically for OS/2, however, expands your communications options. You can change sessions in the middle of a communications operation, and use the system editor or other programs that may contribute to better communication—all while the OS/2 communications session continues unhindered.

One File, One Session

While running a communications program in OS/2 you may occasionally find yourself unable to open, delete, or otherwise manage files you would like to work with. As a multitasker, OS/2 goes to considerable lengths to avoid uncontrolled file changes, and to ensure that two running programs do not change a single file simultaneously.

If you find that you are being unreasonably denied access to a file, the first thing to do is check to see if it is open under another program. Usually you will discover that access is restored after you close the file in the other program.

Suggested Software

The following packages are available at this writing for communication under OS/2:

ABOVE X
ABOVE Software, Inc.
#3 Hutton Centre, Suite 950
Santa Ana, CA 92707
714-545-1181

ChipChat
Cawthon Software Group
24224 Michigan Avenue
Dearborn, MI 48124-1897
313-565-4000

HyperACCESS-PM
Hilgraeve, Inc.
Genesis Center, Suite A
111 Conant Avenue
Monroe, MI 48161
313-243-0576

HyperTerm
Quercus Systems
19567 Dorchester Drive
Saratoga, CA 95070
408-257-3697

CHAPTER TWENTY-TWO

Micro-to-Mainframe Connection

With the proliferation of personal computers in the market, and the increase in power and capacity now available at the desktop, it's easy to get wrapped up in the many applications, functions, and capabilities the personal computer can provide. It's also easy to lose sight of that still necessary and important component in the computer world: the mainframe.

The mainframe plays an extremely vital role in computer communications and will maintain that position for many years to come. IBM's dominance in the computer industry significantly influences the position of the mainframe in that industry. Reliance on the massive amounts of data currently stored on IBM mainframes in corporations around the world is critical to their success. And with the increasing demand to collect, retrieve, analyze, sort, and file data, integrated networks of micros and mainframes are constantly called upon to access, process, and distribute information.

This chapter will help you understand communication and data transmission between a personal computer and a corporation's mainframe. Data is structured and processed differently in these two environments, thus making micro-to-mainframe communication a somewhat complicated task.

Communication between the two computers must involve steps to make the data and processes compatible. The mainframe handles applications requiring large amounts of memory and disk storage, such as corporate database management. In the micro-to-mainframe connection, the microcomputer simply selects a small piece of information from the mainframe and processes it for integration into a spreadsheet, graph, or report.

BACKGROUND

Until the 1970s, a computer system consisted of a mainframe that performed a batch of programs at a time, without direct interaction with the user. Next, the system was a mainframe with "dumb" terminals connected by a terminal controller; this was a time-sharing environment, where several users had access to the computer at the same time. IBM controlled the data communications world at this time with their 3270 network, (mainframe attached to 3270 terminals).

Throughout the 1970s, the concept of *distributed processing* evolved as a result of the need for more computer processing at the local level, the inability of existing information systems to meet user needs, and more independent and geographically dispersed corporate offices. Distributed processing simply means that many of the mainframe's functions can be offloaded to, or distributed among, other local or remote computers. With the introduction of the IBM Personal Computer in August 1981, genuine distributed computer processing at the local, or desktop, level became a reality.

The first personal computers, however, were not designed or equipped for communication with the mainframe. Perhaps this lack was an intentional decision by IBM to thwart any threat to their large installed base of terminals. Then again, the fact that IBM put a cassette port on the early machines may have meant that the company wasn't taking the little PC too seriously. However, as those new personal computers surged into the marketplace, it became apparent that they should be able to communicate with the mainframe; it seemed silly to have both a dumb terminal device *and* a personal computer sitting on the desktop.

This communications need was especially apparent to two engineers from a small company in Atlanta, Georgia. While playing cards one evening, they developed the concept and design for the PC industry's first terminal emulation board and software. Soon thereafter, in late 1982, the first IRMA board was shipped, and IRMA, made by Digital Communications Associates, Inc. (DCA), quickly became an industry standard in micro-to-mainframe communication. In fact, at the end of 1988, over 1.2 million personal computers were connected to their mainframe using terminal emulation products such as IRMA. It is predicted that by 1992 the personal computer will completely displace the dumb terminal as the device of choice for desktop-to-mainframe communication.

Just what does a terminal emulation board do when installed in your personal computer? What is it emulating? And what does it allow your personal computer to do that it cannot do otherwise? This chapter answers these and other questions for you.

THE MICRO-TO-MAINFRAME CONNECTION

Since its introduction, the IBM 3270 computer network has become the backbone of most *Fortune* 500 company networks. A majority of micro-to-mainframe connections are within a 3270 network environment, so our discussion will focus on this type of connection. Over the years, 3270 network capabilities have, of course, evolved with the growth of computer technology. The basic functionality, however, of 3270 micro-to-mainframe connectivity remains the same.

We will begin with a discussion of *local* connections, followed by *remote* micro-to-mainframe connections in the 3270 network. In a local connection, the PC is within reasonable proximity to the mainframe, allowing connection and communication via a cable (typically *coaxial*), rather than modems and phone lines.

The Local Coaxial Micro-to-Mainframe Connection

A local micro-to-mainframe connection involves the *mainframe,* a *cluster controller,* and the 3270 *terminal devices.* The role of each of these components, as well as 3270 terminal emulation and PC communication with the mainframe will be discussed.

The Mainframe

Central to every 3270 network is the mainframe (or host) computer, also known as the CPU or central processing unit. The mainframe in an IBM 3270 network is typically a member of the 370, 303X, 308X, 309X, or 43XX family of host computers. The network processing power and data storage are provided by the mainframe. The mainframe's software components provide overall control of the host resources — specific *application programs* designed for users, such as database management, accounting spreadsheets, and project management. The mainframe also controls sessions between the application programs and end users, and the sharing and routing of information between the mainframe and other devices.

Overall control of the host resources is provided by the *operating system,* the most common being DOS (Disk Operating System), OS (Operating System), OS/VS (Operating System/Virtual Storage), VM (Virtual Memory), and MVS (Multiple Virtual Storage). Mainframe application programs can be standardized packages or customized programs designed specifically to meet the needs of the user. The software components that control the sessions and data flow between application programs and end users are referred to as *transaction processors,* teleprocessing monitors, or transaction control programs. Common transaction control programs are TSO (Time Share Option), CMS (Conversational Monitoring System), CICS (Customer Information Control System), and IMS (Information Management System). Software responsible for sharing and routing of information between the mainframe and other devices is known as the *access method.* Popular access methods include VTAM (Virtual Terminal Access Method), TCAM (Telecommunications Access Method), and BTAM (Basic Telecommunications Access Method). BTAM, the earliest access method, was limited to dedicated networks, that is, networks that only offered one application to the user. VTAM and TCAM were developed later, as it became possible for different applications to access the same network mainframe (multiple application networks). Figure 22-1 shows the relationship between the operating system and the software components.

The Cluster Controller

In order for terminal devices, personal computers, and other devices like printers to connect to the mainframe, an interface is provided by the cluster controller, or terminal control unit. The cluster controller controls data input/output between the end user devices and the mainframe. The cluster controller in local micro-to-mainframe connections may be called a *channel-*

Figure 22-1

Mainframe software components

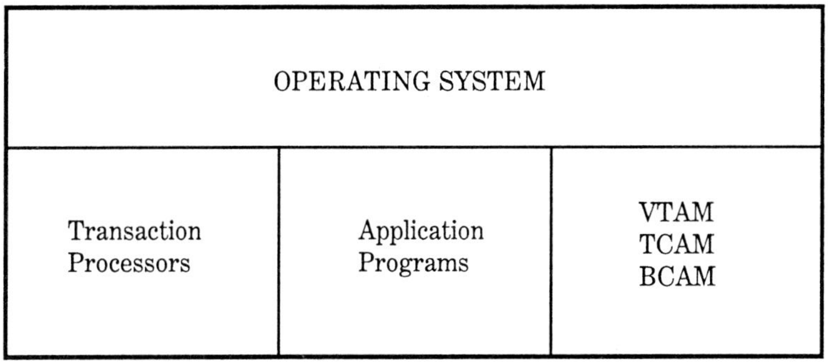

OPERATING SYSTEM		
Transaction Processors	Application Programs	VTAM TCAM BCAM

attached controller when it is attached to the channel of the mainframe, that is, the path through which all data signals travel. The cluster controller is attached by cables, often referred to as *bus* and *tag cables* (see Figure 22-2). These cables are typically no more than 200 feet long. The cluster controller may also connect to the mainframe through the *communications controller*, or front end processor, when direct channel attachments are not available. Further detail on the communications controller will follow in the discussion of remote micro-to-mainframe communication.

In the IBM 3270 network, the most common cluster controllers are the IBM 3274, 3276, and 3174. The 3276 is used only as a remote control unit. The 3274 and 3174 can have from eight to thirty-two end user or terminal devices attached. Twelve different models of the 3274 and nine models of the 3174 are available, each designed for specific environments, data transmission protocols, and numbers of ports. The 3174 has more memory and features than the 3274, including support for Central Site Customization, Asynchronous Emulation Adapter, Intelligent Printer Data Stream (IPDS), and Token-Ring Network 3270 Gateway.

Terminal Devices

Within the 3270 network, there are two major types of end user terminal devices: display terminals and printers. So, what about personal computers?

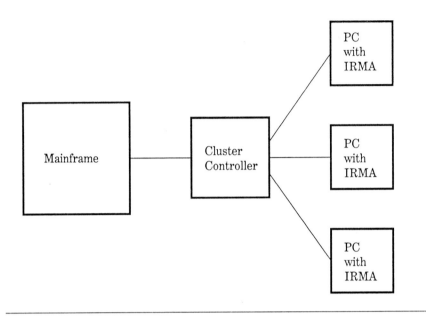

Figure 22-2

Cluster controller connection to mainframe

Remember that PCs must *emulate* a terminal device in order to communicate, essentially fooling the mainframe into believing that it is communicating with a terminal device. Before getting into terminal emulation, let's examine 3270 terminal or display devices.

The many types of display terminals used in a 3270 network can be categorized according to the level of processing capability, screen size (number of horizontal and vertical lines), and either monochrome or color appearance. The purpose of the display terminal is to present the mainframe data for viewing as determined by the mainframe application. The most common 3270 display terminals are dumb terminals known as CUT (control unit terminal) devices. CUT devices have no stand-alone processing capability and rely on the cluster controller to handle all communications processing between the device and the mainframe. CUT devices can access only one mainframe session, or application, at a time. The most common CUT devices are the 3278 monochrome display terminal and the 3279 color display terminal. Other CUT devices include the 3178, 3179,

3180, 3191, 3192, and 3279 S3G for Programmed Symbols (PS) graphics applications.

DFT (distributed function terminal) devices are intelligent terminals that possess limited processing capabilities. They do not have to rely on the cluster controller for processing, but only for communications interface to the mainframe. DFT devices provide support for both PS and APA (All Points Addressable) graphics, and can use multiple interactive screens (MIS). MIS enable the DFT device to access up to five mainframe applications at the same time. The cluster controller must be appropriately configured for multiple sessions, and not all cluster controllers are capable of DFT mode functionality. Common DFT devices include the IBM 3179G (for PS or APA graphics), 3192G, 3193, and 3290. The implementation of DFT has narrowed the gap between the limited CUT terminal and the enhanced processing capabilities of the personal computer. Even so, DFT devices offer far less functionality than the desktop personal computer.

IBM also offers PCs that are specifically designed for use in the 3270 network; that is, they are designed to function as a PC, as well as to communicate with the rest of the network. These include the IBM 3270 PC, 3270 PC/G, 3270 PC/GX, 3270 PC AT/G, and 3270 PC AT/GX. None have met with much enthusiasm.

As mentioned, all these display devices connect to the mainframe through the cluster controller, which serves as the interface. The devices connect to the cluster controller through a cable, typically coaxial cable. *Coaxial cable* (or *coax*) is a high-speed, high-capacity cable for data transmission that is highly immune to electrical interference and signal distortion. It consists of a central wire that carries the data signal, surrounded by insulating material, a layer of copper wire or mesh, and a protective outer coating. The coax cable plugs directly into the terminal on one end and into the cluster controller port on the other end. The common type of coaxial cable is RG62-A/U. Standard recommended cable length from terminal to controller is 1500 meters (approximately 5000 feet) or less. Longer cable connections often result in noise and interference in the line.

Although coax cable has been the cable of choice for computer network connections, *twisted pair cable* has become popular in recent years. Twisted pair cable has traditionally been used for voice transmission only and is the primary carrier in telephone networks. It consists of copper wires twisted together to make a cable, which is covered with insulating layers of material. Twisting reduces interference between pairs of wire when multiple pairs are bundled together. The most common and recommended twisted pair cable matches the Type 3 cable specification by IBM (see Figure 22-3).

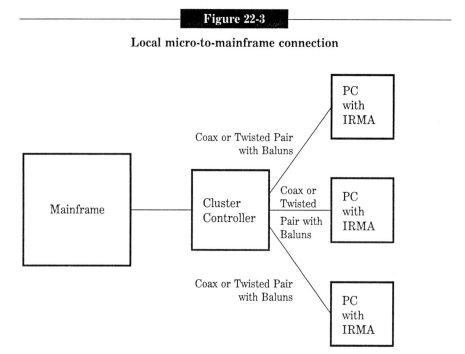

Figure 22-3

Local micro-to-mainframe connection

Twisted pair cable cannot be directly attached to 3270 terminal devices or most cluster controllers without the use of a cable adapter, called a *balun.* For example, twisted pair cable can be used for the distance between the terminal and the controller, but there must be a coax connection into both the terminal and the controller. A balun is used at both ends of the twisted pair to match the signal impedance between it and the coax cable. The use of twisted pair cable for data communications has increased because twisted pair is reliable, less expensive than coax, and readily available in buildings wired for telephones and voice communications. Unless twisted pair is carefully installed according to the manufacturer's specifications, however, problems with interference in data transmission may occur.

3270 Terminal Emulation

Now you know all about the 3270 network and the terminal devices that can communicate with the mainframe, because the mainframe knows how to communicate with and understand them. Suppose, however, that you have a personal computer, such as an IBM PC, Compaq, or other compatible computer, and you need to access mainframe data for a report that you are preparing.

You already know that your personal computer needs to *emulate the terminal device*, making the mainframe believe it is talking to a terminal device, in order for your communication to occur. The most common means of this communication is through hardware and software that is added to the personal computer to provide 3270 terminal emulation capability. (An example of 3270 terminal emulation hardware is the IRMA board mentioned earlier in this chapter, manufactured by DCA.)

The 3270 emulation board fits into an expansion slot in your personal computer and attaches directly to the controller with either coax or twisted pair cabling, in the same manner as terminal devices. Several vendors now offer terminal emulation boards with an RJ11 jack for the direct connection of twisted pair cabling, eliminating the need for a balun. The emulation hardware is brought to life by terminal emulation software that is loaded into your PC's memory. This gives the PC the same functionality as a 3270 terminal device (specifically, a 3278 or 3279 terminal), without sacrificing the PC's independent processing capability.

Terminal emulation software is available for either CUT mode emulation or DFT mode emulation. Most emulation software products also provide file transfer capability, allowing you to not only access and view mainframe data on your PC but also transfer data back and forth between the mainframe and PC. In addition, most of this software supports keyboard remapping, to allow a standard PC keyboard to behave like a 3270 terminal keyboard; printer emulation, so that the PC printer can print data from the mainframe; and support for a variety of PC graphics adapters and compatible display monitors. All 3270 terminal emulation software is typically either IBM-compatible or IRMA-compatible, meaning that it was designed to run on IBM and/or DCA emulation hardware. Most vendors offer emulation software products unbundled from the hardware, so that you can select the hardware and software solution that best suits the needs of your environment.

Let's look at one example of micro-to-mainframe communication through terminal emulation. It's time for Company XYZ to create a new budget for the new fiscal year. Each department, using personal computers emulating terminal devices, inputs their budget information into a central mainframe database. Here it is stored until all departments have completed their budgets. At this point, Corporate Accounting downloads the data from the mainframe to a personal computer using the file transfer capability of the terminal emulation software. The data is now entered into the personal computer's spreadsheet application program. Here the data is combined, the corporate budget allocations are determined, and the final report, complete with charts and graphs, is created for the president. In many terminal emulation applications like this one, the mainframe holds collected data for use by personal computers performing terminal emulation, which have available more applications to manipulate data at a much lower cost than with mainframe applications. Clearly, the micro-to-mainframe connection provides the best of both worlds: a centralized location for data storage and powerful PC applications to enhance the data.

Now that you know how the local micro-to-mainframe connection works, let's move on to the remote connection.

The Remote Micro-to-Mainframe Connection

In the remote micro-to-mainframe connection, the personal computer is geographically remote from the mainframe. For example, Company XYZ's headquarters and mainframe are located in Atlanta, Georgia, but there are branch offices in Birmingham, Alabama and Raleigh, North Carolina. The PCs in these branch offices need access to the mainframe in Atlanta on a regular basis to enter orders, to check inventory, pricing, and shipping schedules, as well as to upload monthly sales figures into the mainframe database.

Remote Connection Components

In the remote environment, several new components are added to the local, channel-attached network environment, to allow the remote devices to interface with the mainframe. Specifically, a *front end processor (FEP), synchronous modems, communications lines,* and a remote cluster controller are now a part of the network.

In the remote location, the personal computers equipped for terminal emulation are connected to a remote cluster controller by either coax or twisted pair cabling, as in the local system. This time, however, the remote cluster controller must reach across the miles to the mainframe. This connection is accomplished across communications lines—either standard dial-up telephone lines or dedicated transmission lines—using synchronous modems. The synchronous modems typically found in the micro-to-mainframe environment are 4800 or 9600 baud modems, either half or full duplex. The modem at the remote cluster controller communicates with a modem at the mainframe end of the connection. The mainframe modem is attached to a front end processor (FEP), which is channel-attached to the mainframe. See Figure 22-4.

The FEP manages the data transfer and transmission between the mainframe and the remote cluster controller and its attached personal computers. With this connection in place, the personal computers at the remote location can communicate with the mainframe, performing terminal emulation as before. This communication requires an appropriate communications protocol to be in place.

Communications Protocols

Since the data in the remote micro-to-mainframe connection is traveling across communication lines that are external to the 3270 network environment, a set of rules for managing the data transmission is needed. These rules, known as *communications protocols,* ensure that errors do not occur in the transmission of data blocks across the communications link.

Figure 22-4

Remote micro-to-mainframe connection

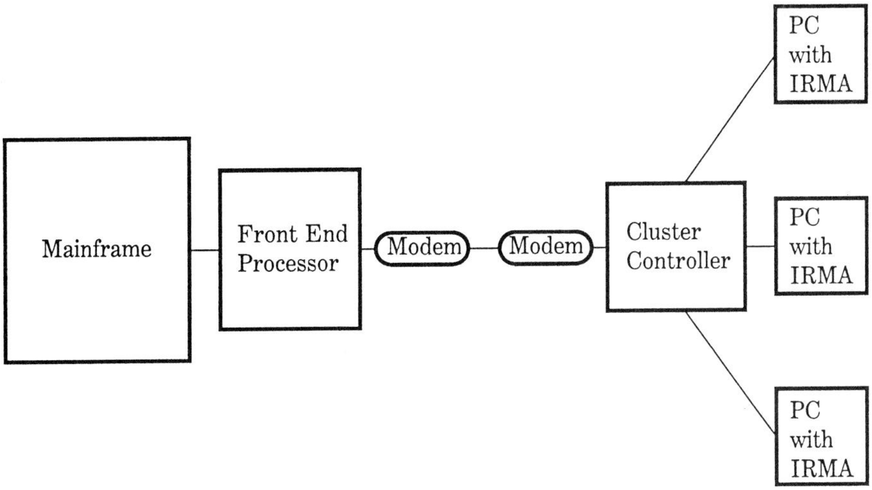

Within the IBM 3270 network, two primary communications protocols exist: *Binary Synchronous Communications (BSC or BISYNC)* and the newer *Synchronous Data Link Control (SDLC)*. BSC was the first protocol used by IBM to allow terminal devices to communicate with the mainframe. The BSC protocol is slower than SDLC, allows for only half-duplex transmission, and requires acknowledgment after each block of data is sent. Although many consider BSC to be obsolete, almost 40 percent of communications networks are still using this protocol.

Most new installations of terminal products within the IBM network environment are using IBM's System Network Architecture (SNA). SNA is simply a layered physical and logical architecture, or design, that defines how components of the network connect and communicate with one another. SNA provides the network manager with greater flexibility in hardware and software utilization, with well-established guidelines that make system integration more efficient and effective. SDLC is the protocol within the SNA environment; it defines the data link between the physical devices of the network, such as the terminals, controller, and FEP. SDLC is more efficient than BSC because it accommodates either full- or half-duplex transmission, and allows up to seven blocks of data to be sent before requiring acknowledgment.

Another communications protocol, used extensively in Europe and becoming more common in the U.S. and Canada, is X25. X25 uses a *packet-switching* transmission, where data is assembled into "packets" and sent like individual "railroad cars" across the communications lines. X25 is typically used for short messages sent over great distances. Personal computers equipped for X25 communication can easily be tied into this type of network with excellent efficiency.

Once the type of communications protocol used by your network has been established, and once the FEP, modems, and communications lines are ready, you can proceed with your micro-to-mainframe connection. Suppose, however, that you have the only personal computer in a small office, remote from the mainframe but needing access to the mainframe. It would not be practical to install a cluster controller in your location for just one connection. But, you are in luck. There are terminal emulation products available that emulate not only the terminal device but also the cluster controller. With this emulator, the FEP believes it is communicating with the cluster controller, when it is really only talking to your PC.

There are many available products for local coax micro-to-mainframe connection, as well as for remote connection. A list of these products and vendors is included at the end of this chapter.

CONCLUSION

The future of micro-to-mainframe connectivity is bright. Both microcomputers and mainframes are vital to today's communications needs. When coupled with any of the micro-to-mainframe products available, the personal computer becomes the most efficient and effective intelligent workstation yet devised. It lets the user process data at the desktop, as well as share the resources of the mainframe without blinking an eye. As new features are implemented, the personal computer will become an even more valuable component of the network. For example, IBM's Advanced Program-to-Program Communication (APPC) will allow users to communicate directly with each other, even if their personal computers are connected to different mainframes. And APPC, also known as LU 6.2, can utilize the existing 3270 emulation hardware platform as the basis for this communication, if desired.

Although not discussed in this chapter, Local Area Networks (LANs) are becoming increasingly important in network communications. LANs and LAN-to-Mainframe connections will also play a significant role in the future, although LAN connections are not expected to exceed the micro-to-mainframe connections described in this chapter until well into the 1990s. Many 3270 micro-to-mainframe vendors recognize LANs as the next logical step and are offering LAN products as well.

This brief description of the micro-to-mainframe connection may have produced more questions than it actually answered for you. Hopefully, however, we have given you a foundation from which you can intelligently explore this interesting environment.

Vendor and Product Listing

Vendor	**Product**
AST Research, Inc. 2121 Alton Avenue Irvine, California 92714 (714) 863-1333	3270/CoaxII - CUT 3270/CoaxIIA - CUT 3270/CoaxII - DFT
Attachmate Corporation 13231 SE 36th Street Bellevue, Washington 98006 (206) 644-4010	Advanced 3270 Coax Adapter EXTRA! Connectivity Software

Digital Communications Associates, Inc. (DCA) 1000 Alderman Drive Alpharetta, Georgia 30201 (404) 740-0300	IRMA 3 Convertible Hardware E78 Plus/E78 Lite Software IRMAX DFT Software DCA 3270 APA Graphics Software IRMA 3279 Graphics Software
IBM	3270 Connection Hardware Personal Communications/ 3270 Software 3270 Workstation Program Software Entry Level Program
Novell, Inc. Communications Products Division 1157 San Antonio Road Mountain View, California 94043	Novell Coax Adapter Hardware PCOX/One Software Netware 3270 MultiWorkstation

PART THREE

A Technical View

CHAPTER TWENTY-THREE

How a Modem Works

Modems are still a mystery to many of the 18 million people who own them. Most of us do realize that modems are the only viable means of communication available today for sending and receiving computer information. This chapter is about the design and operation of modems.

Modems now offer many standard features that were once considered "value added," as well as options such as auto-dial, auto-answer, self-diagnostic capabilities, programmable ROM, and advanced command sets.

Many modem owners choose a modem based on a salesperson's recommendation. Ask your average computer salesperson what a modem is, and you'll hear, "Why, it's a modulator/demodulator. Lets you hook up your computer to somebody else's computer." And that's your answer. We hope to do better in this chapter.

MODEM ADVANCES

Modem technology has advanced tremendously since 1975, when 300bps modems were considered the maximum practical "standard speed" for modems. Built-in limits to copper wire circuits and telephone switching equipment made faster modems practical only for corporate, capital-intensive leased-line networks, or so many thought.

Things have changed since then. We've seen the top speed of affordable modems rise from 300bps to around 19200bps, a factor of 64. These newer modems run faster and more reliably, pack more features, use less power in less space, and cost less. It's the familiar computer pattern of moving toward more power in less space for less money.

Figure 23-1 shows both the *external* and the *internal* types of modem. External modems sit on your desk or underneath your monitor, while

Figure 23-1

Modems come in many configurations. Lower-right is an "internal" modem; others are "external"

internal ones plug into an expansion slot inside the computer case. There are also *acoustic* modems, the oldest modem technology of all.

The next few paragraphs describe the basics of how modems work.

MODEM BASICS

At its simplest, all any modem needs to do is provide a translation service from computer signal to telephone signal and back. Computers "think" in digital, binary form, but copper telephone wires carry signals that correspond roughly to the human voice in loudness, tone, and range. The difference in signal form is shown in Figure 23-2. It's little wonder the two need a translator to communicate.

Figure 23-2

Digital versus analog signals

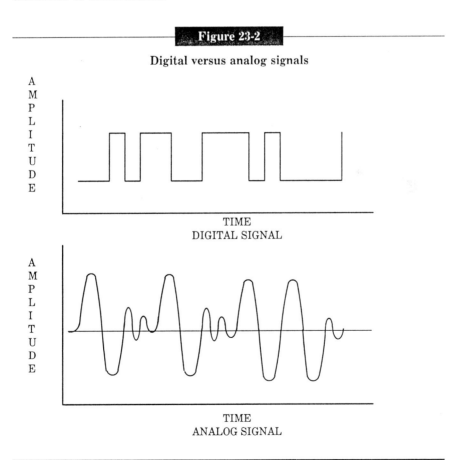

The modem provides this necessary translation. When a computer sends out its data, the modem turns the computer's ON/OFF electrical signals (top part of Figure 23-2) into a telephone's varying or *modulated* audible signal (bottom part of the figure). In other words, the modem modulates the signal—which accounts for the *modulate* part of a modem's name.

The newly *modulated* signal sounds like a whistle or, at higher speeds, like "fuzzy" noise to the human ear. It would make no sense whatever to a computer's logic circuits, but it travels just fine on copper wire. When it arrives at the other end of the phone connection, another modem must turn it back into a digital, ON/OFF (or *dem*odulated) signal. Otherwise the receiving computer won't be able to make sense of it. Hence the rest of the name: *modulate/dem*odulate, or *modem.*

To make this simple idea work, all modems share certain components, like a transmitter and receiver. On a telephone, the transmitter is the mouthpiece and the receiver is the earpiece. Why not just use those? The only other component really needed is something to "talk" and "listen" to the phone while sending and receiving data . . . an electronic translator that can talk over the phone.

Acoustic Modems

Early modems were just about that simple. You placed a normal telephone receiver into a pair of noise-reducing, cushioned cups. These modems, still in use, are called *acoustic couplers* or *acoustic modems,* because they have no direct electrical connection. Instead, they send an audible signal directly into a small speaker, which "speaks" into the telephone mouthpiece. An acoustic modem is shown in Figure 23-3.

Acoustic coupling is not very efficient. In an office environment, the shortcomings quickly become obvious. If someone puts down a coffee cup too hard or drops a spoon during a transmission, it introduces random blips and bleeps into the signal. These get translated at the other end into "garbage" or nonsense characters. At a pay phone, passing traffic can have similar effects.

Direct-Connect Modems

A better solution is to connect the modem directly—electrically, that is, instead of acoustically—into the phone circuit. This eliminates noise, inter-

Figure 23-3

Acoustically coupled modem

ference, and speaker-to-speaker signal loss. It also opens the door to various speed and reliability enhancements.

When direct-connect modems were first used over normal, non-leased telephone lines, the manufacturers needed various official blessings from Ma Bell. The resulting transmissions enjoyed such a dramatic improvement over acoustic coupling that their success was never in doubt. Nowadays acoustic modems are still used, but on PCs they are mostly a traveler's tool. (Teletype Devices or TTDs employed by hearing-impaired users still have them.) For PCs, acoustic modems are handy on pay phones or hotel phones, where you can't just plug in a modem the way you would at home or at the office. If you're the tiniest bit technically inclined, you can get better results with an adapter made of alligator clips, a modular plug, and a short length of phone cord. This adapter involves only two wires and is not complicated to use.) Remember, though, that in most states it is still illegal to connect a modem to a pay phone.

Increased Power, Increased Complexity

The once simple, direct-connect modem is no longer uncomplicated. The technology simply invites too many enhancements. It is normal with PCs for power and flexibility to be directly related to complexity, and modems have been no exception. As they grow in power and complexity, modems get more confusing to use. Some recent high-end products leave the impression that the prize goes to the modem that responds to the most commands.

Even people familiar with modem technology can have trouble with the monthly crop of new bells and whistles.

Some software authors—notably John Friel of Qmodem—smooth the way by providing automatic setup routines for many different modem brands. Friel's approach may become the standard. Meanwhile, users who understand their modems have an easier time, especially when they need to configure a modem for a specific type of task.

Reaching the Speed Limit?

The key to understanding modem communication limits is to remember that the circuit you're using was designed to carry human speech. All the data you send must be stuffed into the same signal space or *bandwidth* as is available on normal voice-grade communication lines.

The maximum theoretical speed that a modem can get on a typical voice-grade line is about 30,000bps. Real-world limits always fall short of theoretical values, however; clearly we cannot expect to see practical modems that greatly exceed the speeds of today's fastest models—at least not using today's voice-grade circuits. ISDN (see Chapter 25) and other innovations may greatly change the face of everyday telecommunications, of course. With ISDN, modems may even be largely replaced by direct digital communication over fiber-optic cables. Communications limits would then depend more upon your PC's processor speed than upon how much data can be crammed onto a voice-grade copper circuit.

For now, we depend upon the modems, and it is likely that they—like the acoustic coupler—will remain useful in PC telecommunications even after something newer comes along. The remainder of this chapter deals with modems, getting more technical as it goes. Choose your own stopping point.

Connecting Your Modem to a Phone Line

Telephone lines are wires, and all wires have resistance. Wires allow electrons to flow from one point to another. The resistance in these wires helps to impede the electron flow.

Impedance is an inherent physical property of wire. The amount of impedance depends on the width of the wire in respect to how much current is flowing, and the length of the wire. At the end of the wires, at the phone company office, are electrical circuits and switches — all designed to permit transmission over these phone lines, but all with limitations on their capabilities.

You can hook up to a phone line in two ways: acoustically or directly. Acoustic modems were explained earlier (see Figure 23-3). Many early portable computers included an acoustic modem, and it is a simple matter to insert the handset into the coupling. Try not to bump or jar an acoustic modem while it's transmitting; this can garble the data or even interrupt the session.

Direct-connect modems connect to telephone lines by means of the familiar RJ11 modular telephone jack (see Figures 23-4 and 23-5). They are less sensitive to noise, and are easy to connect. Back in the old days, before modular phone jacks, you had to cut and splice wires if you wanted a direct electrical connection between your modem and the phone line. This wasn't too popular with the family, as it tended to render the telephone useless.

Most modems are direct-connect (see Figure 23-6). They've become so

Figure 23-4

RJ11 modular telephone plugs

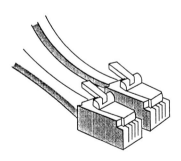

Figure 23-5

An RJ11 telephone jack

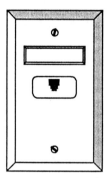

Figure 23-6

A direct-connect internal modem

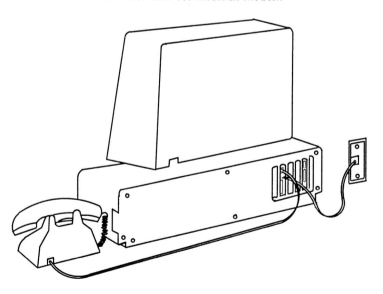

popular that many hotels catering to business travelers now provide an RJ11 jack in their rooms. Electronics stores sell special one-line adapter jacks that allow more complex PBX and key systems to incorporate an RJ11 jack.

Connecting Your Modem to a PC

After successfully connecting your modem to the telephone system, the next step is to make the connection between the modem and your personal computer (see Figures 23-6 and 23-7). Free-standing (external) modems are connected by either a DB-25 or DB-9 cable to the computer's RS-232 serial communications port. Board (internal) modems are connected by plugging a card into one of the computer's expansion slots. Chapter 2 gives more details on installing modems into PCs.

WHEN MODEMS TALK

When two modems communicate, they exchange continuous audible tones called *carrier signals.* Each carrier signal (or carrier) has a frequency

Figure 23-7

The connections at the back of an external modem

established by the modem manufacturer or by a published standard. If one modem detects the absence of a carrier signal for more than a few milliseconds, the connection is broken (the modem hangs up). All this is like a conversation between two people; if Fred doesn't hear anything on the other end of the line—no background noise, no music, no breathing—he hangs up. Fred's modem relays a "carrier lost" message to the user.

Carrier signals are generated as *sine waves*, as illustrated in Figure 23-8. Sine waves start out at a zero voltage level and go to a positive value, then through zero to an equal negative value, and back to zero. The more cycles in a given unit of time, the higher the *frequency* of the signal.

Understanding Digital and Analog Signals

Just as you always suspected, computer book writers cannot produce a book without a discussion about binary numbers. Here it is:

The binary numbering system of 1s and 0s allows each number, letter, and symbol to be expressed in a special sequence of these two digits. Let's take a look at how your computer does its ABCs:

A = 01000001
B = 01000010
C = 01000011

Figure 23-8

A sine wave

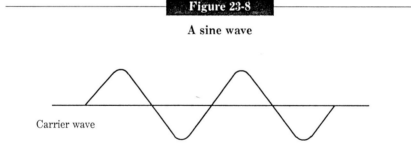

Carrier wave

Each group of eight *bits* (1s and 0s) represents one *byte* or character.

The transfer of information inside a computer is usually handled by a *parallel bus*. If one light bulb circuit can provide two states of information, then you can think of a parallel bus as eight light bulbs operating side by side giving us eight channels of data simultaneously. Eight light bulbs flashing 1s and 0s can thus convey coded information to any onlooker. One channel, or one ON/OFF circuit, gives us one bit of data at a time—a 0 (zero) bit or a 1 (one) bit. Put eight successive bits of data together, and you get a byte.

A byte consists of a predetermined number of bits. Our byte will be equal to eight bits. Thus our eight circuits provide us with one byte of information. For example, 00101010 is eight bits and equals one byte.

Let's return to our eight circuits. Since these circuits provide us with data, we can correctly call them *data channels*. The information on these data channels (numbered 1 through 8) is kept synchronized by a common clock that allows the eight data bits to enter and leave the channel at the same time. How and where these channels connect inside the computer is better left to a computer course.

ASCII Code

Combining eight channels of two states, gives us a total of 256 possible combinations. When you've got some spare time, just count all the different possible combinations that eight channels of 1s and 0s can provide:

00000000	00000100
00000001	00000101
00000010	00000110
00000011	00000111...up to 11111111

A standardized method has been created for using these 1s and 0s as information—two bytes at four bits per byte. This standard is called the American Standard Code for Information Interchange, also known as ASCII (pronounced "az-key"). The ASCII code table is included in Appendix A of this book.

Transmitting Digital Information Using Modulation

At least two states are required to represent digital information. These states are represented by alteration of the carrier signal to represent the binary digit 0 and/or the binary digit 1. Changing the carrier signal is called *modulation.*

Modulation may involve varying any of three attributes of the carrier:

- Amplitude   Magnitude or peak voltage level
- Frequency   Number of complete oscillations of the signal per unit of time
- Phase   Location at which a signal crosses the zero level, relative to the previous signal

---

READ.ME

Different Modems, Different Speeds, Different Frequencies

Modems use different forms of modulation depending on the speed involved. For instance:

- **Frequency Shift Keying (FSK)** is used for speeds below 1200bps. FSK modulation is a two-level technique that represents changes in the binary bit pattern by changes in the frequency of an audio tone. The line is assumed to be in a steady binary 1 state when idle, represented by one particular tone frequency. The modem changes to another tone frequency when the data bit value 0 is sent. See Figure 23-9. These tone changes cause a unique musical effect during transmission.

  Although higher-speed modems (see PSK, described below) do include support for FSK transmission, the lower-speed FSK frequency modulation is seldom used. Today 300bps modems are more commonly found at swap meets, flea markets, or in dusty attics. Although extremely reliable, 300bps limits transmission to about 30 characters per second. Most users can read text displayed on the screen two or three times faster than this and would grow impatient waiting for a 300bps data stream.

READ.ME

Different Modems, Different Speeds, Different Frequencies (*continued*)

- **Phase shift keying (PSK)**   changes the phase of a signal, that is, its timing relationship to a fixed reference, to represent changes in the bit pattern. A reference oscillator is used to measure the phase shift of the incoming signal to determine 0 or 1 bit being transmitted. See Figure 23-10.

- **Differential phase shift keying (DPSK)**   is used in 1200 and 2400bps PC modems and compares the phase angle of the incoming signal to the previously received signal. One change in phase is interpreted as a binary 0 if the preceding phase has been interpreted as binary 1, and so forth. This method does not require a separate reference wave, and needs less electronic circuitry. See Figure 23-11.

- **Amplitude modulation (AM)**   is the simplest modulation technique. Waves of high amplitude are denoted binary 1 and waves of low amplitude are denoted binary 0. AM is highly susceptible to line interference and in practice, is not used by itself.

- **Quadrature amplitude modulation (QAM)**   is the prevailing standard at 9600 bps and higher, and is a combination of PSK and AM. QAM changes both the amplitude (height) and the phase of the wave, allowing twice as much information to be encoded on one wave as does phase shift keying. QAM is essentially a four-phase technique that uses two signals at the same frequency, but the signals are 90 degrees out of phase with each other. For each signal, four possible levels of amplitude can be applied (A1, A2, A3, and A4). By combining two signals that are 90 degrees out of phase, 16 different conditions can be generated, each representing four bits of information. It is possible to represent 32 conditions with the two signal levels. QAM encodes more information on one wave, achieving greater throughput and resulting in faster data communications.

  PC users can upgrade to higher-speed modems. Higher transmission speeds reduce phone call length and expense, increase computer response time, and reduce charges for on-line services.

Frequency shift key (FSK) modulation

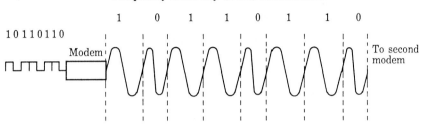

Figure 23-10

Phase shift keying (PSK) modulation

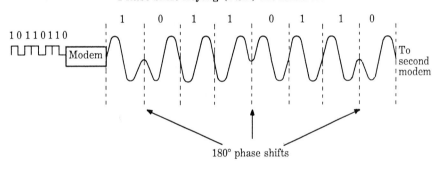

Figure 23-11

Differential phase shift keying (DPSK) modulation

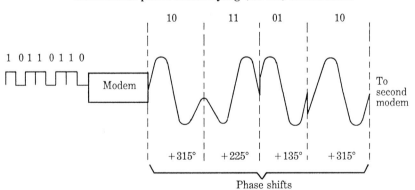

Bandwidth

Bandwidth is the information-carrying capacity of a transmission facility. Bandwidth defines a range of frequencies, measured in Hertz (cycles per second), that it can accommodate without significant signal degradation. The wider the modem's range of frequencies, the greater the capacity to carry data. Most modems use a 300-3000 Hz frequency range in the middle of the bandwidth of a telephone connection.

Think of bandwidth as fidelity. Over the radio, the very high notes and the very low, bass notes are not reproduced very well. In telecommunications, the average telephone line is not very stable in the high or low frequencies. The modem is limited to the center of the bandwidth, which is the clearest and most able to accurately reproduce the modulation.

To move into the higher and lower ranges of the bandwidth, modems often use sophisticated, multiple-bit encoding algorithms to squeeze as much data as possible in both directions. Multiple-bit encoding, unfortunately, also increases data loss during line hits (like static on the line, or a brief voice bleed-through). The goal of effective modem design is to minimize data loss while sending greater amounts of data through a communications link.

Transmission Characteristics: Bps and Baud

The premier buzzword in telecommunications is the odd combination of two small words—*data rate*. Data rate, usually denoted in bits per second, is the correct term for what we usually refer to as "speed." Modems operate either at a fixed transmission speed, or at the speed of the sending device (although that's restricted to a specified range). Some modems are equipped to operate at any of several different speeds. The data rate is controlled by the modem's switch settings, or by changes within the software. The data rate is commonly, but mistakenly in some instances, referred to as the baud rate.

"Baud" and "data rate" do not mean the same thing, yet they are often used synonymously. So what's the difference? The term "bps" expresses the data signaling rate; baud is a measurement of modulation rate. A voice line can accommodate 2400 signal changes per second (baud). Higher-speed modems encode two or more data bits in each signal change. The bps rate corresponds to the number of data bits per signal, multiplied by the baud.

—————————   ██ **READ.ME** ██   —————————

Bps versus Baud

baud = signal changes per second
bps = (data bits/group) × baud

One-Bit Groups	Two-Bit Groups
0	00 10
1	01 11

For two-bit groups, four possible bit patterns (00, 01, 10, 11) exist. In phase shift modulation, for example, a shift of 90 degrees could be represented by 01, 180 degrees could represent 10, 270 degrees as 11, and no shift as 00. By transmitting four data bits into each signal, a modem can support 9600bps. Because medium- and high-speed modems all group data bits for signaling, a modem's bit rate is now rarely equivalent to its baud.

Decibels

One of the most commonly used terms in the communications industry is the *decibel* (DB). The decibel is a unit for measuring the relative loudness of sound, or for expressing the ratio of two amounts of electric or acousticsignal power. Decibels may be a distinct unit of measure; however, they can be converted to voltage potential (volts and millivolts). Transmission and receiving of data occurs at a certain DB level. Interfering noise is measured in DBs and so is frequency response.

READ.ME

The DB Line Load Table

You cannot find the following table in a library or bookstore. These levels represent DBs of a balanced telephone line load. This chart shows DB-to-voltage conversion for power and impedance of the voice-grade line. With this chart, you can measure the actual voltage level of received or transmitted signals, and thus know what DB level you are dealing with. (In the chart headings, "P-P" means "peak-to-peak.")

P-P Voltage	DB Level	P-P Voltage	DB Level	P-P Voltage	DB Level
2.2 v	0	120 mv	−17	16 mv	−34
2.0 v	−1	100 mv	−18	14 mv	−35
1.8 v	−2	90 mv	−19	13 mv	−36
1.6 v	−3	80 mv	−20	11 mv	−37
1.4 v	−4	70 mv	−21	10 mv	−38
1.2 v	−5	60 mv	−22	9 mv	−39
1.1v	−6	55 mv	−23	8 mv	−40
1.00 v	−7	50 mv	−24	4.5 mv	−45
900 mv	−8	45 mv	−25	2.5 mv	−50
800 mv	−9	40 mv	−26		
700 mv	−10	35 mv	−27		
640 mv	−11	30 mv	−28		
570 mv	−12	28 mv	−29		
500 mv	−13	25 mv	−30		
450 mv	−14	22 mv	−31		
400 mv	−15	20 mv	−32		
350 mv	−16	18 mv	−33		

If you measure with an oscilloscope the peak-to-peak voltage at the phone company D mark, and see a signal that is 1 volt from peak-to-peak, you can say your signal strength is −7 DB. On the other hand, if you use a VF Monitor that registers DBs and it registers −7 DB, you know that you have present a 1-volt peak-to-peak signal.

Decibels were originally designed to help determine the rate of change of sound. In data communications, that use is not so consistent. The DB is often used as a reference point, or a voltage level, actually. However, since the DB is the language of the phone company, we are forced to accommodate them. For the phone company, a 2.2-volt, peak-to-peak signal is the zero reference point for our application. It represents the maximum permissible signal level that can or should be put on a phone line. From this point, all voltage levels get smaller. However, since zero is as high as we can go, we represent these smaller voltages in negative DB numbers or minus DB.

Types of Telephone Lines

There are three types of telephone lines: voice grade, conditional voice grade, and leased. The voice-grade line is commonly used for ordinary voice communications. Most modems work reasonably well with this kind of line. Conditional voice-grade lines (switched network lines), which cost more, offer reduced noise levels and provide more efficient data transfer. Leased lines, which are the most costly and complex, offer high-speed, full duplex data transfer.

Line loss can be said to include the impedance of "in-house wiring," added to the distance of the telephone pole outside a house to the nearest phone company office. *Fixed loss loop* (FLL) is a preset factor that the telephone company creates by modifying the existing line loss and adding or subtracting impedance. This is to ensure that your modem's transmit carrier arrives at the phone company office at an acceptable level.

Each phone company office may vary in their acceptable standards. By using a predetermined modem transmit level, however, any phone company may adjust the FLL to suit its own needs. Normally the FLL is set so that if your modem transmits at −9 DB, it will reach the phone company office at the correct level. If your modem transmits at a higher level (say −8 DB), you risk interference of other signals by jamming the phone company with a signal that is too strong. If you transmit at a lower level (−13 DB or −15 DB) there is a risk that the signal will be too weak to be received. Most modems in the PC community are designed to transmit at −9 DB. There are few problems with that level.

The alternative to FLL is the *programmable jack*. The phone company created this phone jack with a resistor that allows your modem to determine a balance of impedance with the phone line. The modem can thus adjust its transmit level as the phone line impedance changes, ensuring a more accurate transmit voltage.

Electrical properties are not stable. The impedance of lines can vary by their length (distance), by their gauge (width of wire), by the temperature, and other outside influences—flocks of birds on the line, for example. If you transmit in the −9 DB range, then what level should you expect to receive as an incoming signal? The phone company is required by law to ensure no greater than a 16 DB loss from transmitter to receiver. Thus, if you transmit at −9 DB you expect the other modem to receive the signal at −25 DB.

Dedicated Lines

When your switched carrier phone line connects long-distance, the call is placed on a trunk line or multiplexer line for lengthy travel. *Dedicated lines* are also used, mostly by industry. They are not accessible by outsiders and are leased by phone companies and common carriers. No dialing is required; the line is always connected to the modems, and the modems are always connected to each other. Both two-wire and four-wire lines are available. A four-wire line is composed of two phone lines. One is exclusively by the transmitter and the other by the receiver.

Dedicated Lines may be set up in two ways:

- **Point-to-Point**   A line running from point A to point B

- **MultiDrop**   A four-wire line connected from a master modem to two or more remote modems (drops), possibly at different locations

A dedicated line always uses the the same circuitry. If the line goes bad, it must be repaired. The repair time can be short, but more commonly is several hours or days. On a dial-up line, if there is a problem you hang up and call again. With a dial-up line, different lines are available.

Satellites

When you call locally, your call goes through the local phone company switch to its destination. When you dial a non-local call that's not going too far (usually in the same telephone operating area), the call goes through microwave or trunk to its destination. When you call a very long distance (coast to coast) or overseas, the call may be routed by satellite. Satellites are poor data communications facilities. There are massive delays in transmission, horrible echoes, and something called the Doppler effect. The Doppler effect is simply a reference to the fact that the satellite is in motion; during prolonged transmissions, this motion can cause the carrier to become distorted.

Satellite communications are discussed in more detail in Chapter 26.

Noise

The biggest threat to data circuits is noise. There are a number of different types of noise.

Impulse Noise   Sporadic, low-frequency voltage spikes typically caused by older phone company equipment. There are still many parts of the country with non-state-of-the-art phone equipment. A VF line monitor or telephone handset can pick up impulse noise. It sounds like a pop, or a crackle.

Background Noise   Present in every circuit, but usually filtered to such a degree that it is rendered harmless. Background noise becomes harmful when its signal strength increases to a point where it can compete with your carrier. It usually has the same sound you hear when you have your radio or TV tuned between stations. When you amplify your data signal, background noise is also amplified. If the data signal is weak and the phone company tries to compensate with a simple increase of the circuit, noise levels will increase as well.

Interference   Outright interference is a real problem. It comes from many sources sneaking in at the phone company office, along the telephone line route, or from the wiring in your house. Military CW, radio stations, foreign exchange lines, and engine noise may interfere with data communications. Ideally, your computer equipment should be on its own circuit breaker— something as simple as an air conditioner turning on and off can do incredible things to your data. Your computer and modem should also share a common ground.

Warning: Do not use a "Ground Eliminator Adapter"! This can be hazardous to the health of your hardware. Interference must be tracked down and eliminated. If the source is the phone company, it is their problem to correct. Otherwise it is your problem.

With a long-distance call, the phone company will sometimes insert an echo suppressor designed to control the amount of echo on the line. This has the effect of shutting down each side of the line in turn to match the reversals in conversation.

The echo suppressor, depending on its type, can have a 100-millisecond delay in leaving the circuit. Carrier generated during that time may be destroyed. Some commercial modems have what is called a "dither tone." The purpose of the dither tone is to deactivate the echo suppressor by keeping both sides of the line in constant use with a low-frequency continuous wave outside the carrier bandwidth. Other modems send a signal tone for a couple of seconds at the start of each call to disable the echo.

Every modem or similar device that is designed to connect to a phone line must conform to FCC standards. One of those standards is the amount of load placed on the line by the device. Most modems and related devices use a *transformer* to not only provide for a balanced load, but also to prevent potentially damaging voltages from passing back and forth. These transformers are designed to provide a 600 OHM balanced load at the line. A 600 OHM load will

- Help minimize echoes

- Provide for proper gain of the received signal

- Insure a proper transmit level

Improper impedance will adversely affect data communications. You cannot control impedance in most cases. More advanced modems and telephone equipment do provide such options; remember that commercial modems are far superior to modems designed for the home PC.

As mentioned earlier, it is illegal to connect an unregistered device to a phone line. Use of homemade filters, equalizers, or amplifiers is subject to severe penalties. Should you desire to connect an unregistered device to a phone line, you must request the phone company to install DAA (Data Access Arrangement) or its equivalent. This device protects the phone line should your equipment not perform as you expect.

Voice-Grade Frequency of Telephone Lines

The phone lines allow transmission of voice-grade signals back and forth, with minimal and predetermined loss. This means the phone company has designed its circuits to allow passage of certain frequencies associated with voice transmissions, and frequencies outside this range are not included or desired. Under ideal circumstances, the *frequency response* of the phone line allows passage of signals between 300 Hz and above 3000 Hz.

How is this accomplished? Amplifiers are designed to amplify any signals between 300 and 3000 Hz, but will not amplify anything outside this range. Signals outside these Hz limits will die off as they travel over the phone line.

Of course, that's the most ideal situation; reality, however, involves *tolerance*—the fly in the ointment, or the bug in the program. Resistors, capacitors, and more have *tolerance*, and tolerances change with temperature and humidity. Two identical pieces of wire will have different resistance levels, if resistance were measured in micro-ohms. As a result, your perfect band pass filter, an amplifier designed to amplify only desired frequencies, has flaws. Some amplification will take place outside the 300 to 3000 Hz dome. The spectrum of desired frequencies is not amplified equally.

Figure 23-12 illustrates that at 2000 Hz, you get maximum output or maximum gain, but at 800 Hz your gain is less, and at 300 Hz it is even less. Although operating at 2000 Hz is the optimum, that leaves only the 2000 to 3000 Hz range within which to operate.

Let's say you connected an audio oscillator to one end of a line and transmitted an exact audio signal. At the other end of the line, you have a

Figure 23-12

Maximum frequency reponse at 2000 Hz

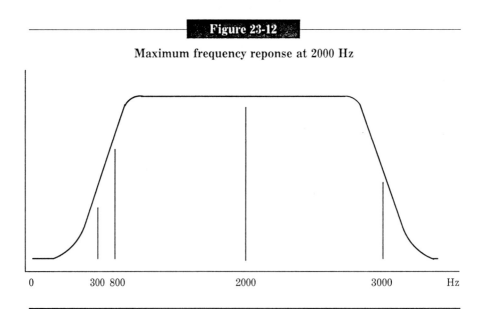

monitor that allows you to see the level of that signal as it arrives. You would see the transmitted signal, *minus* any loss of strength from traveling through wires and circuits. If the line characteristics are as shown in Figure 23-12, you would see a smaller signal arrive at 800 Hz than at 2000 Hz.

When you transmit a 1-volt signal at 2000 Hz, you expect a strong signal to arrive, near 1 volt. When you transmit at 800 Hz, however, there can be less gain or loss, and the signal will probably be below 1 volt. Signals transmitted at 300 Hz, can be well below 1 volt. For example:

Transmit Frequency	Transmit Voltage	Receive Voltage
2000 Hz	1.0	.99
800 Hz	1.0	.85
300 Hz	1.0	.50

Of course, some frequencies are special to the telephone company. For instance, the frequency of 2600 Hz has been set aside as the disconnect frequency. If you were talking on the phone and had an audio oscillator set to 2600 Hz, your call could be disconnected if the tone were picked up by the telephone.

Have you ever wondered how the cable television company is able to send so many different channels over one cable? It's simple—they use a different frequency for each channel, just like a radio uses different frequencies for different radio stations. Computers use FDM (Frequency Division Multiplexing), which spans a wide range of different frequencies (from 300 to 3000 Hz), to send multiple tones or multiple carriers at different, noninterfering frequencies.

The reason why a voice-grade line has a frequency range of 300 to 3000 Hz is because that is the approximate frequency range of our hearing capabilities (but not the full range). A voice-grade line will do just what it implies—operate at voice frequencies. The phone company designed and built phone lines that amplify and carry voice frequencies, but ignore or eliminate outside frequencies.

Frequency Response and Equalization

Frequency response refers to the gain of an amplifier at different frequencies. If it amplifies well across the required bandwidth, the amplifier is said to have a good frequency response; if it amplifies poorly, or is not flat, it has a bad frequency response. Ideally, a telephone line has a consistent response over the entire 300 to 3000 Hz range. However, response varies at different frequencies. If 400 Hz, 800 Hz, and 2000 Hz signals are transmitted at 1 volt, the received results would be something like this:

- 400 Hz received at .6 volt (loss of .4 volt)

- 800 Hz received at .8 volt (loss of .2 volt)

- 2000 Hz received at 1.0 volt (loss of 0 volts)

Since getting the phone company to improve line quality is next to impossible, an alternative is to increase the modem's transmit level at those frequencies where voltage is lost. For example:

Transmit Frequency	Transmit Voltage	Receive Voltage	Loss
400 Hz	1.4	1.0	.4
800 Hz	1.2	1.0	.2
2000 Hz	1.0	1.0	0

Thus you receive a flat frequency response by shaping the transmit signal — adding more voltage where there is loss. This function is called *pre-equalizing the line*. Equalization is accomplished by varying the level of the transmit voltage at the transmitter, or it can be accomplished via a preamplifier at the receiver (altering the levels before it gets to the receiver).

Modems equalize differently, depending on manufacturer and modulation type. However, one way equalization is accomplished is with a *training sequence*. Prior to transmitting a carrier, a modem transmits a test pattern that is something like a "sweep" of the frequency range. The receiving station has stored in ROM exactly what the test pattern looked like when it was transmitted by the originating modem. The receiver compares what it receives against the stored template of the test pattern, computes what the telephone line characteristics are, the voltage loss, and the transmit frequency. It then adjusts its transmitter to vary the transmission voltage at all the different frequencies.

Figure 23-13 shows the response of the phone line, and Figure 23-14 shows how transmit voltage levels are altered to equalize the line. If the voltage is equalized properly, you should ideally get a flat frequency response. Channel characteristics can vary widely from call to call. Serious impairment may occur, such as group delay distortion or amplitude response distortion.

You have seen how we make maximum use of the band pass. We are transmitting out of modem 1 at 1170 Hz, while simultaneously transmitting out of modem 2 at 2125 Hz. The bandwidth of each transmitter is small enough to allow both carriers to coexist on the same circuit without interfering with each other. When we use a different scheme, transmitting in only one direction at a time, we can utilize more of the available bandwidth.

It is this difference that allows us to break the barrier of 600 baud. With

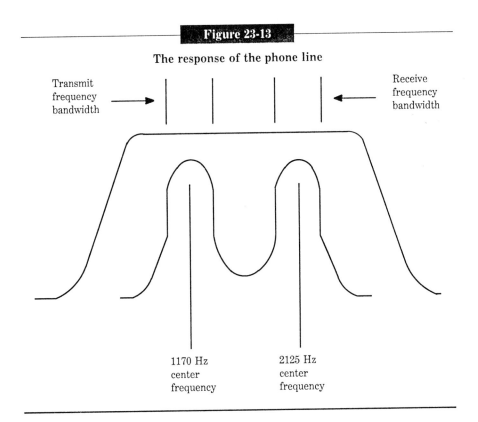

Figure 23-13

The response of the phone line

Transmit frequency bandwidth →

Receive frequency bandwidth ←

1170 Hz center frequency

2125 Hz center frequency

Figure 23-14

A flat frequency response

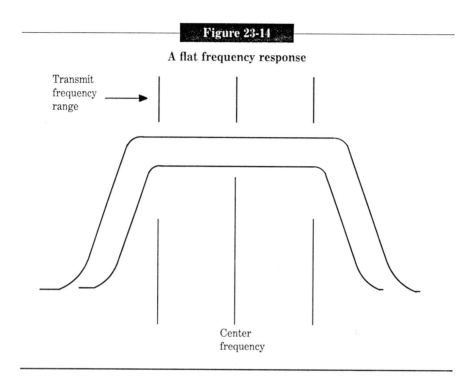

Transmit frequency range →

Center frequency

two modems transmitting simultaneously, each modem takes up half the band pass, and a gap exists between the two bandwidths. Add the two bandwidths and the gap together, and you get a much bigger bandwidth.

Echoes and Other Problems

For short-distance communication, a two-wire line goes in and out of the phone company offices without major transformations. You are probably familiar with the problem of *echo*, where irregularities inherent in transmission cause a portion of the signal energy to be reflected back toward the originating end. This is referred to as *talker's echo*—when using a phone, you can hear your own voice on the receiver but at a much lower level.

From a phone company manual comes this warning: "If the talker's echo encounters irregularities on its way back to the originating end, still another echo is produced which will propagate in the same direction as the desired signal." The hitch is that the echo will be produced on the other half of the line pair, which means your modem's receiver might see its own transmit carrier. Meanwhile, the second echo is aimed at the other modem's transmitter. Luckily, echoes are normally not a problem. Their strength is usually so low that they are not picked up by the receiver. However, if phone line irregularities become prominent enough to generate loud echoes, they will interfere with data. Loud echoes are obvious, so connecting a handset to a line and listening for them is easy.

Distortion occurs when the voltage loss (or delay) of a transmission line varies as a function of frequency. If you transmit a test signal at one end, and monitor the receive level at the other end, you will see a sharp loss when you attempt to transmit through the bad area. As an example, if at 1170 Hz you receive the test signal at 400 mv (millivolts) — or (400×10^{-3}) or (.4 volt) — then at 2125 Hz in the bad area, the receive level might be 100 to 200 mv.

Line Conditions

The telephone network is not a perfect transmission path, even for voice communication. Increased data speed demands ever more precise signaling methods. Problems such as line failure, electrical interference, and random noise may interrupt transmission. The horror stories are common, and really not too interesting.

Random noise is the decrease in signal-to-noise ratio; that is, the ratio between the signal strength, and the amplitude of noise pulses. *Amplitude distortion* is another phrase that strikes terror in the hearts and minds of telecommunications experts. Modems must be able to adjust to the properties of the communications line to prevent the signal from getting too far out of shape. Another source of circuit problems is changes in the analog signal caused by uneven propagation of low and high frequencies. This condition, called *phase jitter*, severely affects high-speed modems whose modulation techniques use phase shift to represent bit patterns.

Some telecommunications experts advise computer users to contact the local telephone company and obtain specially conditioned lines. Conditioned lines require the attachment of signal amplifiers and attenuation or delay equalizers. These lines are a vast improvement, but are still not guaranteed to offer optimum bit-error rates.

The newer model modems now offer a useful feature called fallback. Fallback is the ability to detect poor line conditions and adjust to lower transmission speeds (bps) to prevent data errors. For example, 9600bps modems often offer fallback to 7200bps or 4800bps when the line conditions are unfavorable.

THE INTERFACE

The interface between your computer and the modem (a plug-in printed circuit card) is sometimes called the "adapter" by IBM. It allows different devices to exchange data. There are two standard interfaces used in PCs: parallel and serial.

Parallel Interface

You have learned how eight data channels in parallel can transmit an 8-bit code that represents a single piece of information. Internally, computers transfer data in the parallel format using a *data bus*, as previously described.

With a parallel port, the data is presented at the interface as 8-bit channels or data lines. An additional line is also provided, called a *clock* or *strobe line.* The data is "clocked" or "strobed" out, and the receiving device then uses the clock to synchronize itself to the parallel data being sent. Most PCs are equipped with unidirectional parallel ports capable only of sending data. Since parallel ports are intended for use with the printers, this limitation is not a problem. IBM PS/2s, most laptops, and some other computers have bidirectional parallel ports. With a bidirectional port, the same eight lines are used for incoming and outgoing data.

An interesting feature of the parallel interface is its ability to pass data at fairly high rates of speed. Unlike a serial interface with predetermined data rates, a parallel interface can transfer data at the maximum rate of the device to which it is connected. Figure 23-15 shows a parallel data transmission.

Serial Interface and Asynchronous Communication

The dreaded serial interface is one of the most inefficient and cumbersome methods of communicating. Serial interface was nearly orphaned by the industry in the 1970s.

The serial interface appears at first to be less complex than the parallel interface. Data is transferred in a serialized form; that is, the eight data bits are carried over the serial channel one after the other, in a specific order.

With a parallel transfer each data bit has its own channel. To transfer data using a parallel interface requires a minimum of 11 wires, not including control signals, whereas the serial interface requires only three, also not including control signals. This limitation is one reason why parallel interfacing is not more widely used.

Let's examine the complexity of a serial interface—the oldest form of communication. In serial communication, as in transmitting morse code, one bit of information is sent at a time (see Figure 23-15). Although the serial interface comes in several assorted flavors, the PC serial interface uses the asynchronous (ASYNC) form of transmission only, where data bits are transferred over a single data channel in a consecutive series one after another. (Synchronous communication is covered in the "Digital Interface" section of this chapter.)

Asynchronous transmission requires a stable environment. If there is any irregularity of the line, and something happens to one data bit, subsequent data bits may be misread. For example, say you attempted to send

1110 0000 1110 0000

and the first digit 1 is lost. Then

1100 0001 1100 000 _

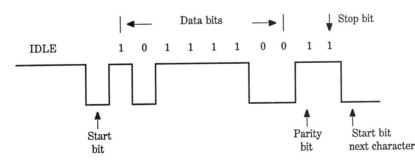

Figure 23-15

Asynchronous data byte interpretation (11 data bits)

| ← Data bits → | ↓ Stop bit |

IDLE   1 0 1 1 1 1 0 0 1 1

Start bit   Parity bit   Start bit next character

is received. All the bits shift over one position, and the integrity of the data is lost.

The Start Bit

When a serial data channel is not used (idle), it rests in the ON or the 1 state. The transmission of a character is begun by turning off the data channel. This removes it from the idle state and sends what is called a *start bit*. A start bit is the first bit preceding every data word (data transmission or transmitted character). Keep in mind that in basic serial, asynchronous communication, each character is transmitted independently. That means each character transmitted requires a start bit.

Immediately following the start bit are the serialized *data bits*. Not all systems use the full eight data bits; some use only seven or six, and others may use nine.

The Stop Bit

In the old days, when serial communication was used on teletype or other ancient devices, the mechanics of the machinery required delay times between characters. For this reason, a *stop bit* was added to the end of the character. Depending on the amount of delay needed, either one, one-and-a-half, or two stop bits were added. Now these do nothing more than mark the end of the character.

The Parity Bit

To help ensure that a character is received properly, a bit is added immediately following the data bits—this is called the *parity bit*. It is not always used. Parity, if used, is either odd or even. Parity is checked by counting up the number of 1s among the data bits. (Start and stop bits are not counted.)

If employing *even parity*, the character must have an even number of 1s between the start and stop bits. If there are an odd number of 1s among the data bits, the parity bit is made a 1 to make the number of 1s even. If the number of 1s is already even, then a 0 is added as the parity bit to keep the number of 1s even. For example, in 01101101, there are five 1s, so we add another 1 to make it even: 011011011. In 10101010, there are four 1s, so we add a zero to keep it even: 101010100.

If employing *odd parity*, the object is to have an odd number of 1s between the start and stop bits. The added parity bit will be a 1 or 0, as required, to ensure an odd number of 1s in the data. For example, in 01101100, there are four 1s, so we add another 1 to make it odd: 01101101.

When a character is received, the number of 1s is counted and compared to the parity bit, thus checking to see if any data bits changed during transmission. If the parity does not match, an error is indicated, and retransmission may occur.

In summary, to send eight data bits, eleven bits of information in all must be sent (eight data bits, one start bit, one parity bit, and one stop bit). This means that the ability to send information has been decreased by one-third.

Bit Length

The start bit that signals the beginning of the data flow is one full data bit long. "And just how long *is* a data bit?" you might ask. That depends on the transmission rate, or how many bits per second you're transmitting. If you are operating at 300bps, then you would divide 300 into 1 to calculate bit length.

Bit Length = 1/300bps

Let's calculate the bit length for 1200bps:

1/1200 = .83 millisecond (rounded off)

The receiving modem *must* be able to differentiate line noise from real data. Otherwise, the modem would see every glitch as a start bit, and wind up out of sync with the real data. Therefore, serial ports typically have a clock that operates a minimum of 16 times faster than the bps rate (the 16× clock).

The 16× clock thus helps the port determine a real start bit from noise. A circuit then remembers the bit time and generates a *spike clock*, which acts as a data sampling window. This spike clock happens in the middle of each bit time. The sample is taken, and the state of the bit (1 or 0) is determined.

You will read more about clocks throughout this chapter.

Data Blocks

In most communications programs, as you type, you are transmitting character by character. You send one start bit, the data bits, parity bit, and stop bit(s) each and every time you press a key. For applications such as file transfer, another way of transmitting is to collect your characters in a buffer, join them together and transmit them nonstop from beginning to end. A *data block,* or a *data packet,* is created when these characters are joined together. Although packets do not require fewer bits, they provide far more efficient data transfer.

The actual size of data blocks or packets of data can vary from eight to millions of bits. There are many advantages to sending data in blocks instead of one character at a time; most of these will be discussed later in this chapter. When data is sent in packets, parity is usually dispensed with and, instead, some extra data such as a *checksum* or a *cyclic redundancy check (CRC)* is calculated and tacked onto the end of each packet.

Checksums and CRC work in different ways, but their essential operation and effect is the same. As each block is sent, the transmitter calculates a *check number* from the data using a predetermined algorithm. The result of this calculation consists of one or more bytes that are appended to the data block. At the receiving end, the data block is treated to the same calculation, which results in the generation of another value. If the result generated upon reception is identical to that carried in the tail of the block, then it is assumed the data block arrived intact. If they do not match, the receiver assumes the data has been corrupted, and a retransmission is then requested.

When either a checksum or CRC is used to determine if the data was received without errors, the parity bit is redundant, and is ignored by the program. (High-end modems that have built-in error detection are another reason why parity is seldom used.)

The UART

How does the parallel data from a computer's data bus get into a serial format? Although this conversion can be done with an array of logical devices, there is one device more commonly used. This device is called a UART (Universal Asynchronous Receiver Transmitter).

The UART is a complete microchip subsystem that converts parallel data to serial data, and serial data to parallel data. UART determines and inserts parity bits, checks received parity bits, creates the start bit, selects the number of (and inserts) stop bits, controls the number of bits per character, and even buffers everything to give itself time to accomplish all these tasks. Much of this work is done through external devices (switches).

READ.ME

Asynchronous Communication in Personal Computers and the UART

There are many methods of communication supported by personal computers, but all can be divided into two general categories: synchronous and asynchronous. Synchronous communication is characterized by high-speed, continuous information transfer, utilizing complex encoding and transfer techniques. Asynchronous communication is characterized by lower-speed, intermittent information transfer, utilizing low-cost encoding and transfer techniques. The standard encoding technique for asynchronous data is typically implemented by integrated circuits called UARTs.

The Universal Asynchronous Receiver Transmitter (UART) converts parallel data into serial data and vice versa, as the data is available (hence asynchronous). It formats the data for transmission, and removes format bits after reception. It can do this while transmitting data, receiving data, and servicing CPU accesses—all at different clock rates.

The NS16450

Personal computers that have the industry standard AT architecture use one particular version of the UART. This is the NS16450. It can interface to the standard I/O adapter card bus and transfer serial data at rates up to 115,200bps. This level of performance allows the NS16450 to meet all requirements for single-tasking systems that communicate with other asynchronous devices.

Typical applications include communications with modems, serial printers, terminals, and direct data transfers between personal computers. These applications are driven by the low cost and simplicity of asynchronous communications. The speed and functionality these applications require is easily exceeded

READ.ME

Asynchronous Communication in Personal Computers and the UART (*continued*)

by the NS16450 in single-tasking systems. As multitasking systems and software develop, designers require more performance from the UART, while maintaining low cost and simplicity. The increased requirements have resulted in a fundamental change in UART architecture and in serial data rate improvements.

The Next Generation UART

The NS16550AF was developed to meet the increasing performance requirements of more advanced systems, and of more sophisticated software running on existing AT systems. There are eight architectural and speed enhancements that result in six performance improvements at the system level. Programmers and hardware designers can use these improvements to significantly increase the efficiency of their serial channels. The eight architectural and speed enhancements are as follows:

1. A 16-byte receiver (Rx) First In, First Out or FIFO to store incoming data

2. A 16-byte transmitter (Tx) FIFO to store outgoing data

3. A programmable interrupt trigger level that activates an interrupt when data in the Rx FIFO reaches the user-selected level

4. Logic to monitor data levels in the Rx FIFO and issue a timeout interrupt to the CPU when appropriate

5. Logic to monitor the data in the Tx FIFO and avoid issuing two interrupts for a closely repeated, empty FIFO condition

6. DMA request strobes for transferring transmitter and receiver data

7. 20 percent faster CPU bus timings than the NS16450

8. A greater than two times increase in the maximum data rate

These enhancements result in six improvements for programmers and designers:

1. The NS16550AF Rx FIFO buffers incoming serial data, resulting in an 8 to 16 times decrease in the number of interrupts the CPU must process, compared to transferring the same amount of data through the NS16450. The programmer can see the performance improvement in multitasking software when considering the overhead involved in context switching to an interrupt handler for each interrupt.

READ.ME

Asynchronous Communication in Personal Computers and the UART (*continued*)

2. The NS16550AF Tx FIFO buffers outgoing serial data, resulting in a 16 times decrease in the number of interrupts the CPU must process, compared to transferring the same amount of data through the NS16450.

3. All systems have a certain amount of latency time when responding to an interrupt. This delay is typically composed of CPU and software context switching. A programmable interrupt trigger level allows the software to adjust the level of system buffering with regard to the CPU speed, serial channel baud rate, and number of active serial channels in the system. This flexibility reduces the probability of data overrun errors in multitasking systems.

4. On-chip support logic for both the FIFOs, in the form of interrupt timers, relieves the CPU of having to directly monitor and control the data levels in the FIFOs. Specifically, the Rx FIFO timeout interrupt ensures that any data entering the FIFO, whether it reaches the programmed trigger level or not, will be transferred by the CPU in a timely manner. The Tx FIFO interrupt delay logic ensures that if the internal data transfer time of the UART is faster than the data transfer rate of the CPU, the UART will not issue another interrupt until the first byte has been completely shifted out over the serial data lines.

5. The DMA request capability of the NS16550AF allows the system to assign data transfer to the DMA controller, thus freeing the CPU for other tasks.

6. The CPU interface speed enhancements allow the NS16550AF to be used in faster systems. The increased maximum baud rate (256K baud) moves the serial data capability of the UART into the range of RS-422A interfaces.

These architectural and speed advantages have allowed the NS16550AF to set a new standard for asynchronous communications in high-performance

READ.ME

Asynchronous Communication in Personal Computers and the UART (*continued*)

computers. Specific examples include all of the personal computers utilizing the Micro Channel Architecture, and workstations from a few manufacturers. This UART architecture was designed to ease the software overhead for any system that will be running multiple tasks involving one or more serial channels.

As the NS16550AF was being improved, maintaining its compatibility with existing software for the NS16450 was the paramount consideration. So, the NS16550AF will appear to software as an NS16450 after power-up or manual reset. In fact, hardware pinout compatibility with the NS16450 was also maintained for all but two pins. These two pins are not used in most NS16450 applications, so the NS16550AF is almost always a "drop-in" replacement for the NS16450 in existing systems. This allows users of existing systems to upgrade to a high performance UART for more efficient file transfers when running programs which use the FIFOs. An example of this is background file transfer via modem. The overall system performance level relative to the serial channel increases five times when using an NS16550AF, compared to an NS16450.

Further Evolution of The NS1655x Series

The industry acceptance of the NS16550AF as a standard has resulted in the design of derivative parts. These parts are higher integration versions of the original UART that include additional functions, higher speeds, and CMOS technology.

The NS16C551 incorporates a UART and a parallel port that are Micro Channel and AT compatible. Another derivative part, the NS16C552, functions as a dual UART, having essentially two NS16550AFs in one package. Speed and power characteristics are similar for both of these parts. The CPU interface is fast enough to allow data transfer at 25 MHz with no wait states. The maximum serial data rate is 1.5M baud. CMOS technology reduces the power consumption to one-eighth that of the NS16550AF.

The NS1655x-series of parts offer clear advantages over the NS16450 for both new and existing systems. These chips provide the hardware basis for high-performance asynchronous communications in IBM and IBM-compatible personal computers.

Electrical Characteristics
of the Interface

This section examines the electrical characteristics of the RS-232 interface. A high voltage is said to be an ON condition, and a ground or negative voltage is an OFF condition. Most troubleshooters use a breakout box or interface monitor that sits between the modem connector and the cable — within the circuit. LEDs are used to indicate the state of each signal: low or high; on or off.

A *voltmeter* can be used to measure the voltage of a control signal. An ON signal measures around 5 to 12. Depending on the manufacturer and logic circuits used, any of three standards are used, but the most preferred and more common ON/OFF voltage standard is +12 volts as an ON condition, and −12 volts as OFF.

The differences in acceptable voltage levels are to accommodate variations in the power supply driving the circuits, resistance in the cables, and the load requirement. The wide variation in acceptable voltage helps to ensure that an acceptable level of voltage will reach the other end. For example, if you talk to a friend across a room, you talk more loudly or softly, depending on factors like noise, other people talking, dogs barking, your friend's hearing, and so forth.

A bad voltage area may indicate the cable is too long, or an output circuit is bad, or an input is overloaded. While some control circuits are always on or always off, others are turning on and off as required. The clocks (in synchronous interfacing) and the data will signal continually going from low to high and high to low. (You would need a Data Scope to see these oscillating signals.)

Signals in the −3 to +3 volt range may make it across the circuit, but there are serious doubts about long-term operation. When you operate at close-to-unacceptable voltage levels, you are more likely to experience problems down the road. Strive for clean, healthy, full-voltage signals. Based on optimum voltage levels and impedance, it is recommended that the cable between computer and modem, when an RS-232 interface is used, should not exceed 50 feet. It is possible to operate beyond that limit, but not recommended.

THE DIGITAL INTERFACE

When two people meet on the street, they greet each other in one of many common forms, and set about talking to each other in a more-or-less orderly way.

"John, hi, how're you doing?"

"Hi! Tim, just great. How 'bout you ?"

When military radio operators engage in communication they use the words "over and out" as a way of letting each other know when their transmission is completed, so the other may transmit. If both operators attempted to transmit simultaneously over the same frequency, their messages would be garbled.

Control Signals

Data communication also uses an orderly process to ensure that data is transmitted only when the receiving party is ready for it. The computer has to be sure the transmitting modem, telephone line, and receiving modem are all ready before attempting a transmission. To ensure that all parties involved are ready to exchange data, there are a number of control signals in the computer-modem interface. Each control signal is used to indicate an ON/OFF condition across the interface. The use of these control signals is referred to as *handshaking*.

In modem etiquette, the relationship between modems and computers is very polite. The control signals clearly indicate who is asking what from whom. Different modem manufacturers use different control signals. The most common are listed here, including alternate (if any) designations.

- **DTR (Data Terminal Ready)** The computer uses DTR to tell the modem that it is powered on, the software is loaded, and it is ready to communicate.

- **DSR (Data Set Ready) or MR (Modem Ready)** The local modem is telling the computer that it is powered on and connected to a phone line in normal operational mode (as opposed to a test mode).

- **DCD (Data Carrier Detected) or CD (Carrier Detected)** An indication that a remote modem is on line and is ready to exchange data. (The presence of a carrier does *not* imply that the carrier has data on it.) This signal is provided *to* the computer *from* the local modem.

- **RI (Ring Indicator)** The modem senses ringing on the line.

- **RTS or RS (Request to Send)** The computer is asking the modem if it is OK to start transmitting data.

- **CTS or CS (Clear to Send)** The modem tells the computer to go ahead and start sending data.

- **TD (Transmit Data)** Data is sent from the computer to the modem for transmission.

- **RD (Receive Data)** Data is received by the modem from the remote modem and is provided to the computer.

The interface between the computer and the modem uses logic signals that represent the control signals. Typically, when the signal is low (ground or negative voltage), the signal is in the OFF state. If the voltage is positive, the signal is said to be ON.

It is important to know that the modem may need a DTR signal from the computer to permit data exchange; and that a communications program may need DSR from the modem before it will begin exchanging data. Furthermore, only after the modem responds with CTS as a response to the computer's RTS can a computer transmit data. When RTS goes high, the carrier is turned on. The transmitter sends all 1s or all 0s until CTS goes high and data begins to flow.

Important: The time between the computer's RTS and the modem's CTS answer is called the "Clear to Send Delay"; this plays an important role later on.

Before we review and move on, it is important to note that although there is a standard that says what is supposed to happen, reality does not always match these standards. It is typical to find in an office environment a cable connecting to a modem with just three wires in it—for Transmit Data, Receive Data, and Ground Signals—nothing more. This means someone has configured the modem and/or computer not to look for any control signals. Occasionally, the control signals may be faked by jumpering connector pins together.

Synchronous Communication

You have already read, earlier in this chapter, that serial interface uses two primary forms of transmission: synchronous and asynchronous. Asynchronous communication (ASYNC) is the transmission mode most people are familiar with, especially in the personal computer market, and has been described at length. There was a time when ASYNC was the one and only method of communication. However, the demand for greater modem speed and efficiency increased because computer users became more sophisticated. Banks began to place terminals in their branches—automated teller machines, account balance terminals, and other nifty devices. Chain stores began to use computerized inventory systems and direct cash register sales information. Credit card companies started hooking large networks of point-of-sale authorization machines into their huge computers. Companies began to share data—employees had take-home terminals, and branch offices used centralized data centers. Modem needs began to increase and become more complex.

Synchronous communication is now the industry standard, featuring high throughput, low overhead, and efficiency. The big difference you will notice in a synchronous interface is the use of two additional signals (Transmit Clock and Receive Clock) of your modem. These clocks are modem outputs that keep the computer interface in sync with the modem. In the ASYNC world, the timing was in bit time, triggered by the start bit. In the world of synchronous communication, the timing information is contained in the Transmit and Receive Clocks. (This may not become apparent to you until much later, but the last piece of news spells disaster for uniformity and compatibility.)

Most manufacturers of 1200 and 2400bps modems built them to be compatible with Bell or CCITT standards. Modems with speeds over 2400bps usually are developed with their manufacturers' own communication techniques. The ASYNC modem manufacturers in the home computer market seem to stress compatibility, but the business modem market is moving further and further from it. What effects the high speed CCITT standards like V32, V42, and V42 *bis* standards will have is not yet clear. In any case, small non-dedicated computers will likely stay with standardized ASYNC communications for the time being.

CHAPTER TWENTY-FOUR

File Transfer Protocols

The ability to exchange files with other systems is one of the greatest benefits of computer communications, and with today's file transfer protocols this task is easier and faster than ever. You can have remote computers transfer documents, database files, spreadsheets, or entire programs directly onto your disks, ready to use. You can transfer files directly from your disks to those of a remote computer. Transferring files this way is faster and cheaper than mailing floppy disks, and is often the only practical way to move data between machines that have incompatible disk formats.

To ensure that data is transferred correctly, computers use *file transfer protocols*, which are established procedures for exchanging data, along with instructions that coordinate the process. Most protocols are *error-correcting*; that is, they sense when data is corrupted or lost due to noise on your connection, and will automatically resend the affected data until it is received correctly.

Of the scores of error-correcting file transfer protocols introduced since the dawn of microcomputing, fewer than a dozen have achieved prominence. Because each of the major communications programs contains a selection of these protocols, you often have a choice—there is no one right answer. Some protocols are good with some modems and awful with others; others are slow and should be used only when the remote computer offers no other choices. Finally, some are outrageously fast, but they exist only in certain programs. To know which protocol will give you the best results, you need some background on how protocols work.

Understanding Xmodem is the first step toward comprehending more recent protocols, which are largely extensions of the original Xmodem concept. Xmodem was invented by Ward Christiansen; it is based on his MODEM7 protocol used on old CP/M systems, and is the oldest EC (error correction) protocol and most widespread protocol. Though Xmodem is slow and limited compared to newer protocols, it is still widely used—particularly because it is often the only protocol that disparate machines have in common.

Xmodem breaks up a file into blocks (or packets) of 128 characters each, and sends each block surrounded by packetization characters that denote the block's beginning, end, and block number, and the checksum of the data contained in the block. The sender then waits for a response from the receiver. The receiver sends back a positive acknowledgment if the block arrives intact, or a negative acknowledgment if the block is corrupted by line noise. To determine whether the block is intact, the receiver computes the checksum of the received data and compares it to the checksum that accompanied the block. If the two agree, the odds are great that the block is intact. When the sender gets a positive acknowledgment, it sends the next block. If it gets a negative acknowledgment, it resends the previous block.

Xmodem spread quickly for a number of reasons. It was far more reliable than simply capturing text that the remote computer displayed on your screen. Also, Xmodem lets you transfer binary files and programs, whereas capturing text limited you to ASCII files. Xmodem came on the scene at just the right time, when modem communications were beginning to catch on. It was public domain (free), and relatively easy to implement in software.

However, along with Xmodem's simplicity came some frustrating limitations. Xmodem is designed for microcomputers and uses 8-bit characters to surround its blocks, which makes it impossible to implement on mainframes that support only 7-bit communications. Xmodem sends only one file, and it doesn't send the file's name, time, or date. Xmodem does not maintain a file's original size (it rounds up to the nearest 128-byte increment). Checksum error-checking lets certain types of errors pass undetected. As microcomputing advanced and people began to send larger files through faster modems, Xmodem's small block size, together with its send-and-wait style of operation, created a bottleneck.

EVOLUTION OF PROTOCOLS

Over the last ten years, hobbyists and entrepreneurs have cranked out a continuous stream of new protocols inspired by Xmodem. While most have faded into obscurity, a few have become important in their own right.

Kermit

Kermit protocol (named after Kermit the frog) was developed by Frank da Cruz of Columbia University in the early 1980s. Kermit, like Xmodem, sends a block (packet) and waits for an acknowledgment, but Kermit doesn't have many of Xmodem's limitations, and it is much more complex. It can send multiple files, with filenames, times, and dates, and it maintains file size data. Its error-checking is more robust than Xmodem's. Most important, Kermit is designed not just for microcomputers, but for mainframes as well. This has brought about wide acceptance of Kermit, which is now installed on more mainframes than any other asynchronous protocol.

However, mainframe compatibility comes at a price: Kermit is substantially slower than Xmodem. Several factors contribute to this. Kermit uses smaller packets (10 to 96 bytes), and each includes more packetization characters than Xmodem. In order to avoid using characters incompatible with mainframe communications, Kermit quotes (encapsulates) many characters, expanding each one into two different characters. Non-ASCII characters may also be quoted. Transfers begin with the exchange of initialization packets; these contain no data, but merely establish how subsequent packets are handled. Finally, acknowledgments consist of several characters, not just a single character as in Xmodem. These factors all add overhead — characters that are not part of the file, but are exchanged just to coordinate the transfer — and this means lower efficiency. On the plus side, Kermit does have a simple compression capability that recovers some of the lost efficiency. Typically, Kermit gives about one-half to two-thirds the throughput of Xmodem.

New, more efficient versions of Kermit have been introduced over the years. A long-packet Kermit expands the packet size up to 9K, and Sliding Window Kermit eliminates the inefficiency of the original Kermit's send-and-wait style of operation.

Of course, mutually compatible file transfer protocols are not the only considerations in communicating with mainframes. For more on making connections between microcomputers and mainframes, see Chapter 22.

Xmodem Improvements

The original Xmodem has also seen a number of enhancements. Xmodem CRC, which uses a 2-byte CRC error-checking code instead of the original 1-byte checksum, became popular in the early 1980s. CRC stands for *cyclical redundancy checking,* which is an algorithm much less prone to allowing undetected errors. Xmodem-CRC is now quite commonly used, and has given rise to another common variation, Xmodem-Auto. This hybrid of Xmodem and Xmodem-CRC uses CRC error-checking when possible, but switches to checksum automatically if the remote computer is capable of only checksum.

Ymodem

Ymodem, introduced by Chuck Forsberg in 1981, offers several improvements over Xmodem. It uses CRC error-checking, sends filenames, times, and dates, and can transfer multiple files. Ymodem also uses a block size of 1K, in contrast to the 128-byte blocks of Xmodem. This increases protocol efficiency, since Ymodem has one-eighth the number of packetization characters, and thus needs to stop and wait for acknowledgments one-eighth as often. The difference is scarcely noticeable in local calls, but through long-distance calls or high-speed modems, Ymodem may be as much as 60 percent faster than Xmodem (for reasons explained later in this chapter).

However, when you've got a poor connection, Ymodem is not a good choice. It takes eight times as long as Xmodem to resend a block damaged by noise. And if your line is bad enough, Ymodem may never get an entire block through without errors.

Will the Real Ymodem Please Stand Up?

There is confusion about the name Ymodem, because at one time many people began to use the name Ymodem to describe another protocol, named Xmodem-1K. Though Xmodem-1K does use 1K blocks, in all other respects it is identical to Xmodem-CRC, and it cannot send filenames, times, dates, or multiple files. When people realized the term Ymodem was no longer definitive, they started calling the real Ymodem (Chuck Forsberg's Ymodem) Ymodem-Batch. And really enlightened people call the mock Ymodem (the one that can't send multiple files) Xmodem-1K. Now that you know all this, the next time you hear the term Ymodem, you'll still be confused.

Ymodem-G, a variation of Ymodem, sends a file in a continuous stream, without stopping for acknowledgments. Ymodem-G offers high efficiency by completely dispensing with error correction; this protocol should be used only through connections that are intrinsically error free, such as with error-correcting modems. If errors do occur during the transfer, the file must be discarded and the transfer repeated.

Blast

Blast, the first bidirectional transfer protocol, was introduced by Communications Research Group in 1983. Blast has gained a following not so much for its ability to send and receive simultaneously, but because it is available for a broad spectrum of computers. Unlike Xmodem, Kermit, and Ymodem, Blast is a "sliding window" compressed protocol, implemented under 30 operating systems. Blast provides high-speed file transfer and remote control, while resisting noise on dial-up phone lines.

Zmodem

In 1986, Chuck Forsberg released Zmodem, the first error-correcting, streaming protocol. Zmodem achieves about 98 percent efficiency, by sending in a continuous stream, inserting error-checking codes at intervals, and pausing only at the end of each file to wait for an acknowledgment. As data arrives, the receiver compares it to received error-checking codes, and immediately requests that flawed data be backed up and resent. Zmodem was also the first protocol to introduce file recovery. This streaming style of operation outran all previous protocols, with no loss in reliability.

HyperProtocol

Hilgraeve introduced HyperProtocol, a true speed demon among protocols, in 1987. It is the first protocol to include truly effective, on-the-fly file compression, capable of blasting data through 2400bps modems at more than 10,000bps, and through 9600bps modems at more than 40,000bps. Its Ziv-Lempel compression algorithm works on files of all kinds, and shuts off automatically with files that have already been compressed. Even with compression off, HyperProtocol gives efficiencies in excess of 99 percent.

Like Zmodem, it is an error-correcting, streaming protocol. But unlike Zmodem, HyperProtocol continues streaming during multiple file transfers, stopping for acknowledgment only after the last file. HyperProtocol maintains its efficiency at higher speeds than most protocols, and has developed a strong following among high-speed modem and ISDN (Integrated Services Digital Network) users.

Lynx

Matthew Thomas released Lynx in mid-1988 as "Lynx: A Full Streaming/ Compression/CRC-32 Batch File Transfer Protocol." He immediately began to implement suggestions from users and released version 2.0 in the spring of 1989. Six months later, after adding handshaking, additional file-handling capability, and a color status window, he released version 3.0 as shareware. The $15 registration fee entitles users to all future versions.

At this point, however, Thomas found that adding more of the features that users wanted would make new Lynx releases incompatible with older ones. He also discovered he had not allowed much room for expansion to higher speeds. Lynx is pretty much limited to 1200 or 2400bps, where it performs wonderfully. At 9600 baud, it slows transfers to about 890 characters per second, much slower than optimum. This disappointed many previously interested users. After much thought, Thomas decided to redesign the protocol entirely and give it a new name. Lynx, unchanged from version 3, would remain the optimum transfer protocol for 1200 and 2400bps transfer speeds. He would optimize the new protocol for higher speeds.

Thus was Puma, son of Lynx, born.

Puma/MPt

Matthew Thomas first released Puma in January 1990. He later renamed it MPt. MPt offers features similar to those of Lynx, such as RLE compression, full-streaming data flow, and hardware handshaking. However, it is thoroughly tuned for modems that operate at 4800bps or higher. It also incorporates "feature flags" that will tell future versions what features to use when talking to another version. According to Thomas, MPt can be expanded to support compression techniques like Lempel-Ziv-Welch and Splay Tree encoding, which would allow further data compression. A chat mode may be included in a future version. All versions, future and past, will be able to talk with one another. MPt has a feature missing from other protocol drivers: a full-screen color display that is both fast and compatible with most multitasking subsystems. The user can select file logging in either of two formats: by an enhancement to the single line format originally specified by Chuck Forsberg in his program DSZ, or by the new Call Data Standard (CDS) that is beginning to gain acceptance. CDS is expected to become the method of choice for logging sessions.

MPt (like Zmodem and BiModem) can resume aborted data transfers from where they were lost due to line noise, communication breakdown, or other failure. No streaming protocol like MPt, however, can reach maximum warp speed on short file transfers. MPt does its best, and is extremely fast, stable, and accurate, on files at least 15KB or larger.

Jmodem

In September 1988, Richard Johnson released a protocol called Jmodem. Jmodem includes data compression similar to Kermit's, but is far easier to implement. It maintains file size, uses an 8- or 16-bit CRC for error-checking, and, additionally, compresses data. It geometrically increases the block size on low-error file transfers up to an 8192-byte maximum. The result in such cases is very rapid file transfers when the phone connection is clean. The Wildcat! BBS and other bulletin board systems have helped spread Jmodem's popularity, primarily because of its speed and accuracy over problem-free lines.

BiModem

John Erickson released an efficient, bidirectional protocol called BiModem in December 1988. It takes advantage of the modem's ability to send and receive information at the same time—a technique that can cut your communications bills in half if you often send and receive files during the same session.

BiModem uses two file recovery methods, allows file updating, and lets you chat or specify additional files while a transfer is going on. Multiple directories can be searched to locate file requests, thus increasing BiModem's flexibility. Like other protocols, BiModem splits files into blocks based on transfer performance, maximizing the block size at 4K, and can recover an aborted file transfer if you lose your connection. BiModem has become popular enough to generate a small "support industry" of its own, which is one way program authors measure their success. Three good examples of BiModem's secondary support program market are BiMark, BiPath, and BiConfig. All are designed to increase BiModem's capabilities and help you tailor the program to your particular needs.

Used at 9600bps, the BiModem protocol is extremely fast and accurate.

PROPRIETARY VERSUS PUBLIC DOMAIN PROTOCOLS

Xmodem was placed in the public domain, where it could be used without charge. Many other protocols have followed the same tradition. Public domain protocols tend to spread quickly, due to their easy availability. However, uncontrolled distribution does cause a few problems. There is no official control over setting or enforcing standards, or of approving changes. So it's not uncommon to find that one computer's Xmodem won't work with another computer's Xmodem. On the other hand, this anarchy does produce some outstanding protocols, and at present Zmodem is the cream of the crop. Figure 24-1 shows a list of the major modem protocols and their capabilities.

Many commercially available communications programs, in addition to supporting public domain protocols, have introduced protocols of their own, called *proprietary protocols.* Proprietary protocols are intended to meet file transfer needs not satisfied by public domain protocols. To use a proprietary protocol, you must generally buy two programs from the same manufacturer; that is, to use Blast, you buy two copies of the Blast communications program. The same is true with Dart protocol (Crosstalk Mk.4), Relay protocol (Relay), and CCDOS protocol (Carbon Copy). HyperProtocol is different. To get HyperProtocol for a PC, you buy HyperACCESS or HyperACCESS/5, but to get it for a bulletin board, minicomputer, or mainframe, you pay only a $1 license fee.

Figure 24-1

Major modem protocols and their capabilities

Capability	Xmodem	Xmodem-CRC	1K Xmodem	Modem7	Sealink	Telink	Ymodem	Ymodem-G	Kermit	Blast	Zmodem	Hyperprotocol	BiModem
1 byte checksum	Y								Y				
2 byte checksum									Y			Y	
2 byte CRC		Y	Y	Y	Y	Y	Y	Y	Y		Y	Y	
4 byte CRC				!							Y		Y
7 bit									Y				
8 bit (with some escaped)											Y		
8 bit (transparency req'd)	Y	Y	Y	Y	Y	Y	Y	Y		Y		Y	Y
Hardware flow control	Y	Y	Y	Y	Y	Y	Y	Y	Y	Y	Y	Y	Y
Xon/Xoff flow control									Y		Y	Y	
Run length compression									Y				
Adaptive compression												Y	
File size maintained				Y	Y	Y	Y	Y	Y	Y	Y	Y	Y
File date maintained										Y	Y	Y	Y
Time maintained										Y	Y	Y	Y
Minimum block size	128	128	128	128	128	128	128		10		64	128	16
Maximum block size	128	128	1K	1K	128	128	1K		9K		8K	2K	4K
Block splitting											Y	Y	Y
Block scaling										Y	Y	Y	Y
Resend when errors detected	Y	Y	Y	Y	Y	Y	Y	Y		Y	Y	Y	Y
Window error - re-transmit										Y	Y	Y	Y
Sliding windows										Y	Y	Y	Y
Remote file requests									Y	Y	Y		Y
Multiple file transfers							Y	Y	Y	Y	Y	Y	Y
Multiple directory search												Y	Y
Add files during sending													Y
Send only new files												Y	
Send files with pathnames												Y	
Build duplicate directories												Y	
Duplicate file rejection												Y	Y
Send using filename lists													Y
Source deletion option													Y
Crash recovery										Y	Y		Y
Crash recovery thru rename													Y
Crashed file deletion												Y	Y
Overwrite existing files												Y	Y
File Verification										Y			Y
File renaming			Y	Y	Y	Y	Y	Y	Y	Y	Y	Y	Y
Abort transfer	Y	Y	Y	Y	Y	Y	Y	Y	Y	Y	Y	Y	Y
Abort individual file									Y			Y	Y
Logging											Y	Y	Y
Full Duplex Chat													Y
Full Duplex Transfers										Y			Y
Direct Connect Peak K Baud	19	19	19	19	19	19	19	19	19	38	38	115	115

BLOCKS OR STREAMING

The trend in protocol development has been away from block-oriented, send-and-wait protocols (Xmodem, Kermit, and Ymodem), toward streaming (or windowing) protocols. The primary reason is speed. As Table 24-1 shows, the speed difference is minor under some circumstances but quite dramatic under others. The newer protocols are clearly much faster in long-distance calls and with high-speed modems. To grasp the reason for this difference, you need to know how newer operating styles differ from earlier protocols, and how the differences help.

Protocols like Xmodem, Ymodem, and Kermit transmit a block of data along with an error-checking code, and then sit and wait for the receiver to send back an acknowledgment. Protocols like Zmodem and HyperProtocol send a continuous stream of data, insert error-checking codes at intervals, and wait for an acknowledgment only once, at the end of the transfer.

As long as there is nothing between the sender and receiver that causes data to be delayed, there is little speed difference between these two styles of operation. But in reality, almost every type of connection (except for a direct, RS-232 cable link) does exhibit some delay. The delay with regular 1200 and 2400bps modems is quite small, but it is significant with any MNP (Microcom Networking Protocol) modem. (See Chapter 26.) With 9600bps

Table 24-1

Seconds Required to Transfer a 10K File

	Xmodem	Ymodem	Zmodem	HyperProtocol	
Local call, 2400bps	44.3	44.1	43.5	43.3	(14.4)*
Long-distance, 2400bps	84.8	52.6	44.0	43.8	(14.9)*
Local call, 9600bps	29.7	11.9	9.5	9.4	(3.1)*
Long-distance, 9600bps	70.2	20.4	10.0	9.9	(3.6)*

These times are calculated from the theory of operation for protocols; actual times are slightly longer, but performance of protocols relative to one another remains the same.

*Times in parentheses include the effects of HyperProtocol's on-the-fly file compression.

modems, the delay can exceed .3 second. Long-distance calls often exhibit delays of .25 to .5 second.

Such delays can decimate the throughput of block-oriented, send-and-wait protocols. Consider transferring a file long distance through a 9600bps modem: It takes Xmodem only .14 second to send a 128-byte block of data, but then it must sit and wait for an acknowledgment. After modem delay (.3 second) and long-distance call delay (.25 second), the block arrives at the receiver's end .55 second later. The receiver immediately sends back an acknowledgment, which takes another .55 second to reach the sender. The total time to exchange the block is 1.35 seconds, though only .14 second was used to transfer data. You get an efficiency of about 10 percent, and an effective throughput worse than 1200bps!

Consider the same transfer with a streaming protocol. The only effect from delays is to slow the file's arrival at the receiver by .55 second, and slow the acknowledgment by another .55 second. This adds only 1.1 seconds to the overall transfer. The resulting reduction to a streaming protocol's overall efficiency depends on the size of the file being sent. With a 100K file, it cuts the protocol's normal efficiency by only 1 percent (say, from 99 percent to 98 percent).

Ymodem-G, a less modern streaming protocol that lacks error-correction, also retains its efficiency despite line delays. But Ymodem-G is no faster, and should never be used instead of Zmodem or HyperProtocol, even for file transfers between error-correcting modems. Using an error-correcting protocol through error-correcting modems is wiser, because the modems cannot correct errors that occur in modem-to-port or port-to-software connection; errors can slip through.

WINDOWING

Windowing is sometimes confused with streaming. In some respects they accomplish the same thing. Windowing allows the transfer protocol to continue sending blocks of a file even if it has not yet received acknowledgments of blocks already sent.

There are two common types of windowing: sliding or fixed. Fixed windowing was the first to be implemented. Its basic premise is that it continues to send blocks of data without acknowledgment, but if an error occurs, it resends the last unacknowledged block and all blocks after it. Sliding windowing, on the other hand, resends only the unacknowledged block, which allows blocks to be acknowledged out of sequence. While sliding windows seems like a nice idea, it tends to be less efficient—kind of like a juggler trying to keep too many balls in the air at once.

BLOCK SPLITTING AND SCALING

What happens when there is an error? Xmodem attempts to retransmit the entire 128 or more bytes of data. On an especially noisy line, you may never be able to get a single 128-byte block of data transmitted successfully. With protocols that send a larger block size, the chance of getting a file sent over a noisy line is reduced even further, unless the program can split and scale.

The *block splitting* rule says all blocks retransmitted because of an error are cut in half. This allows the data to eventually get through. *Scaling* is a similar rule that says when an error occurs, the size of future blocks will be reduced. Of course, line noise can come and go, so block size should gradually work its way back up. Figure 24-1 describes which protocols have splitting and scaling capabilities, and the minimum/maximum block sizes.

FILE COMPRESSION

Compressing files reduces the total number of bytes, allowing the file to be transferred in less time. Compression is an accepted concept, but there is some debate over how and when the compression should take place.

Many products compress files before sending them. The best-known programs for this are ARC and ZIP (formerly known as PKARC). These programs can compress one or several files into a single, smaller file for sending. The receiver of the file then uses the same program to decompress it. These programs can compress spreadsheets or database files to about one-quarter of their original size, text files to about one-half, and program files to about two-thirds. The disadvantage to this type of compression is that it gives you extra work to do before and after a transfer. Compressing and decompressing large files can be time-consuming; it also consumes disk space, because your disk must hold both the compressed and uncompressed form of the file.

Using a modem that compresses files as you transfer them gives you the benefits of compression without the before-and-after work. For example, 2400bps MNP modems let you use a computer-to-modem interface speed of at least 9600bps. The modem accepts data from the computer, compresses it, and passes it into the phone line. The MNP modem at the other end receives, decompresses, and passes the data to the other computer in its original form. Modem compression also has drawbacks. Modems use simpler compression algorithms than do dedicated compression programs, and compress files about half as much, on the average. Compression occurs only if both modems have built-in compression, and such modems cost significantly more than regular modems.

Building file compression into a file transfer protocol could potentially give the same degree of compression as dedicated compression programs, through any type of modem. Most protocols that have incorporated compression have fallen well short of this goal. Kermit and Jmodem, for example, both use a simple compression scheme called *run length encoding*, which replaces any byte that appears four or more consecutive times with a three-byte sequence (an indicator byte, a count, and the character to repeat). This seldom compresses files by more than 10 percent or 20 percent, and does nothing to compress patterns of repeated bytes.

HyperProtocol, on the other hand, uses a highly effective Ziv-Lempel-Welch compression algorithm similar to that of dedicated compression programs. It adapts automatically to each file, compresses any repeated patterns, and works on both ASCII and binary files. In effect, it amplifies the modem's speed. That is, you get throughputs during file transfers that are several times your modem's rated speed. To get this same effect the hard way, most users ZIP or ARC the files before sending them.

FLOW CONTROL

In order for error-correcting modems to work, they have to have data in a buffer that they can manipulate. Normally this is done by having your computer talk to the modem at a faster rate than the modems talk to each other. This allows the sending modem's buffer to fill, so it has data to process and compress. Most modems, however, have a limited amount of buffer space. When the buffer is nearly full, the modem must signal your computer to momentarily stop sending data. There are two methods of signaling: software flow control and hardware flow control.

Software flow control uses two data characters called XON and XOFF to throttle the flow of data. The modem sends the computer an XOFF when its buffer is full, telling the file transfer software to stop sending data. When the modem's buffer falls below half-full, it sends the computer an XON, telling the file transfer software to send more data. Software flow control has some major disadvantages. It takes time to send the XON and the XOFF, which can degrade throughput. Also, if XON or XOFF characters occur in the data, the file transfer software has to somehow tell the other computer that the characters are not coming from the modem. This requires prefixing the character with a control character or escaping to it.

Software flow control does have one advantage. When multiple modems are involved, as is the case for most data networks, there must be a method for the network to inform your computer that its buffer is full, or it is busy. This can only be done using software flow control. (Most networks in use today are heavily buffered and rarely have full buffer conditions.)

Hardware flow control uses two control lines called Clear To Send (CTS) and Ready To Send (RTS). These are physical wires connecting your computer to your modem. The signals can be used two different ways. In the first method, your computer raises RTS to inform the modem that it is ready to send data, and then checks CTS to see if the modem is ready to accept data. This method is half duplex in nature, because it doesn't allow your computer to tell the modem if it is ready to receive data. The second method is much simpler. When your computer is ready to receive data, it raises RTS; when the modem is ready to receive data, it raises CTS. Likewise, your computer must check CTS before sending, and the modem must check RTS. Hardware flow control has the advantage of being fast; the two wires can be raised and lowered at close to light speed, and there are no data characters involved that need to be escaped.

MULTIPLE FILES IN ONE TRANSFER

Xmodem and many of the protocols based on it work like a single-shot rifle; they send only one file each time you initiate a transfer. Since it normally takes a dozen or so keystrokes to initiate a transfer, sending multiple files can be a lot of work. Kermit and newer protocols work like a machine gun; they can send many files, one after another, each time you initiate a transfer. This lets you send multiple files with far fewer keystrokes. Such protocols are often called *batch protocols*.

Most batch protocols specify which files to send by typing a series of specific filenames, or filenames containing wildcards (* and ?). BiModem and HyperProtocol also give you the option to transfer only files with newer times and dates, or to use wildcards to transfer files from various directories. HyperProtocol even lets you transfer all or part of a PC's directory structure to another PC, or transfer files from predefined lists, to avoid having to retype groups of files that you send often.

FILE RECOVERY

Chuck Forsberg was the first to develop file recovery with his Zmodem protocol. File recovery is the ability of the protocol to restart an aborted transmission where it left off. On the receiving side, the protocol first checks to see if the file it is about to receive is already there. If it is, and if the file has the same date and time but a smaller size, the protocol will inform the sender of that fact, and the sending side will pick up where it left off. Unfortunately, some bulletin boards use a file's date and time to reflect when it was uploaded. This causes confusion for the protocols; they think it is a new version of the file.

BiModem has the same file recovery scheme as Zmodem, but it has gone a couple of steps further. A bulletin board sysop who wants file dates and times to reflect the upload time can do this, and yet still get file recovery. An aborted files directory is established to hold aborted, renamed files. Then when the caller tries to finish uploading, BiModem checks this directory to see if it is supposed to restart/recover any files. Then it goes one step further: if a file is not being recovered, it is considered a new version of the program or data.

In new versions, BiModem has a Verify mode for uploading. This mode sends only the CRCs so that the receiver can determine and tell the sender what parts of the files differ. The sender can then send just the pieces that are different. For a transaction log, or a program that only has a couple of modifications at the end, this can significantly reduce the amount of time required to update the file.

THE FUTURE OF FILE
TRANSFER PROTOCOLS

History reveals that file transfer protocols evolve not according to their own agenda, but in response to evolution in the data communications environment. For example, higher modem speeds made block-oriented protocols like Xmodem obsolete, and made high-efficiency protocols like Zmodem inevitable. By examining what is underway in data communications, we can predict the future of file transfer protocols.

Despite high cost and lack of standardization, error-correcting modems have earned a respectable share of the market over the last few years. In coming years they will dominate, as the recently set V42 standard is implemented and prices fall. Today's error-correcting modems (which largely use MNP error-correction) and V42 modems exhibit propagation delays that make block-oriented, send-and-wait protocols bog down. Such protocols will continue to decline, and streaming protocols will flourish.

Another new modem standard, V32, will have an even more profound impact on modem communications. As costs fall for modems that implement this standard, 9600bps modems will become as well known as 2400bps modems are today. Before long, 14,400bps modems are likely to become common, as well. While today's streaming protocols can keep pace with these fast modems, other high-efficiency protocols are sure to join the race. The great bandwidth of these modems also expands the application of bidirectional protocols, such as Blast, Relay, and BiModem.

According to some projections, ISDN will ultimately replace all existing analog telephone service, and is already in use at some corporate sites. Instead of modems, ISDN uses devices called *terminal adapters*; they can support simultaneous voice and data communications at speeds up to 64,000bps. In fact, you can use two 64,000bps channels at once, to get a combined throughput of 128,000bps. Speeds this high demand high-efficiency protocols implemented with great care. ISDN offers exciting potential. Its speed, together with a high-efficiency protocol with compression, can even support real-time transfer of video images!

CHAPTER TWENTY-FIVE

Integrated Service Digital Network — ISDN

This is the future—the complete digitization of the world's telecommunications: ISDN, the Integrated Service Digital Network.

The term ISDN was created in 1973 by the world's telecommunications standards group, the Consultative Committee for International Telephony and Telegraphy (CCITT); however, the scope of ISDN was not defined until 1980. It was then formally defined by the CCITT in 1986. Today ISDN has been implemented only on a very limited basis. These things take time, especially when the phone companies of the world are involved.

THE CONCEPT OF ISDN

The ISDN concept evolved from something called the Integrated Digital Network (IDN). ISDN offers a future worldwide network capable of transmitting voice, data, video, and graphics in digital form at the same time.

ISDN's users are gradually emerging as the necessary equipment is installed in the telephone networks. The goal of ISDN is to provide end-to-end digital communication, in contrast to the current telephone network based on analog signals and modems. This end-to-end digital connectivity will be accomplished through a single standard interface.

The current telephone network provides only voice-grade analog, rather than digital, circuits for end-to-end communications. This makes high-speed communications difficult, because the voice-grade circuits cannot handle the speed that is possible through digital circuits. ISDN does not require new fiber optics to accomplish this high-speed capability, but instead turns copper wires into digital channels. (Although, since more data can flow over fiber optics, it's assumed that they will eventually replace copper.)

ISDN is the result of pressure from both the communications market and from the standards institutions to reduce the cost of voice and data communications. ISDN not only promises lower costs, but also a whole new way of retrieving and accessing information.

There are several key facilities possible with ISDN. First is the ability to connect any computer, telephone, fax machine, or other device to any other ISDN-supported device anywhere in the world. Many other user-oriented services will be provided by ISDN. For example, your telephone number is issued for life; no matter where you move in the world, your ISDN number travels with you.

It is estimated that over 40 percent of personal computers have modems, and this number is increasing daily. This means people want to use their computer to communicate. As computer applications generate larger stores of information, and higher-resolution graphics increase the storage requirements, there is a need for better file compression techniques to send larger, more complex groups of information.

Current modem technology is approaching a barrier to further improvement because of the limited signal bandwidth available in the face of ever higher communication speeds. Already, modem manufacturers are resorting to more efficient compression schemes to squeeze every ounce of performance from today's modems. (See Chapter 24, "File Transfer Protocols," for more details.)

ISDN by its very definition eliminates the need for access to special dedicated, switched, private, or packet facilities. ISDN provides integration of voice, data, and video services over the same connection.

HOW THE TELEPHONE NETWORK WORKS TODAY

The dominant technology used today is based on *circuit switching*. Circuit switching, illustrated in Figure 25-1, usually occurs in three phases, which are described in the following sections.

Figure 25-1

Generic switching network

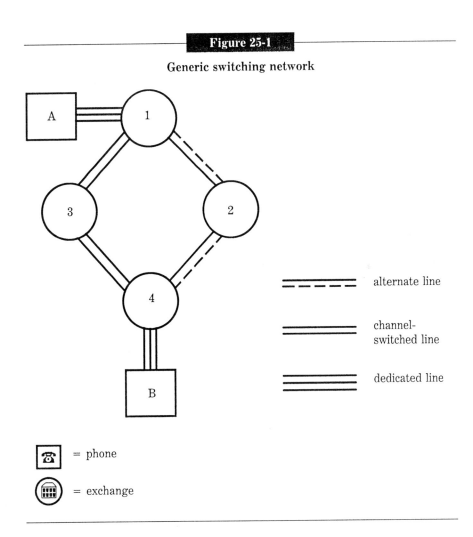

alternate line

channel-switched line

dedicated line

☎ = phone

▦ = exchange

Phase 1: Circuit Establishment

Once you have placed a phone call, through either your modem or telephone, the telephone network must establish a station-to-station circuit. Typically, your telephone or modem (station A) is "hard-wired" to your local exchange office (node 1). Once you have placed the call, this local exchange must send signals to the remote exchange (node 4) nearest the phone you are calling, to set up a circuit.

Node 1 must find the shortest and perhaps even cheapest available link to node 4. Node 1 may choose either node 2 or node 3. Once the node is selected, node 1 allocates a free channel using either FDM (frequency division multiplexing) or TDM (time division multiplexing) through either node 2 or 3. Node 1 then sends a message across this channel to request a connection to station B. In this example, node 1 allocates a free channel with node 3, which receives the message to request communications with station B.

Node 3 allocates a free channel with the local exchange office that handles station B, and forwards the request for connection to node 4 (in this case). Node 4 determines whether station B is busy, and if not, sends the pulse for the phone to ring to station B. Once station B answers, the connection is completed, and a reverse message is sent back to node 1 telling us (eventually) that the call is connected.

This is a very trivial depiction of the call process. As these and other signals are passed back and forth, they create audible feedback on the line—clicks, busy signals, or ringing sounds.

Phase 2: Signal Transfer

Once the circuit has been established, signals can then be transferred from one end to the other. These signals can be analog voice, digitized voice, or binary data. Generally, this connection is full duplex, which means that data transfer can occur in both directions simultaneously. The path for the example is a dedicated link from station A to node 1, channel-switched from node 1 to node 3, channel-switched from node 3 to node 4, and a dedicated link from node 4 to station B.

Phase 3: Circuit Disconnect

When the connection is terminated by either one of the parties, signals are sent along the established link to deallocate the dedicated resources.

MERGING OLD TECHNOLOGY WITH ISDN

Because the telephone network was designed using a series of pulses and tones, most of the equipment in use until the late 1960s could only support a series of tones, or analog signals. This is the main reason modems were invented: the modem is a device that adapts computer signals into the tones and beeps necessary to move information across the telephone network.

ISDN will change all this. Figure 25-2 shows how a typical call is routed on ISDN. The user connection to ISDN is called the "subscriber loop." The user equipment is connected to this subscriber loop, typically twisted-pair wire, and thus to the ISDN switch at the central office.

The ISDN central office connects many other subscriber loops to the ISDN network. The ISDN switch provides circuit-switching, packet-switching, and even dedicated facilities by using the lower layers (1-3) of the

Figure 25-2

ISDN subscriber loop

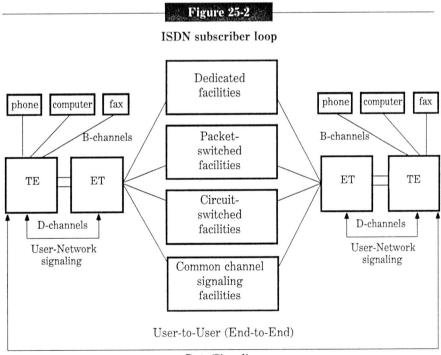

TE — Terminal Equipment
ET — Exchange Equipment

Open Systems Interconnect (OSI) reference model (see Figure 25-3). ISDN is sort of a slow-speed LAN without distance limits. ISDN also provides some of the higher functions of OSI (layers 4-7), to support such applications as Teletex (described later in this chapter), fax, and high-speed transaction processing.

No more will it be necessary to use a modem or rely on a single communications channel to pass computer signals across the country or around the world. A BBS setup on ISDN will be able to provide support for a virtually unlimited number of users. Additional users could be supported by simply adding resources, such as a CPU and additional ISDN connections.

How Does ISDN Work?

The ISDN process begins the minute a subscriber lifts the handset. The phone line will sound just like any telephone line sounds now—there will be a dial tone; the caller will dial and hear the familiar ring. ISDN will be transparent to the user.

—————————   **Figure 25-3**   —————————

The OSI reference model

7	Application	
6	Presentation	Higher layer protocols
5	Session	
4	Transport	
3	Network	
2	Data Link	Network specific
1	Physical	

The major difference with ISDN is that the call is on a *digital* line. The line will carry voice just like a compact disk contains sound – in digitized form. The voice transmission will be much clearer because of ISDN, like the difference between a vinyl and compact disk recording. Because the information on the line is digitized, you won't need a modem. Instead, you'll need what is called a *network interface device.*

Let's look at this concept from a more technical, but simplified point of view. When a caller picks up the telephone receiver, the ISDN protocol checks the D-channel to ensure it's active before generating a dial tone. The subscriber then keys in the number to be called, and the telephone set accumulates all the digits before sending a SETUP message over the D-channel to the local exchange. This message triggers two activities: First the local exchange sends a message through the ISDN network that results in a designated route and allocates resources to handle the call. Then the local exchange sends a CALL PROC message back through the D-channel to the calling telephone. This indicates a call setup procedure is underway.

When the message from your local exchange reaches the remote exchange, a SETUP message is generated and sent to the destination station. If the telephone can accept a call, it sends an ALERT message back through the network that starts a ring tone at the called set. When the caller lifts the handset, a CONN message is sent back through the D-channel to the calling telephone. The B-channel is now available for a telephone conversation.

Why Has ISDN Taken Over 10 Years to Arrive?

The telephone companies have had digital-ready telephone systems and technology for a number of years. The most common use of digital signals today is found in private line (leased line, or *dedicated*) circuits, which are quite expensive and can only be used from preconfigured end points.

The telephone network does carry voice circuits, in a number of cities, over digital lines such as fiber optics, microwave, satellite, and even copper wire. However, the signal is converted to analog before it reaches your telephone by special equipment installed in the network.

If the telephone network is becoming less analog and more digital, why not just make the network all digital? One reason is that digital signals can carry a lot more information than analog, and providing a digital network without some underlying protocol would simply be a waste of resource. In today's digital circuits, voice traffic is carried at a rate of 64 Kilobits-per-second (Kbps)—over eight times the rate of a modern 9600bps modem. A lot of network capability would be wasted with the use of 9600bps signals over a circuit that was designed for 64Kbps.

THE ISDN USER INTERFACE

ISDN is a dynamic system that can change and mold itself to the particular needs of the user at the moment. The signals carried by ISDN may be a mix of voice, data, and video, up to the capacity of the "pipe" circuit (see Figure 25-4). An ISDN subscriber can access circuit-switched and packet-switched services at the same time.

One unique feature of ISDN services is that whereas other services charge on the basis of connect time, ISDN fees are on the basis of pipe capacity. ISDN may very well prove the end of many consumer-based industries such as multiplexors, concentrators, packet-switchers, modem-sharing devices, and the like.

CCITT defines ISDN services as follows:

- Bearer services (low-level communications)

- Teleservices (higher functions of the OSI Model)

- Supplementary services (value added services)

Bearer Services and Teleservices

The CCITT has defined 12 different ISDN services. They refer to these as "bearer services" (in the U.S. we use the term "carrier services"). These are services that the individual telephone companies (the bearers or carriers of the services) should provide in ISDN.

Five bearer services are to define the capabilities of the 64Kbps data transfer. Three are for packet-mode services ("Virtual Call Permanent Circuit," connectionless communications over a D-channel, and user signaling). The remaining four are for *teleservices.*

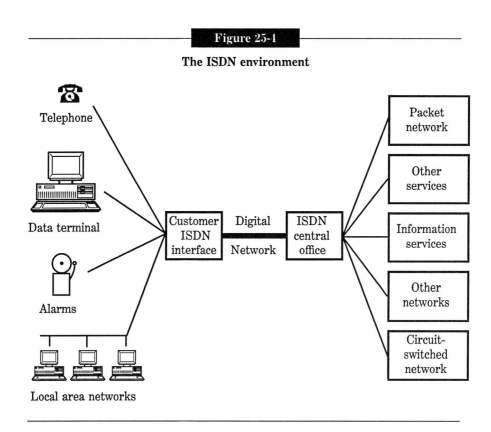

Figure 25-4

The ISDN environment

The ISDN teleservice definitions are currently not well developed. CCITT defined the terms in November 1988, and the definitions have not been completely integrated into the carrier service models. (Also, they are still under the scrutiny of the FCC.) Teleservices may include some of the following.

Telephone Conversations

ISDN would provide a worldwide standard for voice encoding over a digital channel. (As a sales point, the telephone companies like to boast that with ISDN, the caller's telephone number will be displayed at the receiver's end. This would be the ultimate in call-screening.)

Graphics-Based Services

ISDN would also enhance existing graphics-based services. It would allow faster, more practical, graphics-oriented, interactive information utilities. (It would also allow for the Jetsons-style television/telephone that we've all looked forward to since the early 1960s.)

Teletex

Teletex would provide end-to-end computer communications with standard character sets, highlight characters, and communications protocols. This service is designed to transfer electronic documents between office machines with a rich selection of graphic and control characters. It is designed to replace the old telex.

Facsimile

The facsimile standard uses Group 4 for faster transmission of text and graphics images. Group 4 is a black-and-white standard that allows data transfer at 64Kbps, and further resolutions of 200 to 400 pels have been defined. With compression techniques like those used in current Group 3 standards, facsimiles could be sent in a matter of seconds rather than minutes. (See Chapter 26, "Important Technologies and Advancements," for information on fax technology.)

Message Handling

Although the Teletex service offers some features needed to move electronic mail between disparate machines, Teletex lacks some of the features necessary to create, send, route, receive, and store E-mail messages. If you read the section on FidoNet mail in Chapter 5, "E-mail," you may know of some of the problems associated with E-mail systems.

ISDN and CCITT have established some standards for electronic mail systems. Users' needs have been broken down into two main groups: single-system and network E-mail.

Single-System Electronic Mail   This is the simplest and probably the most common type of electronic mail facility, allowing users of a shared system to exchange mail messages. The electronic mail facility is available to anyone logged into the ISDN system.

Network Electronic Mail   Single-system electronic mail can only support exchange of messages between users local to that system. Services to support the routing of mail among like systems, and even systems of different manufacturers, pose a very different set of problems. For this communication to take place, both network mail transfer and mail transfer logic are needed. These standards are provided by the X.400 CCITT protocols.

The X.400 standards regulate many elements involved in transferring a message from one location to its destination. The standard includes the mail header (address), how the mail message is to be encoded and transferred across a network, and how the received message is to be converted and presented to the addressee.

Supplementary Services

Supplementary services are defined independently from the bearer services and teleservices. One possible example would be Caller Identification, which could eliminate the need for login codes and passwords forever. BBS software could pick up this number and log you in automatically. Such an approach might introduce some security problems, however.

Another service might be Busy Call Queuing. After several attempts to log onto a busy BBS, your call could be queued until a channel became available.

ISDN will allow a user to have high-speed access to a gateway through a local area network (LAN). (A gateway is a way to enter another computer system through a computer system—without hanging up and redialing. MCI Mail Service offers a gateway to the Telix system and to CompuServe.) ISDN will provide a gateway to host systems and BBS systems; ISDN calls these systems Enhanced Services Vendors.

You may still call into a BBS that has not yet subscribed to ISDN. ISDN will provide compatibility with analog-based telephone and data communications equipment; in fact, analog users may call an ISDN-based computer, fax, or telephone.

HOW DO I GET ISDN?

ISDN will be sold by telephone companies as a service, although as yet many telephone companies know little about ISDN. Their sales force has been focused principally on the voice/home use, and not the computer angle. (If, after reading this chapter, you do call a telephone company for information on ISDN, you're apt to know more than the service representative.)

To use ISDN, you will need a network adapter or interface. For now, the telephone carrier will supply this device. As ISDN becomes more widespread, outside manufacturers will supply the hardware. Software will also be needed.

BRI and PRI

As has been proposed, the ISDN service will be offered in two packages, Basic Rate Interface (BRI) and Primary Rate Interface (PRI).

The Basic Rate Interface (see Figure 25-5) provides two B-channels (two circuits of 64Kbps), and one D-channel (16Kbps). The D-channel provides status and control information to the ISDN network; however, it may also be used for low-speed data communications. The B-channels are used for applications like digital telephone services, Group 4 fax communications, LANs, data communications, and alarm services.

Figure 25-5

Basic Rate Interface (BRI)

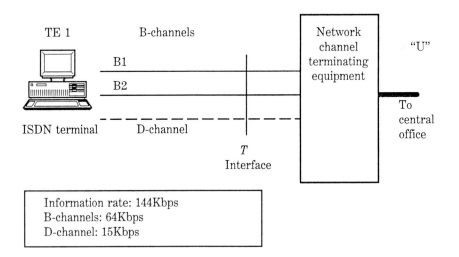

Information rate: 144Kbps
B-channels: 64Kbps
D-channel: 15Kbps

The Primary Rate Interface (see Figure 25-6) is based on the DS1 transmission rate of 1.544 million bps. PRI consists of 23 B-channels, and one 64Kbps D-channel. The B-channels can be used as 23 individual 64Kbps communications lines, or bundled together to form a 3854Kbps H0 channel, or all 24 channels can be bundled together to form a single 1.536Mbps H11 channel. These bundles could be used for bulk data transfer from one computer to another, or for compressed video transfer.

BRI fills the homeowner's need for a telephone and a videotex terminal; PRI offers business users a greater degree of flexibility.

Figure 25-7 depicts the CCITT ISDN reference model. The central office (CO) is linked to your equipment (telephones, computers, fax, and so on) through the *U* Interface. The *U* Interface can run at the basic or primary rate. The basic rate is 160Kbps, consisting of two 64Kbps B-channels, one 16Kbps signaling and control channel, and a 16Kbps channel for framing, synchronizing, and loop control. The total BRI operates at 144Kbps. A primary rate is either 1.544Mbps (North America) or 2.048Mbps (Europe).

Figure 25-6

Primary Rate Interface (PRI)

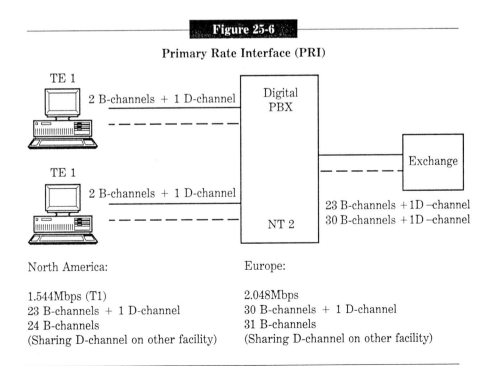

TE 1

2 B-channels + 1 D-channel

Digital PBX

TE 1

2 B-channels + 1 D-channel

NT 2

Exchange

23 B-channels +1D –channel
30 B-channels +1D –channel

North America:

1.544Mbps (T1)
23 B-channels + 1 D-channel
24 B-channels
(Sharing D-channel on other facility)

Europe:

2.048Mbps
30 B-channels + 1 D-channel
31 B-channels
(Sharing D-channel on other facility)

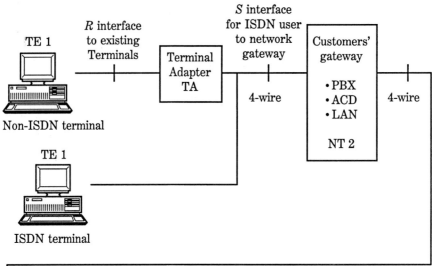

Figure 25-7

CCITT ISDN reference model

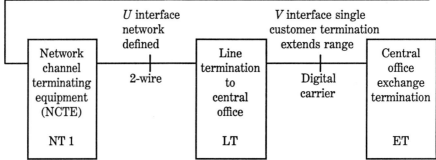

TE — Terminal equipment
TA — Terminal adapter
NT1 — Network
NT2 — Termination
LT — Line termination
+ Reference point

The *U* interface is in turn connected to the four-wire *S* interface. The *S* interface connects the ISDN terminal to the network terminating equipment (NT1). The *S* interface can support up to eight terminals that are accessing the BRI. The *T* interface is used when NT2 equipment is present, typically in the business environment. The *T* interface (see Figure 25-8) allows the customer to connect a PBX (Private Branch Exchange) or LAN to the NT1 device. Non-ISDN terminals (those with RS-232 connectors) may still be used if connected to a terminal adapter (TA), which connects to the *S* interface.

For example, in the typical home the NT2 equipment would be unnecessary because all the services could be provided over a single link. On the other hand, the business network would have a larger number of terminals, so more than one *S* interface would be needed, and the NT2 interface would become necessary to provide intelligence to distinguish between the *S* interfaces. The NT2 equipment would typically be a PBX.

Some other terms you may hear are TE1 and TE2 equipment. TE1 equipment is an ISDN-ready phone, data communications terminal, or a computer interface card that supports ISDN connection. TE2 refers to RS-232 (serial) equipment that must be attached to an ISDN network via a terminal adapter.

THE FUTURE OF ISDN

ISDN currently relies entirely on the 64Kbps building block. The question is: Will ISDN be the telecommunications platform of the future? The answer depends on how well ISDN evolves to meet the increasing demand for

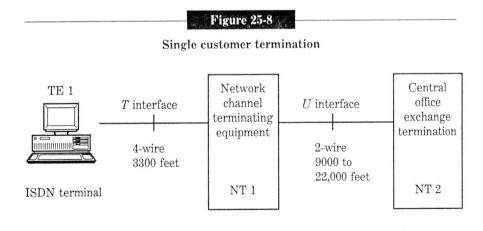

Figure 25-8

Single customer termination

TE 1	*T* interface	Network channel terminating equipment	*U* interface	Central office exchange termination
	4-wire 3300 feet		2-wire 9000 to 22,000 feet	
ISDN terminal		NT 1		NT 2

bandwidth. Many believe ISDN is too slow to handle the demands of video- and graphics-based applications. It remains to be seen how much longer text-based information systems will be the standard delivery system of choice. User interface software is leaning heavily towards graphics. Networks and LANs will be hard pressed to keep up.

Many have dubbed ISDN "I Still Don't Know," or "I See Dollars Now." That communicating in a single environment would be faster and easier via ISDN is the plain truth. Costly software to convert from one format to another, or translate from one protocol to another, would be unnecessary. There would be no problems of international modem incompatibility. Telecommunications would be simplified to a level where anyone could utilize the system.

ISDN offers the most hope for these progressive steps. The OSI model is a good first reference standard, but OSI cannot provide all the versatility that is needed. There must exist some international standard beyond the control of computer hardware vendors that will guarantee the technology to move information in whatever form it may take—unimpeded by costly conversions and unhampered by the inability of one machine to talk to another.

BISDN

One bright spot for the future of ISDN is *broadband ISDN,* or BISDN. BISDN offers low-cost, high-speed transmission facilities. Equipment needed to support BISDN will not likely be available until 1995 and beyond. Broadband ISDN offers support for wide area networks, graphics, video, high-definition TV, and bulk file transfer.

How fast is BISDN? The standards have yet to be written, but BISDN may offer speeds that could deliver the entire written works of all mankind to your machine in less than 60 minutes. BISDN will no doubt bring the additional problem of information overload, and new software will be needed to appropriately distill the data.

SIGNALING SYSTEM 7: TOMORROW'S PHONE

The debate continues on ISDN. Meanwhile, individual Regional Bell Operating Companies (RBOCs) are moving forward because CCITT, the international commission, has issued a standard known as No. 7 Signaling Standard. This is the networking method used internationally to connect ISDN systems. All U.S. RBOCs are using it to avoid compatibility problems.

No. 7 Signaling Standard describes a network system for interconnections. When you pick up your phone to make a call, you generate data signals that tell the network to find a path to the number called. The network finds a path, rings the other party, and then disconnects the path when you are done. That process is called signaling, and under No. 7 Signaling Standard it can do a lot more than just hook your phone up to someone else's.

A CLASS Act

One RBOC, Pacific Bell, now provides Signaling System 7 services under the name CLASS, for Custom Local Area Signaling Services. Other local Bell companies may use other names, but they're all essentially the same because they all use the same System 7 international standard. Here are some brief descriptions of Pac Bell's CLASS services:

Repeat Dialing When you get a busy signal, you'll be able to press a two-digit code to redial the number until you connect. Then you hang up. The system checks both your number and the number you called, every 45 seconds for up to 30 minutes. When both numbers are clear, the system rings you to initiate the call. You pick up the phone and the system rings the number you were trying to reach.

Call Return This service turns your phone into a personal secretary. Have you ever picked up a telephone right after it stops ringing, only to get the dial tone? Maybe you were in the shower or just getting home from the office.

Call Return is a service that tells you the phone number of the caller you missed, and if you wish, returns the call automatically. If that number is busy, you can use the Repeat Dialing function. With this entire process, you never will need to actually dial the number yourself!

Phone Number I.D. A device attached to your phone will display the area code and number of the calling party when your bell rings.

Priority Ringing This service lets you program up to ten different calling numbers into the system, to assign each a unique ring. Use this to monitor the phone for important calls, or to identify calls to specific persons in the household, such as the kids.

Select Forwarding   Select Forwarding lets you specify that incoming calls from certain numbers should be forwarded to another phone number, perhaps a neighbor's house or another office. You can use the familiar Call Forwarding service to send most calls to one number, perhaps a secretary's phone. Select Forwarding can then route other specified callers to a completely different number.

Call Tracing   With Call Tracing you can enter a code to trace disturbing or threatening calls. The system will hold the calling number and call record it in a secure database (to protect everyone's rights). If you then file a police complaint, the information can be released to law enforcement agencies.

Call Blocking   When you do not wish to speak with someone, you can program the phone not to ring for calls from a specific number. The calling party hears a recorded announcement: "We're sorry, the party you are calling is not accepting this call. Thank you." It will be a good way to get the message through to persistent salespeople and other pests.

Call Privacy   This is the other side of the Call Blocking feature—it holds your own number confidential when you place a call. You might use this service when calling, say, an insurance company for quotes, if you didn't want them to have your phone number.

Some Unexpected Wrinkles

A spinoff of Murphy's Law (from a French writer named Jacques Ellul) says that any new technology will create at least as many problems as it solves. Though ISDN and No. 7 Signaling Standard haven't been around long enough to prove Murphy and Ellul correct, some unexpected problems are beginning to show up.

For example, the Phone Number I.D. service is very like the system used by long-distance services to calculate billing information. To turn a profit from this data, these companies will sell the calling number to firms that want to identify instantly the accounts of people who call them.

It's very similar to the System 7 Phone Number I.D. service. So far only 25 companies with active toll-free 800 numbers have bought the pre-System

7 Phone Number I.D. service, and no one has accused them of abuse. American Express discovered an interesting fact, though—people get upset if they think their calls reveal too much about them. American Express service people had to stop greeting callers by name because callers did not respond well to it. Now AmEx representatives first ask for the caller's name, and then seem magically to know all about the account number, balance due, recent payments, and so forth. People like to think that revealing their true name is optional.

Call Privacy will let System 7 callers keep their cover, so this time the new technology brings its own remedy. Ironically, it won't block the older automatic number delivery system that caused such problems for the American Express customer service department.

CHAPTER TWENTY-SIX

Important Technologies and Advancements

As in most books that try to cover everything under the sun, there are some leftover topics that don't fall into a specific category. This chapter covers fax machines, fax modems, packet radio and packet-switching networks, high-speed modems, satellite BBSs, and a few other interesting topics. Don't pass this chapter by without at least reading about packet radio, whatever you do.

FAX AND YOU

Today's fax machines cost a fraction of what their early counterparts did, and with well-defined standards, they are almost universally compatible. Understandably, the fax market has exploded. Now, more than ever, people will pay for immediate information. They are sold on the pitch that the time lost waiting for information can often be the factor that costs them that competitive edge. In fact, fax has become a necessity, period.

Fax transmission has all the immediacy of a phone call. It provides a hardcopy output for the files. Fax machines take advantage of decreased long-distance charges, and many machines offer features that further reduce the costs. It costs no more, per minute, to send a fax than it does to call. (Best of all, there's no chit-chat or music when you're on hold.)

Compare the immediate, inexpensive delivery fax machines provide, with overnight couriers that are usually late. Is it any wonder that in the U.S., 2.5 million installed fax machines transmitted 30 billion pages of information in 1989? The projections are that by 1992, 7 million machines will be in place, and there will be more than 58 billion pages zipping across the phone lines (according to the American Facsimile Association). We'll hardly get a word in edgewise.

A History of the Facsimile

The facsimile machine is on its way to becoming as universal as the photocopier. It seemed to come from nowhere, but it actually has quite a history.

The technology was born in 1842. Alexander Bain, a Scottish physicist and clockmaker, produced the first facsimile device. It was a primitive machine that combined synchronized electrical pendulums to transmit a crude image of a drawing over an electric wire. As the pendulums swung, they created a brown stain on chemically treated paper. Although an astounding device for its time, Bain's Electrochemical Recording Telegraph never made a place for itself in the world of commerce (or anywhere else, for that matter).

A Use for Fax

In the mid-1930s, the facsimile experienced its first commercial application. In 1934, the Associated Press introduced a wire service that distributed both text and photos. Until World War II, this was one of the few commercial applications for facsimile technology. During the war, the government used it extensively in the transmission of maps, orders, and weather charts. After the war this use was adapted to applications in law enforcement.

The use of the facsimile had broadened, although it was still restricted to only a few key markets. The analog device was large, expensive, slow, difficult to use, and produced poor-quality documents. Gradually, the technology improved. In 1952, Dr. Robert Wernikoff developed a way to transmit facsimile digitally. In 1961, with FCC-approved microwave transmission,

AT&T announced a low-cost, wideband transmission service. This made facsimile economically feasible for everyday business applications.

Throughout the 1960s, companies like Xerox, AT&T, and Magnavox announced and improved facsimile machines for general office applications. By 1973 nearly 30,000 facsimile machines were in use in the United States. Not all of these machines were compatible. Users found themselves saddled with an office machine that had a limited range of communication.

CCITT Arrives on the Scene

In the 1970s, the issue of compatibility was taken on as a challenge by The United Nations forum known as the Consultative Committee for International Telephony and Telegraphy (CCITT; see the index for other references). CCITT established a compatibility standard for Group I machines in 1974; these machines used analog transmission to transmit a page in six minutes. Group II standards, set in 1976, applied to machines that also used analog transmission, but transmitted a page in three minutes.

Japan Takes Over

While the CCITT was addressing compatibility internationally, Japan entered the facsimile market to offer technological advancements. Japan's interest in facsimile was based on its need to provide improved image transmission for its pictorial-based alphabet, *kanji*. To write kanji, a person must have command of thousands of characters. Such a language makes typewriters and telex systems virtually useless.

The Japanese needed a more graphic method to transmit written information. The country's success with electronics proved invaluable, as Japanese manufacturers replaced mechanical parts of facsimile machines with complex electronic circuitry. By the end of the decade, Japan was a leading manufacturer of facsimile machines, and many United States companies were marketing the Japanese products. Today, Japan has more facsimile machines in use than any other country in the world.

Meanwhile, Back at the CCITT

The CCITT was still busy establishing standards. In 1980, it set the guidelines for the Group III machines most commonly used today. These machines use digital technology, transmitting a page in less than one minute. They offer superior copy quality and a variety of automated features. Group III was the cause of the facsimile explosion being experienced today.

Facsimile Technology and Today's Market

In its broadest definition, *facsimile* is a way to send an exact copy of a printed document over telephone lines. Fax can be compared technologically to a copier that has its paper plate in New York and its output tray in Chicago. Like a copier, a facsimile machine transmits the image of a document and its content. With a fax you can transmit text, graphs, charts, drawings, photos, and signatures.

The facsimile machine includes a scanner, a transmitter, a receiver, and a printer. The scanner converts the black and white images on a page into a digital bit stream of on/off signals. The transmitter sends these signals over telephone wires to the receiving fax machine. The receiver captures the signal, reassembles it into black and white images, and prints the images on the receiving facsimile's printer.

Group III Facsimile Machines

Today almost all Group III facsimile machines are able to scan, transmit, receive, and print automatically. Many offer a variety of features that make fax machines practically foolproof. Most Group III machines are no more complicated to operate than the office copier. Automatic controls simplify even the most complicated features. Fax machines are also among the most reliable of all office machines. They contain so few moving parts that under normal working conditions there is little to break.

These machines can be categorized and defined by their features and price tags. Some of the features are basic variations, and some are cost-increasing frills.

Image Resolution

Image resolution is a function of the document scanner. The higher the resolution, the clearer the scanned image. Resolution is defined by horizontal lines per inch and vertical dots per inch. Standard resolution is 100 lines by 200 dots. Many machines also offer fine resolution (200 lines by 200 dots), and superfine resolution (200 lines by 400 dots, or even 400 lines by 400 dots).

Logically, superfine resolution is the ultimate. It can offer images clearer than those of a laser printer. Superfine, however, is a feature that only works between two machines of the same brand. So what seems like a real advantage may disappear in practice.

Gray Scale

If your faxing plans include transmitting photographs, you will want to consider a machine that offers gray scale. *Gray scale* is a function of the image scanner. It is available in 16-level and 64-level options. The more levels available, the finer the distinction between shades of gray.

The scanner breaks down the surface of the document into picture elements or *pixels*. Gray scale allows the scanner to assign each pixel a value that corresponds to a shade of gray. These values are stored, and when the image is reconstructed, they provide a representation of the original photo.

Gray scale uses a lot of memory, and will raise the price of the machine. It does provide a very nice facsimile of photographs.

Printing and Paper

All fax machines have a print mechanism, and most of these use thermal printing techniques. *Thermal printing* uses heat to burn an image onto paper that has a heat-sensitive coating. The heated chemical gives the paper an unpleasant odor. The paper comes to the user on large, 98-foot rolls, so it has a tendency to curl. The paper will curl less if you use the 328-foot rolls that some machines accommodate. (This paper smells bad, too.)

The image on fax paper tends to fade over time, so facsimiles are not appropriate for long-term storage. Many fax users use their copy machine to photocopy incoming faxes onto plain bond paper.

Some fax machines use a *thermal transfer ribbon* to print on plain paper. The thermal ribbon is heated by the transfer device, and the heat causes the ribbon to transfer carbon material onto paper. The heating element never directly touches the paper. The paper on these machines also comes in large rolls. The only exception is the Xerox FAX, which uses cut sheets, but even those sheets don't look like bond paper.

Laser Printers

Laser printers in fax machines give you true plain-paper output. Some Group III machines include laser printers; these are among the most expensive of the group. All Group IV machines include laser printers, but these are not yet widely used.

Voice/Data Switch

A voice/data switch can distinguish between voice and data activity on the phone line. If it detects a machine's tones, it activates the fax device. If it detects voice traffic, it ignores the call. A voice/data switch is necessary if the fax and telephone will share the same phone line. It is less important if the fax will have its own dedicated line.

Group III Fax Features

Group III machines offer many features. As usual, you'll find that the more money you spend, the more features you get. Even the most basic machine now comes with a built-in telephone handset. The least expensive devices lack little things like a paper cutter, a document feeder, and advanced phone features.

Paper Cutter

Having to use large rolls of paper without a paper cutter is extraordinarily annoying. If your fax receives a dozen documents of various lengths during the night, your morning then begins with a large, curled pile of thermal paper spilling out of the machine, across the table, and onto the floor. For a few dollars more your fax machine can automatically separate the pages for you as it receives them.

Document Feeder

A document feeder allows the machine to do another mundane task for you. Without one, to send a multipage document, you must stand over the machine, poised to insert the next page at the right moment. It's much nicer to place an eight-page transmission into the document feeder and walk away.

Advanced Phone Features
The advanced phone features are available in more costly models.

Automatic Dial This allows you to dial another fax machine without using the telephone handset. It also stores frequently called numbers for dialing at the touch of a button. There are usually at least five storage slots and often as many as forty.

Automatic Retry Your fax machine will automatically attempt to connect with a busy number. The number of attempts and the interval between them are programmable. This is a boon if you send a lot of facsimiles to corporate numbers, or other frequently busy fax machines.

Delayed Transmission This feature sets your fax machine to transmit a document unattended at some later time. This is a good way to take advantage of lower long-distance rates, and to deliver facsimiles to international offices in different time zones.

Transmission Confirmation This feature notifies you that a document has been successfully transmitted. Some machines can provide a written report of all transmissions that includes information about the quality of the line during transmission and a log of incoming and outgoing facsimiles.

There are still other features available to fax users that may be appropriate or even vital to some fax applications.

Sequential Polling
Sequential polling is a way for your fax machine to call a list of other fax machines and request a transmission. If you are the manager of a company with several branches, you may require a daily or weekly operating report. You can direct your employees to leave the reports in their fax machines. During the night or on the weekend, your fax machine can automatically call and retrieve the reports at off-peak rates.

Memory
The most expensive Group III machines offer memory features. Memory not only raises the cost of the machine, but makes the fax more complicated to use. Memory machines store and forward documents to be broadcast to more than one facsimile machine. You can also use a memory machine as

part of a relay broadcast, in which your memory fax receives a message and then acts as a hub in a wheel of fax machines, distributing the same message again and again. Memory also allows your fax to receive a message even if it runs out of paper during transmission. Absence of paper would otherwise shut a fax transmission down, but a memory machine can store the message in memory until you replenish the paper supply.

This same memory function allows the fax to confidentially receive and transmit messages. Users are assigned codes, and facsimiles are encoded for handling only by those authorized users. (Don't expect to find a memory machine for under $2000.)

READ.ME

Fax Applications

The Philadelphia Inquirer recently recounted the story of a boy who waited too long to finish his homework assignment. He needed information about Charles Barkley of the Philadelphia 76ers, so he used his father's fax machine to send his information request to the team's office. The material arrived 30 minutes later on his father's fax, and he attached it to his book report. He is not the only one finding unconventional uses for the technology.

In New York, office workers fax their lunch orders to the corner deli. A supermarket in San Francisco will accept faxed shopping lists, complete with coupons, and deliver the completed order to the customer's home.

Facsimiles have become popular tools in mortuaries to get an obituary to newspaper offices. Prospective job applicants are invited to fax their resumes. And, finally, the crisis line between Washington, D.C. and Moscow now features a fax machine instead of a red telephone.

Still, these applications cannot account for the 2.5 million machines now in use. According to the American Facsimile Association, fax usage breaks down like this:

Insurance	18%	Government	8%
Banking/finance	16%	Advertising/consulting	7%
Manufacturing	16%	Utility	6%
Law	12%	Construction	6%
Retail/wholesale	9%	Medicine	2%

READ.ME

Fax Tips

As with any communications medium, there are ample opportunities to misuse facsimile transmissions. Some simple fax etiquette guidelines now exist, and it is wise to consider them as standards for using these machines politely.

- Include a cover sheet with each transmission. Make sure the cover sheet includes your name, telephone number, fax number, and number of pages in the transmission, including the cover sheet.

- Make the address as complete as possible. Include the recipient's fax and phone numbers, name, and any other details that will get the facsimile properly routed. Don't assume that the recipient received the message just because the transmission was completed — that only means the fax machine received the message and deposited it in the paper tray. What happens next depends on who picks it up, so the more specific your directions, the more likely that your message will get into the right hands.

- When you prepare a document you know will be fax'd again, use large type and plenty of white space. A third- or fourth-generation fax is difficult to read.

- Pay careful attention when you fax pages that contain color, because dark colors can slow transmission considerably.

- Don't use correction tape or fluid on documents to be fax'd. Instead, photocopy the original and send the copy.

- Be sure to remove any staples or clips that could damage the fax machine.

- Don't send unsolicited facsimiles.

Who's Selling Fax to America?

Today's facsimile market is a volatile one, with models arriving and departing all the time. Not surprisingly, virtually all fax machines are manufactured in Japan. There are about 40 companies offering fax machines now; many of these offer the same machine packaged differently. A few vendors account for most of the sales.

Here are the top five fax vendors:

- Canon USA, Inc.
- Murata Business Systems, Inc.
- Pitney Bowes, Inc.
- Ricoh Corporation
- Sharp Electronics Corporation

These vendors each offer a range of products from the simplest, low-cost machines to the most expensive memory units. For people who want to spend less than $2500, here are details of a representative model for each vendor.

Canon USA Fax-270

This machine offers a standard paper cutter and a 30-sheet document feeder. Telephone features include delayed transmission, automatic redial, speed dialing, and sequential polling. The Fax-270 also offers a 14-page document memory and 64 levels of gray scale.

Murata F25

The F25 offers delayed transmission, automatic redial, and speed dialing. It has a 16-page memory, with confidential mailboxes and relay broadcasting. It offers 16 levels of gray scale and an error correction mode. It has a 5-page document feeder, but no paper cutter.

Pitney Bowes 7100

Phone features offered with the 7100 include automatic redial, delayed transmission, and sequential polling. The 7100 has 16 levels of gray scale and a 10-page document feeder.

Ricoh Fax09

The Fax09 is portable, with phone features that are often found on desktop models, such as delayed transmission and automatic redial. It also has a 7-page memory and 64 levels of gray scale. There is no paper cutter, but a 5-page feeder is standard.

Sharp OF-510

The OF-510 offers automatic redial and alternate redial, which allows an alternate number to be stored in the redial memory as a fallback if the first number is not available. It offers delayed transmission and relay broadcasting. It includes a 13-page memory with an automatic electronic cover sheet feature. The OF-510 has 16 levels of gray scale, a 10-page document feeder, and an automatic paper cutter.

THE FAX FUTURE

Manufacturers introduce new models of facsimile machines all the time. With each new wave of products comes new features. Previously, only the most expensive models included options such as 64-level gray scale and memory. Now these options are beginning to trickle down to the lower end of the product range. Just as the models are improving and becoming more advanced, so is the technology.

Group IV

Group IV facsimile represents the trend in transmission facilities that will lead fax down yet another new road. The CCITT established Group IV standards in 1984, so, in theory, they are not new. However, Group IV machines use private digital telephone lines and Integrated Services Digital Network (ISDN) lines (Chapter 25), which are just now falling into place. Today Group IV machines are used only on private networks. When ISDN standards are set, their application base will expand.

Group IV machines transmit a page in less than ten seconds over 56 Kbps or 64Kbps leased or switched lines. They offer the most advanced memory features, such as store and forward, message handling, and out-of-paper receive. Their scanners offer resolutions that range from 200 by 200 to 400 by 400, and they offer advanced-level gray scale. The output from Group IV machines is on plain paper because they all have laser printers. Group IV also offers interfaces for connection with computers and intelligent copiers.

Have Fax, Will Travel

Personal facsimile is a trend that is building as fax machines become smaller and more feature-packed. These small devices, coupled with cellular phones, make it possible to fax documents from virtually any location. They are popular among reporters, for example, who use them to file stories from the field. Personal fax machines usually weigh less than 15 pounds and often include a carrying case. They are sometimes packaged with a copier and an executive telephone.

Fax Plus Copy Machine

Other fax machines combine facsimile and a photocopier. Their advantages include the convenience of two office machines in one, guaranteed plain paper output for your facsimile, and transmission capabilities for your copier.

Color Faxing

Color faxing is just beginning to appear on the market. StarSignal of Campbell, CA, is offering a machine called ColorFax for a hefty price of $19,900. You can use ColorFax as a color scanner, printer, and copier, as well as a fax device. It prints on plain bond paper from a palette of 256 colors. Transmission must be to another ColorFax machine, but takes less than five minutes.

Dedicated Fax Networks

Aside from technological breakthroughs, people will change the way they use fax. Dedicated fax networks are offered (such as MCI Communications Corporation's MCI FAX). These services offer all fax users the advanced features usually associated with the most expensive fax devices. MCI FAX accepts fax messages from any fax machine. Then the message is sent according to the user's requests for special handling.

Electronic mail services such as AT&T Mail also accept text files from PC owners for transmission as fax messages to any Group III fax machine in the world.

PC-BASED FAX

In 1985, Gamma Link, Inc., of Palo Alto, CA, introduced the first PC-FAX board. This board gives the personal computer the same communications opportunities as the stand-alone office fax. Today more than thirty different manufacturers offer PC-FAX boards.

Fax Board Technology

Fax boards are also called *fax modems*. A fax board is a combination of hardware and software designed to convert computer files to fax format. Fax transmission may be between two fax boards, or between a fax board and a fax machine. Like many other add-on computer devices (such as a hard disk card and internal modem), the fax board fits into an expansion slot on the PC's chassis. The software that comes with the card directs the board to convert, store, send, and receive fax files.

The basic features of the fax board work in the same manner as a stand-alone fax machine, with the exception of the hardcopy provision. The computer's printer may be used to print the fax messages, or the messages may be retained in memory. The fax'd document is stored as a graphic file.

A document scanner may also be added to the computer configuration, allowing facsimiles to be read into the computer. In this way the computer is able to duplicate all the features of a stand-alone fax machine.

To Send a Fax

The fax board encodes the file, much like a stand-alone machine scans a page, converting the file into a bit-map. When the message is sent, the board brings the converted file from the disk into the computer's RAM, dials the receiving device, initiates its handshake, and sends the fax file.

To Receive a Fax

The fax board accepts the incoming call and completes the handshake that establishes a link with the sending device. It then receives the fax message and stores it to disk in the fax format.

Fax Board Versus Data Modem

Much of what a fax board does is similar to the function of a data modem, yet it is different from a data modem. You cannot use a data modem to send fax messages, and vice versa.

Data modems are designed to transfer information between two computers. There are a variety of protocols by which modems may communicate. Fax modems do not have a choice of protocols.

Fax modems are faster. Data modems commonly operate at 1200 or 2400bps. The lowest-priced fax modems run at 4800bps, with most boards now available running at 9600bps. Fax boards and fax machines have the ability to drop their speed to adjust to line noise. The user is unaware of the reduction of speed.

Fax Board Applications

In the United States an estimated 42 million personal computers are in use, and approximately 90 million installed telephone lines. There is a tremendous potential market for the PC-based fax board. In 1988, 40,000 boards were sold. According to CAP International of Norwell, MA, there were 92,000 sold in 1989. The estimate for 1990 is that 178,000 units will be purchased by computer users.

Cost

Many fax boards will be purchased by small businesses and for home offices. The fax boards are priced comparatively with other computer peripherals. You can buy a fax board, complete with software, for under $400. An inexpensive fax machine can cost twice as much.

Selecting a Fax Board

There are some considerations in deciding which fax board to purchase. Perhaps the first is the board's configuration.

The focus so far has been on internal fax boards, but external fax modems are also available. Internal boards are more common, and offer background faxing (an important consideration). The internal boards use an expansion slot in your computer; this may be a consideration if space is limited. External fax modems are excellent for portable or lap-top computers. They plug into a serial slot on the computer, just as a modem does. The disadvantage of an external fax modem is that it cannot operate in the background.

Background Function

Background fax operation is an important consideration. Without it, the fax board will seize control of the computer every time a fax is transmitted or received. This can interrupt work and cause data loss.

Fax boards with a true background operation include their own coprocessor right on the board. Some products claim true background operation; however, they need so much power for RAM-intensive functions such as file conversion that they don't allow other work to be performed while they are in transmission. Without true background operation, a fax board essentially turns your computer into a large, costly, dedicated fax machine.

Transmission Speed

With few exceptions, speed is a price-dependent feature. The lower-priced fax boards often run at 4800bps. More expensive boards offer 9600bps transmission. The faster the speed, the less transmission time. If most of your faxing is long distance, a very fast fax board might pay for itself. If speed isn't a consideration, you can save several hundred dollars on your board purchase.

Software

Friendly software is the key to everyday fax board use. The fax board functions depend on its software, not on its hardware. Unlike the simpler fax machine, fax boards require more user interaction.

Look for FAX software with straightforward menus. Ask for a demo, and try to use it yourself. The software should be easy to understand, logical, and fairly self-explanatory. Remember, the fax board won't do much but take up space and collect dust if you can't figure out how to use it.

Scanner Port

Finally, consider whether the board offers a scanner port. Without a scanner, your fax board can only send resident files from your computer. If the board doesn't have a port, another expansion slot will be needed. With the fax board occupying one slot, your internal hard disk another, plus a modem and perhaps a mouse, your computer chassis would be jam-packed.

Even if you decide now that you don't need a scanner, you may want one in the future. The price has dropped drastically in the last few years; full-page scanners begin at about $700, and are still dropping.

Scanner features vary, but all include software, and can scan a page as large as 8 1/2 by 14 inches. In addition, most offer dithering for scanning gray levels, and optional OCR software for scanning text as well as graphics.

Here are some companies that offer scanners:

Princeton Graphics   They offer the LS-300, at a list price of $1095. It features a full-page scanner with a resolution range of 15, 100, 200, or 300 dots per inch. The LS-300 features scaling, pixel editing, rotation, and 32-level dithering.

Microtek   Their machine is the MSF-300C, at a price of $1595, with 300-dots-per-inch resolution, 64-level dithering, scaling, and rotation.

The Complete PC   They offer the Complete Page Scanner for $699. This is a 200/300-dots-per-inch scanner that includes SmartScan software for cropping, rotation, scaling, sizing, pixel editing, page layout, and image-merging functions.

Other Scanners   Other scanners are available from Hewlett-Packard and Dest. These products cost more than $2000, placing them in a slightly different market from the lower-cost scanners. The H-P Scanjet is the most popular scanner in this category.

READ.ME

Fax Board Vendors and Products

There are five dominant fax board manufacturers that control 73 percent of the market.

The Complete PC They offer the Complete FAX and Complete FAX 9600, both of which offer a true background operation. Other features include delayed transmission, automatic polling, and broadcasting. The Complete FAX runs at 4800bps, and as the name suggests, Complete FAX 9600 runs at 9600bps.

Both models offer simple-to-use menus, and Epson FX printer emulation. (This software feature allows the fax board to emulate an Epson FX printer by use of a "hotkey.") In addition, facsimiles may be converted from and to PC Paintbrush +, Microsoft Windows Paint, and Dr. Halo II.

The Complete Fax 9600 has a configuration option of adding a 2400 baud Hayes-compatible modem with Bitcom software and a voice mail module, for advanced voice mail features. Our advice is to use Telix (see Chapter 4) instead of Bitcom to get full benefits from the modem.

The Complete Fax 9600 sells for $699. The optional modem is $99, and the voice mail option is $199. The Complete Fax lists for $399. Both products have a two-year warranty.

Gamma Link This was the first company to market a fax board. The GammaFax NA features delayed 9600bps transmission, automatic polling, and broadcasting. It does not have an on-board coprocessor. Another product, GammaFax MC, is a Micro Channel version of the GammaFax NA. Micro Channel versions run with IBM PS/2 Micro Channel models. They also offer the GammaFax CP, which has an on-board coprocessor with 256K RAM.

Gamma Link products include some sophisticated features. Software customization allows you to link a database with the fax board, so that the fax directory is automatically updated as your database changes. The command language allows you to integrate fax into other applications. The key drawback of the advanced features is that they are not for the novice. The software features and the operator's manuals assume a high degree of computer experience.

The prices are: GammaFax NA $495, GammaFax MC $795, and Gamma-Fax CP $1095.

READ.ME

Fax Board Vendors and Products (*continued*)

Hayes Microcomputer Products   The Hayes Fax boards were formerly offered by Quadram. There are a range of products, including both internal and external fax modems, and speeds from 4800 to 9600bps.

The Hayes internal modems include the JT Fax 9600 (9600bps), and the JT Fax-Internal (4800bps). JT Fax 9600 also offers an optional 1200 baud modem and a coprocessor. It is the only one of the Hayes PC fax boards that operates in the background. The JT Fax Macintosh and the JT Fax-External are both external modems, and both run at 4800bps. Prices are: JT Fax 9600 $799, JT Fax-Internal $395, JT Fax-External $495, and JT Fax Macintosh $695.

Intel Corporation (PCEO)   The Intel Corporation's Personal Computer Enhancement Operation (PCEO) offers the Intel Connection Co-processor. This is a 9600bps fax board with an optional 2400 baud modem. A Micro Channel version for use with IBM PS/2 Micro Channel models is also available.

The Connection Co-processor includes a 10Mhz, 80188 coprocessor with 256K of RAM. The board also includes a speaker. When used with another Connection Co-processor, a file transfer is possible rather than a fax transmission. The Connection Co-processor comes with a five-year warranty. It sells for $695, with the optional modem listing for $195. Prices have been dropping. To get current prices in the U.S. or Canada, call 1-800-538-3373 and follow the voice-mail prompts to a human being. If you already have a fax machine, Intel offers a very well-executed fax-back service at 1-800-525-3019 or 503-629-7576. One catalog area there covers the Connection Co-Processor and its add-ins.

The Co-Processor system shines brightest when you call another Co-Processor board. Both fax and file transmissions fly along in the background at 9600bps. Transfers can be scheduled for late at night, unattended. The bundled Send-Off! software handles WordPerfect 5.0 and Lotus 1-2-3 files at the touch of a hotkey. This product seems aimed at home offices that need to trade data with far-flung branch offices or employees in the field. With all outposts connected, you get something like the "everything-in-tune" feeling of an LAN without needing the physical LAN hookup.

Note: In the summer of 1988, Intel began a joint operation with Digital Communications Associates (DCA) to establish the Communicating Applications Specifications (CAS) standard. CAS is anticipated to become the communications architecture for future PC communications. Eventually, many soft-

Fax Board Vendors and Products (*continued*)

ware programs will support CAS. Almost any fax board with a coprocessor can be adapted for supporting CAS.

Datacopy This company, now owned by Xerox, offers a complete 9600/1200 Fax modem with software, for about $695. (This was the first fax modem I ever installed in my system.)

Fax Board Trends

The facsimile technology is on the move. The trend is toward more features, with more integration. The future is certain to be more fax-intensive.

Multichannel Fax Boards

Some manufacturers have developed hardware and software that allow several of their boards to run in one machine. One such company is Brooktrout Technology, Inc., which has recently introduced a two-channel fax board. The AT-sized card can support two simultaneous fax transmissions. The manufacturer claims that as many as six of these boards (allowing twelve simultaneous fax transmissions) can run in an AT-class PC.

Fax boards linked together will extend the fax-handling capabilities of the PC. Additionally, you can also expect to see facsimile combined with other communications features to create a complete communications environment within the PC. Fax board manufacturers are already moving in this direction.

Piggyback Slot

Intel PCEO has included a piggyback slot on its fax board. (Right now this is used exclusively for a 2400 baud data modem option.) This slot is designed to accommodate whatever PC communications functions are now in the works at Intel, and it will be ready when they are.

Fax and Voice Mail

The Complete PC offers a product called the Complete Communicator. This board includes the 9600bps fax board of the Complete Fax 9600, and the 2400 baud data modem option. Plus, it includes a voice mail module that allows the PC to handle data, fax, and voice from a single card. Like the other products from the Complete PC, this voice mail module operates in the background. It offers call transfer, message forwarding, and remote operations from any touch-tone phone. It supports as many as 999 password-protected voice mailboxes.

Fax Server

Software is emerging that will allow a single dedicated PC, equipped with a fax board, to serve as a fax server on a network supporting a whole work group. The dedicated PC will send and receive faxes without inconveniencing anyone. It also provides the additional disk storage to store faxes.

Feature Integration

A product such as the Complete Communicator not only integrates three important communications functions into one PC, it creates a system of shared resources within the PC that is greater than the sum of the individual parts. With one expansion slot, you use a single phone line for voice mail, fax, data, and phone calls. The system is able to share a common phone directory, common distribution lists, and one common user interface for all communications functions.

PC communications in the future will continue this type of integration. Users will want all these features to be available, and they will come to expect them to be easily accessed and easily used.

While the fax technology is definitely a mainstream trend, we think you should also know about something very unusual that might become a future trend: packet radio.

PACKET RADIO

Packet radio is telecommunications without the telephone. Thousands of amateur radio operators or "hams" across the country have kissed Ma Bell and all of her Baby Bells good-bye and are using the radio airwaves for data communications instead of the telephone.

Packet Radio BBSs

The key to amateur packet radio data communications is a network of more than 700 *packet radio bulletin board systems* (or PBBSs) throughout the world that are interconnected by shortwave, VHF, UHF, and satellite links. A PBBS provides all the services you expect to find with a typical phone line computer BBS. Bulletins are posted for all to read; files and computer programs may be uploaded and downloaded. Messages may be sent to other users of the system; and since most PBBSs are part of the packet radio network, messages may also be sent to users of other systems anywhere in the world.

Some PBBSs provide other services, as well. For example, current weather information and user directories are accessible on some systems. A recent addition to the PBBS world is the DOSgate, which allows you to use an MS-DOS computer, regardless of what type of computer you may be using to access the PBBS. With DOSgate, a remote user can run any DOS software, as long as it is not graphic-intensive.

Cost and Equipment

What is the cost of using the amateur packet radio network? Would you believe nothing? Using the packet radio network is as close to free as you are likely to get. The only continual cost you will incur is the cost for electricity to run your computer and ham radio equipment. There is no fee for an amateur radio license, nor is there a fee for using a PBBS or the packet radio network. There is the one-time cost of purchasing the equipment necessary to access the packet radio network—about $750. Also, if time is money, then there is the cost of studying for an amateur radio license.

Assuming you already own a computer, the additional equipment required to access the amateur packet radio network includes a VHF transceiver, an antenna, a cable to connect the antenna to the transceiver, and a terminal node controller (TNC).

The transceiver, or "radio," which typically costs $500, is the device that sends and receives radio signals via the airwaves. An antenna, which transfers radio signals between the transceiver and the airwaves, costs approximately $75, and the cable to connect the antenna to the transceiver costs around $25.

The TNC, the brains of the operation, is the device that permits the computer to communicate over the airwaves via the transceiver and antenna. (The TNC, radio, and antenna together are functionally equivalent to a modem used in a typical personal computer communications system; see Figures 26-1 and 26-2.) A TNC will cost approximately $150.

If you are using your computer with a modem to communicate over phone lines, the same software that you use with your modem can also be used with a TNC. However, if you have no modem with software, there is plenty of free public domain software around for packet radio communications.

The Amateur Radio License

To pass the examination for an amateur radio license requires knowledge of electronic theory, amateur radio regulations, and the Morse code. The required level of expertise in these disciplines is higher with each higher class of license. However, to use the packet radio network to its fullest, you only need the next-to-lowest level of license, the Technician class. The required level of expertise for a Technician is minimal for the Morse code, and the study required for theory and regulations expertise should take two to four weeks of work. (For you Morse code haters, there is a proposal in the works for a new license class requiring no knowledge of the Morse code. As proposed, this new class of license will have packet radio privileges and will require knowledge of theory and regulations at a level similar to or slightly above that of Technician class.)

Free Telecommunications

Today, thousands of hams are enjoying worldwide telecommunications for free. This world is also available to you for a small initial investment of time

Figure 26-1

The typical personal computer communications system

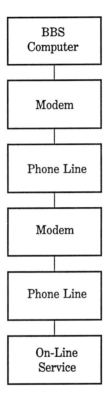

and money. Why not check it out? (You can't afford not to.) For the complete lowdown on amateur packet radio, read *Your Gateway to Packet Radio.* Single copies of this book may be obtained for $15 postpaid from the book's author, Stan Horzepa, 75 Kreger Drive, Wolcott, CT 06716-2702.

The popularity of packet radio telecommunications will be boosted if ISDN and other new services fail to keep the price of telephone data exchange low. Packet radio *is* being boosted by another new technology, the satellite BBS. Let's look at that next.

Figure 26-2

Packet radio computer communications system

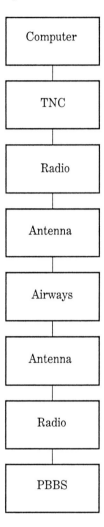

SATELLITE BBSs

Orbiting Bulletin Board Systems or microsats were first conceived on the paper table-napkin of an AMSAT-NA (Amateur Radio Satellite group of

North America) member at a Washington, D.C. meeting in 1987. The discussion that evening centered on producing extremely small, simple, store-and-forward packet radio satellites. The idea was to extend the range of amateur packet radio, and one thing led to another.

Amateur radio satellites go back a lot further than 1987, of course. The first OSCAR (Orbiting Satellite Carrying Amateur Radio) went into space just four years after Sputnik I, in 1961. It was a very simple transmitter that failed within a few weeks. Since 1969, AMSAT groups have launched OSCARs 5 through 13. Two more, which would have been 14 and 15, went up as UOSSATs in January 1990, from England's University of Surrey. OSCARS 16 through 19, the satellite BBSs, went up on that same January 1990, European Ariane launch. The microsats took two years to develop and build, using volunteered material, equipment, and labor.

How Microsats Work

While packet radio is good for point-to-point communications, it takes relay stations to forward data over long distances. With an overhead satellite to gather and transmit messages, global communications became possible.

The microsat orbits the earth four times daily, twice for each hemisphere; to hook up to it, you just wait for the next fly-by in your hemisphere, and listen. When it's overhead, you have 15 minutes to download and upload messages. Someone on the other side of the world can read the message and upload replies when the microsat passes over them. In this way, you can be in touch with any HAM packet radio operator in the world, and it won't cost a thing.

The only limit is the 8MB onboard memory. Messages remain there on a first-in, first-out basis, so if incoming message traffic gets too heavy, the satellite can force messages out before they have been read. In practice, that does not happen, because there are always HAM operators waiting for the next fly-by.

What's coming next? Even now, AMSAT-NA is working on a geostationary packet radio satellite. It will hang in place 23,000 miles up, and allow continuous 24-hour access within its hemisphere. At this writing, its launch date has not been set.

What Microsats Are Made Of

The BBS satellites are miniaturization marvels, weighing about twenty-two pounds packed into a nine-inch cube. Everything about them is elegantly simple—no frills, no waste, no $600 military ashtrays. There are five modules:

- NiCad power batteries recharged by solar cells that cover the cube's surface
- S-Band (70cm) transmitter with up to four watts of power on two channels
- A five-channel receiver
- A fast, XT-class, IBM-compatible computer with 8MB of RAM and a NEC V40 microprocessor, equivalent to an Intel 80186
- A fifth compartment for various experiments

Antennas and Other Materials

Receiving a downlink transmission takes a very simple quarterwave dipole antenna hung out your window, like a coat hanger. The satellite's antennas are much fancier, made from carpenter's tape-measure material donated by the Stanley Tool Company. Everything about these small satellites is a surprise, and everything to make them was donated by individuals and interested companies.

Power

The microsats have no power for maneuvering; everything is done passively. Simple bar magnets keep the satellite oriented to the earth's magnetic field. Photons pressing against the silvered side of the Stanley tape-measure blades keep it spinning at one revolution per hour, fast enough to keep it from getting too hot on one side and too cold on the other.

Equipment You Need to Sign On

To use these orbital BBSs, you'll need a normal transmitter—a two-meter radio will do fine at around 145 MHz. To receive signals you'll need a different unit—a single-side band (SSB), high-frequency (HF), frequency modulated (FM) unit able to receive 70cm (437 MHz) transmissions. (Downlink converters are available if you don't have 70cm coverage.)

A terminal node controller (TNC) does the packetization and addressing required under the CCITT AX25 packet radio standard. You'll need a phase shift keying (PSK) modem that attaches by cable to the TNC, for improved noise resistance.

For More Information

For more information, contact AMSAT-NA, P.O. Box 27, Washington, DC 20055. Other information resources:

BBS   Dr. Jeff Wallack of Carrollton, Texas, runs a BBS dedicated to satellite imaging and to AMSAT-NA activities. Contact the BBS at 1-214-394-7438.

Radio Net   AMSAT-NA sponsors a gathering each Tuesday evening for the latest news and information on the Amateur Space program. Tune to 3840 KHz at 2100 EST, 2100 CST, or 2000 PST. On Sundays, AMSAT-NA nets convene at 1900 Greenwich time on 14.282 and 21.280 MHz.

PACKET-SWITCHING NETWORKS — SPRINTNET, TYMNET, AND OTHERS

On-line information services provide service to thousands of users nationally and internationally. These services use massive mainframe computers connected to an extensive telecommunications network, in addition to the standard telephone system. Direct-dial calls (such as those to an independent BBS) are routed through an ordinary voice-grade line. This is fine for local modem calls—the cost is nominal and the service is usually good. For long-distance modem calls, however, a voice-grade line becomes expensive, and is often of poor quality.

Many on-line services offer an alternative, economical access, such as Sprintnet and TYMNET. Users may dial a local phone number and connect with a *packet-switching network*. The packet-switching network can handle all communications from the caller's local calling area to the location of the on-line service's main computer—at a fraction of the cost of a standard call.

A *packet-switching system* is a way to bundle groups of characters into little electronic envelopes, or *packets*. These packets are marked with an identification number and sent off into the data stream. They are transferred from computer to computer until they reach their destination. The packet-switching network tries to use the most efficient route to the on-line service's computer.

This may sound complicated, but to the user the process is usually transparent. You call a telephone number, and the packet-switching network connects to the on-line service. Packet-switching networks allow low-cost access for many of the commercial on-line services: CompuServe, Dialogue, Delphi, BIX, MCI Mail, GEnie, The WELL, Minitel, and so forth.

Protocols

Some file transfer protocols seem to perform better than others on packet-switching networks. At this writing, Zmodem is the most effective.

Performance

The performance of packet-switching networks varies widely from city to city, and sometimes from call to call. Choose a service based on the results you get. One system might work better than another for your particular configuration.

Several on-line services are building or expanding their own packet-switching networks. One service, MCI Mail, offers a nationwide toll-free (800) number for network access, and yet thousands of their users are still dialing packet-switching numbers out of habit. It's a good idea to check for changes to access numbers, and keep your telecommunications program's dialing directory up to date.

How Packet-Switching Works

As mentioned, the packet-switcher can connect you to the host computer transparently. You can use commands to control its performance. It is possible to increase performance when uploading larger files, by turning off the echoing of characters to your terminal. This half-duplex operation requires less of the system's resources and increases overall throughput. Some packet-switching systems do not recognize flow control commands like XON/XOFF by default, but you can tell the network to respond to these commands, instead of just passing them through and ignoring them. The network may also allow you to enable or disable upload buffers.

Packet-switching networks are a series of nodes set up in cities across the country. Each node is actually a computer system, with two connections to other nodes. If one of these connections fails or is otherwise shut down, the system will automatically use the alternate connection.

A system of hardware and software called a PAD (packet assembler/disassembler) is used to separate data into small fixed-length data packets. By making all these packets uniform and giving them an ID tag, it is possible for large numbers of calls to share the same transmission line. One of the popular protocols, X25, allows for 4095 calls to be active simultaneously.

A PAD consists of a series of "bits" that include the information you transmitted and PAD identification information. The information you send and receive is constantly diced up and tagged, passed along from node to node, and checked for errors. If an error occurs anytime during the process, the entire packet is retransmitted. Each PAD is sent by the best possible route at that instant. Part of your file may come from New York, and another part from California.

Typically, each packing-switching node supports only one speed. You will find that there are different phone numbers for 300, 1200, and 2400bps service. Only a few nodes support 9600bps service. Once your data is in the data stream, the network may transfer the information at speeds as great as 56Kbps. This speed is so fast that it is impossible to tell one route from another. Each PAD appears to take the same time to travel from the host to your PC.

Besides transmitting at speeds greater than your original connection, packet-switching networks operate at 7-bit, even parity. If you are using a packet-switching network to connect to another PC or public BBS, you may need to change your communication parameters back to 8-bit, no parity, before you can connect to the system you are trying to reach.

Packet-Switching Network Commands

Don't issue commands that make changes to your network's control settings unless you are experiencing a particular problem. If the host isn't receiving all the characters you are transmitting, you may be able to set your communications program to add a brief delay after each line it transmits. Turning on your network's half-duplex mode and enabling XON/XOFF flow control will help with large file uploads.

Of course, if you are having a problem and can't figure it out, you can always dial the customer service voice line and ask for assistance.

Sprintnet Command Summary

When you first connect with Sprintnet, you are in the Network Command mode by default. This mode can be identified by the "at" sign (@) prompt. You can connect to any one of the Sprintnet ports by entering **C** for CONNECT, and the port number you want. Sprintnet takes over from there and puts you into the Data Transfer mode.

When you want Sprintnet to do something, go back to the Network Command mode by pressing ENTER, then @, and then ENTER again. You are then back to the Network Command mode. Some of the commands available are

Command	Function
@ HALF	Turns on half-duplex mode
@FULL	Turns on full-duplex mode
ENAB FLOW	Enables flow control
DISAB FLOW	Disables flow control
DTAPE	Disables upload buffer
TAPE	Enables upload buffer
TEST CHAR	Enters Test mode

By sending the break character, you can return to the Data Transfer mode. You will need to check the documentation for your telecommunications program to find out how to do this.

A free booklet with limited explanations of the Sprintnet commands is available from Sprintnet. To receive a copy, write Sprintnet, 12490 Sunrise Valley Drive, Reston, VA 22096; or call them at 1-703-689-6000 or 1-800-336-0437.

TYMNET, Inc. Command Summary

TYMNET is different from other packet-switching networks. The main distinction is that you must press a key to "wake it up." Once connected, ignore any extraneous characters you may see on your screen. Type **a.** TYMNET will respond with the node and port number you are connected to, and a "Please log in:" message. Some of the TYMNET commands are

CTRL-H	Enters half-duplex mode
CTRL-I	Selects shortest path to destination
CTRL-R	Enables XON/XOFF mode
CTRL-P	Even parity enable
CTRL-W	Wide login string
CTRL-X	Enables upload buffer and flow control

READ.ME

Packet-Switching: Pros and Cons

Some of the advantages of packet-switching are

- Greater line efficiency, so more information can be sent in a shorter period of time
- Data concentration
- Priorities can be set up for certain types of packets, so more important information does not have to wait for less important information to be sent

The disadvantage of current public packet-switching networks is that, although they are well-suited to certain kinds of applications, they cannot provide efficient communications as line speeds increase. The problem is the X25 standard, which was published by the CCITT almost 20 years ago when use of 1200bps modems was just becoming widespread. The X25 standard covers public data networks and packet-switchers like Sprintnet and TYMNET. Unfortunately, X25 uses two obsolete concepts:

- **The 128 byte (octet) packet** This packet size is too small a window to efficiently handle the line turnaround of higher-speed modems. In fact, turning the line around can take longer than sending the packet.
- **Virtual circuits** Virtual circuits are set up once for each session and remain in effect until the session is closed by the user. Virtual circuits take time to establish, and cannot avoid congestion delays. If the link fails, so does the session.

A booklet entitled *How to Use TYMNET* is offered free of charge from TYMNET, Inc., 2560 North First, San Jose, CA 95131, 1-408-922-0250 or 1-800-872-7654.

HIGH-SPEED MODEMS

The first modems, typically acoustic couplers, were quite slow by today's standards, capable of transmitting only 110, 150, or 300bps. Later modems operated at a much more usable 1200bps. Not long after that, 2400bps modems appeared on the scene; 2400 and 1200bps modems now make up the bulk of the installed base of PC modems today. Compatibility among 300, 1200, and 2400bps modems of different manufacturers is rarely a problem, since most, if not all, modems use the same modulation techniques. In addition, most 1200 and 2400bps modems are downwardly compatible, switching to lower speeds when required.

Enter high-speed modems. The currently evolving standard is for 9600bps. Using new protocols and data compression techniques, many of these modems achieve an effective speed much greater than 9600bps, and in some cases as high as 18,000bps. Unfortunately, there is not a great deal of compatibility among current high-speed modems. This is due mostly to the lack of a popular standard for manufacturers to follow when these modems were first introduced. And since no modem manufacturer has yet emerged as a clear leader in this area, there isn't even a de facto standard.

As a result, manufacturers have implemented schemes for fast data transmission that are largely unique to each brand and/or model. While this has given us new and creative technology, the drawback is a lack of compatibility among brands, making selection of a high-speed modem a somewhat difficult task. The good news is that there does seem to be some agreement on two: the V29 and V32 CCITT standards. (CCITT standards beginning with X are for packet-switching lines; those beginning with V cover data transmission on regular voice lines.)

Implementing these CCITT standards is still expensive. Until it becomes more affordable for personal use, the high-speed modem will see the most action in the corporate environment, where it is ideal for data transfer and remote PC application support. If your modem use is more casual, perhaps just to browse local BBS systems, you should probably consider a more general purpose modem.

Modulation Techniques: V29 and V32

There are two types of modems: full-duplex and half-duplex. Full-duplex modems simultaneously send and receive data; half-duplex modems transmit in one direction at a time, having to "turn the line around" to reverse the flow of data. Many PC users are already familiar with full-duplex communications if they have used 300, 1200, or 2400bps modems.

CCITT V29 and V32 are the two main modulation standards for 9600bps modems. V29 is the half-duplex standard. V32 addresses full-duplex modulation, and offers more capabilities and compatibility across vendors than V29.

The cost of implementing the technology required to enable high-speed, full-duplex communication on standard telephone networks makes true V32 modems more expensive. However, V32 modem prices have dropped steadily since their introduction and are sure to become competitive with currently popular 9600bps modems.

These more popular 9600bps modems implement clever approaches that use less expensive modulation techniques based on the V32 and V29 standards. The modems that use these techniques emulate full-duplex operation and are sometimes referred to as pseudo-full-duplex modems.

Error Correction and Data Compression: ARQ, MNP, and V42

You have experienced firsthand the noise that can be introduced into a phone conversation. The same type of noise can affect data transmissions. High-speed modem signals are particularly susceptible to telephone line noise, making it necessary to implement methods of detecting and correcting errors. Three commonly used error-correction methods are ARQ, Microcom's MNP, and CCITT V42.

In the past, error correction was largely the job of communications software. With software, however, error detection and correction is usually only in effect when transmitting data using a file transfer protocol (such as Xmodem or Kermit). With high-speed modems, hardware error correction introduced an error-free link during the whole session, not just during file transfers. Software error correction takes processing time and so causes delays; hardware error correction can eliminate delays. Coupled with hardware-based data compression, hardware error correction can actually increase data throughput.

Using an error-corrected link, standard file transfer protocols supported by communications software can still be used, since this type of link is transparent to the file transfer protocol. In some cases, however, it is necessary to adjust the timing of the software protocol so that it is "loose" or "sloppy." This is usually done through a command in the communications program, or with a setup panel, which essentially tells the software protocol to wait a longer period of time for acknowledgment of packets.

ARQ (automatic request for repeat) is a basic error-correction technique utilized by modems such as the US Robotics HST-series and Hayes V-series 9600. In this form of error control, transmission errors detected by the receiver cause it to automatically send a Request Repeat signal to the transmitting device. The data is then retransmitted until it is received correctly, or has been transmitted more than a specified maximum number of times.

MNP (Microcom Networking Protocol) offers several levels of error correction. MNP Classes 1, 2, and 3 provide basic error detection and control. Higher levels add techniques that allow faster data transfer. MNP Class 4 adds extensions that allow it to adapt to line conditions, and Class 5 offers data compression. MNP is in widespread use, and is supported by many on-line services such as CompuServe, GEnie, and MCI Mail, giving those with MNP modems faster and therefore less expensive access to E-mail and on-line information.

MNP works well, but it belongs to Microcom, which sensibly keeps new features to itself for a while before releasing them to competing licensees. Microcom walks a fine marketing line—if few users have MNP, it won't become a standard. If everyone has MNP with no delay, they've obtained without cost what Microcom spent much time and effort to develop. The delayed-release compromise gives Microcom a significant but fair marketing edge. One result is that many modems now offer MNP Classes 1 through 6, but only Microcom modems have MNP Classes 7 through 10. This has helped to keep MNP from becoming a de facto standard like the Hayes AT command set.

What modem vendors needed was a true standard for hardware error control. In 1984, the CCITT appointed a Special Rapporteur on Error Control. Meetings on the topic began in 1985 and have continued since then. Two resulting standards are V42 and V42*bis*; *bis* is a French term denoting an enhancement.

V42, the "parent" standard, sets a streaming error-correction protocol resembling Chuck Forsberg's Zmodem (see Chapter 24). Known as the Link Access Procedure for Modems, or LAPM, V42 is very reliable. V42 Annex A adds MNP Class 1 through 4 error correction to the main body of the standard, allowing V42 modems to talk to MNP modems. Annex A will not be further enhanced. In fact, it may be dropped entirely as the main V42 protocol becomes dominant. Meanwhile, modems that offer only MNP Classes 1 through 4 can advertise V42 compatibility. Although this is not exactly misleading (they can indeed talk to V42 modems), remember the difference when buying a modem.

V42's "Mark II" cousin, V42*bis*, sets a data compression standard that shrinks the size of file transfers by a factor of 3 or 4:1. V42*bis* uses hardware-based Ziv-Lempel compression similar to the popular software compression programs PKZIP and ARC. The Ziv-Lempel technique is patented in the U.S. by Unisys Corporation, which issues licenses in return for what amounts to a token fee. The effect of V42*bis* is to let 9600bps modems transmit effectively at 38,400bps, and 2400bps modems at 9600bps.

When error-correcting modems talk to each other, software protocols like Zmodem actually slow transfers down. If you know the modem on the other end has V42, MNP, or ARQ error correction, use the Ymodem-G software protocol. Ymodem-G leaves error correction to your hardware, and transfers thus go a lot faster.

MNP Error-Correcting Modems

Since MNP error correction is widely used and supported by various information services, it deserves a more detailed discussion here. MNP is designed to conform to the International Organization for Standardization (ISO) Open System Interconnection (OSI) Network Reference Model, known simply as the OSI Model. MNP is concerned with what is called the Link Layer of this OSI schema.

The Link Layer of the OSI Model is responsible for providing reliable data transfer. It uses the Physical Layer to transmit information through the data path. In dial-up data communications, the data transmission of the Physical Layer is performed by "traditional" modems, using standards such as Bell 103, Bell 212A, V22, and V32.

Note: Errors can still creep into hardware-controlled connections. They can occur at either end, in the cable between the serial port and the modem, or in the computer itself. The probability for error is far less than in the phone lines between modems (where errors will be caught), but they will sometimes happen. CRC checking will reveal faulty ARC or ZIP files during decompression, and the occasional blip to ASCII files is not often fatal. Still, you may want to use double care with numerical data, formatted files, or uncompressed binary programs. Several low-overhead protocols like Jmodem (see Chapter 24) can meet this need. Such protocols send large blocks of data between checks and are well-suited for MNP-to-MNP connections.

Performance Comparisons of MNP Classes

MNP is designed for easy implementation on many hardware configurations. Different applications require different cost and performance mixes. MNP is deliberately structured to provide varying levels of performance without sacrificing compatibility. Unlike other protocols, applications that require low-cost solutions can use the simpler, less demanding implementations of MNP; additionally, MNP implementations at all performance levels are compatible with one another. For example, a small application with a simple implementation of MNP can communicate with a more powerful system using a high-performance implementation of MNP.

A description of each MNP performance class follows. The description shows how MNP offers you greater throughput than the basic error-prone communication channel.

Class 1 MNP Class 1 uses an asynchronous, byte-oriented, half-duplex method of exchanging data. Class 1 implementations make minimum demands on processor speeds and memory storage, allowing devices with small hardware configurations to have error-free communication.

The protocol efficiency of a Class 1 implementation is about 70 percent. A device using MNP Class 1 with a 2400bps modem will realize 1690bps throughput. Modern microprocessors have become so powerful that implementations of MNP Class 1 are uncommon in the U.S.

Class 2   MNP Class 2 uses asynchronous, byte-oriented, full-duplex data exchange. Almost all microprocessor-based hardware is capable of supporting Class 2 performance. Common microprocessors selected for MNP Class 2 implementations are Z80s and 6800s.

The protocol efficiency of a Class 2 implementation is about 84 percent. A device using MNP Class 2 with a 2400bps modem will realize 2000bps throughput.

Class 3   MNP Class 3 uses synchronous, bit-oriented, full-duplex data exchange. The synchronous, bit-oriented format is inherently more efficient than the asynchronous, byte-oriented format. In ASYNC, it takes 10 bits to represent 8 data bits, because of the required start and stop bits; the synchronous format does not need these bits. The user still sends data asynchronously to the Class 3 modem; meanwhile, the modems communicate with each other synchronously.

The protocol efficiency of a Class 3 implementation is about 108 percent. A device using MNP Class 3 with a 2400bps modem will realize 2600bps throughput. At Class 3 performance, the MNP protocol "rewards" the user for using an error-correcting modem by producing 8 percent extra throughput over an ordinary modem without MNP.

The MultiTech 224E modem implements MNP Class 3.

Class 4   MNP Class 4 introduces two new concepts, Adaptive Packet Assembly and Data Phase Optimization, to further improve the performance of an MNP modem. During data transfer, MNP monitors the reliability of the transmission medium. If the data channel is relatively error free, MNP assembles larger data packets to increase throughput. If the data is introducing many errors, then MNP assembles smaller data packets. (This is Adaptive Packet Assembly.) Although smaller data packets increase protocol overhead, they also decrease the throughput penalty for retransmissions. The result of smaller data packets is more data successfully transmitted on the first try.

MNP protocol recognizes that during the data transfer phase of a connection, most of the administrative information in the data packet does not change. Data Phase Optimization provides a method for eliminating some of the administrative information. This procedure further reduces protocol overhead.

The protocol efficiency of a Class 4 implementation is about 120 percent. A device using MNP Class 4 with a 2400bps modem will realize approximately 2900bps throughput. With Class 4 performance, the MNP protocol produces 20 percent more throughput than an ordinary modem without MNP.

Microcom's AX/1200, AX/2400, and PC/2400 support MNP Class 4.

Class 5   MNP Class 5 adds Data Compression to the features of Class 4 service. MNP Data Compression uses a real-time adaptive algorithm to compress data. The real-time aspects of the algorithm allow the data compression to operate on interactive terminal data, as well as file transfer data. Data compression also delivers faster screen updates to the user.

The adaptive nature of the algorithm means data compression is always optimized for the user's data. The algorithm continuously analyzes the user data and adjusts the compression parameters to maximize data throughput.

Data compression algorithms, like sort algorithms, are sensitive to the data pattern being processed. Most data being transmitted will benefit from data compression. The user will see compression performance vary between 1.3:1 and 2:1 (some files may be compressed at even higher ratios). The following types of common user files are listed in order of increasing compressibility:

- COM or EXE files (ARC'd files, too)
- Spreadsheet files
- Word processing files
- Print files

A realistic estimate of the overall compression factor a user will experience is 1.6:1, or 63 percent. This is equivalent to having a net protocol efficiency of 200 percent for an MNP Class 5 implementation. A device using MNP Class 5 with a 2400bps modem will realize 4800bps throughput. At MNP Class 5 performance, the MNP protocol produces over 100 percent more throughput than an ordinary modem without MNP.

Microcom's AX/1200c, AX/2400c, and PC/2400c support Class 5. CASE's 4696/VS supports Class 5.

Class 6   MNP Class 6 introduces the new features Universal Link Negotiation and Statistical Duplexing to MNP Class 5 service. Universal Link Negotiation allows MNP to incorporate incompatible modem modulation technology in the same MNP error-correcting modem. Prior to Class 6, MNP was used to enhance current modem technology. MNP Class 6 allows Microcom to create new universal modems.

Important Technologies and Advancements **631**

Most 1200bps and 2400bps modems are designed to be compatible with lower-speed modems. Bell 212A modems operate at 1200bps and incorporate the Bell 103 standard for up to 300bps communications. Likewise, there are V22.*bis* modems that operate as 300bps/103 modems, 1200bps/212A modems, and 2400bps modems. However, high-speed V29 and V32 modems do not provide compatibility with each other or with the lower-speed modulation techniques found in 212A and V22*bis* modems. Before the advent of MNP Class 6, it was impossible for a single modem to operate at a full range of speeds between 300 and 9600bps.

Universal Link Negotiation allows MNP modems to begin operations at a common slower speed and negotiate the use of an alternate high-speed modulation technique. The Microcom AX/9624 modem uses Universal Link Negotiation. Universal Link Negotiation uses the 2400bps/V22*bis* technology to negotiate a link. At the end of a successful link negotiation for Class 6 operation, the modem shifts to operation using 9600bps/V29 technology.

When the high-speed carrier technology uses half-duplex modulation, MNP Class 6 provides Statistical Duplexing. The Statistical Duplexing algorithm monitors the user data traffic pattern to dynamically allocate utilization of the half-duplex modulation and deliver full-duplex service.

An MNP Class 6 modem based on V29 technology delivers maximum performance in file transfer applications; up to 19.2Kbps throughput is possible on dial-up circuits for most applications. In accordance with the principles of MNP, the Class 5 Data Compression is fully incorporated in MNP Class 6. The Class 6 modem will deliver optimum performance even on an interactive terminal using character echoplexing. Screen updates will occur at speeds between 9.6Kbps and 19.2Kbps. Most screen updates will take less than one second.

Microcom's AX/9612c, AX/9624c, and PC/9624c support Class 6.

Class 7 MNP Class 7's Enhanced Data Compression, combined with Class 4, achieves improved throughput with efficiencies up to 300 percent, via the latest data compression technology. Microcom's enhanced encoding technique dynamically adjusts to the type of data being transmitted. This, combined with run-length encoding that sends repeating characters as a single number code, results in the superior compression efficiencies in MNP Class 7.

The Microcom QX/12K supports Class 7.

Class 8 Nothing available.

Class 9   MNP Class 9 utilizes Enhanced Data Compression combined with V32 technology to deliver maximum throughput up to 300 percent greater than ordinary V32 modems. Class 9 also features Enhanced Universal Link Negotiation, which allows connection to both MNP and non-MNP modems at the highest performance level.

The Microcom QX/.32c supports Class 9.

AVAILABLE HIGH-SPEED MODEMS

Listed below are just a few of the high-speed modems available. All of these modems are compatible at the lower speeds (300, 1200, and 2400bps) but, with only one exception, each is unique in the way it achieves higher speeds.

None of these modems is true full-duplex; all of them use a half-duplex scheme that simulates full-duplex communications by turning the line around. This "ping-pong" method, as it is commonly known, works reasonably well if the line does not need to be turned around often, such as when transferring files. The ping-pong method and its speed varies from one brand to another, and in modems with slow turnaround times, the delay can be quite noticeable when using a highly interactive application.

These modems all use the AT command set, and setups for them are included in many communications software programs.

Hayes V-Series Smartmodem 9600

The Hayes 9600 V-series modem uses a Hayes-developed protocol that allows the modem to simulate full-duplex operation. Hayes uses its own enhancement to CCITT LAP-B for error correction, and its own scheme for data compression. While these methods work well, the fact that they are proprietary means they are unlikely to become standard.

A V42 upgrade available from Hayes makes the V-series 9600 fully compliant with the CCITT V42 recommendation. The V42 upgrade also provides compatibility with MNP Classes 2 through 4.

US Robotics Courier HST

US Robotics makes the popular Courier HST modem. This modem is currently used on many bulletin board systems. It uses an asymmetric technique that sends data at high speed in one direction, and at low speed in the other. The directions are reversed as required. The Courier HST will monitor the quality of the connection. If it encounters a noisy line, the speed of the connection is automatically reduced. If the line quality improves, the speed is automatically increased. A V42 upgrade kit is available for $50.

Microcom AX-9624c

Like other high-speed modems, the Microcom adjusts its connection speed according to the quality of the telephone line. This particular model offers MNP Class 6, which is supported by Codex and Digital Equipment Corporation (DEC).

Telebit TrailBlazer

An interesting feature of the TrailBlazer is the way it emulates the Xmodem, Ymodem, and Kermit file transfer protocols, and uses these between itself and the local PC. Employing this scheme allows the TrailBlazer to work with standard communications software that supports one of these protocols, while using its own more efficient protocol to send data to the other modem. Assuming a noise-free connection, the Telebit TrailBlazer can achieve an effective speed of about 18,000bps.

Ven-Tel Pathfinder 18K

The Ven-Tel Pathfinder 18K uses Telebit's TrailBlazer technology (Telebit licensed it to Ven-Tel). Thus, the Pathfinder is the only high-speed modem brand that is compatible with another—it has the same features as the TrailBlazer. While the methods used by these modems are not likely to become the standard, they do provide reliable and fast data transmission.

Changing Times

The CCITT is presently reviewing the techniques used by various modem manufacturers, but a recommendation as a result of these studies is still a couple of years away. For now, anyone wanting to purchase a high-speed modem must take time to study the available products before determining the best choice for a particular application.

Things are changing quickly in this market. More and more companies are producing true V32 modems, which will almost certainly become more popular as the price drops. It is essential to keep up to date by reading periodicals, especially if considering a modem purchase.

As a less expensive alternative to high-speed modems, it may be worthwhile to consider 2400bps modems that implement data compression, such as MNP Class 5 modems offered by manufacturers such as US Robotics, Microcom, and Hayes.

CHAPTER TWENTY-SEVEN

Troubleshooting Your Modem

If your modem doesn't seem to work the way it should when you first hook it up, there are some things you can check. Most problems can be traced to just a few types of snags that are fairly easy to fix.

A list of the most common problems follows (roughly in order by how much inconvenience they cause you):

1. Call Waiting was not cancelled.

2. An external modem cable connection is bad or loose.

3. The phone line is disconnected at wall or modem.

4. The communications (comm) program is set up incorrectly.

5. The modem switches or jumper plugs are set up incorrectly.

6. The modem is competing with another device for a COM port.

7. You have the wrong type of cable.

8. Switches are set incorrectly in the computer (not enough serial ports).

9. There is a problem with the computer Basic Input/Output System (BIOS).

10. The telecommunications program isn't compatible with the modem.

11. Your modem is defective or broken.

PROCEDURES FOR DIAGNOSING MODEM PROBLEMS

The next few pages contain some procedures to help you nail down any problems you've had in getting your modem to work. You'll also be given a list of trouble symptoms, with some actions you can take to correct specific problems. The general rule is try the simple stuff first.

Cancel Call Waiting

You might be surprised at how often people gnash their teeth over repeated loss of signal—and finally figure out that they just forgot to cancel Call Waiting. Call Waiting is a telephone company service that notifies you during a call that another caller is trying to reach you. This is a fine service most of the time. The trouble is that the Call Waiting signal consists of a brief cut-off of all sound followed by a high beep. Your modem interprets this as a lost connection and hangs up.

Most telephone companies that offer Call Waiting service also provide a way to cancel it for times when you don't want the interruption. For example, in some areas you can dial 70# or *70 on your push-button phone to disable Call Waiting. Callers will then hear a busy signal and your data transfers can go merrily forward. If your phone company doesn't offer a Call Waiting disable feature, try setting your modem to **AT S10=255**. This sets your modem to ignore the brief cut-off caused by Call Waiting and prevents your modem from hanging up while on line.

Most communications (comm) programs will let you use prefixes and suffixes to access long-distance carriers or outside lines from an office. Assign the Cancel Call Waiting sequence as a prefix to every number in your comm program's dialing directory and you'll never again wonder what happened to the signal. If your phone company offers Call Waiting but not

Cancel Call Waiting, you might get a second phone line without Call Waiting and dedicate it to your computer. Or you could order Call Forwarding. This service, often offered with Call Waiting, tells the phone company to redirect all callers to a second number—perhaps your office, if you're using the modem at home on the weekend. Finally, you can check your modem manual to see if it will allow you to set the time the modem takes to hang up after it loses the carrier signal. It may interfere with data transmission accuracy if your modem ignores the Call Waiting interruption, but at least you'll still be connected.

Check Your Cables

Before you tear into the machine, take a moment to check your cable and phone connections, the two simplest things to fix. More than one telecommuter has spent hours in search of what went wrong, maybe even sent the computer to the shop, only to discover that the janitors, the kids, or the dog unplugged the phone wire at the wall. Always check your connections first!

Check for a Signal, Any Signal

If you suspect your modem isn't dialing out, there are some quick checks you can make. The simplest is to listen for a dial tone, or for your modem's dial-out tones if your modem has a speaker. If you hear anything when you tell the modem to dial out, the modem is probably dialing out correctly.

If you hear nothing, it's possible your modem simply has no speaker. Check your manual. If you do have a speaker, look in the manual for the command that turns up the volume. (In Hayes modems and many others that use the AT command set, type the command **AT L3** to raise speaker volume.)

If these simple tests seem to show that the modem does dial out, try calling a local node of Sprintnet or TYMNET. To find a local node, you can call Sprintnet Customer Service at 1-800-336-0437; TYMNET Customer Service is at 1-800-336-0149. Both systems have a voice mail system; just press the appropriate numbers on your phone to get to a live Customer Support person. Tell them your location and they'll give you the nearest phone number to access their network. If they ask, tell them the truth— you're setting up or troubleshooting a modem and need the number in order to access information services like CompuServe or GEnie.

Then set your modem to 300 or 1200bps (many nodes will not accept 2400 or higher modem speeds) and call the local access number. If you hear the high-pitched whine of another modem answering your call, that means your modem works fine for calling other numbers. Press ENTER several times to tell the other modem you're ready. If you then start seeing "garbage" characters (such as # $ <) on your screen, that means your modem is working fine and the problem is probably in your communications program settings.

Check Your Hardware Layout

If bad connections aren't the answer, and you get *nothing* back when you try to call one of the network numbers, step back and think for a moment. Is this the first time you've used a modem with this computer? If so, it's a good idea to make sure your system is set up the way you thought it was. Look through the next few paragraphs, and if you're not already sure about the setup, try the simple tests we suggest.

External Modems

Do you have a serial port for an external modem to tie into? Most ATs, PS/2s, and brand name compatibles come equipped with at least two serial ports, one for a mouse and one for a modem or serial printer. Many can handle up to four serial ports in all, if you set the switches correctly.

Look at the back of your machine. Serial ports come in two styles, small ones with 7 pins designed for a mouse, and larger ones, the standard RS-232C port (Figure 27-1) with up to 25 pins. External (stand-alone or desktop) modems usually connect with an RS-232C serial port.

Figure 27-1

Serial port RS-232C connector

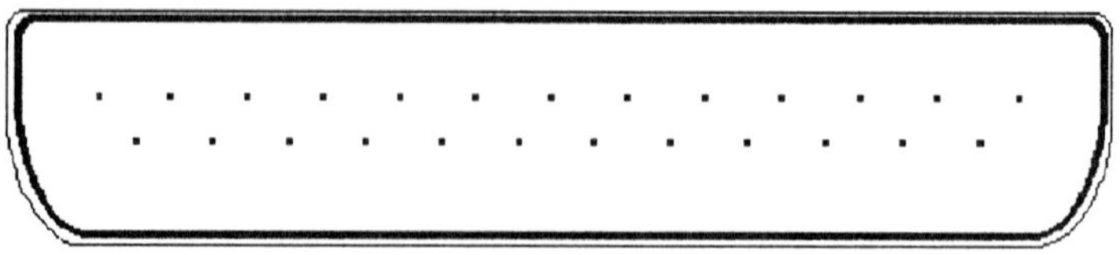

If you see only one connection that looks like Figure 27-1, it may be a parallel printer port rather than a serial port. Printers use the same size connector. You can tell them apart, though, because RS-232C serial ports are male (the *computer*, not the cable, has the copper pins). Parallel printer ports are female.

Internal Modems

Internal modems plug into an expansion slot inside the computer and provide their own modular telephone jacks to connect with a standard phone cord. They don't need a separate RS-232C serial port because the modem itself becomes a new serial port.

Unfortunately, this seemingly simple approach can also lead to problems. Most internal modems these days come set as COM2. If your computer already has two or more serial ports, it may get confused when you add a third port. In the spirit of simplest things first, consult your modem manual and reset the modem to operate as COM3 or COM4 if it can do it. Some modems will only operate on COM1 or COM2. This means you may have to remove or disable one of your serial ports to make the modem work. One way to handle this is to unplug the device plugged into the serial port and then plug in the modem temporarily.

If you do not have a tech manual for your machine, you may have to try a little trial-and-error switch setting. (Some other trial-and-error approaches are suggested a little later.) Or you might take the machine to a shop for an experienced technician to reset.

Locate Existing Serial Ports

If loose or improper cables or connectors aren't the problem, the next thing to do is figure out how many serial ports your machine has. It's best, although not absolutely necessary, to remove your modem from the system at this point. You can unplug the cable or remove an internal modem from its expansion slot. (Once again, keep things simple whenever possible.)

Next, find out how many serial ports your system started with. Several popular and inexpensive programs can help you do this. Figure 27-2 is part of the screen report made by one such program, Peter Norton's SI (System Information) utility. Note that it reports that the computer has two serial ports.

Another program, DEVICE, takes a different approach. DEVICE is part of a memory management system, TSRCOM v. 2.9, made available free to the public by its authors. DEVICE tries to deduce, from the way a

---
Figure 27-2

Norton's SYSINFO report (note the two serial ports)

SI-System Information, Advanced Edition, (C) Copr 1987, Peter Norton

```
          Computer Name: IBM/PC-AT
       Operating System: DOS 3.21
      Built-in BIOS dated: Tuesday, February 3, 1987
         Main Processor: Intel 80286          Serial Ports: 2
           Co-Processor: None              Parallel Ports: 1
  Video Display Adapter: Enhanced Graphics, 256 K-bytes
     Current Video Mode: Text, 80 x 25 Color
   Available Disk Drives: 6, A: - F:
```

computer's memory is used, what basic equipment is installed. In Figure 27-3, DEVICE reports two COM ports among the various devices using the sample machine's memory. (COM ports are the same as serial ports.) REPORT, the "COM-port Sleuth" utility by computer writer Pete Maclean, takes a similar approach but confines its reports to the actual COM ports found active on your system.

Figure 27-3

TurboPower's DEVICE report (note the two COM ports)

Address	Bytes	Name	Hooked vectors
0070:0BB6	–	CON	
0070:0C62	–	AUX	
0070:0C74	–	COM1	
0070:0C86	–	COM2	
0070:0D27	–	PRN	
0070:0D39	–	LPT1	
0070:0D4B	–	LPT2	
0070:0D5D	–	LPT3	
0070:0E3D	–	CLOCK$	
0070:0F17	–	3 Block Units	
0000:2088	37648	NUL	02 0A 0B 0C 0D 0E 27 2F 31 70 72 73 74 75 76 77

If you don't have the Norton Utilities or a program such as DEVICE or REPORT, there is another way to find out how many serial ports DOS thinks a machine has. Copy a short file to various serial ports (COM1, COM2, COM3, COM4). If the computer considers the destination to be a serial port, DOS will issue an error statement or might just sit there, doing nothing (see Figure 27-4). When the computer thinks it has run out of ports, however, DOS stops giving error messages. Instead it creates a file named COM*n* (where *n* is the number where the machine ran out of ports).

Figure 27-4 shows the results of copying a file named NOTES to various COM port numbers on a two-port sample machine.

COM1, a mouse port, gave back the message "Abort, Retry, Ignore?" In this case you can simply press **A** for Abort and go on to the next one. COM2, with nothing attached, did the same. But when we tried to copy NOTES to COM3, DOS took a different course. Since it did not find a COM3 serial port, it created a file named COM3 and copied the contents of NOTES to it. As Figure 27-5 shows, the new file was a copy of NOTES under a new name. That was the tip-off that the machine had no serial port at COM3. It's an unusual procedure, but it works.

To install an internal modem on our sample machine, we could turn off the existing COM2 and replace it with the modem. We could also reset the modem to function as COM3 and plug it in to see if the host computer allows it.

Figure 27-4

Copy a file to count COM ports

```
F:\ ->copy notes com1

Write fault error writing device COM1
Abort, Retry, Ignore? A

F:\ ->copy notes com2

Write fault error writing device COM2
Abort, Retry, Ignore? A

F:\ ->copy notes com3
        1 File(s) copied

F:\ ->
```

─────────────────────── **Figure 27-5** ───────────────────────

DOS runs out of serial COM ports, so it creates a file instead

```
Volume in drive F is DISK1_VOL2
Directory of  F:\

.            <DIR>      8-23-89  11:46a
..           <DIR>      8-23-89  11:46a
NOTES               994  1-03-89  11:24a
COM3                994  1-03-89  11:24a
       4 File(s)    4937728 bytes free
```

Use the Right Phone Plug

Most modems accept standard RJ-series phone plugs (your modem manual will provide a specific list). All modems designed for use in the United States accept a standard RJ11 telephone line plug. The RJ11 is the little plastic clip on the end of the wire that you plug into telephone jacks and wall boxes.

An RJ11 has at least two wires and usually has four. It is designed to accommodate two separate phone lines, but some manufacturers only put in two wires on the theory that most people only have a single phone line. Some modems require all four wires, so check your RJ11 plug. Look for copper bands in the four little grooves in the plug. If your RJ11 only shows two copper bands, get one with all four wires. It may solve your problems.

When you have two phone lines, loose terminal wires can cause leakage from one line to the other. If the leakage is bad enough, it will degrade data transmission. The phone company will install a noise filter on your lines if you ask them. This may help.

Tip: There are two types of phone line filters. One works on your data line, and the other goes on your voice line. If they get installed on the wrong line, that can make things worse. Ask the phone company's technician what type of filter it is and make sure it goes onto the correct phone line.

Tip: Most modems only accept signals from one of the two pairs of RJ11 wires in a two-line system. If your modem is on the wrong line, it's a simple one-screwdriver job to reverse the positions of the two pairs of wires in the wall box. Your modem will now work on the other line.

To Set Up with More than Two Phone Lines   If you have more than two phone lines you'll have a different type of RJ plug, and you'll probably need to reset your modem. For example, the Hayes 1200 Smartmodem is preset for the RJ11 jack; to connect with an RJ12 or RJ13 jack you need to change Switch 7 from UP to DOWN. Check your modem documentation to make sure the modem is set correctly for your home or office telephone system.

Use the Right Modem Cable

If your modem cable came with your external modem, chances are it's the right cable. However, all cables look very much alike. If you have a "spaghetti factory" under your desk or if you got the cable from a box in the closet, take a closer look at the connectors. Standard RS-232C modem cables look much like printer cables and null modem cables, but there are ways to tell them apart. (See Appendix I for detailed diagrams.)

It's easy to tell a printer cable from a modem cable—the two ends of the printer cable are not mirror-image male and female versions of each other. The ends of a modem cable will plug into each other; the ends of a printer cable won't.

If that's not the problem, then look at the connector on the male end of the cable (the end with the copper pins). Most unmodified modem cables have all their pins. If your modem cable does not, that doesn't mean it's the wrong cable—but it's a fair bet that the cable was either modified or nonstandard to begin with. Try a different, more standard modem cable.

A *null modem cable* can be a little harder to identify. Null modem cables connect one computer (perhaps a laptop) directly with another (maybe a desktop model). Because you aren't going through the telephone system, there's no need for modems. To bypass the modem, a null modem cable connects Pin 2 at one end with Pin 3 at the other. This fools each machine into thinking it's connected to a modem. The result is that they'll pass data back and forth at the maximum speed your comm program allows— 9600 or 19200 bits per second, and often at even higher speeds.

That's great for sending data between incompatible systems, such as an Apple and an IBM, or a laptop with 3 1/2-inch disks and an XT with 5 1/4-inch floppies. The problem is that null modem cables won't let a modem and a computer talk to each other—the Data In and Data Out pins are reversed!

If you have a null modem cable, you probably already know about it. If you're not sure, look at each end of the cable. Many null modem cables are simply a standard modem cable with an adapter at one end to "cross" Pins 2 and 3. You'll see the extra hardware at one end of the cable. Simply remove it to get back your standard RS-232C cable.

If the cable was manufactured as a null modem cable, it will probably have a "null" or "null modem" label. Look at the connectors on each end. If you see a null modem label, change to a different cable.

Check Your Software Settings

If you seem to be fine in the hardware department, the next place to look is your comm program. Specifically, you need to match your comm program settings to the computer you're trying to call and to the correct COM port number. You also need to make sure the number you're calling is expecting the call—that the modem on the other end of the line is set to answer calls.

Com Port Number

If your modem is set up as COM2 but your comm program is sending your data to COM1, the signal won't ever get out to your modem. Make sure your software is set to the same COM port as your modem. Your comm program manual will tell you how.

Communication Parameters

You may remember that the main software settings consist of the speed (bits per second sent through the modem), parity, character or "word" length, and number of stop bits. The settings you use depend on who you want to call. If your settings are wrong, your modem won't be able to talk to the modem at the other end. Unless you're in an unusual mainframe-to-micro sort of situation, you should never need more than two settings. The first is 8-N-1: an 8-bit word length, no parity, 1 stop bit. Almost every private bulletin board uses this setting. The other setting is 7-E-1: a 7-bit word length, even parity, 1 stop bit, that works with many mainframe computers. It also works when calling directly to the Sprintnet or TYM-NET transmission networks. You also can reset most comm programs to 300, 1200, 2400, or even higher bps settings. Again, the right setting depends upon whom you call.

Comm Program Settings

All comm programs now give you the ability to change your settings to fit the requirements of the system you're calling.

Sometimes all you need to do is change one setting to make everything work as it should.

- Let's say your comm program is set to 2400bps but the answering modem is set to 1200bps. You'll hear what sounds like the correct "fuzzy" answering tone, but your modem won't respond. Change the setting to 1200bps to solve the problem.

- If you see a lot of "garbage" characters on the screen, try changing to 7-E-1 or 8-N-1.

- If someone needs to call you by modem but your phone won't answer, make sure that your modem is set for the "Auto Answer" mode. If you forget, your modem may report to the screen that someone is calling, but it won't go any further. Check your modem manual for how to set your modem to Auto Answer, and then use your comm program to send the instructions to the modem. On modems that use the AT command set, enter **AT S0=1** and hit ENTER to make your modem pick up the phone on the first ring.

- If you need to call another modem that can't Auto Answer the phone, you may still be able to establish contact. If your modem can communicate solely in the answer mode carrier frequencies, someone on the other end can simply tell the system to go on line after you call. For modems that use the Hayes command set, add the letter **R** after the phone number, as in **ATDT5551234R.** This may solve your problem.

- If you're on a "True Blue" 4.77 MHz machine and using a comm program written in BASIC, you can run into trouble at communication speeds greater than 300bps. You may need to change to a compiled BASIC program or to one written in a faster language, such as C, in order to communicate successfully and at higher speeds.

See Appendix H for some recommended comm programs.

SOME SPECIFIC PROBLEMS AND SOLUTIONS

Problem: I was doing fine, when the screen announced that I had lost the carrier signal.

Solution: Do you have Call Waiting? Disable it before calling out. Check your phone line and modem cable, and reconnect if either is pulled out. If you can't disable Call Waiting but your modem uses the AT command set, try sending it the command **AT S10 = 255**, or the highest number your modem will accept. This will make your modem stay on line longer before hanging up—maybe long enough to get through the false "loss of carrier" signal caused by Call Waiting.

Problem: My phone line is very noisy and I have trouble with accidental disconnections. How do I correct this?

Solution: The phone company will provide you with filters that may help to reduce line noise. It's worth a try. Check your phone and modem cable connections. If they're just a little loose, they can cause noise that's not the phone line's fault at all. If your modem uses the AT command set, try sending it the command **AT S10 = 150**, or try another fairly high number. It will take longer to disconnect even if there is line noise.

Problem: I tried using ATL1 to make my speaker quieter but it didn't work. What now?

Solution: Not all modems use the complete AT command set. Many commands, such as loudness, are optional. Check your modem manual.

Problem: My modem responds with "NO DIAL TONE" even when I know the office PBX wasn't that busy. It worked fine at home.

Solution: There are various levels of "smartness" in modems, from X0 (dumb) to X7 (high school graduate). Read Appendix C on the AT command set for more detailed information on how to take advantage of this setting. Many modems come preset to level X4, which responds with words such as "BUSY" or "NO DIAL TONE" when it detects those conditions on the line. However, many PBX and other office systems have an odd dial tone that modems don't recognize.

Try setting your modem to X0 or X1 (that is, use the AT X1 command with the AT command set). The modem will no longer pay attention to an odd dial tone and won't hang up. (It will also ignore busy signals, so you might want to reset your comm program's time-out to a shorter period.)

Problem: I get two letters on the screen whenever I type in one.

Solution: You are set to half-duplex, so you're seeing not only your own keystrokes but the keystrokes your host (information service, for instance) echoes back to you. Reset your comm program to full-duplex so you only see the host echo.

Problem: When I type something in, I don't see anything on the screen, even though I see responses from the host computer.

Solution: You are set to full-duplex, but your host (a mainframe computer, for example) is not echoing your keystrokes back. Reset your comm program to half-duplex to echo your keystrokes to the screen locally.

Problem: Incoming files don't scroll down the screen; they just keep writing over the top line on the screen.

Solution: Reset your comm program to add a line feed whenever it senses a carriage return. That way, your comm program will make the cursor drop down one line every time the cursor moves back to the left side of the screen. Check your comm program manual to see how to reset line feeds.

Problem: I'm getting an empty line between each line of incoming information, like double-spacing on a typewriter.

Solution: Reset your comm program to NOT add a line feed when it senses a carriage return. The remote computer has added line feeds of its own. Check your comm program manual for how to reset line feeds.

Problem: I'm not getting any response from my modem.

Solution: The most common cause of this is having your comm program set to the wrong serial port. Most new internal modems are preset as COM2, while most comm programs default to COM1. Make sure the modem and the comm program are in agreement. Another possibility may be that your modem conflicts with another serial device (a mouse, or a printer) on a given COM port. Check your modem documentation and reset the modem for a different serial port number — COM3 or COM4, for example.

Problem: My modem does call out, but I can't hear it placing calls.

Solution: Not all modems come with speakers. If yours does, check your modem manual for how to set the volume louder. If your modem uses the AT command set, send it the command **AT L3** to make it louder.

Problem: I just changed to an internal modem and I miss my old external modem's LED indicator lights.

Solution: Lights are handy. They tell you when data transfers freeze, so you can sign off before your phone bill goes through the roof. Fortunately, there are alternatives to the LED display. There is a shareware utility called RS-232 that puts a modem readout on your screen, simulating an external modem's LED display. *PC Magazine* published a similar utility program named LITES.

Problem: My modem won't hang up properly when I finish a call.

Solution: Check your modem manual for the proper switch settings. Some comm programs like to turn off the Data Terminal Ready or DTR signal to force a modem to hang up. Many modems (Hayes, for example) are preset to ignore the DTR signal. Reset your modem and comm program to agree on how to treat the DTR signal.

Problem: My comm program thinks I'm still connected after the modem hangs up the line.

Solution: Check the modem's Carrier Detect or CD setting. Some modems are preset to force the Carrier Detect signal on at all times. Your comm program may use this signal to tell whether you're on line. Reset the modem to reflect the actual state of the Carrier Detect signal.

Problem: Unless I'm on line, my comm program doesn't echo my modem's result codes to the screen when I give the modem instructions.

Solution: Some programs won't read signals from your modem (that is, "OK" to indicate it received an instruction) unless they think the modem is on line. Set your modem to force the Carrier Detect signal on at all times to fool your comm program into reporting all result codes even when you're not on line.

Problem: My 300/1200bps modem worked fine overseas, but it stopped working when I came home to the U.S.

Solution: All 300 and 1200bps modems in North America are governed by Bell standards (Bell 103, Bell 212A). Outside Canada, the U.S., and Mexico, modems use the international CCITT V21 and V22 standards. The main differences are in the frequencies used. Most modems will let you choose which standard to conform to; check your manual and reset it for Bell standards in North America. If you bought your modem overseas, check to see if it's FCC Certified. If it isn't, there's no guarantee that it will hold up very well under normal vibration, temperatures, and humidity. Your modem might simply have failed.

Problem: When I visited a friend, my modem suddenly couldn't access an information service I use all the time. What's wrong?

Solution: The simplest possibility is that your modem is set to tone dialing, but your friend's phone service only accepts pulse (rotary) dialing. Try resetting your comm program to use pulse dialing. Or maybe your normal access number is a toll call from your friend's house. Call the information service to get a local access number from your friend's telephone exchange.

Problem: When I send a message it gets received, but often there are missing words or lines when the recipient reads it.

Solution: Check your comm program's flow control setting. Most programs provide what's called XON and XOFF control so your computer won't send data before the other computer is ready to receive it. If your flow control is turned off, your computer won't pause its transmission when you get an XOFF signal. Data then gets lost "in the wires."

If you're dealing with a corporate mainframe computer, you may need to set your comm program to wait for a "pace character" (such as a colon) before sending the next line. Information services will provide pace characters if you want them to. Setting a pace character guarantees that you won't send the next line before the other computer is ready to receive it.

A third alternative is simply to slow down your transmission rate by inserting a brief automatic pause between characters or between lines. Using character or line pacing takes longer but helps ensure that everything you send gets through to the other end.

Problem: Suddenly I'm getting all garbage characters, or a mixture of garbage and normal ASCII characters on the screen. What happened?

Solution: Check your comm program settings. Specifically, make sure you're on 8-N-1 or 7-E-1 unless you're talking with a corporate mainframe. Getting garbage characters could be the result of accidentally changing some of your communications parameters. If you're trying to communicate with a corporate mainframe, ask your MIS manager if any special settings are required. Also, check Chapter 22 for tips on making a successful micro to mainframe connection.

Problem: I'm trying to change from the telecommunications program that came with my modem to another program, but I can't get the modem to initialize or make any calls out. What am I doing wrong?

Solution: Many times, if you're sure you've selected the correct COM port, the problem lies with the initialization string. Not all modems use a standard AT command set. Check your modem manual for a recommended initialization string. These strings look pretty mysterious, like secret code, and it's important that every character be exactly right. If you specified both the port and the initialization string correctly, you may just have to go back to using the comm program that came with your modem. Some modems, especially inexpensive ones, come with a program (like Bitcom) that has been "tweaked" for that specific modem. Other programs just won't work correctly. The only cure is to buy another modem or to stay with the original program.

PATIENCE IS A VIRTUE

Not everything works right the first time on a computer. Don't be afraid to tinker with the settings. If that's not your cup of tea, don't be reluctant to call on the services of a qualified technician, or to use the support numbers provided with your modem or comm program.

PART FOUR

Appendixes

ASCII Codes for the PC

Decimal Value	Hexadecimal Value	Control Character	Character
0	00	NUL	Null
1	01	SOH	☺
2	02	STX	☻
3	03	ETX	♥
4	04	EOT	♦
5	05	ENQ	♣
6	06	ACK	♠
7	07	BEL	Beep
8	08	BS	◘
9	09	HT	Tab
10	0A	LF	Line-feed

Decimal Value	Hexadecimal Value	Control Character	Character
11	0B	VT	Cursor home
12	0C	FF	Form-feed
13	0D	CR	Enter
14	0E	SO	♫
15	0F	SI	☼
16	10	DLE	►
17	11	DC1	◄
18	12	DC2	↕
19	13	DC3	‼
20	14	DC4	π
21	15	NAK	§
22	16	SYN	▬
23	17	ETB	↨
24	18	CAN	↑
25	19	EM	↓
26	1A	SUB	→
27	1B	ESC	←
28	1C	FS	Cursor right
29	1D	GS	Cursor left
30	1E	RS	Cursor up
31	1F	US	Cursor down
32	20	SP	Space
33	21		!
34	22		"
35	23		#
36	24		$
37	25		%
38	26		&
39	27		'
40	28		(
41	29		)
42	2A		*
43	2B		+
44	2C		,
45	2D		-
46	2E		.
47	2F		/

Decimal Value	Hexadecimal Value	Control Character	Character
48	30		0
49	31		1
50	32		2
51	33		3
52	34		4
53	35		5
54	36		6
55	37		7
56	38		8
57	39		9
58	3A		:
59	3B		;
60	3C		<
61	3D		=
62	3E		>
63	3F		?
64	40		@
65	41		A
66	42		B
67	43		C
68	44		D
69	45		E
70	46		F
71	47		G
72	48		H
73	49		I
74	4A		J
75	4B		K
76	4C		L
77	4D		M
78	4E		N
79	4F		O
80	50		P
81	51		Q
82	52		R
83	53		S
84	54		T

Decimal Value	Hexadecimal Value	Control Character	Character
85	55		U
86	56		V
87	57		W
88	58		X
89	59		Y
90	5A		Z
91	5B		[
92	5C		\
93	5D		]
94	5E		^
95	5F		–
96	60		`
97	61		a
98	62		b
99	63		c
100	64		d
101	65		e
102	66		f
103	67		g
104	68		h
105	69		i
106	6A		j
107	6B		k
108	6C		l
109	6D		m
110	6E		n
111	6F		o
112	70		p
113	71		q
114	72		r
115	73		s
116	74		t
117	75		u
118	76		v
119	77		w
120	78		x
121	79		y
122	7A		z

Decimal Value	Hexadecimal Value	Control Character	Character
123	7B		{
124	7C		¦
125	7D		}
126	7E		~
127	7F	DEL	⌂
128	80		Ç
129	81		ü
130	82		é
131	83		â
132	84		ä
133	85		à
134	86		å
135	87		ç
136	88		ê
137	89		ë
138	8A		è
139	8B		ï
140	8C		î
141	8D		ì
142	8E		Ä
143	8F		Å
144	90		É
145	91		æ
146	92		Æ
147	93		ô
148	94		ö
149	95		ó
150	96		û
151	97		ù
152	98		ÿ
153	99		Ö
154	9A		Ü
155	9B		¢
156	9C		£
157	9D		¥
158	9E		Pt
159	9F		ƒ
160	A0		á

Decimal Value	Hexadecimal Value	Control Character	Character
161	A1		í
162	A2		ó
163	A3		ú
164	A4		ñ
165	A5		Ñ
166	A6		a̱
167	A7		o̱
168	A8		¿
169	A9		⌐
170	AA		¬
171	AB		½
172	AC		¼
173	AD		¡
174	AE		«
175	AF		»
176	B0		░
177	B1		▒
178	B2		▓
179	B3		│
180	B4		┤
181	B5		╡
182	B6		╢
183	B7		╖
184	B8		╕
185	B9		╣
186	BA		║
187	BB		╗
188	BC		╝
189	BD		╜
190	BE		╛
191	BF		┐
192	C0		└
193	C1		┴
194	C2		┬
195	C3		├
196	C4		─
197	C5		┼
198	C6		╞

Decimal Value	Hexadecimal Value	Control Character	Character
199	C7		╟
200	C8		╚
201	C9		╔
202	CA		╩
203	CB		╦
204	CC		╠
205	CD		═
206	CE		╬
207	CF		╧
208	D0		╨
209	D1		╤
210	D2		╥
211	D3		╙
212	D4		╘
213	D5		╒
214	D6		╓
215	D7		╫
216	D8		╪
217	D9		┘
218	DA		┌
219	DB		■
220	DC		▄
221	DD		▌
222	DE		▐
223	DF		▀
224	E0		α
225	E1		β
226	E2		Γ
227	E3		π
228	E4		Σ
229	E5		σ
230	E6		μ
231	E7		τ
232	E8		ϕ
233	E9		θ
234	EA		Ω
235	EB		δ
236	EC		∞

Decimal Value	Hexadecimal Value	Control Character	Character
237	ED		$\varnothing$
238	EE		ϵ
239	EF		$\cap$
240	F0		$\equiv$
241	F1		$\pm$
242	F2		$\geq$
243	F3		$\leq$
244	F4		$\lceil$
245	F5		$\rfloor$
246	F6		$\div$
247	F7		$\approx$
248	F8		$\circ$
249	F9		$\bullet$
250	FA		$\cdot$
251	FB		$\sqrt{}$
252	FC		n
253	FD		^{2}
254	FE		$\blacksquare$
255	FF		(blank)

Modem Switch Settings

The world would be a better place if a clear listing of the modem switch settings were printed on the back of every add-on card or modem case. There's always room for this information, but only recently have vendors provided it. Let's face it, most people lose their documentation. Here are a few of the switch settings of some popular modems, just in case you find one in the bottom of a drawer and want to use it. (You *know* you won't be able to find the documentation.) We've included settings for both host and remote modes.

Hayes Smartmodem

Switch	Remote Modem	Host Modem	Function
1	UP	UP	Support DTR
2	UP or DOWN	UP or DOWN	Digit codes
3	DOWN	DOWN	Send results
4	UP or DOWN	UP or DOWN	Echo commands
5	DOWN	DOWN	No auto-answer
6	UP	UP	Support DCD
7	*	*	Type of jack
8	DOWN	DOWN	Allow commands

* UP for single line, DOWN for multiline.

MultiTech MultiModem 224

For 8-position DIP-Switch:

Switch	Remote Modem	Host Modem	Function
1	UP	UP	Support DTR
2	UP or DOWN	UP or DOWN	Digit codes
3	DOWN	DOWN	Send results
4	UP or DOWN	UP or DOWN	Echo commands
5	DOWN	DOWN	No auto-answer
6	UP	UP	Support DCD
7	*	*	Type of jack
8	DOWN	DOWN	Allow commands

* UP for single line, DOWN for multiline.

For 4-position DIP-Switch:

Switch	Remote Modem	Host Modem	Function
1	UP	UP	CTS forced on
2	UP	UP	Dial-up oper.
3	DOWN	DOWN	Blind dial
4	DOWN	DOWN	Asynchronous

Concord Data Systems 224 Modem

Switch	Remote Modem	Host Modem	Function
OR	ON	ON	Originate
AA	OFF	OFF	Auto-answer
FB	*	*	1200 baud

* ON for 1200 baud, OFF for 2400 baud.

Note: Use factory settings for all internal switches.

Inmac Modem

Switch	Remote Modem	Host Modem	Function
1	UP	UP	Support DTR
2	UP or DOWN	UP or DOWN	Digit codes
3	DOWN	DOWN	Send results
4	UP or DOWN	UP or DOWN	Echo commands
5	DOWN	DOWN	No auto-answer
6	UP	UP	Support DCD
7	*	*	Type of jack
8	DOWN	DOWN	Allow commands

* UP for single line, DOWN for multiline.

Hayes 1200 Baud External Modem (for PC Board)

Switch	Remote Modem	Host Modem	Function
1	UP	UP	Support DTR
2	UP	UP	Digit codes
3	DOWN	DOWN	Send results
4	UP or DOWN	DOWN	Echo commands
5	DOWN	DOWN	No auto-answer
6	UP	UP	Support DCD
7	UP	UP	Type of jack
8	DOWN	DOWN	Allow commands

US Robotics Courier 2400 Modem (for PC Board)

Switch	Remote Modem	Host Modem	Function
1	UP	UP	Support DTR
2	UP	UP	Digit codes
3	DOWN	DOWN	Send results
4	UP or DOWN	DOWN	Echo commands
5	DOWN	DOWN	No auto-answer
6	UP	UP	Support DCD
7	UP	UP	Type of jack
8	DOWN	DOWN	Allow commands
9	DOWN	DOWN	Disconnect with + + +
10	Not used	Not used	For future use

US Robotics 2400-E MNP Modem

Switch	Remote Modem	Host Modem	Function
1	UP	UP	Support DTR
2	UP	UP	Digit codes
3	DOWN	DOWN	Send results
4	UP or DOWN	DOWN	Echo commands
5	DOWN	DOWN	No auto-answer
6	UP	UP	Support DCD
7	UP	UP	Type of jack
8	DOWN	DOWN	Allow commands
9	DOWN	DOWN	Disconnect with + + +
10	Not used	Not used	For future use

US Robotics 9600 Baud HST Modem

Switch	Remote Modem	Host Modem	Function
1	UP	UP	Support DTR
2	UP	UP	Digit codes
3	DOWN	DOWN	Send results
4	UP or DOWN	DOWN	Echo commands
5	DOWN	DOWN	No auto-answer
6	UP	UP	Support DCD
7	UP	UP	Type of jack
8	DOWN	DOWN	Allow commands
9	DOWN	DOWN	Disconnect with + + +
10	Not used	Not used	For future use

Microcom AX9624C 9600 Baud External Modem

Switch settings are the same whether switches are in the front or back of modem.

Switch	Remote Modem	Host Modem	Function
1	UP	UP	Support DTR
2	UP	UP	Digit codes
3	DOWN	DOWN	Send results
4	UP or DOWN	DOWN	Echo commands
5	DOWN	DOWN	No auto-answer
6	UP	UP	Support DCD
7	UP	UP	Type of jack
8	DOWN	DOWN	Allow commands
9	DOWN or UP	UP	Disconnect with + + +
10	UP	UP	Special usage

The AT Command Set

Since the invention of the so-called "smart" modem, the AT command set has been an important factor for those who need to use all the "smarts" their modems have to offer. These commands are the way you talk to your modem. While this Appendix covers the basic AT commands and a few advanced commands, you should use your modem documentation for any commands peculiar to your specific modem. And it is also recommended that you carefully look over the X command in this Appendix to see how it works and its value.

BASIC AT COMMANDS

A reference listing of the common AT commands that you can give your modem follows. Not all modems use the entire command set, and many modems add some of their own (see the section on US Robotics extended commands later in this Appendix). All these commands (unless otherwise indicated) are preceded by the letters AT, meaning "attention!" Some modems respond to the AT in lowercase, and some do not.

If you type **AT** while in the terminal mode of your telecommunications program, the modem should respond with OK. For example, you'd type **AT X4** and press ENTER and receive either the OK message or ERROR, depending on whether the modem supports the X4 level of "smartness." You can also type a string of commands after typing AT, for example, **AT X4F1E0**.

Before you experiment with the AT commands, type just plain **AT**, followed by ENTER, and make sure that you get the OK message.

Command/Options	Function
AT	Attention! Lets the modem know commands are being issued to it. Must precede all other commands except A/, A> and + + +
A	Force Answer mode when the modem hasn't received an incoming call. Example: ATA or AT A
A/	Reexecute the last issued command one time. A/ doesn't take the AT prefix or a Carriage Return
A>	Reexecute the last issued command continuously until canceled by *<any key>*. Dial strings are reexecuted a maximum of ten times. A> doesn't take the AT prefix or a Carriage Return
<any key>	Terminate current dialing operation resulting from an issued Dial command; terminate Repeat mode (> or A>)
B*n*	Handshake options
BØ	(a) V32 modulation, 9600/4800bps (includes V32 answer tones). Not available with all modems *Courier V32:* Default *Courier HST Dual Standard*: Required to answer V32 calls. To call V32 modems, B may be set to BØ or B1. HST modulation remains enabled *Courier HST*: See B1 description. HST modulation remains enabled (b) CCITT V25 answer sequence. Required for all Courier modems answering overseas calls at 1200bps and above

B1	(a) HST modulation, 14.4K/12K/9600/7200/4800 bps (no V32 answer tones)
	Courier HST: Default
	Courier HST Dual Standard: Default. Also calls but does not answer V32 modems
	Courier V32: Calls but does not answer V32 modems.
	(b) Bell answer tone, United States and Canada
Cn	Transmitter enabled/disabled
C∅	Transmitter disabled; receive-only condition
C1	Transmitter enabled (default)
D	Dial the number that follows and enter Originate mode. Optional parameters:

	P	Pulse dial (default); typed as ATDP
	T	Touch-Tone dial
	,	(Comma) Pause for 2 seconds
	;	Return to Command mode after dialing
	″	Dial the letters that follow. Example: ATDT 1800″MCIMAIL″
	!	Transfer call (flash switch-hook)
	W	Wait for second dial tone (with X3 or higher see discussion of X-level settings)
	@	Wait for an answer (with X3 or higher)
	R	Reverse frequencies

DSn	Dial the phone number stored in NRAM[1] at position n (n = ∅ to 3)
En	Command mode local echo (display) of keyboard commands ON/OFF. DIP switch 4 is factory set to Command mode echo ON
E∅	Local echo OFF
E1	Local echo ON
Fn	On-line local echo of transmitted data ON/OFF. Sometimes referred to as the Duplex setting
F∅	Local echo ON. Sometimes called half duplex

---

[1] Nonvolatile Random Access Memory

	Modem sends a copy to your screen of data it sends to the remote system
F1	Local echo OFF (default). Sometimes called full duplex. Receiving system may send a remote echo of data it receives
HØ	Hang up (go on hook)
H1	Go off hook
I*n*	Inquiry
IØ	Display product code
I1	Display results of ROM Checksum
I2	Display results of RAM test
I3	Display call duration or real time (see K*n*)
I4	Display current modem settings
I5	Display NRAM[1] settings
I6	Display link diagnostics
I7	Display product configuration
K*n*	Modem clock operation: Call-duration or Real-time mode
KØ	Return call duration at ATI3 (default)
K1	Return actual time at ATI3. Clock is set using ATI3 = HH:MM:SS K1
M*n*	Monitor (speaker) control
MØ	Speaker always OFF
M1	Speaker ON until carrier is established (default)
M2	Speaker always ON
M3	Speaker ON after last digit dialed and until carrier is established
O	Return on line after command execution
P	Pulse dial (default)
Q*n*	Quiet mode: result codes displayed/suppressed. DIP switch 3 is factory set for result code display
QØ	Result codes displayed
Q1	Result codes suppressed (quiet)
Sr = *n*	Set S-register value: r is any S-register; *n* must be a decimal number between Ø and 255

[1] Nonvolatile Random Access Memory

Sr.b = n	Alternative command for setting bit-mapped registers: r is the bit-mapped register; .b is the bit; n is Ø (off) or 1 (on)
Sr?	Query contents of register r
T	Tone dial
Vn	Return result codes in words or numbers (Words/Numeric mode). DIP switch 2 is factory set for "word" result codes
VØ	Numeric mode
V1	Word mode

X COMMANDS AND THEIR IMPORTANCE

The most interesting AT command function is setting the X command value. This tells the modem how "smart" it should be; the higher the X value, the smarter the modem will act. Some modems accept values up to and beyond X7. You can test your modem in Terminal mode by typing **AT X1**, and observe the result. If you see OK, type **AT X2** and see what you get. Keep increasing the value until you get ERROR for a return message. The last X value that gave you OK is the smartest your modem can be.

Most telecommunications programs initialize the modem with AT X1. This disables smart functions such as determining if a line is busy. After discovering the highest smart level of your modem, type **AT X** *value*, or incorporate it into the initialization string you'll find in the communications program setup. Just change X1 to X4, or whatever X value your modem can handle. Most modems accommodate X4, and most communications programs work better when the modem is set to X4 or above.

The actual reason for the X setting is to establish a level of *result codes* to be used by the telecommunications program. In other words, the modem, if set properly, can tell the program that the line is busy, for example; and the program then knows to reset or redial.

Result Codes Options Table

Not all the higher X values apply to all modems. Use the following table as a guide. As you can see, setting your modem to X6 will make it the most versatile.

Result Codes	Setting							
	X0	X1	X2	X3	X4	X5	X6	X7
0/OK	o	o	o	o	o	o	o	o
1/CONNECT	o	o	o	o	o	o	o	o
2/RING	o	o	o	o	o	o	o	o
3/NO CARRIER	o	o	o	o	o	o	o	o
4/ERROR	o	o	o	o	o	o	o	o
5/CONNECT 1200		o	o	o	o	o	o	o
6/NO DIAL TONE			o		o		o	o
7/BUSY				o	o	o	o	o
8/NO ANSWER				o	o	o	o	o
9/RESERVED								
10/CONNECT 2400		o	o	o	o	o	o	o
11/RINGING						o	o	o
12/VOICE						o	o	
13/CONNECT 9600		o	o	o	o	o	o	o
18/CONNECT 4800		o	o	o	o	o	o	o
Functions								
Adaptive dialing			o	o	o	o	o	o
Wait for second dial tone (W)				o	o	o	o	o
Wait for answer (@)				o	o	o	o	o
Fast dial		o		o			o	o

EXTENDED COMMAND SET APPLICABLE TO US ROBOTICS MODEMS

Most modems have extended commands. With US Robotics modems, you use the AT command, followed by one of the following options.

Command/Options	Function
&An	Enable/disable additional result code subsets
&A0	/ARQ result codes disabled
&A1	/ARQ result codes enabled (default)

&A2	Additional /HST or /V32 indicator in result codes for calls at 4800bps and 9600bps enabled
&Bn	Data Rate, terminal-to-modem (DTE/DCE)
&BØ	DTE/DCE rate switches to follow connection rate (default)
&B1	DTE/DCE rate remains fixed at the DTE setting. Allowable rates are 38.4K, 19.2K, 9600, 4800, 2400, 1200, 300bps
&Cn	Carrier Detect (CD) signal, modem-to-DTE. DIP switch 6 is factory set so modem controls CD and override is disabled
&CØ	CD override (CD always ON)
&C1	Modem sends CD signal when it connects with another modem, and drops CD on disconnect
&Dn	Data Terminal Ready (DTR) signal, DTE-to-modem. DIP switch 1 is factory set for normal DTR operations, and override is disabled
&DØ	DTR override (DTR always ON)
&D1	Reserved
&D2	Terminal must send DTR for modem to accept commands. Dropping DTR terminates a call
&F	Load factory (ROM) settings into random access memory (RAM)
&Gn	Guard tone as part of answer sequence, for 2400/1200bps calls from overseas
&GØ	No guard tone, U.S., Canada (default)
&G1	550Hz guard tone, some European countries
&G2	1800Hz guard tone, U.K., some Commonwealth countries. Requires BØ setting
&Hn	Transmit Data flow control
&HØ	Flow control disabled (default)
&H1	Hardware (Clear to Send) flow control
&H2	Software (XON/XOFF) flow control
&H3	Hardware and software flow control
&In	Received Data software flow control
&IØ	Flow control disabled (default)
&I1	XON/XOFF to local modem and remote computer
&I2	XON/XOFF to local modem only
&I3	Host mode, Hewlett Packard protocol
&I4	Terminal mode, Hewlett Packard protocol

&I5	Same as &I2 in ARQ mode. In non-ARQ mode, XON/XOFF to remote modem for link flow control
&J*n*	Phone line interface
&JØ	Single phone line; RJ11, RJ41S, or RJ45S phone jack (default)
&J1	Multiple phones/modems on line; RJ12 or RJ13 jack
&K*n*	Data compression
&KØ	Disabled
&K1	Auto enable/disable (default). Disabled if modem is set to &BØ and DTE rate switches to match link rate
&K2	Enabled regardless of &B setting
&L*n*	Normal/leased phone line
&LØ	Normal phone line (default)
&L1	Leased line; enables the modem to reconnect if disconnected
&M*n*	Error control (ARQ) and synchronous operation
&MØ	Normal asynchronous mode, error control disabled
&M1	Synchronous mode, error control disabled
&M2	Reserved
&M3	Reserved
&M4	Normal/ARQ asynchronous mode (default). Normal connection if ARQ connection cannot be made
&M5	ARQ asynchronous mode. Modem hangs up if ARQ connection cannot be made
&N*n*	Link Rate (DCE/DCE) variable or fixed. With fixed link rate, modem hangs up if called, or calling modem is operating at a different rate
&NØ	Variable link operations (default). Modem negotiates highest possible link rate with remote modem
&N1	300bps
&N2	1200bps
&N3	2400bps
&N4	4800bps
&N5	7200bps
&N6	9600bps
&N7	12Kbps (HST mode only)
&N8	14.4Kbps (HST mode only)
&P*n*	Pulse dialing make/break ratio
&PØ	U.S., Canada make/break ratio (default)

&P1	U.K., some Commonwealth countries make/break ratio
&R*n*	Received Data hardware (RTS) flow control
&RØ	Delay before modem responds to DTE's RTS signal with CTS signal. Delay is set in S-register 26
&R1	Ignore RTS (default)
&R2	Received data sent to DTE only when RTS is high; used only if DTE supports RTS signaling
&S*n*	Data Set Ready (DSR) operations
&SØ	DSR override, always ON (default)
&S1	Modem sends DTE a DSR signal when it senses a modem tone on the phone line
&S2	On loss of carrier, modem sends DTE a pulsed DSR signal with Clear to Send (CTS) following Carrier Detect (CD)
&S3	Same as &S2, but without CTS following CD
&W	Write current settings to NRAM[1]
&X*n*	Synchronous Timing Source. This specifies whether the modem or DTE generates the timing signals for the Transmit clock during a synchronous call
&XØ	Modem's Transmit clock is the source (default)
&X1	DTE is the source
&X2	Modem's Receiver clock is the source; valid only in V32 mode or for 2400/1200bps connections in HST mode
&Y*n*	Break handling. Destructive Breaks clear the buffer; expedited Breaks are sent immediately to the remote system. Under data compression, destructive Breaks cause both modems to reset their compression tables
&YØ	Destructive, don't send Break
&Y1	Destructive, expedited (default)
&Y2	Nondestructive, expedited
&Y3	Nondestructive, unexpedited; modem sends Break in sequence with data received from DTE
&Z*n* = s	Write the following Dial string(s) to NRAM[1] at position *n* (*n* = 0 to 3)
&Z*n*?	Display the phone number stored in NRAM[1] at position *n* (*n* = 0 to 3)

[1] Nonvolatile Random Access Memory

TYPICAL FRONT PANEL INDICATORS

Symbol	Meaning	Status
HS	High Speed	*All calls above 2400bps:* ON during call progress, after completion of dialing; OFF during HST-mode link negotiations at 2400bps, then ON during connection. Remains ON after disconnect until next call is originated or answered
AA	Auto Answer	*Answer mode only:* ON when your modem is in Auto Answer mode, and when answering a call; in HST mode, goes OFF if the channel is reversed and your answering modem transmits at 450 or 300bps. Also goes OFF when the modem originates a call
CD	Carrier Detect	ON when the CD override (DIP switch 6) is ON (DOWN). ON if DIP switch 6 is UP and the Courier receives a valid data signal (carrier) from a remote modem, indicating that data transmission is possible
OH	Off Hook	ON when the Courier takes control of the phone line to establish a data link
RD	Received Data	Flashes when the modem sends result codes or passes received data bits to the computer or terminal
SD	Send Data	Flashes when the computer or terminal sends a data bit to the Courier
TR	Data Terminal Ready	ON when the modem receives a DTR signal from the computer or terminal. In earlier versions, the status light does not reflect a DTR override (DIP switch 1 DOWN). But in later versions the light goes on at power-on if the override is enabled. The override causes the modem to act as if DTR is always ON

MR	Modem Ready/ Test Mode	ON when the Courier is powered on. Flashes when the modems retrain, including on-line fallback, or while the modem is in Test mode
RS	Request to Send	ON when the Courier is powered on, if your computer or terminal supports RTS. OFF if the Courier is set to &R2 (Received Data hardware flow control) and the computer or terminal lowers RTS
CS	Clear to Send	ON until the modem lowers CTS when Transmit Data hardware flow control is enabled (&H1, &H3). Always ON during synchronous calls
ARQ	Error Control	Automatic Repeat Request. ON when the Courier is set to &M4 or &M5 and successfully connects with another modem under error control. Flashes when the Courier retransmits data to the remote modem
SYN	Synchronous Mode	ON when the modem is set to &M1 and enters synchronous mode

Emoticons

When reading electronic mail or teleconferencing on line, you'll occasionally see little hieroglyphic designs interspersed within text. These are called *emoticons*, and are used to express on line the emotions of normal voice communication—for example, to indicate that the "snide" comment you just made was really a joke, intended to amuse and not offend. Some of the best emoticons are represented here. You can see that most of them use the same few keyboard characters in different combinations. They are normally meant to be viewed from a 90° angle, as most are designed sideways. So tilt your head to the side; you'll see that these are actually little faces.

   emoticon \i-′mōt- -kän\ *n.* A figure created with the symbols on the keyboard. Read with the head tilted to the left. Used to convey the spirit in which a line of text is typed.

Emoticon	Emoticon/Message
:-)	Humor
:-) :-(	Masks theatrical comments
:<)	For those with hairy lips

:<)=	For those with beards, too
:/)	Not funny
'-)	Wink
P-)	Pirate
;-)	Wink II
(@ @)	You're kidding!
:-"	Pursing lips
:-v	Another face (speaking), side profile
:-V	Shouting
:-w	Speak with forked tongue
:-W	Shout with forked tongue
:-r	Bleahhh! (sticking tongue out)
:-f	
:-p	
:-1	Smirk
:-,	Smirk II
<:-O	Eeek!
:-*	Oops! (Covering mouth with hand)
:-T	Keeping a straight face (tight-lipped)
:-D	Said with a smile
:-P	
:-y	
:-o	More shouting
:-O	Still more shouting
:-{	Count Dracula
=¦:-)=	Uncle Sam
7:)	Reagan
:-#	Censored
:~i	Smoking
:~j	Smoking and smiling
:/i	No smoking
:-I	It's something, but I don't know what...
:-x	Kiss, kiss
:->	Another happy face
:-(	Unhappy
:-c	Really unhappy
:-C	Unbelieving (jaw dropped)
:-<	Forlorn
:-B	Drooling (or overbite)
:-¦	Disgusted

:-?	Licking your lips
<:> = =	A turkey
:-) :-) :-)	Loud guffaw
:-J	Tongue-in-cheek comments
:*)	Clowning around
:-8	Talking out of both sides of your mouth
(:-)	Messages dealing with bicycle helmets
@=	Warning about nuclear war
<:-)	For dumb questions
o=	A burning candle
-=	A doused candle
OO	Headlights on a message
:_)	I used to be a boxer, but it really got my nose out of joint
B-)	Batman
B-¦	Michael Keaton Batman
#:-)	Someone with matted hair
:-o	"Oh, noooooo!" (à la Mr. Bill)
#:-o	Mr. Bill II
¦-(	Late night messages
:^)	Messages teasing people about their noses
:-{#}	Messages teasing people about their braces
(:-$	Ill
(:-&	Angry
(:-(	Very sad
(:^(	Broken nose
(:<)	Blabbermouth
:-(=)	Big teeth
&:-)	Curly hair
@:-)	Wavy hair
?-(	Black eye
:	Message about fuzzy things
*:**	Message about fuzzy things with mustaches
%-)	Broken glasses
+ <:-¦	Monk/nun
{0-)	Cyclops
(:-¦K-	Formal message
@%&$%&	You know what this means...
¦¦*(	Handshake offered
¦¦*)	Handshake accepted

< && >	Rubber chickens
> < > <	Argyle socks
2B ¦^2B	Message about Shakespeare
(-_-)	Secret smile
<{:-)}	Message in a bottle
<:-)< <¦	Message from a space rocket
(:-...	Heart-breaking message
< < < <(:-)	Message from a hat salesperson
(O−<	A fishy message
(:>-<	Message from a thief: hands up!
<I==I)	A message on four wheels
:^{	Another mustache
{'	Alfred Hitchcock
@>--->---	A rose

Directory of Modem Manufacturers

The following is a partial list of manufacturers of modems and modem-related products. Phone numbers and fax numbers are provided for your convenience. Of course, all addresses and phone numbers are subject to change.

Acer Technologies Corp.
401 Charcot Avenue
San Jose, CA 95131
(800) 538-1542 (408) 922-0333
(408) 922-0176 FAX

Adaptive Computer Technologies
516 Greer Road
Palo Alto, CA 94303
(415) 324-0121

Advanced Microcomputer Systems, Inc.
1321 Northwest 65 Place
Ft. Lauderdale, FL 33309
(800) 972-3733 (305) 975-9515
(305) 975-9698 FAX

Advanced Transducer Devices, Inc.
(subsidiary of TeleVideo Systems, Inc.)
550 E. Brokaw Road
San Jose, CA 95161-9048
(408) 954-8525 (408) 954-0725 FAX

Amptron International, Inc.
2445 Lillyvale Avenue
Los Angeles, CA 90032
(213) 221-3135 (213) 221-3137 FAX

Anchor Automation, Inc.
20675 Bahama Street
Chatsworth, CA 91311
(818) 998-6100 (818) 407-5330 FAX

Applied Spectrum Technologies, Inc.
450 Industrial Boulevard
Minneapolis, MN 55413-2931
(612) 379-7114

Area Network Products, Inc.
1120 Sycamore Avenue, Suite F
Vista, CA 92083
(619) 727-9600

Artel Communications Corporation
22 Kane Industrial Drive
Hudson, MA 01749
(508) 562-2100

Astrocom Corporation
120 West Plato Boulevard
St. Paul, MN 55107
(612) 227-8651

ATI Technologies, Inc.
3761 Victoria Park Avenue
Scarborough, ON, Canada M1W 3S2
(416) 756-0718 (416) 756-0720 FAX

AT&T
295 North Maple Avenue
Basking Ridge, NJ 07920
(800) 247-7000 (201) 221-2000

Avant Industries, Inc.
12020 Mora Drive, Unit 1
Santa Fe Springs, CA 90670
(213) 946-7706 (213) 946-9476 FAX

Avanti Communications Corporation
184 John Clark Road
Newport, RI 02840
(800) 356-0505 (401) 849-4660

BCH Equipment Corporation
6950 Bryan Dairy Road
Largo, FL 34647
(800) 237-8121 (813) 541-6404

Best Data Products, Inc.
5907 Noble Avenue
Van Nuys, CA 91411
(800) 632-BEST (818) 786-2884

Bizcomp Corporation
522 Mercury Drive
Sunnyvale, CA 94086
(408) 733-7800

Bo-Sherrel Company
36133 Niles Boulevard
Freemont, CA 94536
(415) 792-0354

Burr-Brown Corporation
6730 South Tucson Boulevard
Tucson, AZ 85706
(602) 746-1111

Bytcom, Inc.
2169 Francisco Boulevard, Suite H
San Rafael, CA 94901
(800) 227-3254 (415) 485-0700

Canoga-Perkins
21012 Lassen Street
Chatsworth, CA 91311-4241
(818) 718-6300

Cardinal Technologies, Inc.
New Products Division
1827 Freedom Road
Lancaster, PA 17601
(800) 722-0094 (717) 293-3000

CASE/Datatel, Inc.
7200 Riverwood Drive
Columbia, MD 21046
(301) 290-7710

CASE/Datatel, Inc.
55 Carnegie Plaza
Cherry Hill, NJ 08003
(609) 424-4451

C-Cor Electronics, Inc.
60 Decibel Road
State College, PA 16801
(814) 238-2461

Cermetek Microelectronics, Inc.
1308 Borregas Avenue
Sunnyvale, CA 94088
(800) 444-6271 (408) 752-5000

Chartered Electronics, Inc.
21 Airport Boulevard, Suite G-H
South San Francisco, CA 94080
(800) 882-7475 (415) 875-3636
(415) 877-8048 FAX

CMS Enhancements, Inc.
1372 Valencia Avenue
Tustin, CA 92680
(714) 259-9555 (714) 549-4004 FAX

Codex Corporation
7 Blue Hill Road
Canton, MA 02021-1097
(800) 544-0062 (617) 364-2000

Coherent Communications Systems Corporation
60 Commerce Drive
Hauppauge, NY 11788
(800) 443-0726 (516) 231-1550

ComData Corp.
7900 N. Nagle Avenue
Morton Grove, IL 60053
(800) 255-2570 (312) 470-9600

CompuAdd Corp.
12303 Technology Boulevard
Austin, TX 78727
(800) 531-5475 (512) 250-1489
(512) 250-5760 FAX

Computer Friends, Inc.
14250 N.W. Science Park Drive
Portland, OR 97229
(800) 547-3303 (503) 626-2291
(503) 643-5379 FAX

Computer Peripherals, Inc.
667 Rancho Conejo Boulevard
Newbury Park, CA 91320
(800) 854-7600 (805) 499-5751
(805) 498-8848 FAX

Computer Systems & Technology, Inc.
226 Sherwood Avenue
East Farmingdale, NY 11735
(516) 420-1470 (516) 420-1503 FAX

Comspec Digital Products
2313 West Sam Houston Parkway
Suite 145
Houston, TX 77043
(713) 461-4487

ComStream Corporation
10180 Barnes Canyon Road
San Diego, CA 92121
(619) 458-1800

CTS Corporation
4505 Wyland Drive, Suite 400
Elkhart, IN 46516
(219) 522-8000

CXR Telecom/Anderson Jacobson
521 Charcot Avenue
San Jose, CA 95131
(408) 435-8520

Daetech Computer Technologies Corp.
5512 E. Hastings, Suite 103
Burnaby, BC, Canada V5B 1R3
(604) 294-6135 (604) 294-0349 FAX

Data Race
12758 Cimarron Path, Suite 108
San Antonio, TX 78249
(512) 692-3909

Dataradio Corporation
400 Permeter Center Terrace, Suite 730
Atlanta, GA 30346
(404) 392-0002

DataTrek
4505 Wyland Drive
Elkhart, IN 46516
(219) 522-8000 (219) 522-0822 FAX

DCB of Champaign
807 Pioneer Road
Champaign, IL 61820
(217) 352-3207

DCC Corporation
7300 North Crescent Boulevard
Pennsauken, NJ 08110
(609) 662-7272

DELI
230 North Market Place
Escondido, CA 92025
(619) 743-8344

Dell Computer Corp.
9505 Arboretum Boulevard
Austin, TX 78759-7299
(800) 426-5150 (512) 338-4400
(512) 338-8421 FAX

Develcon Electronics, Ltd.
856 51st Street East
Saskatoon, SK, Canada S7K 5C7

Diamond Flower Electric Instruments Co., (U.S.A.) Inc.
2544 Port Street
West Sacramento, CA 95691
(916) 373-1234 (916) 373-0221 FAX

Digital Data Solutions
872 South Grove
Ypsilanti, MI 48198
(313) 487-4300

Digital Pathways, Inc.
201 Ravendale Drive
Mountain View, CA 94043-521
(415) 964-0707

Dowty RFL Industries, Inc.
Powerville Road
Boonton, NJ 07005
(201) 334-3100

Dynatech Communications
991 Annapolis Way
Woodbridge, VA 22191
(703) 550-0011

EF Data Corporation
1030 North Stadem Drive
Tempe, AZ 85281
(602) 968-0447

Eicon Technology
2196 32nd Avenue
Lachine, PQ, Canada H8T 3H7
(514) 631-2592

Elec & Eltek (U.S.A) Corp.
545 Weddell Drive
Sunnyvale, CA 94089
(800) 428-2839 (408) 734-4223
(408) 734-8352 FAX

Electrodata, Inc.
23020 Miles Road
Bedford Heights, OH 44128
(800) 441-6336 (216) 663-3333

Electronic Systems Technology, Inc.
1031 North Kellogg
Kennewick, WA 99336
(509) 735-9092

Emerald Technology, Inc.
18912 North Creek Parkway
Bothell, WA 98011
(206) 485-8200

Emucom, Inc.
225 Stedman Street, Suite 27
Lowell, MA 01851
(800) 521-1030 (508) 970-1189

E-Tech Corp.
3333 Bowers Avenue, Suite 165
Santa Clara, CA 95054
(408) 982-0270 (408) 982-0272 FAX

Everex Systems, Inc.
48431 Milmont Drive
Fremont, CA 94538
(800) 821-0806 (415) 498-1111
(415) 651-0728 FAX

Fairchild Data Corporation
350 North Hayden Road
Scottsdale, AZ 85257
(602) 949-1155

Fastcomm Data Corporation
12347-E Sunrise Valley Drive
Reston, VA 22091
(703) 620-3900

FiberCom, Inc.
3353 Orange Avenue North East
Roanoke, VA 24012
(800) 423-1183 (703) 423-1183

Fibronics (East Coast)
Communications Way
Hyannis, MA 02601
(508) 778-0700

Fibronics (West Coast)
2091 Business Center Drive, Suite 220
Irvine, CA 92715
(714) 851-1422

Franklin Telecom
733 Lakefield Road
Westlake Village, CA 91361
(800) 327-3850 (805) 373-8688
(805) 373-7373 FAX

Fujitsu America, Inc.
77 Rio Robles
San Jose, CA 95134
(408) 434-6777

Gandalf Data, Inc.
1020 South Noel Avenue
Wheeling, IL 60090
(312) 541-6060 (800) 426-3352

General DataComm, Inc.
Route 63
Middlebury, CT 06762-1299
(203) 574-1118

GoldStar Technology, Inc.
1130 E. Arques Avenue
Sunnyvale, CA 94086
(408) 737-8575 (408) 739-0202 FAX

GVC/Chenel Corp.
99 Demarest Road
Sparta, NJ 07871
(800) 243-6352 (201) 579-3630
(201) 579-2702 FAX

Hayes Microcomputer Products, Inc.
705 Westech Drive
P.O. Box 105203
Norcross, GA 30092
(404) 441-1617 (404) 441-1238 FAX

Holmes Microsystems, Inc.
2620 South 900 West
Salt Lake City, UT 84119
(800) 443-3034 (801) 975-9929
(801) 975-9726 FAX

Honeywell Bull Optoelectronics
830 East Arapaho Road
Richardson, TX 75081
(214) 470-4271

Hyundai Electronics America
166 Baypointe Parkway
San Jose, CA 95134
(800) 544-7808 (408) 473-9200
(408) 943-9567 FAX

INCOMM Data Systems, Inc.
652 S. Wheeling Road
Wheeling, IL 60090
(800) 346-2660 (312) 459-8881
(312) 459-0189 FAX

Inmac
2951 Zanker Road
San Jose, CA 95131
(408) 435-1700

Intel Corp.
Personal Computer Enhancement Operation
5200 N.E. Elam Young Parkway, Mail Stop CO3-07
Hillsboro, OR 97124
(503) 696-8080

International Business Machines Corporation (IBM)
Old Orchard Road
Armonk, NY 10504
Contact your local IBM representative.

International Data Sciences, Inc.
7 Wellington Road
Lincoln, RI 02865
(800) 437-3282 (401) 333-6200

ISC Datacom
1288 Reamwood Avenue
Sunnyvale, CA 94089
(408) 747-0300

Jasmine Technologies, Inc.
1740 Army Street
San Francisco, CA 94124
(800) 347-3228 (415) 282-1111
(415) 648-1625 FAX

Join Data Systems, Inc.
14838 Valley Boulevard, Suite C
City of Industry, CA 91746
(818) 961-7003 (818) 330-6865 FAX

Laser Computer, Inc.
(a Video Technology Co.)
550 E. Main Street
Lake Zurich, IL 60047
(800) 551-5742 (312) 540-8086
(312) 540-8335 FAX

Leading Edge Hardware Products, Inc.
225 Turnpike Street
Canton, MA 02021
(800) 343-6833 (617) 828-8150
(617) 821-0389 FAX

Lightwave Communications, Inc.
650 Danbury Road
Ridgefield, CT 06877
(203) 438-3591

LST, Inc.
(subsidiary of LONGSHINE Electronics Corp.)
2013 N. Capitol Avenue
San Jose, CA 95132
(408) 942-1746 (408) 942-1745 FAX

MacProducts USA, Inc.
8303 Mopac Expressway, Suite 218
Austin, TX 78759
(512) 343-9441

Mastercom Communication Products
24416 S. Main Street, Suite 304
Carson, CA 90745
(213) 834-6666 (213) 549-2920 FAX

Megahertz Corp.
4505 S. Wasatch Boulevard
Salt Lake City, UT 84124
(800) 527-8677 (801) 272-6000
(801) 272-6077 FAX

Memotec
40 High Street
North Andover, MA 01845
(508) 681-0600

Micom Communications Corporation
4100 Los Angeles Avenue
Simi Valley, CA 93063
(805) 583-8600

Micro Electronic Technologies
35 South Street
Worcester, MA 01748
(508) 435-9057 (508) 435-6481 FAX

Microcom, Inc.
500 River Ridge Drive
Norwood, MA 02062
(508) 551-1000

MicroGate Corporation
9501 Capital of Texas Highway, Suite 105
Austin, TX 78759
(800) 444-1982 (512) 551-1000

Mitsuba Corp.
650 Terrace Drive
San Dimas, CA 91773
(800) MITSUBA (714) 592-2866

Multi-Tech Systems, Inc.
2205 Woodale Drive
Mounds View, MN 55112
(800) 328-9717 (612) 785-3500

Mux Lab, Inc.
165 Graveline Road
St. Laurent, PQ, Canada H4T 1 R3
(514) 735-2741

Natural MicroSystems Corporation
8 Erie Drive
Natick, MA 01760-1313
(800) 533-6120 (508) 655-0700

NEC America, Inc.
DCPD, 110 Rio Robles
San Jose, CA 95134
(408) 433-1250

Nu Data, Inc.
32 Fairview Avenue
Little Silver, NJ 07739
(201) 842-5757

Octocom Systems, Inc.
255 Ballardvale Street
Wilmington, MA 01887
(508) 658-6050

Okidata Corporation
532 Fellowship Road
Mt. Laurel, NJ 08054
(800) 654-3282 (609) 235-2600

Optelecom, Inc.
15930 Luanne Drive
Gaithersburg, MD 20877
(301) 840-2121

Osicom Technologies, Inc.
198 Green Pond Road
Rockaway, NJ 07866
(800) 922-0881 (201) 586-2550
(201) 586-9740 FAX

Paradyne Corporation
8545 126th Avenue North
Largo, FL 34649
(813) 530-2000

Patton Electronics Co.
7958 Cessna Avenue
Gaithersburg, MD 20879
(301) 975-1000 (301) 869-9293 FAX

Penril DataCom, Data Communications Division
207 Perry Parkway
Gaithersburg, MD 20877
(800) 638-8905 (301) 921-8600

Plexcom, Inc.
65 Moreland Road
Simi Valley, CA 93065
(805) 522-3333

Practical Peripherals, Inc.
31245 La Baya Drive
Westlake Village, CA 91362
(800) 442-4774 (818) 706-0333
(818) 706-2474 FAX

Prometheus Products, Inc.
7225 S.W. Bonita Road
Tigard, OR 97223
(503) 624-0571 (503) 624-0843 FAX

Racall-Milgo, Inc.
1601 North Harrison Parkway
Sunrise, FL 33323-2899
(800) 327-4440 (305) 476-5609

RAD Data Communications, Inc.
151 W. Passaic Street
Rochelle Park, NJ 07662
(201) 587-8822 (201) 587-8847 FAX

Raycom Systems, Inc.
6395 Gunpark Drive
Boulder, CO 80301
(800) 288-1620 (303) 530-1620

Rockwell International Corp.
Semiconductor Products Division
4311 Jamboree Road, Mail Station 501-300
Newport Beach, CA 92660-3095
(800) 854-8099 (800) 422-4230 (CA)
(714) 833-4700 (714) 833-4078 FAX

S.I. Tech, Inc.
P.O. Box 609
Geneva, IL 60134
(312) 232-8640

Satellite Technology and Research
530 S. Commerce Road
Orem, UT 84057
(801) 224-7000 (801) 225-1660 FAX

SIIG, Inc.
5369 Randall Place
Fremont, CA 94538
(415) 657-0567 (415) 657-5962 FAX

Singer Data Products, Inc.
790 Maple Lane
Bensenville, IL 60106
(312) 860-6500

Sunhill, Inc.
1000 Andover Park, E
Seattle, WA 98188
(800) 544-1361 (206) 575-4131
(206) 575-3617 FAX

Supra Corp.
1133 Commercial Way
Albany, OR 97321
(503) 967-9075

Tailyn Communications Co., Inc.
6100 S.W. State Road 200, Suite 6118
Wocala, FL 32674
(904) 237-1813 (904) 237-4070 FAX

Tandy Corp.
1800 One Tandy Center
Ft. Worth, TX 76102
(817) 390-3011 (817) 390-2774 FAX

Tek-Com/Prentice
2343 Bering Drive
San Jose, CA 95131
(800) 346-6597 (408) 435-9515

Telebit Corporation
1345 Shorebird Way
Mountain View, CA 94043-1329
(800) TEL-EBIT (415) 969-3800

Telebyte Technology, Inc.
270 East Pulaski Road
Greenlawn, NY 11740
(800) 541-0345 (516) 261-0423

TeleMidas, Inc.
49066 Milmont Drive, Bldg. C
Fremont, CA 94538
(415) 226-9888

Telenetics Corp.
5109 E. LaPalma
Anaheim, CA 92807
(800) 826-6336 (800) 822-4267 (CA)
(714) 779-2766 (714) 779-1255 FAX

Terminal Data Corp.
15733 Crabbs Branch Way
Rockville, MD 20855
(301) 921-8282 (301) 921-8353 FAX

Touchbase Systems, Inc.
160 Laurel Avenue
Northport, NY 11768
(800) 541-0345 (516) 261-0423
(415) 856-4268

Transend Corp.
884 Portola Road
Portola Valley, CA 94025
(415) 851-3402

Tri-Data Systems, Inc.
1450 Kifer Road
Sunnyvale, CA 94086-5306

Tussey Computer Products
3075 Research Drive
State College, PA 16801
(800) 468-9044 (814) 238-1820
(814) 237-4450 FAX

Universal Data Systems
5000 Bradford Drive
Huntsville, AL 35805
(800) 631-4869 (205) 721-8000

US Robotics, Inc.
8100 McCormick Boulevard
Skokie, IL 60076
(800) 342-5877 (312) 982-5001
(312) 982-5235 FAX

USAFLEX
135 N. Brandon Drive
Glendale Hgts., IL 60139
(800) 872-3539 (312) 351-7204 FAX

Ven-Tel, Inc.
2121 Zanker Road
San Jose, CA 95131-2177
(408) 436-7400

VIR, Inc.
105 James Way
Southampton, PA 18966
(800) 344-3934 (215) 364-8866

Xtron Computer Equipment Corp.
19 Rector Street
New York, NY 10006
(800) 854-4450 (212) 344-6583
(212) 809-9840 FAX

Zoom Telephonics, Inc.
207 South Street
Boston, MA 02111
(800) 631-3116 (617) 423-1072

GENDER CHANGERS/CABLES

B&B Electronics
RS-232 Interface Equipment
P.O. Box 1008R
Ottawa, IL 61350
(815) 434-0846

Black Box Corp.
Mayview Road at Park Drive
P.O. Box 12800
Pittsburgh, PA 15241
(412) 746-5500 (412) 746-0746 FAX

Cables & Chips
232 Front Street
New York, NY 10038
(212) 619-3132

IntraComputer
101 West 31st. Street
New York, NY 10001
(212) 947-5533

Glossary of Terms

Abort   A procedure to terminate execution of a program.

A/B Switch Box   An external device used to switch between one or more devices such as a modem, a plotter, a printer, or a mouse.

Accelerator Board   A board added onto the computer's main board, via the bus, designed to substantially increase the performance of a PC. This board has an additional microprocessor that runs at a higher speed and takes control of the computer's operation. Accelerator boards often contain additional high-speed RAM.

Acoustic Coupler   Also know as acoustic modem. A type of modem that connects to a phone line through a coupler that fits on a telephone handset. The acoustic coupler converts electronic data to and from audio signals.

Adapter   Also known as add-on card, controller, or I/O card. Adapters are installed in expansion slots to enhance the processing power of the computer or to communicate with other devices. Examples of adapters include printer, asynchronous communication, floppy disk controller, and expanded memory.

Address   A numeric value assigned to a specific memory location permitting reading or writing of data to/from that location.

Address Space   A set of addresses describing accessible memory locations that can be occupied by programs or data. Usually the complete range of memory locations that can be accessed by a microprocessor. The microprocessor in your personal system can directly address one megabyte of space. This space is occupied by both RAM and ROM and can include memory that resides on disk controllers, display adapters, and other peripheral devices.

Analog Signal   A signal with continuous variation, such as the sounds of a voice or music transmitted over telephone lines.

Application   The system or problem to which a computer is applied. The most common applications for personal computers are word processing, business analysis using spreadsheets, and data processing using some form of database program.

Application Program   A program designed to perform a particular task or function, but that does not directly control the computer hardware system functions.

Application Software   *See* Application Program.

Argument   A variable upon which the value of a function depends. The argument entered for a DOS command that regulates the way in which the command operates.

ASCII   American Standard Code for Information Interchange (formerly called USASCII). A standard, seven-bit information coding system that assigns a number from 0 to 127 to each of 128 upper- and lowercase letters of the alphabet, numbers, special characters, and control characters. An eighth bit is invariably added, but its use is less standardized. In telecommunications applications, the eighth bit is often a calculated parity number, most commonly even. Internally, PCs utilize the IBM character set, which employs eight bits to display 256 characters, symbols, a space, and null. This character set is used widely with small computers and terminals and can be transmitted from one location to another using eight bits and no parity.

ASCII Download In general, a download of pure ASCII text. Such a download involves no error checking, but is typically governed by XON/XOFF flow control. *See* Download, Protocol, XON/XOFF.

Assembly Language Assembly language consists of easily recognizable mnemonics and meaningful words, but is a low-level language. It is structured like machine language, but is less prone to coding mistakes. (Machine code consists of only 1s and 0s.) Programming in assembly language allows complete control over the microprocessor, while programs in high-level languages like BASIC and COBOL use only the features provided in those languages. An assembly language program allows control of the computer's instruction set at the lowest level, normally runs faster than a program in the high-level programming languages, and does not require intermediate interpretation.

Asynchronous Communication A type of serial communication by which data is passed between devices. "Asynchronous" means that the timing of each character transmitted is independent of other characters. Also known as ASYNC.

AT Command Set Also known as the Hayes Command Set. This is the industry standard set of commands which the computer uses to control the modem. The commands begin with the prefix "AT"—for instance, AT DT tells the modem to Dial (D) using DTMF touch-tone dialing (T).

Auto-Answer A mode in which the modem answers incoming calls automatically, without your intervention.

Auto-Dial Signifies that a modem is capable of dialing telephone numbers in response to computer commands.

Auto Line Feed A communications parameter that causes a terminal program to automatically perform a line feed (LF) when a carriage return (CR) is seen. *See* Carriage Return and Line Feed.

Auto-Logon Many communications programs are able to perform your logon sequence for you automatically when connecting to a host system. This is done by means of prewritten script files. *See* Logon, Script.

Backup   Refers to equipment or systems designed to provide continued operation when the primary equipment or system fails. A backup diskette stores copies of other diskettes or of data on a fixed (hard) disk, to help prevent loss of data in case of damage and/or system failure.

BASIC   A high-level programming language. The name is an acronym for Beginner's All-purpose Symbolic Instruction Code. Developed at Dartmouth College.

BAT   Abbreviation for batch. Used as the filename extension (.BAT) for executable files containing DOS commands. *See* Batch File.

Batch File   A file containing commands in a particular sequence, allowing them to be processed one at a time, automatically. The filename ends with the extension .BAT.

Baud Rate   The actual rate of symbols transmitted per second, which may represent more than one bit. A given baud rate may have more than one bps rate. *See* Bits Per Second (bps).

BBS   *See* Bulletin Board System.

Bell   ASCII character 7, CTRL-G. This causes the receiving terminal to ring a bell or some sort of alarm sound.

Bell-Compatible   Means that a modem is compatible with the Bell 212A modem specification, which is the standard for 1200bps modems.

Binary   A numbering system with two digits, 0 and 1, used by computers to store and process information.

BIOS   Basic Input-Output System. A collection of primitive computer routines (stored in ROM on a PC) that control the video display, disk drives, and keyboard.

Bisynchronous   Computer communications in which both sides simultaneously transmit and receive data. Also called BISYNC.

Bit   A binary digit and the most basic unit of data that can be recognized and processed by a computer. A bit is either 0 or 1. Bits can be grouped to form larger units of information nibbles (4 bits), bytes (8 bits), or words (usually 16 bits).

Bits Per Second (bps)   The number of data bits sent per second between two modems. This is often improperly referred to as the Baud Rate. *See* Baud Rate.

Block   During file transfers or other error-checked communication, a block is a group of characters sent together, along with some sort of error-checking information. Common block sizes are 128 bytes and 1024 bytes.

Board   (1) Within an on-line service or bulletin board system, a specific message posting/receiving area. Sometimes used to refer to an entire BBS. (2) A printed circuit board, or card. *See* Bulletin Board System, On-Line Service.

Boolean Operators   Based on the algebraic theories of the English mathematician George Boole; used by databases to refine search commands. Operators consist of "and," "or," and "not."

Bootable Disk   A disk containing the DOS (or other operating system) programs necessary to make it "bootable." These include the files for Input/Output and DOS, which are "hidden," and thus transparent to the user. The master DOS diskettes have one disk that is bootable; the others are not. Refer to your DOS User and DOS Technical Reference Manuals for more specific information.

Boot Sector   Sector one of track zero on a floppy or hard disk. This sector contains information necessary for "booting," or starting the computer system.

Bootstrap (Boot)   Comes from the phrase "pulling oneself up by one's own bootstraps," and means the process by which a small program in ROM loads other programs into the computer's memory to start the system.

Bootstrap Loader   A subroutine usually built into the hardware of the computer, capable of initiating the operation of another subroutine. The first instructions are designed to read in the remainder of the subroutine and initiate the total program schedule.

BPS   *See* Bits Per Second.

Break   A command that stops an operation. The keyboard has a BREAK key, but it only works when used with the CTRL key. This keyboard function is programmable and is not always functional or active, depending upon the product.

Break Character   A character that you send to signal a host system to stop what it is currently doing. This is the familiar BREAK key. CTRL-C is a common break character, as are CTRL-K and CTRL-P.

Buffer   An area of memory where the computer or modem stores incoming or outgoing data until it can be processed or sent.

Bug   An error. A hardware bug is an electrical, mechanical, or electronic defect that interferes with the normal operation of a computer. A software bug is a mistake in the code.

Bulletin Board System (BBS)   A computer (generally a microcomputer) set up to receive calls and act as a host system. BBSs allow users to communicate through message bases, and also to exchange files.

Bus   A group of wires used to carry a set of related signals or information within a computer from one device to another.

Byte   A sequence of adjacent binary digits that the computer considers a unit. A byte consists of eight bits.

CAIR   An abbreviation for Computer-Assisted Information Retrieval; the process of accessing and utilizing information stored on a remote computer through your own computer.

Capture   Communications programs often store, or "capture," the data being sent by the remote system. This data may be saved in a disk file, or in a "capture buffer" that you can scroll through and examine.

Card   A small printed circuit board.

Caret   The symbol ˆ, found above the number 6 on most keyboards.

Carriage   A control mechanism for a printer that can automatically control the feeding, spacing, skipping, and ejection of paper or preprinted forms.

Carriage Return (CR) ASCII character 13, CTRL-M. Generated by the RE-TURN or ENTER key, this causes the cursor to move to the first column on the screen. *See* Auto Line Feed.

Carriage Return and Line Feed On IBM-compatible systems and others, this combination is the standard End-Of-Line marker. When displayed on screen, it causes the cursor to move down one line, and also to return to the first column. *See* Auto Line Feed, Carriage Return, Line Feed.

Carrier The basic signal sent over the phone lines which modems use to transfer data. This is the tone that is modulated to signify bits of data. *See* Modulate.

Cartridge A storage medium in its own casing. This could be a hard disk platter for the removable hard disk, or tape if used in a tape drive. There are several different standards for both technologies.

Cathode Ray Tube *See* CRT

CCITT-Compatible Means a modem is compatible with the CCITT (International Consultative Committee for Telephony and Telegraphy) V22bis standard for 2400bps communications. Hayes-compatible 2400bps modems are CCITT-compatible.

Central Processing Unit *See* CPU.

CGA Color Graphics Adapter. A low/medium-resolution color graphics system for personal computers.

Checksum A method of error-checking that involves adding up all characters sent, and comparing the lower byte of the result to an identical checksum sent along with the data.

Chip *See* Integrated Circuit.

Clone A term used to describe an IBM/PC/XT or /AT-compatible computer made by another manufacturer.

Cold Start To turn on the power switch of a computer and begin its operation. If the computer is already on, to turn off the power switch and then turn it on again. After a cold start, all the devices of the computer are reinitialized. Also called cold boot or cold reset.

Color Monitor   A monitor that can display text and graphics in color. The two common types are composite and RGB, with RGB providing the higher quality.

COM   (1) Designation for a serial communication port when followed by a number, as in COM1, COM2, etc. (2) Short for COMMAND when used as a file extension, as in DISKCOPY.COM. Files with the .COM filename extension may be executed by entering the filename without the extension. *See* EXE.

Command   The portion of an instruction word that specifies the operation to be performed. Also, a program that helps you to create, change, analyze, or move data and software. DOS has two types of commands: internal and external.

COMMAND.COM   Also called command interpreter, console command processor, or shell. A file used by DOS to interpret your commands and execute programs.

Command Line   The line on which the system prompt appears, and on which commands are entered into the computer. Also, the command processor supplied with DOS. It acts as the interface between your input and the other components of the operating system, by interpreting all commands and performing executable functions.

Command Mode   A communications program in command mode is ready to accept user commands. *See* Terminal Mode.

Command Stacking   A capability of some systems to send more than one command at a time, rather than entering a single command and then responding to the next menu.

Communications Link   The path of data transfer through the various components involved in communications between two computer systems; for example, the modem, telephone line, and packet-switched network.

Communications Parameters   Settings that determine how your communications software will interpret incoming data, and what type of data will be sent out. The most important parameters are bits per second, parity, data bits, and stop bits.

Communications Software   The software you use to control your modem. This is the software that handles terminal emulation, file transfer, dialing, and all modem input and output.

Compatibility   Being capable of orderly, efficient integration and operation with other elements in a system. IBM products have become a standard in the industry, and for this reason PC manufacturers attempt to produce products compatible with the IBM products. No computer on the market can be 100 percent compatible because of rights owned by IBM regarding their BIOS firmware and BASIC located in ROM.

Composite Color   A color signal that is transmitted to a monitor on one common connector. This method of producing color is adequate, but will not provide high resolution.

Composite Video   The video signals are all combined in one signal and transmitted to the monitor or display.

Computer   Any device that can receive and store a set of logic and arithmetic instructions and information, process the information in a predetermined way, and communicate or store the results.

Computer Language   A programming language; a set of characters or a code used to form words, symbols, or instructions. Language also implies the rules used to combine the characters or code.

Computer Port   *See* COM, LPT1, or Port.

Computer System   A group of hardware. The minimum configuration consists of a computer, video display, keyboard, memory, and storage media. Any number of additional devices may be added to make a system faster and more functional.

CON   Short for console, which historically included both the keyboard and the monitor. In a personal computer, console is often used to designate the keyboard by itself.

Conference   Also called SIG (Special Interest Group). A conference is an area set up as a mini-BBS inside the main BBS. Conferences include separate message bases, file transfer areas, bulletins and doors. Conferences are topic specific and may cover such subjects as politics, desktop publishing, games, and product support.

CONFIG.SYS An ASCII file containing subcommands for the completion of the boot sequence and configuration of certain system characteristics.

Connect The point where two computers connect by modem. Modems usually display a CONNECT message when the two modems recognize each other.

Connect Time The amount of time spent connected to another system. This is generally expressed in hours, minutes, and seconds; sometimes it is expressed in fractions of hours.

Control Character or Key Keyboard character used for a control function. Form Feed and Line Feed are examples of control characters.

CPS The number of characters being sent per second during a communications session.

CPU Central Processing Unit. The central processor of the computer system; the CPU controls the processing routines, performs the arithmetic functions, and has a quickly accessible memory.

CRC Cyclic Redundancy Checking. A method of error checking used in later versions of Xmodem file transfer to cut down on errors when transmitting data.

Crossover Cable *See* Null Modem.

CRT Cathode Ray Tube. An electronic vacuum tube containing a screen on which information is displayed. Most computer monitors, all standard TV sets, and oscilloscopes use CRTs.

CTRL-ALT-DEL A three-key command that resets the PC and initiates a reboot of the system.

CTRL-BREAK A two-key command that generally interrupts a program. This key combination usually has the same effect as CTRL-C.

CTRL-C   A two-key command that generally interrupts a program. This key combination usually has the same effect as CTRL-BREAK.

CTRL-S   A two-key command that generally stops a program, which freezes the screen for viewing. In some programs this is a "toggle"; that is, if you press the combination again, the program continues.

CTS   Clear to Send. An "OK to send data" signal generated by the modem or the serial card.

Cursor   A special symbol on a screen showing the position where a character can be typed or corrected.

Cylinder   A fixed disk drive contains a number of platters, and platters are divided into tracks. A cylinder is collection of all corresponding tracks on all sides of the platters in a disk drive. Read/write heads access the same track on all platters simultaneously.

Daisy Wheel   A printer technology that uses a wheel, or disc, with engraved letters and characters to imprint images on paper. This generally provides the good quality print, called letter quality.

Data   Information of any type, including binary, decimal, or hexadecimal numbers, integers, strings of characters, and so forth.

Database   Any collection of information in any form. The term is generally applied to bibliographic or text information stored on a computer and accessible in a systematic way; a collection of records. On-line services offer databases that a user can search for information.

Data Bits   The bits sent by a modem that actually make up a character of data; this does not include stop, start, or parity bits, which are used only by the modem and not passed on to the computer. As a communications parameter, this specifies the number of data bits the modem will use.

DDD   Direct Distance Dialing.

Debug   The process of finding and correcting errors in a program. Also, a DOS program that is used as a program debugging tool.

Default   The value entered by a program instead of a user.

Default Drive   A drive to which the system looks to read or write information unless you specify another drive name in a command. Initially, the default drive is the one from which DOS is loaded into memory when the system is first booted.

Delete   To remove a file from disk storage.

Delimiter   A character used to separate other characters in a file or command. A delimiter may be a space (one blank character space), TAB (group of spaces), comma (,), semicolon (;), equal sign (=), or a plus sign (+).

DEL/RUBOUT   ASCII character 127. On some systems, this performs the same function as BACKSPACE.

Demodulate   To convert the modulated carrier tone sent by a modem back into data. *See* Modem, Modulate.

Density   The amount of space distribution on a storage medium, such as magnetic storage on a disk, or visual storage on a video monitor (CRT).

Device   A piece of equipment used to input data for processing or to output processed data. DOS provides access to several devices by use of reserved names, such as A:, COM1:, PRN, AUX, and CON.

Device Driver   A program created to control a particular device. DOS loads a device driver into memory at boot-up time. External device drivers are usually listed in the CONFIG.SYS file.

Diagnostic   Diagnostic Program. A computer program designed to first determine if a malfunction exists, and if it does, to locate the malfunction in the computer and/or the attached peripherals.

Dial-Up   To call one modem from another, over telephone lines.

Dial-Up Modem   A modem designed to be used over telephone lines. Due to the problems of phone line noise and signal loss, to be effective a dial-up modem must operate within a low bps range (typically 9600bps or less).

Digital Signal   An electrical signal which takes on only certain values (1 or 0) and is not continuous. A digital signal is either on or off; there is no modulation as with an analog signal. *See* Analog Signal.

Dip   Dual In-line Package. The most popular packaging method for integrated circuits. It has two parallel rows of pins. The number of pins is usually 14, 16, 18, 20, 24, 40, or more.

Direct-Connect Modem   A modem intended to be connected by a dedicated cable to another modem. Since they do not have to operate over phone lines, direct-connect modems can move data much faster than dial-up modems. *See* Dial-Up Modem.

Direct Drive Monitor   A monitor that displays high-resolution text and character graphics, but does not support pixel graphics. This monitor is used by the monochrome adapter.

Directory   A list of filenames and locations of files on a disk. A directory may point to directories called subdirectories, but the DOS master directory is the ROOT directory.

Directory Structure   Refers to how a directory is organized and arranged on a disk.

Disconnect   Also Logoff, Logout, and Signoff. The termination of the connection between two modems. In communications software, the command that causes this termination.

Disk   A circular metal platter or mylar diskette with magnetic material on both sides, which stores programs and data. Disks are rotated continuously so that read/write heads mounted on movable or fixed arms can read or write programs and data from and to the disk.

Disk Drive   The motor that actually rotates the disk, plus the recording/playback heads and associated mechanisms—all in a mountable housing.

Diskette   A diskette serves the same purpose as a disk, except it is made of flexible material and is permanently enclosed in a protective jacket. Also called floppy disk.

Disk Format   Refers to the method in which data is organized and stored on floppy or hard disk. There are many standards in the personal computer marketplace, but the most widely accepted is that used by DOS for the PC family, which is 48tpi, DS/DD (double sided/double density).

Doors   An area found on most bulletin board systems where a user can exit the main BBS program and run any of several stand-alone programs.

DOS   Disk Operating System. A set of programs that controls the communications between the components of the computer. Examples are displaying, reading and writing to a disk, printing, and accepting commands from the keyboard.

Dot Files   Files found in a subdirectory that contain information as to current and parent directories.

Dot Matrix   A type of printer technology that uses a print head to produce text and characters by using arrays of dots.

Download   The information received from the host computer to your terminal; either a noun (the data itself) or a verb (the process of retrieving the data).

Drive D   A reference designator for a drive, which could be drive A or B for floppies, and C for a hard disk. This is commonly used because the software author does not know the reader's or user's environment.

DS/DD   Double sided, double density. These are formats of floppy diskettes, that classify a method of data storage. *See Disk Format.*

DTMF   The touch-tone dialing system used by many phone systems.

DTR   Data Terminal Ready. A signal in your modem or serial card indicating the modem is ready.

Duplex   Data communications that can handle simultaneous two-way communications. Also, a communications parameter used to determine whether or not your computer's keystrokes will echo on your screen or the screen of the computer you are connected to.

EBCDIC Extended Binary Coded Decimal Interchange Code. An 8-bit code similar to ASCII, used primarily by IBM in large computers.

Echo If Echo is set to yes, the character you typed on the keyboard is displayed on the screen and sent to the host.

Echo Network Bulletin board systems often join in a message base exchange where one centrally located board acts as a host. Other boards call to upload messages entered by their users and download messages left by other boards in the network. The effect is that a local BBS user can ask a question and be answered by a user in another state or country.

Edge Connector A connector made of strips of brass or other conductive metal found at the edge of a printed circuit board. The connector plugs into a socket of another circuit board to exchange electronic signals.

Editor A computer program that allows users to create and modify text files, in a process similar to but simpler than a word processor. Often used to create/modify computer programs; hence their output is in a basic text format, without the various control characters that word processors use. EDLIN is the name of the editor provided with the IBM PC and MS-DOS.

EDLIN A DOS utility that enables you to create, edit, and display source programs and text files. EDLIN is a line editor.

EGA Enhanced Color Graphics Adapter. A medium-resolution color system for personal computers.

Electronic Mail (E-mail) The exchange of messages via a bulletin board or on-line service. One user leaves the message on the service "addressed" to another user. When the other user later connects to the same service, he can read the message and reply to it.

Emulation *See* Terminal Emulation.

Entry One item of information in a database, or one item in a list. Also, all the information pertaining to one on-line service in a communications program's dialing directory.

Error Checking Protocol *See* Protocol.

Error Message   DOS displays error messages when it encounters problems while attempting some system functions.

Escape Code   The hex equivalent of ESC is 1B. Normally, what follows is called an escape code. The codes that follow usually have special significance, especially in terminal emulation files.

EXE   Abbreviation for executable. Used as a filename extension in DOS (.EXE) for certain types of executable files, similar to filenames with the .COM extension. *See* COM.

Expanded Memory   Additional memory added to a computer via an add-on memory board with plug-in memory chips using the Lotus, Intel, or Microsoft EMM/EMS standard.

Expansion Chassis   An external system containing a PC bus and power supply, which is used to expand the PC's capacity for adding extra components to the system's bus. Special boards are installed in the PC and in the expansion unit, connected via a large cable, to allow data transmission between the units.

Expansion Slot   Long, narrow edge connectors on the system board, into which adapters and other add-on cards are inserted to expand the functions of the computer.

Extended Memory   Additional memory added to a computer's mother board or add-on memory card, always ranging 1024K and greater. There is limited software support for this type of memory.

External Modem   A modem that is used as a separate unit from the computer, connected through the computer's serial port.

False Drops   Also "false hits"; records retrieved from a search strategy that fit the terms and logic used but are irrelevant to the true intent of the search.

FAT   File Allocation Table. A table stored on the disk to indicate the status and location of every cluster on that disk or partition. Programs can use the FAT to determine the next cluster available for data writing.

Field Within a database or other collection of data, a field is one specific part of a record. For instance, in a database of user information, "name" might be one field, "password" might be another, and so on.

File A collection of related records treated as a unit. In a computer system a file can exist on magnetic tape, disk, or as an accumulation of information in system memory. A file can contain data, programs, or both.

Filename Alphanumeric characters assigned to identify a related set of records that constitute a particular file. DOS allows a filename to have up to eight characters plus an extension name of up to three characters. Certain characters cannot be used in the name or the extension.

File Transfer Protocol *See* Protocol.

Firmware Software stored in a permanently preprogrammed ROM chip. Firmware performs tasks such as hardware diagnostics, initializing the system, and booting.

Fixed Disk Also called hard disk or Winchester. An early IBM disk drive was named the 30-30 (like the rifle)—hence the nickname "Winchester." A bulk storage system with nonremovable, rotating, rigid magnetic storage disks. Typical storage capacities range from 20MB to over 1000MB for personal computers, and much higher for large computer systems. There are some versions of hard disk with removable rigid media in the form of disk packs.

Floppy Disk Also known as flexible disk or diskette. A bulk storage system with removable, rotating, flexible magnetic storage disks. These come in 8-inch, 5 1/4-inch, 3 1/2-inch, and 2-inch sizes. The 5 1/4-inch and 3 1/2-inch disks are most common for personal computers. The 3 1/2-inch and 2-inch disks are found on some laptops. Typical storage capacities range from 360K to 1.2MB on 5 1/4-inch diskettes, and from 720K to 1.44MB on the 3 1/2 and 2-inch diskettes.

Floppy Drive A disk drive designed to read and write data to a diskette for transfer to and from a computer. It is available in 8-inch, the standard 5 1/4-inch, 3 1/2-inch, and the newer 2-inch sizes. The 5 1/4-inch model comes in full height and half height, with the half height size requiring less power and less space.

Flow Control   A method used between two devices to regulate the flow of data. Typically, there is a signal to stop sending data, as well as a signal to start sending again. Between directly-connected devices (such as a computer and a printer) this is usually done by the hardware. Between two modems, software flow control is used.

Format   (1) The structure of an individual database; how the individual records are set up in a database; what fields are available for searching and the contents of each field. (2) The options available for displaying information; most systems use short, medium, or long display formats, and the content of each format varies between systems. (3) A DOS command that records the physical organization of tracks and sectors on a disk.

Framing Bits   Used to describe the bits which "frame" a character sent by modem (the start and stop bits). *See* Start Bit, Stop Bit.

Free Text Search   Similar to the "search" function in a word processor. This is a method of searching a database; it searches the entire item (including title, header, keywords, and body) for a phrase.

Full Duplex   In a full-duplex communications system, characters sent to the host are echoed back by the host to your screen. If your host computer uses full-duplex communication, you should usually set Echo to no.

Full-Text Database   A system that includes the entire text of an article, book chapter, or book; not limited to abstracted information.

Function Key   A special key used by itself or in conjunction with other keys to perform user-defined functions. DOS uses these keys for editing the command line and working in EDLIN.

G   The international symbol for giga, meaning billion. In computer usage it is defined as 1024 times mega and is actually 1,073,741,824, which is also 1K times 1MB. *See* K, M.

Gateway   An ad-hoc connection between two on-line services. A gateway exists when you are provided with a means of accessing one on-line service through another. For instance, users of CompuServe can access MCI Mail.

Half Duplex   In half-duplex communications systems, characters sent to the host are not echoed back to your screen. If your host uses half duplex, set your Echo to no.

Handle   A pseudonym used on a BBS or on-line service in place of your real name, similar to CB radio handles.

Handshaking   The devices at either end getting "in sync" with each other's behavior. This may be a hardware handshake, or a setting of certain software behaviors.

Hangup   The modem "hangs up" the phone line and the "conversation" is terminated.

Hardcopy   A printed copy of machine output in a visually readable form.

Hard Disk   A mass storage device that transfers data between the computer's memory and the disk storage media.

Hard Drive   *See* Fixed Disk.

Hardware   The physical components of a computer.

Hayes Command Set   *See* AT Command Set.

Hayes-Compatible   Hayes compatibility means two things. First, it means that a modem uses the same communications standards as the industry-standard Hayes modems, and second, that the modem also obeys the AT (or Hayes) command set. *See* AT Command Set, Bell-Compatible, CCITT-Compatible.

Hertz (Hz)   A unit of frequency equal to one cycle per second.

HEX   Short for Hexadecimal, a 16-digit numbering system used in computers. Each HEX digit represents four binary digits, hence two HEX digits can be used to represent eight binary digits or one Byte. The 16 digits used are 0-9 and A-F.

Hierarchical Directory   A directory classified by a specific rank or order of items.

Host System   This is, in general, the system to which you are connected when you call a BBS or on-line service. The host system receives calls, presents menus, accepts commands from the local system (your system), and so on.

IC   *See* Integrated Circuit.

ID   Also USERID, USERNAME. The "name" assigned to you by a given BBS or on-line system. This is entered by you when you log onto the system, and identifies you to the system. It may be your real name, a handle, or some string generated by the host system. *See* Handle.

IEEE-448   A standard specification for parallel interfaces between computers and devices. *See* RS-232.

Initialization String   A command or group of commands sent to the modem by a communications program at start-up. This will tell the modem to use a certain setup, which the program needs to correctly communicate with the modem.

Input   (1) Data that flows from external devices to a computer. (2) To send data from external components.

Input/Output   Data transferred from external devices to the computer, or from the computer to external devices.

Integrated Circuit   A tiny complex of electronic components and their connections that is produced in or on a small slice of material (such as silicon). A single IC can hold many electronic elements. Also called a chip.

Intel   A major manufacturer of integrated circuits used in computers. Intel makes the 8086 family of processors and its derivatives: the 8088, 80286, 80386, 80486, and the newer i860. These are the chips used in the IBM PC family of computers.

Interface   An exchange of information between one device and another, or the device that makes such exchange possible.

Internal Modem   A modem that resides inside the computer in the form of an add-on board. *See* External Modem.

I/O Input/Output.

Jumper A piece of wire or conducting material used to connect two terminals on a printed circuit board.

K The international symbol for kilo, meaning thousand. In computer usage it means 2 to the power of 10, or 1024. When applied to individual memory (RAM or ROM) chips, the term usually means 1024 bits. *See* G and M.

Kermit A file transfer protocol designed for maximum portability. Kermit has features that allow it to be used between any two computers that support modems, regardless of system differences. However, because of its emphasis on flexibility, Kermit is very slow and should not be used when faster options are available.

Keyboard Buffer An area of memory that stores information from the keyboard. This memory area can be programmed by the user and by software to enhance editing and control functions.

Keyword/Keyword Search A keyword is a word connected with some item in a database; the keyword can be used to find items pertaining to a specific topic. Many on-line databases allow you to search for items with keywords.

KHz (Kilohertz) 1,000 Hz.

Kilobyte Also K bytes or KB. 1024 bytes.

LAN Local Area Network. A small/moderate-sized network in which communications are usually confined to an area, such as a single building or campus.

Leased Line Modem A cross between a direct-connect modem and a dial-up modem. The modem still works over a telephone or similar line, and across long distances. However, the line is dedicated to this purpose, and is specially conditioned for data transfer. This allows faster communications (greater than 9600bps) with fewer errors. *See* Dial-Up Modem, Direct-Connect Modem.

LED   Light Emitting Diode. An element that is illuminated when an electronic signal is applied (voltage); used as an indicator for the presence of activity.

Letter Quality   This type of printer uses an engraved wheel, or disc, to imprint letters and characters on paper.

Library   A collection of related databases on a system, usually grouped for ease of access on a menu-driven system.

Line Editor   An editor program that allows line-by-line editing. Such an editor may or may not have editing control upon data within a line; however, DOS provides that control with the function key editing features.

Line Feed   ASCII code 10, CTRL-J. This causes the cursor to move down one line. On some systems, this is the complete "new line" sequence, and also causes the cursor to return to the first column.

Line Noise   When you are using a modem over the phone lines, interference and other disturbances cause some noise to creep into the transmission. This can garble characters, cause invalid data to be received, and at worst cause a loss of carrier and disconnection.

Local Area Network   *See* LAN.

Local System   The system initiating a call to a host system (such as a BBS or on-line service). Usually, the local system is your system.

Logical Drive   A drive that has been created by the disk operating system, or DOS. This is done either at the preference of the user or because the physical drive has a formatted capacity in excess of 32MB.

Logoff   *See* Disconnect.

Logon   The act of establishing communications with a host system. This includes establishing a modem connection, and entering your ID, password, and whatever else the system needs to know about you at connection. *See* Auto-Logon.

LPT1   The first parallel port on the IBM PC. *See* Parallel Port.

M   The international symbol for mega or meg, meaning million. In computer usage it is defined as 1024 kilobytes, or 1,048,576 bytes. *See* K, G.

Machine Language   Instructions and data coded in binary numbers. This is the only language recognized by the microprocessor that controls all operations in your personal system. All programs and all data to be processed by the system get translated into machine language.

Macros   The method some communications software has to assign a series of keystrokes to a single key. Once the string of characters has been assigned to a key, you can send a long series of characters to a host system by simply pressing one key. Macros can greatly speed input of commands to a remote computer.

Mainframe   A computer capable of supporting thousands of simultaneous users, which requires substantial resources to operate.

Mass Storage Device   *See* Hard Disk.

Megabyte   One million bytes; abbreviated MB, such as 10MB.

Memory   A device that stores data in a computer. Internal memories are very high-speed and are either read/write random access memory (RAM) or read only memory (ROM). Bulk storage memories are either fixed disk, floppy disk, tape, or optical memories; these hold very large amounts of data but are much slower to access than the internal memories.

Memory Address   A value assigned to a memory location. An address corresponds to the location of a single byte. The address of a memory location may be expressed in hexadecimal or decimal.

Memory Location   A unique address that can be filled with a specific value.

Memory Map   A list describing a block of memory address space that can be occupied by programs or data. It is used as a reference to find the entry points, storage locations, and amount of memory used by stack, data, code segments, or other functions.

Message   A computer "note" left by one user of a system for another (or all) to read.

MHz (MegaHertz)   1000 KHz, or 1,000,000 Hz.

Microchip   Any integrated circuit on a chip. May be a group of electronic components or even a microprocessor (miniature computer).

Microcomputer Chip   Large-scale integrated circuit designed to perform the major functions of a computer (microcomputer or personal computer).

Microprocessor   An IC (integrated circuit) that communicates, controls, and executes machine language instructions.

Milliseconds   One-thousandth of a second. Abbreviated ms, as in 10ms.

Mode   A condition or set of conditions, parameters, or protocols under which an operation can take place. Some examples are color or monochrome display modes, and serial communication protocols.

Modem   MOdulator/DEModulator. A device that allows a computer to communicate with other computers over various transmission lines. Most modems in use with personal computers communicate over telephone lines at speeds of 300, 1200, or 2400bps in a serial mode.

Modulate   Changing the frequency, wavelength or some other characteristic of an analog signal so that it may be interpreted as data by the receiver.

Monochrome   A term used for a video display on which one primary color is available, usually white, with one background, usually black.

Monochrome Composite   A type of video display that attaches to a Color Graphics Adapter (CGA). This display does not provide color, but some models may support "color" in the form of shading.

MS-DOS   Microsoft Disk Operating System. The operating system adapted by IBM for the personal computer family; runs on Intel microprocessor series 8088 and later versions. The operating system controls the components of a computer system, and the system's use and execution of software (application) programs.

Multifunction Board   A PC add-on board designed to provide several functions, allowing the addition of more features to a computer while requiring only one bus slot.

Multiplexer   A device that takes low-speed input from a number of terminals and combines them into one high-speed data stream for simultaneous transmission on a single channel.

Multiuser   The ability to have more than one user access and share a program at the same time, without destroying the integrity of the program.

Near-Letter Quality   A high-quality dot matrix printer that approaches the quality of a letter quality printer.

Nibble   Four bits, or one-half byte. Usually described by one hexadecimal digit.

Nonimpact   A classification given to printers that transfer ink without impacting the paper. The two best known are the laser and ink-jet technologies.

NRAM   Nonvolatile RAM. Unlike normal computer memory, NRAM does not lose its contents when the system is turned off. This is used by many modems (particularly internal modems) to store configuration information (in place of the switches used on other modems). *See* RAM.

Null Modem   A cable used to connect two computers via their serial ports. The cable is wired so that the two computers can send and receive information just as if there were modems at each end.

Object Code   The machine language code that is produced when higher-level languages are translated. This is the code that is actually executed by the computer.

Off Line   The modem state when it is not connected to another modem. Most communications programs display an OFFLINE indicator when not connected. *See* On Line.

Off-Line Printing   The capability of some systems to print the results of a search and mail the results to you as a paper copy, as opposed to your displaying or printing the search results on your terminal.

On Line   The modem state when it is connected to another modem. Most communications programs display an ONLINE indicator when connected. *See* Off Line.

On-Line Service   A service which, for a fee, allows users to connect to its computers and receive or exchange information, messages, and/or files. Many on-line services offer databases, news, shopping services, games, and other services. *See* Bulletin Board System.

Operating System   A set of programs residing in ROM and/or on disk that controls communications between the components of the computer and the programs run by the computer. DOS is an operating system.

Packet   *See* Block.

Packet-Switched Network   A network that transmits data between computer systems using packets of information. These networks typically provide local phone numbers (called nodes) allowing access to on-line services without long-distance charges. Some examples are Tymnet, Sprintnet, and Datapac. *See* On-Line Service.

Parallel Port   A port that transmits or receives eight bits (one byte) of data at a time between the computer and external devices. DOS currently recognizes three parallel ports, named LPT1, LPT2, and LPT3. LPT means "line printer," since the port was originally expected to only be used with a printer.

Parallel Printer   A printer that interfaces with a parallel port.

Parameter   A value selected to specify desired outcomes (from the execution of a command or process).

Parity   A very simple means of error checking. After a set of bits (a character) is sent, another bit is sent to make sure that the total number of 1 (ON) bits sent is either even or odd. With even parity, for example, if three bits were ON in the character, then the parity bit would also be ON (for an even total of four ON bits). Other parities used are mark and space parity (the parity bit is always OFF or ON, respectively), and no parity, which is the most common among microcomputer applications.

Partition   A storage area (on a disk or RAM) accessible to one operating system or process. As MS-DOS is able to access no more than 32 contiguous megabytes on a fixed disk, it is necessary to partition any disk larger than this in order to use all of it.

Password A word used in addition to your USERID to confirm your identity to a host system. While your USERID is public (so that others can send you messages), your password is private—this prevents someone from logging on with your ID.

Path An order to follow when proceeding from one place to another. Used to describe the relationship between files and directories. *See* Pathname.

Pathname A list of directory names that DOS follows to find a given file.

PC Board Printed circuit board.

PC-DOS Personal Computer Disk Operating System. The operating system developed for IBM PCs by Microsoft. *See* MS-DOS.

Peripheral A device that performs a function and is external to the system board. Peripherals include displays, disk drives, and printers. Some peripherals, such as disk drives and peripheral memory, are internal to the system unit.

PGA Professional Graphics Adapter. A display adapter from IBM with a color palette of 256 selections and a very high resolution. It requires a special monitor to match the high-resolution capabilities.

Pixel One element of a video display's resolution, or one dot on the screen. Characters and symbols are made up of many pixels. The number of possible pixels that can be displayed is referred to as the resolution of the screen.

Platen A backing, commonly cylindrical, against which printing mechanisms strike to produce an impression. The platen in a standard-sized printer is about ten inches wide.

Plotter A visual display or board in which a dependent variable is graphed by an automatically controlled pen or pencil as a function of one or more variables.

Polling A computer's act of continuously checking the status of some device or activity, waiting for a certain event.

Populated Occupied by chips. Said of IC sockets and PC boards.

Port   The channel or interface between the microprocessor and peripheral devices.

Post   To leave a message on a host system, intended for another user or group of users. Sometimes used to mean the message itself. *See* Message.

Printed Circuit Board   A board, usually of fiberglass-reinforced epoxy, on which thin layers of metal have been applied and then etched away to form traces. Electronic components are attached to the board and interconnected by the traces.

Print Quality   A term that refers to the sharpness or crispness of printed text and characters.

Profile   Information an on-line system keeps about you, to adjust its behavior when you are logged on. This might include your USERID, password, address, interests, color or terminal selections, and so forth. *See* Bulletin Board System, On-Line Service.

PROM   Programmable Read Only Memory. *See* Memory, ROM.

Prompt   A symbol or message indicating readiness to accept input.

Protocol   A set of "rules" regulating some form of computer communication. This might be a flow control protocol such as XON/XOFF, or an error-checking protocol for file transfers such as Zmodem. The error-checking protocols monitor certain information sent with each block of data; if the received data does not match the check information, the system notifies the sender that an error has occurred, and asks for a retransmission. This continues until all data has been received (the signal for which is also part of the protocol), or the transfer is aborted for some reason.

RAM   Random Access Memory. A storage medium in which access time is effectively independent of the location of the data.

RAM BIOS   BIOS transferred to RAM for faster system operation.

RAM Disk   A disk emulator. A portion of the computer memory is reserved for use as a disk drive. Instead of saving information on a physical disk, the information is saved in RAM. RAM disks pass data more rapidly than physical disk drives, but when their power is turned off all information is lost. A RAM disk is sometimes called a virtual disk.

Read/Write Head   The magnetic head that reads and writes data to and from a disk.

Record   A unit of data.

Remote System   *See* Host System.

Removable Hard Drive   Similar to a hard drive, but uses a cartridge that may be removed. Since there is no standard regarding such cartridges, there is no intercompatibility.

Reserved Names   DOS has certain names that are reserved for its own use, and should never be used for other purposes. Examples are CON for the console, COM for a communications port, and PRN for the printer port. Refer to your DOS manual for a complete list.

Resident Command   A command located in the operating system itself, contained in the file COMMAND.COM.

Resolution   Refers to the number of pixels, or dots, that are displayed on the CRT. The higher the resolution, the more pixels there are, and the better the video display.

RGB   Red Green Blue. The primary colors used by color monitor displays and TVs.

ROM   Read Only Memory. A storage medium in which data is stored permanently. The data in ROM remains intact even when the power is turned off. ROM is used to store important programs such as the BIOS, which interprets the codes sent by the keyboard, self-tests the system, and attempts to read a boot sector on the diskette in drive A each time the power is turned on. *See* BIOS.

Root Directory   Master directory of the DOS operating system. *See* Directory.

RS-232   A standardized serial connection system for computers.

Rubout   *See* DEL/RUBOUT.

Script   A set of commands instructing a program to perform some task automatically. For instance, a script might contain the commands needed to log onto a system, read and capture all messages, download a file, and log off.

Script Files   A capability of some newer communications software. Allows the user to write a series of commands and orchestrate the sign-on, information retrieval, and sign-off activities for various on-line systems. The files, usually composed on a word processor, are saved to disk and read by the communications software when connecting to a remote database.

Scroll   To move the text up or down on a display screen.

SDI   Abbreviation for the "selective dissemination of information;" synonymous with "current awareness." A process by which a database system can automatically run a user-input search strategy at regular (usually monthly) intervals. The system then reports recent additions to the database on that search subject to the user. Generally, the reports are mailed to the user as a printout.

Search   To look for specific information in an on-line database.

Search Strategy   The method used to search a database.

Sector   A pie-shaped portion of a disk. A disk is divided into tracks and sectors. Tracks are complete circles and are divided into sectors. *See* Format, Track.

Serial Communication   Transmission of data between two computers or devices, one bit at a time.

Serial Port   A port that transmits or receives data one bit at a time. DOS recognizes two serial ports, named COM1 and COM2.

Serial Printer   A printer that receives data by asynchronous serial communication; that is, one bit at a time.

Sheet Feeder   A device for printers that allows single sheets of paper to be fed into the printer, such as letterhead paper. This device can be built in or external.

SIG   *See* Conference.

Sign-on   *See* Logon.

Software   Programming tools such as languages, assemblers, and compilers, control programs such as operating systems, or application programs such as electronic spreadsheets and word processors. Software instructs the personal computer system to perform tasks.

Spreadsheet   A software program designed to perform mathematical and financial calculations.

Start Bit   The first bit in a set of data. It signifies that what follows is the data.

Stop Bit   The last bit in a set of data. It signifies that the set of data has been sent.

Storage Device   A place to store data. May be floppy, hard, or optical disk, or tape.

String   A group of successive characters. "ABC" might be a string, as well as "123."

Subdirectory   A directory located in another directory. The number of subdirectories is limited only by the physical size of the storage media. All subdirectories have a dot and dot-dot filename to indicate the current and parent directories.

Subsystem   An external device that contains a system. May include a hard disk, tape drive, modem, and/or other devices.

Synchronous Communication   A system of data transmission dependent on the precise timing of the transmitted data, and on the synchronization of the sending and receiving mechanisms.

Syntax   The rules governing the structure of a programming language or a program to form valid instructions.

Sysop   Short for SYStems OPerator, this is the person responsible for the setup and maintenance of a bulletin board system or other on-line service.

The sysop has complete control over the system—who can log on, how many files can be downloaded, what types of messages can be posted, and so on.

System A generic term for a computer and its peripherals, or for an on-line service or bulletin board service.

System Call Used to tell the system to generate an interrupt for the computer hardware's operation. The system will wait for the computer to acknowledge the interrupt; then it will perform a task and return control to the computer.

Tape Drive Subsystem An external subsystem containing a tape drive product, primarily used for back-up to a hard disk. Such a system may or may not contain an additional hard drive.

Telecommunications In general, the communication of information by electronic means. In particular, the use of computers to exchange data by modems, especially over telephone lines.

Telex An international system of communications by which you can send a message from any Telex terminal in the world to any other Telex terminal, or a computer emulating a Telex terminal. *See* Terminal Emulation.

Terminal An input/output device designed to receive data in an environment associated with the job to be performed. It is capable of transmitting entries to and obtaining output from the system of which it is a part. A "smart" terminal uses a microprocessor to handle the processing; a "dumb" terminal simply handles data input and output, and lacks the so-called intelligence capabilities.

Terminal Emulation A mode in which your PC performs as if it were a terminal, such as the DEC VT100.

Terminal Mode When a communications program is in terminal mode, it is behaving as if it were a computer terminal. Typed characters are passed on to the host system, and host characters are echoed to the screen. *See* Command Mode.

Timesharing System A form of multiuser computer system where each user is alloted a "slice" of processor time. The slices are rotated quickly enough so that to the user, it appears that he or she is the only user of a somewhat slower system.

Track A disk contains tracks and sectors. A track is a circular path on a disk; each track is divided into sectors. *See* Format.

Tractor Feed A device using sprockets to move paper in and out of a printer. Such a device can be built into the printer or can be an external option.

Transmission Rate *See* Bits Per Second.

Truncation Shortening a word with a specific symbol to form a "wildcard" search term (see Wildcard). Expands the term to encompass various suffixes and prefixes. Can be left or right truncation, depending on the system used. After Dark uses the dollar sign ($) as its truncation symbol. For example, to search for computer, computing, and computerized, you would use the single term comput$.

TTY Short for teletype. Also known as a dumb terminal. When a communications program is emulating a TTY, all received characters are displayed on the screen (in other modes, certain characters tell the terminal to position the cursor, clear the screen, and so on).

Turnaround Character In half-duplex communications, this is the character the sending system uses to tell the receiver it is done sending. The two modems then reverse roles until the new sender transmits a turnaround character.

UART An integrated circuit that handles the interface between computer and modem. The UART translates the framing and data bits received by the modem into characters for the computer, and also does the reverse for transmitted characters.

Upload To send data (typically a file) to a host system. This is usually done by means of an error-checking protocol. *See* Protocol.

Utility File A program used to assist in the operation of a computer, such as SORT and CHKDSK. Utilities are usually classified by their purpose, such as working with a hard disk or a printer.

Variable   A word or symbol whose value changes from one repetition of a program to the next, or changes within each repetition of a program.

VDT   Video Display Terminal. The display used on the computer system to provide a means of input and output.

VGA   Video Graphics Adapter. An IBM term for a high resolution color system for personal computers.

Video Mode   A format that defines the display characteristics, including the amount of text that can be displayed, the resolution or detail of the graphics, and the display colors. There are presently over 15 different modes available for the PC, most requiring additional hardware. For example, a screen in mode 3 has 80 columns, 25 lines, 6 foreground colors, and 8 background colors.

WAN   Wide Area Network. Usually a moderate/larger-sized network in which communications are conducted over telephone lines using modems. May also employ gateways and packet-switched networks.

Warm Boot   *See* Bootstrap.

Warm Start   To reinitialize a computer system by pushing the reset button or by holding down the CTRL and ALT keys while pressing the DEL key.

Wildcard   A search word formed by applying a truncation symbol; a wildcard term assumes a wider range of meanings and typically expands what will be retrieved. Sometimes a special wildcard symbol can be applied within a word to expand its meaning, for example, wom?n will retrieve women and woman.

Window   An area of a screen that displays information. Some programs support several windows that can be viewed simultaneously or sequentially.

Word   A set of characters that occupies one storage location and is recognized by the computer circuits as a unit. Word lengths are fixed or variable, depending on the particular computer.

Word Data   A group of bits that is treated by the computer as a unit and occupies one storage location. In personal computers, words are typically 4, 8, 16 or 32 bits long.

WXmodem   Windowed-Xmodem. An extension to the Xmodem protocol. Not widely used.

X25   A standard of error-checked communication between packet-switched networks and their users or other networks.

X400   An international standard of communication between packet-switched networks, especially those using different standards internally.

Xmodem   The grandfather of PC file transfer protocols. Also known as "the modem protocol" or "Christensen protocol" (after its inventor, Ward Christensen). Xmodem uses one-byte control sequences and a simple checksum for error-checking. Although it provides neither great speed nor great error detection, Xmodem's simplicity and ease of implementation have made it by far the most widely implemented PC protocol. Variations include Xmodem-1K (uses 1024-byte blocks instead of 128, commonly misnamed Ymodem), Xmodem-CRC (uses the far more accurate CRC error-checking method), WXmodem, and Ymodem.

XON/XOFF   A simple means of software flow control. During data transmission, if the receiving system needs time to process the data it has received or perform some other task, it sends an XOFF (ASCII character 19, CTRL-S). The sending end will stop sending data until the receiver sends an XON (ASCII character 17, CTRL-Q).

Y Connector   A "split" cable with a connector at one end, allowing one computer to use two modems, or vice versa.

Ymodem   An extension to the Xmodem protocol; uses CRC error-checking, 1024-byte blocks, and an extra block at the beginning of the transfer that contains the filename, actual size, and date.

Zmodem   Rapidly becoming the most popular file transfer protocol in the PC community. Zmodem offers faster transfers with better error checking, greater reliability, restarting of aborted or interrupted uploads and downloads, and other advanced features.

Modem Access: Finding Your Local Numbers

An empty auto-dial directory may seem a bit daunting at first, but it really isn't all that difficult to fill it with local bulletin board system (BBS) telephone numbers. The other local numbers you'll need are for the major packet-switching systems—Sprintnet (formerly Telenet) and TYMNET. Datapac can access U.S. networks from inside Canada. MCI and CompuServe maintain independent access networks inside the U.S.

To find a small BBS in your local calling area will take a bit of digging, but don't give up. Unless you live in the woods, there are probably more BBSs in your neighborhood that you'll ever have time to call. Active BBSs tend to network with each other, so once you find the first one, you're on your way. The trick, of course, is to find the first one.

Local BBSs are not usually listed in phone book, so unless you happen to know a sysop, you could easily feel frustrated. The answer is to use resources other than the phone book—like the following:

Local Computer Stores   Ask your computer store. Whoever sold you your modem can probably put you directly in touch with a local BBS. If you bought the modem by mail, try calling a local computer store anyway. (Many run their own BBS.)

User Groups   Your local user group will have numbers for bulletin boards in your area.

Other Resources

A number of nationwide organizations keep huge lists of BBSs, including location, phone number, sysop's name, area of speciality, and other detailed information. Here are some resources you can use

Computer Shopper   Buy a recent copy of the *Computer Shopper*, a monthly magazine available at large supermarkets. This publication, which carries an inexhaustible supply of ads for computer systems and components, also publishes a large directory of local user groups and BBSs, organized by state and city. These lists are about four to six months old by the time they reach the newsstand, but are considered very reliable.

Fog International   Fog International is the huge "umbrella" group that actually supplies *Computer Shopper* with its list. If you ask, Fog will send you a list of user groups and BBSs local to your area.

The Fog list is exceptional for several reasons. It is organized by state and city. It includes modem speeds available, the name of the sysop, the hours of operation, and a brief description of each system. The list is also as up-to-date as possible. It may not include everybody, but it is one of the most stable and accurate lists available.

To get a list of local numbers, send Fog a self-addressed, stamped envelope together with your area code, phone number, and a request for a local BBS list. Their address is Fog International, P.O. Box 3474, Daly City, CA 94015.

Information Utilities   All of the large information services (Chapter 6) have forums or libraries where you can find local BBS listings. On CompuServe, for example, the IBMNET BBS Forum (GO IBMBBS), Library 7, contains the newest Darwin list. This list, updated monthly, is usually titled

USBBS??.ZIP, where ?? stands for the edition number. On local BBSs you'll sometimes find it listed as USABBS??.ZIP, where the ?? stands for the month. The edition in CompuServe IBM BBS Library 7 is always the most recent available.

In IBM BBS Library 8, BBS sysops are invited to advertise their own systems. It can be fun browsing. Listings usually include information on location, size, hours, and so forth. You may often find new systems advertised there before they ever get included in either Fog International or the Darwin list.

READ.ME

The U.S. BBS Darwin List

The Darwin list originated on the DARWIN board in Gaitherburg, MD. The list is limited to boards with modems supporting 2400bps or faster, that have at least 40MB of storage, and that operate around the clock. Excluded are BBSs that focus on games, "adults only" topics, dating, and similar services or subjects.

While, the Fog International listing is very stable but does not include many new boards, the Darwin listing tries to keep up with changes in the BBS world.

Note: Numbers for BBSs outside the contiguous 48 states, that use CP/M or other non-DOS operating systems, or that charge fees for access, are not verified.

Recommended Software — Shareware and Freeware Programs

There are certain shareware and freeware programs that stand out as "classics" in the PC community. Because of what they do or how well they do it, these programs are considered to be absolute necessities by many computer users. Other shareware programs are relatively new and yet have gained tremendous popularity among users. These are the kinds of programs almost every user should have on their machines. I asked an expert in this field, Mike Callahan (alias Dr. File Finder), to give us a list of the best. You might want to look for them as you move out into the world of telecommunications.

Specific version numbers are included when they refer to details of that particular release, such as a file size. Otherwise, we've left off the version numbers—they simply change too fast. Shareware authors can afford to update their products more frequently than can commercial software vendors, because shareware upgrades do not require promotional hoopla the way their commercial cousins do. As a result, shareware is often in a continual state of change and upgrade. That's great for the user, who may see feedback suggestions for changes instituted in a matter of weeks. A minor drawback is that it's impossible to report current version numbers in a book.

All of the following programs are available both on the major on-line information services and on most file-oriented local bulletin boards. For the most recent versions of each program, download the file from your local BBS and look in the documentation to find where the author keeps the program updated. Most authors keep their most recent updates on CompuServe, Exec-PC, GEnie, or the author's own BBS.

LIST

Author   Vernon D. Buerg

Registration $15 suggested

Description   LIST has become a true classic among computer users. Throw away the primitive DOS TYPE command and take a look at all of the things that LIST lets you do. You can load multiple files and read through them. You can scan for a particular line of text and optionally have your search be case sensitive. LIST will do a Hex dump of any file, strip out the high ASCII characters found in WordStar files, and much more. You can mark a block of text from within LIST and write it to a file or send it to the printer. Looking at program documentation? With LIST you can just print out the portions that you want. Scroll through text a line at a time or a page at a time. You can "clone" your copy of LIST so that it uses all of the colors and defaults that *you* want it to use. While looking at files you can even shell to DOS and do something else and then return to LIST. You can toggle things such as tabs, a printer, EGA 25 or 43 line mode. You can put a ruler on the screen, and go back and find text you found previously. LIST is one of the most complete and versatile text-handling utilities ever written. Your software collection is *not* complete without a copy of Vern Buerg's LIST.

CED

Author Chris Dunford

Registration Donation

Description CED is the best known and most commonly used program among what are known as "DOS command line editors." CED will let you edit previously issued commands by using the arrow keys to recall them. Perhaps CED's most famous feature is its ability to let the user create *synonyms.* Using CED, you can actually create your own, personalized command set. Make **D** do a DIR, or **W5** execute a command such as "CD \WP50^WP." CED's synonyms help you to have total control of your command system, and they don't take up the disk space that multiple batch files do. Another feature of CED is that it can remember the last commands you entered and complete the command for you. CED is compact, versatile, and uses very little DOS RAM. If you really want to feel like you are in control of your computer, then you have to try CED, the DOS Command Editor.

The commercial version, PCED, has much-expanded capabilities. It costs about the same as a midrange shareware registration fee. Try CED, and if you quickly find the program indispensable, as many do, "register" by purchasing PCED.

QEdit

Author Sammy Mitchell

Registration $45

Description QEdit is a small, quick editor that is packed with features and functions. Multiple files can be edited by opening any number of windows. Block operations include Copy, Move, Delete, and Write to File. QEdit has its own box drawing mode that lets you select from a number of styles. QEdit can be configured to be exactly the way you want. All key configurations can be changed so that, if you like, you can make QEdit emulate your favorite word processor. The user runs the configuration program and can set the defaults to suit personal style or taste. With each new release, QEdit just keeps getting better. QEdit has a built-in, configurable Help screen, a pull-down menu system, configurable colors, drop to DOS, column marking, and an Undo function that lets you correct a command that you entered by mistake. QEdit, the choice of thousands of users and programmers, is an absolute must for laptop editing because it's so compact. It's highly recommended.

DSZ

Author   Chuck Forsberg

Registration $25

Description   DSZ is a file transfer protocol driver that can execute many different protocols. It is best known, however, for the Zmodem protocol. Zmodem has excellent error-checking, it is the most resistant to "line noise," and it can even resume a file transfer that was aborted. DSZ itself can drive protocols such as Xmodem-CRC, Ymodem-G, 1K-Xmodem (Ymodem), and more. DSZ is revised constantly in order to keep up with faster modems, faster machines, and a number of other variables. The registered version has certain features that are not available in the shareware version of DSZ. Many users don't realize it, but DSZ even has a built-in "Terminal Mode" so that you can actually dial BBSs, download files, and so on, while using DSZ from the DOS prompt. No one who is using telecommunications should be without DSZ.

PKZIP and PKUNZIP

Author   Phil Katz

Registration $25 to $47

Description   PKZIP and PKUNZIP are versions of what many consider the ultimate utility for packing groups of files into small bundles. PKZIP creates files with an extension of .ZIP and offers a wide variety of features. You can add comments for the .ZIP file itself and for each individual file within a .ZIP file. Files can be added to, deleted from, and moved into existing .ZIP files. Files within a .ZIP file may also be "freshened" by adding newer versions. PKZIP allows a user-selectable packing level so that it can be optimized for speed or for size. The most recent release is even faster than previous versions, and a new algorithm has improved the packing by 15-30 percent. For example, the file that documents PCBoard 14.1 is 805,100 bytes in size, yet, using PKZIP, it is packed down into a 284K .ZIP file. One can also create "self-extracting" files so that the receiver does not need any utility in order to unpack the file. PKZIP and PKUNZIP are the overwhelming choice of sysops and those in the BBS community. If you want to compress your files to save disk space and transfer time, then get PKZIP/PKUNZIP by PKware and Phil Katz, for the ultimate in speed and compression.

TSRCOM Utilities

Author   Kim Kokkonen
        TurboPower Software

Registration $10

Description   The TSRCOM utilities are a group of programs that help the user to manage TSR (terminate and stay resident) programs. The position in memory can be MARKed before a TSR is loaded. Then, if you should later decide to get rid of that TSR, you can RELEASE the MARK and get your DOS RAM back. Over a period of several years, the TSRCOM utilities have become increasingly more sophisticated in their management of TSR programs. TSR programs can easily be loaded and removed. The utilities also contain a program called WATCH, which keeps track of all interrupts and helps in the overall management of TSRs on your system. With so many great TSR programs available, no system should be without the TSRCOM utilities to manage their use. The filename always contains the version number as the last two characters, for example, TSRCOM29.ZIP. The complete Turbo Pascal source code is also available. If you're going to use TSRs, be sure to get the TSRCOM Utilities.

BiModem

Authors   John Erikson and Dave Krause
        Erik Labs

Registration $25

Description   BiModem is the protocol of tomorrow available today. Taking full advantage of the potential of the full-duplex modem, BiModem allows the user to send and receive files at the same time. In addition, there is a "chat" feature so that a conversation can take place during these simultaneous file transfers. With speeds equal to that of Zmodem, BiModem also has the ability to start an aborted transfer exactly where it left off and to check the accuracy of a transfer immediately upon completion. Despite the fact that BiModem is still in its infancy, it has spread quickly around the country. For truly fast and efficient file transfers that can move in two directions at once, get BiModem!

DOORWAY

Author   Marshall Dudley

Registration $25

Description   DOORWAY is a program that allows almost any .COM or .EXE file to be run as a "door" on a bulletin board system. It can also be used as an excellent "drop to DOS" in a host mode. DOORWAY can handle ANSI graphics, QuickBASIC programs, and can require passwords as desired. The most recent versions also support direct screen writes, something that was not possible just a short time ago. DOORWAY has allowed sysops to take interesting programs and make them into doors for the enjoyment of their users. As a drop to DOS, DOORWAY is unsurpassed for its ease of use, security, and reliability. Truly a remarkable program, DOORWAY is in a class by itself.

Newkey

Author   Frank Bell

Registration $55

Description   Newkey is often billed as a "keyboard macro program," but it is that and so much more. Newkey gives you far more for the money than any of the commercial "macro" programs. Newkey *is* a great keyboard macro program, and keyboard enhancer, and it also gives you an extended keyboard buffer. It can increase the typematic rate (the speed at which the characters repeat) of the keyboard, and it can also blank the screen. Newkey also comes in different sizes for those who want to give up some features in order to save on RAM. Thus, if you don't need a pop-up menu, you can use a smaller version of Newkey that doesn't have it. If you want to use macros that are powerful and flexible, use Newkey.

FormatMaster

Author   John Newlin
New-Ware

Registration $20

Description   FormatMaster is a menu-driven utility that facilitates the formatting of floppy diskettes. It formats both 5 1/4-inch (360K or 1.2M) or 3 1/2-inch (720K or 1.4M) diskettes and provides the capability to format multiple disks continuously. In addition, FormatMaster lets you create system diskettes and add volume labels. A unique feature is its ability to sequentially serialize diskettes using a combination alphanumeric volume label. With FormatMaster you can also rapidly reinitialize previously formatted diskettes by clearing the disketted FAT table and directory entry list. Normal diskette formatting and verification are reduced to a single operation to allow the user the option of skipping the verification process to gain speed. This is safe to do with fresh, high-quality diskettes. You can even use special fomatting to set 800K onto a 360K diskette. FormatMaster runs on any IBM PC, XT, AT, PS/2 or compatible and requires approximately 150K of free RAM.

PC Write

Author   Bob Wallace
QuickSoft

Registration $89

Description   PC Write is one of the most versatile word processors to ever evolve in the world of shareware. Steadily growing, changing, and adapting to the needs of its users, PC Write possesses the features of some of the most expensive commercial word processors and has become a very useful and powerful word processing tool. It is used extensively around the United States and the world, and many educational institutions favor it. Sporting a full spell-checker and supporting a wide range of printers, PC Write is also configurable so that it suits the needs of each individual user. If you want a shareware word processor, look for PC Write. Also look for PC Lite, a powerful, yet scaled-down version recently released.

ArcMaster

Author   John Newlin
New-Ware

Registration $35

Description   ArcMaster is a full-featured utility that serves as a control program for the most popular file compression/decompression systems. All of these systems are normally operated with numerous command line switches and filenames that make it difficult to recall the correct command line syntax necessary to accomplish a specific archival task. ArcMaster provides a dual directory display that permits you to mark specific files in one directory and manipulate them by the selected archival system into the other displayed directory.

In addition to standard archival system operations, ArcMaster also provides numerous special operations. These include converting from one system to another, viewing archival system directories, viewing self-extracting compressed file directories, and many others. ArcMaster also lets you copy, move, or delete normal DOS files and view normal DOS files or compressed files through Vernon Buerg's famous LIST program. ArcMaster runs on any IBM PC, XT, AT, PS/2 or compatible and requires approximately 300K of available RAM. It supports ARC, LHARC, ARCA/ARCE, PAK, PKPAK and PKUNP, and PKZIP and PKUNZIP.

SHEZ

Author Jim Derr   California Software Design

Registration $15

Description   SHEZ is a full-featured shell program designed to work with the most popular file compression programs. SHEZ is not as complete a shell as ArcMaster, but it manages compressed files extremely well. The built-in mouse support is well executed. The user interface allows multiple ways to do most things, so you can choose the keystrokes that feel the most natural to you for doing any given task.

The SHEZ program is very easy to configure. You may specify the programs to use with SHEZ—for example, BROWSE or LIST for viewing text files. You can also pick your editor (perhaps QEDIT, VDE, TED or PC LITE) to edit files still in the archive, or a choice of PAK, PKPAK, ARCE or ARC. SHEZ can swap 90 percent of its code out of memory into EMS or to disk when you shell to DOS, edit a file, or run a program contained in a compressed file. This is a program to rely on if you work with compressed files.

LOG

Author   Christopher Laforet

Registration $25

Description   LOG is a program that tracks computer usage, time, and even billing. An excellent tool for the computer consultant, LOG will bill each client based on a rate that you specify. You can print bills, look at individual accounts, fix mistakes, and much more. LOG can also help you keep track of how much time you spend doing different tasks on your computers. Thus, LOG fits the needs of both hobbyists and professionals. You can have multiple log files, export a log file from one machine and import it into the log file on another machine, and more. Very well done and with more exciting features on the way, LOG is fast becoming the best way to track computer usage and time, whether for profit or just for fun. Give it a try.

PC FILE PLUS

Author   Jim Button
         ButtonWare

Registration $69.95

Description   PC File Plus is an excellent database system. It has a very nice user interface that makes it easy for even the novice computer user. There is even a "Learn Mode" that guides you through the program. PC File Plus is full-featured and can do form letters and generate reports based on your specifications. Whether handling a Girl Scout troop, a bowling league, or a small business with 200,000 customers, PC File Plus will fit your needs. It is a complex and comprehensive program that still remains simple to use. I heartily recommend it—PC File Plus is a true classic.

ALT

Author   Instinct Software

Registration $39.95

Description   ALT is a "task-switching" program and much more. ALT will use the EMS (expanded memory), disk space, RAM drive, or all three, and it can dynamically create new partitions. Use Partition 1 as a "working" partition, Partition 2 for your comm program, Partition 3 for your spreadsheet, and so on. You can then toggle easily back and forth between them. ALT, however, has much more to offer: a built-in editor, notepad, three calculators, and a complete Rolodex and appointment system. If that sounds good, wait till you hear the rest. ALT also has a menu system, an excellent cut- and-paste function, complete disk services (similar to XTREE), alarms, and a superb macro capability. The user menu can be redefined so that the functions you use the most are easiest to access, and any features that you choose not to use can be left off the menu entirely. Best of all, these extra functions don't take up any extra DOS RAM. If you want to get much more out of your system and have task switching plus a lot more, try ALT.

Maxi Form

Author   Herne Data Systems Ltd.

Registration $10   Maxi Disk: $19.95 (in the U.S.)

Description   Maxi Form is a utility that lets you get the absolute most out of your floppy disks, depending on the type of drives that you have. It has been tested with DOS 3.2x and later, but cannot be guaranteed to work on all machines. Maxi Form will format a 360K disk to 420K on a 5 1/4-inch drive. It formats a 720K disk to 800K, a 1.2MB disk to 1.4MB, a 360K disk to 800K, and gets an incredible 1.6MB on a 1.44MB disk. In cases where there is some incompatibility with OEM versions of MS-DOS, Maxi Form comes with a small utility, SMAX, that eliminates most problems. There is also a commercial version called Maxi Disk that is menu driven and has all the standard features of Maxi Form, but also supports more disk drives and can create DOS "system" disks. Disk space is always at a premium, and Maxi Form helps you to get the very most out of what you have.

Qmodem

Author   John Friel III
         The Forbin Project

Registration $45

Description   Qmodem is a full-featured telecommunications program. Qmodem has a QuickLearn Script generator to help you easily make logon scripts, and a script language that can handle virtually any situation automatically. The file transfer protocols in Qmodem are solid as a rock, and you can add 10 "external" protocols as well. Automatic Zmodem downloads are available as well. There is a built-in editor, support for EMS, and the ability to configure Qmodem for use on almost any system. Qmodem even has a function that will automatically configure a wide range of modems. The host mode in Qmodem allows a caller to leave messages, read messages, and do file transfers. The protocols available are configurable. Qmodem is a solid and reliable communications program with many fascinating features. The support given by John Friel and The Forbin Project is the best that is available. If you want to check out one of the great telecommunication programs, then get QModem and see what you think.

TELIX

Author   Exis, Inc.

Registration $35

Description   Telix is a full-featured communications program for MS-DOS machines that can meet the needs of almost any user. Its range of built-in file transfer protocols includes Zmodem, CompuServe QuickB, Xmodem, Xmodem-1K, Xmodem-1K-G, Ymodem (TRUE), Ymodem-G, Kermit, SEAlink, Telink, Modem7, and ASCII. Telix allows four external protocols to be defined and called from within, so almost any file transfer is possible.

Other Telix features include a powerful 200-entry multiple dialing directory; an automatic queue redial; DEC VT102 and VT52 terminal emulations; and SALT script language for automated logons and other functions. Telix offers full access to DOS, including a DOS shell, a DOS command option, and full path support. It includes a host mode with file transfers, operator paging, and a remote DOS shell with two access levels. The program also offers a chat mode, keyboard macros, a scrollback buffer, session capture, a usage log, and a translate table.

SMALL UTILITY PROGRAMS

Small utility programs cannot get separate listings here, because they are updated and changed so often. They are, however, a large and important part of the shareware world. They may be found on BBSs and information services worldwide. These small programs are highly useful, and can often be configured for your particular needs. They tend to have lower registration fees than large applications (typically $25 or less). Searching for and finding these gems can be a lot of fun. If you work a lot at the DOS level, they also can make your time more productive. In fact, that's how many shareware utilities got written—the author wanted a faster or better way to do some routine chore and decided to write a program.

Although shareware utility programs often have a rougher feel and a narrower focus than their commercial counterparts, the best of the shareware utilities are phenomenally good. Vern Buerg's LIST is the undisputed leader among ASCII text file viewers. No commercial vendor has beaten the shareware file-compression programs (especially Phil Katz's PKZIP, Yoshio's LHARC, and NoGate Consulting's PAK). QFILER leads every other directory management program for powerful, two-windowed DOS file management. Norm Patriquin's utility programs are famous for flexibility and power, and he's starting to add attractive screens. StupenDOS by Douglas Hays gives Xtree Gold a run for its money as a powerful DOS shell.

One thing to remember—in shareware even more than commercial products, version 1.0 of *anything* is likely to be buggy. This is true of utility programs most of all. Shareware programmers sometimes have limited access to hardware, so utilities that haven't had time to mature can run into compatibility problems.

User feedback can make a big difference. Usually, experience shows that the easier it is to contact the shareware author, the better designed and less buggy the program will be. If you like a program, register—and tell the author what you think—sometimes one or two users bothering to write a note can make all the difference.

Look for these small gems and try them. If you're at all adventurous, you'll quickly build a utility library rivaling the biggest disk vendor's collection.

Cable Diagrams

MODULE PIN ASSIGNMENTS

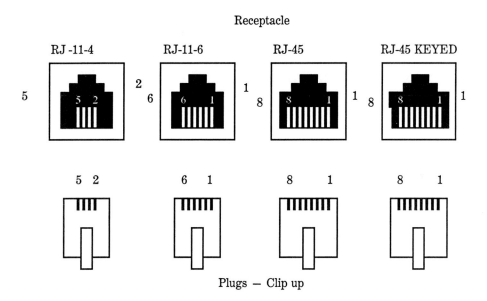

Receptacle

RJ-11-4   RJ-11-6   RJ-45   RJ-45 KEYED

Plugs — Clip up

753

		Table I-1	
		Modem Diagrams Legend	
CCITT	**EIA**	**MNEMONIC**	**DESCRIPTION**
101	AA	GND	Protective frame ground
103	BA	TxD	Transmit Data
104	BB	RxD	Receive Data
105	CA	RTS	Request To Send
106	CB	CTS	Clear To Send
107	CC	DSR	Data Set Ready
102	AB	GND	Reference signal ground
109	CF	DCD	Data Carrier Detect
108	CD	DTR	Data Terminal Ready

MODEM CABLES

For the diagrams that follow, the mnemonics that are used are described in Table J-1.

Standard PC RS-232 Modem Cable, 25-Pin "D"-Shell

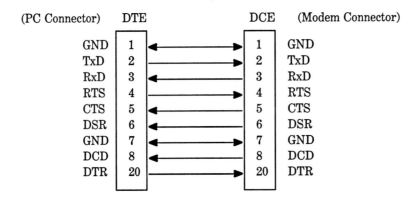

Standard PC DB-9 Modem Cable, 9-Pin

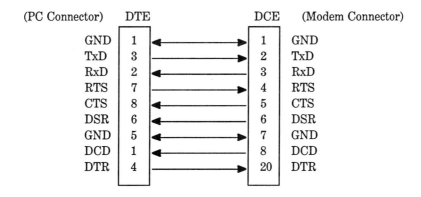

Macintosh Plus Modem Cable, DIN 8-Pin

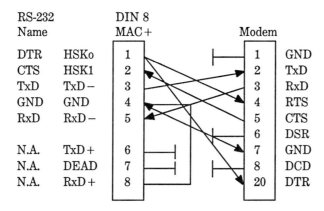

MACHINE-TO-MACHINE CABLES

Null Modem Cable, DB-25 Pin to DB-25 Pin

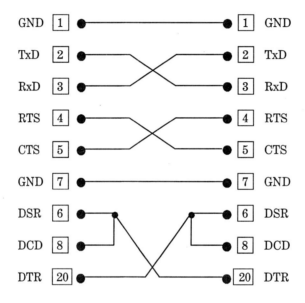

Null Modem Cable, DB-9 Pin to DB-25 Pin

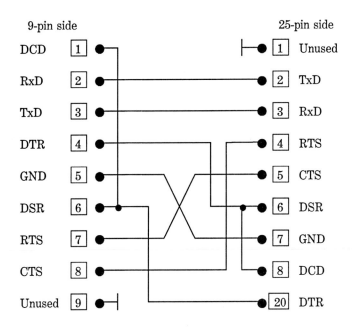

Null Modem Cable, Macintosh DB-9 to IBM DB-25 Pin

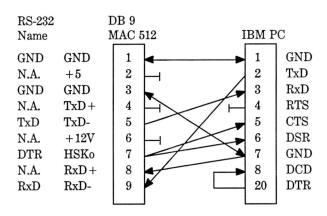

PRINTER CABLES

IBM Parallel Printer Interface

DB25 Female		Centronics Male
1	————————————	1
2	————————————	2
3	————————————	3
4	————————————	4
5	————————————	5
6	————————————	6
7	————————————	7
8	————————————	8
9	————————————	9
10	————————————	10
11	————————————	11
12	————————————	12
13	————————————	13
14	————————————	14
15	————————————	15
16	————————————	16
17	————————————	17
18	————————————	18
19	————————————	19
20	————————————	20
21	————————————	21
22	————————————	22
23	————————————	23
24	————————————	24
25	————————————	25

OTHER CONNECTORS

DB25-Pin Female-to-Male or Male-to-Female Gender Changer

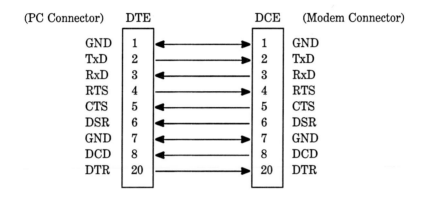

DB9-Pin Female-to-Male or Male-to-Female Gender Changer

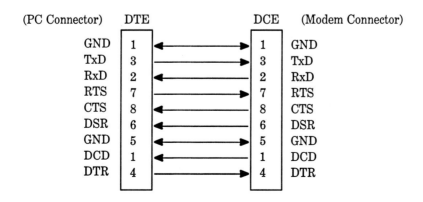

Recommended Reading

There are plenty of good specialty books out there for those who want to know more. Our list is by no means definitive, but it's not bad, either.

The Matrix   John S. Quarterman, Digital Press, 631 pages, $49.95.

This book, a definitive work, outlines all the important accessible computer networks in the world! Want to get a message into Hungary via Bombay via some obscure network? You can do it with this incredible book.

Computer Readable Databases   Edited by Martha E. Williams, Gale Research, updated annually, 1186 pages.

Another fine book that contains more facts about information sources than any book I've seen. Not all databases listed are on line, though.

How to Look It Up On-line   Alfred Glossbrenner, St. Martin's Press, 486 pages, $14.95.

Along with his *Master Guide To Free Software* ($18.95, 530 pages), this will make your on-line life much easier. *How To Look It Up On-Line* is the first and (at this writing) only book specifically designed to show managers, executives, and professionals how to tap industrial-strength databases like those found on DIALOG, BRS, Orbit, and other leading database systems. This book is not for the casual or recreational user, but if your future or fortune depend on information, buy it.

Both of these Glossbrenner Guides are available in bookstores, from the publisher (St. Martin's Press, NYC), or directly from the author. For more information contact Alfred Glossbrenner, FireCrystal Communications, 699 River Road, Yardley, PA 19067 (800-628-7637).

Directory of On-Line Databases   Cuadra/Elsevier, 600 pages, $175.00 annually.

With over 4000 databases available through more than 500 systems, the on-line field cries out for a directory. Several publishers have heeded the call, but this "Cuadra Directory," published by Cuadra/Elsevier, is generally considered to be definitive. Single copies are $75. A one-year subscription ($175) brings you a complete directory issue (about 600 pages) every six months, and two quarterly update supplements. For more information, contact *Directory of On-line Databases*, Cuadra/Elsevier, P.O. Box 872, Madison Square Station, New York, NY 10159.

Online Programming Languages and Assemblers   Edited by William J. Birnes, McGraw-Hill Publishing Company, 1989, 537 pages, $29.95.

A complete documentation manual of all major implementations of high-level language compilers and interpreters available through on-line bulletin boards, shareware interest groups, and freeware information exchanges.

The Modem Reference   Michael A. Banks, published by Brady, a division of Simon and Schuster, N.Y., 1988, 529 pages, $21.95.

A book designed to get you on line as quickly and as easily as possible, and to serve as a continuing reference for your on-line activities. Good book.

Understanding Data Communications, 2nd edition   George E. Friend, John L. Fike, H. Charles Baker, John C. Bellamy, revised by Gilbert Held, Howard K. Sam Company, a division of MacMillan, 1988, 291 pages, $18.95.

All about data communications systems, how their various hardware and software components work, and the interface between telephone network and computer.

Communications and Networking for the IBM PC and Compatibles, revised and expanded Larry Jordan and Bruch Churchill, published by Brady, a division of Simon and Schuster, N.Y., 1987, 511 pages, $22.95.

Part I introduces the reader to fundamentals and applications of data communications for IBM PCs and compatibles. Part II deals with fundamental concepts and practical applications of local area networking for same.

Modems and Communications on IBM PCs W. David Schwaderer, John Wiley and Sons, 1986, 355 pages, $21.95.

Introduction to communications theory and communications hardware, including telephone lines. General instruction in high-performance BASIC programming techniques for writing communications programs.

Using Computer Bulletin Boards John V. Hedtke, MIS Press, 1990, $24.95.

A timely reference for bulletin board users.

Electronic Communication Systems for Home and Office Ronald G. Albright, Jr., Chilton Books (Radnor, PA), 1989, 288 pages, $16.95 (paperback). Available from the author at 1160 Huffman Road, Birmingham, AL 35215 (205-853-8269).

This is the only guide to establishing and using the four major communications technologies available to the small or home business that employs fax, electronic and voice mail, and information retrieval by PC. Each technology is discussed, with profiles of actual users and how the techniques are used in their businesses. A complete and thorough guide.

Other resources:

The Complete MCI Mail Handbook Stephen Manes, Bantam Books (New York), 1988, 498 pages, $22.95 (paperback).

MCI Mail is one of the largest electronic mail systems available, and receives consistently favorable reviews. Manes's book is one reason why MIC should continue to be popular.

How to Get The Most Out of CompuServe Charles Bowen and David Peyton, Bantam Books (New York), $19.95 (paperback), and **Master Guide to CompuServe** Alfred Glossbrenner, Brady Books (New York), 1988, $19.95 (paperback).

These two books put CompuServe's vast resources into clear perspective. Extensive coverage of EasyPlex is included.

Online Steve Lambert, Microsoft Press (Bellevue, Washington), 1985, 320 pages, $19.95 (paperback).

A good introduction to modems, electronic mail, and information access.

The Book of Fax E. King and Daniel Fishman, Ventana Press (North Carolina), 1988.

Essential Guide to Bulletin Board Systems Patrick Dewey, Merkler Publishing (Westport, CT), 1987, 205 pages.

A useful discussion of what BBSs are and what they look like to a user. Several example systems are discussed.

The Telecommuter's Handbook: How to Work for a Salary Without Ever Leaving the House Brad Schepp, Pharos Books (New York), 1990, 242 pages.

An excellent resource book for telecommuters—people who do all or part of their work at home and report in by modem, FAX, or telephone. Includes telecommuting job descriptions and contact numbers for companies that hire telecommuters.

The manuscript for this book was prepared and submitted to
Osborne/McGraw-Hill in electronic form. The acquisitions editor
for this project was Jeffrey Pepper, the technical reviewer was
Werner Feibel, and the project editor was Madhu Prasher.

Text design by Stefany Otis and Martha Conway, using Century
Expanded for text body and for display.

Cover art by Bay Graphics Design Associates. Color separation
and cover supplier, Phoenix Color Corporation. Screens
produced with InSet, from InSet Systems, Inc. Book printed
and bound by R.R. Donnelley & Sons Company,
Crawfordsville, Indiana.